The Triumph of Citizenship

Patricia E. Roy

The Triumph of Citizenship
The Japanese and Chinese in Canada, 1941-67

UBCPress · Vancouver · Toronto

16 15 14 13 12 11 10 09 08 07 5 4 3 2 1

Printed in Canada on ancient-forest-free paper (100% post-consumer recycled) that is processed chlorine- and acid-free, with vegetable-based inks.

Library and Archives Canada Cataloguing in Publication

Roy, Patricia, 1939-
The triumph of citizenship : the Japanese and Chinese in Canada, 1941-67 / Patricia E. Roy.

Includes bibliographical references and index.
ISBN 978-0-7748-1380-8 (bound); 978-0-7748-1381-5 (pbk)

1. Chinese – British Columbia – History. 2. Japanese – British Columbia – History. 3. British Columbia – Race relations. 4. British Columbia – Politics and government. 5. British Columbia – Emigration and immigration – History. 6. British Columbia – Emigration and immigration – Economic aspects. 7. Immigrants – British Columbia – History. I. Title.

FC3850.C5R688 2007 971.1'004951 C2006-906282-X

Canadä

UBC Press gratefully acknowledges the financial support for our publishing program of the Government of Canada through the Book Publishing Industry Development Program (BPIDP), and of the Canada Council for the Arts, and the British Columbia Arts Council.

This book has been published with the help of a grant from the Canadian Federation for the Humanities and Social Sciences, through the Aid to Scholarly Publications Programme, using funds provided by the Social Sciences and Humanities Research Council of Canada.

Printed and bound in Canada by Friesens
Set in Fairfield by Blakeley
Copy editor: Dallas Harrison
Proofreader: Gail Copeland
Cartographer: Eric Leinberger
Cover design: Blakeley

UBC Press
The University of British Columbia
2029 West Mall
Vancouver, BC V6T 1Z2
604.822.5959 / Fax 604.822.6083
www.ubcpress.ca

Contents

Tables and Figures

Tables

Figures

Acknowledgments

Researching and writing a monograph only seems like a solitary occupation; it's a collective effort. This book would not have been possible without the archivists and librarians who collected, arranged, and made available a wide variety of manuscript and printed sources. My thanks go to all of them; alas, including some who are no longer with us. I thank the "anonymous" readers of the manuscript who offered some excellent suggestions to improve it. Not so anonymous are the fellow miners of the archives who passed on little gems to me. They will find themselves thanked individually in the endnotes but I must give a separate thanks to Charles Hou, who shared some of his cartoon collection with me. Thanks too to the University of Victoria, where students asked stimulating questions and colleagues provided a congenial environment.

Like many Canadian scholars, I am indebted to the Aid to Scholarly Publications Program of the Canadian Federation for the Humanities and Social Sciences, which expeditiously handled the manuscript and generously subsidized its publication.

Last but not least I must thank my friends at UBC Press beginning with Jean Wilson, who took a warm interest in the project over many years and did not demur when a projected two volumes became three. More recently, I have enjoyed working with the equally professional and co-operative Camilla Blakeley, who has seen the book through the production process; the copy editor, Dallas Harrison; and the members of the management and marketing team.

A rigorous attempt has been made to find copyright information for all illustrations and to obtain permission to reproduce them. If there are any omissions these are inadvertent and I will be grateful to learn of them.

Abbreviations

ARP	Air Raid Protection
BCFGA	British Columbia Fruit Growers Association
BCSC	British Columbia Security Commission
BESL	British Empire Service League
BNA	British North America
CBA	Chinese Benevolent Association
CBC	Canadian Broadcasting Corporation
CCF	Co-operative Commonwealth Federation
CCJC	Co-operative Committee on Japanese Canadians
CCNC	Chinese Canadian National Council
CIPO	Canadian Institute of Public Opinion
CNR	Canadian National Railway
CP	Canadian Press
CPR	Canadian Pacific Railway
FBI	Federal Bureau of Investigation
IODE	Imperial Order of Daughters of the Empire
IWA	International Woodworkers of America
LPP	Labour Progressive Party
NAJC	National Association of Japanese Canadians
PC	Privy Council
RCAF	Royal Canadian Air Force
RCN	Royal Canadian Navy
SSB	Soldiers' Settlement Board
TLC	Trades and Labour Congress of Canada
UBCM	Union of British Columbia Municipalities
UN	United Nations

The Triumph of Citizenship

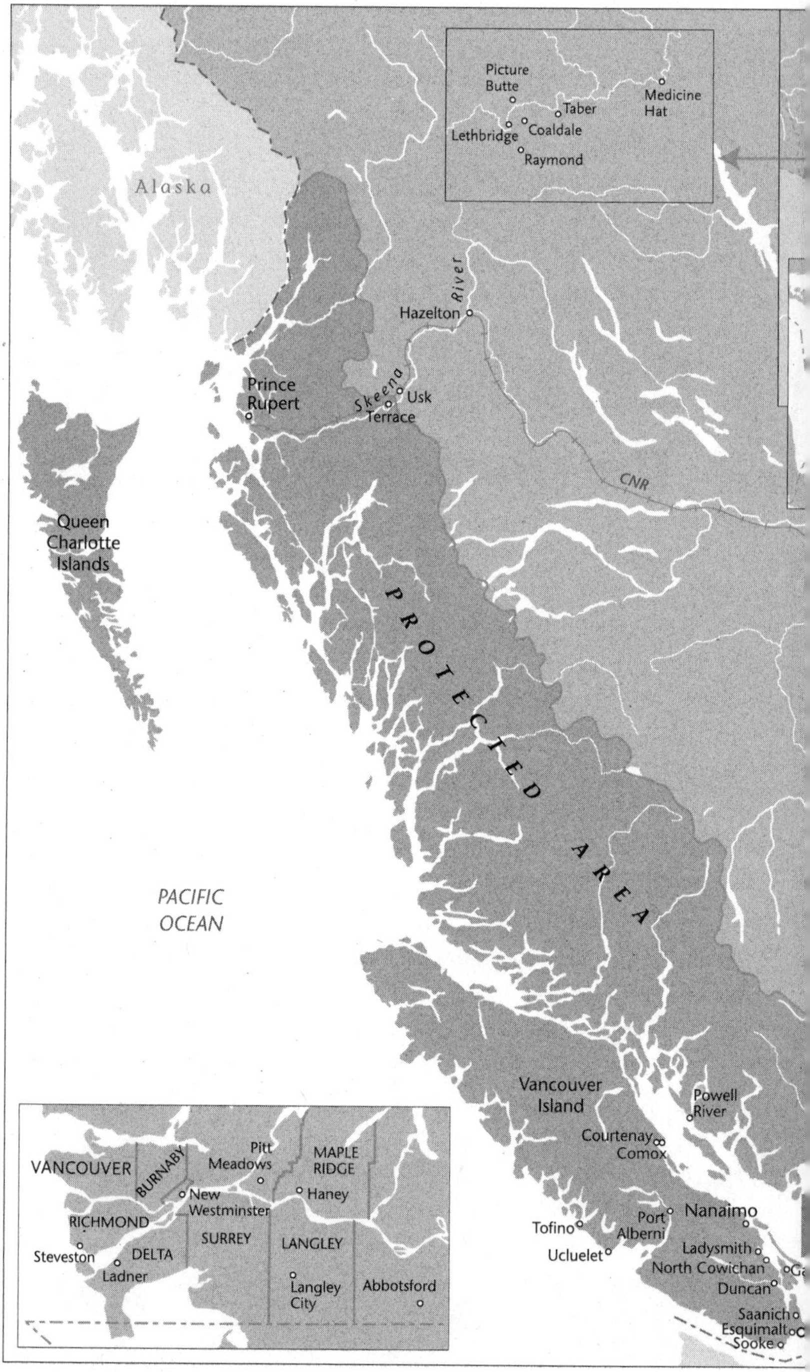

Primary locations and destinations of Japanese and Chinese in Canada, 1942-67

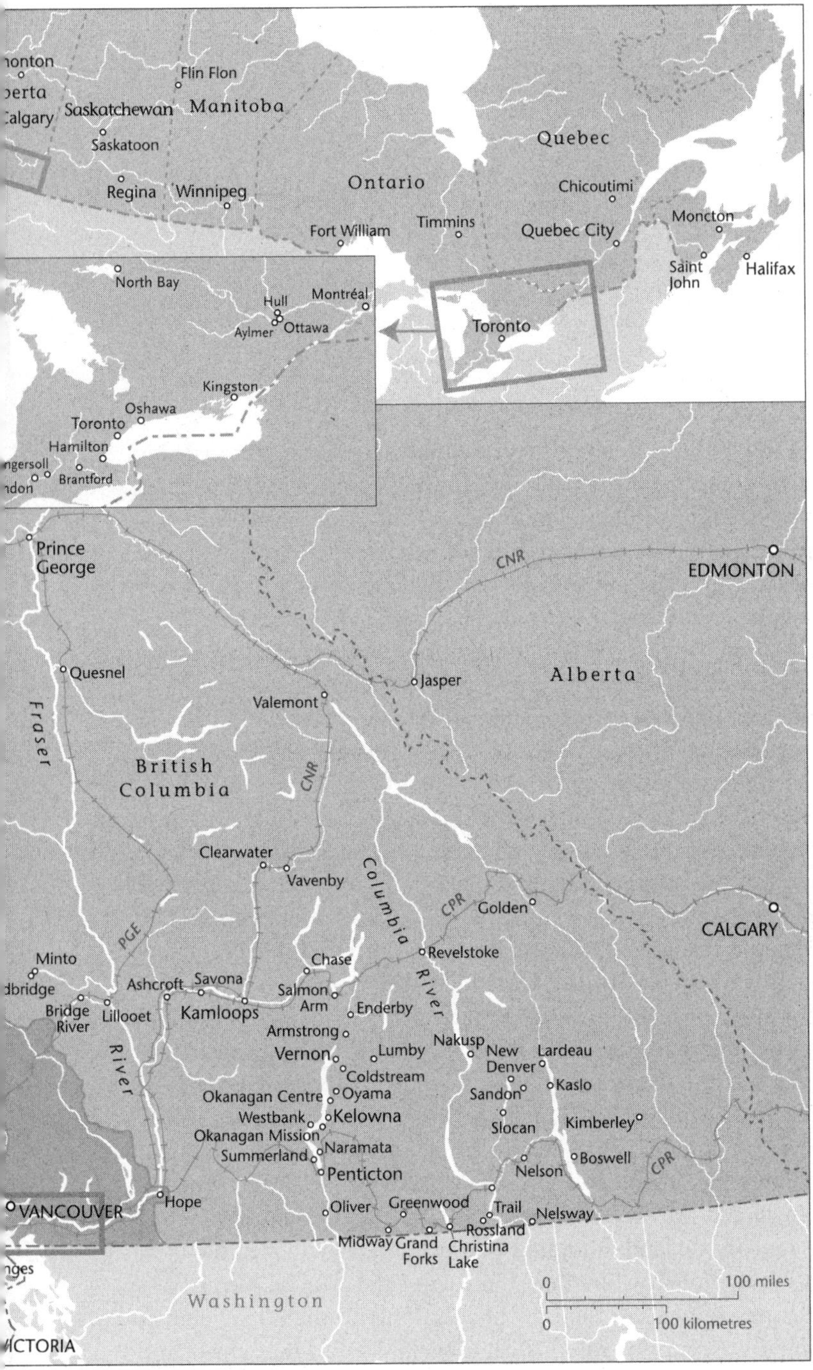
Flin Flon
Saskatchewan
Manitoba
Saskatoon
Regina
Winnipeg
Ontario
Quebec
Chicoutimi
Fort William
Timmins
Quebec City
Moncton
Saint John
Halifax
North Bay
Hull
Montréal
Aylmer
Ottawa
Toronto
Kingston
Oshawa
Toronto
Hamilton
Brantford
Prince George
CNR
EDMONTON
Quesnel
Jasper
Alberta
Valemont
Fraser
British Columbia
CNR
Clearwater
Vavenby
Columbia
CPR
Golden
CALGARY
PGE
Revelstoke
Minto
Chase
Ashcroft
Savona
Salmon Arm
Bridge River
Lillooet
Kamloops
Enderby
River
Armstrong
Vernon
Lumby
Nakusp
New Denver
Lardeau
Coldstream
Kaslo
River
Okanagan Centre
Oyama
Sandon
Westbank
Kelowna
Kimberley
Okanagan Mission
Slocan
Naramata
Summerland
Nelson
Boswell
CPR
Penticton
Hope
VANCOUVER
Oliver
Greenwood
Trail
Nelsway
Rossland
Midway
Grand Forks
Christina Lake
0
100 miles
0
100 kilometres
Washington
VICTORIA

Introduction

In 1968 Premier W.A.C. Bennett of British Columbia took Mayor Peter Wing of Kamloops, the president of the Union of British Columbia Municipalities, to a federal-provincial constitutional conference. While in Ottawa, Wing may have met another Kamloops native and fellow graduate of its high school, Thomas Shoyama, a senior economic adviser to the government.[1] A quarter-century earlier their presence in any governmental role would have been unlikely. In 1941 Wing, born in 1914, was an active member of the Kamloops Board of Trade; Shoyama, born in 1916, had graduated from the University of British Columbia with a degree in economics and commerce, but until fellow Japanese Canadians appointed him editor of their newspaper in Vancouver he had worked as a labourer in a pulp mill.

In 1941 neither Wing nor Shoyama could have worked on a government contract or crown land or practised as a lawyer, pharmacist, or accountant. Many barriers, legal or customary, barred their entry to other occupations. Moreover, neither man could have voted, let alone held public office. The reasons were simple: Wing's ancestors had emigrated from China, Shoyama's from Japan, and both lived in British Columbia. There was no chance that any relatives from China might join the Wing family in Kamloops because of the exclusionary Chinese Immigration Act of 1923, and it was unlikely for the Shoyama family because of the strict limits of the Gentlemen's Agreement between Canada and Japan. By 1941 there was some acceptance of the Chinese in British Columbia, as shown by Wing's membership in the Board of Trade, but after the attack on Pearl Harbor, suspicions of the loyalties of all Japanese in the province escalated, and they were soon ordered to move at least 100 miles inland. Shoyama went with his newspaper, the *New Canadian,* to Kaslo, British Columbia. Until after the Second World War, people of Asian descent lacked the franchise and many other civil rights in British Columbia, the province where most of them lived. How and why the status of Wing and Shoyama changed, and how citizenship triumphed over "racist" ideas, constitute the subject of this book.

Like the two previous titles in this trilogy, this volume emphasizes politics and public opinion.[2] The earlier books, *A White Man's Province: British Columbia Politicians and Chinese and Japanese Immigrants, 1858-1914,* and *The Oriental Question: Consolidating a White Man's Province, 1914-41,* traced the history of discriminatory laws and how politicians fomented and exploited the prejudices of British Columbians. Those books showed that hostility to Asians in British Columbia – and in Canada generally – had multiple causes and that, while many arguments applied to both Chinese and Japanese, British Columbians also distinguished between them. The story of the easing of hostility and the gradual inclusion of Chinese and Japanese into full Canadian society was equally complex.

Objections to both Asian groups began largely as a complaint against "cheap labour" that allegedly undercut white wages, took jobs from white women and men, and did not contribute to the growth of the local economy. Given the notions of "race" that prevailed in the nineteenth century and well into the twentieth century, another objection to Asians was based on the notion that they were inassimilable. That word had several meanings; it could refer to miscegenation – a concept that was as repugnant to most Chinese and Japanese as it was to Caucasians – or to a perceived failure of Asians to adapt to Canadian customs. The latter aspect of the inassimilability argument applied particularly to the Chinese. Because of Chinese migration customs, the head tax imposed on Chinese immigrants between 1886 and 1923, and exclusion from then to 1947, few Chinese established families in Canada. Many sent significant portions of their earnings to families in China and lived in crowded and allegedly unsanitary Chinatowns. Their white critics claimed that they did not contribute to the development of British Columbia and to Canada generally and endangered public health and morality. Given the absence of family life, it is not surprising that some Chinese found companionship in gambling dens or solace through opium. Not only did Caucasians regard both habits as immoral, but they also feared that corrupt Chinese might spread the drug habit to vulnerable young whites, especially young women who would resort to prostitution to support their addictions. The lack of Chinese women also meant that the Chinese population began to decline in the 1920s since few Chinese were born in Canada and older men died or returned to China. Since Western nations regarded China as a populous but weak state with little ability to protect its emigrants, Canada could unilaterally impose immigration barriers on the Chinese.

The same widely held Canadian fear that impelled these immigration policies – that the Chinese by their sheer numbers could overwhelm white society – also applied to the Japanese. Canada, however, saw Japan as a powerful nation and sometime ally that would effectively protest any challenge to its status or insult to its people. Thus, Canada limited, but did not halt, Japanese immigration by diplomatic means. Until its revisions in the 1920s, the

Gentlemen's Agreement negotiated in 1907 placed few restrictions on female immigrants. The Japanese could form families. Japanese women took pride in keeping their children and homes clean, tidy, and moral, so complaints about the Japanese threatening the physical or moral health of Caucasians were rare. By the 1930s a generation of Canadian-born and -educated Japanese, the Nisei, had reached their majority and sought reversal of an 1895 amendment to the British Columbia Registration of Voters Act that added Japanese to Chinese and Native Indians as those who were disfranchised. Since the federal government relied on provincial voters' qualifications, these groups were also disfranchised federally. The Nisei campaign for full citizenship gained some sympathy, but the strength of Japan that had led Canada to treat it diplomatically in immigration matters redounded to the disadvantage of Japanese Canadians as Japan extended its search for a Greater East Asia Co-Prosperity Sphere in the 1930s. Many British Columbians ceased to distinguish among the Canadian-born naturalized Canadians of Japanese origin, Japanese nationals, and the government of Japan. By 1938 war scares were endemic: rumours of illegal Japanese immigration and Japanese plans for sabotage circulated widely, and Canadian government officials warned of riots against Japanese Canadians in the case of war.

This volume is organized in both a chronological and a thematic manner. Because most experiences of the Chinese and Japanese were different, they are generally treated separately. The book begins with the outbreak of the Pacific War on 7 December 1941. Following the shock of Japan's attack on Pearl Harbor and the rapid advance of its military juggernaut southward through Asia, as Chapter 1 documents, panicky British Columbians demanded the removal of all Japanese from the coast. Due to the anti-Japanese propaganda that had long emanated from the coast and because of the war, as Chapter 2 shows, British Columbia's interior and the other provinces were generally reluctant to accept Japanese Canadian relocatees except under strict conditions. In fact, the BC cry that "the east" did not understand its "Oriental problem" reflected ancient rhetoric more than reality. Although few other Canadians had much direct contact with Asians before the war, they shared many prejudices with British Columbians. They readily accepted immigration restrictions, legislatures in Ontario and Saskatchewan tried to prevent Asians from employing white women, and Saskatchewan disfranchised Chinese. By 1941 almost half the Chinese in Canada lived elsewhere than British Columbia but were scattered. Most cities had small Chinatowns, and handfuls of Chinese lived in small towns, especially in the Prairie provinces. Outside British Columbia, however, only Toronto and Montreal, Canada's two largest cities, had more than 1,000 Chinese residents each. In 1941, in contrast, 22,096 of the 23,149 Japanese in Canada resided in British Columbia, and almost all were at the coast.[3]

Because of the war and the government's plan to disperse the Japanese, a provincial question became a national one. Yet after initial hostility, the Alberta, Manitoba, and Ontario communities and the city of Montreal that received the relocated Japanese found them to be good citizens and worthy additions to their populations. As Chapter 3 demonstrates, despite opposition in British Columbia to their return, the revulsion of many Canadians to forcing Canadian citizens of Japanese ancestry to go to Japan after the war stimulated interest in human rights and the value and rights of Canadian citizenship. One of the most telling arguments against "repatriating" Japanese to Japan was its implication for Canadian citizenship since so many had been born in Canada.[4]

The war that brought such upheavals to the Japanese increased the sympathy that other Canadians felt toward China and the Chinese. Since the outbreak of the Sino-Japanese War in 1937, Canadians contributed, for example, to Chinese War Relief. That support continued throughout the war. Meanwhile, the Chinese in Canada bought Victory Bonds, donated money to the Red Cross, and worked in the munitions industry. A few were able to join the armed forces. And despite some concern in British Columbia about the implications for enfranchisement, the army in 1944 began to call up Chinese Canadian men in eligible age groups for military service. The gradual inclusion that led to enfranchisement in British Columbia and the repeal of the exclusionary Chinese Immigration Act in 1947 is described in Chapter 4.

Canada's experience from 1941 to 1967 illustrates how racist ideas can change. In the early 1940s, few Canadians questioned the removal of Japanese Canadians from the coast, the disposal of their property, and the involuntary dispersal throughout the country of those who did not accept "repatriation." Late in the war other Canadians began to pay attention to the civil disabilities imposed on the Chinese, especially their inability to bring wives and children to Canada. With little fuss, British Columbia repealed most of its discriminatory laws and practices affecting the Chinese by 1947; that year Canada repealed the exclusionary Chinese Immigration Act, though it was little more than a token gesture. With memories of the war still fresh in many minds, however, Japanese Canadians, for reasons explained in Chapter 5, had to wait until 1949 to return freely to the coast and enjoy basic civil rights such as the franchise. Even then they did not receive adequate compensation for their wartime property losses. By then Asians within Canada had the same civil and political rights as any other Canadians except in matters of immigration. Gaining equality in that department was a slow process, but as described in Chapters 6 and 7 respectively the Japanese and Chinese communities used their newly acquired political voices to help replace a Canadian immigration policy that depended largely on country of origin with one that privileged skills and the ability of an individual to contribute to Canada. Together the last three chapters show how the Chinese and Japanese who were once excluded gained inclusion as full Canadian citizens.

The reasons for this change vary and, like the reasons for the original antipathy toward Asians, were multifaceted or intertwined. Some years ago in "British Columbia's Fear of Asians, 1900-1950," I argued that "the feelings of insecurity and inferiority underlying the assorted anti-Asian arguments" could be listed under headings such as "the challenge to morality, overwhelming numbers, the Japanese military threat, 'unfair' economic competition, and, especially, inassimilability."[5] By the time the Pacific War broke out, British Columbians had for the most part, except for the external threat from Japan, overcome those fears through legislation and practices that regulated morality, the labour market, and immigration. By the summer of 1945, a badly beaten Japan was no longer a military threat; once it regained its independence, it was a demilitarized ally and an important trading partner.

The concept of inassimilability was still alive in 1941 but gradually disappeared. Chinese Canadians by their contributions to Canada's war effort and Japanese Canadians by their determined loyalty to Canada despite the harsh treatment inflicted on them proved that they were good, loyal Canadians. Dispersal – whether voluntary in the case of the Chinese or enforced in the case of the Japanese – eased pressure points in coastal British Columbia. Moreover, in their day-to-day encounters with Caucasians in many parts of the country, the Chinese and Japanese demonstrated that they were capable of being full, contributing members of Canadian society. The atmosphere for including them in the Canadian polity was eased by the revulsion that the Western world had developed to racist ideas, the growing appreciation of the importance of human rights, and the pride of Canadians in their new citizenship. Thus, people who were once excluded could be included.

That openness of spirit, however, did not immediately extend to potential immigrants from Asia; old fears that their countless numbers could overwhelm Canada revived after the war. Both Japanese and Chinese Canadians had to exercise their new political rights and, in association with sympathetic Caucasians, lobby for changes in immigration laws to permit family reunification. Although made easier by the fact that the Chinese voters were a factor in several federal constituencies, it was a long process. In the meantime, some Chinese resorted to creating fraudulent documents and "paper families" to circumvent the law. By the 1960s, a prosperous and confident Canada could afford to be generous. After permitting illegal Chinese immigrants to "adjust" their status, Canada undertook a general review of its immigration policy and in 1967 removed its racial barriers. Now Asians who had once been excluded could, if they had the necessary skills, be included as Canadians.

These changes were part of a sea change in Canadian attitudes that had been developing for some decades but whose denouement was accelerated by the Second World War. That change can be seen in the greater concern for the collectivity of Canadians as demonstrated by the introduction of a variety of new social security measures, including unemployment insurance, the family allowance, the universal old age pension, and the beginnings of medicare. In addition Canadians relaxed many of their ideas about morality, easing liquor laws in many provinces and allowing gambling. They once regarded gambling as an immoral habit and cited the proclivity to play games of chance as a reason for halting Chinese immigration; by the 1960s, governments were sponsoring lotteries![6]

Constance Backhouse, a legal historian who defines the term "racism" as "the use of racial categories to create, explain, and perpetuate inequalities," argues that racism "remained hauntingly static."[7] For the years before the Second World War, the period on which her study concentrates, she is largely correct; however, as the waning of discrimination and the acceptance of Chinese and Japanese as full citizens after the war demonstrate, racism ceased to be static at least in these circumstances. Indeed, like others throughout the Western world, Canadians realized that "race" was a social construct rather than a biological fact. As historian James St.G. Walker observed, Canada saw "an apparent watershed, even a 'paradigm shift,' during and just after World War II."[8] This volume has many examples of how "race" or more specifically concepts of "race" were mutable. How else does one explain such diehard "racists" as H.H. Stevens appealing to Chinese voters or Halford Wilson working with the Chinese to preserve Vancouver's Chinatown from redevelopment? Or columnist and later politician Elmore Philpott describing the Japanese as potential fifth columnists in 1943 but championing their civil rights after the war or Victor Odlum, who ran (unsuccessfully) on a White Canada platform in the 1921 federal election, urging an end to Chinese exclusion in 1945 when he was Canada's ambassador to China?

Before the war ended, Canadians were questioning notions of racial superiority and expressing concern about the need to protect human rights. Asians, especially the Japanese, became the focus of this shift. Historian Ross Lambertson has shown how the Co-Operative Committee on Japanese Canadians (CCJC), a group formed to assist Japanese Canadians resettle in Toronto, evolved to become "the first major human rights coalition of the immediate post-war period" and an exemplification of "the new interest in human rights that was emerging out of the struggle against totalitarianism."[9] In educating the public and the politicians, Canadian civil libertarians made good use of references to "universal human rights" in the Charter of the United Nations (1945) and the subsequent Universal Declaration of Human Rights (1948). The sentiment in those documents – that there were "fundamental human rights" – built on the Atlantic Charter that Prime Minister Winston Churchill and President Franklin D. Roosevelt issued in 1941. The Canadian government, though sympathetic to human rights, had problems with the Universal Declaration. Its concerns included the limited powers of federal states to deal with such matters, the tradition of relying on statute law and judicial interpretation rather than general declarations of principles, the lack of precision in the document, and the inclusion of economic and social rights in a document protecting political and civil rights. Nevertheless, Canada believed in its general principles and, facing the embarrassment of being grouped with Communist nations and some others with repressive regimes, did sign.[10]

While concern for human rights is an overarching theme in the story of changing Canadian attitudes to Asians, a strong economy and labour shortages rather than unemployment made it easier to accept Asians as equals. By the time the Pacific War began, the Canadian economy was generally operating at near-full capacity. Jobs were plentiful, and wages were good. Old arguments about "cheap Asian labour" no longer had any basis. In the immediate postwar years, despite some short-term unemployment as soldiers returned and industry converted to peacetime production and a continuation of some wartime economic controls, Canada as a whole prospered. Employment and the national income were at high levels. The *Canada Year Book* described the 1.5 percent unemployment rate in 1947 as "close to an irreducible minimum." During the war, Canada had become highly industrialized; afterward, with wartime savings in their pockets, Canadians were keen to buy consumer goods that had been unavailable during the war or unaffordable during the Depression. In addition exports were high as Europe needed Canadian raw materials to rebuild its economy. The population was growing with the beginning of the "baby boom" and the resumption of immigration, mainly from Britain and continental Europe. Indeed, when the press criticized immigration policy, it was to complain that the government was not doing enough to bring in new immigrants, but it insisted on a selective policy. Canadians wanted to choose their immigrants, though as described in Chapters 6 and 7 the public and many elected politicians were more willing than the officials in the Department of Immigration to include Asians.[11] The campaigns for a relaxation of immigration laws and against Japanese repatriation nicely illustrate how governments respond to public pressure. Indeed, the interplay between elected politicians and the public and between the government and its civil service advisers is a secondary theme throughout this volume.

Historiography, Sources, and Nomenclature

Historiographically, this volume breaks new ground in that it brings the stories of both the Chinese and the Japanese and of both the war and the postwar periods between a single set of covers. Several scholars have examined the wartime experiences of the Japanese. The first book-length study, *The Canadian Japanese and World War II: A Sociological and Psychological Account* by sociologist Forrest E. La Violette, was based largely on readings of the public press and observations of the Japanese community itself.[12] As Japanese Canadians concentrated on re-establishing themselves, their wartime story faded from public memory. The BC centennial of 1958 encouraged the national Japanese Canadian Citizens Association (JCCA) to sponsor the writing of a history of the Japanese in Canada. The association commissioned Ken Adachi, a journalist, to write it and sent him across Canada to interview Japanese Canadians. The process was time consuming, and funding was often a problem, so the book did not appear until 1976. Relying almost entirely on interviews and published sources, Adachi produced what is still the definitive history of the Japanese in Canada.

A few years later a young scholar, Ann Gomer Sunahara, intrigued by the reasons for the removal of her husband's family from British Columbia to Ontario, delved into the rich resources of the National Archives of Canada to produce *The Politics of Racism: The Uprooting of Japanese Canadians during the Second World War.* Her work gained more than scholarly attention since the JCCA relied to a large extent on her research to document its case for what became the successful campaign for redress. Although his main interest was the prewar period, W. Peter Ward included a chapter on the Japanese evacuation in *White Canada Forever: Popular Attitudes and Public Policy toward Orientals in British Columbia.* The first edition had only a brief overview of the postwar era; the second has a short preface further analyzing that period. His conclusions are not dissimilar from mine. Several works on the Redress Movement, of which the most important is Roy Miki's *Redress: Inside the Japanese Canadian Call for Justice,* include some historical background.[13]

In collaboration with two scholars from Japan, Masako Iino and Hiroko Takamura, and Canadian historian J.L. Granatstein, I was one of the authors of *Mutual Hostages: Canadians and Japanese during the Second World War.* Although that book describes the rising hysteria in British Columbia immediately after the attack on Pearl Harbor, some reviewers seem to have based their comments on an earlier article by Granatstein that they interpreted as suggesting that there were doubts about the loyalties of Japanese Canadians. It is true that Canadian officials had limited knowledge of the Japanese in Canada, but the police and military were quite convinced that by interning fewer than forty Japanese nationals immediately after Pearl Harbor they had put everyone of doubtful loyalty out of circulation. *Mutual Hostages* argued that the fear of physical attacks on the Japanese in Canada might have given the Japanese military an excuse to take reprisals against Canadian and British prisoners of war and, that this concern, rather than doubts about the loyalty of Japanese Canadians, explains the removal of the Japanese from the coast. That is also argued here.[14]

Readers seeking a detailed study of the wartime experiences of the Japanese in Canada here will be disappointed. Because those experiences have been well documented and memoirs continue to appear, Japanese "voices" appear only occasionally, but references appear at appropriate points. In the postwar era, when Japanese Canadians actively sought full civil rights and a relaxation of immigration restrictions, their voices became an important part of the story through important sources such as the *New Canadian* and the records of the JCCA and related organizations.

Since the story of the Chinese is less well known, I have included as much English-language evidence of their views and actions as I have been able to find. Perhaps because their experience was less dramatic – though separation was painful for the Chinese men in Canada whose families were in China – the Chinese in Canada so far have been less well served by historians, though younger scholars such as Lisa Rose Mar are doing promising research. In *The Concubine's Children: Portrait of a Family Divided,* Denise Chong described her own family, which had members in both China and British Columbia. Both historian Anthony Chan and sociologist Peter Li have written brief overviews that are strongest on the prewar and post-1967 years. Several prominent members of Vancouver's Chinese community produced the most thorough overview, *From China to Canada: A History of the Chinese Communities in Canada,* under the editorship of Edgar Wickberg. It focuses on organizations within Canadian Chinese communities. Two historical geographers have also studied Chinatowns. David Chuenyan Lai has examined the physical features of a number of Chinatowns within Canada; Kay Anderson, who has a strong theoretical bent, has written a well-researched study of how outsiders saw Vancouver's Chinatown. In *The Chinese in Vancouver, 1945-80: The Pursuit of Identity and Power,* Wing Chung Ng used Chinese- and English-language sources in a study of the internal politics of Vancouver's Chinese community in the postwar years. A more popular history is Paul Yee's *Saltwater City: An Illustrated History of the Chinese in Vancouver.*[15]

As Ng's work demonstrates, it is wrong to assume, as Caucasians often did, that the Chinese community thought as one. While Caucasians tended to think of Foon Sien, who made many pilgrimages to Ottawa in search of a relaxation of immigration laws, as the chief spokesman for Chinese in Canada, within his own community he was controversial. Some of this internal division appears in Chapter 7 in the discussion of Douglas Jung's political career, but a study of the internal politics of the Chinese communities in Canada would require another book or books. Similarly, Caucasians erroneously saw the Japanese Canadian community as monolithic and failed to distinguish between those who were legally, though not necessarily intellectually, enemy aliens and those who were proud Canadian citizens. Moreover, there were social and economic divisions within Japanese Canadian communities, but that too is the subject for another study.

In the earlier volumes, I drew heavily on newspapers as a source of public opinion. While editorials represent only the opinions of the editor and publisher, most newspapers want to stay in business and are unlikely to offend large segments of their potential readership. Whether the newspapers made or reflected public opinion is, of course, a moot point, but in some cases the influence seems to be clear. The liberal *Toronto Daily Star* and the *Winnipeg*

Free Press, for example, probably deserve considerable credit for generating opposition to the postwar "repatriation" of Japanese Canadians, and Foon Sien suggested that only after Canadian newspapers and periodicals "took up the struggle" did the campaign for the repeal of the exclusionary Chinese Immigration Act go well. At the same time, in expressing opposition to the return of the Japanese Canadians to the Pacific coast, Vancouver and Victoria papers reflected public opinion. Yet we must also remember that in the first weeks after Pearl Harbor the public paid scant attention to their calls to "keep calm." The fact that many people wrote letters to the editors, however, suggests that they believed the press did influence opinion.[16]

This time I have again drawn on the press, but because this volume deals with the Chinese and Japanese nationally rather than solely provincially I have had to sacrifice comprehensiveness of coverage in order to provide some regional breadth. In researching *A White Man's Province* and *The Oriental Question,* I was able to read most BC newspapers in their entirety. Most were weeklies, and many early ones were essentially advertising sheets with only a page or two of news and editorial comment. For this volume, and particularly after 1945 or so, I have relied largely on the major provincial dailies. That, however, is not the problem that it might appear to be. With better transportation, the metropolitan dailies circulated widely in the hinterland, and hinterland journals focused largely on purely local issues or merely carried wire service reports of national and international news. As for the press outside British Columbia, I have dipped into representative major newspapers at times when there was reason to believe that some issue relating to Chinese or Japanese Canadians would elicit a comment. I sampled the French-language press, but the few examples of opinion that I found tended to be similar to those in the English press.

As the notes reveal, I have benefited from the selected translations from Chinese-language newspapers, especially the *Chinese Times,* prepared by the team headed by Edgar Wickberg that did the research for *From China to Canada.* The Chinese Canadian Research Collection at Special Collections in the library at the University of British Columbia also includes transcripts of interviews, questionnaires, and translations of some other Chinese-language sources. The papers of Foon Sien, who long acted as a spokesman for Chinese Canadians, are also at UBC, but many of the boxes are filled with clippings and other printed matter available elsewhere.

Most of the records relating to Japanese Canadians apart from personal diaries, memoirs, and the like are in English. The *New Canadian,* which began as the Nisei newspaper, was published once or twice a week during the war, when it operated under censorship (the records of the press censor at Library and Archives Canada [LAC] are interesting in their own right) but was able to express editorial opinions and report the activities of Japanese Canadian organizations. It continued to publish for many years after the war.

The records of the JCCA located at LAC include some files from predecessor organizations and are especially strong on the post-1947 period. Because the files include correspondence as well as reports from its branches and records of conventions, they offer excellent insight into the Japanese Canadian community and clearly demonstrate divisions within it. The records of the CCJC and of F. Andrew Brewin at LAC supplement them.

As the notes indicate, this book also draws heavily on government records, the papers of politicians, and the files of various organizations. The published debates of the House of Commons and, to a lesser extent, the Senate are a very useful and easily accessible source of political opinion. Since provincial governments had relatively little to do with Asians or immigration, most of the relevant manuscripts are located in LAC. Before the day of the photocopier, the government used the mimeograph machine, copy typists, and carbon paper to generate copies of many of its documents. Thus, the same letter or report often appears in more than one collection, but usually I have provided only one citation.

Records of the federal government's major policy decisions, including some background information, can be found in the Records of the Privy Council Office, especially the Cabinet War Committee. For Japanese Canadians, the records of the Department of External Affairs are important since it coordinated many aspects of policy relating to their wartime and immediate postwar treatment. And because Prime Minister King was also the secretary of state for external affairs until 1947, much correspondence that passed through that department often also appears in his own papers. The day-to-day administration of matters relating to Japanese Canadians during the war and for several years after is recorded, sometimes in great detail, in the records of the relevant divisions of the Department of Labour, which took over the duties of the British Columbia Security Commission, the agency responsible for moving the Japanese from the coast. Information about external security during the war can be found in records of the Department of National Defence. The most concentrated collection of material opposed to the presence of Japanese Canadians in British Columbia is found in the papers of Ian Mackenzie, but there is material along the same lines in the Halford D. Wilson papers at the British Columbia Archives and the Howard Green papers at the City of Vancouver Archives.

Immigration policy and practice are recorded in the files of the Department of Citizenship and Immigration and its predecessor, the Department of Immigration. Unfortunately, because of privacy legislation, many of the files listed in the Finding Aids are not open, but the file titles suggest that many of these are individual cases. General policy and practice can be discerned from the open files. Departmental records can be supplemented by the papers of several cabinet ministers responsible for immigration (J.W. Pickersgill, Ellen Fairclough, and E. Davie Fulton) and especially those of

Prime Ministers W.L. Mackenzie King, John Diefenbaker, and Lester B. Pearson. These papers, along with those of leaders of opposition parties such as John Bracken and M.J. Coldwell, often include letters from constituents with opinions on policy generally and occasionally poignant concerns about individual would-be immigrants. The Louis St. Laurent papers are disappointingly thin both for the period of his prime ministership and for his earlier career as minister of justice and secretary of state for external affairs. Despite the wealth of documentary material, historians have only begun to scratch the surface of the many aspects of the fascinating subject of immigration policy.

Increasingly, scholars have used the Japanese word *Nikkei* to refer to the Japanese people collectively whether they be of the immigrant generation (Issei) or Canadian born (Nisei), Japanese nationals, or Canadian citizens. During the war and immediate postwar years, the common term was simply "Japanese" or more pejoratively "Jap," a favourite term of headline writers, without regard to birthplace or national status.[17] Unless context makes such distinctions necessary, I have often simply used the word *Japanese*. Throughout the war years, the removal of the Japanese from the coast was referred to as an "evacuation," and this term is still in common usage. Like others, Roy Miki has noted that it was a euphemism. He is partially correct; the Canadian government did not expect to return Japanese Canadians to the West Coast after the danger had passed; however, as Chapter 1 argues, the term was correct in the sense that Japanese Canadians were being removed from potential danger. That danger, of course, was not an external military threat but the fear that frightened and angry white British Columbians might violently attack Japanese Canadians and their property. I have generally used the terms "evacuation" and "evacuee" for the war years and "relocation" and "relocatee" for the postwar years. By 1945, when it seemed to be unlikely that the Japanese would be permitted to return to the coast, "evacuation" and "evacuee" were no longer appropriate terms, though contemporaries did not always appreciate that. The word *internment* has been loosely used; even the formal apology of the Canadian government to Japanese Canadians in 1988 referred to their "internment." In fact, only about 800 men were interned because, in a few cases, the Canadian government had reason to suspect their loyalty to Canada and more commonly because they refused to co-operate with the evacuation process to protest the breakup of family groups.[18]

The apology and redress payments to Japanese Canadians in 1988 and to Chinese head tax payers in 2006 epitomize the theme of this volume. From 1942 to 1949, Canada excluded Japanese Canadians from coastal British Columbia, and excluded Chinese immigrants from 1923 to 1947. How these once-excluded peoples were gradually included in the Canadian polity demonstrates the triumph of citizenship.

1

A Civil Necessity: The Decision to Evacuate

> It is going to be a very great problem to move the Japanese and particularly to deal with the ones who are naturalized Canadians or Canadian born. There is every possibility of riots. Once that occurs, there will be repercussions in the Far East against our own prisoners. Public prejudice is so strong in B.C. that it is going to be difficult to control the situation.
>
> W.L.M. King, Diary, 19 February 1942

That comment of Prime Minister Mackenzie King followed Japan's surprise attack on Pearl Harbor and quick military successes in Asia, which stimulated white British Columbians' long-standing fears of Japanese aggression. Within days of that observation, King's government ordered all people of Japanese ancestry, including those born in Canada, to leave the coast of British Columbia. In 1947, in its final report on the re-establishment of Japanese in Canada, the Department of Labour attributed "the decision to evacuate persons of the Japanese race from the coastal areas of British Columbia" to "considerations of military necessity." "Military grounds" were also the official reason Canada gave to Spain, the protecting power for Japan's interests in Canada. That interpretation persisted. In 1961, Louis St. Laurent, who had been justice minister in 1942, claimed that there was reason to fear that Japanese forces might try to land on the BC coast and doubt about the "loyalty of persons of Japanese descent in B.C."[1]

The explanation was deceptive; military authorities did not demand the removal of *all* Japanese from the coast. The chiefs of staff in late February 1942 did not consider an invasion from the Pacific "a practicable operation of war," though raids or bombing attacks "to contain North American forces in America" were possible. They made no mention of the Japanese in British Columbia, though the Joint Services Committee, Pacific Coast Command, was anxious to remove Japanese men from certain defence areas, namely Ucluelet-Tofino, Prince Rupert-Skeena River, the Queen Charlotte Islands, and Quatsino Sound. Many civilians appreciated that moving the Japanese was not a military necessity. In mid-February 1942, the Vancouver *Daily Province* frankly conceded that "a good deal of the agitation for the removal of the Japanese had nothing whatever to do with the war or the necessities of defence, but was promoted by agencies that had political axes to grind or selfish interests to serve." Given the nervousness of coastal British Columbians about a possible Japanese attack, especially after the fall of Singapore, their long-standing suspicions of the Japanese, complaints of economic competition, and the vociferousness of the province's politicians, Prime Minister King had reason to fear trouble. His government ordered the evacuation of *all* Japanese not for any real military reason but to prevent a greater evil, hysterical attacks on Japanese residents of coastal British Columbia. Of that likelihood, there was ample evidence.[2]

On 6 December 1941, the *Trail Daily Times* asked rhetorically, "how will Canada react to the war in the Pacific which now seems inevitable?" Japan's bombing of Pearl Harbor was a shock but not a surprise. After discussing the wording of the order in council declaring war on Japan, the Cabinet War Committee considered the "desirability" of "counselling against any anti-Japanese demonstration in B.C." and, in line with a recommendation of the Special Committee on Orientals in British Columbia (the committee, set up in 1940, was composed of Ottawa-based officials), expressed its belief in the loyalty of the Japanese in British Columbia. General K.C. Stuart, chief of the general staff, assured cabinet that coastal defences were in order and that the RCMP had the situation "in good control." The original plan was to ask Premier T.D. Pattullo to warn British Columbians of the danger of "irresponsible anti-Japanese demonstrations," but Pattullo was in the process of resigning, so the Cabinet War Committee decided not to send a message to him. Despite his lame duck status, Pattullo issued a press release about Japan's "treacherous surprise attack" and exhorted British Columbians to "completely defeat the enemy abroad" and co-operate with the authorities to defend "our country." It said nothing of Japanese Canadians. Similarly, in a fifteen-minute-long speech that was broadcast in both Canada and the United States on 8 December, King stressed Canadian co-operation with Britain, the Commonwealth, and the United States. His only mention of the Japanese in Canada was to the effect that "competent authorities are satisfied [that the] security situation is well in hand and are confident of the correct and loyal behaviour of Canadian residents of Japanese origin." He noted that the Japanese had been registered and fingerprinted and the "dangerous" ones interned. As for Japanese nationals and those naturalized after 1922, he said that, like Germans and Italians, they would be required to report regularly to the RCMP. He made no special mention of the Canadian born.[3]

More calming was RCMP Commissioner S.T. Wood, who broadcast a plea to British Columbians to treat local Japanese with "courtesy and fair play." To reassure the public, the RCMP publicized the detention of thirty-one "Japanese nationals who had been previously listed as potentially dangerous." Wood reported that, despite thorough investigations, the RCMP had found no evidence of subversive activity among Japanese in British Columbia who could not be blamed for the war. Following advice from the Standing Committee on Orientals[4] that "over enthusiastic or irresponsible Occidentals" might cause disturbances, the RCMP encouraged Japanese-language schools and newspapers to close lest their existence cause "suspicion and irritation" among people unable to read or speak that language. When the press implied that the government had ordered the closures, the white population seemed to be pleased. The Standing Committee's most sweeping recommendation was to immobilize the Japanese fishing fleet. The navy began doing this on 8 December. Cecil E. Hill, in charge of the RCMP in British Columbia, believed that this action had avoided a "public uproar" and protected the BC coast from small boats that "were undoubtedly a menace."[5]

On 12 December, Hill reported that "public reaction" had not "crystallized," but despite police patrols in Vancouver and New Westminster "alarmed" Japanese feared "irresponsible Occidentals." Apart from a brick thrown through the window of a West End store and a blazing oil-soaked rag tossed into a boarding house on Powell Street, there was no violence. Mayor J.W. Cornett urged citizens "to keep their feet on the ground"; General R.O. Alexander took the emergency calmly and assured Ottawa that "his forces were not 'panicky.'" Japanese Canadians publicly reaffirmed their loyalty to Canada, but the Okanagan resident who said "pretty soon this will be all Japan" undercut their work. He was fined $200 and jailed for two months under the Defence of Canada Regulations for uttering statements likely to be prejudicial to His Majesty.[6]

Much of the press heeded the censor's request to "do nothing to promote over-excitement." All three Vancouver dailies urged readers to "Be Calm!"; they recognized that most local Japanese residents were Canadians and were not responsible for the actions of Japan, and warned of the dangers of "hot-headed activity of a minority among the Japanese and among our own people." Under the headline "Show Them Consideration," the Vancouver *Daily Province* stressed that "our quarrel is with Japan, not with Japanese nationals here or people of Japanese blood," and it urged people to "abide by the law." The *Federationist,* the CCF paper and the voice of the BC Federation of Labour, admonished that "encouraging racial or color prejudice or ... vandalism of any kind" would hinder the war effort. Outside Vancouver, the *Comox District Free Press* urged "Let's Keep Our Heads" and let the authorities, not "rash souls," take any necessary action against local Japanese who had no part in starting "such an unprovoked war." When the postmaster at Oliver said that the arrival of two Japanese families affronted "our long standing policy of no Orientals," the *Vernon News* hoped that "none of the hatred for their Imperial cousins will be visited on these hardworking, industrious people." Kelowna's acting mayor, O.L. Jones, was confident that the 332 local law-abiding Japanese would enjoy the benefits of British justice. The *Kelowna Courier* urged, "let them alone, give them a little sympathy, and let the police handle the bad actors whom undoubtedly they are watching closely."[7]

Japanophobes, however, did not distinguish between Japanese Canadians and the government of Japan. Thus they interpreted assertions that "*most* local Japanese were loyal to Canada" as implying that some might not be. That theme ran through newspapers from Prince Rupert to Penticton. The *Nanaimo Free Press* hoped that the loyalty of the Nisei, the Canadian-born Japanese, would be "equal to the strain." Other editors did not give Japanese Canadians the benefit of the doubt. The *Kamloops Sentinel* asserted that "any representative of a nation that would act as Japan has acted in relation to the United States is not to be trusted; not at any price." The *Ladysmith Chronicle* hoped that "the horror of war may clear the air ... by sending these to the third and fourth generation back to the Japanese gardens where they can do least harm." Mincing no words, the *Creston Review* admitted that interior residents had had "very little contact with these apes [who are] ... sly, treacherous, dishonest, and hate white men." More politely, the *Victoria Daily Times* declared that Japan's recent "treachery" meant that the Canadian government must "re-examine the status of all Japanese in this country." Apart from warning of incendiary bombs, its local rival, the *Daily Colonist,* said nothing on the Japanese until late December.[8]

Efforts to assure British Columbians that police and the military had the situation in hand were thwarted on 8 December when Western Air Command warned of surprise Japanese attacks "directed by lights." As one of his last acts as premier, Pattullo announced an indefinite blackout. Radio stations went off the air at 5:30 p.m., night shifts were cancelled, air raid wardens went to their posts, and householders scrambled to buy blackout curtains, plywood, flashlights, and candles. In Prince Rupert, it was said that nearly fifty enemy planes had been seen near San Francisco, but a story that nearby Sitka, Alaska, had been bombed was quickly denied. Mayor Andrew McGavin of Victoria announced that "the Japanese are reported off the Aleutian Islands. We expect them here any time. The situation is very grave." G.W. McPherson, who arrived in Vancouver on 10 December to act as custodian of Japanese property, found that the blackout had caused more concern about an "immediate attack" than the presence of Japanese. The censor blamed emphasis on an "imminent" air raid for the "jittery state." Nevertheless, the next morning a resident recalled that "the sun came up to find us all intact and unmolested, but panic did not diminish immediately."[9]

On 10 December, on request of the provincial police, the federal government declared the "entire province" a vulnerable area. Ian Mackenzie, the only BC member of the federal cabinet, told the new premier, John Hart, that areas around Prince Rupert, Vancouver, and Vancouver Island south of Port Alberni were "in greatest hazard," but the whole coast and much of southern British Columbia east to Fernie was "liable to a lesser degree to enemy attack." That was worrisome given the state of defences. G.G. McGeer (Liberal MP, Vancouver-Burrard) facetiously suggested that, knowing there were no air raid defences, the Japanese were unlikely to raid "at night when they could do so with much more safety in the daytime."[10]

A few days later, while inspecting Pacific coast defences, General Stuart told the press that an invasion was an "extremely remote" possibility and that his forces could cope with "hit and run" attacks. Those calming words were overshadowed when the naval provost marshal at Halifax said, "the impossible has happened too often in this war to consider a Japanese invasion of the west coast of Canada impossible." Mayor Cornett and Vancouver's ARP (air raid protection) committee sought federal funds to plan the evacuation of civilians and the care of bombing victims. The censor suppressed such stories as tending "to nervousness, in some cases frenzy, and toward mass hysteria." The *Vancouver Sun* called for co-ordinated efforts to arrange emergency shelters and sandbagging but saw "wholesale evacuation, or a desertion of our cities and countryside," as "a miserable, contemptible theory." Well inland, residents of Prince George and Kamloops complained of inadequate protection. In Prince Rupert, the most exposed city, the *Daily News* concluded, "military and naval authorities are fully entitled to warn" civilians of an imminent attack on the Pacific Northwest. The next day it published a full page of photographs of Canada's Pacific coast defences.[11]

Many worried about local Japanese acting as fifth columnists. R.H.B. Ker, a prominent Victoria businessman, complained, "we can't trust these yellow devils one foot ... they ought to be behind barbed wire ... in a place where they can do no harm." As a postscript, he added, "we must purge this country of all Japs after we have won the war!" A Vancouver school principal advised the prime minister that the Japanese "are not thinking or working for Canada ... They are not to be trusted." Letters to the editor included an almost daily dose of suggestions about fifth columnists. The false claim of US Secretary of the Navy F.A. Knox that "the most effective fifth column work of the entire war was done in Hawaii, with the possible exception of Norway," reinforced the idea. A few British Columbians proposed repatriating all Japanese who were registered with the Japanese consulate; others proposed interning all Japanese or at least strictly supervising their activities or shipping them to Ontario and Quebec for the duration of the conflict. McPherson reported "a rather explosive situation as between the Japs and the whites" and thought even "reasonable thinkers ... generally feel that the security of the Province is in grave danger from a fifth column." One Vancouver resident claimed that

80 percent of the people wanted the "immediate internment of all Japanese nationals" and warned that, "when Hong Kong falls, or we lose any big battles or if Japanese bombers ever come over B.C.," there "will certainly be rioting and bloodshed in Vancouver." The head of the Pitt Meadows ARP wrote of "courting disaster" by not dealing with "the internal Jap situation." Saying that it was impossible to distinguish between loyal and disloyal, he proposed interning all adult males, with the "repatriation of all" as the final goal.[12]

General Alexander informed the Joint Services Committee, Pacific Coast, of growing demands for interning "the entire Japanese-born community" and the "obvious" "dangers of such agitation." He asked F.J. Hume, chairman of the Standing Committee, "to explain the situation" and seek the co-operation of Vancouver newspapers. Hume privately told the prime minister that Japan's military successes "inflamed public opinion against the local Japanese" and that "a very small local incident" could cause "most unfortunate conditions between the whites and Japanese." In a joint press release, the Standing Committee, army, navy, and RCMP said that they had taken "adequate measures" such as closing Japanese-language schools and newspapers, registering Japanese, restricting the movement of Japanese nationals, and immobilizing the fishing fleet. The Canadian Broadcasting Corporation (CBC) advised radio stations that the Japanese "have so far proved themselves to be loyal Canadian citizens" and that "inflammatory statements in regard to them are not in the general interest."[13]

The press garbled the joint statement and gave it little prominence. Not all editors were convinced that the situation was in hand. The Victoria *Daily Colonist* observed Japanese nationals with short wave radios; the *Chilliwack Progress* noted that countries that had "been over-run by Axis gangsters felt the same way about their security until it was too late." Possibly because the Standing Committee approached them directly, the Vancouver papers counselled against violence. The Vancouver *Daily Province* agreed with the difficulty of forgiving fifth column work at Pearl Harbor, in Thailand, and in Malaya or the Nazi-like methods of the Japanese government, but it agreed that it was "neither logical nor wise to indulge in the same resentment" against the local Japanese. The *Vancouver Sun,* sensibly observing that putting 23,000 people behind barbed wire would require "colossal" effort and expense, advised against interning Japanese who "behaved well." It repeated advice "to be calm" and warned that "violence ... will be repaid by worse measures applied to our own people in Japanese prisons." Jack Scott of the Vancouver *News-Herald* urged treating local Japanese with intelligence, not hatred.[14]

After Hong Kong fell on Christmas Day, the public needed more assurance. Having been told that Hong Kong could be defended for months, the *Victoria Daily Times* asked if there were sufficient defences to "discourage the common enemy from an attack on say, Victoria, Prince Rupert, Vancouver,

New Westminster, or even on such communities as Kamloops and Nelson." The Vancouver *News-Herald* reprinted a Dr. Seuss cartoon that had originally appeared in New York's *PM*. It showed a long line of stereotypical Japanese coming down the coast from Washington and Oregon to California, where another stereotyped Japanese, complete with buck teeth and round eyeglasses, was standing at a counter handing out packages of TNT. Over his head was a sign reading "Honorable 5th Column," and on top of his little warehouse another Japanese looked out over the ocean with a spyglass. The *News-Herald* added its own caption: "B.C. Is Further North…" Mackenzie reported "restlessness and disquiet" and "a feeling" that the government was "not taking a sufficient interest in this problem." Howard Green, the Conservative MP for Vancouver South, told his father at Kaslo, "I am getting hotter under the collar every day about Canada's attitude to this Pacific war – by the time I reach Ottawa I will have a sizzling speech under my belt. We are sitting here like a lot of pheasants the day before the hunting season opens." News of a Japanese naval attack on five ships off the California coast compounded fears.[15]

Military and police officials thought that the situation was "well in hand" but worried about "the danger of serious anti-Japanese outbreaks by the white population." On 30 December, General Alexander noted that "public feeling is becoming very insistent, especially in Vancouver." He cited letters to the editors, individuals – "both calm and hysterical" – who were bombarding him to do something, and conversations with Premier Hart and Lieutenant Colonel A.W. Sparling of the Standing Committee. More ominously, Alexander noted that planned "public demonstrations and street parades against the Japanese" could "lead to very serious inter-racial clashes involving considerable damage, bloodshed and possibly fatal casualties." Recognizing the need to treat local Japanese humanely and "in conformity with the Geneva Convention" and to protect Canadian prisoners of war, he urged interning Japanese males between the ages of eighteen and forty-five, removing them from the coast, and organizing them for paid employment on public works or similar projects. In the meantime, he arranged for a mobile reserve and for troops to assist the police if needed to protect "the Japanese against those who wish to do them violence." Because he could not protect Japanese in isolated places, he endorsed the recommendation of the commanding officer, Pacific coast, to remove all Japanese from the Queen Charlotte Islands. Premier Hart concurred and wired Prime Minister King about a "very serious" situation. H.L. Keenleyside, the Department of External Affairs specialist on the Japanese Canadian situation, feared "public demonstrations against the Japanese" in Vancouver and asked the chief of the general staff to instruct Alexander to co-operate with the police to make "absolutely certain" that no such demonstrations developed.[16]

While the military was concerned mainly about the Vancouver area, the

RCMP on Vancouver Island predicted "very strong demands ... for the complete internment of all Japanese, irrespective of their place of birth." Although only slightly more than 1,000 Japanese lived on southern Vancouver Island, and only 275 were in greater Victoria, that city's residents believed that geography made them especially vulnerable. Moreover, many British expatriates in Asia sent their children to boarding schools on the island and, since the Sino-Japanese war, often sent their wives. Others, retired in the area, claimed special knowledge of Asian affairs and had time to write letters. A legislative reporter observed, "the war has come so close to Victoria, there's a new rumour about submarines, air planes or sabotage every day."[17]

After hearing a suggestion that 5,000 enemy troops might attack British Columbia, the Victoria Kiwanis club circulated a resolution to other service clubs, public bodies, and the government. It cited old stories of fishermen being Japanese naval officers, fifth column activities at Pearl Harbor and in the South Pacific, the likelihood of local Japanese aiding invaders, the danger of sabotage, and difficulties in distinguishing "between the loyal and disloyal" among "people who have recently given ample demonstration of their treachery and deceit." The Kiwanians claimed that the only way "to overcome the menace" was "to intern the entire Japanese population of British Columbia ... preferably east of the Rockies, where it would be impossible for them to engage in fifth column activity." In a slightly less sweeping manner, Esquimalt Municipal Council called for interning "all enemy aliens, especially the Japanese population of the coastal regions." Other organizations on southern Vancouver Island, including the Native Sons of British Columbia, the Native Sons of Canada, Oak Bay and James Bay ARP wardens, Britannia Branch No. 7, the Canadian Legion, the Saanich Board of Trade, the Capital City Commercial Club, Saanich Conservatives, the Victoria Rotary Club, and the Local Council of Women, demanded the removal of all Japanese from the coast, interning or placing them in protective custody and in some cases removing them from Canada after the war. In Duncan, the Legion, Elks, and Rotary Clubs sent wires to Prime Minister King. At a mass meeting sponsored by the Chamber of Commerce, 250 people demanded the immediate removal of all Japanese. The *Ladysmith Chronicle* warned that, if they were not moved to inland provinces under supervision, wartime conditions might "arouse greater prejudice against Japanese in B.C. and lead to attacks against them."[18]

Both Victoria daily newspapers published letters to the editor favouring the removal of Japanese from the coast. Editorially, the *Victoria Daily Times* questioned the state of coastal defences and warned of sabotage. Columnist Elmore Philpott suggested that forest fires made great "potential opportunities for fifth column sabotage." H.T. Matson of the Victoria *Daily Colonist* avoided "taking much of an editorial stand" because "it would not require much to detonate a physical explosion against local Japs." Nevertheless, his paper asserted that after Pearl Harbor, Thailand, and Hong Kong "it would be folly to leave free and untrammelled in a vital defence zone those who, though friendly enough on the surface, may in fact be enemy aliens under orders to create mischief." The *Daily Colonist* urged "decisive action now." Major General E.C. Ashton, retired chief of the general staff, who lived in Victoria, told Minister of Defence J.L. Ralston, "men who know the Japanese" said that they could probably raise 6,000 or 7,000 trained fighting men from among the Japanese born. "This," he said, "is a real fifth column." R.W. Mayhew, the Liberal MP for Victoria, recommended moving "all Japanese except Canadian born to the interior of the province [and] giving them work to support their families." King agreed that "their own safety as well as ours is at stake."[19]

Few voices spoke for the innocent Japanese. Nellie McClung, an author and well-known social reformer, who lived in Victoria, wrote in the *Victoria Daily Times* that "all precautions must be taken ... but we must not sink into Hitler's ways of punishing innocent people, just because we do not like their country." Similarly, the student newspaper at the University of British Columbia asked, "we don't like Jew-baiters and Jew-baiting. When did Jap-baiting become patriotism?" The *Peace River Block News*, the only BC newspaper published east of the Rockies, insisted on turning "the full fury of Canada ... against the Japanese Empire" but warned that "it is just as important we keep our heads and not unjustly hurt innocent people." These were voices in the wilderness.[20]

While fears of fifth column activity inspired demands for the removal of the Japanese from the coast, an immediate concern was the fate of Japanese fishermen, whose approximately 1,200 vessels had been tied up. Security considerations neatly dovetailed with old desires of white and Native fishermen to be free of Japanese competition. If the government was so sure of their loyalty, A.W. Neill (independent, Comox-Alberni) facetiously asked, why was it necessary to take the "really rather drastic" step of tying up their boats? Neill was not disappointed; he only wished that "it had been in the middle of the fishing season!" The winter fishery was limited, so there was time to consider means of supplying the British Ministry of Food and providing a livelihood for the fishermen. After initially warning that white or Indian fishermen could not take up the slack, particularly in the shrimp fishery and salmon gill netting of the very productive Japanese, local fisheries department officials reported that apart from some temporary disorganization the departure of the Japanese would not cause serious difficulties. The executive of the British Columbia Fishermen's Protective Association, an organization of gill netters, recommended that its members refuse to fish if Japanese were allowed to do so. Saying that reissuing licences to Japanese "would seriously endanger the safety of the Canadian people," the United Fishermen's Federal Union proposed making Japanese boats available to experienced white or

Native fishermen. The Fishermen's Protective Association suggested that, if its members could buy Japanese fishing equipment, they, along with Indian fishermen and men who had left the industry because it was overcrowded, could pick up the slack. The *Fisherman,* a Communist newspaper that spoke for several unions, denounced racial prejudice and violence but demanded removing the Japanese from fortified areas, cancelling their fishing licences for the duration of the war, and making their vessels and gear available to white fishermen. Similar representations by other fishermen's unions led General Alexander to accuse them of seizing "an opportunity ... to secure absolute monopoly of the fishing industry." That too was the observation of a Ladner pioneer, who recalled that "the greatest clamor" for removing the Japanese came from those who wanted the competition out and who "had covetous intentions toward the equipment of their hated rivals." The fishermen were not alone in wanting the Japanese out of the industry. Saying that they must be removed to avoid opportunities for treachery, Alan Chambers (Liberal MP, Nanaimo) asserted that it was time to ensure that the Japanese "be forever excluded from the woods and mills, the farms and from industries" to make places for returning veterans. Inland, the *Penticton Herald* mused, "it would be marvellous ... if the Oriental fishing population could be replaced by men of our own color and heart."[21]

The decision to remove Japanese Canadians from the fisheries was well received for relieving "any temptation" to assist Japan. Indeed, it was one of the rare occasions when fishermen and canners agreed. The Fisheries Institute of British Columbia, representing over 90 percent of the canners and packers, denied asking for their return. So too did H.R. MacMillan, the president of BC Packers. Richard Bell-Irving, a prominent canner, privately said that losing an "efficient fishing fleet" was a "blessing in disguise since the Japanese were becoming more independent each year," and their absence would give white and Indian fishermen a larger share of the catch. Similarly, George Anderson, secretary of the Halibut Fishermen's Association at Prince Rupert, retailed old stories of Japanese fishermen being naval officers in disguise and warned that they would be a serious postwar problem. The Native Brotherhood there complained of Japanese at coastal canneries endangering the industry and "our Native people." When a rumour circulated that Ottawa might let some return, F.J. Hume reported "a state of uneasiness," the Vancouver *Daily Province* warned that feelings "might easily get out of hand," and a fishermen's union predicted "a Hell of a row." Police discouraged the United Fishermen's Federal Union from holding a meeting at Vancouver lest it lead to "precipitous action," but an RCMP special patrol of Steveston saw no evidence of disturbances. The Vancouver Zone Council of the Canadian Legion studied ways of using the Japanese fishing fleet to rehabilitate veterans of both world wars. Alderman Halford D. Wilson tried to abet the agitation, but the censors hindered him.[22]

Advised of "the need to humour the white population until such time as they calm down a bit," General Stuart recommended against letting Japanese return to the fisheries. Although the military had plans to aid the civil power in case of emergency, like General Alexander, Stuart worried about "protecting the Japs against an unruly faction of the white population." Perhaps to assuage such sentiments, the press published photographs of masses of Japanese fishing vessels tied up "somewhere" on the BC coast. Meanwhile, J.A. Motherwell, the chief supervisor of fisheries in British Columbia, announced that he would issue fishing licences only to whites and Indians until further notice.[23]

Japanese fishermen had lost their livelihoods. Provincial police feared that rumours their boats might be transferred to whites would "not tend to harmonious conditions" among 1,500 unemployed Japanese at Steveston, where the situation was "delicate." The Vancouver *Daily Province* and the *Vancouver Sun* urged Ottawa to find other employment for them. Most members of the Standing Committee favoured selling Japanese equipment to white fishermen but saw a serious unemployment problem after Japanese discharged from employment because of "public indignation" moved to Vancouver and New Westminster, where "public resentment" was greatest. The committee suggested putting all male Japanese aged eighteen to forty-five in "volunteer" work units inland, where they could "further our War Effort" by work such as building air raid shelters and the Hope-Princeton road.[24]

Fearful of displaced fishermen taking up farming, white Fraser Valley farmers sought legislation to prevent Japanese from buying or renting more farmland or buying or renting crops. They said nothing of fifth columnists but rehearsed an old claim that Japanese "peaceful penetration of farming and other primary industries plus the raising of large families constitutes a serious political, economic and social menace to this country." Several municipal councils and boards of trade endorsed the resolution, but the attorney general said that such a law would be *ultra vires*. Nevertheless, many saw the war as a way to end Japanese competition and solve the "Asiatic problem." The *Langley Advance* honestly admitted that many who demanded the removal of the Japanese were "not so much interested in a military sense as they are in getting rid of Japanese competition from commercial and agricultural ranks." The Prince Rupert *Evening Empire* observed, "whites cannot compete with them." In the roundup of the fishing fleet, it saw a loosening of "the roots of Japanese penetration." At a mass meeting in Duncan, C.F. Davie, a former Conservative MLA, referred to the Japanese "saturation" of lumbering and fishing; another speaker suggested that "loyal Canadians" could "remedy their infiltration" of industry by refusing to employ or work with Japanese. A plea by Dr. W.B. Clayton for "British justice" for local Japanese who had done nothing wrong elicited a strong attack; his argument that Germans had not been interned drew a telling shout, "but they're white."[25]

Dr. Clayton was one of the few to question removing the Japanese. Another was the *Federationist*. Its first editorial after Pearl Harbor referred to the Japanese as economic competitors but concluded that removing "low standard groups" would not end unemployment, bring social security, or "necessarily bring us closer to the co-operative commonwealth." It soon changed its mind, endorsed interning Japanese nationals and individuals of doubtful loyalty, and urged watchfulness for possible fifth columnists. Yet it stressed that the Canadian born "deserve more consideration, if not different treatment," and the necessity of remembering that "we are fighting against racial persecution." Similarly, delegates to the International Woodworkers of America (IWA) convention in Vancouver approved essential defence measures but warned against "racial prejudice and mass hysteria." Individually, many labour leaders favoured removing the Japanese to prevent fifth column activity. Harold J. Pritchett, president of the IWA, wanted to evacuate all Japanese but claimed that doing so didn't "mean embarking on a policy of racial hatred, or opening the way to anti-Japanese riots." At a CCF-sponsored conference of trade unions associated with both the rival American Federation of Labor and the Canadian Congress of Labour, delegates decided not to debate the Japanese question, but they represented only a small portion of British Columbia's labour force.[26]

In the meantime, H.F. Angus, a University of British Columbia professor of economics and political science and a prewar champion of the enfranchisement of the Canadian-born Japanese who was temporarily working for the Department of External Affairs, worried about retaining the goodwill of the Japanese. He proposed inviting Hume and provincial government representatives to a conference in Ottawa to discuss problems arising from the presence of "Canadians of Japanese race and resident Japanese nationals" and the "particularly urgent" question of fishermen. F.J. Mead of the RCMP suggested including MacGregor Macintosh, who for some years had claimed that the Japanese were taking over British Columbia, to avoid giving "Jap-baiters" an excuse to criticize the government. The government hoped to formulate "a definite policy" that all would co-operate to implement. The invitation was issued on 3 January; the next day Sparling, Hume, and Macintosh of the Standing Committee, T.W.S. Parsons of the Provincial Police, Jack Barnes of the RCMP, and George Pearson, provincial secretary and minister of labour, boarded a Canadian Pacific Railway train in Vancouver. Hume, Pearson, and Barnes had at least one formal meeting on the train, but the four-day-long journey undoubtedly provided occasions for informal discussions.[27]

By then the fisheries were a secondary consideration. A trickle of resolutions calling for interning all Japanese began in Victoria and became a flood from individuals, veterans' organizations, service clubs, and municipal councils in the Vancouver Island communities of Nanaimo, Duncan, Courtenay, Ladysmith, and Alberni. Despite espousing "the apparent truth that many Japanese in British Columbia dislike the conduct of the men of Tokyo as much as we detest it," the *Victoria Daily Times* refused to believe that the government proposed "to wait until a few railway bridges, a few power plants, a few water systems, have been destroyed before they are convinced these Japanese – or at least some of them – are actual enemies in our midst." Vancouver Island weeklies reported "definite uneasiness" over Ottawa's handling of the situation, distrust of the Japanese, and inability to distinguish between those who were loyal to Canada and those who were not. "The innocent," conceded the *Cowichan Leader,* "have to suffer with the guilty." The Japanese "may be all right," said Alderman W.T. Grieves of Nanaimo, "but we do not know. It is our duty to adopt 'safety first.'" The military was also concerned. Air Commodore L.F. Stevenson, in charge of Western Air Command based at Victoria, agreed with popular sentiment that "our national security cannot rest on precarious discernment between those who would actively support Japan and those who might at present be apathetic." He recommended moving "all male Axis Aliens between 16 and 50 years" from the coast and interning them or keeping them "under careful surveillance." In the meantime, Hume announced that the Standing Committee would urge removing "all male Japs" between ages eighteen and forty-five and disposing of the fishing fleet. Hume and Sparling added to apprehension when their comment that several hundred Japanese fled during registration was interpreted to mean that Keenleyside's 1938 report on illegal immigration was based on false information.[28]

Not all British Columbians believed RCMP assurances that the Japanese had surrendered their guns and had nothing "much stronger than a peashooter." Commissioner Hill informed his superiors that the Standing Committee's discussions with businessmen, canners, and fishermen revealed "unanimous sentiment" that the government should take "strong action" immediately, that the Occidental population thought that it had "reason to fear the Japanese, and the Military authorities, for your confidential information, admit that in the event of an attack here, they would be unable to handle the large number of local Japanese should those Japanese assist the enemy."[29]

Mayhew was less pessimistic. After discussions with Mackenzie in Ottawa, he told the press that the government had taken "very definite safety measures," which could not be disclosed for security reasons. Explaining the need to consider "our own security" and "the safety of the loyal Japanese," Mayhew suggested letting Canadian-born Japanese men prove their citizenship by joining the Canadian army for training and service in eastern Canada. He would send the rest "far inland ... where they would not be a problem in case of an attempted invasion" and "could be properly protected" while doing useful work such as road construction. Despite its Liberal leanings, the *Victoria Daily Times* disagreed. It argued that "the comparative handful of Japanese who might be trusted to wear His Majesty's uniform would not be worth one-tenth of the risk involved by their recruitment." Reporting the Japanese atrocities in British Malaya, it thought that it would be "kind to the [BC] Japs by segregating them on sensible lines" to ensure their safety and "decent treatment under the circumstances."[30]

Both major Vancouver newspapers worried about sabotage but considered the internment of *all* Japanese to be an unnecessarily strong measure. The *Daily Province* would accept the word of those who said they were loyal to Canada but insisted on protecting vulnerable points against sabotage. The *Vancouver Sun* agreed that the Japanese must not be "treated harshly or unkindly" because many Canadians were in Japanese hands but deemed it impossible to separate the loyal from the disloyal. The censor kept the papers on a short leash and quashed plans of both dailies to gather more stories for "'steam-ups' on the Jap situation." Yet the *Vancouver Sun* repeatedly called for removing all male Japanese at least 100 miles inland "for their own protection and for the future goodwill of the Japanese colony here." Asserting that the "beastly nature" and shocking "treachery of Pearl Harbor and the Manila murders" had "prejudiced the case of hard-working, right-living Japanese everywhere in the world," it warned that local Japanese would "be suspected and distrusted if hit-and-run forces of the enemy" ever assaulted the city. It attacked the *New Canadian,* the English-language newspaper published by Japanese Canadians, for "sneering" at jitters after Pearl Harbor. Similarly, the New Westminster *British Columbian* recommended moving Japanese inland to prevent fifth column activity in case of an air attack and "a popular outburst" that would be a "blot on Canada's record." The next day it cynically responded to comments from Ottawa that moving the Japanese east of the Rockies was "silly" by averring that Ottawa was unlikely to "welcome an opportunity to make a close acquaintance with the little brown brother."[31]

Meanwhile, Alderman Wilson, who had campaigned against potential Japanese fifth columnists since at least the spring of 1940 but who had been fairly quiet since Pearl Harbor, reappeared even though the censor considered him "a menace, a nuisance and a pest." A syndicated Ottawa columnist reported that the mildest description of him was a "thoroughly bad influence" whose agitation might incite anti-Japanese riots and put "a mess on our hands." Wilson had two proposals. Varying an old theme, he proposed requiring Japanese to show evidence of renunciation of their Japanese citizenship before they could get trade licences. The city's legal advisers said that the Defence of Canada Regulations gave enemy aliens the protection of the law. Citing Knox's allegations of fifth column activities in Hawaii, Wilson planned to ask city council to demand the removal of all Japanese east of the Rockies. His "fans" encouraged him with comments such as "when the Japs begin their sabotage all that needs to be done is to start a fire in one of their own yards to sweep everything along the water front." Because it added little new "fuel to the rising anti-Japanese sentiment of this coast," the censor let the Vancouver *Daily Province* report Wilson's proposal. In supporting Wilson, Alderman Jack Price suggested that the Japanese should welcome a move for their own protection, for "if a bomb dropped here there is no telling what might happen."[32]

Despite dismissing Ottawa's disapproval of his campaign lest it incite "anti-Japanese riots," Wilson realized that he had little sympathy from the press, and most city councillors thought it "presumptuous" to interfere while Ottawa considered the matter. Thus, he proposed to introduce only a notice of motion but, "yielding ... to pressure of public opinion," sought immediate passage of a motion to remove Japanese to work camps east of the Rockies. Mayor Cornett asked citizens "to refrain from 'rabble-rousing'" and to deal with the situation "calmly and judiciously." Cornett anticipated problems; a week earlier he had reminded Justice Minister Louis St. Laurent that "ambitious politicians" had "fanned" anti-Japanese sentiment. Seeking an indication of government policy, he warned that "a good many serious thinking citizens have sensed a potential danger here as Japan's ambitions grew." Since he was waiting for a reply when Wilson introduced his motion, Cornett "smothered" it procedurally. Buoyed by supportive phone calls and telegrams, as members of the Standing Committee left for Ottawa, a dauntless Wilson told them that a mass meeting was being organized and that "if something isn't done there are going to be riots." Wilson was not alone in warning of riots, though others blamed him for the situation. Ira Dilworth, the BC representative on the CBC, worried that by setting "themselves at the head of movements to take direct action" Wilson, Macintosh, and their like were endangering "the whole constitutional framework of our State." "I shudder to think," he told Angus, "what might happen" if there were "bad news concerning the Pacific situation." Grey Turgeon (Liberal MP, Cariboo) confidentially advised the prime minister that, without "drastic action, the situation will get out-of-hand. The Government will suffer, and so will the Japanese personally and through destruction of property."[33]

Wilson was already organizing what was tentatively called the "Pacific Coast Defence League." Under the chairmanship of Tom Burnett of the Ex-Servicemen's League, it first met on 9 January. It planned a mass meeting to discuss resolutions for removing all Japanese from the coast, forming a home guard "to teach men street fighting and bush fighting," providing for unemployed whites "before we worry about the Japanese," and making "some adequate use" of idle Japanese fishing boats. Representatives of several unions of fishermen, truck and laundry drivers, civic employees and street railwaymen, the Canadian Legion, the Army and Navy Veterans, and "The Flying Column," a self-appointed defence group, allegedly attended. The committee was quite secretive, however, about its membership. Wilson told the meeting that "an expression of public feeling regarding the situation here will influence Ottawa in minimizing the claims of some members [presumably Angus] of the Standing Committee on Orientals now in Ottawa." Wilson called local Japanese a "potential reservoir of strength" for the enemy. He denied wanting "any mass hysteria or rabble-rousing," but Burnett told reporters that "perhaps it was time there was some of that." In fact, as Jack Scott of the Vancouver *News-Herald* revealed, only sixteen people attended the meeting, and the only one to speak from the audience, C. Wilmott Maddison, was best known for wearing a pith helmet! Maddison claimed that "the Japanese here were out to get him" because he had planned to write "an exposé of conditions" in Japan for *Maclean's* and *Liberty*. Scott noted that Maddison's writings were confined to his own local magazine, *The Parashooter*. The *News-Herald,* the only daily to comment on Wilson's scheme, warned against "private zealots" trying to solve the "Japanese problem" instead of leaving it to proper authorities such as the RCMP.[34]

Similarly, in commenting on rumours that Ottawa thought it too costly to move the Japanese, the Vancouver *Daily Province* advised letting military and naval authorities deal with local Japanese "unclouded by the performance of agencies who are riding the storm of public restlessness for their own selfish advantage." Writing from Ottawa, Bruce Hutchison, a Victoria-based reporter, argued that an "unofficial spokesman" who feared "anti-Japanese riots and bloodshed ... underestimates our intelligence. Anyone who would do violence to the Japanese of British Columbia is not only mad but criminal and should be locked up immediately." Nevertheless, he noted that, if there were 24,000 Germans in a small area on the Atlantic coast, Ottawa might not think British Columbians were "so crazy ... in asking that the male Japanese be moved quietly, without violence, without hardship, with courtesy and decency to some other part of the country where they can work for a living at reasonable wages and support families."[35]

In reporting the departure of members of the Standing Committee, the press indicated that the Ottawa meeting would deal with possible fifth column activities. It quoted Premier Hart as saying that he and Attorney General R.L. Maitland had urged Ottawa "to remove the menace of fifth column activity" and had met senior military officials. The press correctly reported that the federal government was investigating how the United States was coping with a similar problem, but reports were sketchy. The *Victoria Daily Times* said coastal states were strictly controlling Japanese; the Vancouver *Daily Province* reported that no large coastal city had urged a wholesale transfer of Japanese inland and that Seattle was tolerating them.[36]

On 8 January at 2:30 p.m. in Room 123 of the East Block in Ottawa, several federal cabinet ministers and officials from concerned federal departments met the Standing Committee and provincial government representatives.

Perhaps not so coincidentally, a number of the federal representatives were past or current residents of British Columbia.[37] Mackenzie opened the meeting by outlining "the peculiar position of the Japanese population in Canada," notably their concentration in one province close to a theatre of war and the apparent absence of any strong group among them opposed to the government of Japan. He described the tendency of Canadians to believe that their loyalties were racial. He admitted "intense economic jealousy of the Japanese, and a wish in some quarters to appropriate their property," and he noted their existing economic and political disabilities and the lack of a long-term policy on their future. Keenleyside then reviewed recent policies emphasizing "just and decent treatment for Canadians of Japanese race," including normal employment insofar as it was compatible with defence needs. He noted co-ordination with American policies, the importance of avoiding excuses for retaliation against Canadians under Japanese control, the desire to maintain "a reasonable attitude" among civilians," and the need to use "the full force of the law to prevent anti-Japanese demonstrations and to protect Japanese Canadian communities."[38]

The agenda provided time to discuss postwar problems, the position of Canadians of Chinese and East Indian descent, censorship, and ways of making the policies "known to the public of Canada in order to insure their intelligent co-operation." Those at the meeting accepted most of Keenleyside's principles but would not allow all Japanese to remain in their normal employment. For "reasons of national defence and security," they decided that the Japanese should not engage in the coastal fishery and that their boats and equipment should be made available, "on equitable terms," to white fishermen. Those at the meeting also agreed that the RCMP should strictly control the sale of gasoline and blasting powder to persons of Japanese racial origin and that Japanese nationals should be kept under surveillance and not be allowed to possess or use short wave radios, radio transmitters, or cameras. In a rare effort to distinguish between nationals of Japan and nationals of Canada, the meeting participants accepted offers from Canadian Japanese to perform wartime service. They suggested encouraging them to enlist in the Canadian army, calling up others under the National Resources Mobilization Act for service outside British Columbia, and forming a Civilian Corps to work on projects of national value, presumably in British Columbia since a suggestion that these projects be in central or eastern Canada was crossed out in the final draft.[39]

According to Mackenzie, "the real difference of opinion" arose over a proposal to remove all persons of Japanese origin, or at least males of military age, to areas east of the Rocky Mountains. Mackenzie estimated about 2,000 to 2,500 able-bodied adult males fell into this category. Calling the debate a "difference of opinion" was an understatement. General Pope recalled how Pearson, Hume, and several committee members were "breathing fire," and at one point "all hell broke loose." A "vitriolic" Pearson accused Keenleyside "of knowing nothing" about his "own province and of being uninterested in the fate of the people living in great danger there," even though Pearson, a family friend, knew that Keenleyside had many close relatives at the coast. Henry Angus admitted antagonizing some attendees by protesting the molestation of "Canadian citizens on grounds of race" but accepted any movement recommended by the military or police for security reasons. Escott Reid recollected "the physical presence of evil" as the British Columbians "spoke of the Japanese-Canadians in the way that the Nazis would have spoken about Jewish-Germans."[40]

Despite emphatic protests from Pearson and Hume, the majority decided that removing all persons of Japanese racial origin or at least males of military age from the coast was unnecessary for national defence and security, would contradict Allied professions of justice and humanity, would "be answered by vicious cruelties" on Canadians under Japan's control, and would be at variance with American policy. Mackenzie suggested that Pearson and Hume submit a minority report. He agreed on the difficulty of convincing British Columbians that there were no problems with defence and security; he favoured compelling Japanese nationals to move from the coast and giving them suitable employment in secure areas under surveillance. Giving more weight to the views of the British Columbians than to those of government officials, Mackenzie warned the prime minister, "unless we take immediate action, our white people may resort to unwise tactics in Vancouver." He urged the government to make its policy public. The prime minister endorsed restrictions on fishermen, believed that Japanese nationals "must be treated differently with no possibility of treachery," opposed enlisting any Japanese in the army, endorsed the Civilian Corps, and according to an unsigned note favoured "evacuation to points in the interior of Japanese Nationals (able-bodied)." Agreeing with the difficulty of dealing with a panicky and sceptical public, Angus suggested that King and a government spokesman speak to British Columbians over the radio, state the policy, and generally "convey the atmosphere of sober deliberation" at the meeting to "impart confidence and carry conviction." He thought that representatives of the Standing Committee, the Armed Services, and External Affairs should have "off-the-record" discussions with the press in Victoria, Vancouver, and Ottawa. The meeting participants accepted variations on these ideas, but the Prime Minister's Office rejected a radio talk.[41]

Without firm information, the press speculated about what had gone on. The Department of External Affairs promptly denied a press report by Charles Bishop that the meeting seemed to favour moving Japanese from the province, but the press got a good sense of the meeting. It reported that the BC representatives and the Ottawa officials disagreed on the danger but would recommend measures to guard against both "potential treachery by the few Japanese residents who may be inclined toward subversiveness" and "possible riots by civilians against Japanese nationals in case of an enemy air attack." It quoted Pearson as saying that British Columbians wanted "all Japanese moved well inland to prevent them from linking up with their countrymen in the event of a Japanese attack on the west coast."[42]

After the meeting, several participants spoke to the press. In a telephone interview from Ottawa, Hume refused to reveal details but said that the government had been very fair. Later in Vancouver he explained that hundreds of enemy aliens would be removed from the coast, while Canadian-born and naturalized Canadians could volunteer for works projects. He said that Ottawa accepted his committee's recommendations, and with Mackenzie's help the committee overcame "tremendous obstacles," including the failure of federal authorities to plan immediate action. In Victoria, Pearson emphasized the desire "to avoid compulsion in dealing with the Canadian-born Japanese," who "think Canada is a pretty good country and do not want Japan coming here to disturb things." Yet, he speculated, if Japanese forces landed, "it might be a different matter." He thought that Ottawa did not realize the seriousness of the situation but would act on military advice "as to what constitutes a military danger" and was "most anxious" to protect the Japanese "against any riots."[43]

By then the recommendations of the Ottawa conference were public knowledge. The press release had been delayed, possibly because of a two-day debate in cabinet in which Mackenzie believed "we went as far as we could possibly go in regard to the Japanese situation." Later King made some "slight changes in construction" in Keenleyside's draft press release. Significantly, he asked for "specific mention" of the "real danger of [the] situation being provoked by citizens other than Japanese," since such trouble would "be greatly exaggerated and misunderstood in Japan, where many Canadian soldiers and others are obliged to rely upon the protection of the Japanese Government." In slightly different words, the published press release noted, "the full force of the law will be invoked to prevent anti-Japanese demonstrations and to protect Canadian residents of Japanese race." It promised that there would be no action to give Japan an excuse to mistreat Canadians under its control. Anyone who read the entire press release, a rather long document that few papers published in full, would see the distinction between those Japanese who were Canadian nationals and those who were not, but an ambiguous reference to taking "utmost precautions ... to see that no illegal acts are committed by Japanese or other enemy aliens" was often misinterpreted.[44]

Premier Hart was satisfied with plans to deal with the "very disturbing situation." For most British Columbians, the main point was that "Japanese and other enemy aliens" would be removed from the defence areas. The phrasing was unfortunate. Although the Vancouver *Daily Province* congratulated the government for putting "a premium on Canadian citizenship," many British

Columbians regarded *all* Japanese, including the Canadian born, as "enemy aliens" or "Japanese nationals," and this view was reflected in press commentary. The *Vancouver Sun* commended the "common sense decision," but its praise seems to have been based on a faulty premise that all Japanese, except those granted police permits, would be removed from the coast. That also seemed to be the understanding of the *Victoria Daily Times,* which, in referring to hostages in Japanese hands, ominously added that "two can play at reprisals if need be." The *Comox Argus* urged "a long view" that a condition of peace with Japan be the exclusion of its nationals from British Columbia. Other editors were generally pleased but prophetically warned that "extremists, who were calling for immediate internment," would not be satisfied and expressed concern if Ottawa did not act promptly.[45]

No better evidence of that was Alderman Wilson. He doubted that the plan went "far enough" but claimed that making the coastal strip "a protected zone" would end anti-Japanese talk, satisfy public opinion, and cause the cancellation of a proposed mass meeting on exclusion. Wilson told city council that he would await clarification of Ottawa's policy before formally seeking support for a "campaign to induce the Dominion Government to exclude Japanese from British Columbia for all time, either under a redistribution of Nipponese among the various provinces, or repatriation to Japan." In the meantime, responding to the prime minister's desire to halt Wilson's "inflammatory statements," the censors prepared to impose "a fairly complete 'black-out'" on him.[46]

Wilson's proposal for postwar repatriation was extreme, but other politicians demanded the removal of all the Japanese from British Columbia. Provincial Conservatives in convention on 10 January resolved that the Japanese should be sent east of the Rocky Mountains to places where they would not be a danger and be given adequate maintenance. Delegates spoke of the imminent danger and of fifth column activities. J.A. Paton (Coalition-Conservative, Vancouver-Point Grey) said that high military authorities in Victoria wanted all Japanese removed from the coast; in the legislature, he urged the government to press Ottawa for their immediate removal "lock, stock and barrel" to a place where they could not act as fifth columnists in case of an attack. Retired Brigadier J. Sutherland Brown predicted that "every little slant-eyed Jap will wave the flag of the Rising Sun if his countrymen invade this coast."[47]

Such rabble rousing led the Vancouver *News-Herald* to impose an interregnum on the debate; its silence lasted two days. The Vancouver *Daily Province* attacked Howard Green, the association president, and Paton as "definitely discreditable." Green, however, sincerely believed what he said. A few days later, "very much concerned about the situation in the Pacific," he put "a great deal" of himself into a speech to the Ad and Sales Bureau of the Vancouver Board of Trade, where he declared that British Columbia "must take the lead in acquainting the rest of the Dominion of the deadly peril on the coast" and warned that, if potential fifth columnists were not removed, the province could become another Belgium. Green was making a political point, but he was genuinely frightened. He arranged railway passes for his family "just in case" and told his parents, "Each morning I wonder whether there has been a raid."[48]

Some Liberals agreed with these views. A few days later, referring to Okanagan demands that no coastal Japanese be allowed to stay there after the war, the *Vancouver Sun* averred, "our people will not again stand for Japanese domination in any industrial activity. The short-cut may be to send them all home after the war." Several Liberal associations in Vancouver suburbs wrote to Ian Mackenzie urging the removal of all the Japanese, including the Canadian born. North Burnaby Liberals favoured seizing their property but compensating them once they left the country. At a meeting of several Burnaby Liberal associations, Tom Reid (Liberal MP, New Westminster) claimed that there was "not a military secret on this coast the Japanese did not know" and proposed deporting all of them. Nanaimo Liberals unanimously endorsed Chambers' earlier demand for the "total exclusion" of Japanese from coastal waters, woods, mills, farms, and industries and the detention of all males of military age who were Japanese nationals. Mayhew told Victoria's Chamber of Commerce that he favoured more drastic steps than recommended by the committee but would "wait and see if that was a preliminary measure or a full control program." He privately advised Mackenzie of "every indication of organized effort on Vancouver Island opposing your Committee's action," including a proposal to boycott the Victory Loan to force the removal of all Japanese from the coast. That body was the Defence of Canada League, which Reginald Hayward, a former Victoria mayor and former Conservative MLA, explained was a 100 percent Canadian organization "composed of native born white Canadians." Citing Japanese knowledge of the coast and opportunities for sabotage, the league urged the government to remove all Japanese, the "Yellow Peril," from defence areas. Veterans' groups, the United Commercial Travellers, the Victoria Kinsmen Club, and others continued to demand the removal of all the Japanese. Individuals such as Ker congratulated Mackenzie on his success "so far" in clearing "from this coast ... all Japanese (and other enemy aliens as well) who might be potential fifth columnists should an attack occur from across the Pacific." The Vancouver *Daily Province* ominously cautioned, "the order about the local Japanese seems to have satisfied everybody – for the moment."[49]

"For the moment" was the operative phrase. After a brief decline in the number of letters to the editor and to Ottawa, disenchantment returned as the government seemed to do little to remove anyone. As historian Ken Adachi noted, the government did not follow up with any publicity to reassure the public. Ottawa correspondents could only speculate about government plans and the location of labour camps. At the coast, there was confusion. Members of the Standing Committee had been quoted as saying that the government did "not intend to force naturalized or Canadian born Japanese to move," but Pearson, in suggesting that "force" had a special meaning, implied that "all loyal Japanese will volunteer." No one would say what would happen to those who did not. Delay was inevitable. The government had no detailed plans, it did not know which department would be in charge, the extent of the "Protected Area" had not been defined, and the press release – the only written record of government policy – could be misinterpreted.[50]

The government's work was complicated by the petty concerns of some BC members of Parliament. A minor distraction was uncertainty over the future of the Standing Committee. Angus and Mead had resigned because of their duties in Ottawa, and the MPs, particularly Reid, were jealous of local references to "Mayor Hume's Standing Committee" and of Hume's alleged use of his work on the Standing Committee in a recent civic election.[51] Reid complained that he had been "kept entirely in the dark" about what was happening. He said that he had been "very discreet" and made no public statements after Japan entered the war, but Hume's activities had "somewhat undermined" him in the constituency. Describing what he must have considered the most heinous political crime, Reid suggested, "it would not surprise me if Mayor Hume accepted a C.C.F. nomination at the next election." Neill objected to the lack of restrictions on "the naturalized Jap [who] is often the most dangerous class" but seemed more angered by the fact that Angus, "a man whose violent and extreme pro-Japanese tendencies through long years have become a byword and reproach in the minds of 90 percent of the people of British Columbia," had signed the reply to his complaint. Moreover, Neill disputed Angus' assertion that Pearson and the Hume committee fully agreed with government policy. Mackenzie reported that the BC MPs were "very antagonistic" to the Standing Committee and to Hume, who had been "of no use" at the meeting of 8-9 January.[52]

After considering personnel changes,[53] the cabinet accepted Keenleyside's advice that, rather than debate the committee's membership and role, it should dissolve, explaining that the government had decided on its policy and was "taking over direct control of the situation." Two weeks passed before that decision was announced. No one much noticed the committee's demise, although the *New Canadian* thanked it for the "relatively orderly and smooth manner in which the problem is being solved, the absence to date of violent outbreaks of any kind." Hume graciously told the press, "we have done all we can do. I'm quite satisfied with the new arrangement provided they give us some action on our recommendations." Dissolving the Standing Committee assuaged backbenchers, but Mackenzie continued to propound their sentiments. After rejecting a suggestion to put Colonel B.R. Mullaly, a Japanese-speaking officer of the Canadian army, in charge of the Civilian Labour Corps, Mackenzie reminded civil servants that a cabinet committee of himself and the ministers of agriculture and labour must approve any policies and that the BC MPs must be informed of any changes.[54] These were procedural niceties; the real difficulty was Mackenzie's understanding that "all able-bodied, adult enemy aliens" and "all able-bodied Canadian Nationals" would be removed from the protected areas, although Canadian nationals could volunteer for the Civilian Corps. The civil servants recalled that no one, "not even Colonel Macgregor Macintosh," had suggested compulsion of Canadian nationals and that "a clear distinction" had been made between them and Japanese nationals. Keenleyside observed that, after the BC MPs returned to Ottawa, the belief developed "that all persons of Japanese racial origin are to be treated alike" and that Canadian nationals would be required to move. That, Keenleyside feared, could lead to pressure "to carry out a policy" that had been rejected since "compulsory deportation of Canadian nationals, based on the colour of their skins, would be used for propaganda" in Asia and might harm Canadian and British prisoners of Japan.[55]

A memorandum, probably drafted by Keenleyside and designed for distribution to the BC MPs, outlined the situation. It explained that responsibility for policy had been assigned to the Department of Labour and the actual placing of Japanese, German, and Italian nationals in suitable employment outside the defence area to the Unemployment Insurance Commission. The RCMP was notifying nationals who would be required to leave and was considering applications to remain from women, children, men over military age, and "special cases" who had good reason for remaining and posed no public danger. The government expected that movement would begin soon and would probably set a deadline of 1 April 1942 for departures. As for the Civilian Corps, plans were still being formed, but it expected to treat enlistment as a "patriotic act," that pay and allowances would, like those of the army, be sufficient for decent maintenance of dependants, though it might involve a "financial sacrifice," and that the work should relate directly to the war effort against Japan. The memo reported that the Japanese were "eager to co-operate" but wanted definite information and advice about subscribing to the war loan or conserving their cash for emergencies. It also noted that Japan, through the protecting power, had inquired about its nationals. Yet, the memo pointed out, much still had to be done to stress to the Japanese that "subject to military requirements" they, and their property and occupations, would be treated with justice. The memo advised that the prime consideration was destroying "the military power of Japan, Germany and Italy," that the Department of National Defence had not asked for the removal of "either Canadians of Japanese race or Japanese nationals," and that men were often of greatest use to the war effort by remaining in their normal employment or replacing someone serving in the Armed Forces. Moreover, the memo stressed, Canadians should not "display fear or anger" against the Japanese in Canada since Japan could easily interpret that as a "white" versus "Asiatic" conflict and use it for propaganda purposes in China and India and similarly that talk of "fear of reprisals" could make the Japanese feel that "protection against harsh treatment" lay not in "British tradition and Christian ethics" but in Japan's military strength.[56]

The memo was submitted to cabinet but apparently not to the BC MPs, who, Mackenzie reported, "seem to insist on the compulsory evacuation of Canadian nationals if they do not volunteer" and who thought that the wages offered in the Civilian Corps were too high. He warned that, if the prime minister did not have a "full and frank" conference with them, there could "be an unpleasant discussion" in Parliament. Mackenzie may have exaggerated their anger. In Parliament, the MPs had been silent except for two brief questions and had not protested the vague answers they got. Responding to Grote Stirling (Conservative, Yale) about the placement of Japanese labour in the interior and removing women and children, Mackenzie said, "that is not definitely determined." When Reid asked three days later about an official statement on the removal of the Japanese from the coast, the prime minister merely said that he would give a statement but did not know when.[57]

On the coast, however, federal officials reported a deteriorating situation. J.H. McVety, the regional superintendent for the Unemployment Insurance Commission, "heard certain threats and rumours" that if any part of the coast were bombed and lives lost "the vengeance of the population would be taken out on Japanese regardless of the category to which they belong." Thus, he warned, it might be necessary "to provide troops to protect Japanese from our own people. If the males are removed, the natural chivalry of our people, I think, would prevent attacks on the Japanese women and children." Major H.C. Bray, an intelligence officer with Pacific Command, reported that the "good effect" of the mid-January announcement about removing enemy aliens had "been more than counteracted by the fact that no further action appears to have been taken nor plans prepared." Moreover, he claimed that the Japanese were becoming insolent, that British Columbians were becoming "hysterical," and that the government intended to do nothing further. He reported a growing movement to withhold subscriptions to the coming Victory Loan "until such time as every Japanese irrespective of age, of sex or place of birth has been removed East of the Rockies." In passing the report to Minister of Labour Humphrey Mitchell, Minister of Defence J.L. Ralston said that he had "done all I can" by signing the order creating the protected areas, but physically moving the Japanese was up to the RCMP and the Department of Labour.[58]

Initially, there were so many proposals for employing Japanese that finding work was not a problem. One of the most bizarre was that of George Murray, former Liberal MLA for Lillooet, who would dress them in Native costumes and employ them as gardeners in provincial and national parks to serve as a tourist attraction. Most proposals were more realistic. The provincial government offered to find suitable public works projects but left open the question of who would pay for these projects. Interior communities promoted pet projects such as building or improving roads between Hope and Princeton, Terrace and Prince Rupert, Usk and Hazelton, Nelson and Nelway, Sicamous and Revelstoke, and Blue River and Valemont. So many Okanagan fruit growers wanted Japanese labour, the *Victoria Daily Times* observed, that "there aren't enough Japs to go 'round." That too was the conclusion of Angus, who thought that Ontario would take 2,000 farm workers and that "opportunities for normal employment [were] so great, the proposed Civilian Corps might be unnecessary."[59]

National magazines agreed that it was a national problem; British Columbia did need safeguards "against stabs in the back." Some eastern papers also expressed sympathy for British Columbia's demand that the Japanese be removed from the province. As well as almost daily front-page news of the war in the Pacific, they carried wire service stories of the situation in British Columbia and of the parliamentary speeches of BC MPs. The farther east, however, the fewer the stories. The *Halifax Herald* and the *Star,* the *Gazette,* and *Le Devoir* of Montreal, for example, had plenty of news on the Pacific War and, in the case of the *Gazette,* expressed concern about the vulnerability of the Pacific coast given the fall of Singapore but only scattered reports on British Columbia. Major dailies in Ottawa and Toronto had news reports and occasional editorials, though curiously, given its later interest in the matter, the only editorial comment in the *Toronto Daily Star* was a Les Callan cartoon depicting the "strategic withdrawal" of the Japanese from the coast. Editorially, the *Ottawa Journal,* the Toronto *Globe and Mail,* the *Saskatoon Star-Phoenix,* and others shared the view of the *Winnipeg Free Press* that precautions were necessary. After erroneous reports of fifth columnists in Hawaii and Asia, they commended the federal government for acting "to guard against potential fifth columnists" by making registration compulsory, incarcerating potential saboteurs, and rounding up the fishing fleet. Yet they also thought that the government should "not be too severe with the Japanese in general" since most Japanese in Canada were loyal to Canada. In commenting on the unwillingness of other provinces to accept the Japanese, the *Star-Phoenix* suggested that British Columbians were perhaps too alarmist in demanding the removal of the province's entire Japanese population.[60]

In any case, central and eastern Canada was no more amenable to accepting Japanese workers than the interior of British Columbia. Officials in Ottawa had hoped to send most Japanese nationals to Ontario to help solve an acute shortage of bush labour, but problems soon arose. Early in February, one lumber operator who was anxious for their labour cancelled the plan because

"Strategic Withdrawal to Prepared Positions," *Toronto Daily Star,* 21 January 1942. Les Callan, the *Toronto Star* cartoonist, was well aware of the situation in British Columbia as he had previously been the *Vancouver Sun*'s cartoonist. By permission of the *Toronto Star.*

the Ontario government warned him that he would lose its business if he employed Japanese. At the same time, Ontario's labour minister informed his federal counterpart that the provincial cabinet did not want any Japanese "brought in for any kind of work" under any "conditions or circumstances" and would not give any business to their employers. When the Department of Labour abruptly cancelled departure arrangements for a group of Japanese nationals, it cited "unforeseen difficulties with the lumber company." The Vancouver press variously interpreted that to mean logging camps no longer required workers or that problems had arisen with accommodation, but the truth soon came out. Keenleyside suspected Premier Mitchell Hepburn of making the decision as part of his campaign against Ottawa. Other provinces, though less belligerent, were also unwilling to accept Japanese. In Alberta, for example, the Medicine Hat City Council protested moving "enemy aliens from one part of Canada to another for employment in private industry."[61]

In commenting on this rejection, Attorney General R.L. Maitland drew on an ancient BC theme as he asserted, "Ottawa says that there is difficulty in getting other provinces to take Japanese from British Columbia … [since] we are at war; we are in the front line. It is not a question of who wants them or who does not. The Dominion Government must see that they are placed in safe areas as will assure the safety of this coast." Echoing that sentiment, the Vancouver *Daily Province* described the war as "the problem of all Canada" but admitted that other provinces were probably reluctant to take Japanese because of assertions by "the most vociferous of the agitators that once the Japanese were outside the province" they would not be allowed to return.[62]

Residents of British Columbia's interior were equally hostile to accepting Japanese. Okanagan residents resented the desire of those on the coast to be rid of the Japanese and often behaved much like people on the coast. Despite shortages of agricultural labour, few wanted to add to the local Japanese population of somewhat under 1,000. With rare exceptions, even those who wanted Japanese labour wanted it strictly controlled and only for the duration of the war. In the southern part of the valley, there was little debate. Oliver residents had long ago decided "No Japs." In Summerland, the Municipal Council, the Board of Trade, and the local branch of the British Columbia Fruit Growers Association (BCFGA) unanimously protested importing "any Japanese whatsoever into the Okanagan Valley" lest they infiltrate "into the Summerland district." Some mention was made of possible sabotage of fruit and vegetable crops, but the main objection was economic. Penticton Municipal Council utterly opposed "the mass importation of Japanese unless in the opinion of the federal government it is vitally necessary to the defence of Canada." At a public meeting, Mayor R.J. McDougall argued that if Japanese "must be brought in" they should not bring wives or families. Others suggested admitting them only under guard. The president of the Board of Trade warned that Japanese would want to stay and would, as in the Fraser Valley, "endanger our fruit growers' interests." The past president of the Junior Chamber of Commerce declared that nothing would stop them from buying land, settling permanently, and creating "a half-Jap community." Fearing the arrival "of Japanese who elsewhere by their economic standards and group solidarity have ousted all but themselves," the *Penticton Herald* agreed. A Penticton resident who took in a Japanese friend faced so much protest that he sent the friend away.[63]

Several hundred Japanese already lived on agricultural land around Kelowna. When fruit and vegetable growers said that they could employ about 1,200 Japanese labourers, the Board of Trade invited service clubs and the Canadian

Legion to join it in sending a telegram to Ottawa demanding that evacuees be kept in "concentration camps" and let out to work seasonally only under "strict police supervision." As in Penticton, there was concern that once in the Okanagan they would remain there. Kelowna City Council unanimously opposed their entry. At nearby Winfield, a public meeting was 100 percent in favour of not bringing in Japanese from the coast. By early February, as some "well-dressed and educated young Japanese" drove into the district in "large, private automobiles" and sought information about buying land, Kelowna residents feared that it would be "extremely difficult to prevent a substantial influx." The Board of Trade urged the prime minister to "take immediate action to prevent Japs settling here to forestall any possible unfortunate action by resentful citizens." Kelowna City Council warned of violence and asked other municipalities to sign a demand that all male Japanese of military age be interned, that Japanese be prohibited from purchasing, leasing, or renting land or other real estate, and that evacuees be strictly supervised. As for demands from Vancouver that the Japanese be moved east of the Cascades, the *Kelowna Courier* asked, do coast people "not care what happens to the rich Interior country as long as the Japanese are moved out and kept out of the coast area?" As for the eastern provinces that would not accept the Japanese, it asked, "are we part of Canada?" Kelowna lawyers, like Penticton realtors, promised not to help the Japanese acquire land.[64]

In the Vernon area, where some Japanese had long resided, opinion was divided. The *Vernon News* deplored using the war as an excuse "to put these unfortunate peoples to work" on projects designed to help develop certain areas and to interfere with their contributions to growing food for Britain. Later it admitted that Okanagan residents did not necessarily agree, but reminded them that Canada professed "British ideals of freedom, tolerance, and personal liberty," that precautions were necessary, but that persecution must be avoided. Members of the Vernon Board of Trade were somewhat ambivalent about evacuee labour, but the executive and some prominent growers sought Japanese labour "under guard" for agricultural work and construction projects such as the Monashee road. When some city councillors opposed bringing in Japanese under any circumstances, Vernon City Council adopted a compromise accepting Japanese only for highway work and under military supervision. The Okanagan Municipal Association noted that the valley already had "too great a percentage" of Japanese and asked the government to stop their infiltration and enact laws, retroactive to 7 December 1941, preventing them from buying, renting, or leasing land or crops. Possibly as a sop to those who wanted roads or agricultural labour, it suggested that "a properly controlled evacuation" under military supervision for useful work in less dangerous areas would "cause local indignation to subside." Ottawa was already moving to restrict the acquisition of land by Japanese.[65]

While urban residents did not want more Japanese in the valley, vegetable

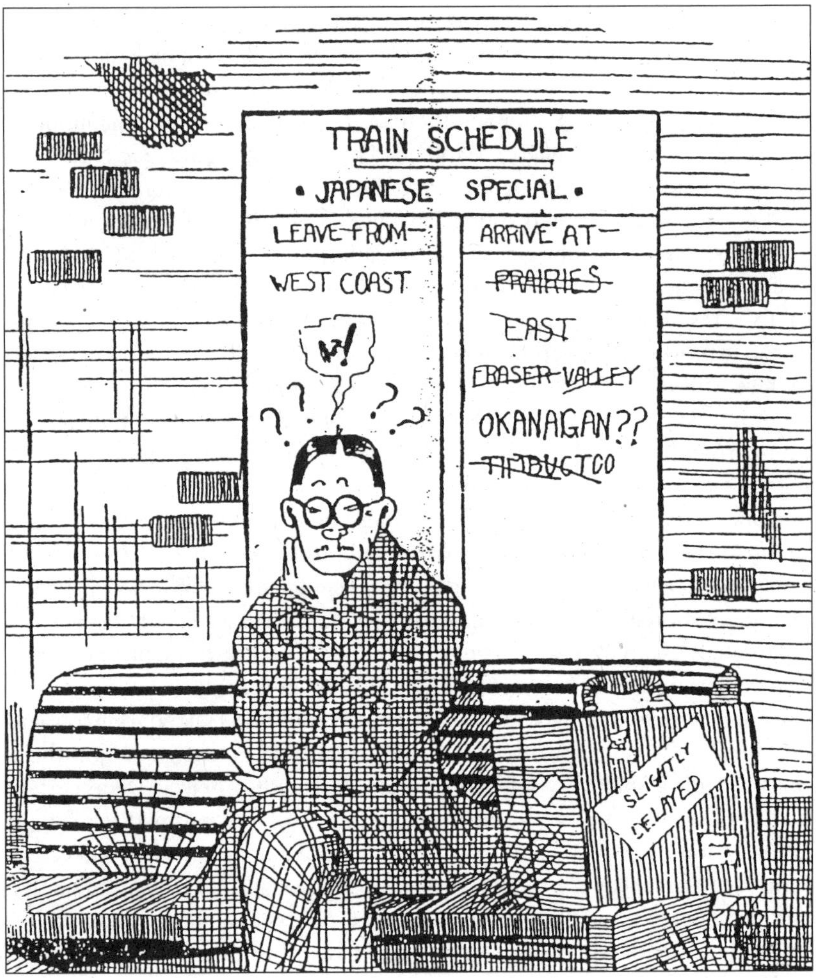

"When Does the Train Leave?" *Vernon News*, 29 January 1942. At the time this cartoon was drawn by an unknown artist, only adult male Japanese nationals had been told to leave coastal British Columbia. Finding destinations for them delayed their departure.

growers complained that townspeople and small orchardists were stirring up the issue without solving a labour shortage. Many fruit growers also needed labour, but southern delegates at the BCFGA convention generally opposed the use of Japanese labour. The meeting applauded provincial Minister of Agriculture K.C. Macdonald's assertion that he would not support moving any Japanese to the Okanagan "even for the rescue of your crop" since "once they were allowed in it might be hard to get rid of them." Nevertheless, after hearing J.B. Shimek of the Coast Berry Growers Association say that the Japanese were good workers and loyal members of co-operatives but should be prohibited from buying or renting land, the convention voted thirty-six to nine to admit Japanese to help handle the fruit crop under certain conditions – namely, that they would be under supervision, could not buy or lease land or crops, and had to leave after the emergency. Three southern interior MLAs, Frank Putnam (Coalition-Liberal, Nelson-Creston), C.S. Leary (Coalition-Liberal, Kaslo-Slocan) and T.A. Love (Coalition-Conservative, Grand Forks-Greenwood), however, opposed their entry lest they become permanent residents. At Grand Forks, the Canadian Legion and the Junior Chamber of Commerce also objected, but the Nelson Junior Chamber – saying that it was "purely a military matter" – refused to support a Grand Forks resolution. Just after Ottawa announced that all Japanese would be leaving the coast, a delegation of Kelowna-area residents headed by W.A.C. Bennett (MLA, Coalition-Conservative, South Okanagan) and including the mayor and representatives of the Kelowna Board of Trade, the BCFGA, the BC Federation of Agriculture, and the Interior Vegetable Marketing Board, warned that "something drastic is going to happen" unless "the present alarming uncontrolled infiltration of Japanese from [the] coast" was stopped.[66]

Kamloops City Council, fearing that Japanese labour would increase local unemployment, recommended that "the only safe method of dealing with enemy aliens is to place them in internment." The *Kamloops Sentinel* agreed that this would allay fears of their becoming permanent settlers. When Japanese, who allegedly demonstrated a "very truculent and insolent" behaviour, began drifting into the area, the Kamloops City Council and Board of Trade demanded the immediate internment of all male Japanese of military age and "strict police supervision" of others. The Kamloops and District Liberal Association wanted to ensure that no Japanese could buy or lease land during the war, a proposal that Ian Mackenzie endorsed as "the unanimous opinion of the people of British Columbia." After returning from the Okanagan Municipal Association meeting, Mayor George R. Williams reported a sense there "that they would take the law into their own hands" rather than have Japanese. He complained of the "scurvy trick" of the coast people who "do not care who gets the trouble so long as they are free of it." Aldermen agreed. They rejected a Victoria resolution for the removal of "all persons of enemy races" from the coast as "too much milk and water." After inserting the word *immediately,* they adopted a resolution prepared by the local Canadian Legion complaining of the "apparent unsupervised infiltration [of] Japanese to interior points" and called for the internment of males of military age and the "humane evacuation" of all Japanese from the coast under "strict supervision." The *Kamloops Sentinel* attributed intense feelings to delays in moving the Japanese from defence areas, a lack of supervision, and the absence of concern by coast residents about anything except getting "the Japanese away from the coast, irrespective of what trouble may ensue elsewhere." T.J. O'Neill (Liberal MP, Kamloops) quoted a prominent Kamloops businessman as saying that it would not be surprising "if the citizens decided to take the matter into their own hands if Ottawa does not act soon and definitely."[67]

During January and February, only male Japanese nationals of military age were under orders to move, though Ottawa encouraged all Japanese men to move inland. Given the refusal of other provinces to accept them, building the Yellowhead Pass highway and other roads in the interior of British Columbia seemed to be the most likely employment, but arranging accommodation took time. When the Canadian National Railway objected to having potential saboteurs working adjacent to its rail lines, the RCMP said that suspected subversives had been interned and promised to protect the railway from sabotage. In mid-February officials announced that the movement would begin imminently, but repeated delays in the departure of the first 100 Japanese nationals did not ease public doubts. Finally, on 23 February 1942, amid publicity designed to "demonstrate to the public that the Government had actually instituted the Jap exodus," the first Japanese nationals left for the Jasper area.[68]

In the meantime, daily news of Japan's military successes increased tension. Hong Kong fell on Christmas Day, Manila on 2 January. By mid-January, Japanese forces were rapidly taking over the Netherlands East Indies and had invaded Malaya. On 15 February, they captured Britain's supposedly impregnable fortress of Singapore. Adding to the jitters of coastal British Columbians was the observation of the liaison officer between the U.S. Army Air Corps and the Royal Canadian Air Force that "the fall of Singapore would leave the west coast of North America exposed to attack by sea and land." In Vancouver, rumours circulated that the local Japanese celebrated the victory with feasts and were dressing in "flashy new clothes to impress their countrymen when they arrive." British Columbians increasingly felt insecure. The *Cowichan Leader* declared, "military authorities know that, even as you read this, the B.C. coast may be subjected to what may be described as a nuisance attack. If Japan's drive southward is not stopped, ... she will ere long ... extend the scope of her operation towards this coast." Elmore Philpott suggested that "if Singapore falls a Japanese attack on Alaska is much more than a possibility." In Vancouver, St. Paul's Hospital organized a blood bank "exclusively for use of air raid victims in British Columbia," and Mayor Cornett took full control of the local air raid protection program "to relieve public anxiety and eliminate internal friction" in the organization. Vancouver City Council asked Minister of Defence Ralston to visit the Pacific coast. "If adequate precautions have been taken to protect Vancouver and other coast cities against attack by air, land or sea," Cornett averred, "it is only right our citizens should receive assurance of this." Ralston's reply that coastal defences were being constantly reviewed, could be reinforced, and were planned to meet any expected attack temporarily satisfied Cornett.[69]

Concern about defences extended east of the Rocky Mountains, where politicians and editors recalled how the United States had claimed that its defences were in good order before Pearl Harbor and how the British had said the same about Singapore. After Premier Hepburn told an Ontario agricultural group that Japanese forces might invade Canada within three months by coming "down the prairie side and not the Pacific," the press envisioned a scenario in which Japan might seek to take over Alaska and British Columbia as a "buffer" against American might. Vendors of Victory Bonds had already suggested this possibility. For example, a full-page advertisement published in both English and French across the country portrayed sinister-looking Japanese and Nazi figures on either side of a map of Canada with the slogan "Ils menacent le Canada à l'est et à l'ouest," or, in English, "They menace Canada on both coasts."[70]

The BC MPs stressed the need for better coastal defences. Green repeated earlier assertions that "Canada is in deadly peril" because Canadian forces on the Pacific coast were "hopelessly inadequate" to cope with the situation in which Japan controlled the ocean and might seek Aleutian bases from which to attack "Prince Rupert, the Queen Charlotte Islands, and even Port Alberni," the whole of British Columbia, and even Edmonton and Calgary. Trying to score points in the concurrent conscription crisis, he emphasized that home defence conscripts could not even be sent to the San Juan Islands to defend Victoria. He claimed that 1,800 Japanese fishermen could "guide enemy naval forces to every bay, every landing place and perhaps every gun on the Canadian coast." If that happened, he expected that "our generals would make another of those strategic retreats with the remnants of our forces to the mountains, leaving the people on the coast to their fate, and in the result thousands of Canadians would have to die to get back what need never have been lost." Pacific coast residents, he declared, were entitled to "protection from being stabbed in the back," with "the only complete protection" being removal of the Japanese population from the province. British Columbia, he concluded, was waiting "rather impatiently" to know if the government would implement its announcement of 14 January to define protected areas and move the Japanese from them, though it had not said whether that applied to the Canadian born and the naturalized as well as Japanese nationals.[71]

BC Liberals were equally concerned. George Cruickshank (Fraser Valley) followed with a brief admonition: "We cannot afford to take chances after Pearl Harbor," or "everybody in British Columbia will, in a few years, be speaking Japanese." Tom Reid, noting that the "many optimistic reports" of "high military men and authorities" were "certainly not justified" by later events, suggested that people could "hardly be blamed for being rather sceptical." Asserting that coastal residents were "greatly perturbed with respect to Pacific coast defences," he asked, if Singapore falls, where "will Japan strike next?"

Victory Bond advertisement, 1942. With its menacing figures of both a Japanese and a Nazi soldier, this advertisement appeared in many newspapers, in both English and French, throughout Canada in early February 1942.

Grey Turgeon was less "afraid of a direct attack, unless it be of a sporadic nature against Vancouver and Esquimalt," than of a "positively planned attack across Alaska or over the Aleutian Islands." He proposed completing highways from Prince Rupert to Edmonton and from Vancouver to Edmonton via Blue River and constructing airports that would, incidentally, benefit his constituency. R.W. Mayhew asked, "we have the Japanese, the counterpart of Hitler; starting in Malaya, working their way to Singapore, into the Philippines, into the Indies and to Australia and New Zealand; and how do we know that Canada is not the next?" He did not think that Japan was interested in bombing BC cities but saw the Esquimalt dry dock, the Pacific Cable, the Trail smelter, and links with the rest of Canada as possible targets.[72]

The press was also worried. In reminding readers of the protection provided by the Pacific Ocean and air defences, the Port Alberni *West Coast Advocate* was in line with the thinking of senior military officers but was exceptional among its provincial counterparts. Citing Reid's speech, the *Vancouver Sun* implied that the government had been unable to offer Reid private information to "diminish his anxiety" about inadequate defences. It opposed sending the fourth division overseas until it could be replaced in British Columbia by a unit of similar size. The *Trail Daily Times,* noting the two-hour flying time from Vancouver to Trail, suggested that Green's allegations about neglected defences "cannot be thrust aside ... 'Too little too late' has become more than a catchword in many parts of the world." Similarly, the *Victoria Daily Times* asserted that experience elsewhere showed that "it can happen here"; the *Cowichan Leader* observed, "here we are on Vancouver Island like the neck of a chicken stuck out ready for the next axe, while an apathetic government at Ottawa still in effect chants those same damning words, 'It can't happen here.'" The *Evening Empire* described Prince Rupert as the "nearest neighbor to that militant power, over yonder." Well inland at Kaslo, the *Kootenaian* warned that Japanese fishermen would be valuable "in establishing sub-nests with which to wreck our shipping and ports."[73]

Provincial legislators joined the cry and largely set aside partisan differences. CCF leader Harold Winch was as concerned about the Japanese presence as were any of the coalition members. He warned that, unless his party got "certain facts on the state of preparedness in B.C. to meet a possible Japanese attack," he would seek a closed sitting of the legislature to examine coastal defences. Now that Japan's forces were "within one hundred miles of Australia," J.A. Paton said, "this part of the Empire [must] not be allowed to become a danger spot." Attorney General R.L. Maitland, who did not "feel safe while the Japanese are on the coast," claimed that "we have every reason to fear attack and to fear fifth-column activities" since to strike the rest of Canada Japanese invaders would have to "pass over our dead bodies, our fields, our timber, our homes." The legislature passed a motion, introduced by H.G.T. Perry, the minister of education, and seconded by Winch, calling Ottawa's attention "to the immediate necessity of completing the strongest and fullest measures of defence against our enemies." Premier Hart expected that the Japanese would soon be leaving vulnerable areas but promised to go to Ottawa if its action was "insufficient." Amazed that the legislature had to remind Ottawa about defence, the *Victoria Daily Times* exhorted readers to "remember everything – not only Pearl Harbor and Singapore!"[74]

The fall of Singapore was crucial. As Bruce Hutchison wrote from Ottawa, "when Singapore fell, Canada's conception of the war fell with it." Paton described British Columbia "as the meat in a Japanese sandwich, with landing parties in front and 'quislings, fifth columnists, and enemy aliens' in the rear." Walter Sage, a University of British Columbia historian, wrote to his friend Henry Angus that "the fall of Singapore has certainly changed things ... We are anxious and trust that Ottawa will waken up fully to our danger." The *Vancouver Sun* suggested that Canada establish a well-equipped mobile striking force of 15,000-20,000 men to repel "any Japanese landing attempt from Alaska southwards." Then President Roosevelt warned that Alaska was in danger and that the United States could not defend it. The *Vancouver Sun* asked, did the prime minister "not realize that a Canadian division might be the salvation of British Columbia or Alaska?" The Vancouver *Daily Province* complained of the government's "equivocation and evasiveness" since Pearl Harbor, the lack of military forces at the coast, and the presence of local Japanese. Inland, the *Trail Daily News,* inspired by Howard Green's speech to the Toronto Conservative Club, suggested that Japanese forces might be at the "northern gates of British Columbia" within a month, launch bombing raids, and use Japanese residents of the province as effective fifth columnists, as they had done in Malaya. Green got so many letters about defence and the Japanese that it seemed "the people are now thoroughly roused to their danger, which is very encouraging for it means that something may be done." Some approached the prime minister directly. The Vancouver local of the Canadian Brotherhood of Railway Employees, citing "a great general feeling of unpreparedness," wanted fortifications up to and including the Rockies, a call up of all persons aged eighteen to sixty, the formation of guerrilla and home guard units, the commandeering of property to prepare for an invasion, tightened regulations on the freedom of movement of enemy aliens, and guards for industrial plants and public utilities. Arthur Turner (MLA, CCF, Vancouver East) told the prime minister that waste, incompetence, delays, and "general unpreparedness" against any kind of attack were "having such a dangerous effect on the people of B.C. that responsible officials cannot settle down to their work while the condition lasts." The secretary-treasurer of the Associated Property Owners of Vancouver cited "the possibility of a Japanese invasion" to argue for reduced city taxes![75]

In Ottawa, Hutchison found the BC MPs in a state "bordering on revolt because they are not satisfied with the government's military preparations," and Roosevelt's warning had persuaded other MPs of their case. Citing the minister of national defence as admitting that "preparations on the Pacific Coast are entirely inadequate," Mackenzie opposed sending more troops "overseas until we have adequate defences for our coast." Green told his family, "this Singapore business is devastating"; if British Columbians "place any value whatever on their lives [they] had better not be satisfied until every individual in the Province is in his or her place for the defence of every inch of our territory – and is planning to strike out at the Japs away from our shores." Such claims garnered sympathy elsewhere in the country. In commenting on one of Green's statements, the *Brantford Expositor,* for example, suggested that such "apprehension" was "entirely logical," that "Vancouver must never be another Pearl Harbor."[76]

In fact, the government was planning a secret session of Parliament to discuss the military situation. Ralston's speech notes for the session mentioned possible nuisance raids but said nothing of the Japanese in British Columbia. A somewhat alarmed Hutchison reported that the "brass hats" persisted in seeing only occasional bombing raids. Claiming that "Nero would be quite at home in Ottawa," he sketched a scenario in which "Nero supplies the music. The Japanese will supply the background, the flames and the sound effect in Vancouver." He suggested that the BC MPs would use the secret session to demand the total evacuation of the Japanese. "Never before," he alleged, "have B.C. members acted so unitedly in any issue." Editorially, the *Vancouver Sun* suggested that "Mr. King is not doing everything he can to defend Canada." Visually, the *Victoria Daily Times* and a number of other Canadian newspapers published a syndicated cartoon of the "Wishful Thinker" mounted on a rocking horse, "Japan Can't Get the Raw Materials Needed for a Long War," and gazing out over a fallen horse, Singapore, and about to be hit by "Attacks on the Dutch Indies." In urging British Columbians to buy Victory Bonds, the Vancouver *News-Herald* reported a story of Japanese shelling California and warned of Japan's plans to invade British Columbia. Lieutenant Governor W.C. Woodward expected a raid soon.[77]

News of Japan's military successes and stories of fifth column activities increased suspicions of all Japanese, including the Canadian born. Although it did not appear in the Vancouver press, possibly due to censorship, adding to the sense of foreboding, as it did in the United States, was the comment of the influential American columnist Walter Lippman that enemy aliens on the Pacific coast were holding back on sabotage until they could strike the blow "with maximum effect." British Columbians impatiently observed the government's apparent inaction in implementing plans to remove male Japanese nationals from the coast. All the prime minister did in early February was dissolve the Standing Committee, summarize the policy announced in mid-January, and urge other Canadians to deal with Canadian citizens of Japanese race with "tolerance and understanding." Not until 14 February were male enemy aliens – Japanese, German, and Italian – told that they must move east of the Cascades by 1 April and, along with all Japanese nationals, no matter their age or sex, surrender cameras, radios, firearms, and explosives. From Vancouver, Senator J.H. King advised that the "somewhat confusing" reports of the mid-January policy statement would make it necessary to announce officially "that the removal will be thorough." For "peace of mind and assurance to the public," he urged that it "be done at the earliest possible moment and there should be few exemptions."[78]

The government was well aware of such feelings. General Alexander and the Joint Services Committee, Pacific Coast, warned that "the continued presence of enemy aliens and persons of Japanese racial origin in the Protected Area constitutes a serious danger and prejudices the effective defence of the Pacific Coast of Canada." That committee recommended moving male Japanese from the west coast of Vancouver Island, the Prince Rupert-Terrace area, and the Queen Charlotte Islands but within days urged removing *all* Japanese, regardless of sex or age, from those areas by 1 April 1942. Commissioner T.W.S. Parsons of the Provincial Police confidentially advised Attorney General R.L. Maitland that existing regulations for removing Japanese were "ineffectual." "With these people," he argued, "neither Canadian birth nor naturalization guarantees good faith. Something to remember in the case of invasion or planned sabotage." To support his claim, he cited specific cases of Japanese, including overage Japanese nationals, still living near air bases or important communications links such as the Victoria telephone exchange. Maitland immediately sent the report to Mackenzie with a covering letter saying that "nothing short of immediate removal of the Japanese will meet the dangers which we feel in this Province." G.S. Pearson told the press that federal and provincial authorities intended to undertake "a progressive removal of *all* persons of Japanese origin from coastal British Columbia" but advised Arthur MacNamara, the federal deputy minister of labour, that moving adult males quickly would avoid "a very serious situation ... through the bitterness of the whites at the dilatoriness of the Federal Government's action" and prevent "an insistent demand for the removal of every Japanese of every category from this province." Harold Winch asked Premier Hart to press Ottawa for "immediate action to move all Japanese from vulnerable areas of the coast." After conferring with Hart and General Alexander and talking to Mackenzie on the telephone, Winch reported that Hart had done all that he could, but federal officials were "passing the buck."[79]

Some British Columbians wrote directly to the prime minister. Lieutenant Governor W.C. Woodward sent a three-page letter on the "appalling" "lack of precautions" about "the Japanese menace on our coast." Colonel Macintosh publicly and privately "earnestly" entreated the prime minister to remove all Japanese from the Pacific defence area immediately. "With every enemy success," he contended, "local Japanese of all categories are becoming more arrogant and white citizens comparing measures taken by United States on their Pacific Coast with lack of decision here are preparing to take drastic action themselves." On 19 February, the day before Macintosh wrote his letter, President Franklin D. Roosevelt had signed Executive Order 9066, which, though not naming them, effectively authorized the removal of all Japanese from designated military areas.[80]

Tales of "truculent" Japanese increased. Stories of Japanese schoolchildren in the Fraser Valley saying that their parents expected Japan to invade in April became urban legends. Richard Bell-Irving told of a foreman finding some Japanese workmen sitting in a circle around a large map and gloating as they put "rising sun" flags on points taken by Japan. One incident hardened opinion. After Ian Mackenzie announced that the departure of Japanese nationals would begin on 18 February, about 100 Japanese nationals refused to board a train bound for interior work camps apparently because they knew that they did not have to leave until 1 April and thought that they were not wanted anywhere, as demonstrated by Ontario's reaction to their employment. Japan's military successes may have strengthened their resistance.[81]

Editorial opinion reflected the desire to remove potential fifth columnists and dissatisfaction with Ottawa's inaction. As the *Victoria Daily Times* commented, "if even half the yarns about the activities of the Japanese which filter, directly or indirectly, into the office of this newspaper are true, there is much to justify the apprehension which Mr. Mayhew has just voiced in the House of Commons." It complained of Ottawa's failure to recognize experience elsewhere that "anything can happen here." Similarly, the Victoria *Daily Colonist* noted that public opinion had "crystallized in favor of removal of 'all' Japanese" and that Ottawa's inactivity was not tempering "the antagonistic attitude of the Pacific Coast Canadians towards the Japanese." It repeatedly called for public pressure to "insure safety within the country" by interning alien enemies outside the province. The *Nanaimo Free Press* agreed that continued pressure was necessary to "complete removal of these people from the protected areas which are likely to be the scene of invasion." Newspapers in Comox, Duncan, and Ladysmith agreed that the Japanese were a danger and complained of Ottawa's inaction. Such sentiments were not confined to Vancouver Island. The *Trail Daily News,* in reporting FBI seizures of "vast quantities of contraband" from Japanese in the United States, observed that "a Jap does not change his color when he steps from the American to the Canadian side of the border yet ... the benevolent government is allowing the dear little yellow man to remain at the coast a few weeks longer meanwhile giving them opportunities to do a little more dirty work for their emperor." Both Prince Rupert newspapers questioned the loyalty of local Japanese. The *Vernon News* claimed that there was "more danger" in delay than a scheme "to give British Columbia absolute safety and treat the Japanese fairly." In the Fraser Valley, the New Westminster *British Columbian* urged Ottawa to "get on with the job"; the *Chilliwack Progress* contended that international relations were no excuse to "pussyfoot" around the Japanese. Similarly, the Vancouver *Daily Province,* which had tried "to steady public opinion" against rabble-rousing MPs, MLAs, and other newspapers, described "growing impatience" with Ottawa's failure to say what it was going to do. In the Vancouver *News-Herald,* Philpott wrote that there was no way to prevent Japan "from planting or employing active fifth columnists to do whatever it wants done. The entire Japanese population should be moved from this coast as soon as it is humanly possible. That means now – before an actual military action can take place." His editors called it "no service to democracy when the interests of minorities are allowed to prevail against the interests of the majority." The *Vancouver Sun* claimed that "all authorities regard it as unthinkable that any colony of Japanese males should remain" on the coast and that moving them east of the Cascades would "satisfy most" British Columbians. As the military situation deteriorated, it demanded the immediate removal of all Japanese and an end of incidents that let them "snap their fingers at Canadian authority."[82]

As individuals and in groups, British Columbians sent their views to Ottawa and especially to Ian Mackenzie. They represented a wide variety of interests, as a random list suggests: the Vancouver South Conservative Association; the Victoria Rotary Club; the Vancouver Kinsmen Club; the Fraternal Council of British Columbia; the Provincial Council of Women; the United Commercial Travellers, Vancouver; the Maple Ridge Citizens League; the Lynnmour-Dollarton Liberal Association; the Canadian Corps Association (representing several regimental organizations in Vancouver); the union of Canadian National Railway Sleeping and Dining Car Workers; the Prince Rupert Chamber of Commerce; the North Fraser District Board of the British Columbia Women's Institutes; the North Vancouver, New Westminster, and Powell River Boards of Trade; the Provincial Command of the Army and Navy Veterans of Canada; the Vancouver Real Estate Exchange; the Vancouver Gyro Club; the Prince Rupert and Revelstoke Women's Canadian Clubs; and the Housewives League of British Columbia. A few, such as the Imperial Order of the Daughters of the Empire (IODE) in Prince Rupert, the Nanaimo Board of Trade, and the Fraser Valley Milk Producers Association, worried about the presence of Japanese in places offering easy opportunities for sabotage. Some warned of violence if the Japanese were not removed. A Prince Rupert church group suggested that removal from the coast was "for the safety of Canada, for the safety of the Japs themselves." A Victoria resident predicted that if his city was bombed its people "would kill every Jap they could lay their hands on." Most resolutions simply demanded the removal of all Japanese, regardless of age, sex, or citizenship, from the coastal area or in some cases east of the Rockies. "Do not let the color of card or age of Jap stand in your way," admonished the British Columbia Poultry Industries Committee. "Remember Singapore and the consideration their troops gave the civilian population." More influential was a resolution unanimously passed by over 800 men and women at a special Victory Loan luncheon in Vancouver where Dr. Hu Shih, China's ambassador to the United States, spoke. Referring to the "imminent danger" of an enemy attack, and the "alarming" lack of effective measures to relieve problems caused by the presence of enemy aliens, the resolution urged the immediate evacuation of "all enemy aliens and all people of Japanese origin from Defence Areas of Pacific Coast."[83]

Municipal councils also sent resolutions to Ottawa and asked other BC municipalities to do the same. On 13 February, Victoria City Council unanimously resolved that "the experience of countries overrun by our enemies has shown us the menace of allowing persons of enemy races to live in any place that may be open to attack." It called for "prompt action" to relieve "the apprehension ... and to assure that our women and children are to be safeguarded from grave jeopardy" by removing "all persons of enemy races from the coast of British Columbia without further delay." Within two weeks, Saanich, Duncan, North Cowichan, Surrey, Alberni, Port Alberni, Chilliwack, Esquimalt, New Westminster, West Vancouver, Prince George, Nanaimo, Courtenay, Langley, Trail, and Enderby and Canadian Legions in Delta and Sooke had endorsed the resolution. Yet as far as Victoria City Council was concerned, the resolution had had no effect on Ottawa. On 20 February, on behalf of the city and adjacent municipalities, Mayor Andrew McGavin wired the prime minister urgently requesting action: "Unanimous opinion that enemy action will develop against this coast and people alarmed at lack of defence precautions and complacent attitude of your government." Three days later council reminded the prime minister of its dissatisfaction and asked for Mackenzie's "resignation in view of the 'slaphappy way' in which the Japanese situation has been handled on the Pacific Coast." Coming to the defence of a fellow Liberal, Mayhew told the *Victoria Daily Times* and Victoria City Council that Mackenzie had "done everything he possibly could" to secure the removal of "all Japanese" from the coast "at the earliest possible date" but was only one voice in cabinet. Mackenzie himself accused council of acting "without knowledge of the facts." He accused other parts of British Columbia and Canada of refusing to accept Japanese and reminded the city of the need to act sanely and humanely because many British subjects were in Japanese hands.[84]

In the meantime, an umbrella group, the Citizens' Civil Defence Committee, and its affiliate, the Immediate Action Committee of the Victoria and District Canadian Legion, began planning a mass protest meeting. Mayhew cautioned that the "many old people" in Victoria "are liable to think that a Mass Meeting is an indication that danger is more imminent than appears on the surface. Then one never knows how far some people who are excited might help to excite each other." Mayhew's advice had no effect. By 20 February, the Victoria Kinsmen Club had got other interested organizations to support a resolution demanding the removal of "all Japanese from the coastal area" and threatening to boycott Japanese individuals and businesses. Twenty-four groups sent representatives to a meeting that set up a temporary executive of what was renamed the Citizens' Security Council. The representative of the CCF District Council argued that "the things we suggest doing to the Japanese are what the Nazis did to the Jews and the Poles," but the meeting unanimously demanded the removal of "all Japanese of all ages and both sexes" within thirty days. A resolution sent to MPs warned that "the feeling of the people of British Columbia is rapidly becoming uncontrollable and will undoubtedly lead to violence." Three days later the president of the Victoria Chamber of Commerce cited a planned "open air mass meeting" on 1 March to buttress arguments for immediate action to deprive Japanese on Vancouver Island of "the right of free movement" and to put them under strict surveillance until quarters could be prepared for them elsewhere.[85]

The Immediate Action Committee prepared a handbill, "News Flashes after We Are Dead," which urged people to read it "commencing with the evil Japanese face and hands in the left-hand top corner, menacingly regarding any and all of our coast cities and the foundation of their community life, and even their means of escape," and to use their influence "towards the total elimination from the Pacific Coast, of the Japanese of all ages and all sexes." It circulated the leaflet widely. The Montreal *Gazette* reproduced it; others used it as inspiration for sympathetic editorials. In Victoria, the committee planned a parade from downtown to the Beacon Hill Park bandstand on Sunday, 1 March, where Colonel Macintosh, Colonel Ross Napier, and Tom Barnard, provincial president of the Canadian Legion, would speak on behalf of a resolution similar to that of the Citizens' Defence Committee.[86] The prospect of such a meeting was frightening. The Chamber of Commerce did not support it lest it cause anti-Japanese demonstrations similar to the anti-German riots after the sinking of the *Lusitania* in 1915. Mackenzie warned the national headquarters of the Canadian Legion that the "firebrands" who circulated the literature might "try to organize mob action" that could lead to reprisals against Canadians in Japanese hands or sabotage in Canada. Since the government had just announced the removal of all Japanese from the coast, the Canadian Legion withdrew its support, and Barnard did not speak. Neither did Macintosh, a member of the active army. Mackenzie asked the minister of national defence to hold members of the services in quarters during the proposed mass meeting lest uniformed personnel "become associated with riotous and destructive behaviour" or be "required to quell disorder." The military declared the park off limits for the day, and military police saw that no one in uniform entered it. The meeting passed without incident.[87]

A similar movement emerged in Vancouver. Vancouver City Council moved cautiously, but its actions escalated in the first three weeks of

February as discontent with federal inaction rose. On 2 February, council, taking a "wait and see" policy, tabled a resolution from an Army and Navy Veterans Association branch endorsing any city action "to guarantee transfer of all Japanese residents out of the coastal district." A week later council agreed to Alderman Wilson's requests, sought federal authority to cancel the trade licences of enemy aliens and Japanese, and resolved that "speedier action on part of the Government ... will not only provide greater security for defence areas but will allay fears of Vancouver citizens generally and will be in the best interests of the Japanese residents." In forwarding this to Minister of Defence Ralston, Mayor Cornett reported "increasing irritation and criticism" over the government's "apparent failure" to implement announced policies. One reporter suggested that council had set itself up as "the unofficial successor" to the Standing Committee as "watchdog on the Nipponese situation." The next week, after a vigorous debate, it beseeched Ottawa to re-establish the Standing Committee. Unlike Victoria's generic reference to "enemy aliens," Vancouver specifically named the Japanese. Citing the danger of "a potential reservoir of voluntary aid to our enemy," it implored Ottawa "to remove all residents of Japanese racial origin to areas of Canada well-removed from the Pacific Coast" under conditions that would give them "a reasonable livelihood." Minister of Justice St. Laurent replied that the government did not want to inflict "unnecessary hardship" on people who were being moved "as a precautionary measure only." He indicated that the volume of departures from the coast would increase in the next week. Council listened. It refused, for example, to endorse a housewives' plan to boycott all things Japanese.[88]

Meanwhile, Alderman Wilson was the principal speaker at a meeting on 12 February sponsored by the United Commercial Travellers and attended by delegates from sixty organizations, mainly veterans' groups such as the Army and Navy Veterans and The Flying Column; "patriotic" British and Canadian bodies such as the Royal Society of St. George, the IODE, the Canadian Daughters' League, the Native Sons of BC, and the Primrose Club; and fraternal orders such as the Lady Foresters and the Elks. Wilson attacked Canadian-born Japanese, most of whom, he alleged, were trained in Japanese-language schools, "the chief instrument of propaganda of the Imperial Education Department of Japan." He quoted one of them saying in the *New Canadian* on 31 July 1940 that "some day a Japanese Hitler will arise which will wreck vengeance upon Canadians." Such a sentiment was quite out of keeping with the fiercely Canadian editorial policy of the *New Canadian*, but its columnist "K.W.," in commenting on the inability of Nisei to practise as lawyers, suggested that such denials could sow "seeds of bitterness" that in the future might "see a group of brilliant Nisei who have emigrated to Japan, leading a virulent anti-Canadian movement in Japan, because they have been abused here in early and tender years. After all, most of us have heard of an embittered Austrian house painter whose name is Adolf." The meeting unanimously called for organizing a council to preserve and promote "the British way of life in Western Canada" and to co-ordinate activities to impress on "Ottawa the necessity for immediate action in removing British Columbia's entire Japanese population east of the Rockies."[89]

Since this group seemed to be under the influence of Wilson and The Flying Column, members of Vancouver's business and political elite became alarmed. Twenty prominent residents – including Austin Taylor, an industrialist; Grant MacNeil and Harold Winch, CCF MLAs; Mrs. F.J. Rolston, a coalition MLA; Birt Showler of the Vancouver Trades and Labour Council; P.A. Woodward and Victor Spencer, whose families owned two of the city's largest department stores; Henry Macken, a prominent lumberman; W.G. Murrin, president of the BC Electric Railway; and J.A. Clark, a retired general and former Conservative MP – formed a Citizens' Defence Committee. "With a view to stabilizing public opinion and in the interest of public safety," the committee circulated a petition for immediate removal of enemy aliens from all points that the military thought essential for defence and public safety and the immediate "evacuation of all those of Japanese origin from the Pacific Coast." Within a day, the Vancouver Labour Council, the Kiwanis and Rotary Clubs, and the BC Command of the Canadian Legion endorsed it. As the preamble to the petition hinted, committee members saw a need for leadership and co-ordination "to prevent untoward action and expression." They were particularly worried that The Flying Column's proposed mass meeting on 4 March might cause "unfortunate incidents," a euphemism for a riot. The Canadian Legion executive warned that a "trifling incident" could require a call out of the reserve army "to protect the Japanese against the Canadian white people." By then Wilson claimed that about 150 associations were co-operating in his council. He also subscribed to a theory that there was a move afoot to create a disturbance so that the military would have to take over.[90]

Mackenzie viewed the mass meetings as part of a "calculated plan to incite riotous actions against Japanese." Moreover, the idea was spreading. In the Fraser Valley, Reeve S. Mussallem of Maple Ridge warned that "riot and bloodshed" might follow indignation meetings planned "to condemn the dilatory Government action" and that the Japanese had been "openly hostile since Singapore." Mackenzie again explained why the movement of the Japanese had been delayed and asked Mussallem to tell people that resolutions were welcome but in view of the danger to "use your authority to discourage such public assemblies." Mussallem was able to cancel the meeting, and the White Citizens League of Maple Ridge organized a petition instead. Commenting on the agitation, the editor of the *Maple Ridge-Pitt Meadows Weekly Gazette* suggested that the hysteria "being dished up" was "not altogether groundless," that "people's tempers are getting frayed," and that "in fairness to them and to the Japanese" "something should be done at once."[91]

Concerns about a Japanese invasion persisted. The *Cowichan Leader* admitted the possibility of "some exaggerated tales about Japanese activities in our midst" but cited plans allegedly found in California for a Japanese invasion via Canada to claim that not all stories were "pipe dreams." Even the editor of the Vancouver *Daily Province* asked why Prime Minister King had not taken British Columbians, who were "living in the midst of alarms," into his confidence. "Vancouver will be patient if Mr. King will be frank," it asserted, and "make allowance for unavoidable setbacks and disappointments if they are clearly disclosed. What is desperately needed is authoritative assurance that the government recognizes the dangerous situation and is proceeding with all possible haste to meet it."[92]

In Ottawa, BC MPs continued to draw attention to provincial sentiment. Only Angus MacInnis, who observed that most Japanese in British Columbia were Canadian citizens, thought that the situation was in hand. Others agreed with Cruickshank, who had "not the faintest idea which branch of the government is handling the Japanese question – nor has any other British Columbia member." They criticized inadequate coastal defences, referred to the danger of fifth columnists, and stressed the difficulty of distinguishing between the loyal and the disloyal. Mayhew, for example, complained that Japanese could still move freely about and suggested that they might have cached munitions along the coast. While agreeing that they must have "proper shelter and proper care," he asserted that "blood is thicker than water" and concluded, "I would not want to be the one responsible for sorting out the loyal Japanese from the disloyal." Olof Hanson (Liberal, Skeena), claiming that fishermen were the "greatest potential danger," urged removing "all Japanese of military age" from coastal areas. Other MPs referred to the Japanese question in the throne speech debate, but Neill, "a cantankerous fellow" in King's eye, focused on it entirely and implied, "I told you so." Spy and sabotage stories figured in it, but Neill also anticipated buying out and expatriating the Japanese to "settle once and for all this canker in the life of Canada which prevents us from being a united white Canada." McGeer expressed concern about defences and the trustworthiness of the Japanese race. Mayhew privately apprised King of proposed mass meetings, of the plans of "experienced hunters and woodsmen" to act against potential saboteurs, and of many calls from Victoria and Vancouver "expressing considerable alarm" that Japanese had not been moved from strategic sites. Senator J.H. King reported, "people in Vancouver and Victoria are very nervous." He was certain that Japanese government agents all along the coast would "strike whenever the opportunity occurs." Ian Mackenzie approached cabinet colleagues. On 14 February, for example, he told Minister of Justice St. Laurent that the date of 1 April for removing Japanese nationals was "far too remote, and public opinion at the coast will demand much quicker action." By then Mackenzie was taking credit for carrying "British Columbia's fight for action on the Japanese problem" against fellow cabinet ministers who did not want Japanese in their parts of the country.[93]

On 19 February, in answering Grote Stirling's question about Japanese in the interior, the prime minister emphasized the necessity of restrained language in order to "prevent hasty and unwarranted action" by individuals who might not appreciate the consequences of their actions. He neither clarified policy nor satisfied BC MPs. On 21 February, six Liberal backbenchers plus A.W. Neill and G.E.L. MacKinnon (Conservative, Kootenay East) drafted a letter to him expressing frustration at the lack of government responses to their representations. They complained that King had not referred to "many of the Japanese who would be dangerous to us and helpful to our enemies" and demanded the removal of all Japanese to points east of the Cascades. Perhaps realizing logistical problems in placing evacuees, they asked only for their immediate removal from sensitive areas near airports, military installations, and power plants and the removal of the rest as rapidly as possible, beginning with able-bodied males and concluding with families. They asked too that regulations concerning curfews, radios, cameras, explosives, motor vehicles, and the like be applied to naturalized and Canadian-born citizens. They also wanted a prohibition, retroactive to 7 December 1941, on Japanese acquiring land anywhere in British Columbia.[94]

Events rapidly overtook these requests. Two days earlier cabinet had discussed the Japanese situation. Musing in his diary, King agreed that the problem had drifted because no one minister was responsible and two who were, Mitchell of Labour and St. Laurent of Justice, had been absent fighting by-elections to get into Parliament. St. Laurent, however, had been thinking about the subject. On 21 February, he told the Ontario section of the Canadian Bar Association that, while many Japanese were Canadian born and most Japanese in Canada were normally "entitled to full recognition of the same fundamental rights we claim for ourselves," the crisis made "preventive" but not "punitive" measures necessary. "After the treacherous attack on Pearl Harbor," he did not think the white population could "be expected to pursue their war effort with singleness of purpose and confidence if something was not done at once." In a statement that might have emanated from British Columbia, he added, "we know that the oriental mind differs from ours, and we know what disasters have overtaken others because of the twists and quirks of that oriental mind." He believed that it was necessary "to safeguard the interests and perhaps even the lives of those we are surely entitled to look upon as the real Canadians of that territory."[95]

King was convinced that "public prejudice is so strong in B.C. that it is going to be difficult to control the situation." The next day the Cabinet War Committee discussed the matter. Stressing the need to regard Japan as a potential aggressor on North America, King convinced the committee to pay more attention to defence and air raid preparations. Home defence, of course, would increase the need for soldiers in Canada and "probably avoid any necessity of conscription and meanwhile will help to quiet the feeling in Canada." Conscription was King's main concern, but his fear of riots was real. His main personal experience with Japanese in British Columbia was investigating damage claims after the 1907 anti-Asian riot in Vancouver. Since at least 1938 and especially since 7 December 1941, officials watching British Columbia had warned of anti-Japanese riots. On 23 February 1942, Mackenzie told Ralston that Premier Hart reported that "feeling" was "simply aflame." Without immediate action to remove all Japanese from near power dams, gun emplacements, and the like, Mackenzie feared "an outburst of feeling." As evidence, he enclosed the telegram from Vancouver's Citizens' Defence Committee. The next day he reinforced his warning with a clipping about Victoria City Council's demand for his resignation because of the "'slaphappy way' in which the Japanese situation had been handled." Although Mackenzie had no sympathy for the Japanese, he was the messenger, not the decision maker.[96]

On the afternoon and evening of 24 February 1942, Parliament met in a secret session. Defence was the main theme, but the prime minister spoke "more or less freely about the Japanese situation and the need to be very much on our guard in dealing with the Japanese." Earlier that day cabinet had authorized the minister of justice to "exclude any or all persons regardless of their citizenship, from protected areas as defined under the defence of Canada regulations." On the morning of 25 February 1942, the prime minister issued a press release announcing the new policy. That afternoon, as he tabled an order in council, he noted the need for haste "in the interest of law and order out on the Pacific coast."[97]

Five days earlier the United States had announced a similar program. The coincidence of timing is striking; however, despite the agreement of the Permanent Joint Board on Defence in the fall of 1941 that the two nations "should follow policies of a similar character in relation" to their "populations of Japanese racial origin," there is scant evidence of consultations. Nevertheless, H.F. Angus, who was close to the decision-making process in Ottawa, declared in his memoirs, "the fate of persons of Japanese race in BC was sealed by the panic action taken by the United States, in spite of its famous bill of rights." In both countries, race had trumped citizenship. The prime minister, who eighteen months earlier had viewed the real problem with the Japanese in Canada as making them and especially the Canadian born "good and loyal citizens," now yielded to pressure from the West Coast and his own fear that hostility to the Japanese could lead to outbursts against them.[98]

Curiously, the press reported the momentous decision to remove all Japanese from the West Coast with less than banner headlines. The handful of editorial comments tempered relief at Ottawa's response with complaints that the government should have acted earlier and concern over the need for vigilance to ensure that the government did not change its mind. While the *Vancouver Sun* suggested that British Columbia should unanimously state that the Japanese should never be allowed to return, others warned of "dangerous emotionalism" and "hysterical clamour" against "helpless" Japanese who, "as a military measure, are required to leave their homes and their occupations at the coast." Indeed, Angus MacInnis, a later champion of the rights of Japanese Canadians, told a correspondent, who wanted all Japanese removed from the coast, that most were Canadians whose "rights as Canadians must be respected." Then he added a qualifier: "in so far as it is compatible with adequate defence and public safety." Few questioned the decision, though a suburban newspaper, the *Marpole-Richmond Review,* wondered if fear or economic jealousy explained the outcry against the Japanese and if this is "Hitler's country or a democracy."[99] Once the government announced that all Japanese would be leaving the coast, the volume of protests rapidly declined. Nevertheless, hysterical outbursts were still possible, and the Provincial Police kept a close watch.

If all Japanese were removed in order to prevent riots and demonstrations, the policy succeeded. Mayhew was relieved because he thought that British Columbians, especially in Vancouver, Victoria, and New Westminster, "would have taken the matter into their own hands." In Vancouver, the Citizens' Defence Committee and its subcommittee, the Citizens' Defence Council, welcomed the news but warned of the urgent need to stabilize public opinion by announcing when the movement of Japanese "from strategic areas of defence and public safety" would begin. It promised to co-operate with the British Columbia Security Commission that Ottawa established to manage the removal of the Japanese and said that "mass meetings or other demonstrations" were "at present unnecessary." On 2 March, Mackenzie sent a wire to Maddison, expressing the hope that "you and other experienced men will have sufficient influence to restrain any excitable elements." The United Citizens' Defence Council, which seems to have been separate from the Citizens' Defence Committee, also offered co-operation and recommended postponing protest meetings until "reasonable time has elapsed" to permit execution of the general evacuation orders.[100]

Nevertheless, some planned mass meetings went ahead. In Victoria, despite sanctions by the Canadian Legion and the Armed Forces, the Immediate Action Committee, with Victoria City Council's support, held a meeting but promised that there would be no inflammatory speeches. Colonel Napier, the chief speaker, rehearsed old arguments about difficulties in distinguishing between loyal and disloyal Japanese and denied that such meetings could lead to violence. The meeting quietly endorsed resolutions for a sunset-to-sunrise curfew for all Japanese and immediate implementation of plans to remove the Japanese from the protected areas. Most present were well dressed, middle aged, or elderly; they sat politely as if listening to a dull sermon. At Mission, an overflow crowd attended an anti-Japanese meeting sponsored by the Canadian Legion on Sunday, 1 March. After Reverend G.L. Collins called for a "white" Fraser Valley and Alderman Wilson said that some Nisei sympathized with Japan's aspirations, the assembly, fearing "imminent danger of attack," urged the government "to expedite the enforcement of the orders" to remove all persons of enemy alien origin, not just enemy nationals, by 1 April 1942.[101]

The official announcement on 10 March of Japanese atrocities against Canadian and other British subjects at Hong Kong raised the possibility of reprisals against Japanese Canadians. The Montreal *Gazette,* for example, warned that such talk was useless; it would not hurt the Tokyo warlords, and the notion of "punishing one man for another's crime" was repugnant. Nevertheless, it urged the government to act more swiftly in placing restrictions "upon those 25,000 potential fifth columnists of the West." Naturally, the greatest concern was in British Columbia. Expecting the "ugly" story to "shock public opinion," the Department of External Affairs asked the RCMP, the local police, and the military to work "to prevent the indignation which must follow on the publication of reports from Hong Kong, venting itself on persons of Japanese origin in Canada." In Vancouver, the army confined soldiers to barracks to have them on hand in case of "reprisals against Japs." Mackenzie proposed banning public meetings protesting "Government war measures" because of the "danger of disorder."[102]

The Department of External Affairs was right about indignation. News of "unspeakable atrocities," "sadistic vengeance," and "barbarities" shocked the public. A Victoria *Daily Colonist* columnist said that it was time "to cease cuddling and coddling our potential coastal jackals"; the *Powell River News* proposed killing one Japanese for every Canadian killed in Hong Kong, but that measure was extreme. Other editors confined ideas of reprisals to interning all Japanese, speeding up the evacuation, or more constructively making a greater effort to win the war. In fact, most people took the news quietly and heeded advice to provide no excuse for reprisals against Hong Kong prisoners. The *Vancouver Sun* contended, "because the Japanese military have made beasts of themselves is all the more reason why our treatment of Japanese in Canada should be completely exemplary of the rights and principles expected of a Christian country." "As our indignation burns," said the Vancouver *Daily Province,* "we must keep our heads." Similar calls for "British fair play" appeared elsewhere. "We are," said the *Nanaimo Free Press,* "treating the Japanese rather in the code of a Christian country, merely placing them where they can earn a living, and be removed from a region which is too close to the Pacific Ocean to be occupied by combatants of an alien race, in fact removing them for their own safety."[103] That damning comment on white British Columbians was true. Removing the Japanese from the coast was evil, but there were no riots.

In a brief for redress in the late 1980s, the National Association of Japanese Canadians (NAJC) rightly denied "military necessity" as a cause of removal but erred by completely rejecting the concept of "Protective Custody." Protective custody, or removing the Japanese from the coast for "their own good," had two meanings. One was the notion expressed, for example, by John Shirras, assistant commissioner of the BC Security Commission, that Japanese were moved because they "would be compelled to join the invading forces" in the remote event of an invasion by Japan. In 1942, however, protective custody reflected concern that a "public seething with hatred and hysteria, demanding the removal of Japanese Canadians," might physically attack Japanese people and property. Since at least 1938, federal officials had warned of riots if something were not done to appease anti-Japanese sentiment in British Columbia.[104]

H.F. Angus remembered believing that the idea of possible "bloodshed" in British Columbia if the Japanese were not interned was "absurd," but others who were also sympathetic to the Japanese accepted the need to protect them from white hysterics. A lawyer hired by some Vancouver Japanese who wanted to move in family groups noted that "feeling" was so "very tense" they feared "violence," "accepted evacuation as a necessary evil," and wanted to co-operate. The BC Security Commission told a Lethbridge alderman that it had concerns about spying but emphasized the need "to avoid civil disorder" and observed that sabotage was not a concern "as most of the Japanese are far more frightened than our own people." A CCF speakers' handbook advised, "persons of Japanese origin were removed from the defence areas of British Columbia as much for their own safety as for the safety of the state." The *Western Recorder,* the United Church newspaper in British Columbia, mentioned "military reasons" for moving the Japanese but also cited "possible danger from extreme individuals." That too was the recollection of officials. In later interviews, F.J. Mead of the RCMP and Colonel A.W. Sparling, who represented the Department of National Defence on the Special Committee on Orientals, recalled fear of "riots or racial clashes" that would "cause bloodshed in B.C.," with "fatal consequences in Jap prison camps in retaliation." Hugh Keenleyside, who was sympathetic to the Japanese Canadians, recounted how, "given the temper of the times and the irresponsibility of some of the leaders of the anti-Japanese forces," there was a "real danger of riotous attacks." Minister of Labour Humphrey Mitchell "vividly recalled" discussions in 1942 when Howard Green, Harold Winch, Birt Showler, and other British Columbians warned of "bloodshed" unless the Japanese were moved. As the Pacific War was ending, Mitchell told a delegation from the Co-Operative Committee on Japanese Canadians that it had been necessary to move the Japanese in 1942 because "Canada is a democracy and the Government has to take some notice of public pressure." To the latter comment, *Nisei Affairs,* a new magazine, commented, "what he did not state was that this 'pressure' came from a reactionary racist group which is definitely not a majority opinion." *Nisei Affairs* was partly correct; there was public pressure, but it reflected what appeared to be majority opinion.[105]

Early in 1943, G.E. Trueman of the Department of Labour's Japanese Placement Division told a Toronto audience that "mass hysteria and race prejudice" forced the mass evacuation. British Columbians knew that this version of protective custody reflected poorly on them. The New Westminster *British Columbian* thought his explanation "mischievous because it sails close to the truth without actually touching it." It denied "mass hysteria" but admitted that "hotheads" could have incited "the mob spirit." Other angry editors called Trueman's comments "foolish"; "the product of woeful ignorance of the situation here, or direct misrepresentation of the facts"; "stupid"; an "insulting slander"; and, in the word of the *Vancouver Sun,* "nonsense." In Parliament, Tom Reid denied that "mass hysteria and agitation by some members of parliament" had caused the removal of the Japanese. After Pearl Harbor, he argued, no one "knew what might happen in British Columbia. Here were 23,000 Japanese, hundreds of whom had bought new trucks which they had filled up with gasoline and loaded with gunpowder. They had the finest maps of the coast and they have [sic] eleven hundred fishing boats." After the excitement over Trueman's statement faded, the *Vancouver Sun* conceded that the Japanese had been removed "as much for the safety of the Japanese themselves, as for reasons of national prudence for Canada." Sadly, in early 1942, so strong were suspicions and hatred of all things Japanese that violence was possible. In almost identical words, Harold Winch and R.W. Mayhew said that all Japanese must leave the coast for the protection of the province and themselves. Mayhew feared that news of ill treatment of prisoners of war in Hong Kong would "cause serious trouble" and an embarrassing local situation; certainly, fears of riots permeated the thinking of officials in Ottawa.[106]

Moreover, the Japanese had few friends who were willing to speak out on their behalf. In his history of the Japanese in Canada, Ken Adachi, a teenager in 1942, asserts that white Canadians raised "not one effective voice of protest" against evacuation. That statement was almost totally correct. The Pacific Co-Operative Union, a Fraser Valley berry growers' organization, told Ottawa that the Japanese were important food producers, that farm work was available for unemployed fishermen, and that the Standing Committee on Orientals had not considered the cost of moving thousands of Japanese. The union was not disinterested; many of its members were Japanese, but others noted the importance of the Japanese to the berry industry. Leo

Sweeney, whose Vancouver cooperage supplied the barrels in which a large part of the crop was shipped to England, reminded agitators of the key role of the Japanese in the berry industry. Nevertheless, he endorsed precautions against fifth column activities.[107]

The few Christian church leaders who spoke merely called for "Christian principles and British fair play" and warned against "ugly Hitlerian methods" of race prejudice. Reverend Hugh Dobson of the United Church's British Columbia Conference opposed sending Japanese men away from the coast lest doing so "breed such a resentment that Japanese women might become as dangerous as men." Church leaders could not easily go beyond the feelings of their congregations. After a talk by Reverend W.R. McWilliams, pastor of the Japanese United Church in New Westminster, some members of Vancouver's St. John's United Church agreed that many Japanese were loyal to Canada, but others favoured removing those of military age from the coast. Several members of the Ladysmith United Church ignored their pastor's advice that work among the Japanese was more necessary than ever and questioned the advisability of ministering to the Japanese. Like United Church leaders, the Anglican Provincial Board of Missions to Orientals in British Columbia declared that "the safety of the Country is the first consideration" but called for "the true British tradition of justice and fair play" in "any protective measures the Government may feel necessary" toward the Japanese.[108] Such ambivalence reflected traditional views of BC Christians toward Asians in their midst.

In sum, although economic factors cannot be ignored, a major reason for moving Japanese Canadians from the West Coast was to protect them lest physical violence follow verbal attacks. As Japan's military machine seemed unstoppable in Asia, civilians increased their fears of a Japanese invasion, forgot the early advice of the press and politicians to keep calm, and ignored the distinction between Japanese who were nationals of that country and those who were Canadian citizens. Adding to the unease of British Columbians were the sometimes ambiguous statements of the Canadian government about its policy toward Japanese Canadians, and its seemingly dilatory action in removing male Japanese nationals after announcing in early January that it would do so. It is also true, of course, as the National Association of Japanese Canadians later asserted, that government policies were "motivated by political considerations based upon racist traditions accepted and encouraged by politicians." Indeed, Austin Taylor, who was in charge of the evacuation, said in May 1942 that "political pressure" made the government deem "it necessary to evacuate all Japanese from the coastal area."[109] In January and February 1942, the politicians did not have to encourage anti-Japanese feelings; they had only to respond. Alas, the anti-Japanese cries emanating from the coast spread to the interior of British Columbia and to the provinces to the east; that seriously complicated the efforts of the British Columbia Security Commission to resettle the Japanese.

2

Adverse Sentiments beyond the Coast

> The [BC Security] Commission was deluged by protests from private citizens and public bodies alike; not only from British Columbia but from widely scattered places all over the Dominion, and very largely on account of this the process of Evacuation was considerably hampered.
>
> BC Security Commission, *Removal of Japanese from Protected Areas*, 1942

Finding new locations for the Japanese was not easy. People who resided east of the Coast Mountains, informed by years of coastal propaganda, cited security concerns and the likelihood of Japanese becoming permanent residents to argue against their coming save possibly as workers under military guard. Even after any military threat passed, most jurisdictions were reluctant to accept evacuees. Local farmers and businessmen feared competition. Only in fading mining towns where new residents might maintain the local economy or among Prairie sugar beet growers who were desperate for labour was there a desire to accept evacuees, and even there opinion was split. Many Japanese Canadians, of course, believed that their evacuation was only a temporary measure.

Given "the magnitude of the task of implementing" the removal of the Japanese, the federal government had to act quickly. In the United States, the army took charge, but neither the Canadian army nor the RCMP had the necessary personnel to do so in Canada. Concluding that more than departmental effort was required, Prime Minister W.L.M. King suggested creating a special organization administered by men from British Columbia. The cabinet agreed and asked Austin Taylor, a prominent industrialist, to chair it. Taylor's appointment was announced later that day.[1] His assistant commissioners, F.J. Mead of the RCMP and John Shirras of the British Columbia Provincial Police, had extensive experience with the Japanese question. Twenty-one British Columbians served as an advisory board. Nine, including the attorney general, the federal minister of labour, and Harold Winch, leader of the CCF opposition, were Taylor's nominees.[2] The others, nominated by some BC Liberal MPs, reflected geographic interests. Ian Mackenzie thought the committee "reasonable" in representing all three parties but giving "the government a majority of friends." Then, to his consternation, Taylor appointed Grant MacNeil, a CCF MLA and former MP, and Mackenzie's "most inveterate political enemy," as commission secretary. MacNeil's politics were helpful. After he spoke, the provincial CCF convention called for a "speedy and humane" evacuation with each province taking a quota of Japanese. From the outset, Taylor asked the public to be "patient" and treat Japanese as "humanely and considerately" as they expected Canadian soldiers and civilians interned by Japan in Asia to be treated. Echoing that sentiment, Minister of Labour Humphrey Mitchell said in Vancouver that he hoped the movement would be handled with "the traditions that have made the British Empire great" – that is, common sense and not hysteria.[3]

That briefly pacified British Columbians who had been agitating for faster action given the deteriorating military situation. After General A.G.L. McNaughton warned that a diversionary raid on Canadian territory was likely, the press in Vancouver and Victoria resumed discussing the inadequacies of local defences. Premier John Hart said that people were "very worried." Lieutenant Governor W.C. Woodward expected Japanese bombs within six months. In Parliament, Howard Green (Conservative, Vancouver South) pictured Japanese invaders bayoneting prisoners of war and "raping and murdering our women as they did in Hong Kong"; he advised his parents not to move to Vancouver from their Kootenay home "now that there is such a likelihood of attack." Eventually, the Vancouver *Daily Province,* which had said that an attack was possible, concluded that "alarmist propaganda" had gone too far and welcomed news that the army would send two mobile divisions to the coast for its "psychological value"; the *Vancouver Sun* saw it as "vindication."[4]

By mid-May, Premier Hart denied that British Columbians were "jittery" about an invasion; nevertheless, a Canadian Institute of Public Opinion poll in June revealed that 50 percent of Canadians believed that a Japanese attack on the West Coast was likely within the year. In early June, Japanese planes attacked Dutch Harbor in the Aleutians, a Japanese submarine torpedoed an American merchant ship at the entrance to the Strait of Juan de Fuca, and the Japanese army captured the Aleutian island of Attu. On 20 June, Canada suffered the "first armed attack" on its soil when a Japanese submarine shelled the Estevan Point lighthouse and the nearby Hesquiat Village. Air raid protection personnel went on alert, reminded the public of air raid and gas attack precautions, demanded more equipment, imposed radio silence for several nights, briefly blacked-out Prince Rupert, and began planning to evacuate women and children from Vancouver Island.[5]

Demands for stronger defences continued along with speculation: was the attack on Dutch Harbor a feint to draw attention away from a later attack elsewhere, a reconnaissance raid, or simply "an audacious nuisance raid" to save face after an American raid on Tokyo? Not just the coast was concerned. The Edmonton *Bulletin* declared, "the Japanese dagger is pointed straight at Canada"; the Calgary *Albertan* asserted that the Dutch Harbor raid "should bring home to Canada that our country is by no means immune to attack." Yet after the attack on Estevan Point, there was no panic at the coast. The *Vancouver Sun* suggested that the submarine had attacked a "lonely lighthouse" because every other target "had ample protection." Both Mayor Andrew McGavin of Victoria and Premier Hart denied that people had the "jitters." The American success in the Battle of Midway in early June temporarily reduced fears of an invasion of North America. Censors did not stop speculation about raids but muted the talk of the lieutenant governor, premier, and provincial forestry service about "Jap bomber raids" that scared "nervously inclined" British Columbians. Most significantly, the removal of Japanese Canadians from dangerous areas eased fears except in Vancouver, where many still resided. By late April 1942, the Japanese had been removed from up-coast points and Vancouver Island; by early June, most had left their Lower Fraser Valley homes. The commission temporarily housed them at its central clearing station at the Hastings Park Exhibition Grounds. When it opened Hastings Park in mid-March, the commission had only general ideas about long-term placements. In April Taylor told the *New Canadian* that neither he "nor anyone else knows what the future of the evacuated Japanese will be except there is no intention to prevent families from being reunited."[6]

Despite the popularity of road-building schemes in the interior of British Columbia and in Ontario, plans to move large numbers of men to road camps were impeded by dissent within both the white and the Japanese communities. Some whites claimed, without foundation, of lax supervision, of Japanese earning more than veterans on relief or army privates, and of not working very hard. Although the Department of National Defence and the RCMP initially thought that the benefits of new roads outweighed the minimal risk of sabotage, American military officials and the joint chiefs of staff recommended closing camps near railway lines. Minister of Labour Mitchell was anxious to avoid having the Permanent Joint Board on Defence order their removal. Although Commissioner S.T. Wood noted that the Japanese workers were not detained or interned and were not considered dangerous, he reluctantly agreed "to play safe." However, what really curtailed the road camp scheme were the refusal of dissidents such as members of the Nisei Mass Evacuation Group to report because they insisted on being evacuated in family groups and the sit-down strikes of camp workers to protest grievances, especially separation from families and property losses. The strikes

"Don't Wait till Then," *Calgary Herald*, 26 March 1942. As cartoonist Stew Cameron depicted, the Rocky Mountains did not protect Albertans from worries about a Japanese invasion. Courtesy of the Provincial Archives of Alberta.

were effective. Over a decade later, a columnist in the *New Canadian* called it a "critical decision" that "more than any other single thing ... laid the foundation for our successful post-evacuation struggle to win our way back to greater freedom in a broader Canadian citizenship." In June the government let married men join their families in the interior and arranged to move single men to Ontario lumber camps. By the fall of 1942, fewer than 1,000 men were in road camps.[7]

By the time Hastings Park was closed on 30 September 1942, about 8,000 Japanese had passed through it; their most vivid memories were of crowding, a lack of privacy, and a stench that betrayed the normal use of many buildings as livestock barns. Hastings Park was never intended as anything more than a clearing station. Assuming the "immediate" removal of all Japanese from the "protected area," Vancouver City Council had commended Ottawa for its action but soon fretted over rumours that the park would be "a permanent depot to which Japanese from all over the Province are being sent and that a very long time may elapse before all of them are removed." The editor of the *Federationist* wondered what would happen if Japan invaded Australia and committed atrocities. To allay public concerns, Mackenzie promised Vancouver City Council that all Japanese would be out of the park in a few weeks and that, as long as he was in public life, they would not return to the coast. Taylor complained that the latter claim "sabotaged" efforts to dispel rumours among evacuees that men were being removed "so that women and children can be machine-gunned, etc., etc." Trying to reassure Japanese Canadians, he told the *New Canadian* that Mackenzie's statement lacked foundation. The *Federationist* facetiously suggested that, as the logical conclusion of his argument, the Scottish-born Mackenzie should consult the "Red Indians," who might "repatriate" him along with many others "whose forebears were unquestionably 'aliens.'"[8]

In any case, Mackenzie did not relieve apprehension in Vancouver, especially that of Alderman Wilson. When Minister of Labour Mitchell explained that the government was moving Japanese first from "dangerous and vulnerable points" and seeking suitable placements, Wilson accused him of showing no intention of removing the Japanese "entirely" after the war and of being governed by "influences" who wanted the Japanese to keep wages down. Wilson believed that Ottawa "would not go to the expense of removing Japanese from the Pacific Coast unless they had proof" that they were not loyal to Canada and could not be trusted if Japan invaded. Calling Vancouver a Japanese "dumping ground," he warned that public dissatisfaction could cause "undesirable occurrences." The RCMP already feared that "any open demonstration" by the Nisei Mass Evacuation Group might arouse a demand for "immediate and speedy action. Taylor agreed that inaction could revive "hysteria." So did Mackenzie, who quoted Wendell B. Farris, the new chief justice of the BC Supreme Court, as saying, "people are getting impatient." When detainees in the immigration shed rioted, the Vancouver *News-Herald* asked, "why are these potentially dangerous 'guests' left where they could conceivably co-operate with the Japanese raiding force, especially if the latter were working in co-operation with a local Fifth Column?" It called it "utterly and completely ridiculous" to have more Japanese in the city than ever before despite almost daily warnings of probable attacks on the coast. Taylor called the fracas "more playful than anything else," but the rioters were quickly interned.[9]

Most Japanese in Vancouver in the summer of 1942 were women, children, and older men who had been left in their own homes until they could be removed from the coast. Some employers laid off Japanese workers. The Vancouver General Hospital dismissed three student nurses; St. Paul's Hospital retained its one student and one staff nurse since few white patients complained. Although "Little Tokyo" started to look like a ghost town, some stores still operated, the Japanese worked in some sawmills, walked freely about, and even fished in the harbour. Vancouver City Council, accusing the commission of being "too soft," demanded that military authorities take over its responsibilities. Reporting that council was "getting restive and truculent," Mackenzie urged the commission to move the Japanese before seeing what it could do for them.[10]

Several BC Liberal MPs were also unhappy. George Cruickshank objected to Japanese logging or working in lumber mills near Hope, where the proximity of the Trans-Canada Highway and the Canadian Pacific Railway made opportunities for sabotage "obvious." R.W. Mayhew (Victoria) and G.G. McGeer (Vancouver-Burrard) attacked the commission's "bureaucratic incompetence" and Taylor's unwillingness to listen to advice. By June Taylor was so frustrated by press demands "for a statement on complete evacuation" and the government's failure to decide on a "definite policy" that he threatened to resign. He expected that continued separation of families would increase dissent among the Japanese and feared that the attack on Alaska might lead a "disgruntled public" to make "an all-out demand for complete evacuation proposals."[11]

As the Security Commission slowly moved the Japanese out of Vancouver, the Vancouver City Council and the Canadian Legion continued to complain of what the *Vancouver Sun* called the "fiasco" of Japanese "contempt" for regulations and their seeming trickle away from the city because of Ottawa's "fatal inability to move out of the usual departmental groove." Claiming that "the Japanese are now virtually upon the coast of Canada," BC MPs said that British Columbians were "extremely disturbed." They accused the commission of "pussyfooting" and of not being insufficiently stern in disciplining or guarding men in the road camps, controlling Japanese at the coast, or preventing them from acquiring land in the interior. They wanted to give the job of moving the Japanese to the military, as in the United States. Minister of

Labour Mitchell's admonition that painting Japanese in such colours impeded arrangements with other provinces and might lead to retaliations against "our young men in the Straits Settlements and Japan" did not please them.[12]

On 21 July, thirteen BC members met in the minister of labour's office to complain that the Japanese were "running us instead of us running them."[13] Mackenzie warned of "sabotage" and mass protest meetings unless "drastic action" was taken to move the Japanese from Vancouver. Looking ahead, he wanted all Japanese, including Canadian nationals, sent to Japan after the war. When they got no satisfaction, the members appealed to Parliament. In opening the debate, Howard Green suggested that evacuation plans were "breaking down" since – as of 9 July – 9,191 Japanese were still in the protected area, and some worked on the waterfront. Predicting "trouble" if they were not removed "without further delay" and repeating complaints about dissident road workers, he proposed that, rather than scatter the Japanese through the interior, the government adopt the American plan of setting up special towns for them. Others declared that it was a national problem, presented particular grievances such as the "seepage" of Japanese into the Okanagan, Cariboo, or Kamloops, and called for greater supervision of evacuees in the Kootenays, where W.K. Esling (Conservative, Kootenay West) admitted that the Japanese had been accepted. A.W. Neill (Independent, Comox-Alberni) attacked eastern Canada's "utter ignorance" of BC conditions and favoured turning the evacuation over to the military. As part of the peace settlement, he would repatriate all, including the Canadian born, who were "more aggressive and the more dangerous." "If some atrocity took place in Japan," he warned, "there might be a riot in Vancouver and fifty or a couple of hundred Japs might be killed."[14]

Such alarms captured attention at the coast. Mayor Andrew McGavin of Victoria and the reeves of the adjacent municipalities of Oak Bay and Saanich wired Mayhew: "Lack of ordinary foresight on part of government appears about to plunge population of British Columbia into irretrievable and horrible disaster." In a panic, they declared that "time is very short" and demanded that "internment by military [is] only solution irrespective of financial standing." Mayhew wisely ignored their request to read the telegram in the House of Commons. In Duncan the *Cowichan Leader* called for interning "the whole lot"; the Union of BC Municipalities approved a Kelowna resolution that the Japanese be put under charge of military authorities and, "with all reasonable despatch," be moved east of the Rockies or interned "at such places and under such conditions as shall ensure full military security."[15]

In fact the MPs were out of step with some of their constituents. There was sympathy for the commission in Vancouver. The Anglican Synod expressed appreciation of its "skill, care, and courtesy" in dealing with the evacuation, as did the Roman Catholic archbishop. The *Vancouver Sun* admitted that the commission had done a good job given Ottawa's failure to make plans to move the Japanese before coastal residents insisted on it. The Vancouver *Daily Province* agreed and accused the MPs of being out of touch. "Otherwise," it declared, "they would not talk about the likelihood of anti-Japanese riots in Vancouver or the turning of British Columbia into another Hong Kong." Some civility survived. At Chilliwack, two young people's groups had farewell parties for Japanese members who were leaving. Similarly, several white residents of Mission presented departing Japanese with gifts, and the *Fraser Valley Record* remarked that "through their honesty and co-operation these Japanese men, women, boys and girls won the admiration of many white citizens and these people were indeed sorry to see them go."[16]

THE SECURITY COMMISSION initially hoped to put about 2,500 Japanese in Alberta's sugar beet industry, about 5,000 in road camps and 1,000 in lumber camps in the BC interior, and about 3,000 women and children in or near ghost towns such as Lumberton, Kaslo, and Greenwood. It knew that the Okanagan wanted evacuees only as temporary labour under control. There and elsewhere, opposition related to fears of sabotage also reflected concerns about competition and permanent settlement. At one point, when the commission was short about 12,000 placements, a frustrated Austin Taylor urged Ottawa to make all parts of Canada outside the restricted area take a certain number of Japanese. Nevertheless, the commission would not "arbitrarily place Japanese in locations where the sentiment of the resident population was adverse to them."[17]

When the evacuation proceeded slowly in the spring and summer of 1942, British Columbians readily blamed the "bottleneck" on "some of our sister provinces" that were "fighting a 'delaying action' against accepting them" and displaying a "terrible lack of Canadian unity" by not respecting national security needs. After chastising "Canada east of the Rockies" for not accepting "its responsibilities except after long and painful negotiation," the *Vancouver Sun* later decided that "the enforced migration elsewhere of the Coast Japs ... will make it easier for the rest of Canada to come around to our view." When Toronto refused to admit Japanese, the Vancouver *Daily Province* observed, "isn't that characteristic of good old Toronto? It clings to the war industries; they provide profit and a payroll. It rejects the Japanese, even if the safety of the country requires their removal from the coast defence area ... Toronto wants all the advantages that come from war, but passes the disabilities on to somebody else." Complaints against the "east" were not confined to the press. United Church leaders attributed agitation in Vancouver for sending all Japanese to Japan to "growing despair for eastern support of fair and comprehensive national policies of geographic and occupational dispersion." They urged the president of the BC conference to press on eastern delegates that the "numbers involved are small in relation to population of Canada but too great for absorption and assimilation by this province." The *New*

Canadian complained of the failure of the rest of Canada to accept evacuees as a matter of "national importance."[18]

Given their failure to co-operate with the placement of male Japanese nationals, the unwillingness of other provinces to accept Canadian-born Japanese was not surprising. In any case, few Japanese wanted to go farther east than Alberta. The commission did not consider the Maritimes but briefly looked at Quebec, where the French-language press had shown interest in the Pacific War and West Coast defences but had limited interest in Japanese Canadians. Premier Adelard Godbout was prepared to have a few, specifically two gardeners that the MLA for Chicoutimi wanted to hire, but reminded federal officials that the Lac St. Jean region was home to large hydroelectric power facilities and the Aluminum Company of Canada. A few hundred Japanese, mainly young adult Nisei, later moved to the province, mainly to Montreal, where jobs were plentiful but housing was scarce and expensive. They entered a variety of occupations, and some opened their own businesses.[19]

With its many employment opportunities and Premier Mitchell Hepburn's offer to accept 2,000 Japanese, Ontario was more promising. That attitude won grudging praise in British Columbia, where some editors thought that "dumping" 10,000 to 15,000 Japanese on Ontario "poetic justice" and "a useful contribution to the solution of a national problem." When the Ontario cabinet rejected plans to employ Japanese in lumber camps and beet farms, *Maclean's* reported "ironical smiles" in British Columbia. Hepburn was not amused. Concerned about a serious lack of agricultural labour, particularly in the beet fields of southern Ontario, he believed that admitting Japanese would "assist our fellow Canadians in British Columbia" who wished to move the Japanese eastward "not because of any overt act on the part of the Japanese" but because of their concentration at the coast. Indeed, Hepburn believed that the prospective agricultural labourers were "Canadian-born and our way of life is their way of life." As for any who might be dangerous, Hepburn would move them to locations where they could do little harm and contribute to the war effort. He said that his government would co-operate fully with Ottawa but that Ontario farmers would have to decide if they wanted Japanese labour. As for himself, he employed eleven evacuees on his farm.[20]

The reluctance of Ontarians to accept Japanese was partly the fault of BC propaganda about potential fifth columnists. As Stephanie Bangarth has shown, southwestern Ontarians had many of the same anti-Japanese sentiments as British Columbians. The *Brantford Expositor,* for example, in commenting on the Immediate Action Committee leaflet circulated by the Victoria branch of the Canadian Legion, repeated West Coast suspicions of potential fifth columnists. While criticizing the government for acting so slowly, it admitted that the delay might be attributable to the unwillingness of other provinces to take Japanese. The Ontario executive of the IODE got that group's national convention to demand that the Japanese be kept under "strict supervision" for security reasons. The National Council of Women, however, merely called for the immediate removal of all Japanese from the Vancouver area. The Toronto District Trades and Labour Council endorsed the petition of the Immediate Action Committee that questioned the loyalty of the Japanese in Canada. A leader of Toronto's Chinese community said that "a Jap is always a Jap at heart, no matter where he was born. It would be very, very dangerous to let even one run loose in this city." When six Japanese families representing twenty-six individuals, all self-supporting members of the United Church, and including several University of British Columbia students and graduates, applied to move to Toronto, Mayor Fred Conboy had a private meeting with members of the Board of Control, the RCMP, the Trades and Labour Council, the IODE, the Local Council of Women, the Canadian Manufacturers' Association, the Board of Trade, and the manager of an insurance company. Despite the fine credentials of the applicants, who had mentioned their contributions to Canada's war effort, the mayor thought it inadvisable for Japanese families to move to the city because of its many war industries. Church groups offered to sponsor young female domestic workers, but the council of Forest Hills, an upper-class village within Toronto, reversed its decision to admit Japanese workers after a veterans' association protested and several councillors questioned the Canadian patriotism of the evacuees. James McRuer, a Toronto lawyer sympathetic to civil rights, told the mayor that Japanese girls would help women who were doing war work and could be "as safely kept in Toronto as any other place" if "under proper supervision." In 1942 a few Japanese with local sponsors did settle in Toronto, where at least one recalled that he found no "extreme discrimination." London City Council was concerned about the lack of surveillance of Japanese, who were seen walking around after dark. In Ottawa municipal authorities objected. When a resident applied to bring a Japanese couple, formerly in the employ of the lieutenant governor of British Columbia, to work as domestic servants, the Board of Control sympathized with his inability to find other workers but unanimously agreed that, although the Japanese were good servants, "and some were faithful Canadians," it was impossible "to tell those who would be faithful from those who would be spies."[21]

Economic considerations often outweighed security concerns in shaping Ontario attitudes. Some northerners were anxious to have new highways or workers in isolated lumber camps; however, as one member of the legislature suggested, after the atrocities in Hong Kong Ontario's roads could wait. In Fort William, city council initially protested that placing 3,000 evacuees in nearby pulpwood camps would endanger local munitions plants and the transcontinental railways. However, when a serious labour shortage developed, the Fort William City Council and the Trades and Labour Council agreed to their employment in essential industries if no other workers were available, provided that they were paid prevailing wages and that the government guaranteed their removal after the war. Pulp and paper workers' unions in northern Ontario, however, objected to Japanese labour. And, once they learned of the region's isolation and lack of family accommodation, few Japanese would accept the work. The lack of family housing also made farm placements unattractive. The few single men recruited to work in sugar beet fields around Chatham satisfied their employers, but city residents resented their presence. The hostility of urban residents, low earnings because of poor weather, difficult work, and restrictions on their activities encouraged Nisei labourers to seek other employment in Ontario.[22]

In 1943 and 1944, attitudes to Japanese in Ontario "fluctuated" according to the state of the war or reports of atrocities in Asia. Ottawa's propaganda efforts did nothing to ease hostility. For example, late in 1942, a National Film Board production, *The Mask of Nippon,* portrayed the Japanese as a race that "could practise deceit and treachery in such a manner that their every action held a double meaning." Early in 1944, the Wartime Information Board issued a pamphlet in which historian A.R.M. Lower asserted that the Japanese who had "a knack for getting themselves disliked" might have to be deported after the war. In the summer of 1945, McGill University sociologist Forrest E. La Violette observed that "pre-war stereotypes of Japanese character," though in "the process of change," were "still basic to some proposed solutions for the settlement of the so-called Japanese problem."[23]

Local circumstances also affected sentiment. In Beamsville, the Department of Labour attributed strong anti-Japanese feeling to two employers with reputations for using cheap labour. At Aylmer, the rotten eggs that Royal Canadian Air Force personnel from a nearby base brought to a demonstration and the "intimation" that Royal Australian Air Force trainees would use violence if Japanese were employed in a laundry created a potentially dangerous situation. Fourteen employees refused to work when the laundry hired a Japanese national and his wife. About 250 citizens and airmen gathered at a city council meeting to demand their removal. So tense was the situation that the mayor sought to put the Japanese couple in the county jail for their own protection. A clergyman temporarily defused the mob, but the only long-term solution was the removal of the couple. Ingersoll actually sought Japanese help, but a mob tried to invade a fertilizer factory that hired some. The town council, however, refused to ask for their dismissal. Violence, threatened or actual, was exceptional.[24]

Elsewhere a desperate labour shortage made Japanese workers more acceptable. In Hamilton, at the beginning of 1943, only three or four firms would hire Japanese; by August twenty or so companies, including major ones such as the Steel Company of Canada, did hire Japanese despite protests by a local veterans' association against "spreading British Columbia's problem throughout Canada and most particularly Ontario." It favoured sending those whose loyalty could not be proven to Japan but would let individuals of "proven loyalty" remain. At Oshawa, unions rejected the idea of Japanese co-workers, but in London some Nisei were elected to a union executive.[25]

Toronto maintained its opposition to the Japanese, but the BC Security Commission sought to place young men and women in the city in the hope that their families would follow. To assist in the resettlement process, the commission had one of its officials, Mrs. C.V. Booth, explain to a group of Toronto women, most of whom were associated with the Young Women's Christian Association, that the commission was encouraging the Japanese not to "collect in one part of the city." A men's subcommittee was also set up. Both committees endorsed the idea of scattering Japanese families around the city and encouraging the Nisei to join church, athletic, and other groups where they might mix with other Canadians. When some Japanese arrived, two controllers (elected members of the municipal government) demanded an investigation; the *Toronto Daily Star* and the *Evening Telegram* said that they were "running around Toronto." As the labour shortage increased, hostility waned but revived with stories of atrocities early in 1944. In March 1944, the Board of Control asked the federal government not to put any more evacuees in the city; in November the Police Commission refused to issue business licences to Nisei. Forest Hills still refused to admit Japanese domestics. By the spring of 1945, Premier George Drew suggested that Ontario could exclude any newcomers, a point that the Vancouver *News-Herald* quickly noted was contrary to the British North America Act, as British Columbia had long ago discovered. Thus, while Japanese continued to move to various parts of Ontario, including Toronto, their numbers were few partly due to their reluctance to move to areas where they might not be welcome and where they would be separated from family and friends. They were widely dispersed and employed in a variety of occupations, mainly in small factories or the service industries. A few did highly skilled work, but many found themselves in demeaning jobs. Former fishermen, for example, found it difficult to take orders from a foreman; few girls could get white-collar work, and those who worked in domestic service disliked "'rigid class distinctions' in this part of Canada where they are looked down [on] as 'housemaids.'"[26]

In the immediate wake of the announcement that all Japanese would be required to leave the coast, the *Winnipeg Free Press* wondered why, since a few Japanese might try to aid the enemy, the government was so slowly moving them. In Manitoba, as elsewhere on the Prairies, opinions about accepting Japanese varied, but urban areas were generally reluctant to have them, while areas of intensive agriculture such as sugar beet production wanted labour. Early in February 1942, Manitoba's minister of agriculture called a meeting to discuss having Japanese labour assist with the beet and other crops. Many Winnipeggers did not want Japanese residents, and some members of the Trades and Labour Council feared the Japanese as a "menace" who would be cheap labour and who would aggravate a housing shortage. Mayor John Queen, however, indicated that if there were "some mighty good reasons" the city might admit a few if Ottawa covered the costs of education and public assistance and ensured that they did not become "cheap labour." Indeed, he warned that, if word got out that one firm already employed Japanese at less than going wages, "there would be an outcry against the Security Commission supplying cheap labour to certain employers." He need not have worried; the Security Commission was unwilling to let Japanese even meet occasionally in Winnipeg. Residents of a market gardening area twenty miles north of Winnipeg opposed the entry of Japanese, presumably because they foresaw competition. In the north and south, however, there were demands for highway workers and sugar beet workers respectively. Flin Flon's municipal council unanimously endorsed the idea of importing Japanese to do highway work. When the federal government scotched that plan without explanation, local residents speculated that the reason might be fear of sabotage in the area's copper and zinc mines. If removing Japanese from British Columbia was in the national interest, then Premier John Bracken offered to co-operate. He asked Ottawa to assume full financial obligations, provide protection from sabotage, and remove the Japanese after the emergency, but he regarded the offer of a formal agreement as an unnecessary courtesy. Attorney General James McLenigan explained that Manitoba was willing to "fit in" if Ottawa thought that placing Japanese there would assist the war effort. J.B. Shirras of the Security Commission surveyed possible placements and helped to prepare the way by telling the press that the Japanese were "educated, clean, law abiding," experienced agricultural workers who had "shown themselves to be superior residents" and had enjoyed a higher standard of living than they were likely to experience during the war. To ease doubts about their loyalty, the commission emphasized that they were either Canadian born or naturalized. When Lockport and St. Andrews, two rural communities, the homes of many of the Winnipeg Grenadiers who were prisoners of war in Hong Kong, raised strong objections, the Security Commission quickly moved the evacuees to other places. Generally, however, Manitoba sugar beet growers welcomed Japanese workers, and to keep their families together some Japanese accepted the work. By October 1942, 1,053 individuals had moved to Manitoba. Their numbers did not increase greatly, and Manitobans, who were short of labour, appear to have tolerated them. By 1944 the province seemed likely to co-operate in any permanent dispersal policy.[27]

Farther west the predominance of grain farming in Saskatchewan meant that the province had no need for large numbers of farm workers. Thus, Premier W.J. Patterson indicated that his province would deal with families on a case-by-case basis. A few Japanese had already arrived. In April the RCMP reported that nine had come to Regina, where there were already a few Japanese who, despite the adverse effects of the war on their businesses, were doing everything they could to help the war effort. In Saskatoon it was another story. When George Tamaki, a native of New Westminster and a graduate of the University of British Columbia who had attended the University of Saskatchewan as an exchange law student from Dalhousie University, asked permission to bring his two high-school-age brothers to the city so that they might attend the collegiate, the *Saskatoon Star-Phoenix* interviewed thirteen representative citizens. Four were willing to see at least a few Japanese come to the city. Some of the other nine cited no particular reason for their opposition, but two cited potential economic competition. After pondering the matter for over a month, Saskatoon City Council bowed to pressure from a number of local individuals and organizations that expressed concern for the safety of military and industrial establishments, fear of labour competition, and resentment of an enemy race. It refused to admit them and rejected the application of Taira Yasumaka despite bank references showing that he could support his family and pay school fees for his children and church references that he had been the superintendent of a United Church Sunday school for many years. A few weeks later it took no time to inform Y. Takashi, a fourth-year engineering student who had permission from the university, the BC Security Commission, and the police to attend the University of Saskatchewan, that it would not admit him to the city. Almost all members of the council shared the view of Alderman F.B. Caswell: "We have two Japs in town now and that's two too many."[28]

Alberta, the most westerly of the prairie provinces, had had Japanese settlers since 1906. As of October 1941, 551 Japanese, of whom 264 were children, were registered as residents. About 350 lived in the Lethbridge district, especially in farming areas around Raymond, with about forty in Raymond itself. Another forty or so lived in Edmonton. The rest were scattered. Many were farmers who owned their own land and raised a variety of crops but principally sugar beets. Like their counterparts at the coast, they had been registered and fingerprinted before Pearl Harbor; unlike the coastal Japanese, they could vote if they were naturalized or Canadian born, but they were not a political force since many of the Canadian born were too young to vote. Nevertheless, they were keen to express their loyalty to Canada by taking pledges of loyalty, donating to the Red Cross, and in the case of some Nisei, enlisting in the Canadian army. At Raymond, when twenty-six residents in the Canadian army, including three Nisei, came home on Christmas furlough in 1941, the Canadian Legion, Lions, and Rotarians sponsored a banquet in their honour, and Harry Hironaka gave a speech stressing his loyalty to Canada. A few days later the Japanese community held its own banquet in their honour. Among the guests were James H. Walker, the local MLA, the mayor, and other Caucasians who praised the Raymond Japanese as a "fine type of citizens."[29]

Security concerns predated the decision to move all Japanese from the coast. As early as 8 December, Edmonton took precautions against air raids. The Edmonton *Bulletin* noted that a modern bomber could easily fly in from the coast and that the Aleutians provided a "stepping stone" to Canada; the *Lethbridge Herald* thought that its city's airport and railway facilities could be targets for bombers operating from aircraft carriers. In January and February, the *Calgary Herald* ran several editorials on the possibility of fifth column activity by Canadian Japanese and the inadequacies of coastal defences. Reflecting concern that Alberta might be vulnerable, it even ran a cartoon about building bomb shelters in Calgary backyards. While sympathizing with security concerns on the coast, the *Calgary Herald* did not think it "practicable" to move the entire Japanese population of British Columbia east of the Rockies, but in the immediate aftermath of the mid-January announcement that Japanese male nationals of military age would be moved from the coastal zone the paper focused on the defence of the coast rather than on the movement of Japanese to Alberta.[30]

In contrast, the Edmonton *Bulletin* stressed that prairie residents would oppose any such movement and suggested placing the Japanese in secluded valleys in British Columbia's interior from which they could neither escape nor do damage. As it reflected on the desire of beet growers for labour and the need of the Japanese for a "chance to earn a living," the *Bulletin* conceded that despite potential fifth column activities it might be possible to deal with the Japanese individually and treat them like other enemy aliens – that is, interfering only with those who invited "actual suspicion" and allowing "trusties" to work in the beet industry. "Any unusual or discriminatory" action, the *Bulletin* warned, could give Tokyo an excuse for reprisals against Canadians.[31]

Even when only the evacuation of Japanese nationals was planned, Lethbridge City Council objected to the entry of any coastal Japanese even if they were usefully employed in the beet industry. Medicine Hat City Council believed that evacuees should be employed only on government work projects and under close supervision. The *Calgary Herald* thought that, since the Japanese were "good workers," they might be usefully put to work building roads in the Peace River or the Alaska Highway or in the sugar beet fields.[32]

The announcement that all Japanese residents would be moved from the coastal defence zone created what sociologist Forrest La Violette called "the dilemma of economic need versus social rejection." Beet growers and processors in southern Alberta wanted Japanese labour, but urban boards of trade, chambers of commerce, and Canadian Legion branches worried about security and costs of education, relief, and health care. They did not want Japanese even as visitors. The Edmonton *Bulletin* immediately recognized the problem: "No province wants them, and no community seems even willing to tolerate them ... Tokyo's treachery has made the Japanese name very positively detested all over Canada, where it was already unpopular." Yet it

"Taking No Chances," *Calgary Herald,* 15 January 1942. In the aftermath of Pearl Harbor, even Prairie residents became concerned about air raid protection. Courtesy of the Provincial Archives of Alberta.

admitted that "they must be moved somewhere" and be allowed to earn a living or be supported at taxpayers' expense; it also noted the need to avoid discriminatory treatment lest Tokyo use that as an excuse for reprisals. The *Calgary Herald* continued to see benefits in having Japanese build roads or even the Alaska Highway, but it still worried about security.[33]

Despite urban qualms, a delegation representing beet growers, Canadian Sugar Factories, the federal Department of Agriculture, and Lethbridge City Council consulted the BC Security Commission in Vancouver. The commission was anxious to place Japanese in the beet fields, especially since housing was available. It promised to select experienced agricultural workers who had been vetted by the RCMP, to pay for education, health care, and social services, to provide "strict supervision," and if necessary to provide additional police protection. On their return, the delegates told a representative gathering in Lethbridge that they had made no commitments about accepting Japanese labour. After several members of the audience complained that more than fifty Japanese had recently moved into the Raymond area without the authority of the Security Commission, the meeting called for the removal of all "unauthorized immigrants" before any controlled movement could be considered. That caveat created an opening to discuss the arguments presented by the delegates who had gone to Vancouver. They explained that the Security Commission had offered up to 500 families of five each whose movement would be controlled. One delegate, A.E. Palmer of the Dominion Experimental Farm, who spoke as a citizen and not as a government employee, said that the "Japanese problem" was a national one and that while their presence posed "some real dangers" Alberta was in a better position to handle them than the coast. Similarly, Mayor David H. Elton of Lethbridge did not favour having enemy aliens in the area but said that, "if the government of this country wants us to take the Japs and help solve the problem, that is the thing we ought to do." An RCMP observer reported that the latter argument reflected the meeting's tone. A few days later Philip Baker, president of the Alberta Beet Growers, informed Minister of Labour Mitchell that "regardless of considerable opposition we believe saner citizens for patriotic reasons would support [the] policy of bringing Japanese families here under strict supervision" if assured that "both Japanese Canadian citizens and Japanese aliens sent would be removed" after the emergency. Support was mixed. At Picture Butte, beet growers unanimously agreed that it was their "patriotic duty" to assist in moving the Japanese and offered to "cooperate in every way with the Dominion government in bringing Japanese labor to this district."[34]

Other communities, however, strongly opposed the Japanese. In the legislature, James Walker, who in late December had praised the good citizenship of Raymond's Japanese, said that people there were "up in arms" about Japanese who had come from British Columbia on their own or to join friends and relatives among the approximately seventy-two Japanese families who had lived in Raymond for many years. Premier William Aberhart replied with an RCMP statement that there was no reason for alarm, that those who had arrived or were coming soon had jobs, and that the established Japanese settlers in the province were "well behaved and apparently loyal." That statement did not relieve the situation. A few days later the Raymond branch of the Canadian Legion expressed "strong opposition" to an influx of Japanese except under government supervision and an agreement that they not remain permanently. Rumours circulated that "a stream" of Japanese had "poured" into the district; in fact, by early March only twenty had arrived and all with RCMP permission. Yet some Raymond residents claimed that more than fifty had come looking for work. To strengthen their hand in protesting "any open movement of Japanese" from British Columbia and the expansion of Hutterite land holdings, a delegation of Raymond residents secured the support of the Lethbridge Board of Trade. Since news of atrocities at Hong Kong had just been released, one Board of Trade member said that, "if we must accept Japs into this district, they should be behind barbed wire."[35]

The Raymond Legion and Citizens Committee also organized a mass meeting "Re: Hutterites and Japanese" on Sunday, 15 March. Despite six inches of slushy snow, about 500 people from around the district attended. It was not wholly a protest meeting, for Philip Baker and Frank Taylor, who had been in the delegation that interviewed the Security Commission, explained that any Japanese brought to the area would help with a critical labour shortage, be under supervision, and be returned to British Columbia after the war. Nevertheless, the meeting protested "the unrestricted influx of Japanese to the district and the Hutterite acquisition of further lands." The resolutions suggested that an increased Japanese population would endanger the coal mines, air fields, railways, sugar factories, and irrigation works. The *Lethbridge Herald* declared that every Japanese was "a potential fifth columnist" and must be kept under "thorough surveillance," but it believed that southern Alberta should accept a number of Japanese agricultural workers and let them earn their own livings and "not be a deadweight on the Federal Government." Beet growers around Raymond, Picture Butte, and Coaldale welcomed Japanese families as a source of labour and to assist the Security Commission.[36]

At nearby Taber, residents also reluctantly accepted the Japanese. The *Taber Times* warned that the Japanese might solve the labour problem but that turning them loose in southern Alberta "would almost certainly create a great deal of disturbance." It urged keeping them in military camps and bringing them to the beet fields under guard. Taber residents filled the local theatre "to overflowing" at a mass meeting organized mainly by businessmen and farmers. Although A.E. Palmer answered many questions about the Vancouver meeting, other speakers, claiming that the district was "already overloaded with many aliens," opposed the entry of Japanese labour. An RCMP observer, however, concluded that people would "make the best of it in the interests of patriotism and loyalty." A few days later the Taber-Barnwell Sugar Beet Growers said that they would "loyally" support the government by taking sufficient Japanese to meet their labour needs – but only "for the duration of the war as their unpleasant duty." They also asked that no enemy alien be allowed to purchase, rent, or lease lands for the duration of the war and for five years afterward. The local branch of the Canadian Legion was still unhappy, particularly when some Japanese found work in the local cannery; its motives were not wholly economic, for it also opposed Japanese children "mingling or associating under any pretence with our children."[37]

Thus, although Premier Aberhart believed that British Columbia was "the best place" for the Japanese, he did not protest their arrival if the federal government guaranteed to supervise them and covered all costs, including maintenance, education, and medical care. After Aberhart informed the federal government of these terms, Roy Lee (Social Credit, Taber), who opposed employing the Japanese in the beet fields, introduced a motion declaring that an "influx of substantial numbers of Japanese into Alberta might create serious complications and impose burdens upon Albertans" and must be "entirely removed from the province at the end of the war." The legislature unanimously passed the resolution. Although Austin Taylor assured Aberhart that the commission would control any Japanese moved into Alberta and cover any relief payments, Aberhart was not convinced that the commission had sufficient power to do that and especially to remove them after the emergency. Thus, Prime Minister King agreed to pass orders-in-council giving the commission adequate powers to fulfill its promises to remove the Japanese after the war. Although Alberta and Ottawa did not formally conclude an agreement until 6 May 1942, by early April the press was reporting the arrival of Japanese families destined for the beet fields.[38]

While the beet-growing areas grudgingly accepted Japanese agricultural workers, many Alberta cities and towns were not prepared to have Japanese in their midst. The situation was not improved by the *Calgary Herald*'s repeated attacks on the federal government for not moving the Japanese more quickly from the "vital defence areas of Canada's Pacific coast." It demanded that the federal government "exercise its sovereign authority by distributing these undesirable aliens all the way from the Rocky Mountains to the Maritime provinces, but always under strict police control and continued surveillance." When the Canadian Legion national convention in May 1942 passed a resolution that any peace treaty must provide for the return of all Japanese nationals to Japan as soon as possible after the war, the *Calgary Herald* noted, "now that the coast Japanese are being spread in these other provinces there is a growing recognition of the validity of British Columbia's protest against the presence of aliens whose ideas are diametrically opposed to democratic principles. Ontario, Alberta, and so forth do not want a permanent Japanese population." The Calgary Trades and Labour Council urged interning all Japanese for the duration and denying them employment until veterans and other citizens were fully employed and then only under supervision. Calgary councillors, claiming that they did not want people who had been "forcibly removed by the authorities," and noting that their city was an important military and munitions centre, rejected the application of two Japanese to reside in the city even though one of them had been educated in Calgary and could work in his father's store. In a case of the "pot calling the kettle black," when the City of Ottawa refused to admit Japanese domestic servants, both the

Calgary Herald and the Calgary *Albertan* suggested that Ottawa was "selfish" in not accepting any Japanese.[39]

Before the announcement of a mass evacuation, Lethbridge City Council expressed its opposition to a transfer of "enemy aliens" from British Columbia to southern Alberta. After the announcement that all Japanese would be moved from the coast, the Lethbridge Trades and Labour Council, citing possible sabotage of the many military bases on the Prairies and the possible lowering of labour standards by cheap Japanese labour, called for the internment of all Japanese in an isolated area. Similarly, a Board of Trade member said, "if we must accept the Japs into this district, they should be behind barbed wire." Once the mass evacuation was under way, like the *Lethbridge Herald,* the board felt a patriotic duty to co-operate with the federal government to solve "a serious problem" but opposed the employment of enemy aliens by private individuals. After Alderman J.A. Jardine got the assurance of the Security Commission that the city would not be responsible for them, aldermen accepted the advice of Mayor Elton that "we must subdue our personal feelings and co-operate with the government." Those feelings toward the Japanese were bitter. During the discussion, aldermen referred to Japan as "the most treacherous nation on earth" and claimed that all Japanese were loyal to the emperor. The local chapter of the IODE got the provincial chapter to call for "constant vigilance" over Japanese nationals and the internment of all adult Japanese nationals brought east of the Rockies." Given such sentiments, the city's co-operation was limited. It remained "positively opposed" to the employment of Japanese "in any capacity whatsoever" within city limits. When twenty beet workers began working at the Broder Cannery, the council reluctantly let them stay for the week when their labour was urgently required. Similarly, Medicine Hat City Council refused to let a Japanese resident of twenty years standing bring his brother and family from Vancouver to the city for the duration of the conflict. In so doing, the council reiterated its policy that it would "not assist in any way in bringing Japanese into this area" and reaffirmed its view that "all Japs should be kept together under government supervision."[40]

Since northern Alberta farms were not labour intensive, there was no suggestion of placing Japanese there, but the City of Edmonton was another matter. Nine Japanese families representing eighteen individuals asked Edmonton City Council for permission to reside there. Reverend J.T. Stephens, superintendent of the United Church's All People's Mission, supported their application and said that all were Christians and "patriotic Canadians." The applicants assured the city that they had sufficient funds to support themselves. Two, for example, Mr. Shimotakahara, the proprietor of the Modiste Fashion Shop, and Mr. Kuwahara, the manager of Silkolina, Ltd., were Vancouver merchants. Mr. and Mrs. Kato explained that they particularly desired to settle in Edmonton since their son was a house surgeon at the

Edmonton General Hospital. Mayor John W. Fry was sympathetic to their application and those of similar individuals but feared the establishment of "a Japanese colony" in a strategic air centre. The Edmonton *Bulletin* insisted that any evacuees be kept under police supervision. Only two aldermen objected: one was concerned about security, while the other thought that the Japanese might take jobs "badly needed by city residents." After being assured that the evacuees would cover their own costs, including the education of their children, council accepted them. It later admitted a few other families, but only three actually arrived. Some may have been discouraged by the inhospitality of the Chamber of Commerce's objection to "individual infiltration" lest it "lead to the opening of loop-holes through which application for individual treatment might be made" and provide "opportunities for 'unfortunate' acts which may have a bearing upon the nation's welfare." Edmonton City Council also began questioning the admission of individual Japanese. Citing a serious housing shortage, in June it stopped admitting them.[41]

Although there were no evacuees in Jasper, the Geikie and Decoigne work camps were nearby. "Feeling" in Jasper was reported to be "very high" because the workers were not under guard and could sabotage the railway. Although only five at a time were allowed to come to the town for recreation, railway workers and the Canadian Legion protested their presence. Residents were so nervous that local veterans had armed themselves with borrowed rifles and made themselves available if needed to assist the police. Canadian National Railways was concerned about publicity given to their presence. Rumours circulated about laziness, drunkenness, strikes, and the raising of a Japanese flag in the camps, but the RCMP ascertained that the stories had no foundation. Nevertheless, the RCMP reported that recent arrivals, mainly clerks and storekeepers, were unfamiliar with manual labour and inclined "to crab and make trouble." Troublemakers were promptly removed.[42]

By the end of October 1942, 2,585 Japanese had been moved to Alberta sugar beet farms, and others followed.[43] Albertans' acceptance of the Japanese was a slow process. Although farmers praised their hard work, the Security Commission admitted that "the main object of the Alberta farmers is to exploit Japanese labour." It reported that a number of Japanese had asked to go to the interior housing settlements because of poor living conditions and inadequate incomes from seasonal work. The provincial government, probably responding to a resolution from the Union of Alberta Municipalities, forbade the Japanese to patronize beer parlours and liquor stores. Bitterness did not disappear. When the University of Alberta admitted three Japanese students in 1943, the Edmonton *Bulletin* attacked it and Edmonton City Council, saying that it was impossible to distinguish between loyal and disloyal Japanese. Lethbridge City Council opposed the request of local hospitals to hire Nisei domestic workers, and only in January 1946 were Lethbridge residents permitted to hire Nisei girls as domestic servants, although not all the girls could obtain permits to work legally. W.S. Wallace, a local resident who had been seconded to the American army during the war to learn the Japanese language, on returning to Lethbridge in March 1946, observed how "Japanese were made to feel unwelcome in every sense of the word." He was one of the Lethbridge residents who formed a Consultative Committee on Japanese Canadians to enlighten the public about the situation of Japanese Canadians. The committee noted that the Japanese were good customers for local merchants and an important labour supply but would leave southern Alberta if they could not live and work in the city. Although some local Nisei were somewhat impatient with the Consultative Committee, which in their eyes was not pushing for change, they reported that the names of the "girls" employed in the city had appeared on the municipal voters' lists and that six Canadian Japanese had been admitted to the carpenters' union. Many years later Wallace noted that the city's hostility gradually faded, and "the despicable ordinance died a natural death." In 1944, Calgary City Council rejected a request to admit 100 Japanese to relieve a severe labour shortage in packing plants, and Edmonton denied the applications of two Japanese to reside in the city. Calling them a source of "cheap" labour, the Alberta Federation of Labour wanted Japanese removed from the province. After the dispersal program was announced, Ernest C. Manning, who became premier of Alberta after Aberhart's death, reminded the federal government that his province's agreement with the BC Security Commission had provided for the removal of the Japanese after the war, but federal officials found that his real concern was the cost of educating Japanese children.[44] In sum both urban and rural Albertans and both employers and workers at best grudgingly accepted the Japanese and only for the duration of the war.

While coastal British Columbians chastised fellow Canadians for their reluctance to accept the Japanese, that reluctance also appeared in their own province. The Vancouver *Daily Province* rightly attacked interior communities for acting like eastern centres in refusing to accept Japanese. The *Vancouver Sun* tried to ease concerns by avowing that Vancouver had "no plan to unload our problem on their doorstep." Some interior residents wanted Japanese labour to build public works such as roads or airports. A few observers, such as the *Similkameen Star* of Princeton, counselled "dignified restraint" and fairness toward the Japanese; it wanted to close the gap in the Hope-Princeton road. Other interior residents worried that the Japanese would remain after the war. Hostility persisted in some places, but in the smaller communities that received relatively large numbers of Japanese propinquity led to neighbourly relations.[45]

The Okanagan Valley, which offered the most employment opportunities, was the only inland area with a significant prewar Japanese population. Approximately 1,000 Japanese lived mainly in rural areas around Kelowna and

Vernon. Between 7 December 1941 and the formation of the BC Security Commission, an unknown number of their friends and relatives from the coast, the "Pearl Harbor Japanese," joined them. In an exaggerated claim, W.A.C. Bennett (MLA, South Okanagan, Coalition-Conservative) said that about 2,000 had moved into his constituency since registration in March 1941 and that hundreds more were expected. There were so many objections to their coming that an RCMP officer warned that there might be no place for them. Bennett said that public feeling was "running high." Grote Stirling (MP, Yale, Conservative) feared that "disorder" would follow a mass meeting called by the Kelowna Board of Trade "to discuss the menace of Japanese infiltration." He wanted the entire valley declared a protected area into which no Japanese could enter. At Vernon the *Vernon News* warned that "a threatening storm is brewing." The Board of Trade seriously considered not sending a representative lest "heat rather than reason" prevail. The "boisterous" two-and-a-half-hour meeting on 5 March provided a "safety valve"; there was no disorder. The 750 representatives of City Councils, Canadian Legion branches, boards of trade, British Columbia Fruit Growers Association (BCFGA) locals, and other organizations from Armstrong to Oliver unanimously agreed that the "alarming ... infiltration" would imperil the safety and living standards of valley residents. They demanded that the entire valley be made a protected area and that "Pearl Harbor Japanese" be removed.[46]

On 9 March, seventy delegates from municipal councils, boards of trade, and agricultural organizations met at Kelowna. Claiming that all Japanese were "potentially dangerous" and warning of "public disorder" after continued "uncontrolled migration," delegates demanded that the "Pearl Harbor Japanese" be put under military guard. That was a compromise: southern delegates wanted to intern all Japanese; many delegates favoured evicting recent arrivals, some Vernon delegates wanted Japanese labour under military supervision, and a few, such as Captain C.R. Bull, former Liberal MLA, said that Okanagan residents were "safe and sound." The meeting formed the Okanagan Valley and Mainline Security Committee. A few days later R.G. Rutherford, a Kelowna accountant and Okanagan representative on the BC Security Commission, told a stormy commission meeting that the Okanagan did not want "to evade a proper share of responsibility for the national problem" but that a Japanese influx might gradually eliminate "the white man from the Okanagan" and cause an "explosion" against local Japanese. Taylor replied that neither he nor the commission could be pushed around. Later that day some civility returned. The commission would not let Japanese migrate freely or send evacuee children to white schools, hinted that it might remove non-agricultural labourers among the recent arrivals, and promised not to issue permits for the Okanagan without the consent of the local Security Committee. That was not wholly satisfactory because Japanese could still enter from intermediate points. After hearing

Rutherford's report, however, the committee realized that it could not expect "priority" in removing the "Pearl Harbor Japanese." It did ask that they be put under curfew and that their vehicles and radios be confiscated. Its main demand remained "definite assurance" that the Okanagan Valley would not be designated an area to which Japanese might be evacuated or reside.[47]

Without such assurance, the committee warned that it might not be able "to check overt action of a sort which we are particularly anxious to avoid." Many Okanagan residents were "deadly serious" that "the free movement of Japanese to the valley must stop." Predictions of "a spectacle of lawlessness" persisted. The Kelowna Junior Board of Trade planned a mass indignation meeting and posted signs such as "Coast Japs, You Are Not Wanted. Keep Out" at the ferry terminal and other places. Roadside signs at Summerland said, "Japanese and Germans Keep out of Summerland." Curiously, the Canadian Japanese Association in 1940 had claimed that by means such as not working on Sundays the handful of Japanese there had "established a very friendly relationship with the White farmers in the village." Kelowna City Council, calling the Japanese a military danger, incapable of assimilation, and a threat to economic health wherever they congregated, encouraged them to leave by denying them electric light, water, and civic licences.[48]

Recognizing the extent of the hostility, the commission assured Rutherford that no more Japanese would be permitted to go to the Okanagan, and any who did would "be dealt with when major problem worked out here." No publicity was supposed to be given to this, but an inexperienced acting editor of the *Kelowna Courier* called it an "insult" that would not halt the "brown boches" from "creeping" into the valley. That, and a report of fears of Ku Klux Klan tactics and vigilante action, led the Vancouver *News-Herald* to predict possible "mass violence" in Kelowna "against Japanese refugees." In fact, news of the halt to the influx and satisfactory discussions with the federal minister of labour led the Junior Board of Trade to cancel its proposed indignation meeting. In its next issue, the *Kelowna Courier* denied any hysteria and called the situation "eminently satisfactory." When Grote Stirling was home at Easter, he found a decline in the "resentful and dangerous state" of public opinion that existed after "the arbitrary and even insulting treatment" given the Okanagan delegation when it tried "to present its views to the Commission."[49]

Calm did not prevail everywhere. At Salmon Arm, over sixty representatives of area municipal councils and farmers' institutes attended an emergency meeting, sponsored by the Chamber of Commerce. They viewed "with alarm" the arrival of thirty Japanese and their "possible invasion into the business and commercial life of the city." The meeting unanimously resolved that no more Japanese should be admitted; that those already present should be denied business and driver's licences and the right to sublet land; that they should be put under curfew; and that after the war all evacuees should be removed and Japanese nationals deported. Yet not everyone was opposed to them. One strawberry grower asked that two evacuees working on his farm be allowed to bring in their families. He got no sympathy, but the *Salmon Arm Observer* noted that local Japanese were "honest, industrious, law-abiding [and] always willing to help good causes." Such divided opinions persisted. When a Japanese mother and her five young children arrived with a commission permit, the municipal council told her sponsor, a white berry grower, that she could not stay, but a few neighbours signed a petition in her favour. A year later, when local farmers experienced a labour shortage, the district council heard the Japanese described as "very fine" workers who would be removed from the area within six months after the end of the war. In an informal ballot, however, ratepayers emphatically rejected the entry of Japanese. Council remained firm; when a mill at nearby Canoe hired Japanese to build new bunkhouses, it asked the commission to withdraw them. Yet individuals developed friendly relations with the Japanese through means such as basketball games and, in 1945, a mammoth Dominion Day picnic.[50]

In other communities too, opinions were divided. At Okanagan Mission, near Kelowna, "tempers threatened to boil over" when the secretary of the local branch of the BCFGA castigated employers of Japanese as "Quislings" and resigned because the president employed them. Yet at the mass meeting in Kelowna, some fruit growers said that they needed Japanese labour, albeit under supervision. The conflict simmered. In presenting the Okanagan and Mainline Security Committee's resolution against Japanese in the Okanagan, Thomas Wilkinson, its chairman, admitted that "certain" fruit and vegetable growers wanted Japanese workers. That revived conflict between northern and southern growers and between farmers and urban dwellers; an exasperated commission said that the two factions "virtually tied our hands." Asserting that their needs should not be prejudiced by what was probably "a smaller element in the town than is commonly supposed," BCFGA locals at Vernon and at nearby Coldstream asked the BCFGA, the Vernon Board of Trade, and the Security Committee to relax their positions on seasonal Japanese labour. The BCFGA District Council approved, and the Board of Trade was prepared to consider it, but the *Vernon News* argued that "rightly or wrongly" most Okanagan citizens "still adamantly opposed" employing the Japanese under any conditions. Vernon City Council referred to the Security Committee after several aldermen complained that the Japanese would stay. Alleging that fruit growers only wanted cheap labour, Alderman David Howrie feared that the Japanese would make it impossible for "our boys" to get jobs after the war. Stirling told the Department of Labour that the Japanese might "get such a liking for those surroundings" they would not want to leave.[51]

The issue brought the Okanagan and Mainline Security Committee, which claimed that it did not oppose supervised Japanese labour, to a "crossroads" with a "definite cleavage" between urban and rural residents and among rural residents. Vegetable growers broke ranks with fruit growers by insisting on the admission of thirty women and children whose husbands, working on a share crop basis, had threatened to quit if their families could not join them. Fruit growers, however, made "a brittle truce" with townspeople by devising a "local option" whereby districts that requested it could temporarily bring in supervised male labour to thin and harvest the 1942 crop.[52]

Chastising Okanagan residents for believing that they should be "the Heaven sent chosen few," entitled to "privileges contrary to every other place in Canada," Taylor told fruit growers that the commission was "not an employment bureau" and would provide labour only if growers supplied family housing and a living wage for the duration of the war. Minister of Labour Mitchell agreed that such labourers should not purchase or lease land or lease crops and implied that arrangements could be made to remove them after the war. In the meantime, the commission was not disposed to move "Japanese into the Valley in opposition to local determination to keep them out." As harvest season approached, Vernon-area groups broke away from the Okanagan and Mainline Security Committee. While taunting Okanagan fruit growers about changing their minds, Taylor made a "radical change" and let "responsible" north Okanagan growers bring in temporary labour from Greenwood and self-supporting settlements in return for room, board, medical care, and going wages.[53]

Vernon City Council, which still belonged to the Security Committee, did not want Japanese living in the city lest they open stores but accepted their temporary work on nearby farms and orchards under police supervision. By mid-September, over 300 Japanese were picking apples in the area. Despite an incident at Coldstream in which pickers shook apples off the trees and struck for higher wages, growers were generally satisfied with their new workers. By spring the *Vernon News* observed that "the whole situation has been so quiet for many months now that the public agitation of last spring and summer has been largely forgotten" and that, if a problem had existed, it had been "settled on as equitable a basis as common sense could devise." The *Kelowna Courier*, however, predicted "a Frankenstein defying eradication" if the north Okanagan did not check the Japanese problem. No such monster appeared, but Vernon City Council barely tolerated the Japanese. Mayor David Howrie simply didn't like the Japanese, who, according to him, were "no asset to any community." The city let Japanese in to shop but not on Saturday night. After hearing more complaints about "damn brazen" young Japanese coming to shop, the mayor warned of "serious trouble" if the Japanese and soldiers at the army camp decided to fight. He rejected one alderman's suggestion that the Canadian born could not be kept out of the city. Indeed, council recommended deporting the Japanese to Japan. Not all Vernon officials were so hostile. The school board was willing to admit

Japanese children to its schools if space were available. And the editor of the *Vernon News* sensibly observed that the situation called for "wise restraint" since growers needed Japanese labour to harvest their fruit.[54]

Division persisted in the Okanagan and Mainline Security Committee even after Vernon-area members withdrew. For four hours in November, in a "disorderly and heated pell-mell of argument" and "mental savagery," the committee debated the matter. Southern regions did not want Japanese; municipalities around Kelowna were divided. Those who opposed Japanese labour feared that they would not leave after the war; those who wanted them worried about immediate labour needs. Finally, delegates voted fourteen to four, with twelve abstentions, to bring in Japanese labour. Saying that the committee was no longer useful in dealing with labour issues and predicting that permanent Japanese settlements would sabotage the economy of existing orchards and farms, James D. Pettigrew of Kelowna resigned as chairman. A delighted *Vernon News* editor, taking a pot shot at his Kelowna rivals, hoped that the committee, which had "ceased to serve any useful purpose," would "not be heard from again."[55]

In the meantime, the BCFGA, expecting a serious labour shortage, reaffirmed its "local option" policy. The Okanagan Mission and Oliver locals firmly opposed using Japanese; one Oliver fruit grower said bluntly, "we don't want any Japs in this district, and anyone who has any truck or trade with them should be boycotted." At Naramata, a poorly attended BCFGA meeting voted seven to three to use Japanese labour, but residents secured signatures from 155 of the municipality's 210 voters opposing it. Yet practical needs made some people change their minds. After "a long and stormy meeting," Penticton-area growers decided to use Japanese if the labour shortage did not ease. Some Penticton city councillors understood the need, but others feared that the Japanese, with an allegedly lower standard of living, might be the "thin edge of the wedge" of serious economic competition. After a heated debate, council refused permission to import Japanese labour. At a similarly "stormy" meeting, the Board of Trade, with some members abstaining to express sympathy with growers, voted thirteen to twelve against employing Japanese. When the CPR wanted a few Japanese to do track work, Penticton City Council denied them entry, so they had to remain on railway property even when off duty. Thus, Penticton had no Japanese residents.[56]

Kelowna, which had a few Japanese, was hostile to newcomers. When four women with three children joined their husbands on vegetable farms near the city, local protests led the commission to fear "a serious situation." The *Kelowna Capital News* deplored concern for keeping Japanese families together when nothing was heard about the family lives of "our people" away fighting the war. The *Kelowna Courier* complained of a "considerable influx" of Nisei, whom it called "just as much a potential danger as their fathers or uncles who were born in Japan." When the farm labour plan was announced in the summer of 1942, Kelowna City Council would not let Japanese reside in the city. Residents provided some harvest labour by closing stores two days a week and excusing students from high school. The *Courier* thought the BCFGA plan satisfactory for temporary help but wanted a guarantee that they would leave after the war. At the annual meeting of the BCFGA in mid-January 1943, however, only Summerland and Oliver opposed the "local option." Nevertheless, the *Courier* claimed that few growers wanted Japanese families, and the convention generally felt that the Japanese "must be removed from the fruit areas at the conclusion of the war." So strong were fears of permanent settlement that, when the minister of fisheries denied allegations by MP George Cruickshank that "certain interests" had sought the return of Japanese to the fishing industry, the *Courier* interpreted that to mean the Japanese might stay in the interior.[57]

The Kelowna Board of Trade favoured aiding growers, including vegetable growers who could provide employment during most of the year, but Kelowna City Council, the Junior Board of Trade, and the Canadian Legion insisted that growers guarantee the departure of any Japanese after the crop season. Indeed, when a Japanese family en route from Tashme to a placement at Westbank, across the lake from Kelowna, stopped, a "vigilante committee" from those three bodies gave them twelve hours to get out of Kelowna. By the time an RCMP officer told the vigilantes that "it was not their privilege to take the law into their own hands," the family had left. Their presence, explained the *Kelowna Courier,* "was the spark which brought the realization that there is no control of Japanese infiltration." Twenty-three families with "duration permits" had recently gone to work on Westbank farms, where it was suspected that they would stay and turn the Okanagan "white man's country" into another Steveston. At Westbank feeling ran "high over the uncontrolled infiltration of Japanese families." After hearing Kelowna Alderman George Sutherland aver that 23,000 could enter the valley within hours, the BCFGA local stopped approving applications for Japanese labour. The Women's Institute unanimously opposed the entry of Japanese during the war.[58]

Trying to reconcile the needs of fruit and vegetable growers for labour with the views of Kelowna residents, Alderman Sutherland convened a meeting that drew up a four-point program repeating the demand for the removal of all Japanese who had entered since 7 December 1941 and the exclusion of all Japanese except males over the age of sixteen who might enter under special permits for seasonal work. It recommended appointing a three-member committee with a representative of the fruit growers, of the vegetable growers, and of city residents to be responsible for procuring Japanese seasonal labour and organizing city residents to help with the harvest. The commission surprised Kelowna residents by saying that it would not send Japanese labour until white residents "got their house in order." As a conciliatory measure, W.A. Eastwood of the Department of Labour visited Kelowna and promised that there would be no "duration settlement" and that he would recommend removing the "Pearl Harbor Japanese." Nevertheless, Mayor G.A. McKay claimed that only an "immediate settlement of this problem" would prevent "disorder." The commission tried to call the local committee's bluff by announcing that it would remove the 112 men, women, and children identified as "Pearl Harbor Japanese" but only if they were moved at once. Growers in nearby Oyama, Winfield, and Okanagan Centre were keen to get their labour. The local committee had a "dilemma." Since most worked for other Japanese, their absence would not directly affect white growers but would substantially reduce production. The committee asked that they not be removed until after the harvest, and the Security Commission gave in. In the words of the *Kelowna Courier,* "the fight to keep the Central Okanagan white has been long and, at times, bitter, but it has apparently been successful."[59]

The "victory" announcement was premature. Japanese from the coast "struck" and proposed to leave immediately to protest being removed at the end of the season. The timing was crucial; it came when tomato and onion growers most needed labour. Some growers, fearing the loss of their tomatoes, favoured changing the recent agreement; others preferred to let the tomatoes rot and not yield to the Japanese. Alderman Sutherland refused to grant them "duration" permits but got the Japanese to return to the fields by letting them remain until November and allowing growers to apply to keep them over the winter. That temporarily resolved the problem. Sutherland later said that he would judge cases individually but would not grant family permits; the men said that they would not stay, the BCFGA instructed its representative on the committee to resign, and it insisted that Sutherland resign too.[60]

After a new committee chaired by W.A.C. Bennett began administering permits, both sides made concessions. The city agreed to have some family permits; growers agreed that all permits would be issued on their own merits and subject to cancellation. In fact, the new committee rejected only fifteen of eighty-six applications for permit extensions. Given that many applicants had dependents, this meant that 169 "Coast Nips," as the *Kelowna Courier* called them, remained in the Kelowna area over the winter. Animosity in the city remained high. News of atrocities in the Far East so inflamed resentment that the police advised Japanese to stay out of Kelowna except on Mondays, when they were required to report to the police. Kelowna City Council considered abolishing all permits for "Pearl Harbor Japanese" after 15 November 1944, but the Board of Trade rejected that as "too drastic."[61]

During the 1944 season, fruit growers arranged to bring in about 700 Japanese men and women as temporary workers. An RCMP officer predicted "another storm of protest from the anti-Japanese elements" but anticipated "no serious dispute" because everyone recognized the importance of harvesting a bumper crop, and "anti-Japanese activity in the central Okanagan " had been dormant for some months. Sentiment had not mellowed. Feelings were intense when ninety-eight Japanese who had been picking fruit at Vernon drifted into the Kelowna area after the harvest. When the commission did not immediately remove them, Kelowna City Council reaffirmed its opposition to their infiltration, and the Board of Trade protested its failure "to honour its obligations to Kelowna." At "the most single-minded meeting on the Japanese question ever held in the district," the board, without dissent, expressed "grave concern" that the "definite stand" of coastal residents not to allow the Japanese to return meant that "the only place where these people may congregate after the war will be in the interior of B.C." After explaining why it believed that the Japanese were inassimilable and of doubtful loyalty, it circulated a resolution demanding "repatriation of all peoples of Japanese origin after the war to Japan."[62]

Some other municipal councils endorsed the resolution, but Kelowna City Council narrowly decided not to participate in a "political football." The smaller of the city's two newspapers, the *Kelowna Capital News,* thought that, "much as most people would like to have all the Japanese deported to Japan after the war," this was unlikely. In any case, it argued, the Canadian born had been educated in Canada, were loyal to it, and were assimilating. By then a commission representative had met the Security Committee, which was "resolutely determined" to have the "Pearl Harbor Japanese" removed. The commission agreed to remove Japanese without permits and promised to remove the "duration" settlers as soon as feasible. That, said the *Kelowna Courier,* provided a "considerable element of relief." Once the war ended, the commission ordered the seventy-three evacuees who wished to remain in Canada to leave the Okanagan by 15 November 1945, but it let ninety-four who signed for repatriation remain until that could be arranged.[63]

In a postwar protest of the repatriation policy, a Kelowna fruit rancher noted that the Japanese had "added greatly to the development of this territory." Along with other growers, he accepted local control by the Security Committee "to avoid adding fuel to the flames of racial hatred which burned fiercely enough and also as a compromise to secure assistance from the city to harvest our crops." That, in a phrase, was the story of the Okanagan's wartime experience with the Japanese. Racial hatred was always simmering. Occasionally, it threatened to boil over, and in the one instance when it did a Japanese family quickly heeded the vigilantes and left town. Yet economic factors also had a role. City residents, aware of years of complaints at the coast, feared that Japanese might settle and open competing businesses. Assured by federal regulations that Japanese could not buy or lease agricultural land for the duration, fruit and vegetable growers had no such immediate fears. Moreover, they needed labour, and the Japanese had a reputation as hard workers. North Okanagan residents had had good experiences working with Japanese in co-operative marketing schemes and so were more amenable to accepting Japanese labour than their southern neighbours, who had never permitted Asians to settle in their communities and who believed coastal and California propaganda that once Japanese settled they would be followed by more.[64]

Kamloops residents also protested the possible coming of Japanese; however, given the limited employment opportunities in the city and its immediate environs, relatively few came, and most arrived independently of the Security Commission. They were not welcome. In March 1942, Kamloops City Council sponsored a mass meeting at which a number of residents complained that bringing in Japanese would merely shift a problem from the coast to the interior. They asked that people of Japanese origin not be allowed to buy, lease, or rent any land or business anywhere in Canada and be placed in federal work or internment camps under armed guard. The publisher of the *Kamloops Sentinel* privately asked T.J. O'Neill, the local member of Parliament, "who is to say any Japanese is not a potential enemy? We have only to read of what has happened in the southwest Pacific where the most quiet and innocuous little shopkeeper did his bit for the fatherland when the time came." Publicly, his objective was "all Japanese under military guard." When the Security Commission seemed to pay no attention to complaints from Kamloops, the Board of Trade wrote directly to Minister of Justice St. Laurent complaining that it was "intolerable" to see "arrogant" Japanese displaying "ready money" and driving around the countryside in "high-powered cars." Moreover, the board noted that Kamloops was only thirty minutes flying time from the coast, and in case of an attack it would be easy to parachute arms to the road workers, who could cut off communications between the coast and eastern Canada. Because the board wanted new roads, it did not call for the removal of the camp workers, only that they be placed under effective military guard.[65]

Nearby municipalities did not go quite so far as to demand armed guards but did not welcome the Japanese. In Chase, some residents considered leaving, and 130 individuals, including Natives, enemy aliens, and people who rented land to the newcomers, signed a petition against the "infiltration" of three or four self-supporting families. A Provincial Police officer, however, convinced them that it was better to scatter Japanese "through the country than to have them packed into camps separated from their families." Within Kamloops, the Council of the Board of Trade, while pleased to have the Japanese "doing road work," protested their movement into the area, except under guard, and demanded their removal to Japan after the war. It alleged that Japanese were buying land through third parties and asked other boards of trade to seek a law to prevent them from owning land in British Columbia after the war. Through the Resistance Association that raised funds for China's war effort, local Chinese residents urged Chinese farmers not to employ Japanese or to work on farms employing Japanese. Kamloops City Council was also concerned about third-party land transactions and a continuing influx of Japanese contrary to the promises of the commission. Tension mounted. While admitting that Japanese watching the Rocky Mountain Rangers drill at Riverside Park was only a minor incident, the *Kamloops Sentinel* warned that "the outward mildness of Canadians may be covering the smoulderings of a fire that will burst into flames" and "the horrible bloodshed, pillage and burning of race riots." In Parliament, O'Neill cited the incident to buttress his argument that the commission was "pussy-footing" with the "yellow devils" and was neither properly guarding nor disciplining road camp workers north of the city who staged a sit-down strike. The commission, however, refused to increase its supervision.[66]

Gradually, some Kamloops-area residents tried "to make the best" of the situation and accepted the employment of Japanese. O'Neill urged the government to retain them on the Sicamous-Revelstoke project, where there had been little unrest; the *Kamloops Sentinel* suggested employing the Japanese in logging camps to overcome a severe labour shortage. No one complained of the Japanese who planted and harvested 768 tons of tomatoes and 54 tons of potatoes and other vegetables at Ashcroft. Within Kamloops, however, opposition to any Japanese settlement persisted. When the *Vancouver Sun* said that Vancouver had learned to get along without them, the *Kamloops Sentinel* accused Vancouver of being "parochial" in thinking that the Japanese had left the province; in fact, the *Vancouver Sun* sympathized with fears among Kamloops residents of a Japanese takeover of local industry and agriculture. Kamloops City Council denied permission to Japanese who wanted to settle in the city. D.B. Johnstone, an elderly real estate and insurance agent, and the Board of Trade of which he was secretary persistently called for sending all Japanese to Japan after the war. Johnstone claimed that, since coastal residents would "unite in refusing" to have the Japanese return, the unorganized districts in the "beautiful country" of the interior would "be flooded with these creatures." Johnstone had influence. When Kamloops City Council resigned from the Okanagan and Mainline Security Committee, saying that it had become a labour exchange, he persuaded it to rejoin so that some agency would tend to the Japanese after the war.[67]

Apart from Johnstone, most of the comment on the Japanese question came early in 1944 when R.H. Carson (MLA, Coalition-Liberal) suggested that "the Japanese are planning on making a stand in some of the sunny valleys of the interior." He alleged that "certain individuals," acting as agents, were buying "some of the best farms" in the area for transfer to Japanese after the war. The reference may have been to a Chinese tomato grower who sold the unexpired term of a lease to a white grower who wanted a Japanese to operate the tomato ranch; the RCMP could find no evidence of agents for the Japanese buying land.[68]

A situation that reminded commission officials of Kelowna reflected conflicting interests. Faced with a severe labour shortage, some canners entered crop share agreements with Japanese, and lumber operators sought more Japanese workers. In 1944 the Provincial Police reported that the 339 Japanese in the Kamloops area were mainly in the nearby farming communities of North Kamloops and Brocklehurst. O'Neill claimed that North Kamloops "looks like little Tokyo"; the Board of Trade alleged that 400 Japanese had taken up land and might control the South Thompson Valley. With Kamloops City Council and the Canadian Legion, the board organized two well-attended indignation meetings to demand the withdrawal of the Japanese and the creation of a protected area extending fifty miles in all directions. Some residents were so bitter that law breaking seemed possible. In oblique references to lumber operators and farmers, speakers claimed that "the Japs … are being brought in by people whose greed exceeds their patriotism." Much rhetoric at meetings and in *Kamloops Sentinel* editorials exploited old ideas of Japanese owing allegiance to Japan and of being potential saboteurs. "We cannot forget that the Japanese are a race apart when it comes to allegiance to the land of their birth or their ancestors," added the *Sentinel*.[69]

Revelations of Japan's atrocities against Allied prisoners of war raised emotions, as did the designation of a nearby ammunition dump as a protected area. Minister of Defence J.L. Ralston, however, said that additional security measures were unnecessary "from the military point of view." That was not news. In an interview with the RCMP, Dr. R.W. Irving, who was on the platform at the protest meetings, admitted having no knowledge of Japanese buying land but used a security pretext to make people "more alive to the desirability of banning the Japanese from the Kamloops area" than a mere economic argument. Sergeant J.K. Barnes of the RCMP observed that the loudest condemnations of Japanese labour came from individuals who were not employers and had no direct link with agriculture or lumbering. Some Board of Trade members proposed boycotting businesses employing Japanese. The Interior Lumber Manufacturers, however, urged the federal labour minister to let them hire Japanese seasonally to produce lumber "desperately needed for the war effort" but to remove them after the war. Trying to resolve the problem and ease public opinion, the Department of Labour reluctantly set up a semi-official local advisory committee to provide an "orderly method of handling Japanese labour." The real concern at Kamloops, as in many other interior centres, was not seasonal labour but the possibility that the Japanese, with no incentive to return to the coast, where their property had been sold, would remain if they acquired property.[70]

Despite hostility to their presence, some Japanese continued to come into the area, and that kept anger toward all things Japanese alive. O'Neill revived old stories in telling the Board of Trade that troubles in the road

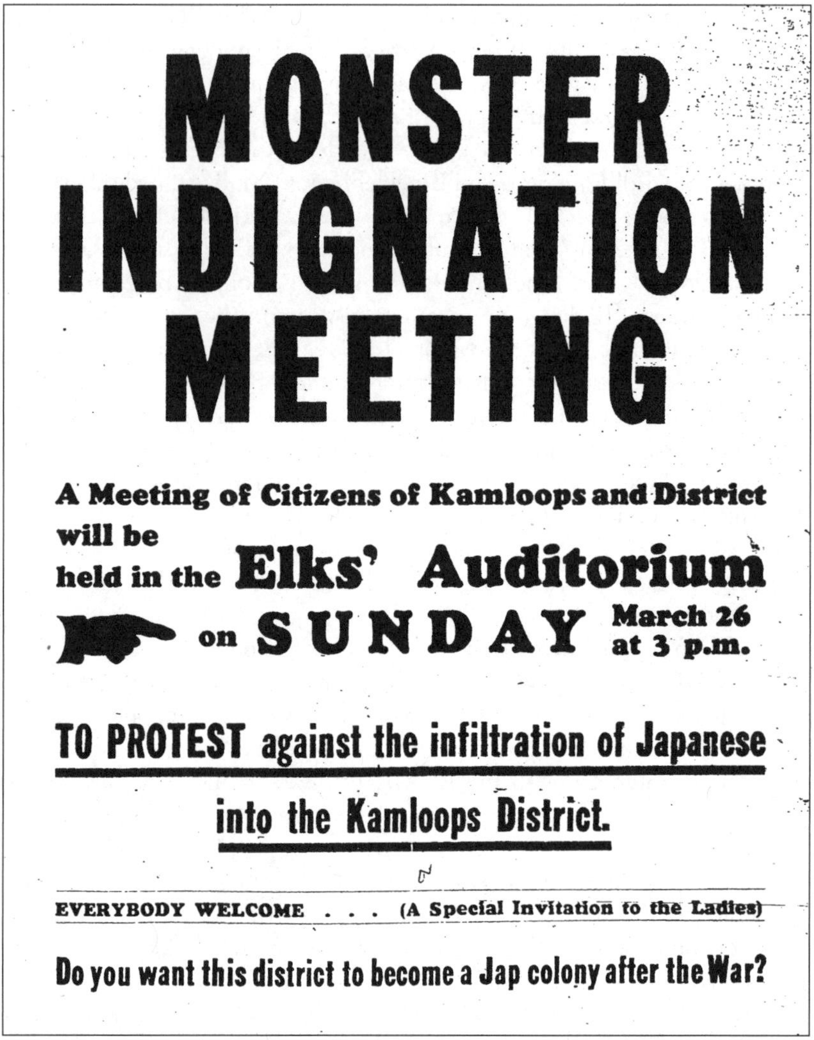
MONSTER
INDIGNATION
MEETING
A Meeting of Citizens of Kamloops and District
will be
held in the Elks' Auditorium
on SUNDAY
March 26
at 3 p.m.
TO PROTEST against the infiltration of Japanese
into the Kamloops District.
EVERYBODY WELCOME . . . (A Special Invitation to the Ladies)
Do you want this district to become a Jap colony after the War?

"Monster Indignation Meeting," *Kamloops Sentinel,* 22 March 1944. Note the "special invitation to the Ladies" and the question, "Do you want this district to become a Jap colony after the War?"

camps had been "acts of disloyalty" and that no one could be "loyal to two countries." When Angus MacInnis told a CCF meeting that many Japanese were loyal Canadians and could not be deported, he was applauded, but amid mutterings of protest several people walked out. The strength of local anti-Japanese feeling was further demonstrated late in 1944 when an Ashcroft resident bought one of the best houses in Savona, a village a few miles west of Kamloops, and began putting Japanese on the property. All seventy-three adult residents of Savona signed a petition declaring that, "in view of the diabolical and treacherous way in which the Japanese started their war, the beastly atrocities marking their conduct of it," they could not see any Japanese "or endure the thought of them" except "with horror and extreme antipathy." Calling the advent of Japanese in their community a "gross outrage," they demanded their removal. When the commission and the RCMP authorized the employment of an elderly couple as caretakers of a summer resort, Savona residents broke forty-seven windows in the building. That tactic backfired. The commission left the couple in place to demonstrate that violence would not be tolerated, and O'Neill lost interest in the case.[71]

Attempts to secure Japanese labour continued, but many Kamloops residents remained hostile. Just after the Pacific War ended, the *Kamloops Sentinel* repeated sentiments of 1942: "Given the right circumstances the unknown enemies among these Japanese could have sprung into action and the plight of the people in British Columbia would have been comparable to that of the unfortunate victims in the Far East. The fact that this situation never developed does not lessen the responsibility of those who exposed us determinedly over the protests of the people."[72]

NOT ALL JAPANESE went to existing communities. Because it could not find sufficient existing accommodation, the Security Commission leased a ranch fourteen miles east of Hope where it adapted existing farm buildings and built a number of small cabins to house almost 3,000 evacuees in the community of Tashme, which, except for a few administrators and church workers, was entirely Japanese. Some, generally the wealthier evacuees, moved on their own with the commission's blessing. Despite the Lillooet Board of Trade's opposition and the claim of Margaret "Ma" Murray of the *Bridge River-Lillooet News* that introducing Japanese would "annoy and excite the white people," some well-to-do Japanese families proposed setting up a self-supporting settlement at Lillooet for about 450 individuals. At a public meeting organized by the agent for the Japanese, some of the fifteen residents present looked forward to new business; others were suspicious. The meeting made no decision. Recognizing their unpopularity, the Japanese did not accept employment in Lillooet, and the Provincial Police saw to it that they came to town only during daylight hours.[73]

Austin Taylor, who had extensive interests in mines around Bridge River, thought that vacant hotels and houses at the Minto and Goldbridge townsites "would be an ideal spot" especially since they were accessible only by a single road. Rumours that a local sawmill would hire Japanese workers led the handful of residents to organize an indignation meeting. Some liked the prospect of money being put into circulation and of help in paying local taxes; others believed that guards would be required to prevent espionage. When they learned that the Japanese would be coming, many residents, especially those at the Minto townsite who had to move to make a place for them, were "up in arms." The *Bridge River-Lillooet News* warned of sabotage and suggested that any Japanese were "liable to be met with a stick of dynamite instead of a welcoming hand." E.C. Carson (MLA, Coalition-Conservative, Lillooet) claimed that miners in the Bridge River Valley might "take the law into their own hands." When a Lillooet merchant sold lumber and supplies to the newcomers, the Board of Trade asked him to resign. Despite Mrs. Murray's repeated admonitions, few residents saw the Japanese as "potential enemies"; one accused Mrs. Murray and her husband, G.M. Murray, ex-Liberal MLA, of "rabble rousing" in an effort to profit politically or personally. Whatever the reason, Mrs. Murray was disappointed when the arrival of hundreds of Japanese elicited "no outward sign or recorded view of dissension," that all except one white merchant were dealing with "an alien enemy," and that three-quarters of the population was "supporting the invasion." By April 1943, most residents who had opposed the coming of Japanese had changed their minds, but the Provincial Police officer at Goldbridge expected criticism because Japanese girls, employed as maids in the homes of the telegraph operator, the postmaster, and the baker, could easily tamper with messages, the mail, or more ominously the bread. His superiors anticipated no trouble and thought the notion of tampering with the bread "ridiculous in the extreme." About 1,000 Japanese settled in the Bridge River-Lillooet area, where the commission gave them no financial support and limited supervision.[74]

Because Taylor had little faith in education or compulsion to eliminate hostility that might end Japanese co-operation with the evacuation program, he sought sites where there would be little protest. An expensive possibility was locating Japanese on "isolated crown grant lands" where families could re-establish themselves as farmers or in limited industrial enterprises. More practical were communities such as Greenwood, Kaslo, New Denver, and Lumberton, where a decline in mining or forestry had left vacant buildings that could be made habitable. Even then he knew that it would be necessary "to consider community protests." Ian Mackenzie stressed that "the security of our people on the coast" was the first consideration and that "public clamour outside protected areas" was only secondary. Mitchell agreed but urged the commission to "do more to allay public feeling" by issuing "a series of carefully prepared statements" noting that the Japanese were forbidden to buy or lease land and that Japanese nationals had to report regularly to the RCMP. The federal cabinet agreed and advised the commission to select "the best place to move women and children within B.C." and to move them there.[75]

Even while the Security Commission was seeking resettlement sites within British Columbia, four major Christian churches – Anglican, Roman Catholic, Salvation Army, and United Church of Canada – that were ministering to the Japanese at Hastings Park suggested moving them to the interior in groups organized by religion. A Roman Catholic missionary from Vancouver had already scouted the possibility of settling adherents of his faith at Greenwood. The United and Anglican Churches liked the idea of faith-based settlements; so did the Security Commission, which assigned Greenwood to the Catholics, Kaslo to the United Church, and Slocan to the Anglicans. Problems in matching the number of adherents of a particular faith to the availability of housing and of moving thousands of people from many communities meant that the resettlement plan soon broke down. Although the churches provided kindergarten and high school studies and spiritual services in their assigned communities, they did not have a monopoly, and adherents of more than one faith as well as non-Christians resided in every community, save for the small and isolated settlement of Sandon, which was almost entirely Buddhist.[76]

The availability of housing led the commission to look to the Kootenays in southeastern British Columbia. Public opinion meant that it could not "consider places adjacent to railways or vulnerable areas," though there was no "possibility of sabotage," but as in the Okanagan and Kamloops economic concerns underlay many protests. Some groups, such as the Boswell and District Farmers' Institute, simply did not want any Japanese. Others wanted them under specific conditions. The Nakusp Board of Trade wanted road workers or paying guests at a nearby resort under "proper supervision." After receiving "numerous resolutions and protests" from local organizations, Revelstoke City Council asked Ottawa not to move any more Japanese into the interior except under military guard, but like the local Board of Trade and Canadian Legion it wanted Japanese under guard to repair the Trans-Canada Highway. To ensure that Japanese did not settle in town, it forbade anyone to rent houses or tourist camps to them. In time the city welcomed the money spent by road camp workers. The West Kootenay Council of the Canadian Legion demanded that Japanese be removed at the end of the war so that they could not develop local colonies. A columnist in the *Arrow Lakes News* of Nakusp suggested that the Japanese "are here, not to remain humble citizens, but to be masters, all in good time ... To open up the heart of the country to them will be bitterly rued."[77]

Anticipating that the commission might move Japanese to the Kootenays, on 26 February 1942 Ian Mackenzie and the MPs for Kootenay East, Kootenay West, and Yale asked Minister of Justice St. Laurent to protect certain areas. The areas around the lead and zinc smelter at Trail and the related hydroelectric system of the West Kootenay Power and Light Company were quickly added to the protected area. When S.G. Blaylock, president of the Consolidated Mining and Smelting Company, learned that evacuees might be placed at Lumberton, an old lumbering community, he protested that it was on the railway and near power lines serving the company's Kimberley mine. The commission did not use Lumberton but moved families to several "ghost towns" in the Slocan Valley, including Sandon, which was "practically uninhabited"; Slocan City, which had no more than 350 residents; and Kaslo, which had a population of about 1,000. Blaylock, already upset by Ottawa's public refusal to guard his plants, was horrified. The Japanese, he alleged, were capable of suicide attacks, and the company had large quantities of powder on hand. Since mountains separated Kaslo and the Slocan Valley from the company's installations, the commission paid scant attention to his plea. He pressed the government to equip the local militia with machine guns "to make some show of resistance" to potential saboteurs and to install anti-aircraft guns in case Japanese planes from an aircraft carrier hidden in coastal fogs attacked the Columbia River Valley. Eventually, the Department of National Defence placed three armoured troop carriers and two armoured Bren gun carriers at the Bonnington power plant, where it could "cut off the Japs should they come down from the Slocan country." Although recognizing that the Japanese were "industrious, frugal, and generally speaking, good citizens" who had generously contributed to war savings drives, to avoid giving "any Japanese sympathizers" an opportunity to aid the enemy, the Trail Board of Trade recommended moving all Japanese east of the Rockies and closely supervising them, but saying that it was "no permanent solution" it did not endorse a resolution against Japanese acquiring land but suggested that they develop agricultural land for postwar settlement by veterans.[78]

Like the editor of the *Trail Daily Times* who noted that Trail "fortunately" had no Japanese evacuees, communities in the protected area were pleased that they need not worry about Japanese in their midst or, as the *Creston Review* crudely put it, "the brown termites from the coast." The *Nelson Daily News* insisted that Japanese must be "scrupulously fairly treated in accordance with international law" but must not displace Canadian workers, bear down wages, or operate their own businesses. Board of Trade members were already seeking to provide supplies for the settlements![79]

Outside the protected area, opinions were mixed. At Golden, the Board of Trade asked that 500 Japanese be sent to the area; 200 citizens passed a protest resolution. Residents of Nakusp were "entirely complacent" because the absence of empty buildings meant that it was unlikely to be a relocation centre, but if the government placed Japanese there citizens "would consider it unpatriotic to protest." At New Denver, a resident recalled, after "much hot discussion, ... even those who felt disposed to oppose their coming into the town on personal grounds, began to see that the poor Japs had to go somewhere, and that they had better surrender their own prejudices and make a virtue of necessity. So the City fathers and the Board of Trade signified their willingness to receive these unfortunate outcasts." In what W.K. Esling called a unique document, the New Denver Canadian Legion said that the influx of Japanese into the Slocan Valley was "a very necessary

War Measure." It was "quite willing to accept the situation, in a spirit of Democratic Co-operation, and true Christian spirit." Since few buildings were available at New Denver, the commission constructed a number of its rudimentary houses there.[80]

About twenty miles to the south along Slocan Lake at Slocan City, the commission rehabilitated forty-nine abandoned houses and built 629 new ones there and at nearby Lemon Creek. According to the secretary of the Slocan Board of Trade, the few objections were soon "swept away" as their behaviour proved that the Japanese were "worthy of the courtesy extended to them by so many residents of the Slocan." Mrs. K. Popoff, a resident of Slocan City, told several Women's Institutes that the Japanese were welcomed as customers for dairy and garden products, making Slocan a thriving agricultural and supply centre, and undertaking community tasks such as fencing the war memorial and erecting a flag staff from which flew the Union Jack. They were so honest, she said, that there was "no need to lock doors any more now than before the arrival of the Japanese." Evidence of the acceptance of the Japanese in Slocan came late in 1943. When the Nelson Board of Trade asked the federal government to move Japanese from the Kootenay before the end of the war or "with the greatest expedition at the end of hostilities," the Slocan District Board of Trade disagreed. It thought that dispersal was probably a good idea but opposed wartime action and argued that British Columbia must accept its share of Japanese. In other words, daily contact showed Slocan residents that the Japanese were not the evil people portrayed by coastal propagandists.[81]

Because Nelson was within the protected area, its residents had had little contact with the Japanese. Kootenay residents, asserted the *Nelson Daily News,* accepted Japanese only as a war measure. Had they thought the settlement would be permanent, it said, "there would have been such an uprising of public opinion" that the government would have had to distribute the Japanese across the country or intern them in concentration camps. Initially, the Board of Trade considered demanding the removal of Japanese from Canada after the war but called only for their removal from the district after H.D. Dawson, the city engineer, suggested that forced expulsion would be Hitlerian. A few months later it again claimed that it "would be manifestly unfair to leave this district saddled with these undesirable people of foreign race." Several times the *Nelson Daily News* predicted "furious and unrelenting opposition" to letting "a single Japanese to remain in Kootenay after the war." It believed that they would form a "horrifying" proportion of the population, break down the economic structure, and "reduce portions of the West Kootenay to the level of the least desirable part of East Vancouver." Ignoring one alderman's protest that Japanese had served in the Canadian Expeditionary Force and that the proposal would only protect business and professional men, Nelson City Council and Esling endorsed a resolution from the Retail Merchants' Association for legislation to prevent Japanese from owning or leasing property or acquiring business licences.[82]

Regional differences in attitudes toward the Japanese were also evident at a meeting of the West Kootenay-Boundary Farmers' Institutes. Delegates from Nelson and the restricted area sought the immediate removal of the Japanese, but districts with Japanese residents spoke well of them. Indeed, when the provincial Advisory Board met early in 1944, the West Kootenay delegate explained that the Japanese had been useful to district farmers, and he alone opposed a resolution for the "total expulsion and exclusion of Japanese from the province." Similarly, the Kaslo *Kootenaian,* in attacking the Nelson Board of Trade, asked, "does it not occur to these men that the people to decide such a question are the people who are living in the areas with the Japanese?"[83]

Kaslo was the first centre to suggest that it would accept Japanese evacuees. On 4 March 1942, the Board of Trade offered the use of several hotels to house a work party of 200 or more Japanese to build the Lardeau highway and other public works. Initially, the Kaslo Board of Trade and the City Council wanted them under government control and without families. When some residents protested, Mayor F.E. Archer called a public meeting. At this overflow gathering, the city clerk pointed out that most Japanese were Canadian citizens and had caused no disturbances at the coast. Moreover, he and others spoke of the new business that they would bring. Reverend H.J. Armitage of the United Church suggested the "obvious duty as Canadians" to help the government. About 95 percent of those present agreed to have a work party reside in the city; the Kaslo *Kootenaian* suggested that a possible inconvenience would be for the "benefit of Canada." Not everyone agreed. When the commission decided to send women, children, and elderly men to Kaslo, some residents organized a petition against it. Howard Green advised his parents, long-time residents of Kaslo, that a thousand Japanese would "completely over-run" the town and that "if you ever get them into Kaslo you will never get them out." He urged them and their friends "to save Kaslo" by protesting to the commission and the MLAs on its Advisory Committee. Green's uncle secured about 115 signatures on a petition protesting a Japanese influx as "the most sickening of all blows" to fall on the "helpless residents" of Kaslo. The Legion and IODE also protested. In Ottawa Green lobbied Ian Mackenzie, who cited the protest to argue that the commission was so unpopular among BC MPs that it should be abolished and the government should act directly.[84]

Green's prejudices, not popular opinion in Kaslo, guided his actions. The Kaslo Board of Trade and City Council agreed to accept families. At a public meeting, L.E. Boultbee of the commission explained that moving women, children, and older men from the coast for the duration of the war was "absolutely necessary for national safety" and that the commission would provide education, medical care, and other services as well as a subsistence allowance that would be spent in local stores. Moreover, the Japanese would be subject to curfew and could not leave the city limits, hunt, fish, drive a car, or own a radio. Extra police would patrol the city. And, the Kaslo *Kootenaian* added, "best of all, the Commission covenants to remove the whole party after the war." When an advance party of construction workers arrived on 25 April, the *Kootenaian* admitted that there had been much "idle talk" on the pros and cons of accepting Japanese but admonished, "let us be grown-up enough to refrain from any demonstration of our own feelings, for or against the will of the Government." It urged residents to consider the "lot of the evacuees" whose property and homes had been seized and who had been "deported in a body to strange new places." "Let us not treat them as alien enemies," it cautioned, "until they prove themselves as such. It's a fine chance to demonstrate if Christian British Columbia can practise what it preaches."[85]

Within months the Kaslo *Kootenaian* noted that some opponents had "withdrawn their disapproval, because the Japanese have proved to be a patient, industrious, cleanly people, and have won the respect of everyone by their submission to the hardships that were bound to attend such wholesale evacuation." The Japanese soon settled in to the "livest 'ghost town' in the West." They participated in sports days and the annual flower show, joined the volunteer fire department and Girl Guide companies, planted gardens and picked cherries, attended services and social activities at the United Church, and generally integrated well with the white community. Except for a "storm of indignation" and warnings of "serious disorders" from the Canadian Legion when the commission turned the drill hall into a recreation hall for Japanese, the white community had few complaints. The *Kootenaian* saw "no sign of real friction" because the evacuees had "the sympathy of everyone," and most residents put up with any inconvenience as a patriotic gesture. While urging precautions against sabotage and describing their presence as "a temporary expedient till [the] coastal danger of invasion is over," C.S. Leary (MLA, Coalition-Liberal, Kaslo-Slocan) noted that many Japanese were "our own citizens" who had been "driven from their homes and businesses through no fault of theirs." Moreover, "better times" had come; Kaslo was no longer in a state of "suspended animation." In October 1944, the *Kootenaian* claimed that at least three-quarters of the population favoured having the Japanese. Somewhat surprisingly, early in 1945 Kaslo City Council endorsed the Kelowna Board of Trade resolution for the repatriation of all Japanese; the Board of Trade and the *Kootenaian* urged it to rescind the motion, and it did.[86]

The Board of Trade was particularly embarrassed because at a public meeting its members had asked that the Japanese be allowed to remain until permanent homes were found for them in the east. The meeting had agreed that "these people have shown themselves to be good living people causing no trouble, and have established themselves here, and are content to stay," and could find employment in lumbering and road building. Kaslo City Council reported high feeling "against the continued prodding our Japanese have taken by B.C.S.C. officials here, who obviously take their orders from the Jap-haters at the coast." One alderman privately suggested that officials had "been affected by the race hatred inculcated by politicians such as Howard Green and Ian Mackenzie." The *New Canadian,* then published in Kaslo, agreed that given adequate employment "people would be glad to remain in what is assuredly one of the finest spots in the country." But, the Kaslo *Kootenaian* admitted, there was "nothing in Kaslo to appeal to the Japanese people as a permanent home" since there were no opportunities for market gardening or commercial fishing. After the war, the Department of Labour accelerated dispersal but, acceding to pressure, abandoned plans to remove all Japanese from Kaslo and let those with employment remain on an individual basis. Given limited employment opportunities in 1953, only eight Japanese families remained. Yet Kaslo had been, in the words of the *New Canadian,* "a graphic illustration of how the artificial barriers of race will crumble under the influence of good-neighborliness."[87]

To the west, in the Boundary district, similar situations developed. There lumbering and agriculture, much of it undertaken by Doukhobors, sustained Grand Forks, the major centre. A few miles to its west, Greenwood, once the site of a copper smelter, was now almost a ghost town with 150 residents; a few miles to the east was a summer resort, Christina Lake. Initially, the area did not expect Japanese because it thought that it was in the restricted area, but by early March half a dozen or so Japanese had come to work on farms. When a member suggested sacrificing the economy to keep the Japanese out, the Grand Forks Board of Trade cheered and demanded that the movement of the Japanese, their destinations, and their occupations "be under strict military control." When about 100 self-supporting Japanese took over the Alpine Inn and some other properties at Christina Lake, "a raging storm of indignation" erupted at Grand Forks. The *Grand Forks Gazette* worried about Japanese "without guard or discipline" being within striking distance of the Trail smelter, Canada's "biggest war-producing machine," and perhaps having radio signalling devices. Some owners claimed that the Japanese presence would prevent them from using their summer homes and depress property values. Some permanent residents welcomed Japanese business to replace normal summer trade reduced by the tire shortage, but the School Board was unwilling to enrol Japanese children. When the commission told protesters that the evacuation was a national problem, the *Grand Forks Gazette* suggested that this comment reflected "contempt for the common people." Nevertheless, the Japanese remained at Christina Lake.[88]

At Greenwood, in March 1942, the Board of Trade, claiming that Japanese could never be completely assimilated and were a problem in terms of defence, favoured the postwar repatriation of all Japanese. When Father

Quigley visited the community to see if it would be a suitable site for his parishioners, he had to disabuse local residents of the idea that the Japanese would murder their children. He explained that the Japanese Canadians were law abiding and posed no danger. When the commission indicated that it would settle Japanese at Greenwood, a public meeting on 6 April cleared the air slightly. The *Grand Forks Gazette* reported that those with "visions of the skulking Oriental, similar to those who had caused atrocities to Canadians at Hong Kong running at random through the district," were reassured to learn that males of military age would not be coming and that most were Canadian born, anxious to show their good conduct, and often had private means. Area farmers were of two minds. Some thought that the Japanese would be useful if under military guard and probably more efficient than Doukhobors; others opposed any "truck or trade with the Japs" and feared that their "menace" would not end with the war. The *Grand Forks Sun,* however, opposed converting Greenwood "into a Jap town" and suggested that even women and children had "been taught loyalty to Japan." In fact, many were Roman Catholics who moved with missionaries from Vancouver who provided educational and religious services. Despite some early resentment, white residents quickly welcomed newcomers with friendly gestures such as gifts of garden vegetables and freshly caught fish. Mayor W.E. MacArthur told the Southern Interior Boards of Trade that Greenwood was "getting along fine" with the 900 Japanese residents that it had accepted for reasons "of humanity, patriotism, and business." Nevertheless, he added, they should be sent to Japan after the war, with the buildings that they were restoring used for convalescing veterans. The board called for a royal commission to determine the basis on which enemy nationals might remain in Canada.[89]

The evacuees quickly became part of the community. Most Japanese children attended the Catholic school set up by the Atonement order, but some attended the public school. Both Japanese and Caucasian children performed in a Christmas concert organized by the Canadian Girls in Training, a United Church young women's group. Japanese adults and children joined community celebrations such as Labour Day festivities. Indeed, the *Grand Forks Gazette* was "impressed by the smooth and friendly atmosphere evidenced between the residents of Greenwood and the Japanese who are their visitors for the duration." The availability of railway and lumbering jobs meant that most families were self-supporting. By the spring of 1945, the Greenwood Municipal Council, saying that Japanese were law-abiding and good citizens, refused to endorse Victoria City Council's request for a referendum to let voters decide which classes of Japanese should be sent back to Japan. Greenwood councillors suggested that the Japanese should be dispersed but given normal rights and privileges.[90]

Meanwhile, at Grand Forks controversy remained. Grand Forks City Council decided not to admit any Japanese, even women whom local farmers wanted as harvest help, and asked the commission to remove those already present. It would only let Japanese enter the city to conduct necessary business. As more Japanese seemed to arrive on every train, the *Grand Forks Gazette* wondered if residents were doing their job "by encouraging this same race of people to settle among us, as if heroes, and enjoy the fruits of comparative peace resulting from the Canadian blood that flowed at Hong Kong." Buttressing such arguments, the paper published letters from local men serving in the Armed Forces that "we are over here ready to fight Germans ... and those of our enemy race are being protected and palavered over in the land we call home." The local RCMP officer reported that most residents had decided to "make the best" of the situation, but T.A. Love, editor of the *Gazette* and Coalition-Conservative MLA for Grand Forks-Greenwood, was taking "every opportunity to aggravate the condition" because of "racial hatred" and was inflaming the situation with "reports of Japanese atrocities committed on allied prisoners." For example, when three evacuees were arrested near the hydroelectric plant for fishing without a licence, the *Gazette* suggested that "they might have had other designs than seeking fish."

By the spring of 1943, antagonism was abating. The schools offer a good example. Fears of health problems were easily dispelled, but parents and taxpayers worried about costs until the commission agreed to pay half and to guarantee payment of tuition fees by Japanese parents. When some parents and taxpayers proposed a separate school for Japanese, the School Board warned that removing them from the high school would so reduce enrolment that it might lose a teacher. For administrative reasons, grade school Japanese students initially attended a segregated class but in September 1943 moved into regular classes. Japanese students participated in extracurricular activities such as the maypole dances, though not in the May Queen's suite, the high school basketball teams, and the annual concert. In 1948 the Grand Forks School Board hired a Nisei graduate of the Victoria Normal School to teach in its public school.[91]

While young people easily mingled, in the summer of 1943 Grand Forks City Council became concerned when it seemed that a Japanese might buy a house in West Grand Forks. Such a purchase was contrary to a federal order-in-council; he had only leased the property. At the end of 1943, council reconsidered its ban on letting the Japanese work in the city and early in 1944 issued permits for domestics and certain agricultural workers. In the meantime, the Japanese Farm Laborers Association reported that the Japanese employed on district farms spent about $70,000 in 1943 at Grand Forks businesses. Their contributions to the local economy made them more acceptable, as did a change in the ownership of the local newspaper. T.A. Love retired from the *Grand Forks Gazette,* though not the legislature, in February 1943. His successor, Stanley Orris, a newcomer from the Prairies, argued that it was unfair "to take what money we can from him in our stores and businesses and give him no part of our community life in return." He urged letting Japanese who wished to be "good Canadian citizens" remain if they were educated "in the ways of Canada," did not segregate themselves, spoke English, and gave up any responsibilities to Japan.[92]

EVACUATION WAS AN INTERMEDIATE STAGE in dispersing the Japanese across Canada. For Japanese people who were moved, it was at best an unsettling experience. Yet it was necessary once Ottawa decided to remove them from the coast. Decades of anti-Japanese propaganda had infected inland residents. Thus, in 1942 the commission could not find long-term homes for them. Other provinces took Japanese evacuees on the understanding that they would be removed after the war; so did the interior of British Columbia. The absence of Japanese did not change opinions in Vancouver. Nor did their presence change all minds in the interior. Districts that took them under protest, such as Kelowna and Kamloops, or had none, such as Nelson, were no more sympathetic in 1945 than in 1942, but communities such as Kaslo, New Denver, and Greenwood accepted them and learned to appreciate them.

This chapter has rehearsed many reasons for objections; a more interesting question is why some communities accepted Japanese and were reluctant to see them leave. Without newcomers, Kaslo and Greenwood were likely to become ghost towns, but local leadership – political, economic, and religious – was also a factor. Municipal leaders in Kaslo and Greenwood encouraged co-operation with the Japanese. So did Kaslo's newspaper editor and, after a change in ownership, the *Grand Forks Gazette*. In Kaslo, which the commission designated as a United Church settlement, religion formed a bond between white and Japanese residents of that faith. Religion was also a factor in Greenwood, though the situation was slightly different since white Roman Catholic missionaries came with their communicants.

In eastern Canada, especially in Ontario, church members modified their views as they worked with young adult Nisei who, encouraged by the commission, were moving there to seek employment. There, as in British Columbia, the *New Canadian* cheerfully observed, many Canadians had "formed their concepts of Japanese individuals only from highly colored cartoons, news reels, and news reports ... As an ever-growing number comes into personal contact with us, a warmer tolerance, if not an active goodwill, gradually replaces many false prejudices."[93] The beginning of co-operation with the dispersal program and protests against repatriation are the subjects of the next chapter.

3

"Repatriation" to Japan and "Non-Repatriation" to British Columbia

> We must not permit in Canada the hateful doctrine of racialism which is the basis of the nazi system everywhere. Our aim is to resolve a difficult problem in a manner which will protect the people of British Columbia and the interests of the country as a whole, and at the same time preserve in whatever we do, principles of fairness and justice.

In these words read in the House of Commons on 4 August 1944, Prime Minister King tried "to balance all the conflicting views" and summarize postwar policy for the Japanese. His statement was ambiguous. He condemned "racialism," stressed the need to "deal justly with those who are guilty of no crime, or even of any ill intention," admitted that "for the most part" they had "refrained from acts of sabotage and obstruction," and reiterated that the government must treat loyal Canadian citizens "fairly and justly." Yet he condoned "racialism" by accepting that strong anti-Japanese feelings in British Columbia and the "extreme difficulty" of assimilation would make it "unwise and undesirable" for them to congregate there or for new immigrants to come for many years. In the short run, he announced that, after a quasi-judicial committee investigated both Canadians and Japanese nationals, the "disloyal" would be deported, but the loyal could remain if they dispersed and did not form "an unassimilable bloc or colony which might again give rise to distrust, fear and dislike."[1] In conceding that it was a national question and that Japanese must not congregate in British Columbia, King yielded to provincial prejudice. Most British Columbians were happy to see the Japanese leave the coast; some were determined that they should not return. A few spoke for justice and fair treatment for Japanese Canadians, particularly for Canadian citizens, and often cited the Atlantic Charter and antipathy to Hitler-like racial prejudice as their reasons.

As soon as the BC Security Commission was set up, the provincial government shed all responsibility for Japanese residents, even denying them access to its liquor stores or permission to buy beer by the glass. More ominous was its attitude toward schooling. After Pearl Harbor, public school officials resisted expelling Japanese children as "an act directly aimed at the yellow race," but Minister of Education H.G.T. Perry refused to educate "children who were arbitrarily taken ... (presumably in the national interest) from their regular places of domicile." His department told school boards that they did not have to enrol evacuees. Responses varied. Lillooet assessed Japanese for taxes on improvements to rented land but denied their children access to its schools. At Grand Forks, "malcontents" said that Japanese children might carry tuberculosis, but the board admitted them after the commission and parents paid tuition fees. Early in 1943, Perry introduced an amendment to the Public Schools Act to bar Japanese children. Many people welcomed this way of ensuring that "Jap families" would not return; a few worried about humanitarian ideals. Harold Winch, the CCF leader of the opposition, called it an "uncivilized step, contrary to the high ideals for which we are supposed to be fighting"; Reverend W.H.H. Norman, a former United Church missionary in Japan, warned that children would suffer. While sympathetic to interior school boards, the Vancouver *Daily Province* cared about visiting "upon innocent children born here" the consequences of inflamed public sentiment. The federal cabinet rejected a "veiled threat" of disallowance, but the province withdrew the amendment after Prime Minister King reminded Premier John Hart of Ottawa's heavy wartime responsibilities and promised to pay to educate evacuees.[2]

Nevertheless, the province adamantly refused to educate Japanese children. Perry supported school districts that refused to admit Japanese students. The greatest test was in Westbank, across Okanagan Lake from Kelowna, where some orchardists hired Japanese families. W.A.C. Bennett (MLA, Coalition-Conservative) protested "any deviation" from plans to make evacuee children study by correspondence. Fearing that an infiltration of Japanese children might "cause considerable public protest," Perry told the local school inspector not to admit them without consulting the department. The children remained in school until term end. When their father asked about correspondence courses, he was told that he could buy lessons but not the answer sheets. When Grace MacInnis (CCF, Vancouver-Burrard) asked why Japanese students had to pay nine dollars for correspondence courses for which others paid only a dollar, Perry answered that their education was a responsibility of "the Dominion government [that] moved them at a time of peril." When asked if British Columbia had requested payments from Ottawa, Perry replied, "No, why talk about selling your birthright for a mess of potage? I would be selling the whole school system for $65 a kid." Despite the recommendation of a federal royal commission that the province take over educational responsibilities, Premier Hart saw "no reason" to change.[3]

Ottawa yielded to British Columbia and set up an elementary school system that relied on hastily trained Japanese Canadian teachers but overrode the province on the employment of Japanese on crown timber lands. In the fall of 1942, Okanagan fruit growers feared that a severe labour shortage in interior logging camps and sawmills would impair the supply of wooden apple boxes. After lumber manufacturers lobbied him, C.D. Howe, minister of munitions and supply, asked Victoria to relax the rule. The provincial lands minister favoured putting "idle" Japanese to work but refused to lift the ban, as did Minister of Labour George S. Pearson, who feared sabotage. Representative fruit growers along with box and lumber manufacturers discussed the problem with MP Grote Stirling and MLAs W.A.C. Bennett and Bernard G. Webber (CCF, Similkameen). Stirling and Bennett feared sabotage, but the industry said that the Japanese would be "under proper supervision." Many Kootenay residents also favoured letting Japanese earn a living and ease a labour shortage. Frank Putnam (Coalition-Liberal, Nelson-Creston) blamed "agitation" on people who let "their judgement ... be warped by prejudice." Although Premier Hart and some cabinet ministers were sympathetic, the caucus was "absolutely" opposed. Under the War Measures Act, the federal government ignored provincial objections and on 23 February 1943 authorized the employment of Japanese in interior forests. The provincial labour minister conceded, "it is Ottawa's decision and we must accept it."[4]

Responses were mixed. Both the Vancouver *Daily Province* and the *Vancouver Sun* saw the need to ease a labour shortage and let the Japanese earn a living. Vancouver City Council gave qualified approval to any measure putting Japanese in gainful work away from the coast; Victoria's Trades and Labour Council protested placing Japanese in the woods. Okanagan lumbermen were pleased, but the *Kelowna Courier* reported fears of sabotage and of Japanese remaining after the war. Grudgingly, it admitted that if properly supervised and discouraged from permanent settlement their use might "be justified by the pressing need for increased production." In Nelson the Board of Trade changed its mind and accepted Japanese in the lumber industry. Even if labour shortages had not trumped prejudice, the federal government would not abide interference with the war effort.[5]

The rhetoric immediately preceding the decision to remove all Japanese from the coast only occasionally mentioned economic reasons for their removal. Yet the comment by the Vancouver *News-Herald* columnist Barry Mather in the fall of 1944 that the debate over the future of the Japanese had "nothing to do with the insignia of the rising sun or the Union Jack, it has to do with the sign of the dollar," bore considerable truth. Once the Japanese were going or gone, certain industries were anxious to see that they not return to compete. The fisheries are an example. By rounding up the Japanese fishing fleet, Ottawa gave priority to security, but both cannery operators and other fishermen were anxious that the Japanese not return. Unlike interior lumbermen who desperately needed labour, canners were happy to see the Japanese go. The president of the Canadian Fishing Company, expecting that "the last of the vermin will be out of our sight by the end of the summer," planned to manage without them. Some observers, ignoring the cyclical nature of salmon runs, attributed good catches to their absence. The *Vancouver Sun* claimed that everyone in the industry earnestly hoped "the tricky yellow men are out for good." A Vancouver *Daily Province* columnist found a certain truth "in the joshing remark an Indian made when boats, laden to the gunwales with sockeye, came in to Steveston. Said he: 'You see! When the Japs go the salmon come back. If the white men go the buffalo will come back!'" A *Daily Province* cartoon echoed this. Several fishermen's unions repeated demands to exclude Japanese permanently. So did politicians.[6]

Replacing the Japanese on Fraser Valley farms, however, was problematic. They grew about two-thirds of the labour-intensive strawberry crop that had British markets. Provincial Minister of Agriculture K.C. Macdonald and the press feared that their departure would reduce production. With the approval of the custodian of enemy property, some farmers arranged privately or through the Pacific Co-Operative Union to have white neighbours lease their farms for the 1942 season. Few tenants, however, could maintain production. Municipal leaders worried about tax payments. Yet in calling for the sale of all Japanese-owned land, the Union of British Columbia Municipalities was more concerned about repatriating "all Japs" after the war. The Maple Ridge Board of Trade wanted it sold to "properly selected white settlers" – that is, neither Mennonites nor Doukhobors – with the "ultimate aim and object" being the total exclusion of Japanese. Even before the full evacuation was announced, the British Columbia Federation of Agriculture endorsed a resolution from Saanich urging "in the interest of post-war reconstruction" an immediate expropriation of Japanese-owned land "on a fair basis."[7]

Saying that "these excellent small farms would be suitable for soldier settlers" under the proposed Veterans Land Act, Ian Mackenzie favoured leasing them temporarily to suitable tenants. However, T.A. Crerar and officials in the Department of Mines and Resources who were responsible for the land considered "justice and equity" for Japanese owners. To prevent sales or leases at sacrifice prices, Crerar persuaded the government to forbid anyone from purchasing, leasing, or otherwise acquiring any Japanese-owned agricultural land in a protected area without approval from a federally appointed referee. That officer turned out to be G. Murchison, the director of soldier settlement. A survey revealed that only about half of the 939 properties were suitable for soldier settlers and that holding strawberry and poultry farms and greenhouses for veterans would be costly. Murchison recommended selling the land "to approved persons as soon as possible, under [the] best terms possible," and in simple "justice and equity" compensating owners based on values established by the survey. Nevertheless, in June 1943, the Soldiers' Settlement Board (SSB) bought Fraser Valley farmlands.[8]

Japanese also owned stores and homes. The custodian did not want to appear to confiscate property, and the Department of External Affairs wanted to avoid any excuse for reprisals against Canadians in Japan. Members of the Security Commission's Advisory Committee criticized whites who high-pressured Japanese owners to sell property for "a song." Given a housing shortage, the custodian expected no difficulty in renting houses in Vancouver, but some city councillors, keen "to obliterate the last vestiges of Jap control over Little Tokyo and reclaim it for all time as a white residential section," urged Ottawa to sell the property to whites who could renovate it. Mayor J.W. Cornett believed that this would help to ensure that Japanese would not return, since "we couldn't throw the whites out to bring the Japs back." The city condemned many houses as fire hazards, for defective wiring, for insufficient baths, or for having cockroaches. Since the properties were unlikely to earn sufficient rent to cover repairs or pay taxes, the custodian advised liquidating them or slum clearance. Either policy, he noted, implied that "the Japanese owners will not be permitted to come back and establish themselves in Vancouver or at any rate in this particular area."[9]

On 11 January 1943, the Cabinet Committee on Japanese Problems recommended liquidating urban and rural property. For Japanese owners, that caused "mental turmoil" and disappointment since Ottawa had implied that it had taken property "as a protective measure only." Indeed, in explaining the property sale to the Spanish consul, the protecting power for Japan, the Department of External Affairs explained that the property was sold to safeguard the owners' interests since it "would be subject to rapid deterioration in value during their prolonged absence." In raising funds for a legal challenge, the *New Canadian* appealed to the "democratic tradition" of the right to own property. F.G. Shears of the custodian's office cautioned that sales did "not necessarily mean the Japanese will not be allowed to re-establish themselves on the Pacific coast." His view was atypical. In the legislature, Grant MacNeil (CCF, Vancouver-Burrard) warned that 16,000 Japanese would return to British Columbia after the war since eastern provinces did not want them. Noting the need to apply the principles of the Atlantic Charter and the impossibility of repatriation for many years after the armistice, he suggested encouraging relocation within Canada by selling property and sending the proceeds to "the evacuated Nipponese," who could stay where they were. When Premier Hart mentioned that former Japanese lands would be made available to veterans, the press concluded that evacuees would not return. Reeve Hugh Cunningham of Maple Ridge bluntly said that his municipality "will be much better off with the farms being operated by white people."[10]

Not all British Columbians agreed. One editor asked rhetorically, "if we believe in confiscation of property for one enemy race, why do we not apply it to all enemy races?" When church workers reported Japanese Canadians' distress over property sales, an ecumenical group of national religious leaders and civil libertarians protested, as did some BC church groups. The Baptist Convention of British Columbia said sales that violated constitutional rights and "the spirit of the Atlantic Charter" would bear "much bitter fruit." United Church members in the Fraser Valley protested selling property without its owner's consent. Some politicians were unmoved. A.W. Neill told the BC Conference of the United Church, "we are at war with Japan and it is the law of nature to seize the property of the enemy and, if necessary, sell it." Claiming that the government was selling land because of its strategic location, not its owners' race, he questioned the churches' wisdom in prejudicing the government's case.[11]

No one wanted the Japanese to acquire new holdings. If that happened, the *Kelowna Courier* feared, the Okanagan would "find itself in the postwar years with a racial problem which it will not be able to solve." The *Nelson Daily News* demanded a careful watch and severe penalties to prevent Japanese from buying land under cover of a lease or share-cropping arrangement since "we do not wish to have left with us after the war a large residue of the Japanese whom we agreed to accept purely on a wartime basis." Then in December 1943, to encourage the re-establishment of the Japanese elsewhere in Canada, Ottawa decided to let them, with permission, lease property for business or productive purposes. At the time, rumours were circulating that the Japanese were using agents to buy "choice land for farms after the war."

Attorney General R.L. Maitland was determined that Japanese should not get title to land. In the spring of 1944, he went to Ottawa and persuaded the federal government to "tighten up" regulations against their acquiring land by passing an order in council (PC 3797) imposing a penalty of $500 or three months in jail on any non-Japanese who acted as an agent to hold land for any Japanese. The Victoria *Daily Colonist* claimed that most British Columbians would endorse the move, albeit belated, because, "defeated in the war but unrepentant, the Japanese at peace would have begun their slow and steady infiltration of every land where they could secure a fresh foothold." Early in 1945, a Fraser Valley representative on the Farmers' Institute Advisory Board told the legislature's Agricultural Committee that the Japanese had been "bred to hate Canadians" and had planned "to kill us all." The board demanded that no Japanese be allowed to settle in Canada and that "no person of Japanese ancestry [should] be allowed to carry on business in B.C., either directly or indirectly," or "hold any land." The Agricultural Committee recommended making it illegal for Japanese to own, hold, or lease land. The house almost automatically adopted the report but then, realizing that such a measure would be *ultra vires,* merely received it.[12]

Denying them the right to acquire land would not keep the Japanese out of small business. One of Halford Wilson's correspondents wrote in the spring of 1942 that, "having eliminated unfair business competition, the next move should be to make sure this cankerous growth should never again be allowed to take root." Before leaving for military service in the summer of 1942, Wilson urged Vancouver City Council to continue seeking licensing powers to prevent Japanese from returning. At a brief visit to council while on leave, he noted that arguments about straining international relations no longer applied. Without Wilson, council did not pursue the matter, but others took up the idea. The Vancouver Barbers' Union increased efforts to legalize the five-day work week lest Japanese "again invade" the barbering trade and block improvements in working conditions. The provincial Barbers' Association sought to amend its act to bar Japanese and their "cut-rate methods" from the trade. Burnaby Municipal Council, following a request from the Canadian Legion, appointed a committee to determine if it could legally deny Japanese the right to own or rent property or conduct a business.[13] However, during the war, these were academic questions.

G.E. Trueman of the Department of Labour, who had much to do with the administration of the resettlement program, later recalled, "early in the evacuation process, the Government had seen, in the movement of the Japanese Canadians from the west coast, a chance to settle once and for all the Japanese Problem."[14] What was the solution? Despite consensus in British Columbia that the Japanese should not return to the coast, there was disagreement over what should happen after the war. Two basic ideas, with variations within them, emerged. One was "repatriation" to Japan. Some of its advocates wanted to send all Japanese to Japan; others would only deport Japanese nationals and those who could not demonstrate loyalty to Canada. The other option, dispersal across Canada, with British Columbia possibly taking a quota, was also the second choice for all but the diehards among those who wanted repatriation.

Many British Columbians wanted, in the words of Attorney General Maitland, to get the Japanese out of Canada "forever." R.H.B. Ker, a Victoria industrialist and member of the Security Commission's Advisory Committee, insisted on getting "rid of the last one of this treacherous breed." The Victoria *Daily Colonist* agreed that repatriation "would create a new and thoroughly welcome opportunity to put British Columbia men into British Columbia jobs." The *Vancouver Sun* was delighted with a hint that Ottawa would consider "sending all the Japanese back to Japan." Mayor Cornett of Vancouver, saying that it would be impossible for the Japanese, "a constant source of irritation," "to expect sympathetic consideration from our own people," asked Vancouver City Council to pass a resolution calling for the postwar repatriation of all Japanese. Yet there was some resistance to such a drastic measure. Dr. Norman F. Black and the Consultative Council, a group of Caucasian civil libertarians and clergymen formed initially to assist in easing tensions between Issei and Nisei, likened that proposal to "the characteristic Nazi concept of race." Subsequently, Vancouver City Council tabled Cornett's motion. A month later it agreed with many of Cornett's allegations about Japanese labour and business practices and the impossibility of assimilation but called only for the repatriation of the Japanese born and those Canadian born whose loyalty to Canada was in doubt. It did insist on "a fair distribution" across Canada of the remainder.[15]

Federal MPs had differing but predictable responses to council's "middle of the road" resolution. A sympathetic Ian Mackenzie intimated that the matter should not now "be discussed unduly" but advised council to demand the peace conference guarantee that Japanese would not return to the province. Admitting that this went "fairly far in regard to those born in Canada," he asserted that "the main thing is our security." Neill was unequivocal; he would ship all Japanese to Japan because scattering them across Canada "would be comparable to dispersing a leper colony." Angus MacInnis, however, reminded council that the Canadian born and naturalized Canadians were not responsible for Japan's imperial government and described a proposed loyalty tribunal as "Hitler-like." Other members made very general comments.[16]

Undaunted, during December's municipal election, Cornett called for repatriating all Japanese. "If we lose this chance to be rid of them," he averred, "we may never have another." His opponent, Don Brown, noting that the Japanese were a federal responsibility, opposed repatriating the Canadian born and favoured dispersal. Cornett won over two-thirds of the popular vote, but the Japanese were only one of many civic issues. Six weeks later, at a YMCA public forum entitled "After the War, What of the Japanese in BC?" Cornett predicted "bloodshed" in the streets unless the Japanese problem was settled.[17]

Cornett's prediction of bloodshed may have been exaggerated, but many others favoured repatriation. At both its 1942 and its 1943 conventions, the Union of British Columbia Municipalities demanded the return of all Japanese to Japan and their "permanent exclusion from Canadian soil"; in 1943 the Canadian Federation of Mayors and Municipalities endorsed the resolution. So many British Columbia organizations wanted repatriation that a Japanese Exclusion League was redundant; a pamphlet was the only legacy of its brief existence. Twelve groups and individuals presented briefs for repatriation to the legislature's Committee on Post War Rehabilitation. Premier Hart gave them credibility by telling the prime minister that the resolutions expressed "the feeling of the people of the province generally."[18]

Liberal and Conservative organizations also called for repatriation. The 1944 provincial Liberal convention heard forecasts of civil war if the Japanese returned and old arguments about their ties to Japan, domination of certain economic fields through "starvation wages," and "treachery" at Pearl Harbor. They unanimously called for the immediate postwar removal from Canada of "all persons of Japanese ancestry" and in the meantime forbidding employers to hire them and not allowing them to carry on business in British Columbia or "hold, own, or lease land." Provincial Conservatives agreed with repatriation. Their executive resolved that no peace treaty should be signed unless there was "a definite policy" for returning "all people of Japanese origin to Japan." Attorney General Maitland opposed their return to the province, not because of "hatred but with full regard to our self-preservation." Neill, though no Conservative, privately suggested that a pledge by Conservative leader John Bracken to "do his utmost ... to repatriate all the Japs" would be "immensely popular."[19]

In the legislature, Coalition members agreed that Japanese did not belong in British Columbia but did not agree on what to do with them. Some favoured their repatriation to Japan; others, recognizing that this might not be possible, demanded their dispersal throughout Canada. Nancy Hodges (Coalition-Liberal, Victoria) set the theme by asserting that these "unassimilable people" should be treated kindly and humanely until they were repatriated to their "motherland." Predicting that men returning from Hong Kong and other theatres of war would not "take kindly to the continued presence ... of these representatives of an enemy country which has wrought unspeakable indignities upon white men and women," she claimed that repatriation would be cheaper than letting Japanese remain to become "a serious racial problem." R.C. MacDonald (Coalition-Conservative, Dewdney), vowing that he would fight to the end "against the continuation of Japanese in British Columbia after this war," added that the Japanese had "penetrated seriously into every conceivable industry in this province." A few months earlier in the Salmon Arm by-election, he had called Japanese farmers unfair competitors. Now he attributed the success of the previous fishing season to the absence of Japanese fishermen. James Mowat (Coalition-Liberal), whose Alberni riding had many fishermen, warned of "civil war" if the Japanese returned to the west coast of Vancouver Island. Another Coalitionist-Liberal from a constituency where fishing was important, E.T. Kenney (Skeena), believed that sending Japanese to Japan would "make it truly Asia for the Asiatics – and having rid ourselves of them – we might make our slogan, 'Canada for the Canadians.'" If repatriation were not possible, he demanded that all provinces take a quota and that Japanese be forbidden to engage in industry or acquire property.[20]

Repatriation became a political football. J.A. Paton (Coalition-Conservative, Point Grey) accused the CCF of "giving comfort" to the Japanese by promoting their enfranchisement and questioned how it could represent labour and fight for the Japanese who were cheap labour and "unassimilable, racially and nationally." Earlier in the session, other Coalition members had accused MacNeil of rejecting repatriation by calling for dispersal; his colleague Herbert Gargrave (Mackenzie) explained that MacNeil only opposed immediate repatriation. Gargrave believed that loyal Canadian-born Japanese should not be repatriated and should be allowed to serve in the Canadian army. Other

CCFers took up the fight. Laura Jamieson (Vancouver Centre) charged that "race prejudice and color discrimination" would cause a "terrible" war "of the colored peoples against the white." E.E. Winch (Burnaby) shouted across the floor, "I have wondered what the attitude of professing Christians would be if on arriving in heaven they found the Japanese there?" At that, a reporter observed, some Coalitionists "looked askance at each other."[21]

The CCF did not speak as one. Some members criticized Angus MacInnis' repeated protests against repatriation of the Canadian born and his denunciations of the Liberals' "Nazi tactics." At the 1944 provincial convention, Sam Guthrie (MLA, Cowichan-Newcastle) urged delegates to speak to mill workers "who have had to work against Japanese competition." Warning that the public remembered Pearl Harbor, Hong Kong, and Japanese atrocities, he predicted that MacInnis' Japanese policy would defeat a number of CCF members at the next election. Prince Rupert delegates agreed that the Japanese must not return to the coast. Like Grace MacInnis, the majority believed that political defeat was better than lowering "the flag on this issue of equality for all races." After a prolonged, "heart-burning" discussion, the party reaffirmed its policy that not all Japanese should be sent to Japan and that the matter must be settled internationally.[22]

As the debate within the CCF demonstrated, opinion in British Columbia was conflicted. The Vancouver *Daily Province,* which had criticized "the uncompromising repatriation of all our Japanese to Japan," praised the moderation of the CCF policy. More typically, the *Vancouver Sun,* under the heading "Keep the Japs Out," sided with Guthrie. When Winch and CCF stalwarts such as MacNeil and Dr. Norman Black argued that the Japanese should be spread across the country and given a chance to develop economic opportunities and "educated up to Canadian levels of citizenship," the *Victoria Daily Times* facetiously suggested that the new Saskatchewan government demonstrate "its devotion to C.C.F. principles" by letting all the Japanese settle there.[23]

Parliament, where BC members had once been almost as one on Japanese matters, also saw division. At one extreme, Neill said, "let us at least take advantage of this one opportunity to correct our error and make for all time a white British Columbia and a civilized, Christian Canada." He demanded that the prime minister insist on "repatriation of all Japanese" as part of any peace treaty. If British Columbia's wishes were not respected, he supported separating the western provinces from eastern Canada. At the opposite pole, MacInnis said that it was not repatriation but "deportation or exile." Most members took positions somewhere between these extremes; they did not want the Japanese at the coast but would not necessarily deport all of them. George Cruickshank said that every BC organization except the CCF was "demanding that the Japanese be sent out of the country after the war" but insisted only that they not return to the Fraser Valley. W.K. Esling and

Thomas Reid conceded a need to respect the citizenship of the Canadian born, but Reid stressed that they were "unassimilable" and should prove their worthiness by cutting themselves completely "from the control and authority of Japan and its emperor." In a speech so general that both Mackenzie and MacInnis commended it, Howard Green, who privately thought that "the only hope the Japanese have of getting the problem settled is to scatter them across Canada," praised younger Japanese for re-establishing themselves in the east but warned of "grave trouble" if they returned; but he did not explicitly demand repatriation.[24]

Like the politicians, provincial editors were of several minds. The *Victoria Daily Times,* for whom Nancy Hodges was a columnist, implicitly favoured repatriation, attacked the pro-Japanese sympathies of CCF MLAs, and repeatedly referred to Japanese atrocities in Asia. The other major Liberal paper, the *Vancouver Sun,* said that other provinces did not understand the Japanese question and reiterated its "ideal policy": repatriation of "all people of Japanese blood." It reported receiving letters warning that "a reception committee armed with machine guns" would greet any returnees. Yet a new idea was slowly emerging as other editors began to distinguish between Japanese nationals and Canadian citizens. The *Nanaimo Free Press* might exempt the Canadian born from repatriation but argued that "the Old Country Japanese is Nipponized so deeply" that he cannot shed his loyalty to Hirohito. The Vancouver *Daily Province* questioned the practicality of repatriation especially of Canadian citizens and emphasized national and international aspects. The relatively liberal Vancouver *News-Herald,* saying that talk of mass deportation was premature and unwise before the peace conference, called for compensation for the property losses of repatriates and, most importantly, distinguished between the Japanese and the Canadian born. It even argued that forming combat units of Japanese Canadians would do more to win the war than outbursts in Victoria. Yet it warned that, if Ottawa did not relieve British Columbia's Japanese burden, "it will be taking the quickest and surest step to foment national disunity in the Dominion."[25]

Similar divisions of opinion occurred in boards of trade. The New Westminster Board of Trade's Post-War Rehabilitation and Reconstruction Committee warned that the return of the Japanese to the coast would build up "trouble and possible bloodshed" and set "the stage for the eventual exclusion of the white man from B.C." Not all boards endorsed unqualified repatriation. In the spring of 1942, for example, Cranbrook and Nanaimo endorsed Kamloops' demand that there be no peace settlement until all Japanese were returned to Japan, but Vernon and the Associated Boards of Trade of Eastern British Columbia rejected that as too drastic. The Associated Boards of Trade of Vancouver Island in 1943 refused to act on a Tofino repatriation resolution because international affairs were government, not board, matters. Delegates to the 1944 British Columbia Junior Chamber of Commerce convention rejected resolutions from Surrey and Kelowna demanding the removal of all Japanese from Canada after some delegates spoke of the need to show that Canadian citizenship meant something and that the peace treaty would have to deal with its international complications.[26]

As was evident in many arguments, Canadians were becoming conscious of the concept of citizenship; references to the citizenship rights of Canadian-born Japanese were a telling argument against wholesale repatriation. Although his district was hostile to Asians, the editor of the *Penticton Herald* said that, "to meet international rehabilitation and concord ... and to give sensibility to the word 'victory,' ... we should retain our own citizens of Japanese parentage, while ridding the country of non-citizens." The *Nelson Daily News* noted the impossibility of deporting a Canadian citizen without rewriting international law and departing "from basic British principles of citizenship of which we are proud." The Kaslo *Kootenaian* warned that problems of racial minorities must be resolved calmly after the war if Canadians were to develop their citizenship. Even S.G. Blaylock conceded difficulties in deporting Canadian citizens. His "cheap solution" was a bribe, a cash grant of $500 to $1,000 to any Japanese who would go to Japan. The New Denver Board of Trade also supported the Canadian born and, probably due to its firsthand experience with the Japanese, was willing to retain Japanese nationals who had been good citizens but warned that the Japanese must not be allowed to "become a minority group with a persecution complex."[27]

The Christian churches protested repatriation but recognized BC sensitivities. Archdeacon F.H. Graham told the Nelson Board of Trade that it was impossible to repatriate Canadian citizens. The Anglican Synod of Kootenay agreed. The 1943 and 1944 BC Conferences of the United Church affirmed that deporting a large number of Canadian citizens was "contrary to the Christian conscience" and in 1944 endorsed the admission to citizenship of all persons born in Canada regardless of their race or parental national origin. However, BC delegates to the General Council of the United Church in September 1944 discouraged the national body from making pronouncements on an issue that "was vitally identified with necessary war regulations and precautions." The Consultative Council, in which United Church members were prominent, organized an ecumenical resolution signed also by representatives of the Anglican, Baptist, and Roman Catholic Churches. Calling the expulsion of "all persons of Japanese stock" "wicked and preposterous" and characteristic of Nazism, it warned that policies based "on national and racial prejudices, exacerbated by wartime passions," would prejudice future trans-Pacific commerce, "play into [the] hands of those who would like to see interracial quarrels within the British Empire," "increase animosities which might lead to World War III," and "do violence to the conscience of a very large section of the Canadian people." It warned against overstating "the anxiety" with which British Columbians

"How Do You Tell a Loyal Jap from a Disloyal Jap?" *Vancouver Sun,* 1 June 1943. The suspicion depicted here underlay much of the hostility to Japanese Canadians.

viewed "the implications of the sudden reappearance of thousands of poverty-stricken Orientals returning to homes and occupations no longer available to them." The council recommended dispersing the Japanese, settling them, and making them self-supporting and reasonably content before the war's end.[28]

While that argument was predicated on the belief that most Canadian-born Japanese were loyal to Canada, some British Columbians found it difficult to distinguish between the loyal and the disloyal. The *Vancouver Sun* alleged that many still regarded Japan as their homeland and that many born in Canada had been educated in Japan and used their Canadian citizenship as a "stunt" to "cloak" "intentions and aspirations which are totally foreign to the ideals of Canadian citizenship" such as fifth column activities. Its columnist, Elmore Philpott, suggested that their prewar cultural activities had been "subversive" training for fifth column activities and "the cult of Emperor worship." The Victoria *Daily Colonist* made similar allegations, as did the *Kelowna Courier,* which demanded the "expulsion of all Japanese," who "would always be an alien race." Two old-time political foes and anti-Asian agitators joined the debate. H.H. Stevens said that, if Japan had attacked the coast, "every last Japanese, Canadian-born, naturalized and alien, would have been expected to proclaim their Japanese citizenship, and participate in the ravaging of our cities and homes." Victor Odlum admitted that repatriating all Japanese would be unjust to "loyal Canadian citizens" but thought it "better to be unjust to this small number than to permit the whole group with their anti-Canadian and pro-Japanese sentiments to remain in Canada" as he revived his 1921 election campaign arguments about problems caused by inassimilability.[29]

The most important statement on repatriation came at the meetings of the Provincial and Dominion Commands of the Canadian Legion in Vancouver in June 1944. Despite some references to Hitler-like racial hatred, the BC Command called for the postwar repatriation of all Japanese. Three days later at a meeting of the Dominion Command, Ian Mackenzie made a vitriolic rallying cry that he would "not remain 24 hours in any government or any party which allows the Japanese on B.C. shores." Making the old cries of inassimilability and "unfair" economic competition, he spoke specifically to veterans: "We want the fruit lands and the fisheries of the Pacific Coast – not for any member of this race that plunged the stiletto of treachery – into the heart of our great neighbour nation at Pearl Harbor – we want the fruit lands and the fisheries of this great Province – for the men of Ortona – for the men of the Air Flights – and the hard sea trails for our own white – battling – fighting – enduring – Canadian men!" Although reported in the local press, in the short run his speech was overshadowed by news of D-Day, but it was not forgotten.[30]

Mackenzie was not the only one to speak to the Canadian Legion on the Japanese question. Mayor Cornett told the Provincial Command that by opposing his 1942 resolution to send all "Nipponese" to Japan after the war aldermen favoured "the Japs remaining here." The aldermen took umbrage at this insinuation. To put their views on record, Cornett asked them to pass a resolution for the postwar repatriation of *all* Japanese, no matter where born. Few aldermen opposed the principle but, after "a stormy session," tabled the motion because several were absent and some wanted unanimous support for the resolution. Despite Cornett's efforts to revive the matter, it remained on the table for some months.[31]

In sum no one in British Columbia wanted all evacuees to return. There was some consensus that Japanese were inassimilable and potential economic competitors. Opinion about postwar policy, however, was mixed. There was support for sending all Japanese to Japan; however, given growing awareness of the value of Canadian citizenship and the realization that one of the objectives of the war was a fight against racism, there was also recognition that "repatriating" Canadian citizens was impossible. A solution might be repatriating Japanese nationals and the disloyal and dispersing the others across Canada.

"From the Mountains to the Sea," *Vancouver Sun,* 18 October 1944. In such statements, Mackenzie pandered to what he believed were the wishes of his constituents and British Columbians generally.

Dispersal was not a new idea. Almost as soon as the general evacuation was announced, some British Columbians called for permanent dispersal across Canada. Even a mellowed Macgregor Macintosh suggested that if widely dispersed the Japanese would be scarcely noticed and be better Canadians. He was not optimistic about other provinces agreeing but said that Canada could not send the Canadian born to Japan and must deal with them equitably. He was not alone. The executive of the Union of British Columbia Municipalities, the 1942 CCF convention, and the *Kelowna Courier* favoured dispersal. "Distributed in small groups" east of the Rockies, said the Vancouver *News-Herald,* the majority of these "decent, law-abiding Canadian citizens" would be transformed "from a potential wartime menace to a real peacetime asset." In contrast, the *Vancouver Sun* predicted that the Japanese would, "by hook or by crook, concentrate again in Vancouver and the adjacent area, to become a community menace not capable of assimilation, very capable of maintaining rival Japanese national aspirations in defiance of Canadian unity." Although it preferred "wholesale repatriation" as the "right solution," it encouraged the Japanese "to spread themselves widely" and would let perhaps 3,000 reside in British Columbia.[32]

Dispersing Japanese to provide "every necessary labour in essential industries across Canada" and reducing their "undue concentration ... in particular areas and occupations on the Pacific Coast" were the Security Commission's watchwords. Arthur MacNamara of the Department of Labour hoped that gradually giving each province a share of the Japanese would ease a long-standing "sore point" in British Columbia. RCMP Commissioner S.T. Wood was confident that in "comparatively small groups" hardworking Japanese families, "given reasonable opportunities," would "make homes for themselves" and "be acceptable" in their new communities. The *New Canadian* also saw dispersal as "the very real hope of a new and fresh start and the building of a firmer and happier future." Similarly, a number of Nisei who settled in Montreal reported in the summer of 1944 that "our own relocation experience has taught us that we can now become a better integrated part of the total Canadian population than was formerly possible." But for a variety of personal reasons and uncertainty about their reception in provinces that grudgingly accepted evacuees, few Japanese wanted to cross the mountains. Moreover, although the government offered a placement allowance, those without additional funds of their own found it insufficient to re-establish themselves in the east.[33] Dispersal, at best, seemed to be only a partial and temporary solution.

In making postwar policy, Ottawa was influenced both by public opinion and by what it understood to be American policy. Thus, in August 1943, Norman A. Robertson prepared a memo "in the vain hope" that Prime Minister King would discuss the Japanese question with President Franklin Roosevelt at the Quebec Conference. If the Americans took "more drastic measures," he expected that Canadian public opinion would "probably compel us to go along with them." Robertson proposed assisting volunteers to go to Japan, deporting internees and those who put themselves under the protecting power, and revoking the Canadian citizenship of any who left. He recommended no further immigration. He thought that loyal Canadians of Japanese ancestry, mainly British subjects and Canadian nationals, should be allowed to stay in Canada without any special restrictions. King had no opportunity to raise the matter with Roosevelt but authorized the Department of External Affairs to ascertain American plans.[34]

Canadian officials noted a major difference between Canadian and American policy; Canada did not clearly distinguish between its own citizens and Japanese nationals, whereas the United States did. Moreover, a frustrated official complained that government departments worked at cross-purposes. The Security Commission had told the provinces that evacuation was a temporary measure; by selling Japanese property, the secretary of state made the return of Japanese to their former homes unlikely. Although the War Relocation Authority admitted that "the wartime handling of evacuee property is a sorry part of the war record," the American government had not sold real property on a large scale. In Canada, the Placement Division of the Department of Labour tried to relocate Japanese on a permanent basis, but the Department of Justice would not let them buy or lease property. By freezing Canadians in their jobs, the Department of Labour made it difficult for Japanese to leave sugar beet projects. And by proposing to disfranchise Japanese outside British Columbia, the secretary of state removed one attraction of the east. So dismayed was A.H. Brown of the Department of Labour that his memo for the prime minister concluded that Canada's policy was "total repatriation and expatriation of all Japanese irrespective of nationality," a policy that he opposed. He favoured having a commissioner investigate the loyalty of Japanese and giving full citizenship rights, including the right to live anywhere outside the protected area and to own or lease property and acquire licences for those who were loyal.[35]

As far as the public knew, Ottawa was doing little. In November 1943, Bruce Hutchison found that Ottawa was "not in the least excited by the Japanese problem." He condemned demands for repatriation as "racial prejudice" but warned the prime minister that returning Japanese to the coast might "create the worst racial situation Canada has ever known." King agreed that the problem "cannot be viewed with too much circumspection." Tom Wayling, a *Vancouver Sun* correspondent, reported that Ottawa officials were "disinclined to tackle" the postwar fate of the Japanese since Japan could refuse to accept the Canadian born, and there seemed to be no "constitutional means of expelling them." In any case, it was questionable if Canada would engage in the mass deportations that Hitler had made into "a black art." Individuals who were helping to resettle Japanese Canadians in London, Ontario, told the prime minister that deporting people born and educated in Canada and "imbued with Canadian ideals" and Japanese nationals who obeyed Canadian laws "would be a gross miscarriage of justice." Yet support for mass deportations was not confined to British Columbia. The Toronto *Globe and Mail* claimed that Japanese would "remain an alien isolated element, discontented with their environment and perennially disloyal at heart." When readers said that "wholesale deportation" was "cold-blooded," the *Globe and Mail* agreed that it departed from tradition but called the Japanese a special case. Citing Howard Green's speeches, not an objective source, as evidence, it claimed that a "substantial" number had engaged in subversive activities since the war began and were loyal to Japan.[36]

As the press speculated, the Departments of Labour and External Affairs considered policy. They proposed adapting the American model of segregating the "disloyal" from the "loyal" to ascertain who would be subject to deportation. It would then free "innocent Japanese," mostly Canadian nationals, whose only offence was "having Japanese ancestry," from racially based restrictions on their activities and "prepare the way" for their postwar acceptance "as proper persons to remain in Canada." Gordon Robertson, the civil servant who co-ordinated these discussions, suggested that most opposition to the Japanese returning to the coast might "be coming from a vociferous minority who are loudly supporting a completely unjust policy." He cited a Canadian Gallup Poll released in mid-February 1944. It showed that 80 percent of Canadians would return Japanese nationals to Japan but that 59 percent would let Canadian citizens remain. Significantly, opinion in British Columbia was similar to that elsewhere. A wire service story observed that, "however thorny the problem," authorities could be consoled by the fact that it was the "one issue" in which public opinion divided in the same way across the country and that people agreed citizenship was the test of whether Japanese should be allowed to stay. Yet the poll could be interpreted another way. While 59 percent of Canadians might let Canadian citizens of Japanese ancestry remain and 8 percent were undecided, 33 percent wanted to send Canadian-born Japanese to Japan.[37]

About the time the poll was taken, the press revealed additional news of Japanese brutalities against Allied prisoners of war. In condemning the atrocities, few newspapers mentioned the Canadian Japanese. A notable exception was the *Victoria Daily Times*. It urged the legislature to ask Ottawa "to expatriate all Nipponese citizens who expect to resume their pre-war activities in this province." Austin Taylor claimed that the BC public would not "tolerate any compromise on the part of the Government to allow the Japanese to return to the coast," and Lieutenant Governor W.C. Woodward told a Chinese War Relief banquet, "we are not supposed to forgive the Japs."[38]

Without a firm policy, the government could not announce anything, although the Cabinet War Committee approved the principle of segregating the loyal from the disloyal. In May 1944, Green and some other BC MPs accused the government of "drifting." Minister of Defence J.L. Ralston's promise of a full statement, insofar as it could be forecast, temporarily halted their "sharp revolt" and rekindled eastern press attention. Opinions were still divided. *Saturday Night* called the doubts cast by BC members on the Canadian citizenship of persons of Japanese ancestry "very, very Nazi," but several eastern newspapers sympathized with allegations of Japanese espionage and loyalty to the emperor of Japan. "There is not room for them in British Columbia, no room for them in any province of this Dominion," declared the Montreal *Star*. Its competitor, the Montreal *Gazette*, said that "the rest of Canada can not remain aloof to the problem that faces British Columbia. It concerns us all!"[39]

In refining aspects of earlier proposals, Norman Robertson suggested emphasizing the Japanese question as a national problem and the undesirability of having all evacuees return to British Columbia. To answer charges of inassimilability, he proposed stressing that "unjust persecution ... of innocent individuals," mainly Canadian citizens, was contrary to "British traditions of justice and fair play." Moreover, he reminded the prime minister, there had "not been one single case of sabotage by persons of Japanese race in this country during the war," and a few thousand Japanese could not "possibly constitute a menace" to Canada. He repeated the idea of having a commission determine loyalties, revoking the status of the disloyal as British subjects, and sending them to Japan as soon as possible after the war. To encourage the loyal to disperse, he would impose a quota on the number allowed to return to British Columbia for several years but lift restrictions on their acquiring property elsewhere. Robertson warned, however, that making a "liberal and realistic policy" had become more difficult because of continued anti-Japanese agitation, Ian Mackenzie's promise to resign if Japanese were allowed to return to British Columbia, and the proposal to disfranchise Japanese outside British Columbia.[40]

While British Columbia's federal politicians pressed for a statement on postwar policy, a more immediate issue was the franchise. Early in 1944, M.J. Coldwell, parliamentary leader of the CCF, told a West Coast questioner that, unless Canada treated Japanese Canadians as citizens and enfranchised them, it would be "denying them the basis of Christianity and democracy." In the legislature, W.W. Lefaux (CCF, Vancouver-Centre) proposed enfranchising Asians serving in the Armed Forces. The numbers were few since Canada was not calling them up for military service. Other CCF members, Dorothy Steeves and Grace MacInnis, continued to speak for Japanese enfranchisement. There were reports that some Coalition members supported the idea, but the likelihood of the legislature enfranchising Japanese was slight.[41]

The focus shifted to Ottawa with the introduction, in the summer of 1944, of Bill 135 to amend the Dominion Elections Act to let Canadian soldiers, including prisoners of war, vote in a wartime election. A parliamentary committee drafted the bill. Before the House of Commons approved it, the cabinet took advantage of King's absence in England and, apparently at the instigation of Ian Mackenzie and Secretary of State Norman McLarty, added Section 5 to the bill. It disfranchised anyone, except Canadian war veterans, of enemy racial origin who had been disqualified by race from voting in any province. Thus, because British Columbia disfranchised them, no Japanese Canadian, including those who had voted in other provinces before the war, could vote in a wartime federal election. Opposition members, who had no opportunity to examine the bill's final version, were surprised when the *Winnipeg Free Press, Saturday Night,* and other journals drew attention to Section 5. Equally surprised and indignant was Mackenzie King, who had condemned Robert Borden's Wartime Elections Act, 1917, for limiting the rights of British subjects. Moreover, Senator Norman Lambert warned that the bill could affect Liberal support in Ontario and the Prairies by affecting individuals of German origin, and, though it might preserve two or three BC seats, letting "the C.C.F. become the champion of fair treatment for minorities may well have an influence even in Quebec." The CCF was doing well in Saskatchewan and Ontario, had won former Liberal seats in federal by-elections in Manitoba and Saskatchewan, and was slightly ahead of the Liberals and Conservatives in a September 1943 national public opinion poll. That was a peak, but a June 1944 poll still gave it 24 percent of the national popular vote.[42]

Many liberal-minded Canadians opposed plans to disfranchise Japanese outside British Columbia. As soon as Forrest La Violette, a McGill University sociologist studying the Japanese in Canada, alerted them, civil libertarians, church groups, and Japanese Canadians deluged the prime minister with requests to stop the bill. On one day alone, the Prime Minister's Office received thirty letters and telegrams protesting the measure as undemocratic, un-British, and un-Christian. The Japanese Canadian Committee for Democracy, a Nisei organization, described the proposal as "contrary to British justice, and contrary to the expressed war aims of the United Nations." The United Church Board of Evangelism and Social Service warned that it would "greatly nullify" efforts of the Christian churches to resettle Japanese and "endanger" postwar Pacific international relations; the *United Church Observer* called it "racial discrimination with a vengeance" and "too much like Hitler's doctrine of blood and soil." The National Interchurch Advisory Committee, to which G.E. Trueman belonged, reported resentment among Canadian Japanese "who know no other home and who had hoped to live and die in this country and who by this bill will be left without nationality." Army intelligence reported that Bill 135 ended the desire of Canadian Japanese to enlist in the Armed Forces. The *Globe and Mail* and the *Toronto Daily Star* condemned the denial of democratic rights to Canadian citizens.[43]

Several Liberal senators attacked the clause as representing "the most hateful feature of Hitler's Nazi doctrine of racialism," but the majority (thirteen to nine) apparently agreed with a Conservative claim that the Japanese were "constitutionally unable to understand the principles of democratic government" and refused to delete Section 5. Given the protests that were flowing into the Prime Minister's Office, the government used an ambiguous amendment by the Senate to let the House of Commons revisit the bill. King said that it had overlooked the Japanese who had voted outside British Columbia before the war and who should still vote. Drawing on a memo prepared by McLarty, King suggested that riots might result if large numbers of Japanese appeared at the polls in British Columbia; he did not mention McLarty's observation that evacuees, concentrated in a few areas, might "conceivably influence the result in certain constituencies." King wanted to remove racial discrimination from the franchise but did not want to give BC Japanese a right that they would not have if they had not been required to leave. Several CCFers attacked racial discrimination; to King's surprise, the BC members, except Neill, were virtually silent. In the Senate, J.H. King as house leader explained the changes. Another BC Liberal, J.W. de B. Farris, forecast that enfranchising inassimilable people would tempt politicians in "close elections" to seek a block vote. "And so concessions are made, step by step," he argued, "until the prospect of a white British Columbia is destroyed." Other senators were not impressed; they approved the government's amendment.[44]

Not all British Columbians approved of the proposed disfranchisement but for differing reasons. The United Church, the CCF, civil libertarians, and a few journalists criticized any attempt to disfranchise all Japanese. The *Penticton Herald* admonished, "citizenship in Canada must have a meaning, not alone for folk of Japanese ancestry but for all of us." The provincial executive of the CCF said that Section 5 resembled the racial persecution against which the United Nations was fighting. Elmore Philpott called it "proof of the folly of basing public policies on hatred, bigotry, or racial arrogance." However, he predicted that if Japanese were treated as outcasts elsewhere they would return to the coast. The Vancouver *Daily Province* said that it would be "repugnant" to see the Japanese vote but did not think that race should be the basis of citizenship.[45]

The main opposition to Bill 135 had come from eastern Canada, while the usual opponents of the Japanese in British Columbia simply did not want to see the Japanese enfranchised. The *Globe and Mail* found "no defense for legislation based on the thesis that Canadian citizens can at any time be stripped of their rights without any investigation of their character or conduct, merely on account of racial pedigree." Describing it as "one of the most cowardly devices" in Parliament's history, *Saturday Night* claimed that the bill was intended to "gratify" British Columbia by extending its racially based franchise to other provinces. It warned that Canadian citizens could be deprived of rights at any time simply because of their grandfather's racial origins. An angry Tom Reid informed the editor that if Japanese voted "the voice of Japan will then be heard in our legislative halls, as all Japanese are completely under and subservient to the Japanese government." When J.A.

Paton wrote that the Japanese had the sinister motive of helping Japan to "command a beach-head on this continent," a point also made in *Vancouver Sun* editorials, several BC newspapers reprinted his article, "Japanese Sent to Canada as War Party." If that were true, said *Saturday Night,* the right to vote was "the least of the instruments" with which to advance Japan's interests. It rightly concluded that disfranchisement was an excuse to attack the CCF and strengthen the campaign for repatriation. With minor variations, the Vancouver *News-Herald,* the *Vancouver Sun,* and the *Victoria Daily Times* shared the view of the Victoria *Daily Colonist* that "all Japanese in Canada cannot be blamed for what had occurred at Tokio ... [but] who can testify as to the inner loyalty of man's heart. The vote is the last thing to give men and women so circumstanced, and for whose loyalty not even the C.C.F. can vouch." More vividly, the *Vancouver Sun* alleged that if Japan had invaded British Columbia "99 out of 100 B.C. Japs would have received their countrymen with loud banzais." A few days later the Victoria *Daily Colonist* remarked that the franchise was not quite as important as having "a definite policy ... to return the Japanese to their own land."[46] Given conflicting views from east and west, the government compromised by allowing anyone who had the franchise before the war to retain it.

Officials in Ottawa saw a link between disfranchisement and postwar plans for the Japanese. Under the direction of Norman Robertson, Gordon Robertson of the Department of External Affairs legal division, who was working on postwar policy, suggested that the prime minister use the debate on Section 5 to indicate plans "for the general disposition of persons of Japanese race." The prime minister agreed. His speech on Bill 135 included a promise of an early statement on the larger question. He told Roy Brown, editorial director of the *Vancouver Sun,* that the government sympathized with British Columbia but had to consider both domestic and international implications.[47] Early in August, King announced the policy based largely on Norman Robertson's memorandum. After noting that there was no evidence of disloyal acts by any Japanese in Canada, King issued the new policy giving the Japanese in Canada a choice: they could sign up for "voluntary repatriation" to Japan after the war or agree to dispersal by moving out of British Columbia.

THE REACTIONS OF BC MPs to King's August announcement foretold provincial reaction. A.W. Neill, who doubted that the loyalty of the Japanese could be determined, firmly stated that British Columbia wanted "to get rid of the Japs, dead or alive." Since other provinces seemed to be unwilling to keep them after the war, he expected Japanese to drift back to British Columbia and re-enter its industries. However, Howard Green reflected a more moderate and common opinion in commending King for recognizing the Japanese problem as one "for the whole of the Canadian people." He suggested extending the protected zone after the war to the whole province and starting to resettle the Japanese in family groups at once. The press described initial reaction as "generally favorable"; former premier T.D. Pattullo called it "very sensible." Such responses reflected what the Wartime Information Board had discerned, "the existence of a considerable, if quiet, body of opinion which was distressed by the amount of undiscriminating prejudices and by the readiness of most local politicians to foster and exploit it." Many individuals repeated traditional objections to the Japanese, but the unmitigated hostility of 1942 was breaking down. Some observers agreed that British Columbia must accept a share of Japanese; a few had concerns about violating the rights of Canadian citizens.[48]

Nevertheless, opposition to the possibility of Japanese remaining in Canada persisted. The national Imperial Order of the Daughters of the Empire, for example, endorsed the request of its BC chapter that the peace terms make provision for "the total exclusion" of Japanese from Canada, including those born in Canada. In British Columbia, concerns were greater. In his successful bid for re-election in December 1944, Mayor Cornett warned that any Japanese who returned would require police protection when soldiers came home. He declared that "our children's children will regret that all Japanese were not sent back to Japan." Several aldermen agreed. The first vice president of the Provincial Command of the Canadian Legion said, "they should all be kicked out, lock, stock and barrel, and sent to where they came from." The provincial cabinet declined comment, but Coalition-Liberal backbencher Nancy Hodges contended that there was "no place for Japanese in Canada. They cannot be trusted, and have by their barbarity, proved such to be the case." The *Nanaimo Free Press* unequivocally declared, "we never want to see them back here." Groups such as the Native Sons of British Columbia demanded that all Japanese "be expelled from Canada" as soon as possible. Mayor David Howrie of Vernon thought that the Japanese were "no asset to any community" and told the Department of Labour that his city "strenuously" objected to their presence. He "strongly" recommended sending them to Japan.[49]

Many observers questioned the ability of the proposed loyalty tribunal to distinguish between the loyal and the disloyal or wondered how a peacetime government could enforce regulations to prevent large numbers of Japanese from returning to the coast. The Victoria *Daily Colonist* doubted that it was "humanly possible to segregate those who would die for the emperor-god and those who might not, once they are free in Canada, how can they be controlled?" In subsequent editorials, reminiscent of prewar propaganda, it alleged that the Japanese had "openly plotted and worked for the downfall of this land" and called for their total exclusion from Canada. After initially claiming that the government had had "special information" and "excellent security reasons" for moving the Japanese, the *Vancouver Sun,* perhaps recalling its Liberal leanings, observed that the Security Commission could put "the finger on the trouble-makers, the malcontents and the disruptive propagandists." It later explained its support for dispersal by asserting that democracy called "for the sharing of common burdens," though it claimed that only a minority of Japanese had abandoned their loyalty to Japan and wanted to become "good Canadians."[50]

Realizing that "the great bulk of Japanese cannot simply be dumped into their homeland," many British Columbians welcomed dispersal. An unscientific public opinion poll indicated that 65 percent of Vancouver residents favoured it. Proclaiming that it "practically" meant preserving British Columbia "as a white province," the *Vancouver Sun* grudgingly admitted that the province would have to accept some as the price of King's "promise to repatriate the disloyal and ban further immigration." The *Ladysmith Chronicle* believed that some Canadian-born Japanese were "more fanatically Japanese than their ancestors" but admitted that dispersal might produce "a much better feeling." The Victoria Builders' Exchange argued that if the government could not deport all Japanese at least it should discourage them from returning to British Columbia by denying them the right to own property or acquire fishing or trades licences. Some Okanagan residents feared that dispersal would mean a continued Japanese presence. The *Kelowna Courier* endorsed King's policy in general but warned that British Columbians would view dispersal "with a jaundiced eye" until they knew there was a "sound scheme of preventing the drift back into British Columbia."[51]

What was most striking in the comments was recognition by people such as Mayor McGavin of Victoria that Canadian citizens had rights and, if loyal, should be allowed to remain in Canada. "We are," he told the press, "supposed to be fighting for higher ideals than those of our enemies." The Vancouver *Daily Province* called King's policy "a curious mixture" that seemed to exploit popular feeling for electoral purposes. It asked, "if we are going to recognize any man as Canadian, ... on what principle of Canadianism or citizenship" are we going to deport him or restrict his movements, his place of residence, or his occupational opportunities? A more telling example of the growing sense of the rights of Japanese Canadians as Canadian citizens was the debate at the Annual Convention of the Union of BC Municipalities. The resolutions committee approved a resolution, similar to ones passed in 1942 and 1943, that after the war "ALL JAPANESE BE DEPORTED TO JAPAN." Many delegates referred to the inassimilability of Japanese and their propensity to drive white men out of industries, but some delegates, notably W.R. Beamish of Burnaby, argued that deportation would mean the departure of men in Canadian military uniforms and that the federal government had no power to deport Canadian citizens. One delegate called the resolution unconstitutional, "inhuman, undemocratic and un-Christianlike." After a long debate and a suggestion that the issue was becoming a political football, the convention tabled the resolution.[52]

Pending federal and provincial elections provided occasions for further debate. In Kamloops, which federal Progressive Conservative leader John Bracken knew was "very antagonistic to the Japanese because many have been sent there," and again in Victoria, he said that all Japanese must be removed from British Columbia after the war, a point that Howard Green continued to make at Conservative meetings. At his nominating convention, Grote Stirling, Conservative incumbent for Yale, attacked the Liberal policy as "unrealistic" since there was no way to keep Japanese in particular areas or determine their loyalty; he wanted to deport all of them because they were "disloyal" and could not be assimilated. Conservatives in the Coalition government also had little sympathy for Japanese. The provincial government, especially Premier Hart and Liberal cabinet members, kept quiet, but Attorney General R.L. Maitland found no "desire for friendship or co-operation with that yellow race." He told the British Columbia Fruit Growers Association that he was "sick and tired of being told by others who shall live here," a comment that was interpreted to mean the government would demand the removal of all Japanese from the province. E.C. Carson, another Coalition-Conservative minister, told the *Fisherman* that because Japanese could not be assimilated they should be excluded from Canada and particularly British Columbia. Tilly Rolston (Coalition-Conservative, Vancouver-Point Grey) asked rhetorically, "have we spent millions of dollars putting the Japs in a safe place only to have them come back?" Telling a tale of how before the war "Great Japanese Characters" appeared on Mount Douglas, "the No. 1 hill of the Victoria district," she claimed that Japanese settlers had been an advance guard for a Japanese military attack. R.C. MacDonald insisted that "the only clean cut business-like" solution was to deport all Japanese "to their own country where they belong." "To give them a vote," he asserted, "would be surrender." After Laura Jamieson suggested that Asians could be assimilated as well as Scotsmen, MacDonald appeared in the legislature wearing a kilt and playing the bagpipes. Other Conservatives, including W.A.C. Bennett, assailed the CCF for being sympathetic to the Japanese and especially for demanding their enfranchisement.[53]

A few Liberals questioned the policy as they prepared for a federal election. At a nominating meeting in Penticton, some Liberals, notably C.R. Bull of Kelowna, attacked a recent provincial Liberal anti-Japanese resolution as "typical of the Nazi spirit against the Jews." The split convention referred the matter to a committee, but Yale Liberals remained divided on repatriation. Several young Vancouver Liberals attacked the "fascist attitude" of such solutions, but their softened attitude was exceptional. Most Liberals worried about the electoral strength of the CCF. A Vancouver Liberal admitted, "we have made capital (Political) over the fact that the present Government would stand absolutely opposed to any return to former conditions with the Japanese." Similarly, Senator Farris urged the Fraternal Council of British

Columbia, an organization whose members included the Loyal Order of the Moose, the Elks, the Knights of Pythias, and B'nai Brith, to work to defeat the CCF and prevent the return of the Japanese to the coast. In Vancouver East, speakers at a federal nominating convention "served notice" that they would use the Japanese question to defeat Angus MacInnis. Not surprisingly at New Westminster, Tom Reid said that the Japanese must be sent to Japan. At the Fraser Valley meeting in Mission, the incumbent, George Cruickshank, stressed using the opportunity "to see that the Japanese do not come back." The meeting urged Ottawa not to "allow any future settlement of Japanese," to forbid their employment or owning or leasing of land, and to remove "all persons of Japanese ancestry" from Canada immediately after the war. Six weeks later, at a panel discussion organized by the CCF in Mission, the audience applauded Cruickshank when he said that he would "send every Jap back to Japan" or at least east of the Rockies. When Cruickshank asked anyone at Chilliwack who wanted the Japanese back after the war to rise, no one did.[54]

Mackenzie, the province's leading federal Liberal, had no qualms about keeping Japanese out of the province. Shortly before his nominating meeting, Arthur MacNamara, director of the National Selective Service, visited British Columbia. According to the Canadian Press, MacNamara said that Japanese would not be allowed to congregate in "Little Tokyos" after the war but could fish, farm, and log at the coast. MacNamara's immediate, less newsworthy, denial got little attention. Mackenzie quickly clarified government policy. Speaking not as a cabinet minister but "as one British Columbian to another," he said that he approved King's policy but would go further with his slogan "no Japanese from the Rockies to the sea." British Columbians, he declared, must insist that the other provinces "recognize our unique – and special danger." Saying "remember Pearl Harbor," he based his argument not "on racial considerations but on the security of our own people." Aware of the electoral threat of the CCF, Mackenzie referred to "our Socialist friends" who would enfranchise the Japanese.[55]

He did not go unchallenged. Bruce Hutchison, a friend of the Liberals, answered, "if pure and uncurbed racial prejudice" against innocent people became the election issue, we would "reduce our politics to the level of our enemies." Hutchison was referring to enemies overseas, and CCF speakers tried to turn the tables on the Liberals. On several occasions, Angus and Grace MacInnis and Grant MacNeil called on Mackenzie and BC Liberal MPs such as Reid to resign from Parliament because their views on the Japanese question contradicted those of Prime Minister King. M.J. Coldwell told an Ontario audience that Liberal politicians were "trying to climb back into power on the backs of the Japanese Canadians" using the same tricks as Hitler had used against the Jews. Angus MacInnis, the province's only CCF MP, agreed. He endorsed a halt to Japanese immigration but at Kelowna, in answering a question planted by W.A.C. Bennett, said that Japanese must have the human right of being able to move freely within Canada. As for repatriation, "decent people" did not deport citizens. His wife, Grace MacInnis, an MLA, urged CCFers to "knock the hyphens out of Canadian citizenship."[56]

The CCF, however, had divisions in its ranks. Herbert Gargrave (Mackenzie) denied that the party would enfranchise the Japanese and said that most favoured dispersal because, in the words of MacNeil, any mass return to the coast "would create serious problems and social tension." Harold Winch had to deny that the claim of Mildred Fahrni, a party member, that intermarriage would solve the Japanese problem was party policy.[57] The CCF was also embarrassed when some International Woodworkers of America (IWA) locals passed resolutions favouring repatriation. At a meeting sponsored by the Chemainus local, the chairman avowed that no one in the community, which had a significant prewar population of Japanese, had "any use for the Japs ... If it is the wish of the people of B.C. to kick them out, then kick them out." However, at its annual convention in January 1945, District Council Number One, which covered British Columbia, advised all political parties "to stop kicking the Japanese question around for more vote-getting purposes." While favouring returning the disloyal to Japan and keeping all Japanese out of the coastal defence area "until the last threats of Japanese fascism and aggression have been completely eliminated," it endorsed the plan to disperse the "loyal and Canadian-born Japanese across the country." So did the United Fishermen and Allied Workers Union, which deplored attempts to make the question a "political football" that intensified "racial hatreds and prejudices."[58]

Discussions of dispersal and repatriation continued in the fall and winter of 1944-45. When the United States announced that it would let loyal American citizens return to the coast in January 1945, several editors explained that Canada had not yet determined who was loyal, but others did not want the Japanese back. The Victoria *Daily Colonist*, for example, declared, "nobody in this Province wants to see the Japanese back in control of the off-shore fishing industry, or the small-fruits industry on the Lower Mainland," which was "military occupation in all save name." The *Vancouver Sun* claimed that the Japanese government had "sent" immigrants "to pre-empt certain industries" and that industry had managed well without them. Similarly, the provincial president of the Canadian Legion warned that their return would threaten "our standard of living," and given the state of resentment and prejudice "it would be better for their own sakes if they did not return."[59]

Meanwhile, municipal councils and local boards of trade circulated petitions for repatriation. The Kamloops Board of Trade told King that his policy was "indefinite, futile, conciliatory, and impossible to carry out." Alleging that many Japanese had come to Canada as "agents" to form a "bridgehead" for the Japanese government, it believed that repatriation of "every person of Japanese origin" was the only solution. Its widely distributed circular got limited response, though in endorsing it the Princeton Board of Trade added their "serious competition" in agriculture, fishing, and logging to the reasons for repatriating all Japanese. A resolution initiated in January 1945 by the Kelowna Board of Trade drew considerably more attention. Its executive largely endorsed an idea proposed by a local magistrate, T.F. McWilliams. Although somewhat similar to the government's announced policy, McWilliams would require all Japanese desiring to stay in Canada to promise to remain for at least ten years in the province to which they were assigned but would give them full citizenship rights, including the franchise, after five years. The full board, dissatisfied with the Security Commission's failure to remove Japanese without permits, did not discuss McWilliams' plan but, after what the *Kelowna Courier* called the "most single-minded meeting on the Japanese question ever held in the district," demanded the "repatriation of all peoples of Japanese origin after the war to Japan." It circulated the resolution to municipal councils and other organizations throughout the province.[60]

Response to the resolution, which the Vancouver *Daily Province* called the result of "blind prejudice," was mixed. Forty-eight municipalities or groups endorsed it. Esquimalt, Mission Village, North Cowichan, Ladysmith, and Salmon Arm District did so with little or no debate, but Victoria proposed to ask voters at the next federal election if they favoured repatriating all Japanese or only the Japanese born. Eleven recipients, including Penticton Municipal Council and the Mission and District Board of Trade, filed it partly because they did not believe that the Canadian born could or should be deprived of their status as Canadian citizens. Surprisingly, despite strong arguments for repatriation from Mayor Cornett and some aldermen, most Vancouver aldermen opted to co-operate with Ottawa and tabled the resolution. That meshed well with a recent Vancouver *Daily Province* observation that it was "as futile to talk of sending Canada's Japanese to Japan as it would be to make plans for locating them on Mars," because it would require approval of the Allies.[61]

Significantly, seven recipients of the Kelowna Board of Trade's resolution rejected it, including Kelowna City Council after Alderman Hughes-Games called the subject a "political football." That too was the sentiment of Courtenay aldermen, who would not even second a motion to adopt it. One of them facetiously suggested that it could be applied to Germans and almost everyone else. "Then," he said, "we'd have to give the country back to the Indians." Ironically, among those protesting Courtenay's decision was the secretary of the Native Brotherhood of British Columbia. Acting on behalf of Native fishermen, he questioned council's right to take action directly opposed to the almost unanimous public support for repatriation. Over the protests of Mayor George Muir, who claimed "a Jap is a Jap," Nanaimo narrowly rejected the resolution, with some aldermen referring to the rights of the Canadian-born Japanese and the Atlantic Charter. Although some Prince Rupert aldermen claimed that "the only good Jap is a dead one," and Japanese were "the lowest form of human beings on the face of the globe," the council rejected the resolution because of its political motives, its lack of constitutionality, and the citizenship rights of Japanese who had been "exploited as cheap labour." The Associated Boards of Trade of Vancouver Island shelved a repatriation resolution because they did not think that it reflected the ideas of most boards.[62]

There was no regional pattern to the actions of municipal councils and boards of trade. In greater Vancouver, the press censor noted that "the anti-Japanese forces" were "becoming more vigorous than ever." The White Canada League reappeared under a new name, the Japanese Repatriation League, because the name "'White Canada' brings up the Chinese and Hindoo questions which might be somewhat controversial, whereas the Japanese question is a problem to itself." Its goal was "the repatriation of the Japanese, now in Canada to Japan." Representatives of fishermen but not the Fishermen's Union, cannery executives, farmers, fruit growers, and the Native Brotherhood attended the initial meeting at Steveston. One organizer asserted that if the Japanese came back they could "go fishing but we'll see to it that they never get ashore again." Well-known Japanophobes, including Mayor Cornett, Alex Paton, Tom Reid, and C.E. Hope, spoke at its meetings. Ian Mackenzie was on its Advisory Board, as were A.W. Neill and F.J. Hume. The organization expected to have to work to "crystallize public opinion" lest even the Japanese east of the Rockies "be shuttled back to our province." It proposed to use the radio, publish a paper, and circulate petitions. From headquarters in downtown Vancouver, the league hoped to raise money from the business community. It circulated petitions as far east as Moncton (whose city council endorsed it). Despite its claim that 90 percent of the public was behind it, the league got little publicity in the Vancouver press and faded from view soon after the end of the Pacific War.[63]

The sense of Japanophobes that they needed a Japanese Repatriation League and the mixed support for the Kelowna repatriation resolution suggested that there was some sympathy for Japanese who were loyal Canadians and antipathy toward or embarrassment over racist ideas and actions. Although Grace Tucker, an Anglican worker among the relocatees, complained of the church's voice being silent "or extremely feeble," some church leaders publicly expressed sympathy for the Japanese. At a general synod of the Church of England in Canada, Canon Wilberforce Cooper of Vancouver called Canadian Japanese "good neighbors and good parishioners," while Archbishop W.R. Adams of Kootenay asserted that Canadian-born Japanese wanted "to grow up with Canada." At Prince Rupert, Reverend James A. Donnell, pastor of First United Church, withdrew from seeking the Liberal nomination in Skeena because he believed that the nominating convention's resolution favouring exclusion of Japanese from the coast and their deportation was "illiberal." Not all United Churchmen agreed. In September 1944, several BC delegates persuaded the General Council not to criticize repatriation and dispersal as "unchristian and undemocratic" lest that be interpreted as a desire to have the Japanese back in British Columbia. However, at the annual provincial conference in May 1945, the Evangelism and Social Service Committee opposed the "wholesale or indiscriminate deportation" of people who had not been proven disloyal.[64]

A prominent friend of the Japanese was Dr. Norman Black of the Vancouver Consultative Council. In speeches and in letters, he attacked racial hatred as a possible cause of another war and the annihilation of the white race, supported a halt to immigration, endorsed dispersal as a way of preventing a "resurgence of very serious racial difficulties in British Columbia," and called for enfranchising Canadian citizens and letting them buy real property. In the spring of 1945, the Consultative Council published a pamphlet by Reverend W.H.H. Norman refuting many racially biased allegations against the Japanese and stressing the Canadian citizenship of three-quarters of them. The Vancouver branch of the League of Nations Society endorsed voluntary dispersal but urged ending restrictions on the Canadian born.[65]

In the fall and winter of 1944-45, discussions of the fate of the Japanese were largely academic. Apart from encouraging individuals to move to the east, Ottawa took no real steps to implement the plan outlined in August. Officials undoubtedly knew that a Canadian Institute of Public Opinion poll had shown 33 percent support for returning all Japanese to Japan, a figure that was the same as a finding a year earlier, and that 41 percent would let loyal Japanese remain. The pollsters also reported the somewhat surprising fact that opinions in British Columbia were similar to those elsewhere. Then in mid-March 1945 the Canadian government "stunned" Japanese in British Columbia and caused them much anguish by announcing that they must leave the province or sign up for "voluntary repatriation" to Japan. Federal officials asked newspaper editors not to interpret "this programme as a means of ridding B.C. of the Japanese" lest that cause Japanese to resist relocation, but most people interpreted it to mean that the Japanese would be leaving. Posters clearly advised "Persons of Japanese Racial Origin Now Resident in British Columbia" that if they wished to "remain in Canada [they] should now re-establish themselves East of the Rockies as the best evidence of their intentions to co-operate with the Canadian government in carrying out its policy of dispersal."[66]

That too was the impression in British Columbia, but response was mixed. The *Victoria Daily Times* suggested that "in the main" British Columbians would approve any plan that removed the Japanese permanently. Mayor Cornett, who had recently suggested giving Canadian-born Japanese gratuities and sending them to Japan as "missionaries: for the Canadian way of life," was "jubilant." He called for regulations to ensure that Japanese sent east of the Rockies would not return. Others were sceptical about the effectiveness of dispersal given the reluctance of the Japanese to move and of other provinces to accept them. The politicians interviewed by the press answered predictably. Premier Hart, saying that he had not had time to examine the plan, refused to comment, as did prominent CCFers Harold Winch and C.G. MacNeil. Herbert Anscomb and E.C. Carson, provincial cabinet ministers, were not reticent; they believed that the Japanese must leave Canada since their movement could not be controlled after the war. Howard Green wanted no Japanese in the province but suggested that repatriation was a matter for the forthcoming San Francisco Peace Conference. As for those Japanese who were not resettled east of the Rockies or repatriated, he urged giving them adequate financial resources and settling them in some Pacific Ocean territory under United Nations auspices. Many who favoured removing the Japanese from Canada or at least from British Columbia still urged Ottawa to do so; those who knew the law recognized that Canada could not do so unilaterally. Attorney General Maitland told provincial Conservatives that the solution would have to be found in the peace treaty with Japan, a point also made by Senator Farris, the leading constitutional lawyer in the province. However, a Vancouver *Daily Province* editor wrote from the San Francisco Peace Conference that if Canada sought to send Japanese home "she will stand alone," since most Americans believed in giving law-abiding Japanese, citizens or aliens, "the fundamental freedoms for which all the United Nations pledge."[67]

Prime Minister King left the San Francisco conference early to launch the federal election campaign in Vancouver. He spoke about the war against Japan, but there is no evidence that he mentioned Japanese Canadians. He was the only party leader or prominent Liberal not to do so in British Columbia, although in no constituency was the Japanese question the only issue. At Liberal rallies, Ian Mackenzie urged, "this is your last chance to see that the problem of Japanese population of the coast and B.C. is settled," and voting for the CCF is "voting to re-install the Japs in economic competition with your returning servicemen." He promised to resign if they were not removed. Tom Reid accused King of having civil service advisers who had been bribed by the Japanese. Reid urged total repatriation. Like Mackenzie, he suggested that a vote for the CCF would give relatives of "our Japanese enemies" the "full rights of Canadian citizenship including the right to vote and to stand for public office." Liberal candidates in Vancouver East, Vancouver-Burrard, and Fraser Valley declared that the Japanese must not return to British Columbia. Senator Farris, speaking for Liberal incumbent T.J. O'Neill in Kamloops, criticized the CCF for wanting to enfranchise the Japanese, who, he claimed, were "not equal to the requirement of democracy."

When hecklers called out that "the Japs are human beings," an unperturbed Farris replied, "no sensible person wants to compare those of German or Italian descent with the 'heathen' Japs."[68]

At Kamloops Progressive Conservative leader John Bracken attacked the King government for supplying scrap metal and other products to Japan even after the start of the Sino-Japanese war. In Vancouver and Victoria, he declared, "in the interest of national safety, and in the interest of the standard of living of our fishermen and other workers, as well as the long-term interest of the Japanese themselves, they shall no longer remain on or adjacent to the Pacific coast." He would not permit persons of the Japanese race to reside anywhere in the province even in peacetime. Howard Green agreed that there should be "no half-way measures ... The Japs must never be allowed to return to British Columbia." He attacked the Liberals for wanting to scatter them and the CCF for wanting to scatter them and give them the vote. In Angus MacInnis' Vancouver East constituency, on Vancouver Island, and in the Lower Mainland, Conservative speakers and advertisements opposed the return of any Japanese. In Nanaimo, a constituency lying between the suburbs of Victoria and the southern limits of Comox-Alberni, Conservative candidate George Pearkes reminded audiences of CCF policies and avowed that "never again must a Jap be allowed in our province to exploit our fishing and lumbering industry to the disadvantage of the white men." He would "get rid of all the Japs, and send them back to Japan," whether or not they were Canadians. In Comox-Alberni, independent Jack Gibson, who sought to replace the retiring A.W. Neill, "would not care to win an election by appealing for racial discrimination," but he doubted the loyalty of the Japanese and promised to work for the return of all to Japan as "the only real solution to their problem and ours."[69]

As well as facing the thunder of Liberals and Conservatives, the CCF had to contend with attacks from the far left, namely from the Labour Progressive [Communist] Party (LPP), whose candidates in New Westminster and Skeena opposed the return of the Japanese to the coast lest they re-enter the fisheries. The LPP candidate in New Westminster said that the Japanese could not return "because of prejudice, that dispersal is best." At the other extreme, the CCF had to deal with its own members who put justice for the Japanese ahead of political considerations. Some members knew that their attitude to the Japanese "is going to cost us a lot of votes but we are on the side of right." In Yale, for example, O.L. Jones asked, "are we going to stoop as low as Hitler and Mussolini to pass laws to victimize racial minorities?"[70]

To meet Conservative and Liberal assaults, the CCF widely advertised a "True and False" statement of its platform and the attacks on it. The fifth item under "False" was "the CCF will bring all Japanese back to the Coast." Across from it under "True" was this statement: "A lie. The CCF will resettle Japanese Canadians in small groups in all the provinces. The CCF is the only party with a policy that will end the Liberal and Conservative policy of using these people to undercut wages and increase profits for big business." A second advertisement, "Humbug or Honesty," noted contradictions between Ian Mackenzie and Mackenzie King: "All CCF candidates" are pledged to "one honest, practical policy, to protect and advance Canadian living standards" by resettling the Japanese across Canada, making it possible for them to live there, to prevent the "interests" from using them as cheap labour, and "to avoid a mass return of Japanese to the Coast."[71]

CCF speakers, including MacInnis and M.J. Coldwell, the parliamentary leader, accused other parties of race-baiting. They dared Liberals and Conservatives to state unequivocally "that they would send every person of Japanese origin out of Canada." MacInnis suggested that Mackenzie would "stick with the cabinet policy like a burr to a bull's tail" on the Japanese question; provincial leader Harold Winch erroneously claimed that Laurier was "the first to bring Japanese to the country" and correctly recalled that Mackenzie, in 1920, was the first to call for Japanese enfranchisement. As for the CCF's own policy, MacInnis said that it was "not pro-Japanese, it is pro the human race." Coldwell agreed that the disloyal and those who wished to go should be repatriated, but loyal Japanese must be treated as other Canadians. Many CCF speakers, after asserting that the major powers would not let Canada deport the Canadian born, claimed that the Liberals had adopted the CCF policy of dispersal. Nevertheless, some CCFers, including MacNeil, complained of Japanese in the interior taking jobs from veterans, a point also made in a party advertisement in Nanaimo, where candidate Dr. J.H. Thomas opposed deporting Canadian citizens but avowed that the "CCF would eliminate the Japanese 'forever' as 'unfair' competition" in the fisheries and forest.[72]

British Columbians divided their votes largely at Liberal expense. The CCF retained Vancouver East and gained Kootenay East and Kootenay West from the Conservatives and Cariboo and Skeena from the Liberals. In the Kootenays and Cariboo, the Japanese were not an issue. In Skeena the Liberal candidate would exclude them from the coast and if possible deport them to Japan; the Conservative candidate cited Bracken's promise to keep them out of the province; and the LPP candidate wanted to keep them at least 150 miles away from the coast. If H.G. Archibald, the CCF candidate, said anything on the matter, the Prince Rupert *Daily* News, a Liberal paper, did not report it. However, in pre-election talk, a speaker at a CCF meeting in Prince Rupert said that he did "not like Japs," but the CCF believed that there should be "no discrimination on grounds of race, creed or color" and that deportation on racial grounds would be illegal. Archibald got only 36 percent of the vote, but with three others splitting the remainder he won. In a postmortem letter to the prime minister, G.G. McGeer, who had not run again, explained that he had expected the CCF's attitude "on the Jap issue would have eliminated that party as a factor in British Columbia politics" but that the conscription crisis had turned many Liberal supporters against King. Personal factors may also have been at work. In Kamloops, Nanaimo, and Burrard, Conservatives ran popular military figures, E. Davie Fulton, George Pearkes, and C.C. Merritt respectively. Howard Green retained Vancouver South, but "a low chorus of hoots" greeted him election night when he visited a town hall meeting and explained the Conservative "no Jap pledge."[73]

While the election was in progress, the Japanese in the interior were making the agonizing decision of signing for repatriation or agreeing to move east of the Rockies, where the welcome might be unfriendly. From time to time, the press reported their "slow but steady" movement eastward and speculated on the percentage that would sign for repatriation. The *Vancouver Sun* suggested that the willingness of some to go to Japan confirmed suspicions "that their most natural and abiding loyalty is to the Japanese homeland." Indeed, so unwilling was the paper to concede that many Japanese were Canadians that it criticized them and particularly the *New Canadian* for not apologizing for Tokyo's actions. In fact, Japanese Canadians complained of "government authorities ... [being] convinced by racist propaganda emanating from British Columbia that the more people of Japanese origin they can induce to sign for expatriation, the smaller will be the so-called 'Japanese problem,' for them to solve." While proclaiming the loyalty of Japanese Canadians, *Nisei Affairs*, in its first issue, asserted that despite this and the disabilities imposed on them many Japanese Canadians were "determined to be recognized as full and loyal Canadian citizens, and all the race-baiters and race-haters cannot alter the fact that they are CANADIANS." It expressed the hope that the "spirit of the Charter of the United Nations" would enable such Japanese Canadians to participate "in the development of our national life." More specifically, Thomas Shoyama, editor of the *New Canadian*, and G.E. Trueman had been trying to get publicity for the enlistment of more than 100 Canadian-born Japanese in the Canadian army for service in the Pacific theatre in psychological warfare and as translators and interpreters. Fearing that Japanese intelligence might exploit this information or that as Canadians they would be endangered if captured, the censor, though sympathetic to the domestic advantages of publicity, refused to permit it. Only after the Pacific War was effectively over did their service become public knowledge.[74]

After the election and the beginning of the segregation of interior residents who would be going to Japan from those moving east, protests against repatriation revived. A few came from church workers and others in the interior settlements, but the main agitation came from eastern Canada. The Toronto-based Co-Operative Committee on Japanese Canadians (CCJC), which worked with the Japanese Canadian Committee for Democracy, took the lead by lobbying in Ottawa. Formed in Toronto in 1942, it gradually became a broad-based organization whose members included civil libertarians, pacifists, representatives of various church groups (mainly the United Church), trade unions, and women's organizations. United Church members sent a "large number of letters and resolutions" to Ottawa urging tolerance of the Japanese. Many letters endorsed the encouragement of dispersal by lifting restrictions on property ownership, indemnifying property losses, giving assistance in re-establishment, and granting full citizenship rights to all Japanese with a "clean record"; others wanted to let people who signed for repatriation under duress change their minds. The *Toronto Daily Star* endorsed the CCJC's efforts "to prevent in Canada what is said to be a Nazi-like action against a minority group." That editorial appeared the day after the United States dropped an atomic bomb on Hiroshima. The war was almost over, but some British Columbians had not changed their minds about the Japanese. On 14 August 1945, the *Vancouver Sun,* concerned that the repatriation might not be permanent, asked, "what kind of a bomb has to be detonated under the Dominion government to get it to act on its own policy for dispersing the concentration of Japanese in British Columbia?"[75]

Two wrongs never make a right, but Nazi horrors in Europe alerted Canadians to the evils of racialism. As Canadians debated deporting all Japanese to Japan, some critics described it as "Nazi-like." They expected any peace treaty to include provisions against the ill treatment of minorities and racial discrimination. "In the face of that," Bruce Hutchison asked in November 1943, "how can Canada attempt the deportation of all Japanese?" The popular radio program *Town Meeting of Canada* in November 1943 asked, "What Should We Do with the Canadian Japanese after the War?" In an argument that he repeatedly used, J.A. Paton accepted that exclusion on racial grounds would be akin to "the tactics of Hitler" but asserted that Japanese should be repatriated as soon as possible because they were inassimilable and had come "not as colonists, but as invaders with evil intent." On the other side, Reverend G. Hayden Stewart of the Disciples of Christ described racial prejudice as the fundamental cause of the problem, favoured dispersal, and called repatriation of any but the proven disloyal as "Nazi-like" in its "un-British, unscientific and barbarous" concept of race.[76] While some British Columbians were keen to send all Japanese to Japan, one positive result of the debate was a realization that Canadian citizenship should mean something and that people born in Canada and loyal to it had rights.

If moving all Japanese from the coast was a necessary evil, much of their subsequent treatment was an unnecessary one. The inadequate handling of their personal and real property and the hardships of camp conditions can be explained, but not excused, by wartime conditions. The long postwar delays in permitting their return to the coast and letting "repatriates" change their minds about going to Japan were unnecessary evils arising mainly from atavistic attitudes of politicians who were more racist than their constituents. Yet as the evolving story of the Chinese in British Columbia suggests, racism could be selective, and racist ideas could change, although Ottawa did not always realize that.

4

The Effects of the War on the Chinese

> We cannot expect to insult the Chinese and keep them as friends.
>
> Bruce Hutchison, *Vancouver Sun*, 12 January 1943

For Chinese Canadians, the Second World War marked a real turning point in their relationships with the larger Canadian community. As a contributor to Vancouver's *Chinatown News* noted in 1966, "it took a world disaster to enable the Chinese Canadians to win this partial acceptance." Similarly, an elderly Chinese resident of Timmins, Ontario, recalled many years later, "before the Second World War, the Whites thought and believed that we Chinese were parasites contributing nothing to society. They thought that we just want to make money and did not care. But, when China fought against the Japanese who were also Canada's enemies, the Whites in Timmins came to their senses ... It is a sad thing to say that it took a war for them to turn around and consider the Chinese worthy humans." After the war, the sympathy that had been developing for them since the end of their immigration in 1923 and through the Sino-Japanese War had practical manifestations: Canada repealed the exclusionary Chinese Immigration Act, though it maintained discriminatory immigration practices. The provinces – mainly British Columbia – repealed laws and ended customs that had limited the opportunities of Chinese to earn a living. By enfranchising the Chinese who were Canadian citizens, British Columbia and Saskatchewan allowed them to participate fully in civic life. At a personal level, the 1958 claim of the *Vancouver Sun* that a Chinese child could "grow up unaware that there's such a thing as racial discrimination" was probably too pollyanna-ish, since prejudice persisted among a few people. Nevertheless, friendships between individual Chinese and Caucasians gradually extended to the whole community as they participated together in the workplace and other activities. So much assimilation took place, especially among the Canadian-born Chinese, that by the 1960s the Chinatowns of many Canadian cities had disappeared, and the survival of the large ones of Vancouver and Toronto was in question.[1]

On V-J Day, the Chinese and Caucasians shared the festivities. That sharing symbolized the goodwill that they had been developing over the long course of the Pacific War. The more than 100 Chinese residents marching behind a banner, "United in War, Let Us Be United in Peace," were the highlight of Victoria's civic parade. At Vernon, a Chinese dragon led an impromptu parade when victory was announced; the next day at the official parade the Caledonian Pipe Band went through Chinatown. In Kelowna a contingent of Chinese "got a great ovation." "Groups of Chinese joined with whites who gave vent to their joy" by dancing in New Westminster's streets. A "special feature" of Trail's civic parade was "a Chinese contingent arranged by Harry Wong, to honour the people who suffered the longest under the Japanese threat." In Prince Rupert, Mayor Harry Daggett invited Chinese residents to join the parade since they had "the best reason of all to rejoice over the defeat of Japan." The Chinatown celebrations, part of Vancouver's organized festivities, "led all the rest in color and gaiety." After a fifteen-minute demonstration of fireworks and firecrackers, the prelude to a three-day celebration, "the crowds broke in" for a joyous party, though it was the younger Canadian-born Chinese, with "youthful hopes and dreams of a future full of possibilities, one that ignored the reality of lingering discrimination," who mostly joined in the festivities as older people worried about future conflict in China.[2]

Similar phenomena occurred throughout the country. In Halifax, for example, hundreds went from the main celebrations on Barrington Street "to watch and encourage the Chinese celebrants," who "were probably the happiest people in the city and showed their rejoicing in a noisy celebration which featured the din of a drum, tom-toms and heavy Chinese cymbals and the popping of firecrackers." In Montreal, Chinatown, where "there were more French- and English-speaking Canadians than Chinese," was "the real backdrop" of the celebrations. "Ultra-conservative Toronto," reported the *Globe and Mail*, "went to Chinatown ... The Chinese themselves watched stoically for a few minutes, then suddenly a dragon parade started and the street erupted in the long-saved firecrackers ... Occidentals jumped up and shook hands with Orientals with wide grins and mutual congratulations." The "most colourful activity" of Hamilton's two-day celebration was the dragon head with its "flapping ears, smacking lips and rotating eyeballs" that headed the nearly 100 members of the Chinese community who, accompanied by a drum and cymbals band, marched through city streets followed by "hundreds" of other citizens. In Regina the Chinese actively joined a civic parade. Winnipeg and Calgary did not have parades, but many local celebrants joined the festivities in their Chinatowns.[3]

The celebrations were indicative of the sympathy that had been growing for the Chinese since the mid-1920s, but in British Columbia, where slightly over half the Chinese in Canada resided, there had been no change in their legal status. Thus, it was in that province that the war brought the greatest changes. The Second World War had brought prosperity to British Columbia. The population grew as wartime industries drew people from elsewhere in Canada. At the end of the war, many of those industries were converted to meet peacetime needs. In 1945 the provincial Department of Trade and Industry reported another year of "vigorous industrial activity" as it commented on how "business is moving to British Columbia." Both the privately owned BC Power Corporation and the provincially owned BC Power Commission were building new hydroelectric power plants; the traditional primary industries of forestry and mining were doing extremely well. The value of forest production in 1947, for example, hit an all-time peak due to high volume and high prices, and the related pulp and paper industry was expanding with several new mills under construction. Mining, after a brief dip due to war conditions and strikes, regained in volume by 1948 and continued to expand with the reopening of old works in the Kootenays and some new discoveries. Business was moving to British Columbia, but Canada as a whole was also prospering.[4]

The Sino-Japanese War created sympathy for China, stimulated the tolerance for the Chinese that had been emerging since the end of their immigration, and sharpened distinctions between Chinese and Japanese. After Canada declared war on Japan, the Chinese Benevolent Association (CBA) in Vancouver advised Chinese people to be "cool" and sold over 8,000 small Chinese national flags that they could wear to avoid being mistaken for Japanese; the Chinese consul urged Victoria Chinese to wear Chinese national buttons or other emblems because some Chinese in Vancouver had allegedly been beaten by whites who thought they were Japanese. Others put "Me No Jap" signs in shop windows. Governments also gave new status to Chinese. Early in 1942, the attorney general returned guns surrendered in August 1940 to Chinese who were Canadians by birth or naturalization. As local Chinese noted, it was unjust and "illogical" for Canada to send arms to Chinese across the Pacific but take them away from Chinese in Canada. The National Film Board produced a sympathetic film, *Inside Fighting China*. Yet there were cases of Canadian soldiers from the military camps at Nanaimo and Vernon beating up Chinese.[5]

After Pearl Harbor, support for China and the Chinese as victims of Japanese aggression increased. In January 1942, as Allied forces rapidly retreated in the Pacific theatre, the *Toronto Daily Star* took some comfort in "the wonderful spirit and splendid military effectiveness of the Chinese people" as they inflicted heavy losses on Japanese forces near Changsa. To underscore the point, the next day it noted how, unlike the Japanese, the

Chinese were not contemptuous of the white race, and despite different colour there was "between us … an understanding and respect." Service clubs and church groups organized social events to bring Chinese and whites together. Rotary clubs in all parts of the world sponsored a Chinese Day or Week in early February 1942; throughout Canada they had local Chinese as special guests or speakers, as did some other service clubs. The press praised the Chinese for contributing both to the Chinese War Relief Fund and to the Red Cross, Victory Loans, and hospitals; urged Caucasians to contribute to Chinese War Relief; and praised the spirit and military effectiveness of the Chinese whenever they defeated Japanese forces. The Vancouver *News-Herald* and many newspapers across Canada underscored the importance of China as an ally when, early in January, they published a cartoon by the noted syndicated American cartoonist Rollin Kirby that showed a Chinese infantryman, bayonet in hand, striking down Japanese soldiers, with the caption "52,000 Japanese Casualties at Changsha."[6]

In 1944 the New Westminster *British Columbian* commented that various factors, particularly "China's stand against the Japanese aggression," had largely overcome the race prejudice, which would "continue to fade away." Such feelings were not universal. Having received "a spate of letters" complaining of Chinese driving automobiles, not responding to the war effort, and not paying income taxes, the *Vancouver Sun* suggested that "the sparks of intolerance are beginning to fly." While cautioning Chinese residents to remember that "their conduct is under close scrutiny by a number of unsympathetic persons" and warning that "the smallest fires sometimes give off the most smoke," it admitted that most complaints were based on misinformation, that the generally industrious, honest, and law-abiding Chinese had made praiseworthy contributions to war work. Roy Mah, who was hired by the International Woodworkers of America (IWA) to organize Chinese workers, blamed anti-Oriental attitudes on "social stereotypes," ignorance, and race-baiting by "professional" politicians. The City of Victoria, for example, prosecuted some aged and infirm Chinese for not vacating premises condemned by the sanitary inspector. Overall, the medical health officer found that Chinatown was overcrowded with war workers, but living conditions had materially improved, and younger Chinese, educated in local schools, were moving away from its congestion. Yet a university student of Chinese descent told a CCF meeting that he expected existing racial prejudice to increase after the war. The Vancouver Parks Board, for example, refused requests to let Chinese use its Crystal Pool for more than one two-hour period each week.[7]

The workplace did accept Chinese. In New Westminster, they took over fruit and vegetable stalls at the city market when the Japanese left. When Vancouver could not find a white merchant to rent a fishmonger's stall in its city market, only one alderman opposed renting it to a Chinese. About

10 percent of the members of the Dock and Shipyard Workers Union in Victoria were Chinese, who got the same pay as white workers in similar jobs. Mary Lim was chosen to launch HMCS *Capilano*. The approximately 3,000 Chinese employed in shingle mills and shipyards in the Vancouver area received the same wages as white workers but threatened to strike because of unequal treatment in pensions and income tax for those whose families were in China. The affected unions advised them not to demarcate "workers' organizations and actions ... on racial or ethnic grounds" and took up their cause. Eventually, the Chinese ambassador persuaded the federal government to let Chinese claim overseas dependents on their income tax.[8]

Some unions were keen to have the Chinese become members. The IWA had Roy Mah prepare a Chinese-language edition of its newspaper and successfully protested to the War Labour Board when a mill at Youbou on Vancouver Island paid Chinese and East Indian workers ten cents an hour less than whites doing similar work. The importance of the board's action, said the *BC Lumber Worker,* "cannot be overestimated" since Asians had been paid substandard wages and housed in quarters that white workers deemed uninhabitable and a danger to health. The Fish Cannery, Reduction Plant, and Allied Workers' Union organized Chinese cannery workers. When provincial Minister of Labour George Pearson questioned the co-operation of Chinese and East Indians with British Columbia's labour laws and their honesty and reliability, Mor Cheolin of the Chinese Publicity Bureau said that the Chinese wanted "to live on the same level but are not privileged to enjoy the same economic right." The Chinese Youth Association of Victoria warned that Pearson's comments would hinder Chinese support of the next Victory Loan. Cannery workers and the Vancouver Trades and Labour Council attacked Pearson; the *BC Lumber Worker* called his ideas contrary to the Atlantic Charter and the Allied cause.[9]

Occasionally, old complaints against the Chinese reappeared but got little sympathy. For example, the *Kingston Whig-Standard* attacked an alderman who proposed a by-law to prevent white women from working in Chinese restaurants. "We are all glad to see that Canadian opinion is definitely on our side," noted the Chinese embassy in Ottawa. When the League of Women Voters in Vancouver asked if their city had a similar by-law, the city solicitor reported that a provincial law prohibiting the employment of white or Indian girls in Chinese restaurants had proven "unworkable." No more was heard of the complaint.[10]

Although the Chinese engaged in war work and participated in civil defence by organizing air raid protection units and practising first aid, firefighting, and other useful skills, service in the Armed Forces was problematic. In 1940 the government decided not to call up Asians for military service under the National Resources Mobilization Act. As a Chinese woman explained succinctly in 1944 when some Caucasians complained that Chinese were not required to do military service, "they are not drafted ... because they have no vote." Nevertheless, some Chinese men and women were able to volunteer, and a few – such as Roger Cheng, an electrical engineer, of Vancouver and Frank Ho Lem of Calgary – gained commissions. The Royal Canadian Navy did not lift its colour bar until March 1943, so a few young Chinese Canadians sought to enlist in the United States Navy. One Chinese Canadian, Douglas Sam of Victoria, enlisted in the Royal Canadian Air Force, was shot down behind enemy lines, escaped, and became a hero in Victoria. Meanwhile, the press had complimentary stories of individual Chinese men and women enlisting for service, winning commissions, and performing heroics.[11]

The army did consider forming all-Chinese units. Soon after Pearl Harbor, the third battalion of the Canadian Scottish regiment in Victoria began testing Chinese recruits for what it expected to be a complete platoon composed of Chinese. W.B. Seto, who was in the officers' training program at the University of British Columbia, suggested that a battalion of Canadian-born Chinese could express their "devotion and fulfill our responsibility towards our adopted country" and, at the same time, "eliminate a sense of strangeness and a pronounced inferiority complex that will handicap Chinese recruits." Similarly, Frank Ho Lem, who took his officer's training in Victoria, reported that a number of young Chinese "would like to see a Chinese Canadian unit." Major General R.O. Alexander of Pacific Command was sufficiently interested to inquire about possible numbers. Yet he regarded them more as Chinese than as Canadians, for he approached the Chinese consul in Vancouver, not the Chinese Canadian community. The consul thought that the number was too low to form a battalion but that forming one or two companies would contribute to better understanding between the two groups of people and be visible evidence of the alliance of Canada and China in the United Nations. He noted that such a unit could fully operate in English, but the army, claiming language difficulties and small numbers, rejected requests for an all-Chinese unit.[12]

The political argument against recruiting Chinese for the Armed Forces was that service would lead to a demand for enfranchisement. In December 1942, Victoria's Chinese Youth Association, after noting how the province's 23,000 Chinese contributed to the war effort, asked the provincial cabinet to cancel legal disabilities such as disfranchisement. Could its members be blamed, the association asked, for wondering if "all the professed ideals we are fighting for are, after all, but mere hollow illusions and that the land for which he is willing to lay down his life can never be truly called his own?" Acting premier R.L. Maitland argued that wartime was not the time for controversy and that the province had the "right" to deny the franchise to any group that might vote en bloc. The Vancouver *News-Herald* disagreed but was almost alone in commenting on the subject. Meanwhile, in the spring of 1944, as one of its last acts, W.J. Patterson's Liberal government of

Saskatchewan restored the franchise that that province had withdrawn from the Chinese in 1908. The Chinese had not complained much, for few were naturalized, but they considered the law a slight since the approximately 100 Japanese in the province could vote. In commenting on the measure, the Regina *Leader-Post,* under the condescending heading "Charlie Gets Vote," expressed satisfaction with a step that would "further solidify and increase the feeling of good will between Canadians and these brother members of the Allied Big Four" as it noted the good citizenship of local Chinese. In Parliament, Angus MacInnis (CCF, Vancouver East) asked how the other members would "square themselves with the Chinese, our gallant allies," when they went back to British Columbia and told them, "you were good enough to fight the Japanese but you are not good enough to have the vote in British Columbia."[13]

Once the army began calling up Chinese for military service in the summer of 1944, some Chinese "cheerfully" accepted service. As one recalled, "it wasn't an easy decision to enlist ... but it's still our country, even if we're not treated well." In contrast, approximately 400 Chinese youths and men in Vancouver protested, saying "no vote, no fight." Foon Sien asked Premier John Hart for a special session of the legislature to enfranchise Chinese. That session was not forthcoming, but in February 1945 the premier and cabinet received a delegation composed of Foon Sien and several other prominent Chinese Canadians. At the same time, the Chinese Canadian Association, which denied any link with the protesters, sent a petition bearing 726 signatures to Hart and the cabinet. The accompanying brief complained that, while "not exempt from full citizenship responsibilities," they lacked "rights enjoyed by all citizens of a democratic country." They asked for the franchise "on moral grounds" so that they could make Canada, their home, "worthy of being called a home." It cited their standard of living, scholastic successes, and contributions to the war effort, including the participation of about 250 Chinese British Columbians in the armed services, the purchase of Victory Bonds, and work in the munitions industry, as proof of their ability to serve Canada "in any capacity with full responsibility." The Chinese Youth Association in Victoria favoured the call-ups if they received full civil rights. It discussed how it might "seize the right to vote." The Wong Kung Har Tong Society in Vancouver had earlier reminded Premier Hart how Chinese Canadians were co-operating with the war effort. Because "the Chinese in Canada have been given the privilege to serve in the armed forces in Canada," it asked that the province enfranchise all Chinese who were Canadian citizens.[14]

By then the army, or at least General George Pearkes, who was in charge of Pacific Command, was keen to have the Chinese particularly to use as specialists in the Asian theatre. Forming a special training unit for them, he claimed, would mean that they would "not be treated in any way different from the normal soldiers serving in the Canadian Army," yet he would keep them together to obviate "difficulties arising from racial characteristics and language considerations and, at the same time, promoting esprit de corps." The General Staff, however, was less certain. Saying that the Department of External Affairs agreed with him, Lieutenant General J.C. Murchie advised, "from the National standpoint it should be a good thing to mix them with their fellow Canadians and from the start of their military life wean them from any peculiar habits or customs they may have." Some draftees were put in regular units, but twenty-five Canadian-born Chinese members of the Canadian army were loaned as wireless operators to British forces in India and Australia, where they distinguished themselves. When Britain asked for 125 more, the Cabinet War Committee doubted that it could secure that many volunteers but approved their despatch. Unfortunately, their service got little publicity because of its nature behind the lines. When an "All-China Troop Comforting Association" held an embarkation ball to honour Chinese Canadians proceeding to active duty, military officials requested that no mention be made of their destination or duties. Only after the war, when Private Louis R. Chow of Vancouver wrote from Ceylon to his brother, did the public learn that Secret Force 136, composed of 200 BC Chinese paratroops, had been dropped behind Japanese lines in Malaya to collect information, commit sabotage, and train natives to fight.[15]

Once the call-up went out to Chinese Canadians, the BC press speculated on the relationship to the franchise. The legislature's only wartime concession was to enfranchise all persons, including Chinese and Japanese, who had served or were serving in the Canadian Armed Forces. The Vancouver *Daily Province* endorsed that but emphasized that "the basis of [the] franchise should be citizenship and not military service." Similarly, when the Montreal *Standard* ran a photograph of a returning Chinese Canadian veteran being greeted by his father and brother with the caption that he could vote but they could not, the Vancouver *News-Herald* suggested that British Columbia was "being held up to ridicule all across Canada because it denies full rights of citizenship to those minorities which had colored skins."[16]

The province's reluctance to make more than token gestures toward enfranchisement was echoed in Ottawa's restraint in relaxing immigration regulations. Late in 1940, a Chinese resident of Duncan, who acted as a court interpreter, suggested that if Canada allowed Chinese to bring in their sons the community would contribute $1,000 for each immigrant. A.L. Jolliffe, the chief controller of Chinese immigration, curtly replied that the labour market could not absorb them. Not even the prime minister could budge immigration officials. In the summer of 1941, Ghe Chuey, who served King as he travelled by private railway car in western Canada, asked the prime minister to intercede to let him bring his wife and two children to Canada.

He had come to Canada in 1912, had worked for the Canadian National Railways since 1918, had become a Christian and a Canadian citizen, and had testimonials from prominent citizens as to his fine character. The prime minister offered to do what he could, but the Department of Immigration said that admitting Chuey's family would be contrary to the intent of the Chinese Immigration Act.[17]

Noting a "change of sentiment" in Canada toward China after "the conflagration spread to the Pacific," the CBA in Vancouver sought a modification of the Chinese Immigration Act to admit bona fide merchants and professional men, students, and wives and children of Chinese already in Canada and an annual quota of 150-200 immigrants. Their request got only a routine acknowledgment, but encouraged by China's consul general in Canada individual Chinese wrote to newspaper editors in Canada's major cities as a "trial balloon" to test public opinion.[18]

Indeed, a desire to improve its standing with China led Canada to reconsider exclusion. When T.A. Crerar, the minister of mines and resources, suggested repealing the act to remove a "badge of inferiority" and develop goodwill for postwar trade, Prime Minister King was "wholly sympathetic" even if it led to "unfortunate" things being said in Parliament. In a chat with Victor Odlum, before Odlum took up his post as Canada's first ambassador to China, King, apparently forgetting that the 1923 exclusionary act had abolished the head tax, suggested considering its removal. King had undoubtedly misinterpreted a suggestion from H.L. Keenleyside that it would be useful if Odlum's "first act" in Chungking was to discuss a reciprocal agreement that would "spare Chinese sensibilities" by admitting businessmen, missionaries, and the like on renewable two-year permits. Their children born in Canada would not acquire Canadian nationality, but the third generation and beyond might obtain it. Norman Robertson agreed and reminded King of the harshness of making the Chinese "the only members of the human race who are not allowed to bring their wives and children to Canada." King approved "very strongly." The Department of Immigration liked the idea but advised that without such an agreement "discriminatory legislation of some kind is the only course open." Jolliffe warned that female immigration would intensify "the problem in British Columbia." Keenleyside knew that China might not "accept what is essentially an exclusion agreement," so he advised Odlum to explain that Canada must control "its own policies" and that, while some people thought the 1923 act a mistake, political feelings in British Columbia made "it impossible to accept Chinese immigrants."[19]

In what may have been a test of the public mood, journalist Bruce Hutchison, who had good contacts in Ottawa, told *Vancouver Sun* readers, "we cannot expect to insult the Chinese and keep them as friends." Noting that the *Winnipeg Free Press* had demanded an end to immigration discrimination, he proposed solving a "very difficult" problem by a "token" measure such as admitting a few under a gentlemen's agreement. The article went unnoticed by British Columbians, who rarely discussed Chinese immigration but whose opinions were divided. When the convenor of the Vancouver Local Council of Women's Immigration Committee recommended denying entry to Canada to "nationals of any race who can not be assimilated by marriage, ... this applying equally to Chinese and Japanese," the Victoria Local Council responded to the complaint of Victoria's Chinese Youth Association by dissociating itself from the Vancouver motion.[20]

Mme Chiang Kai-shek's eloquent address to Parliament in June 1943 stimulated one Vancouver editor to suggest revising "our attitude toward China and her people" and devising a reciprocal scheme that without permitting "a wholesale influx" would "go far to remove the present feeling of injustice under which the Chinese smart." The press wondered if Mme Chiang, who did not mention immigration in her speech, had discussed it with King. His diary does not refer to such a discussion, but he later told Parliament that she had indicated that China "would not misunderstand an arrangement" recognizing Canada's need to preserve "certain economic standards" but believed that her people were "entitled to be dealt with as equals and not as inferiors." King, who favoured ending exclusion, saw "no reason" not to adopt a gentlemen's agreement or a reciprocal arrangement. Meanwhile, Q.P. Jack, president of the CBA, publicly chastised the government for extending "the hand of friendship to China" and simultaneously making "certain the hand remains a closed fist" as he reminded Vancouver residents that China was part of the United Nations and that the Chinese were good citizens of Canada.[21]

At about the same time, the United States prepared to repeal its exclusionary act and put Chinese under its quota system. That system would admit only about 100 Chinese annually, but the symbolism gave the United States considerable credit in China. The *Ottawa Journal* suggested that President Roosevelt's pressing of Congress to admit Chinese and grant them full citizenship rights made Canada's position not "too creditable." Similarly, the *Vancouver Sun* and the *Victoria Daily Times* noted that the new American policy would "probably force the issue" and remove discrimination without permitting the entry of a significant number. From China, Odlum offered conflicting advice. In early December, he said that, by not acting before the United States, Canada lost an opportunity to gain goodwill. He urged Canada to join Australia in opposing any change in policy; within the month, he complained that Canada and Australia were still injuring "the self-esteem of the Chinese." Nevertheless, in the summer of 1945, he told three members of the Legislative Yuan, who were about to visit North America, that, "high as was Canada's regard for China and for the Chinese, Canada could not allow a large inflow of migrants from any country, particularly from one the assimilation of whose people had already proved so difficult." A few months later he told the prime minister, "we must not exclude a man because he is Chinese; but we may control his movement to Canada because he represents a migratable group beyond our capacity to assimilate." Odlum recommended accepting a token number, about thirty-five a year.[22]

Aware of "rising resentment" about exclusion, King wanted to put a statement on Chinese immigration in the 1944 throne speech. The Department of External Affairs presented the Chinese minister with a draft reciprocal treaty that it hoped would "meet Chinese susceptibilities without causing opposition in any part of Canada" by granting temporary permits to merchants, doctors, clergy, and the like. Odlum thought the proposal "generous," but China saw it as discriminatory because it singled out Chinese and might set a precedent for other nations seeking to prevent Chinese immigration. Given opinion in British Columbia, Keenleyside argued for retaining the exclusionary law if China rejected the treaty. In that eventuality, Odlum suggested saying that China had rejected a "generous treaty."[23]

BC editors recognized the need to promote good relations with China, especially in light of postwar trade opportunities, but did not favour significant Chinese immigration. When reports circulated that Canada was preparing a treaty that would end exclusion, the Vancouver *News-Herald* suggested that it "might well be called an act of Chinese Inclusion – confirming the fact that China has taken her rightful place as a full sovereign nation" and ending the "fiction" of Chinese inferiority. However, it cautioned that neither was Canada ready to receive a "flood of immigrants" nor were the Chinese "ready to become part and parcel of our country through the process of absorption that is necessary in the creation of a homogenous population." Believing that the treaty would halt Chinese immigration, the *Victoria Daily Times* bluntly declared that it would "be highly satisfactory to those of us who believe in total exclusion" but admitted the need to do something if the Chinese already present were to stay permanently. When it realized that the United States was ending exclusion and making Chinese eligible for citizenship, the *Daily Times* stepped back lest a law that was more discriminatory than that of the United States impede postwar trade with China. Similar opinions appeared nationally, although not every newspaper mentioned it or made much comment. The *Toronto Daily Star*, for example, simply appended a brief description of the proposed treaty to an editorial on the mutual aid treaty that Canada and China had recently concluded. The *Globe and Mail* complained that the government had done nothing "to right a wrong and do justice to a people who have fought so nobly on our side for so many years." Yet the liberal-minded *Saturday Night* claimed that no Canadian newspaper "would advocate in plain language the free and unlimited admission of Chinese into the Dominion at the present time." The *Winnipeg Free Press* suggested that, by respecting "the principle of equality," the proposed agreement might "be a happy solution of this immigration question"; without directly saying so, it indicated that it would mean the entry of only a few specified groups and only on a temporary basis.[24]

With the end of the war, Chinese Canadians increased their campaign for a new immigration policy. In a widely publicized letter, Foon Sien, on behalf of the BC-based Hoysun Ninyung Benevolent Association (a locality organization), asked the government to repeal the 1923 act and admit a limited number of Chinese annually "in view of China's great contribution to the success of the United Nations" and "the great friendship that has grown up between Canada and China." He proposed a quota system as in the United States. A few Chinese Canadian groups expressed concern for possible competition from newcomers for jobs and in business, but many Chinese Canadian organizations petitioned for at least the admission of wives and children of Canadian residents. The CBA, the Chinese Chamber of Commerce, and others appealed to China's diplomats in Canada and to President Chiang Kai-shek of China for assistance to support their request that Canadian politicians repeal the exclusionary law.[25]

The government was responsive. Early in 1946, its officials concluded that "all immigration measures involved some form of discrimination" but that a reciprocity treaty would have the "least unfavourable effects." China again indicated that it would not accept such an arrangement. When Canada announced that Canadians could apply for the admission of first-degree European relatives – an almost meaningless gesture since Canada lacked facilities to process them and shipping was in short supply – China's ambassador saw the announcement as further evidence of discrimination against "the people of a country which has been Canada's faithful ally during a long period of stress and strain." He refused to withdraw what the Department of External Affairs considered an "intemperate and unfair" protest note even after being told that Canada was only dealing with a short-term problem affecting Europe. The department prepared a "stiff note" of reply but apparently did not send it, probably because Prime Minister King suggested that Ambassador Liu Shih Shun might have a point. Dr. Liu was anxious to resolve the "unsatisfactory situation." Despite difficulties in implementing a quota, which his government favoured, he sought admission of "next-of-kin." Canadian immigration officials, however, feared intense pressure if each of the approximately 35,000 Chinese in Canada applied for three or four relatives and were concerned that any concessions to the Chinese would lead to similar demands from "East Indians" and Japanese. In any event, discussions were set aside pending an overall review of immigration problems.[26]

Almost half of Canada's Chinese population in 1941 lived in Ontario, Alberta, Saskatchewan, and Quebec, but the editor of the *Chinese Times* of Toronto reported that British Columbia was the "toughest nut to crack" in the campaign to repeal the act. Yet scant public comment in 1946 and early 1947 suggested that British Columbians would not be upset by *limited* Chinese immigration. Like the eastern press, the *Nelson Daily News* suggested that the Chinese Immigration Act violated the spirit of the United Nations Charter and was a trade "barrier more lofty than any tariff wall." Although it cautioned that there was "a limit ... to the number we can assimilate economically" and that China's "colossal millions" could "swamp our whole economy," the *Vancouver Sun* observed that, while the Japanese came "as a directed invasion, ... in many cases financed by their home government," the Chinese "as a class [had] fitted themselves into the general economy, [and] were never objectionable."[27]

As some long-time residents took advantage of opportunities to return to China after the war, there were some poignant stories. In reporting how 600 Chinese men had recently sailed to China, Mary Quan wrote that many were middle aged and active in the community, but a combination of "discouragement, dissatisfaction or disgust" had caused their departure. She asserted that "no law ... makes a white man better than a colored one. There is no justice in robbing a man of his civil rights while forcing the accompanying responsibilities on him." Yet the many farewell tributes and parties showed how well liked some of them were. In Peterborough, Ontario, for example, Hum Hoy, the proprietor of the Paris Café, retired to China in 1948; the press reported that he had "made friends with young and old from every walk of life." In Saskatchewan, the Regina *Leader-Post* reported sympathetically how eight Chinese operators of a café in Swift Current were planning to sell their business and return to China. Similar stories appeared in British Columbia. Over 100 residents of Chase gave Yip Num, a restaurateur who had lived in the community for thirty-four years, a leather travelling bag and billfold as he left for China. He in turn donated $1,000 to the community hall building fund. According to the *Kamloops Sentinel*, "their best wishes came from the heart for he had been with them, through thick and thin, during many years and they had come to know him not as a Chinese restaurateur but as a man, a man from China who was part of Chase." Nearly seventy Kelowna businessmen had a farewell dinner for Lee Bon, who had operated a grocery store for thirty-five years. Neighbours and friends, both Chinese and white, had a party for Toa Yat Chim, a vegetable grower who had resided in Surrey for forty-five years, and gave him $100.[28]

As the farewell tributes suggest, the Chinese population of British Columbia was declining. Once shipping became available, the government expected that about 30 percent of the Chinese would leave. That was an overestimate, but during 1946 and the first half of 1947 about 2,000, mostly men over the age of sixty, returned to China. These departures profoundly affected Victoria's Chinatown since most of its residents were aging men; the young men were marrying Canadian-born women and following a Canadian rather than a Chinese diet. The departure of market gardeners, warned the BC Coast Vegetable Marketing Board, might significantly reduce vegetable acreage. Similarly, Vancouver's licensing department reported that, during six weeks in the fall of 1945, of the dozen plus applications for transfers of business licences from Chinese corner stores, only four of the new owners were Chinese.[29] As the Chinese role in the provincial economy waned, concern about them as economic competitors declined.

Diplomatic importuning from China, the lobbying efforts of Chinese in Canada, the imminent expiry of the wartime orders in council extending the time under which visitors to China might remain out of Canada, and fears that a proposed meeting of Asian nations might lead to complaints at the United Nations about racial discrimination in Canada led the federal cabinet to discuss the Chinese Immigration Act in December 1946. In a committee, Louis St. Laurent, the minister of external affairs, observed that, "under the United Nations Charter, Canada had undertaken to avoid discrimination based on religion, race, colour or sex, and to respect fundamental human rights." "The right of a man to live with his wife," he said, was "fundamental, and the present policy of exclusion of these relatives could not be successfully defended in United Nations discussions."[30]

The cabinet knew that a recent public opinion poll had shown that a majority of Canadians favoured selective immigration, that only 24 percent believed Chinese should be kept out, and that many supported repeal of the exclusionary law.[31] In Toronto Caucasians and Chinese had established a Committee for the Repeal of the Chinese Immigration Act that reminded King of his 1943 admission that the act was "a mistake" and violated the United Nations Charter. The Canadian Council of Churches called for an end to "discrimination against the Chinese people"; indeed, in his Sunday sermon, a prominent United Church minister in Toronto urged that Canada arrange immigration restrictions with the government of China rather than have Canadian immigration officials enforce them. In Winnipeg, after hearing from local Chinese members of the Repeal Committee that the law conflicted with United Nations obligations and was contrary to principles of humanity, morality, and social welfare, the Trades and Labour Council endorsed repeal of the act.[32]

When the Toronto and District Labour Council called the Chinese Immigration Act "an insult not only to an Allied nation but to one of the great civilizations of the past," editors from various parts of the country agreed, though not always for the same reasons. *Saturday Night* lauded the "gratifying progress" of the movement for repeal. Most arguments opposed discrimination. The Toronto *Globe and Mail* attacked "unjust" discrimination, while the *Toronto Daily Star* reminded readers that exclusion was contrary to "the principles of democracy" and conflicted with Canada's United Nations obligations by discriminating "against the Chinese as a race." The *Winnipeg Free Press* suggested that the Chinese Immigration Act insulted "a proud race" and by preventing "newcomers from living normal lives is not unlike Hitler's own methods"; its rival, the Winnipeg *Tribune,* which had noted how the city's 800 Chinese residents had won "the admiration of all" for "their thrift, industry and spirit of service," agreed that it was "high time" to repeal the act "as completely out of keeping with Canadian feelings toward a gallant and friendly ally." The Montreal *Star* reminded lawmakers of "a strong new nationalism" emerging in the Orient as it noted past discrimination; the Montreal *Gazette* called for a policy to "modify the discriminatory and unreasonable regulations which virtually exclude all Chinese." In a feature report, it showed that the city's Chinatown was no longer an "old slum" but one of "the more progressive business like and better lighted districts in the metropolis." The North Bay *Daily Nugget* opposed a law that discriminated against people who had "proved themselves industrious, hard-working, and thoroughly commendable citizens." The *Ottawa Citizen* presented humanitarian and commercial reasons for repeal. Economic reasons of another kind influenced the Toronto *Evening Telegram.* It agreed with appeals to the four freedoms promulgated by President Roosevelt in 1941 but suggested that a stronger argument was Canada's need for Chinese to operate laundries and restaurants. In a similar vein that reflected lingering thoughts in British Columbia, the *Vancouver Sun,* though friendly to the Chinese for doing useful work that no one else wanted, shared ancient beliefs that most Chinese were sojourners and that a reciprocal immigration arrangement could result in their "swamping" Canada.[33]

Given the diplomatic situation and general support for the move, the cabinet ignored immigration department warnings of problems in identifying Chinese and a possible influx of several thousand Chinese, most of whom would settle in British Columbia. It decided to repeal the Chinese Immigration Act to let Canadian citizens have their wives and unmarried children under the age of eighteen join them. Late in January 1947, Mackenzie King invited Ambassador Liu, "a very great friend," to tea, where he told him that the Chinese Immigration Act would be repealed, though Canada would still "control the numbers" through the general Immigration Act. Liu, according to King, "regarded the matter as having great international significance," and his manner became "a little more formal."[34]

Meanwhile, support for ending exclusion mounted. Chinese from Victoria to Halifax and in small centres such as Flin Flon, Manitoba, and medium ones such as Calgary, London, and Windsor met on 26 or 27 January 1947 to pass resolutions for repeal of the act and its harsh "43 restrictions" so that they could bring wives and children to Canada. In Toronto a placard proclaimed *Gung Do Chin Yuen Day* ("Petition for Justice Day"). In some cities, non-Chinese attended the meetings. In Quebec City, for example, the editor of the *Quebec Chronicle Telegraph* and the police chief were among those signing the resolution.[35] The meetings were redundant; on 27 January

"Insult Expunged," *Windsor Daily Star,* 28 January 1947. Knight of the *Windsor Daily Star* neatly captured a widespread sentiment. Courtesy of the *Windsor Star.*

1947, a few days before the new parliamentary session began, Prime Minister King announced that the government intended to repeal the act.

The overarching theme of press comment and letters to Ottawa was commendation for ending a long-standing injustice against the Chinese or, in the words of *Le Droit* of Ottawa, this "unjust and stupid" law. Other Roman Catholic journals, such as the Ontario-based *Canadian Register,* praised the decision on moral grounds because the denial of a "normal family life in a country which frowns upon miscegenation" had left the way "open for all kinds of tensions and unnatural situations." That sentiment was echoed by *L'Action catholique* of Quebec City and by the secular *Toronto Daily Star,* which also referred to Canada's obligations under the United Nations Charter. Yet journals such as the Montreal *Star,* the *Ottawa Citizen,* the Regina *Leader-Post,* and the *Saskatoon Star-Phoenix* added that repeal should not mean "a renewed influx of Chinese." In Victoria, the *Daily Times* reported that Chinatown residents expected "no surge of Chinese women coming to Canada" since most younger Chinese men had married Chinese Canadian women and "probably would not like the girls brought up in China." Nevertheless, Chinese informants suggested that future immigrants would bring their families to avoid "the hardship suffered by so many older Chinese here." The Vancouver *Daily Province* agreed that an influx was unlikely as it welcomed the removal of "discrimination against a great and friendly nation" and criticized the BC MPs who feared that repealing the act "would open the door to a flood of Chinese immigrants." It argued that the Chinese should not be subject to a discriminatory and "cruel" law but should be under the same immigration act as everyone else. Canadian Chinese agreed. The "extreme pleasure" of "The Assembly of Chinese Residents of Vancouver" and the "deep sense of gratitude" of the Kingston Chinese Community Centre were representative messages to Ottawa.[36]

While most Canadians, including British Columbians, welcomed or at least did not protest repeal of the Chinese Immigration Act, J.A. Glen, whose Department of Mines and Resources was responsible, while noting principles enunciated at the United Nations, told Parliament that because "so many opinions were expressed throughout the country" the government would "proceed surely and steadily" in removing "discrimination against the Chinese." Only the wives and unmarried children under the age of eighteen of Canadian citizens would be admitted. Of the approximately 26,000 Chinese in the country, Glen estimated that only 8,749 were Canadian citizens and hence eligible to bring in their wives and children.[37]

The BC MPs, though not adverse to giving justice to Canadian citizens of Chinese ancestry, thought that the minister underestimated the potential numbers. Howard Green calculated that there were 22,000 more married male Chinese in Canada than married female Chinese. Their wives and eligible children, he suggested, could double Canada's Chinese population.

"Welcome Home!" Montreal *Star,* 28 January 1947, by Reidford. The narrowness of the door's opening implies how few Chinese were able to enter Canada as a result of the end of exclusion.

After pointing out that 53.7 percent of the Chinese in Canada resided in his home province, he briefly traced the history of their immigration and problems with assimilation and living standards. Nevertheless, he conceded that the Chinese were "scrupulously honest" and "loyal friends" who were "very well liked" in British Columbia, but he warned "that opening the gates to an influx" would probably destroy the good feeling that was likely to lead to their enfranchisement in British Columbia. Green concluded by asking for "full details" about future Chinese immigration policy. Other BC MPs, three Liberals, Thomas Reid, George Cruickshank, and James Sinclair; the independent J.L. Gibson; and Angus MacInnis of the CCF followed in the debate. All, including MacInnis, echoed Green's demand for further details. In the words of Reid, "what of the second or perhaps third step?" They decried past injustices in immigration policy, especially in comparison to those applied to the Japanese, they praised China as a good ally and the Chinese "as a people of honesty and integrity," and they endorsed BC plans to enfranchise eligible Chinese. Cruickshank even claimed that, if BC law permitted, a Chinese man would nominate him at the next election. Nevertheless, most members rehearsed arguments about inassimilability and the danger of an influx imperilling the "white Canada that we have here." Davie Fulton, who did not speak in the debate, told constituents that the BC MPs feared being "accused of racial discrimination" but felt "very strongly" that, with their province being most affected, they were "entitled to know what measure of immigration will be allowed." They wanted the assurance requested by MacInnis that removing discrimination did "not imply that we are compelled to allow every Chinese who so wishes to come here." One rumour suggested that the BC MPs had threatened to bolt from their parties without such assurance. In sum, the BC MPs, no matter their party affiliation, theoretically favoured removing discrimination against Canadian citizens, but opposed the admission of a significant number of Chinese.[38]

King had to try to please both those "who did not want to do anything that might make their position in B.C. more difficult" and "those who wanted to serve United Nations ends," including himself. His cabinet was equally perplexed as to how and where to draw the line in discriminating "between different races and people who wish to come to Canada." King believed that "there should be no exclusion of any particular race" but equivocally observed that "a country should surely have the right to determine what strains of blood it wishes to have in its population and how its people coming from outside have to be selected." In cabinet he asked about admitting near relatives of Chinese who were residents of Canada but not citizens. St. Laurent suggested devising "a general immigration policy which, within prescribed limits, would avoid discrimination on racial grounds," possibly by a quota system that would preserve the existing proportions of all racial groups in Canada. Cabinet asked the Interdepartmental Committee on Immigration to report on these ideas as soon as possible. The committee, however, refused to consider a quota mainly because the Department of Immigration lacked the necessary administrative machinery. The committee also thought that some beliefs, so "widely and strongly held," particularly in British Columbia, were "a political factor that cannot be overlooked." King's immediate concern was the Liberal caucus. Although in analyzing the initial debate J.W. Pickersgill said that Sinclair and the other BC Liberals only wanted "some assurance that the door is not going to be opened to large scale Chinese immigration," the prime minister complained that the BC Liberals, who had won their seats by slim majorities, were demanding "individual legislation to suit their different constituencies." In caucus, Sinclair "went after Glen without gloves" for neither consulting the BC MPs nor explaining what would replace the exclusion act. By explaining the government's plans, St. Laurent was able to satisfy Sinclair, but Reid remained unhappy.[39]

Reid soon discovered that he was out of touch with opinion in British Columbia, where the only public opposition to repealing the Chinese Immigration Act came from small groups with anti-Asian traditions, such as the Delta Board of Trade, the Saanich Progressive Conservative Association, the Newton Branch of the Canadian Legion, and the Native Sons of British Columbia. The Vancouver *News-Herald* reprinted a *Toronto Daily Star* editorial observing that repeal would not end discrimination since, unlike others, Chinese had to be naturalized before they could sponsor immigrants. Thus, when Reid visited his constituency in April, he advised the Surrey Liberal Association that repealing the act "did not mean opening the door to Chinese immigration," but Canada had to consider opinion at the United Nations; he told the New Westminster Rotary Club that the exclusion act had been an "insult to the Chinese nation as a whole."[40]

For some left-wing and labour groups and civil libertarians, the new Chinese immigration policy did not go far enough. The BC Federation of Labour, the IWA, the Victoria Labour Council, the British Columbia Labour Progressive Party, the Victoria-Oak Bay CCF organization, the Canadian Congress of Labour, as well as the Vancouver and Manitoba branches of the Canadian Civil Liberties Union welcomed the elimination of discrimination inherent in the act but complained that repeal did not end discrimination. Outside British Columbia, that support was not confined to the left wing. The Anglican and Presbyterian Churches urged that the lack of Canadian citizenship should not prevent Chinese from bringing in their wives and children. The Montreal *Gazette* expressed disappointment at the narrowness of the proposed changes, while the Toronto *Globe and Mail* suggested that the limited concession was a manifestation of the "streak of race prejudice, which has for so long colored the immigration policy of this Government. Writing in the *Saskatoon Star-Phoenix,* James H. Gray described the repeal bill as "no more than a gesture" since orders in council still restricted Chinese immigration.[41]

Chinese groups across the country were disappointed that the new policy was still discriminatory. They asked for the same status as Europeans in immigration matters, namely that the government cancel PC 2115, which allowed only Asians who were Canadian citizens to sponsor family members as immigrants, and that it put the Chinese under PC 695, which permitted the entry of the wives, unmarried children under the age of eighteen, and fiancé(e)s of legal residents of Canada. At a reception hosted by the Hoysun

Ninyung Benevolent Association in honour of T.C. Davis, who was about to take up his post as Canadian ambassador to China, retired ambassador V.W. Odlum said, "we want Chinese who come to Canada to make this country their home for all time." He encouraged his audience to press for necessary changes in the Chinese Immigration Act. Indicative of how attitudes had changed over the past quarter century, Odlum, who had campaigned unsuccessfully on a White Canada platform in the 1921 federal election, now admitted, "there was no cause for this law originally."[42]

Almost three months later, in announcing the general immigration policy, the prime minister told Parliament that the government would repeal both the Chinese Immigration Act and the 1931 order in council that denied naturalization certificates to people of Chinese or Japanese origin who could not prove that they had renounced allegiance to their native land. He emphasized, however, that, because "large-scale immigration from the orient would change the fundamental composition of the Canadian population" and cause social and economic problems with serious international complications, the changes would be limited. King was pleased with the reception given to his statements, though he admitted in his diary that he would have gone "a step further" and let all Chinese send "at once" for their families, as in the case of Europeans, but he had to deal with a "fear of an influx" and the "situation in B.C." Nevertheless, he enjoyed the subsequent parliamentary debate that indicated his policy statement had "met with all but complete approval on the part of the different groups in the House." What once appeared to be "the most difficult measure of the session" had been resolved. Significantly, no BC Liberal spoke, possibly because, as R.G. Robertson of the Prime Minister's Office observed, the promise of no change in the "fundamental composition of the Canadian population" eased worries about a Chinese influx. Four Progressive Conservatives, Fulton, Cecil Merritt, Pearkes, and Green, had no objections to removing discrimination against Canadian citizens who had made many contributions to the country. Pearkes' account of his wartime meeting with Chinese Canadians who had volunteered for military service in the South Pacific moved even the prime minister, who thought it "a very reasonable statement. Well balanced." Conservatives did complain of a lack of clarity in plans for effective control of Asian immigration. Specifically, they worried that, if all Chinese Canadians brought in their wives and children, there would be "considerable" immigration. William Irvine (CCF, Cariboo) stressed that the Chinese must be treated like any other immigrants, but Angus MacInnis asserted that, "if the Chinese are put on the same basis as other people so far as their right to enter this country is concerned, that does not mean that Canada must allow the entry of every Chinese who comes within the regulations and asks to come here."[43]

With the exception of some Social Credit members from Alberta; a Progressive Conservative from Kingston, who wanted Canada to remain

British and Canadian, and one from Calgary who worried about admitting large numbers of people who could not be assimilated; and a Quebec Liberal who feared the possibility of Chinese Communists coming to Canada, members of Parliament from other provinces welcomed the repeal of the Chinese Immigration Act. Moreover, many chastised the government for retaining discrimination, though no one proposed a completely open door for Chinese immigrants. M.J. Coldwell (CCF, Rosetown-Biggar, Saskatchewan) called it "a cruel hoax" for Chinese since discrimination remained. The Liberal civil rights activist David Croll (Toronto-Spadina) declared that it was only a half measure, that Canada must give "people of colour in Canada ... the same rights that I enjoy." John Diefenbaker (Progressive Conservative, Lake Centre, Saskatchewan), like many other opposition MPs, warned that the proposed law might require Canada to prove to the United Nations that "we are not discriminating against any race and proceeding contrary to our pledged word." Parliament agreed, without division, to repeal the Chinese Immigration Act. Soon after, during a free-time political broadcast on the Canadian Broadcasting Corporation, J.A. Glen reviewed the changes in Chinese immigration policy, noting that only the wives and children of Chinese in Canada would be admitted for the present.[44]

The press outside British Columbia approved the removal of blatant discrimination or, as *L'Action catholique* put it, the end of an "injustice of which the Chinese were the victims." The Regina *Leader-Post* commended the government for wiping out a "racial stigma." The *Calgary Herald*, the *Edmonton Journal*, and the Toronto *Globe and Mail* were pleased that the doors were not being flung open, but the *Toronto Daily Star*, noting that the cost of bringing in family members and supporting them in Canada meant that few Chinese were likely to send for families, complained of continued discrimination since Chinese who were not Canadian citizens had to wait five years for their families to join them.[45]

Within British Columbia, there was little immediate comment. Six weeks later, however, the *Vancouver Sun*, inspired by the call of Percy Bengough of the Trades and Labour Congress of Canada to a Senate Committee on Immigration and Labour for "the exclusion of all races that cannot be properly assimilated into the national life of Canada" and apparently thinking that Canada might adopt a quota system, claimed that the government had granted entry rights to 12,000 Chinese wives and children of Canadian citizens. In an editorial that it could have copied from one published decades earlier when Bengough was a founder of the Asiatic Exclusion League in 1921, the *Sun* predicted that British Columbia could have a Chinese population of a quarter of a million by 1960. It admonished that "large-scale admixtures of alien cultures cannot be achieved without setting up serious stresses." The Saanich branch of the Canadian Legion shared that sentiment, but it and the *Sun* were virtually alone in their concerns.[46]

In China the *Central Daily News* of Nanking lauded the new law for showing "Canada's friendly attitude towards our new China and her respect for the dignity of China as a sovereign state and for the equal treatment of the Chinese people." It did not see the restrictions as particularly discriminatory since they applied to all Asians. China's government welcomed a "step in the right direction" but complained that only Canadian citizens could bring in wives and families. Since China was not interested in a reciprocal agreement, St. Laurent accepted a departmental recommendation to tell China that Canada could not see its "way clear to making any further proposals with regard to Chinese immigration at the present time." Ambassador Davis reported that China's "intellectual classes" had "hard feelings" about discriminatory immigration laws, but the "non-intellectual class," estimated to be at least 80 percent of the population, was more concerned with getting enough food and probably did not "even know where Canada is, let alone that our country had enacted any type of legislation of a discriminatory type against them."[47]

Until they received that message, government officials had actively contemplated how to control Chinese immigration. H.L. Keenleyside, now deputy minister of mines and resources, warned that, if all the male Chinese in Canada took advantage of the new regulations and each had two children, there could be 66,000 immigrants. A movement of even half of that number, he suggested, would "arouse a new storm of anti-oriental feeling in British Columbia," where about half of them would probably settle. As "the only practicable way of avoiding the grave influx of Chinese men and women now threatening the country," he recommended a quota on the wives of Chinese who were not Canadian citizens at the time of the act's implementation. Neither his new department nor his old one, External Affairs, favoured that idea. Lester B. Pearson, the undersecretary, thought that a quota would arouse "serious criticism" and suggested limiting the flow through existing regulations such as delaying medical examinations, imposing standards on ocean travel; and requiring husbands to demonstrate that they could maintain certain standards of health and accommodation for their families in Canada. Given the apparent lack of interest in Canada among the Chinese in China, when China's chargé d'affaires called, Keenleyside merely quoted Mackenzie King's statement of 1 May and told him that China should take the next step since it had turned down Canada's earlier "reasonable and fair proposal."[48]

So slightly was the door opened that the Chinese in British Columbia complained. The *New Republic,* a Chinese daily newspaper published in Victoria, urged the Senate to consider relaxing the restrictions since only 3,500 Canadian Chinese would be eligible to send for their families. Victoria's Chinese community predicted that its numbers would fall by half within five years since many of its residents were over sixty years of age and were returning to China rather than sending for families despite inflation that made the cost of living higher there than in Canada. During 1946 and the first half of 1947, about 2,000 individuals from across Canada returned to China even though some had to borrow their fares. Yee Chew Ping, secretary of the conference of the Western Division of the Chinese Nationalist League of Canada, told the press that many were market gardeners who had no one to take their places and asked for equal treatment for Chinese and European immigrants.[49]

Few Chinese residents of Canada could afford to bring in their families, and in any case no passenger ships operated directly between China and Canada, and Canada lacked adequate facilities in China to make medical inspections and investigations. Thus, by 1 December 1947, only sixty-six Chinese had applied to bring approximately 200 family members to Canada. Almost a year after the repeal of the act, Joseph Hope, a spokesman for Victoria Chinese, said that "not a single wife or child of a Chinese-Canadian citizen" had yet arrived. He even cited the case of a naturalized businessman whose wife had lived in Victoria for fifteen years, where she had given birth to their children, but could not re-enter Canada after a visit to China. An Ontario MP warned that delays in medical inspections risked the loss of any goodwill that the government may have gained among Chinese Canadians for liberalizing immigration laws. Officials in the Department of Citizenship and Immigration did not expect an immediate mass movement, nor did the Committee for the Repeal of the Chinese Immigration Act as it urged that non-citizens be allowed to send for their families, especially since both Chinese law and Canadian custom had made it difficult for Chinese residents of Canada to become naturalized. By mid-June 1947, only sixty-eight Chinese had applied for naturalization, a number that was much smaller than anticipated. The repeal committee appealed directly to the cabinet, presented a brief to the Senate Committee on Immigration and Labour, secured the support of a number of newspapers that objected to discrimination on moral and humanitarian grounds, and, most importantly, persuaded the Senate committee that Chinese residents of Canada, citizens or not, should be allowed to bring in their wives and children. When the Cabinet Committee on Immigration Policy considered the matter, an immigration department official advised that this could allow as many as 13,000 Chinese to bring in wives and families. The cabinet committee decided not to change the law.[50]

When it seemed likely that the Communists under Mao Zedong would defeat the Nationalist government of Chiang Kai-shek, Canada sped up processing in Hong Kong by using airmail rather than sea mail to send documents across the Pacific and sent an additional immigration officer to Hong Kong but did not relax examination procedures. It also made it easier for Chinese to become naturalized by dropping the requirement that they first divest themselves of Chinese nationality and excusing those with more than twenty years of residence in Canada from demonstrating a command of English or French. The defeat of Chiang Kai-shek's Nationalist forces in China and the victory of the Communists under Mao Zedong in 1949 increased the desire of Canadian Chinese to bring in family members from Hong Kong, where they lived in "unnatural conditions" and were quickly becoming destitute. By late November 1949, 625 Chinese women and children had been admitted to Canada, another 429 cases had been approved but were unable to get transportation, and about forty per week were applying. The number of Chinese in Canada applying for naturalization rose to an average of 150 per week.[51]

The CBA in Vancouver asked that unnaturalized residents be allowed to bring in families who had fled to Hong Kong. The director of Chinese immigration predicted that admitting other than the wives and children of Canadian citizens would lead to "a flood of applications for citizenship," and the Hong Kong office would be unable to cope with an estimated 2,800 families that might apply. Cabinet adopted a compromise on 21 December 1949. To assuage the CBA, many of whose members were qualified Canadian voters, as a humanitarian gesture it agreed to admit wives and families who had reached Hong Kong by 1 December 1949 and whose sponsors had applied for naturalization before that date; to satisfy the Department of Immigration, it would not consider any others. The *Vancouver Sun* reported that Canada had "extended a helping hand" to several hundred refugees who were relatives of Canadian Chinese. A few weeks later, after learning that many refugees lacked passports or other travel documents, cabinet recommended that the immigration department accept affidavits "to avoid hardship to admissible wives and children of Canadian citizens of Chinese race." No public objections were evident, but as of June 1950 Canada had admitted only 1,386 Chinese immigrants, most of whom had arrived in the previous six months. Repeal of the exclusionary Chinese Immigration Act had been only a token gesture toward citizens of Chinese ancestry. Foon Sien rightly declared in 1950 that Canadian Chinese "still smart under the indignity of statutory discrimination which make[s] them 'second class citizens.'"[52]

THAT WAS CERTAINLY TRUE in immigration matters, but many other barriers to full citizenship had been abolished. The most important one was enfranchisement in British Columbia. During the war, when the Chinese Canadian Association and other Chinese groups sought enfranchisement, the provincial government said that wartime was not the time for controversy. Whenever he met a provincial cabinet minister, Foon Sien, who was living in Victoria as editor of the *New Republic*, "harped on the question of giving the franchise to Orientals." The Chinese branch of the Army, Navy, and Air Force Veterans, however, took the lead in reminding British Columbians that, since all Chinese Canadians had been subjected to military and civilian service under the National Resources Mobilization Act, "they should not now be denied the full rights of citizenship, including the vote." The Vancouver *Daily Province* agreed: "Every Canadian citizen should, by virtue of that citizenship, have the right to vote." In the fall of 1946, with the backing of a dozen non-Chinese organizations, including the United Church, the United Nations Society, and the Vancouver Consultative Council, the Chinese Canadian Association again appeared before the legislative committee on the Elections Act. The question attracted little notice, but there was sympathy for enfranchising all Canadian citizens no matter their racial origin. Indeed, of the groups presenting briefs to the committee, only the Japanese Repatriation League opposed Asian enfranchisement. The Vancouver *News-Herald* complained that British Columbia was the only province to ban certain citizens from the polls. The *CCF News* noted that despite the Citizenship Act Asians in British Columbia were second-class citizens who could not "take part in choosing the government." The *Vernon News* asked, "what clearer breach of the intent of the citizenship act could there be than this?" In the "new light" of the Citizenship Act, the *Vancouver Sun,* which had harboured reservations about enfranchising Chinese "remittance men" who had dual citizenship and whose immigration could "swamp our whole economy," nevertheless found the disfranchisement of "Orientals" "anomalous." With the proclamation of Canada's Citizenship Act on 1 January 1947, the enfranchisement of the Chinese became, in the words of Jack Scott, "an indication of enlightened public opinion." At its next session in the winter of 1947, the legislature, in what one editor described as a "foregone conclusion," readily struck out "Chinese" and "Hindus" from those who were ineligible to vote. Indirectly, that gave them the right to vote in federal elections and removed barriers to professions such as accountancy, law, and pharmacy whose members had to be on the voters' list.[53]

Although the Chinese branch of the Army, Navy, and Air Force Veterans complained in 1946 that some of Vancouver's laws, including denial of the municipal franchise to Chinese Canadians, were "chaotic and deplorable," granting of the provincial franchise did not immediately lead to the municipal vote. In the fall of 1948, a lawyer for the CBA told Vancouver City Council that Chinese paid taxes on "millions of dollars" worth of property and were the largest group of property owners without a vote. Despite "spirited opposition" from Alderman Halford Wilson, who said that it would give Ottawa an excuse to lift the ban on Japanese at the coast, Vancouver City Council agreed that, if the Union of British Columbia Municipalities (UBCM) approved enfranchising Asians municipally, it would seek the necessary amendment to its charter to let Asians vote. At the 1948 UBCM convention, Foon Sien and Denis Murphy, the CBA lawyer, asked for the municipal vote. J.W. Fletcher of West Vancouver was almost alone when he claimed that extending "the franchise will lower the bar and allow all Orientals to move here by the millions." With only two dissenters, the convention endorsed granting the municipal franchise to Chinese. In March 1949, the provincial legislature amended the Municipal Act and the Vancouver City Charter and enfranchised Japanese and Indians provincially. With rare exceptions, the press welcomed this erasure of "a blot from British Columbia's record," "an encouragement to better citizenship," conforming to "principles of freedom of opportunity," the culmination "of a long and uphill struggle for the cause of civil liberty," and the removal of "the stain of unjust discrimination," in short "a good thing," while from across the Rockies the Calgary *Albertan* called it a "victory of common sense and justice."[54]

Chinese Canadians first took advantage of the franchise with the 1948 Vancouver Centre federal by-election. They were keen to get on the voters' list. All three parties opened campaign offices in Chinatown and suggested that they would do the most to promote Chinese equality. For example, George Pearkes, speaking for the Conservatives, said that he had been fighting restrictions such as those limiting the immigration of family members. The Liberals held a party in Chinatown, and their candidate, Ralph Campney, provided transportation from Chinatown to his rally in the Hotel Vancouver. The CCF, which won, claimed that it got the majority of the approximately 600 Chinese votes, but of 195 votes in a poll in Chinatown 87 went to the Liberals, and the remainder were almost equally divided between the Conservatives and the CCF. That Liberal success may have been due to the work of Foon Sien, who campaigned actively for the party and who was later a guest speaker at a Vancouver Centre Liberal function. After the election, the Liberals invited the Chinese to their summer picnic. In the June 1949 federal election, after a nine-year absence, H.H. Stevens attempted to get back into politics as an independent candidate in Vancouver Centre. He was first elected to Parliament as a Conservative in 1911 on a platform that promoted a White Canada policy and was re-elected in 1921 with a similar plank. In 1949 he spoke to 700 Chinese Canadian voters at the New W.K. Gardens in Vancouver's Chinatown and promised that, "if I am elected, I will represent you as my fellow Canadian citizens. There will be no discrimination, no difference."[55] Stevens lost, but his change of stance and the new electorate vividly demonstrated changed sentiments in British Columbia.

By enfranchising Chinese, the provincial government automatically removed a number of disabilities such as the right to vote in school board elections, to be called to the bar, or to qualify as pharmacists. A new Act to Regulate the Working of Coal Mines made no mention of Chinese, whereas its predecessor had made it an offence to employ them. In practice as well as in the law, provincial and municipal governments ended discriminatory practices. The provincial government appointed a Chinese Canadian as a sales tax inspector to work with Chinese merchants, and the Victoria School Board hired at least one Chinese woman as a teacher and another as a secretary. When informed that old regulations forbade it to patronize firms with Asian employees, Vancouver City Council cancelled the practice. When criticized for not hiring Chinese, the city replied that the Department of Health employed both a Chinese doctor and a Chinese nurse and that no Chinese had applied for other positions. Council in 1950, however, rejected a suggestion that the Vancouver City Police hire a Chinese Canadian to help combat crime against the Chinese. Alderman Wilson claimed that such a hiring would be to admit "discrimination which doesn't exist," but as late as 1961 both the *Chinatown News* and the *Vancouver Sun* complained that the city still had no Chinese police officers. Private enterprise, however, hired Chinese. The Hudson's Bay department store in Vancouver, for example, had a Chinese model in a fashion show for teenagers.[56]

According to Foon Sien, the right to vote "proved to be a wonderful weapon with which we were able to fight off racial discrimination." Such a fight was still necessary, for some everyday discrimination remained throughout the late 1940s and the 1950s. Indeed, in congratulating John Diefenbaker on introducing a Bill of Rights, Foon Sien, on behalf of the CBA, asked that it include something to protect Canadian Chinese. "Too many times," he explained, "we have been shunted off the line of labour because of our ancestry ... and never because of our qualifications." Moreover, though admitting that a Bill of Rights could probably do nothing about the prejudices of individuals, he asserted, "we have been slighted socially." A number of BC examples illustrate the reasons for his concern. Vancouver's Kerrisdale Arena denied access to the Connaught Skating Club because it had six Chinese Canadian members. In Toronto the Chinese Canadian Association complained of the use of stereotypes in a National Film Board production. In Victoria the director of vocational training at Victoria High School could not place some top students in suitable employment simply because they were Chinese, and engineering graduates of the University of British Columbia reported problems in getting appropriate jobs because of their race. A Chinese person was refused admission to two private clubs in Victoria because of his race, but there was a turnabout of sorts since a short time later a Chinese club in Vancouver refused admission to a Westerner.[57]

Despite such discrimination, the striking thing to emerge was the almost immediate challenge that it elicited. The College of Physicians and Surgeons reprimanded a Vancouver eye specialist who refused to treat a boy because he was Chinese. Acting on the initiative of trustee Waldo Skillings, who said "he could not understand why Orientals who had no vote, should get the business when 'white' firms did not," the Victoria School Board discontinued buying fruits and vegetables from a Chinese supplier and, over the protests of several trustees, decided to patronize only "white firms." Such racial intolerance "shocked" both local newspapers, which said that as "good citizens and equally good merchants" the Chinese were "entitled to all of their rights in a free land." The Canadian Legion also protested. The School

Board quickly and unanimously rescinded its decision. When a missionary from the Chinese Catholic Centre in Vancouver charged that young Chinese Canadians were having problems getting jobs, Tom Alsbury, president of the Vancouver Trades and Labour Council, denounced employers who hid their own prejudices behind a claim that employees would not want to work with the Chinese. In 1956, however, Attorney-General Les Peterson – following the lead of other provinces (notably Ontario) and the federal government, and recognizing the interests of his constituents in Vancouver Centre – introduced a Fair Employment Act. Citing the Universal Declaration of Human Rights, he told the legislature that there were employers who refused to hire Chinese and landlords who refused to give them accommodation simply because of their colour.[58]

The legislature passed the Fair Employment Act, but did not bring in a Fair Accommodation Act until 1961. Landlords did practise discrimination. In New Westminster, Susan Chew, a Victoria native, owner of the popular Waffle House restaurant, and leader of a cub pack at an Anglican church, put a deposit on a suite in a new luxury apartment building. Soon afterward, the prospective new owner of the building, an American, refused to have her as a tenant. The mayor, while decrying the fact that "colour and race should not enter into our daily life," did not think that the city could do anything. A New Westminster alderman described Miss Chew as one of the city's finest citizens, and the city's medical officer cancelled his lease in the building, and others were prepared to follow. The local radio station, CKNW, and the local newspaper, the *British Columbian,* also stood up for Miss Chew, and Vancouver newspapers joined the campaign. Faced with this protest, within a day the building owner withdrew it from sale, apologized, and asked Miss Chew to be a tenant in a gesture welcomed by the *British Columbian* as the removal of "the stain of racial discrimination" from the city.[59]

Even old problems of poor living standards and gambling got a sympathetic hearing. At Prince Rupert, when Chinese restaurant workers complained that they could not always understand English, local health authorities provided an interpreter at a short course on food handling. In Kamloops, however, the Royal Café advertised that by changing to "All White Help" it could "offer the best in service efficiency and cleanliness" after the medical health officer closed four Chinese restaurants. Yet in that city, following reports of "aged, indigent, and ill Chinese ... crowded into doss houses," the mayor recommended that the city establish a community boarding house for them. Kamloops City Police did raid Chinese gambling houses, but as in the past Vancouver was the centre of such activities. A lawyer acting on behalf of two Chinese who were convicted of keeping a common gaming house complained, with reason, every time there was a change at City Hall the Chinese expected newspaper headlines and "kudoes" to those who were going to clean up gambling. Within days of taking office in January 1947, Mayor G.G.

(Gerry) McGeer, as head of the Vancouver Police Commission, suggested reorganizing the police force and replacing all members of the gambling, liquor, and morality squads. The target was alleged corruption within the police, not Chinatown. The day before the police chief gave McGeer a list of gambling houses, bootleggers, and houses of ill repute police warned the owners of the approximately thirty-seven Chinese gambling joints that they would be shutting them down. The gambling business seemed to die down, but in March police searched and closed many of the joints and arrested their inmates. As Vancouver City Police continued to raid Chinese gambling houses, Magistrate Mackenzie Matheson promised that he would "have something to say pretty soon if this court continues to be used for collections from Chinese." The *Vancouver Sun* followed with an attack on such "prosecution or persecution" and suggested letting the Chinese form social clubs where gambling could take place under proper controls. "Surely," said the paper, as enfranchised citizens "the Chinese have the same rights as other citizens in this matter of recreation."[60]

Nevertheless, in 1949 a relatively new mayor, Charles E. Thompson, announced a ban on the playing of *fan tan* and *chee fah* at fifteen licensed Chinese clubs. That, said Foon Sien of the CBA, might "mean the end of clean, organized gambling in Chinatown," where gambling was an outlet for many older Chinese who had no home life. On the whole, the authorities were more interested in cracking down on organized crime and police corruption than in the small Chinese gambling houses, though police in Vancouver and Victoria continued to raid them from time to time. In 1964 British Columbia's attorney general released a report about widespread gambling among elderly Chinese in Vancouver; the following spring the gambling squad ordered many of the clubs closed until they used chips rather than cash. In Toronto, in a story that could have come out of the early twentieth century, the morality squad smashed a hole in the wall of a Chinese social club, from which several occupants fled by running across the roof. The police charged three men with keeping a common gaming house. Yet there was sympathy for the gamblers. A *Globe and Mail* columnist said that, though he realized the law must be enforced, the police should look the other way and let some Chinese engage in "a little betting among themselves."[61]

In the community at large, the Chinese were being accepted as full members. The Rotary Club maintained its interest in China and in promoting good relations with Chinese Canadians. In Kelowna it invited representatives of the local Chinese community to an International Chinese Day; in Kamloops one of the club's own members, Peter Wing, introduced another member, William Louie, who gave "a keen analysis of Sino-Japanese relations over the years." In Vancouver, after King Edward High School students formed a private swimming club so that Chinese classmates could swim with them, the Vancouver Parks Board opened the Crystal Pool to the public without respect to race, colour, or creed. Throughout the province, the press reported on Chinese Canadians succeeding in academics and athletics, winning talent and beauty contests, serving in the Canadian army, contributing to Victory Bond drives and hospital funds, and sharing with whites in church socials and service clubs.[62]

By the 1960s, there were even a few instances of intermarriage. More commonly, Chinese were advancing in the professions. In reporting the appointment of Dr. Wah Leung as founding dean of the University of British Columbia's Faculty of Dentistry, the Vancouver *Daily Province* remarked, "60 years ago, he would not have had the chance of a snowball in July. He could neither have achieved professional success in North America, nor if he had, could he have hoped to occupy his present new position." "For all practical purposes," it added, "persons of Chinese ancestry are now fully accepted Canadians in British Columbia, overlooking some medieval survivals like our iniquitous immigration laws." The Vancouver press was reporting how Chinese Canadian physicians were being appointed to local hospitals and serving both Chinese and Caucasian patients; the graduation of Morley Chang as the top student in the Institute of Chartered Accountants exams; the naming of Ralph Long as an assistant city prosecutor; the appointment of George Wong, a bank manager, to the Board of Governors of the new Simon Fraser University; and the elections of Peter Wing as mayor of Kamloops, George Yip as alderman in Fort St. John, Edward Lum to the Saanich Municipal Council, and Tan Lim to the Golden Village Council. Such integration was not confined to British Columbia. An Ottawa restaurant owner served as president of the Canadian Restaurant Association; Ying L.K. Hope was elected to the Toronto School Board; and near Timmins, Fred Wong was elected to the Tisdale Township Council with the slogan "a Wong vote is a right vote." Even groups that four decades earlier had been blatantly anti-Chinese accepted Chinese. The Retail Merchants Association that had vigorously lobbied for the exclusionary Chinese Immigration Act of 1923 twice elected Wilson J. Lee of Edmonton as its national president.[63]

Politically, Chinese Canadians made a major mark through Douglas Jung, a native of Victoria, lawyer, and veteran, who became the first Chinese Canadian to seek a legislative seat. Running as a Progressive Conservative, he came second with 28.45 percent of the votes in a 1956 provincial by-election in Vancouver Centre, losing to Les Peterson, the candidate of the Social Credit government, who made a special appeal to Chinese voters. Peterson told *Chinatown News*, a biweekly magazine, that not only had his law firm handled many immigration cases but also, if elected, he would seek "to oppose and expose any discrimination on the grounds of race, color, or creed." Jung, who may have lost votes because of a "whispering campaign" against him in Chinatown, moved to federal politics, where he ran as a Progressive Conservative in the 1957 federal election. Jung used his Chinese ancestry to advantage. In appealing to the electorate at large, he said that 99.9 percent of the population treated him "just like other Canadians," but he was "deeply concerned with the future of Canada and her position in the world of nations," and his background would give him an edge in dealing with Far Eastern problems. The historian Wing Chung Ng argues that Jung's victory in 1957 boosted the claim that the younger generation, the *tusheng*, were leading Chinese Canadians into "full acceptance" and was a "milestone in the decline of the traditional brokerage of the CBA" that was dominated by the immigrant generation. In the pivotal 1957 election, which saw the Conservatives under John Diefenbaker form a minority government, Jung won 41 percent of the vote and defeated a Liberal cabinet minister, Ralph Campney. Jung was re-elected in the Conservative sweep of 1958. Jung, however, was acutely conscious of representing a minority and told Prime Minister Diefenbaker that, "because of my racial background, I feel that whatever I say is subject to closer scrutiny. I want very much to establish myself as a parliamentarian rather than to have others think of me as Chinese, and while this latter aspect has its attractions at the proper places, I do not want to capitalize on that fact."[64]

An unpleasant incident in Parliament that centred on Jung nevertheless illustrated that racist terminology survived in the vocabulary of a few atavistic British Columbians. In the Senate, J.W. de B. Farris, a one-time provincial Liberal attorney general, attacked Jung for allegedly telling a North Atlantic Conference of Political Youth at NATO in Paris that Canadian and American governments primed youth groups going to Russia and made them biased against the USSR. Although Jung later asserted that he had been misquoted, what drew attention was Farris' gratuitous remark: "What right," he asked, "has this Chinaman to make these statements in Paris on behalf of the Canadian people?" Although no senator objected to the use of the demeaning term "Chinaman" and Prime Minister Diefenbaker had no comment for the press, Lester Pearson, leader of the opposition in the House of Commons, expressed "regret and disapproval," and the CCF constituency association in Vancouver Centre had a special meeting to discuss the "utterly shocking remarks." The *Vancouver Sun,* which reported the incident over several days, made no editorial comment but reprinted editorials from the Toronto *Globe and Mail* declaring that such "bigotry" had no place in Canadian life and from the Hamilton *Spectator* reminding Farris that Jung had been elected by the voters of Vancouver Centre, a snide allusion to the fact that Farris had been appointed to his position.[65]

While most of those who were making a mark in mainstream society were Canadian born and educated, opportunities also existed for the new immigrants of the 1950s and 1960s. In Vancouver the *Chinese Bulletin* exhorted new immigrants to take advantage of opportunities such as English-language classes and trades and vocational training offered by school boards and advised them that flexible schedules at the Vancouver Vocational Institute would allow them to work and study.[66]

Labour unions, once among the most vociferous critics of Asian "cheap labour," had organized Chinese workers for some years. The Communist-dominated IWA and the breakaway Woodworkers Industrial Union of Canada hired Chinese organizers to recruit members at coastal sawmills. Local 89 of the Fish Cannery, Reduction Plant, and Allied Workers Union began organizing Chinese cannery workers in 1944 and fought the Chinese contract system. That approach backfired. Canners began eliminating Chinese employees; by 1949 few were left in the industry. In Vancouver Foon Sien launched a drive to sign up 10,000 Chinese workers, mainly restaurant and hotel employees, who would affiliate with the Trades and Labour Congress (TLC). Alderman R.K. Gervin, who was also secretary of the provincial council of the TLC, encouraged them because a Chinese trade union would "end the threat of 'cheap' labor" in the province. Alderman Wilson, who before the war had led the campaign against Asian economic competition, offered to assist the proposed union on any matters of civic legislation. However, the BC Federation of Labour, noting that several major unions already had a number of Chinese members, opposed the idea of a separate union, and the plan apparently faltered.[67]

Although Chinese vegetable growers in the Okanagan complained that agricultural marketing boards had discriminated against them and hindered co-operation among producers, Chinese fruit growers seem to have got along with their white competitors. Early in 1945, for the first time, a Chinese grower attended a meeting of the BC Fruit Growers Association. Perhaps white fruit growers felt the same way as white potato growers on the coast, who expected many of their Chinese competitors to return to China once the situation there stabilized. Chinese vegetable growers, however, were declining in number as few younger Chinese wanted to take up that hard work. At Ashcroft, for example, before the war Chinese growers shipped out as many as thirty carloads of potatoes a day, but after the war they were unable to get workers and sold out. Some returned to China, while others went to Vancouver or Kamloops.[68]

Given the revolutionary situation in China, Canadian citizenship became increasingly important for Chinese. As the Communists took over, a few feared that if trouble developed between China and Canada they might be uprooted as the Japanese had been in 1942. Some Chinese Canadians in Toronto founded the Canadian Chinese Association to strengthen their position, to secure "fair play and justice," to promote good citizenship and better relations with "fellow Canadians," and to better the Chinese standard of living. When some Chinese Canadians in Vancouver voiced similar fears, the *Vancouver Sun* advised them to "forget their fears of wholesale dispersal if war comes between Canada and China. Such an idea hasn't even occurred to anyone else. The fact that Chinese residents have been given the right to citizenship is the best testimony to the public's high regard for these industrious and law-abiding people. Their loyalty to Canada has never been in question, much less any suspicion that they might be infected by the Peiping brand of Communism."[69]

ALTHOUGH NEW IMMIGRATION revived some Chinatowns, such as that of Edmonton, most were declining. In smaller communities, they often faded away as the older men, the core of their populations, aged, died, or returned to China and as younger people sought better accommodations in other parts of the city. Despite the admission of some wives and children, in the 1940s and early 1950s the Chinese population was declining as the death rate exceeded the birth rate. In British Columbia, for instance, the registrar of vital statistics recorded 276 births in 1952 and the deaths of 335 males and 29 females. The case of Nanaimo dramatically illustrates the problem. After fire in 1960 destroyed what had sometimes been a lively community, the Chinese community built two seniors' residences to house about seventy elderly men. The younger Chinese had already moved to various parts of the city. One Caucasian businessman claimed that "there is no color bar in Nanaimo. The modern Chinese live anywhere and everywhere here." Other Chinatowns across Canada just faded away.[70]

Even the large Chinatowns of Vancouver and Toronto were under siege because of urban renewal. In 1955 Toronto City Council announced that it would expropriate nearly two-thirds of Chinatown to build a new city hall and civic square. Although many Chinese residents were unhappy, the *Globe and Mail* was surprised at how little protest there was. It called on the city to provide a suitable site to relocate Chinatown, which, reduced to about a third of its size, continued to shrink. With increased immigration in the 1960s, four new Chinatowns emerged to replace the original one, but in 1964 several candidates for municipal council called for the preservation of a Chinatown in the heart of the city. Maxine Ma, a native of Toronto and a teacher in one of its public schools, believed that Chinatown should stay. Yet she observed that most Chinese of her generation had "blended into the Canadian way of life," speaking English as their first language, mixing socially with Caucasians, and eating Canadian food. Yet not all in the Caucasian community realized that. A Toronto *Evening Telegram* columnist suggested that the Chinese in Toronto and some other Canadian cities "have never been integrated, yet they do not seem to mind" and had philosophically accepted the demolition of part of Chinatown. Even the new immigrants were eager to integrate. When the Board of Education, at the behest of the Italian community, organized English classes for adults, most of the students were Chinese who had been encouraged to attend by the Mon Sheong Foundation, a service club. The most striking evidence of integration was the observation of a *Toronto Daily*

Star reporter that "far from the fear of segregation is the fear of disappearing into the white community by intermarriage, by moving outside of Chinatown, by being influenced by the material benefits of the non-Chinese mode of life, and by forgetting their language and traditions." By then approximately 12,000 individuals of Chinese ancestry resided in Metro Toronto, but fewer than seventy-five lived in Chinatown. Indeed, Wes Lore, the editor of a new Toronto-based publication, the *Canadian Chinese Association Journal,* declared that "the death of Chinatown is more of a reality now than it ever was. I can see a Chinatown existing in Toronto only as a pseudo oriental, western controlled mall with an outward façade of China and an inward organism of North America." He accused fellow Toronto Chinese Canadians of being indifferent and apathetic. As he wrote, the situation was changing. An influx of Chinese from Hong Kong and growing interest in preserving "Old Chinatown" among some more established members of Toronto's Chinese community gave it a brief reprieve.[71]

From the earliest days of Vancouver, its Chinatown had an image of crowded living conditions, doubtful sanitation, and an aura of mystery. The younger generation of Chinese were moving away from Chinatown and scattering themselves around the city. In some areas, white residents discouraged Chinese from buying properties in their neighbourhoods, but gradually Chinese families found themselves accepted as good neighbours. As the *Chinatown News,* the voice of the *tusheng,* observed in 1962, Chinatowns had done much to assist new arrivals, but the new generation was "imbibing the freedom and the greater economic opportunities now taken so much for granted" so that only "a few, mostly oldtimers, are content to remain within the confines of Chinatown." Most oldtimers were elderly single men. Some families still lived in the nearby Strathcona district, but Chinatown itself became largely a commercial centre with stores and restaurants catering alike to Chinese and to white residents and tourists. With its various association buildings, it also served as a social centre for the Chinese community. In lauding the founding of the Vancouver Chinese Association of Commerce, the *Vancouver Sun* regretted "the passing of the picturesque old Shanghai Alley" but observed that "the smartly turned out Chinese families from homes scattered throughout the city are testimony of a great advance" as it described Vancouver's Chinese community as "a splendid example of the development of the Canadian mosaic. Retaining so much of their own heritage, retaining their language to a degree probably unmatched, supporting three daily newspapers of their own, the Chinese-Canadians are nevertheless an integral part of this land. And Vancouver is the better for it."[72]

Nevertheless, as historical geographer Kay Anderson noted, city planners and politicians shaped their ideas about urban redevelopment by "inherited ideas about a Chinese race and place." Since 1948 city planners had been calling for slum clearance. By 1957 they were devising schemes to replace what they considered the slums of Strathcona, the home of over 4,000 Chinese, with subsidized, high-density public housing. Community leaders and organizations protested that the plan would break up a viable community and cause great hardship, especially to the elderly who would be displaced. Yet some Chinese community members favoured development. Through the pages of the *Chinatown News,* some Canadian-born Chinese argued that the "desirable features of Chinatown" should be retained to make it "an outstanding tourist attraction," but "the Chinese people, given the opportunity and the means, would turn their backs to this congested area." That was a sentiment shared by the *Vancouver Sun,* which saw slum clearance as "Chinatown's opportunity" while calling for its preservation if the Chinese themselves helped "to make it a better and finer Chinatown." Given such division, Vancouver City Council paid scant attention to the protests. Mayor Thomas Alsbury bluntly said that he hoped for co-operation; however, "in the interests of a planned city, the redevelopment must go ahead." The city expropriated six city blocks, demolished buildings housing about 300 Chinese, and built the first stage of the new housing project.[73]

By the early 1960s, when it came time to make plans for the second stage of the project that would displace more people, the government considered the opinions of its Chinese residents. Thus, Mayor Alsbury appointed George Wong, a banker, to chair a redevelopment consultative committee, and the provincial government named Kim Tim Louie, a wholesale grocer, and Faye Leung, a realtor, to the seven-member Vancouver Housing Authority. Commenting on Louie's appointment, Alderman Wilson said he believed that Louie was chosen not only for his business abilities but also to demonstrate to the Chinese that there would "be no prejudice in their relocation." In its initial stages at least, the committee received only a few inquiries and no complaints. As planning evolved, this changed. On behalf of the Chinese Property Owners Association, Harry Fan called for a halt to redevelopment since it would cut off the future development of Chinatown and "strangle Chinese business activities." Moreover, he argued that Chinese liked to raise families in homes in which several generations lived together, and if families had to leave children would be unable to attend Chinese schools, and many Chinese organizations would have to disband. Thus, he proposed that homeowners be allowed to redevelop their own houses and that government agencies build proposed apartments some blocks to the east.[74]

After "dramatic protests" at a public meeting on slum clearance, Mayor William Rathie, who, the *Chinatown News* later complained, never attended Chinatown functions despite repeated invitations, accepted the idea that Chinese families preferred to live in houses rather than apartments. Nevertheless, he angered many Chinese when he called on Chinese architects to draw up a plan that would suit family life, in other words to build a new Chinatown that would be separated from Chinatown's natural residential area. Saying that the plan was tantamount to building a Berlin Wall and comparable to "the forced evacuation of Vancouver's Little Tokyo," Foon Sien resigned from the mayor's consultative committee on planning for Chinatown. The Vancouver *Daily Province* was sympathetic to the Chinese. While favouring a halt to "creeping decay," it recognized that a "prosperous and colourful Chinatown" would be valuable for tourism and could not be "planned" since it had "slowly grown into what it is." It urged the city to exercise "more than the usual tact, understanding and foresight." Initially, Dean and Faye Leung gave only qualified approval to the mayor's plan since homeowners did not want to move into low-cost suites and would receive insufficient funds for their expropriated homes to buy new ones. Then they devised a scheme that looked very much like an answer to the mayor's request. On behalf of the Vancouver Chinatown Development Association, they proposed to build rows of Oriental-style houses with pagodas, moongate windows, and rock garden landscapes that would resemble a Chinese village. The plan gained the endorsement of the *Vancouver Sun,* which asserted that "the Chinese know what type of homes they want to live in." There was one problem; many Chinese Canadians did not want to live in a Chinese village. Gilbert Eng, an architect, called the scheme "anti-social and outright commercialism"; he proposed rehabilitation without pagodas that would not segregate the Chinese into a distinct area or, as the *Chinatown News* later put it, isolate them "from the mainstream of Canadian life." Seeing the split within the Chinese community, the *Vancouver Sun* noted that City Council would need "the wisdom of Confucius to keep all these admirable people happy." Although somewhat condescending, the comment did show that local politicians had to pay attention to the Chinese as citizens. Controversy over the future of Chinatown continued. The federal government's Central Mortgage and Housing Corporation, however, saved the city from having to exercise its wisdom by refusing to authorize a proposal that was inconsistent with the overall development plan. The city's Technical Planning Board also warned that the small lots on which the Leungs' scheme was based could eventually become blighted themselves.[75]

During the 1964 civic election campaign, two mayoralty candidates, Marianne Linnell and Alsbury, actively sought support in Chinatown. Linnell, who was accompanied by Dean Leung when she visited the *Chinatown News,* said that she would push for redevelopment of the business district and set aside several blocks for private developers to construct self-owned homes for Chinese families. Alsbury was more general but promised to improve Chinatown. Chinatown did not seem to be a major issue in the Chinese community or in the city as a whole, judging from the candidates' advertisements in the *Chinatown News.* Meanwhile, planning and the acquisition of property proceeded slowly, but Alderman Wilson apparently persuaded the Department of Planning to delay expropriating private homes until it could find alternative properties for residents. Nevertheless, as the city acquired their properties, more people had to move.[76]

In addition to attempting to change the residential nature of Chinatown and Strathcona, the city wanted to revitalize the commercial section of Chinatown to enhance it as a tourist attraction. At a dinner meeting at a popular Chinese restaurant, the W.K. Gardens, to which many leaders of the Chinese community had been invited, Mayor Rathie in April 1966 announced a major program to "improve the overall appearance of Chinatown." The *Chinatown News* agreed that the Chinese Canadian community had abdicated its responsibilities in this matter, but when a Hong Kong journalist described Chinatown's streets as "somewhat dirty and evil smelling," with its residents not realizing their poverty, it took umbrage at this insult and declared that "Vancouver is proud of its Chinatown."[77]

By then Chinatown was facing perhaps its greatest threat ever. While undertaking initial planning for the final and largest stage of the redevelopment plan in 1967, the city announced that a new freeway would require the demolition of a number of commercial buildings and separate Chinatown from the rest of the downtown commercial district. Local architects, University of British Columbia architecture and planning students, the Town Planning Commission, the Board of Trade, and others who wanted to maintain Chinatown as a civic asset joined the protest against the freeway. The *Chinatown News* observed that the issue was "galvanizing the long-divided, fragmented and quarrelsome" Chinatown into a united front. "Chinatown," it explained, "has always been a landmark of character and culture to this city. It gives Vancouver that sophisticated cosmopolitan atmosphere unmatched by any other metropolis in Canada. In the midst of our jungle of concrete, steel and high rises, Chinatown stands out with its unique pattern of excellent restaurants and shops and pagoda styled buildings."[78] This time Vancouver City Council listened and abandoned the freeway project; following protests from residents of Strathcona, both Chinese and non-Chinese, Ottawa froze the funding for the third stage of redevelopment and the freeway.

Whereas Japanese Canadians had suffered because of the actions of their ancestral land, Chinese Canadians benefited from the war because China was a loyal ally. By V-J Day, Chinese Canadians had demonstrated their loyalty to Canada by buying Victory Bonds, working in war industries, and volunteering for the armed forces despite initial discouragement. In return, they rekindled their campaign for full citizenship especially the right to vote. Their loyalty was rewarded – in part. Saskatchewan enfranchised them in 1944; British Columbia followed suit in 1947. Ottawa even relaxed its exclusionary Chinese immigration policy, but only ever so slightly. As Chapter 7 shows, the Chinese had to exercise all of their new-found political opportunities over the next twenty years in order to achieve full equality as Canadian citizens.

5

Toward First-Class Citizenship for Japanese Canadians, 1945 - 49

> The orders [in council restricting the liberties of Japanese Canadians] are out of keeping with the principles of Canadian citizenship, the Charter of the UN (which we signed), and the draft proposals of the International Bill of Rights. There is no room in Canada for a second-class citizenship.
>
> Toronto *Globe and Mail*, 17 March 1948

V-J Day, enthusiastically celebrated by so many Canadians and especially by Chinese Canadians, made little immediate change in the lives of Japanese Canadians. Over the next three and a half years, their plight saw tension between advocates of human rights and equality of citizenship on the one side and, on the other, those whose antipathy to all Japanese had been reinforced by the war. The likelihood of "repatriation" loomed over the heads of many Japanese in Canada. Those in the BC interior who had chosen to stay in Canada faced the need to move east of the Rockies even though Caucasian friends were often unhappy about the prospect of their departure. At the coast, however, opposition to their return remained strong in some quarters and especially among BC MPs. Yet given prosperity and widespread support for human rights and citizenship – much of it encouraged by revulsion at the injustice of deporting loyal Japanese Canadians – all but the most atavistic Japanophobes gradually changed their minds. The federal government cancelled the repatriation orders and in 1949 finally granted Japanese Canadians freedom of movement throughout the country, and the BC legislature removed the legal disabilities that had made them second-class citizens. Even then Japanese Canadians were not quite first-class citizens.

The excesses of the Second World War and particularly those of the Nazis under Hitler stimulated international interest in human rights. The Atlantic Charter of August 1941 in which Prime Minister Winston Churchill of the United Kingdom and President Franklin D. Roosevelt of the United

"Canada's Racial Minorities," *Nisei Affairs,* November-December 1946. An unknown cartoonist for *Nisei Affairs* portrayed the hope that Japanese Canadians and other racial minorities had of eliminating prejudice, insecurity, and restrictions on their activities.

States spoke of the need to protect human rights was probably the most significant single statement of that need until the 1945 United Nations Charter included the concept of "fundamental human rights," a belief later incorporated into the Universal Declaration of Human Rights. In addition to these international actions, as historian Ross Lambertson notes, with prosperity and political stability Canadians became more accepting of ethnic diversity and formed organizations to fight discrimination.[1]

The phrases "human rights," "civil liberties," and "United Nations Charter" pervaded the rhetoric around the campaign for full civil rights for Japanese Canadians. Civil libertarians such as B.K. Sandwell of *Saturday Night* magazine reminded the government that the UN declaration provided "the right to freedom of movement and residence within a country." In a pamphlet prepared for *Citizens' Forum,* a radio broadcast with related discussion groups, the Canadian Association for Adult Education observed that "the treatment of Japanese Canadians, both during the war and since the peace, has given rise to a searching inquiry into the state of civil liberties in Canada today." Although Prime Minister King chastised the University of Toronto Liberal Association for saying that Canada's policies affecting Japanese Canadians made it among democratic countries "the most persistent violator" of the United Nations Charter and its pledge to protect human rights, the federal cabinet recognized the possible implications at the United Nations. Canada's treatment of its Japanese residents caused embarrassment when the *Washington Post* called plans to "repatriate" Japanese a treatment that cheapened Canadian citizenship and, most grievously, "an odious manifestation of racism."[2]

The plight of Japanese Canadians was a major stimulus to the development of a human rights movement in Canada. With the end of the war, civil libertarians gained new strength. In August 1945, a week before Japan's surrender, about a dozen business and professional men and women in Vancouver, including some who had been involved in the Vancouver Consultative Council, formed the Institute for Inter-Racial Friendship. To promote "understanding and good-will between the various racial groups comprising the community," the institute sponsored workshops on international relations, secured widespread publicity through the press and the CBC, published a pamphlet entitled *Our Refined Race Hate,* showed films on race relations, and provided programs for church and other groups. Its luncheons featured internationally known speakers such as Paul Robeson, Eddie Cantor, Dr. D.P. Pandia, and Dr. T.Z. Koo. The institute formed branches in Calgary, Moose Jaw, and Victoria. In addition individual British Columbians, such as R.M. (Bob) Millar, a past president of the Vancouver Rotary Club, told Rotarians in Vernon and Victoria that "race prejudice" was "the greatest menace facing future world peace." In an open letter published in the Montreal *Gazette* and sent to fifty-four other newspapers, McGill law professor and civil libertarian F.R. Scott declared that asking the Japanese to decide on repatriation during the war was "like offering a condemned man a pistol so that he may choose swift suicide to a public hanging." "The real problem," he concluded, "has nothing directly to do with the Japanese at all; it is the problem of racial intolerance. The problem is only aggravated by deportation ... We should be generous to this harmless minority whom we previously admitted to our shores, and apply fully to them the principle that race, religion and color are no bar to full citizenship in this democracy." The real strength of the human rights movement, at least as it applied to Japanese Canadians, was in Toronto, where the Co-Operative Committee on Japanese Canadians (CCJC) played a major role in seeking recognition of their citizenship rights.[3]

Under the "repatriation" scheme, almost half of the Japanese in Canada would be sent to Japan. In the spring and summer of 1945, 10,511 or 43 percent of the Japanese in Canada signed for "voluntary repatriation." That number included 2,524 Canadian-born adults whose 3,740 dependent children under the age of sixteen were also subject to "repatriation." The Department of Labour was anxious to send them to Japan as soon as possible to increase public support for lifting restrictions on those Japanese, mainly Canadian citizens, who chose to remain in Canada. With the war's end, the CCJC hit a responsive chord. It distributed thousands of copies of leaflets across the country and gained the support of many church groups to develop opposition to sending Canadian nationals, who did not want to go, to Japan and to demand removal of restrictions on Japanese in Canada. Whereas in the first half of 1945 the Prime Minister's Office received only four requests for a moderate policy on Japanese Canadians, in July and August it received thirty-six, and from September through late October it received forty-five form letters and thirty-seven individual letters and telegrams. Seven arrived on 20 October alone. The Departments of External Affairs, Labour, and Justice had similar experiences. Congregations and associations affiliated with the United Church sent the most protests, but so did interdenominational bodies such as the National Interchurch Advisory Committee and groups within the Anglican, Presbyterian, Baptist, and Mennonite Churches. Some letters even came from British Columbia. Most communications alleged that many Canadian-born Japanese signed for repatriation under duress, a claim denied by government officials. The correspondents also asked that Canadians of Japanese origin be given full citizenship rights and be encouraged to disperse throughout Canada by the removal of restrictions on property purchases and the acquisition of business licences, assistance in re-establishment in their lines of work, and indemnification for property losses. The campaign had secular support. With "compulsory deportation," admonished the *Winnipeg Free Press,* "we have as a nation given way to racialism and this dangerous and dreary road is one which has a precipice at its end." The *Toronto Daily Star* and *Saturday Night* and others echoed such views. The *Ottawa Journal* warned that "repatriation" would mean that "our naturalization laws," "our professed ideals about democracy," and the Atlantic Charter and its pledge to abolish racial discrimination would not have much meaning. A small-town Ontario newspaper suggested that the treatment of Japanese who were Canadian citizens would test "Canada's racial tolerance and sense of British fair play." Lorne Greene, the CBC news announcer known as the "voice of doom" for his wartime broadcasts, rightly reminded Canadians that "repatriate" was not a fitting word since most likely repatriates had "never seen Japan."[4]

Such ideas did not always resonate well in British Columbia. Old antipathies died slowly. Moreover, in the fall of 1945, newspapers had almost daily stories of returning prisoners of war and civilian internees telling of beatings, brutality, and inadequate food and medical attention in the "living hells" of Japanese prison camps. Since some British Columbians lumped all "Japanese" into a single category, such accounts discouraged acceptance of Japanese Canadians. The Victoria *Daily Colonist,* after charging that it was "common knowledge" that they had "not renounced their allegiance to the Japanese throne," asserted that any place the Japanese had had in Canada was "forfeited by the cruelty of their fellow countrymen in Asia." An early manifestation of this baleful response to atrocity stories was the action of the Union of BC Municipalities (UBCM). After tabling a similar resolution in 1944, its 1945 convention overwhelmingly called for the repatriation of *all* persons of Japanese origin because, given the "Japanese national doctrine, outlook and expressed intention," they would "never fit into the Canadian scheme of life." Many delegates who had been prepared to see the Japanese return to the coast changed their minds after hearing of atrocities.[5]

The *Winnipeg Free Press* damned the "incredible" UBCM resolution for deporting people who were "Canadians in everything except the pigmentation of their skin" as undercutting the war's aim against racial crimes and "Nazi principles." It warned that catering to British Columbia's racialism would set a dangerous precedent that could be used "against any other racial minority," yet it admonished provinces that would not accept Canadian Japanese not to protest "the apparent racial animus in British Columbia." The *Halifax Herald* agreed "that before any Canadian begins to talk about the Japanese question he or she should have a reasonable understanding of the facts – and the viewpoint of the British Columbia people."

British Columbians, who had been complaining that "the East" did not understand the "Oriental Question" since the 1870s, agreed that eastern Canadians must accept Japanese Canadians before chastising British Columbians. Declaring that British Columbians could "be as high-minded, as noble and as altruistic as Manitobans or Nova Scotians or Ontarioites," the *Vancouver Sun* complained of other Canadians showing "more consideration ... to the Japs than to British Columbians" and of failing to accept Japanese. The Prince Rupert *Evening Empire* suggested that if eastern Canadians lived in British Columbia "they would think it over again because there are circumstances that are not always what they seem." When *Saturday Night* alleged that the anti-Japanese campaign was really directed against all non-whites, C.C. Merritt, a war hero and recently elected Conservative MP for

Vancouver-Burrard, appealed to Torontonians to accept the same proportion of Japanese as were in prewar Vancouver. Even the Vancouver *Daily Province,* which believed that sending "thousands of these helpless and pathetic people back to Japan" would do "violence" to the foundations of Canada's "own nationhood," told eastern Canadians that, if they took "steps to keep the Japanese in Canada," they must "help look after them." A Department of Labour official neatly explained the situation in a private note to a colleague: "There are a remarkable number of people who apparently don't want the Japanese to leave Canada, [but] none of them are willing to have them as next door neighbours unfortunately." By then, however, the *Ottawa Evening Citizen* was observing "an encouraging disposition to tolerance and fair play on the part of many groups in Eastern Canada."[6]

Yet tolerance was limited. The *Halifax Herald* again noted that the real test of those who opposed "repatriation" was their willingness to take Japanese "into their own midst." In the neighbouring province of New Brunswick, representatives of several unions in Saint John had protested the purported arrival of nine Japanese and the anticipated coming of another thirty-six to forty-five to work at a mink farm in Black's Harbour lest they "break down labor standards" in the province. The manager of Connor Brothers, the employer, said that only one man, his wife, and their several children had arrived, and no more were expected despite a labour shortage. The province had no policy because it had not expected an influx of Japanese; nevertheless, the local registrar of the National Selective Service warned that "by importing Japs" Connor Brothers "would create a Frankenstein." No more Japanese went to New Brunswick, but news of the protest buttressed the *Vancouver Sun*'s assertion that neither the federal nor the BC government had done anything to promote dispersal.[7]

British Columbians had other evidence of the unwillingness of other provinces to accept Japanese Canadians, but it was not conclusive. Lethbridge would not allow Japanese other than female domestic servants to live or work in that city; Premier Ernest Manning insisted that the federal government remove relocatees from Alberta. In Ontario Essex and Oxford counties passed resolutions against the entry of Japanese; Toronto attempted to do so. In fact these were isolated incidents, and Manning, like Premier Stuart Garson of Manitoba, simply wanted temporary help with costs of education and welfare. Moreover, Edmonton City Council asked that Japanese Canadians be given treatment equal to that of other citizens and that Alberta accept Canadians of Japanese origin as equals. Ontario's attorney general declared that no municipal government could restrict the free movement of Canadian citizens. The *Calgary Herald,* while repeating many prewar shibboleths about sojourning, security threats, and the evils of miscegenation, criticized eastern cities for adopting a "superior moral tone" on the matter while refusing to accept Japanese Canadians. That, too, was federal policy. A form letter sent

"Awaiting an Extraction," *Vancouver Sun,* 18 August 1945. R.N. Meadows reflected a long-standing British Columbia sentiment that the rest of Canada did not understand their concerns about Asians.

to church groups that protested deportation advised them "to accept without racial prejudice either family groups or young people of Japanese ancestry" and assist them in re-establishing themselves and finding employment.[8]

On the coast, hostility to the Japanese remained high over the fall and winter of 1945-46. One illustration was the October 1945 provincial election. Although the main theme was the traditional "free enterprise or socialism," some Coalition candidates alluded to atrocities as they attacked the Co-Operative Commonwealth Federation (CCF) for its supposed sympathies for Japanese Canadians. Gordon Wismer, a Coalition candidate in Vancouver Centre, warned that, "if the CCF comes back, you will have the Japanese back on your hands ... those same men who used our soldiers for bayonet practice, the same men who kicked the teeth of half the poor devils who have been coming back to us recently." If the Japanese returned, he predicted a "perpetual CCF government" since "the Japs will vote" as their "bosses" dictate. In the affluent Victoria suburb of Oak Bay, Herbert Anscomb, a cabinet minister, declared, "nothing we could do would be more tragic in the light of atrocities perpetrated by Japanese in the Pacific war" than the CCF policy of bringing some Japanese back to British Columbia and enfranchising them. Declaring that it was a federal matter, Attorney General R.L. Maitland advised voters to show Ottawa their disapproval of the CCF policy since the Japanese "problem" would probably arise at a peace conference. Other Coalition speakers, including Senator J.W. de B. Farris, who toured the province on behalf of Coalition candidates, presented variations on the theme. In Cowichan-Newcastle, Macgregor Macintosh rehearsed old claims of Japanese pushing white men aside in industry and predicted that if they returned they would "form an indigestible core in our society." He repeatedly avowed, "the place for the Japanese is in Japan, since they cannot be assimilated." Similarly, J.A. Paton, who was seeking re-election in Vancouver-Point Grey, favoured deporting the Japanese because "the way in which they infiltrated into the countries they so ruthlessly attacked is evidence enough of what goes on, even now, behind their smiling faces." In Delta, which included much of the lower Fraser Valley, Reeve A.C. Hope of Langley, who was seeking election there, denied using the Japanese question as a vote getter but suggested that their return would sabotage the chances of veterans to settle on Fraser Valley farms. In Comox, A.W. Neill, speaking for the Coalition candidate, said that the only solution was to send all the Japanese to Japan. At Prince Rupert, independent candidate former premier T.D. Pattullo advertised, "a vote for the C.C.F. is a vote for the Japs." One ad featured a verse:

> How courteous is the Japanese,
> He always says, "Excuse it please."
> Then climbs into his fishing smack
> As on the river he has left his track.
> He smiles and says, "I beg your pardon."
> He bows and gives a friendly grin,
> Then calls his buddies, his countrymen.
> He grins again, and the C.C.F. does bow,
> Beware you fishermen, do your duty now.

Fishermen did not do their "duty" for Pattullo. There was no Coalition candidate, but he lost to the CCF. By voting for the CCF, his campaign manager mused, fishermen "approved" the return of the Japanese.[9]

The issue, however, had embarrassed the CCF. Provincial leader Harold Winch (Vancouver East) and other CCF speakers tried to evade it by saying that it was a federal matter. In fact, contrary to what Coalitionists claimed,

THE ISSUE IS ...

JOBS NOT JAPS!

CCF RECORD

Always opposed Japanese immigration to Canada.

Demanded end of shipment of Canadian war materials to Japan.

Urged Japanese be moved from coast.

Always opposed return of Japanese to coast, urged dispersal across Canada.

Urges deportation of Japanese not Canadian citizens.

Plans to remove threat to white living standards.

LIBERAL-CONSERVATIVE RECORD

Voted in Parliament to allow Japanese into Canada.

Refused to stop war aid to Japan.

Acted only on public pressure.

Has at last adopted CCF plan.

Will not and cannot deport Canadian-born Japanese.

Wish to continue using Japanese to reduce white wage levels.

DO NOT BE FOOLED—

VOTE CCF FOR PROGRESS

"The Issue Is ... Jobs Not Japs!" *Victoria Daily Times,* 24 October 1945. Although many CCF members championed the right of racial minorities such as Japanese Canadians, the party perceived a need to appeal to the prejudices of Victoria-area voters in the October 1945 provincial election.

the CCF's Japanese policy was not dissimilar from theirs. Winch eventually explained that the party favoured dispersal and opposed the mass re-entry of Japanese to coastal areas. On election eve, the CCF ran a display ad in both Victoria daily newspapers under the heading "The Issue Is ... JOBS NOT JAPS!" The ad claimed that the CCF had urged the removal of the Japanese from the coast, had always opposed their return, had urged their dispersal across Canada, and had favoured the deportation of non-Canadian citizens. The CCF claimed that Coalitionists would use the Japanese "to reduce white wage levels," whereas the CCF would remove any threat to white living standards. In a campaign postmortem, Grant MacNeil, who, with his running mate Grace MacInnis, was narrowly defeated in Vancouver-Burrard, cited the Japanese question as a factor in the party's defeat in some constituencies and especially in Vancouver.[10]

About the time of the election, a newly arrived journalist in Vancouver expressed puzzlement at "the fiercely blazing anti-Japanese intolerance," of "trade unionists, journalists, artists, hand laborers and businessmen … [who] stubbornly uphold one opinion in common, kick out the Japs," a sentiment that he claimed was "deeply rooted in the pocket book." Evidence of that sentiment continued. In March 1946, Ian Mackenzie told a meeting of cabinet ministers, civil servants, and representatives of the CCJC that the feeling of British Columbians against the Japanese was only partly racial, that it was "economic in origin." He contended that Japanese had forced white fishermen out of the industry and had mapped the coast for the benefit of Japan. Similarly, George Cruickshank told veterans who were anxious to get on former Japanese farms in the Fraser Valley that if the courts gave Japanese the rights of citizenship they could demand the return of their farms; he warned the BC Coast Growers Association, "you can't compete with them, in strawberry growing at least." In the legislature, A.C. Hope explained that competition was impossible because "a Japanese woman goes into the fields with a baby on her back and works all day." Although it also referred to inassimilability by colour and culture, the *Surrey Leader* urged readers to organize to prevent the return of the Japanese to the Fraser Valley. "The low standard of living," it asserted, "is the economic reason why we in Surrey don't want the Japs back." In setting out its reasons for opposing their return to the coast, the *Vancouver Sun* said, "frankly, it is an economic question." With reason the editor of the *Grand Forks Gazette* claimed that those who wanted to send the Japanese away did so not because of their racial origin but because "they have learnt from a vociferous minority that the Japanese are bad people to have in competition with white men in business." That phrase – "competition with white men" – reveals the difficulty in separating motives for hostility to the Japanese. For example, in November 1946 Mackenzie, while speaking to the McGill University Liberal Club, alleged that two Japanese had been shot for disloyalty. When the Vancouver *News-Herald* accused him of "whipping up hatred and unfounded suspicion against a Canadian minority," Mackenzie replied, "I want British Columbia for our own white people." Yet while referring to a racial concept, he based his "whole reply on economic, not on racial, lines" and repeated tales of Japanese fishermen acting as spies.[11]

Although there was no longer any danger from Japan, wartime bitterness still provided Japanophobes with a rationale. "Too many things have happened since Pearl Harbor," Mayor J.W. Cornett of Vancouver said, "for us to accept the Japanese people on the same basis as before." Several Liberal and Conservative constituency organizations in Vancouver and Victoria as well as groups such as the Courtenay-Comox Board of Trade, the Port Kells Ratepayers Association, the Vancouver and Gulf Islands Farmers' Institutes, the Ganges chapter of the Imperial Order of the Daughters of the Empire (IODE), the Associated Boards of Trade of the Southern Interior, and the Orange Lodge of British Columbia called for repatriation. A spokesman for

"Be Careful, Mister!" Victoria *Daily Colonist,* 20 January 1946. Hugh Weatherby conveys two sentiments here: suspicion of the loyalty of Japanese Canadians to Canada, and British Columbia's long-standing but misplaced resentment of "the East" for not understanding its "Oriental Problem."

the Native Brotherhood of BC (whose members were mainly north coast First Nations fishermen) favoured deporting all the Japanese; the Native Sons of BC suggested re-establishing Japanese with any claim on Canada at Canadian government expense somewhere in the South Pacific![12]

Others realized that it was impossible to "repatriate" Japanese who were Canadian citizens, had not signed for it, and had shown no sign of disloyalty, but few wanted them back at the coast. The *Vancouver Sun* and the New Westminster *British Columbian* insisted on dispersal, and if a share remained in British Columbia they must not congregate at the coast. The idea of "repatriating" Canadian-born citizens appalled the Vancouver *News-Herald,* but it did not want them all at the coast or in interior "ghettoes." It chided Ottawa for letting other provinces dictate who could live within their borders. The BC Command of the Army and Navy Veterans asked that these "threat[s] to our Canadian way of life" be barred from the coast for at least ten years. Federal Liberal and Conservative politicians took a hard line. Howard Green and the Progressive Conservatives were determined that they "should never get dug in again in this Province." Ian Mackenzie called for "effective measures ... to prevent persons of the Japanese race ever again residing on the Pacific Coast of Canada."[13]

THE FATE OF THE JAPANESE who had signed up for repatriation was in Ottawa's hands. In trying to satisfy the opinions represented by Green and Mackenzie and those of the advocates of civil liberties and human rights who demanded justice for Japanese Canadians, the federal government temporized. Early in October 1945, it introduced Bill 15 relating to the Emergency Powers Act. This omnibus bill gave the government legal authority to continue some of its wartime powers into peacetime. Section 3 (g) gave the cabinet power over "entry into Canada, exclusion and deportation and revocation of nationality." Once its implications for deportation and the removal of citizenship were realized, the CCJC informed MPs of its opposition to "all legislation proposing to cancel or deny to loyal citizens of Japanese ancestry, or of any other descent, the rights and duties of their citizenship and threatening them with deportation." *Nisei Affairs* argued that the provision would mean "no citizen is safe during this emergency period." The *Ottawa Journal,* citing protests from varied groups such as churches, the Canadian Legion, and chapters of the IODE, reminded the government that the measure would remove any meaning from naturalization laws or "our professed ideals about democracy." In reporting the many telegrams and letters that he had received, CCF federal leader M.J. Coldwell urged that, in the "interests of Canada's reputation among the nations of the world," the government not act until members of Parliament could ask questions about the policy.[14]

In response to the probability of a "full-dress" debate, on 21 November Minister of Labour Humphrey Mitchell announced a policy that had been considered as early as 12 September, namely that the government would accept written requests for cancellation of repatriation applications submitted by Canadian citizens before 2 September, the day of Japan's formal surrender, and would review later submissions by the Canadian born. That modest gesture, in the words of the *New Canadian* "a step in the right direction," did little to mollify Japanese Canadians or their sympathizers. Within a week, the Prime Minister's Office received "a large number of letters," mainly from church and civil rights groups, complaining of deportation, accusing the government of "racialism" or inconsistency with "liberal British traditions," and causing "hardship, heart-break and injustice" to individuals. The *Winnipeg Free Press* noted the need to define Canadian citizenship and the right to remain in Canada in law; a professor at Regina College wrote in the Regina *Leader-Post* that for six years Canada had fought to defeat the "ugly phases" of Nazism and had denounced as "the most degrading the Hitlerian theory of racism." "That theory," he added, "was not to die with Hitler. It reigns in Canada today in the treatment of the Japanese-Canadians." The public agreed. A national Gallup poll late in December found that 49 percent of those polled had no reservations about letting Canadian citizens remain in Canada and be treated as such, another 13 percent would let them stay under certain circumstances, and only 25 percent would send them to Japan. However, 60 percent of those polled would repatriate non-Canadian citizens.[15]

Some British Columbians also objected to a precedent that could deprive any Canadian of citizenship. As in eastern Canada, the United and other major Protestant churches led the opposition, but even the White Rock branch of the Canadian Legion protested, as did some individuals and newspapers. The *Vernon News* declared, "the guiding principle … in regard to all minorities, the Japanese included, is summed up in two words – British justice." Similarly, the *Grand Forks Gazette* asserted "either Canadian citizenship is valid for all Canadians, regardless of color or creed, or it is valid for no citizen of Canada whatever." Yet the government's modest concession displeased the *Vancouver Sun,* whose headline suggested, "Japs Can All Return to British Columbia."[16]

The *Vancouver Sun* was mistaken. The cabinet only agreed that Canadian-born Japanese would not have to prove their loyalty or be forced to go to Japan. For other Japanese, Minister of Justice Louis St. Laurent tabled three orders in council on 17 December 1945. PC 7355 permitted the deportation of Japanese nationals who had applied for repatriation or who had been interned; of naturalized Canadians who had not revoked a repatriation request before 2 September 1945; and of Canadian-born Japanese who did not revoke a request before an individual repatriation order was issued. It also covered their wives and children. A second order, PC 7356, revoked any status that a deportee might have as a British subject or Canadian national effective the date of departure from Canada. The third, PC 7357, provided for the establishment of a so-called loyalty commission to examine the loyalty of Japanese nationals and naturalized British subjects who sought to remain in Canada. St. Laurent explained that only Japanese nationals or naturalized Canadians who had asked to be deported would "be forcibly dealt with." As for the Canadian born, he said ominously, "we can arrange to have them go," but Parliament would decide.[17]

Many petitioners, including some poignant requests from Japanese children, complained that the new orders would break up families. *Nisei*

Affairs asserted that the orders meant "little change" from earlier plans of "mass deportation" and would have a "disastrous and abortive effect on the most basic aspects of personal and social relations." Outside the Japanese Canadian community, the main arguments against the orders in council referred to principles of citizenship and justice. The *Toronto Daily Star* warned that the orders raised serious questions about the value of Canadian citizenship for immigrants and recalled that deporting civilians "on racial and religious grounds" was one of the crimes charged against the Nazis. The Toronto *Globe and Mail,* however, regarded the stripping of Canadian citizenship from those who chose to be repatriated as "an obvious step" but that sending the Canadian born against their will to a foreign country would be stooping "to the moral level of the Nazis themselves." It welcomed the orders for honouring "the principles of British freedom" and respecting "the natural birthright of the native Canadian," but declaring that "racial discrimination has no place in this country" it urged the government to go further and give those Japanese who were citizens of Canada the basic rights of "freedom of movement, freedom to work and earn a living in any honest way." Similarly, the *Maple Leaf,* a newspaper published for Canadian soldiers still serving in Europe, declared that the treatment of the Canadian-born Japanese "had overtones of racial persecution and intolerance camouflaged by the war."[18]

The CCJC described the orders as "a particularly flagrant denial of justice and the basic rights of citizens." Within a week of their being tabled, a group of citizens – including B.K. Sandwell, J.E. Atkinson of the *Toronto Daily Star,* George Ferguson of the *Winnipeg Free Press,* and members of the CCJC – launched a writ in the Ontario Supreme Court. Their lawyer, Andrew Brewin, argued that the proposed "deportations of citizens on the grounds of race" was "a new departure in civilized countries expressly disapproved by recent developments in the field of international law." Noting the urgency of the matter, given the imminent departure of the first ship carrying deportees to Japan, Brewin asked the federal government to avoid a multiplicity of actions by referring the orders to the Supreme Court. The government obliged and in January 1946 asked the court to rule on the validity of the orders in council. That did not end debate. By the end of February 1946, the Prime Minister's Office had received between 700 and 1,000 letters and petitions of protest, many of them from Protestant churches and civil liberties groups. The CCJC asked Toronto-area clergy to have public prayers for the success of their suit and distributed a leaflet prepared by the Vancouver Consultative Council inviting people to protest the orders that "Threaten Your Citizenship!"[19]

While many protests against the orders, including ones from labour unions such as the United Steelworkers of America, which had some Japanese Canadian members in Ontario, and from the Roman Catholic bishops of Quebec, came from eastern Canada, a surprising number came from British Columbia. Most were from United Church congregations and organizations, but some also came from Anglicans. From all parts of the province, individuals sent letters and telegrams of protest or signed petitions. The *CCF News* endorsed the leaflet, and secular groups such as the Mine, Mill, and Smelter Workers Union at Kimberley, the Vancouver Secondary Teachers' Association, and the Mainland Branch of the Canadian Association of Social Workers, also protested.[20]

Although support for deportation was limited, doubts about the loyalty of Japanese Canadians persisted. The Toronto *Evening Telegram* said that Canadians "cannot forget the trickery and deceit and cruelty of which the Japanese showed themselves capable in the late war. Any Japanese man who wanted to forsake Canada when he thought Hirohito and Tojo were going to win cannot be trusted to be loyal in this country in the future ... [and] certainly should be thrown out." Despite the lack of any evidence of disloyalty or sabotage on the part of the Japanese in Canada, some British Columbians were still convinced that given a chance many Japanese Canadians would have committed disloyal acts. The Victoria *Daily Colonist,* claiming that there would be "sincere concern in British Columbia if the government reversed its Japanese policy," accused the King government of temporizing. It was sure that the loyalty of the Japanese could not be determined. Sparing no venom, the *Vancouver Sun* rhetorically asked, "if Japan had won the war, would the Japanese in the Dominion now be asserting their rights under Canadian citizenship and demanding that Tojo treat them as defeated nationals?" The Prince Rupert *Evening Empire,* recalling the shelling of Estevan Point and the landing of incendiary balloons, wondered "if Honourable Toronto has ever thought of these things." A trade magazine advised, "let's not make ourselves silly in the eyes of these Japanese who knew full well where their sympathies lay and which way they'd shoot if an invading army put rifles in their hands." In a similar vein, the *Langley Advance* attributed the absence of sabotage to the Department of National Defence's safeguarding of vital installations, the police roundup of Japanese known to be "under the influence of the Emperor," and the removal of all Japanese from the coast. In Parliament a new member, J.L. Gibson (Independent, Comox-Alberni), joined Howard Green, Tom Reid, and George Cruickshank (Liberal, Fraser Valley) in questioning the loyalty of the Japanese.[21]

According to R.W. Brown of the *Vancouver Sun,* at the dominion-provincial conference in November 1945, only Premier Hart called for retaining Clause 3 (g) in Bill 15 as "the only way to give integrity to the government's policy of controlling the Japanese during the first few years of peacetime." Several of his cabinet ministers vehemently opposed the presence of the Japanese or at least those who had signed for repatriation. Herbert Anscomb asserted that "all must go back to Japan." Attorney General R.L. Maitland said that the government would not take a stand on a purely dominion matter but later told the Supreme Court that Japan had shelled the coast and launched bomb-laden balloons and that, even after the war was brought home to them, these "menace[s] to Canada" still desired to go to Japan. When the Supreme Court in February 1946 ruled the orders valid, Maitland urged Ottawa to proceed with deportation immediately.[22]

Press opinions about the court's decision varied along predictable lines. The Victoria *Daily Colonist* wondered why the King government had bothered referring the orders to the court because, if it had the right to "intern" the Japanese in the first place, it "surely had the right to send them back to the land of their allegiance." The *Vancouver Sun* greeted the decision as "vindication" and suggested that those Japanese who claimed that citizenship was "their most sacred possession" had played "fast and loose" with it during the war. The Prince Rupert *Daily News* was pleased that people who had been unfriendly "in action and heart" would not be allowed to remain "as a potential if not an active fifth column." Two Montreal papers, *La Presse* and the *Gazette,* saw the court's decision as a solution to "a difficult problem" by letting some Japanese stay but removing others. The *Toronto Daily Star,* however, regarded the issue as a matter "of humanity" and claimed that most Canadians would not want to "emulate the Nazis in the treatment of minorities." Similarly, the *CCF News* warned of the consequences of "action based purely on racial grounds." More significantly, the Vancouver *Daily Province,* reflecting an emerging tolerance, warned that if it stood the decision would let the government "deport or exile any Canadian" and make Canadian citizenship "not worth a farthing."[23]

The Supreme Court decision, however, was not clear-cut. The judges unanimously agreed that the government could deport Japanese nationals, and a majority ruled that it could also deport Canadian-born and naturalized citizens. The court also said that wives and children could not be included in deportation orders. Regarding the last decision as a moral victory, the CCJC urged the government to withdraw the orders or amend them to ensure that no one would be sent unwillingly to Japan without a full enquiry into his or her loyalty. Because the decisions were "confusing," it urged the government to appeal to the Judicial Committee of the Privy Council in London. After consultation with Ian Mackenzie, who wanted to proceed with deportation as far as the Supreme Court rulings permitted, the government facilitated an appeal to the Privy Council. The CCJC and Saskatchewan's new CCF government, with its concerns about civil liberties and Canadian citizenship, represented the other side. Premier Tommy C. Douglas believed it "pitiful" that, "because a race had committed a crime, individuals in a Christian country should be treated like lepers." To show its good faith, Saskatchewan offered to accept some Japanese relocatees and appointed two Japanese Canadians to senior positions in its civil service. In introducing a Bill of Rights in March 1947, Attorney General J.W. Corman cited among the reasons for it the "alarm felt by all freedom-loving Canadians [about] the orders-in-council deporting and denationalizing British subject Japanese." The Saskatoon Ministerial Association and the University of Saskatchewan's student council shared that positive view of the Japanese. The *Sheaf*, the student newspaper, had distributed 27,000 copies of an extra protesting Bill 15 and plans to deprive Japanese Canadians and others of their Canadian citizenship.[24]

The BC government was displeased by the reference to the Privy Council. Gordon Wismer, who became attorney general after Maitland's sudden death in March 1946, worried that for "highly technical" legal reasons the Privy Council might find the orders in council *ultra vires*. He urged Ottawa to put the orders into statutory form lest the return of all Japanese create "a most serious situation in our province." After visiting Ottawa, he said that he expected the federal government to legislate "to compel Japanese who are Canadian citizens to live in certain designated parts of Canada," an idea that the Vancouver *Daily Province* called "subversive and dangerous." Wismer was primarily concerned with the coastal region, but the Vancouver Liberal Association wanted to exclude the Japanese from the whole area west of the Rockies, as did the *Nanaimo Free Press*, which frankly stated that "British Columbia will be a better place without the Japanese." In Parliament J.L. Gibson tabled a petition signed by 8,000 British Columbians asking for legislation to "ensure that all persons of Japanese descent be deported from Canada to Japan." The BC Command of the Canadian Legion convention rejected a resolution "deploring the action of organized and unorganized individuals who are appealing the verdict of the Supreme Court," and the Provincial Council of Women complained when its national body asked the government to suspend or rescind the orders in council without consulting local councils on a "highly controversial question."[25]

In the meantime, the prime minister, responding to the "present flow of letters and protests," announced that the government would deport only those who wanted to leave and would defer appointing the loyalty commission. The Vancouver *Daily Province* praised the government for doing the "sensible and decent thing," namely halting deportation until the Privy Council ruled. In contrast, the Toronto *Globe and Mail* saw parading "the case before the Privy Council" as an admission that the government preferred "a refuge in legalism, rather than face the broader aspects of the issue" and put "a poor value on Canadian citizenship."[26]

In retrospect, the government's announcement that it would deport only those who wished to leave was the end of the repatriation program, but that was not known at the time. Realizing that the judgment could go against them, the CCJC had second thoughts about an appeal to the Privy Council. In late March, a CCJC delegation interviewed members of the cabinet, including the prime minister (who deemed their hour-long discussion "interesting"), St. Laurent, and Mackenzie. The CCJC urged the government to cancel orders "exiling" Canadian citizens. Mackenzie said that British Columbians strongly believed the Japanese who had been economic competitors and whose fishermen had mapped the coast "to the advantage of the Japanese government" should not be allowed to resettle at the coast. An initial report in the Japanese Canadian Citizens Association newsletter suggested that King and St. Laurent had indicated a desire "to drop the entire deportation issue" but preferred to wait until the Privy Council ruled and public opinion changed; that optimistic report was erroneous. A less sanguine revised report merely said that the government had indicated that if legal means failed to halt the deportations political action would be necessary. The CCJC subsequently appealed to members of Parliament to rescind the orders that put "the value of Canadian citizenship into contempt," violated international law that defined "deportation on racial grounds ... as a crime against humanity," and contradicted "the language and spirit of the United Nations Charter."[27]

The CCJC also pressed the government to lift restrictions that discouraged Japanese Canadians from dispersing across the country. It was concerned that the Japanese who remained in Canada, even Canadian citizens, lacked many civil rights and could not return to coastal British Columbia. As early as August 1945, a delegation had interviewed various government officials and Minister of Labour Mitchell asking that Japanese Canadians be permitted to purchase property east of the Rockies and secure trades licences so that they could open businesses. Mitchell suggested that opening a business "was the worst thing a Japanese could do" since it "would immediately arouse the antagonism of the public." The delegates replied that it was the government's responsibility to educate the public against such antagonistic views and noted how the United States was doing "a very fine job" of educating its people in this respect. The CCJC circulated a leaflet, *Our Japanese Canadians: Citizens Not Exiles,* that, in addition to seeking financial aid for the appeal to the Privy Council and asking for letters to Parliament against deportation, stressed that Japanese Canadians were still "denied basic human rights," including "freedom of movement and the right to purchase land and homes." It called for "an adequate" rehabilitation program, including restitution for property losses. "The Japanese people in Canada," a writer in *Nisei Affairs* explained, "want only to be allowed to live as other Canadians, free citizens in a free country," and argued that continued restrictions demonstrated that the "forced movement" was not related to "military necessity" but to the "political considerations" of "certain racist politicians."[28]

Even in British Columbia, there was some sympathy for ending restrictions. A writer in a provincial mining trade magazine reminded readers, "the question is not to decide whether or not the Japanese help or hinder the economic life of British Columbia ... Neither is it a question of assimilation into Canadian life, though that is important enough. Some Japanese are good Canadians and others are not. But what has that got to do with telling a Canadian citizen that he is not a Canadian citizen after all?" The writer criticized those who wanted to deny Japanese Canadians the right to reside at the coast. Similarly, the editor of the *Grand Forks Gazette,* after quoting the *Ottawa Journal* on the Atlantic Charter, noted that "either Canadian citizenship is valid for all Canadians, regardless of color or creed, or it is valid for no citizen of Canada whatever." Dozens of petitions, printed in Vancouver, arrived in the Prime Minister's Office from across the country. One Vancouver correspondent secured 120 signatures on "a hit-or-miss" basis and met only eleven people who refused to sign because they were hostile to the Japanese. Under the heading "Relative to Canadian Residents of Japanese Ancestral Stock Who Are Not Subject to Deportation," the petition asked that to reabsorb them quickly into economic life they be granted "full rights and privileges normally incidental to citizenship or residence in Canada," especially the right to own or lease property and to move freely within Canada. The realistic petitioners recognized that "in the present circumstances" it might be advisable to govern their return to the coast by permit, but to promote dispersal they recommended prompt and generous adjustment of economic losses. The petition concluded by requesting that any measures "relative to any racial minority" be in accord with the government's commitments to "human rights" and "fundamental freedoms" under the United Nations Charter.[29]

References to citizenship were timely. In the spring of 1946, Secretary of State Paul Martin introduced legislation "to avoid many complexities and confusions" in existing laws, reflect pride in Canadian achievements and "aspirations as a nation for the future," and "establish clearly a basic and definite Canadian citizenship ... upon which the rights and privileges of Canadians will depend" by bringing in a Citizenship Act. British Columbia's Liberal and Conservative MPs feared that the new act would preclude restricting the movement of the Japanese who were Canadian citizens. Howard Green set out the case by recalling a litany of atavistic arguments for maintaining British Columbia's "right" to exclude Japanese. "If the government caves in," letting them remain in the province, he contended that in forty or fifty years "there will be forty or fifty thousand Japanese on the coast, again in contact with Japanese merchant ships, going back and forth to Japan, again under domination of the Japanese consul, still worshipping the Japanese emperor and still a menace." In a widely quoted statement, he warned of "bloodshed" if Japanese returned to the fishing industry. The Victoria *Daily Colonist* claimed that he did not overdraw the picture; the *CCF News* accused him of encouraging "violence and lawlessness." Grote Stirling (Progressive Conservative, Yale) said simply, "we should boldly undertake the removal of the Japanese from Canada." Other Conservatives questioned the loyalty of Japanese to Canada. E. Davie Fulton (Kamloops) said that, contrary to "the wave of hysteria and ill-considered agitation which is sweeping the country against these orders in council," many Japanese so affected were "certainly not subjects or citizens, nor were they loyal Canadians." "The people of British Columbia," he said bluntly, "do not want to have them." Stirling and Liberals Thomas Reid (New Westminster) and James Sinclair (Vancouver North) stressed the alleged dual citizenship of the Japanese. They asked how Canadian-born Japanese who were registered with the Japanese consul and subject to military service in Japan could be unequivocally loyal to Canada. Some MPs simply did not want the Japanese back in the province. Cecil Merritt declared that British Columbians would not accept having "this red-hot shot dumped back into their hands to carry again alone." George Pearkes (Nanaimo) cited letters from constituents pleading, "do not let the Japanese come back," mainly because "they are not assimilable." Yet Pearkes, who appreciated the value of Canadian citizenship, recognized the conundrum in "the principle that Canadian citizens must live somewhere and not be allowed to live elsewhere." He urged the Japanese to take "every opportunity to go back as quickly as you can to Japan." His neighbour from Comox-Alberni, J.L. Gibson, would accept legislation to keep Japanese from the coast for twenty years but warned of "trouble" if they came back. While the allusions were to physical violence, Cruickshank revealed an underlying motive by predicting that no Liberal or Conservative in the province would be re-elected if the Japanese returned to the coast. The other BC MPs so insisted that the government not use the citizenship bill to abandon plans to deport the Japanese that H.G. Archibald (CCF, Skeena) accused them of suffering "from violent attacks of yellow fever," while Angus MacInnis (CCF, Vancouver East) suggested that they seemed to be discussing "the perpetual racial discrimination act." Martin said that the citizenship bill did not alter the effects of any orders in council affecting persons with a "certain status" but yielded to the British Columbians and amended it to clarify this.[30]

While the fate of Japanese Canadians was in the hands of the Judicial Committee of the Privy Council, the deportation orders were not widely discussed. Then, in December 1946, the Judicial Committee ruled them valid. Predictably, those who were concerned about civil liberties and the rights of Canadian citizenship said that deportation would "make a mockery" of the new Canadian Citizenship Act, accused the government of Hitler-like racialism, and called for a Bill of Rights. After noting that the Privy Council ruling meant "that these extraordinary powers of the state extend to all Canadians of whatever ancestry," the Montreal *Star* rightly observed that "wider support can be expected for the point of view of the courageous few who held to the principle despite the hysteria of war." It suggested that "it would be liberal in the true sense of the word, to wipe out the past, to make a fresh start and to do so quickly in order to end the corroding uncertainty to which these unfortunate people have lived for so long." Again letters urging abandonment of the deportation policy filled government mailboxes.[31]

"Dual Personality," *Vancouver Sun,* 3 December 1946, by R. Meadows. Although the war had ended over a year earlier and Japan had been thoroughly defeated, suspicions of the loyalty of Japanese Canadians lingered in some quarters.

Like their eastern counterparts, the editors of the Vancouver *Daily Province* and the *CCF News* fretted about implications for Canadian citizenship. Attorney General Wismer, however, was "gratified" that the dominion had the power to protect the nation in time of war. The *Vancouver Sun* was satisfied that "ex-aliens who repented of seeking Canadian citizenship ... when Japan was winning the war" had found that they could not "work both sides of the street." Yet that comment reflected a moderation in tone, for it correctly assumed that the government would not exercise its right to deport the Canadian born. Moreover, in a despatch from Ottawa, *Sun* editor Roy W. Brown said, "the status quo would probably suit British Columbia" as long as the Japanese remained dispersed. J.W. Pickersgill, the prime minister's special assistant, sent the column to King, noting that it was "presumably a significant change of the attitude in Vancouver, which may well have a bearing on future policy."[32]

In mid-January the Canadian Press reported that the highest levels of government in Ottawa were studying the "recurring headache" of Canada's Japanese problem "with a view to a final and complete cleanup of the issue." Reporter John Leblanc speculated that the government would not send more Japanese to "the war-wracked islands across the Pacific" since the policy of breaking up the Japanese concentration at the coast was working. When the cabinet discussed its response, it knew that fewer than 7,000 Japanese remained in British Columbia. The Cabinet Committee on Japanese

"Who's Next?" *Winnipeg Free Press,* 22 February 1946. One of the main arguments against the "repatriation" policy was its implication for other naturalized Canadians.

Problems, whose members included Mitchell, Mackenzie, and a number of civil servants, recommended taking no further action on deportation other than assisting voluntary repatriates. According to King's diary, the cabinet meeting on 22 January 1947 was "most interesting." St. Laurent, who believed that the Japanese "would never really work into Canadian life and their numbers might become troublesome," worried that once Japan became "a settled country" it would, through the United Nations, demand that Japanese in Canada have "the same rights as the white population." Thus, St. Laurent "fought strongly and bravely for deporting practically all who could be deported, including some Canadian citizens." King and other ministers answered that in the interests of "good-will and peace" "it would be a crime" to send people who had behaved well during the war to Japan. Even Mackenzie, who, King admitted, would "have [the] most to lose," grudgingly agreed to make the decision unanimous, not, he said, because it was right but because "they would not be able to get support to carry it out." King expected that the government could not easily defend itself against agitation aroused by civil libertarians. The Liberal Party, he mused, was already "in a false position in the minds of many people through our ill-Liberal treatment of different persons. We would probably raise a real issue if we sought to oppose what now seemed to be general public opinion in the matter of dropping the question of deportation, though holding the right to control the movement of the Japs in Canada for some time to come." It was, he thought, the only decision "that we could really hope to get successfully through Parliament and which, on humanitarian grounds, is right." Moreover, he correctly believed that British Columbia had "changed its attitude considerably." Two days later the prime minister announced the end of the deportation program. As R.G. Robertson, one of his secretaries, observed, neither the press nor any letter writer had suggested retaining the deportation policy.[33]

If any good came out of the whole deportation story and the attempt to revoke the citizenship of Japanese Canadians, it was the contribution to a growing awareness of the importance of citizenship both as a general concept and in a legal sense and of the need for a Bill of Rights. Indeed, the throne speech opening the 1947 parliamentary session announced plans for a parliamentary committee "to inquire into ways and means of protecting people in this country against racial, religious and economic discrimination" and to examine how Canada could implement the obligations that it had accepted under the United Nations Charter in the field of human rights. When Prime Minister King chose Ian Mackenzie to introduce the bill, the press noted the irony since, as Bruce Hutchison wrote, Mackenzie had "chiefly promoted the most serious recent interference with Canadian liberties – racial discrimination against Canadians of Japanese origin."[34]

Advocates of a Bill of Rights continued to cite the experiences of Japanese Canadians as evidence of the need for such a bill. Some erroneously believed that the American Bill of Rights had protected the rights of Japanese Americans;[35] most simply referred to the Canadian situation and the threat that Bill 15 had made to citizenship. In a column accompanied by a disclaimer that the *Vancouver Sun* did not endorse it, Hutchison warned, "if any government is ever given the power to say where any Canadian shall live, then no Canadian will ever be safe again." He argued that, "when government[s] seek such powers it is high time that we had a bill of rights written into our constitution." Others, including B.K. Sandwell and the editors of the *Winnipeg Free Press,* agreed. A Citizens' Forum leaflet listed the treatment of Japanese Canadians as a reason to inquire into civil liberties and a Canadian Bill of Rights. In calling for such a bill, *Nisei Affairs* expressed the hope that the new Citizenship Act might begin a new era in which "people will become less involved in matters of race and color," but it saw no evidence of Canada giving certain racial minorities "the right to full elevation of citizenship." The founding convention of the National Japanese Canadian Citizens Association (JCCA) in September 1947 asked for the inclusion of a Bill of Rights in the Canadian Constitution. Its Race Relations Committee noted that other groups also suffered discrimination in matters such as immigration for Chinese and the "reserve complex" for Indians and that Ontario had had to pass a law prohibiting the publication of any sign indicating discrimination against particular groups, such as Jews. When Prime Minister John Diefenbaker introduced his Bill of Rights in 1960, he recalled how the 1945 orders in council provided for deporting and stripping Canadian citizenship

"What's Wrong with This Picture?" *CCF News,* 5 June 1947. Despite advertising in the 1945 provincial election that it opposed the return of the Japanese to the coast, the CCF did support a bill of rights that would protect minorities such as Japanese Canadians.

from people whose "only offence … in 99 percent of the cases, as it turned out subsequently, was their colour." Harold Winch (CCF, Vancouver East) and John Taylor (Progressive Conservative, Vancouver Centre) agreed. J.W. Pickersgill (Liberal, Bonavista-Twillingate) denied that there was anything about "colour" in orders issued while Canada and Japan were technically at war but urged that a Bill of Rights provide that, "under the War Measures Act, the governor in council may not for any reason whatever exile any person from Canada, citizen or otherwise."[36]

Accepting the formal end of the deportation program was relatively easy for most British Columbians. A few former prisoners of war still spoke of atrocities, and the press occasionally reported Japan's secret plans to conquer North America, but wartime memories were fading. It was also difficult to ignore publicity about the United Nations Charter and its references to the promotion of human rights and the new Canadian Citizenship Act. Moreover, the Japanese population of British Columbia rapidly declined in 1946. Between 1 January and 1 July 1946, it dropped by 3,878, while that of other provinces, chiefly Ontario, increased by 2,295. By 1 January 1947, British Columbia's Japanese population was only 6,776, almost all of whom were in the interior. In the words of the *New Canadian,* the movement east was "growing into a steady stream." It accelerated after Ottawa let those who had signed for repatriation relocate east of the Rockies. The *Vancouver Sun* happily reported that, since "the evacuated Nipponese appear to be complying" with dispersal, British Columbia's main "minority problem" was advancing "toward permanent settlement." The Vancouver *Daily Province* thought that cancelling the proposed loyalty tribunal and deportation plans and offering amends was the least the government could do "if it has regard for justice at all," but it recommended that Japanese Canadians not concentrate at the coast.[37]

Having accepted similar advice from the Department of Labour "to ensure that the redistribution would take permanent roots," the cabinet retained certain restrictions on movement and fishing licences "for a limited period." As Mackenzie resignedly told the press, lifting some controls and providing compensation were "fair to all concerned"; he took refuge in the continued ban on the entry of Japanese to the coastal region. The *Vancouver Sun* was confident that his presence in the cabinet would guarantee that. Similarly, Attorney General Wismer found little fault in withdrawing the repatriation orders provided that the Japanese did not enter the coastal zone or the fisheries.[38]

East of the Rockies, several editors complained that the lack of freedom for Japanese made "a farce of citizenship." The new policy, in the words of the Montreal *Star,* told Japanese Canadians that "anywhere else you can be a Canadian to your heart's content, but you can't be a Canadian in British Columbia," and complained of their "second class" status. Their situation, it suggested, was akin to the "servitude" associated with totalitarian countries such as Russia, a view echoed by the *Calgary Herald.* "Either the Japanese-Canadians are citizens, or they aren't," it proclaimed and called for full citizenship rights, including the right to move freely. In observing the absence of Japanese Canadians at ceremonies inaugurating the Citizenship Act, the *Toronto Daily Star* noted how they were still subject to the restrictions of the War Measures Act and argued that, unless justice were done and "police rule" removed, "the value and honor of Canadian citizenship will be less than complete." In complaining how the government had not given equality to Japanese Canadians, the Toronto *Globe and Mail* suggested that the government's "vauntings about Canadian citizenship will mean much more when it treats that privilege as sacred beyond anything political conniving might demand." The Japanese, said the *Saskatoon Star-Phoenix*, "will enjoy a citizenship somewhat less complete than other Canadians in that residence in one province will be barred to many of them"; a second editorial suggested that, if Mackenzie were "the only obstacle to a just and liberal policy," he should be allowed to "die on the barricades of intolerance." The Regina *Leader-Post* neatly summarized the argument: "Freedom of movement is the right of Canadian citizens."[39]

The Alberta government had regarded the Japanese relocatees as temporary residents only. Thus, it denied them benefits such as the franchise, free maternity care, the full old age pension, and equal treatment in the schools. Early in 1948, the conclusion of a two-year cost-sharing agreement between Edmonton and Ottawa led Alberta to recognize the approximately 3,000 Japanese Canadians so affected as full citizens, a move welcomed by the *Calgary Herald* as a wise action as it praised their "useful and even essential contribution to the life of the province." Yet, it mused, "they could have made a much greater one, had they not been handicapped by blind prejudice on the part of many non-Japanese. We do not expect to see this prejudice disappear overnight, but we hope it will melt away gradually, so that the industry and ability of these new citizens can be fully utilized." At the same time, the *Herald* criticized the 149 MPs who were absent when the House of Commons rejected a CCF proposal to allow Japanese to move freely to and within British Columbia.[40]

Some British Columbians, however, were adamant that the Japanese must not return to the coast. As Tom Reid left for the 1947 parliamentary session, he said that British Columbia "must make a last ditch stand against any resettlement of the Japanese on the Coast or they may not get another chance." He was not alone in this view. Diehards such as the editor of the Victoria *Daily Colonist* warned that "twenty years from now all Canada, and not merely British Columbia, will have a Japanese problem on its hands, with the time past when anything practical can be done about it." When the CCJC called for revoking all restrictions, the *Vancouver Sun* mused that, if it were true that the Japanese had no desire to return to the coast, the restrictions would be no hardship, "and if they don't come back, they can have no need for fishing licenses." The Native Sons of British Columbia, several Liberal and Conservative constituency associations, and the Army, Navy, and Air Force Veterans also opposed the return of the Japanese. After a heated debate, the Provincial Command of the Canadian Legion rejected a resolution condemning "the fomenting of racial or religious prejudice among Canadians" and narrowly voted for "closer scrutiny of Japanese colonies in B.C."[41]

Yet these sentiments no longer reflected widespread opinion. Some British Columbians actively called for full citizenship rights, including freedom of movement, for Japanese Canadians. The Vancouver Consultative Committee was in the forefront. It told MPs of its indignation at the impression that

British Columbians were "substantially unanimous in favouring discriminatory measures," that hundreds of them had made its work possible, and that individual members and official bodies of the Anglican, Baptist, United Church, Presbyterian, Unitarian, Salvation Army, and other communions had taken "virtually identical" stands, while Archbishop W.M. Duke had recently named a Roman Catholic priest to serve on its executive. The Vancouver branch of the Canadian Civil Liberties Union distributed circulars condemning restrictions on Canadian citizens of Japanese origin as a threat to "civil liberties" and the role that Canada "should play in the United Nations and the world" to newspapers across the nation. Several prairie editors used it to emphasize that "discrimination is repugnant to the principles of the British North America Act, to the pretensions of the Canadian Citizenship Act and to the United Nations charter." More significantly, the Burrard Young Conservative Association called for the "unrestricted movement" of Japanese in Canada. The New Westminster *British Columbian,* while wary of a revival of "intense concentrations of Japanese at certain points," admitted that "anyone who is fit to stay in Canada is just as fit in one place as another."[42] Opinion in the province had shifted remarkably since 1945 when sentiment was strong for sending all Japanese, Canadian citizens or not, to Japan just as soon as ships could be found to carry them.

In mid-April 1947, Ottawa finally lifted restrictions on the movement of Japanese east of the Rockies. In British Columbia, they still required permits to travel more than fifty miles, change residence, or enter the coastal area. Without such restrictions, asserted the *Vancouver Sun,* 13,000 Japanese would "trickle back." The Victoria *Daily Colonist* agreed that, "until sentiment" changed and time erased "the memory of a danger that seemed real enough" after Pearl Harbor, they should be excluded from the province. In Parliament, Mackenzie, who a few months earlier had replied to a Vancouver *News-Herald* editorial accusing him of "whipping up hatred" by declaring that "I want British Columbia for our own white people – for the soldiers, sailors and airmen who saved us – saved freedom and Christianity for us," boasted that the province's Liberal and Conservative MPs stood as one on the need to continue restrictions for another five or ten years to maintain "the security of our own people along the security zone of British Columbia."[43]

When Parliament debated the Emergency Powers Bill to allow continued controls, Mackenzie stressed what he called British Columbia's right to "adequate conditions for its own internal security along the coastline." Howard Green also pursued the "security" theme and revived stories of the fishing fleet having been a front for Japan's navy. Concerns about Japan as a military threat were odd given the country's thorough defeat, but Reid believed that "when Japan rises again ... these Japanese will be useful to Japan." A Vancouver Liberal senator, S.S. McKeen, recited stories of prewar spying, contended that the Japanese had come to take over the country, and predicted that they would continue "their explorations" if they came back. He warned that riots and even bloodshed might follow their return "at this time." Angus MacInnis easily challenged the security theme by pointing to the ridiculous picture of "a few old men and old women and children … being kept east of the Rockies or east of the coastal defence zone in order to protect British Columbia from invasion." However, the old-timers – Mackenzie, Reid, Green, Stirling, and Senator Farris – had a full reservoir of anti-Japanese arguments. Stirling bluntly stated that his constituents opposed any "further intrusion" of inassimilable Japanese since that would mean two equally unattractive situations, either nesting "themselves in cells" or intermarriage and the consequent "dreadful … creation of an Eurasian cast." "Intermarriage," echoed Reid, was "the crux of the question." Even the young Conservative and Victoria Cross winner Cecil Merritt thought that "difference in colour" made "assimilation almost impossible." Like most MPs, including those from other parts of Canada, he thought dispersal better than facing "the condition that might arise in some of the centres of British Columbia" if restrictions on their movement to the coast lapsed. Similarly, Farris told the Senate Banking Committee that cancelling controls on the Japanese would bring the problem to an "acute" head. Two younger members of Parliament, James Sinclair and Davie Fulton, both war veterans and elected in 1945, endorsed dispersal as the only "practical way" to give the Japanese "the chance to become good Canadians." Unlike their colleagues, they recognized problems in reconciling limitations on persons of Canadian nationality with "the unfairness" of letting Japanese congregate in the province.[44]

Contrary to what the MPs seemed to think, interest in the Japanese was fading. The Victoria *Daily Colonist* still called for the exclusion of the Japanese from the coast, but the *Vancouver Sun* and *Daily Province* merely reported the debate as part of their parliamentary coverage. The Vancouver *News-Herald,* however, mocked the MPs who claimed that "B.C. fears the Japanese for military security reasons" and criticized Parliament for "pandering to … race-baiting politicians." Jack Scott, a *Sun* columnist, suggested that "the hatred of some of our white citizens against our brown citizens has cooled into apathy" but attacked the racial prejudice that British Columbia's white economic interests had established with the help of the politicians such as ex-alderman Halford Wilson, Mackenzie and Reid, and the "splendid co-operation" of the King government. That too was an argument of CCF MPs. J.H. Matthews (Kootenay East) told Parliament, "the question is not merely a racial one, but one that has its economic side. British Columbia objects to the presence of the Japanese because in the fishing industry, in logging and in agriculture, they hold down jobs which white men need."[45]

While some British Columbians ascribed economic causes to past policies, eastern Canadians focused on racial issues. In the *Winnipeg Free Press,* Bruce Hutchison wrote a damning critique: "Sheer racialism, the doctrine of Hitler, has thus been written deliberately into the laws of Canada by men who are constantly mouthing their slogans of One World and universal peace." Suggesting that the Russian government would exploit Canada's discrimination against the Japanese because they were "yellow," he focused his animus on Mackenzie and the BC MPs "who hate the Japanese simply because they are Japanese." That was also the sentiment of *Nisei Affairs,* which noted that "a more observant eye than the prejudiced glaze of Mr. Mackenzie would see many barriers which would prevent any, if any, large scale return to the west coast." It cited the loss of homes, stores, businesses, boats, farms, and savings and the expense in moving to British Columbia and restarting there. It warned that the continued controls were "dangerous precedents" for other minorities. In protesting the restrictions, the CCJC agreed that few Japanese Canadians were likely to return to British Columbia but opposed the principle of "preventing any group of law abiding citizens from travelling anywhere in Canada if they so desire." The JCCA asked the prime minister "why British Columbia should be the only Province in the Dominion, not upholding the Citizenship Act, and classifying Canadian Citizens, because of racial origin."[46]

In 1947 Parliament had extended the restrictions on the Japanese for one year. As the restrictions were due to expire, the cabinet considered letting them lapse on 31 March 1948. Minister of Justice J.L. Ilsley warned that Parliament was unlikely to extend restrictions that were probably *ultra vires.* Unable to reach a conclusion, the Cabinet Committee on Japanese Problems referred the matter to the cabinet as a whole. In the meantime, Mackenzie retired to the Senate, a move hailed by the Vancouver *News-Herald* as perhaps permitting the erasure of a blot on Canada's record. Shortly thereafter British Columbia's new premier, Byron "Boss" Johnson, visited Ottawa. Johnson warned King that repealing the orders might cause the Liberals to lose the by-election created by Mackenzie's retirement. BC MPs and Ralph Campney, the Liberal nominee in Vancouver Centre, agreed that repealing the orders would mean not "a chance in the world" of winning that by-election or one in Yale caused by Stirling's retirement. Despite Ilsley's protest that "history would denounce the Party for having continued these Orders," caucus agreed with King that "history would condemn a govt. standing for certain principles if it allowed itself to be defeated by an enemy govt … when it was within its power to still carry on." In Vancouver Mackenzie said that the Japanese should not return to the coast to protect "our fisheries for our returned men" and that current "international discussions" made security a consideration. Two weeks later, trying to reconcile differences within a "completely divided" caucus, King asked if it wanted to protect "the minority constituted by the handful of Japanese, or the minority constituted by the entire population of B.C." The latter minority, in fact, were mainly Liberal members of the House of Commons and the Senate.[47]

While the cabinet and the Liberal caucus were considering the matter, George Tanaka, "a quiet-spoken young war veteran" and the executive secretary of the JCCA, lobbied cabinet ministers and MPs. The CCF supported him, and Davie Fulton expressed hope for continued "progressive revocation of certain restrictions" while warning against arousing "old feelings of hostility." Minister of Labour Mitchell presented Parliament with a compromise as he sought authority to regulate the entry of Japanese into British Columbia for another year to provide time "to ensure stability of resettlement elsewhere in Canada." He understood that few Japanese desired to return to the coast but feared that "the precipitate return of even a limited number" might "resurrect racial issues and animosity which have existed over many years," but he expected such animosity to disappear in a few years.[48]

In the relatively short debate, only five British Columbians spoke. Citing the hostile response to the province's attempt to ban the employment of Asians on crown timber lands, MacInnis accused the minister of assuming that "there is tremendous race prejudice in British Columbia." In a rambling speech, Reid disagreed. He revived old arguments about the Japanese not being assimilable and quoted constituents at Steveston who said that if the Japanese returned they would "get even with them" for the torture that Japanese forces inflicted on Canadian prisoners of war. Pearkes alluded to atrocities, the arrogance of some Japanese in Canada in 1942 who "laughed" at coastal defences and boasted of a quick return, and warned of "crimes of revenge." J.L. Gibson said that his "own people" "bitterly opposed" the Japanese, but neither he nor Cruickshank, the other BC MP who spoke, offered any real reasons. Both Liberals and Conservatives admitted that "time is healing many of the sores … There is not the same bitterness of feeling there was three years ago." The resolution passed, though a CCF MP added, "on division."[49]

In the *Vancouver Sun,* Elmore Philpott praised MacInnis. "It was time," said Philpott, that "somebody from B.C. nailed the downright lie that British Columbia is mostly inhabited by bigots," since most British Columbians believed in "fair play." That and the Vancouver *News-Herald*'s comment that Canadians could not "be proud of their democracy" because Parliament had approved of discrimination contrary to "the principles" of the new Citizenship Act were the only editorial notes in British Columbia, although several eastern journals attacked the decision for endorsing racial discrimination and violating principles of Canadian citizenship. Contrary to some eastern Canadian observers, however, high prices, austerity, and freight rates were the by-election issues, not the Japanese question. When Humphrey Mitchell spoke for the Liberal candidate in Vancouver, he said that "extremely few" Japanese would return to the coast.[50] That was the only recorded comment on the subject in either Vancouver Centre or Yale. In both the CCF won.

The MPs who spoke on the final extension of limitations on the Japanese represented coastal constituencies. Interior communities were of two minds about retaining Japanese. Those who had come to know the Japanese during the war tended to favour giving them full citizenship rights; those who had not initially shared many of the same ideas as coastal residents. Even those who had brief encounters with the Japanese were impressed. A.R. Lord, the principal of the Vancouver Normal School, who spent parts of three summers helping to train Nisei teachers at New Denver, told the New Westminster Rotary Club that his students "had language, social adaptability, and all the essentials that make good Canadians – they were Canadians of Japanese descent, just as good Canadians as I am a Canadian of Scotch descent." In Kaslo, the *Kootenaian* suggested that Japanese Canadians knew that their future depended on dispersal. It believed that "their industry, thrift, cleanliness and adaptability will quickly win them friends wherever they go, and as a result our Japanese problem will solve itself."[51]

In Kaslo, New Denver, Slocan, and Greenwood, where relocatees had formed a significant portion of the population and established friendly relations, many white residents were unhappy to see them go. J.C. Harris, who had leased land at New Denver to the Security Commission, informed the prime minister that he and his family had "continued to live there & found the Japanese most friendly & ready to co-operate." At Slocan the mayor was one of nine residents who wrote to all MPs opposing the deportation of Japanese Canadians against their will. They noted that "many of us ... at one time from ignorance received these people in our midst with suspicion and dislike. But, when we got to know them, we found them to be respectable law abiding Citizens, whose living standards and decorums are equal to the occidental Canadians in similar walks of life." The Japanese, the Slocan residents asserted, are "suffering from the petty spite for the sins of the ruling Caste of Tokio, on account of the colour of their skin." When H.W. Herridge (CCF, Kootenay West) told Parliament in 1947 that a majority of interior residents "would like to see the Japanese treated as Canadian citizens," he was correct, at least for the Kootenay and Boundary districts. As the orders barring the Japanese from the coast expired, the mayor of Greenwood, who admitted that his city depended on the Japanese, who formed three-quarters of its population, said that it wanted them to stay. "We gave them a square deal," he explained, "and they showed they were good citizens and good workers ... We figured they got a raw deal on the coast and showed them plainly that they are Canadian citizens." Kootenay residents sometimes influenced other British Columbians. In 1946, for example, their delegates persuaded the provincial Advisory Board of Farmers' Institutes to table, until the Supreme Court decided, a lower Fraser Valley resolution calling for the deportation of all Japanese.[52]

Propinquity encouraged toleration in other communities where relocatees had settled. At Lillooet sixty Japanese tomato growers, members of the Lillooet Co-Operative Association, joined local white growers to purchase a tomato cannery and packing house. The *Bridge River-Lillooet News* had earlier welcomed a plan of Japanese businessmen to manufacture soybean products at Ashcroft and now praised the co-operation as pointing to "prosperous horizons." The only objection was from Indians, who complained that there and in Kamloops Japanese farmers would not employ them.[53]

Some interior residents with limited contact with the Japanese did not want them in their region. In the fall of 1945, the *Nelson Daily News* feared that the approximately 10,000 Japanese still in the West Kootenay might remain. It wanted only a "fair proportion," which it calculated at about sixty. The Nelson Board of Trade, however, refused to endorse a Kelowna resolution calling for measures to prevent Japanese from congregating in British Columbia. One member observed, "we now have a Citizenship Act. Many of these Japanese are third generation in Canada and have as much right as you and I to be Canadians."[54]

North of Kamloops, at a public meeting, fifty-three residents of the tiny communities of Birch Island, Vavenby, and Clearwater said that they would "not be responsible" for maintaining peace and order if Japanese were settled in the district. Their concern may have been the approximately 120 Japanese who had been building the Yellowhead Highway. In Kamloops itself, the Board of Trade repeatedly called for the repatriation of all who requested it, the removal of the several hundred "special permit" Japanese from the district as soon as possible, and the retention of no more than the prewar Japanese population of thirty-three. The Local Council of Women opposed relaxing the repatriation policy, but the Women's Missionary Society of the United Church endorsed a petition from Nisei at Tashme asking that they be permitted to cancel their applications for repatriation. With the passage of time, Kamloops residents slowly accepted Japanese Canadians. Late in 1947, the Royal Inland Hospital let Dr. M. Uchida admit his patients to the hospital but not treat other patients. A year later Dr. A.J. Fujiwara moved to North Kamloops from Bridge River and Lillooet and set up a dental practice. At a social level, Nisei had considerable success integrating with the local community, particularly by participating in athletic teams. In the summer of 1949, Frances Kato, a student at Kamloops High School and a candidate of the JCCA was elected Queen of the BC Round-Up.[55]

Since early in the century, the south Okanagan had refused to accept Asian settlers, but the north was more tolerant partly because of its need for agricultural labourers. That division continued. C.W. Morrow (Coalition, North Okanagan) told the legislature, "we don't mind assimilating our share," but we do not want the large number we had during the war. Others did not want the Japanese to acquire land. When a Japanese resident bought an orchard at Coldstream (near Vernon), a white orchardist predicted that the Japanese would eventually "oust the white race." The Vernon Board of Trade referred the matter to the Associated Boards of Trade. By late 1947, Vernon City Council, after an extended discussion, gave a building permit to a Japanese who had bought a residential lot. Vernon had about 200 Japanese residents before the war; by 1949 it had about 400 who were well established in the community.[56]

Again reflecting the local divisions within the Okanagan, W.A.C. Bennett (MLA, Coalition, South Okanagan), whose constituency included Kelowna, claimed that the valley was "alarmed" because as long as Japanese were excluded from the coast "the valley being [the] next warmest section in all Canada will have [the] major portion of all Japanese when free movement is allowed." In the legislature, he denied any "feeling of race hatred" but said that for economic reasons Okanagan residents "did not want 10,000 of the Orientals to remain permanently." The Kelowna Board of Trade believed that the valley already had "too many" inassimilable Japanese. By early 1947, the board could discuss the matter "without heat" and took it to the Associated Boards of Trade of the Okanagan and Mainline, which expressed concern about an influx of Japanese after the restrictions on their movement expired. In the legislature, Bennett repeated these arguments; in Parliament, Grote Stirling outlined the case. These were the last gasps, however, of old prejudices. By 1947 Japanese were being accepted as Okanagan residents. At the founding meeting of the JCCA in September 1947, a Kelowna delegate reported that the situation was "gradually improving." As the orders restricting the movement of the Japanese expired, the editor of the *Kelowna Courier,* in recalling "one of the most distressing episodes in the life of this community," observed that the Japanese had taken "their place in the community and in the whole will make good Canadians. With little or no prospect of any further influx, it would seem that 'finis' might well be written to the Japanese problem in the Okanagan and our efforts turn to living in peace and harmony."[57]

The coast too was becoming less hostile to Japanese. Letters opposing the return of the Japanese still arrived in Ottawa, but their number was falling, and they came from traditional sources such as a past grand factor of the Native Sons of British Columbia, the North Burnaby and Prince Rupert Liberal Associations, and a Canadian Legion branch in New Westminster. More significantly, the *Vancouver Sun,* the last major critic of the Japanese presence on the coast, had recently written that the province had "outgrown" racism. "Their reception [at the coast] may be warmer than their welcome in certain quarters," it warned, but it expected that the 6,000 Japanese remaining in British Columbia could "be absorbed in the fast-expanding economy of this great province" if they did not congregate in certain occupations. In this apparent turnabout, the *Sun* was responding to a decision of the provincial cabinet to revive a 1902 law forbidding the employment of Asians on crown timber lands. During a severe wartime labour shortage, a federal order in council suspended the provincial law, and a number of Japanese secured jobs in the interior forest industry. Even as the war was ending, the International Woodworkers of America (IWA), whose membership had grown exponentially during the war, was organizing Japanese workers in interior sawmills – a measure that drew protests from a Vancouver Island local – and demanding that they be granted full citizenship rights. The IWA saw that employers could exploit the Japanese and so lower the wages of white workers. Ottawa revoked the order in council in March 1947, but not until early 1948 did the provincial Department of Lands and Forests announce that it would enforce the ban on the employment of Asians on crown lands. About 350 Japanese had been employed "illegally" as loggers, and another 550 or so were affected either as workers in related sawmills or as dependents. Within the province, enforcement of the law set off protests that united disparate interests: interior lumber operators feared losing an important labour force; the IWA worried about violations of its collective agreement. The operator of the Boundary Sawmills at Midway, for example, reported how sawmills depended on the Japanese to cut the logs needed to "produce the still vitally needed lumber." He attacked the order as "a discriminatory measure directed at the Japanese people, of whom most are Canadians by birth," and an imposition on employers' rights. "We do not feel justified that we should be told that we cannot employ the Japanese in the woods any more than a farmer can be told that a Japanese workman cannot work on his farm." The JCCA, civil libertarians, church groups, and the CCF were in the forefront of those condemning a violation of human and citizenship rights and protesting what reminded Harold Winch of "Hitler's brutality against racial minorities."[58]

The provincial press uniformly criticized the violation of human rights and a policy that by making the interior less attractive would encourage the Japanese to return to the coast. The Vancouver *News-Herald* described "this cruel and arbitrary act" as showing that "the mentality which presents in persecuting these people is still very much alive in the government of this province." Similarly, the Vancouver *Daily Province,* under the heading "A Ruling to Make Canadians Blush," attacked a policy "based on racial and economic prejudice" for violating "the principle of equality which the Citizenship Act seeks to establish." The *Victoria Daily Times* wondered how the Citizenship Act could have "full meaning" if British Columbia maintained the attitude that it was "dealing with enemy aliens." Some objections were based on fear that Japanese forced from interior woods would go to the coast. The Prince Rupert *Daily News* accused the provincial government of "chasing" the Japanese "from pillar to post." The *Vancouver Sun* also saw the forestry ban as "a piece of needless aggravation that merely cuts their new roots and induces them to drift back into their former haunts and habits." It called the ban an "act of deplorable discrimination" and affirmed that the province had "long since outgrown the kind of racism of which this order appears to be a reflection." An unscientific public opinion poll in Vancouver indicated that 62 percent of the population disapproved of the ban.[59]

Realizing the unpopularity of the policy, within four days Acting Premier Anscomb announced that the notice of exclusion had been a routine matter in contracts going back to 1902, but the government would suspend enforcement until the legislature decided future policy. Critics welcomed the retreat. The New Westminster *British Columbian* was heartened because "the furore" demonstrated "that B.C. has made a notable recovery from war hysteria and is prepared to do reasonable justice to members of this unloved race within its borders." Elmore Philpott suggested that British Columbia had now grown up. The *Vernon News* was pleased that the public was "awakening to the injustices perpetrated and to the dangers inherent in adoption of any race dogma." From the east, the *Toronto Daily Star* observed that the government's prompt response to public opinion "should encourage all who are trying to combat racial prejudice in this country."[60]

Groups and individuals such as the IWA, the BC Federation of Labour, boards of trade in several interior communities affected by the ban, and church groups, including the Anglican House of Bishops and the Board of Evangelism and Social Service of the United Church, had opposed the ban. Although their immediate concern was logging, George Tanaka and Hydese Onotera of the JCCA, with the assistance of Vancouver lawyer T.G. Norris, presented a brief to the cabinet listing the things that Japanese could not do in British Columbia. When the legislature met, Attorney General Wismer proposed to eliminate racial discrimination in government contracts, including employment on crown lands. The legislature unanimously agreed to let Canadians of Japanese origin work on crown timber lands east of the Cascades but rejected Winch's motion to remove all racial discrimination against Japanese. The *Winnipeg Free Press* praised "a remarkable victory" for civil rights that indicated "a deep change in the public thinking of British Columbia" while chastising the province for not enfranchising the Japanese.[61]

The legislature's refusal to withdraw all restrictions on the Japanese reflected lingering concerns about their future role in the economy, especially in fishing. E.T. Kenney, the minister of lands and forests, had many fishermen, both white and Native, in his Skeena constituency. He claimed that the return of the Japanese "would be a detriment to our own people" and to "Indians [who] had never been so prosperous as today because the unfair competition of the Japanese in the fishing industry had been removed." The fisheries posed an embarrassing dilemma for two CCF MLAs, Herbert Gargrave (Mackenzie) and Samuel Guthrie (Cowichan-Newcastle), who also had fishermen constituents. They "sidestepped" the matter by saying that fishermen must decide if Japanese should return to the industry.[62]

From time to time, fishermen in communities such as Ucluelet on the west coast of Vancouver Island, Sunbury on the lower Fraser River, and Pender Harbour on the Sechelt Peninsula expressed opposition to the return of the Japanese. Leaders of the United Fishermen's and Allied Workers Union (UFAWU) did not necessarily agree. Like the IWA, during the early postwar years the UFAWU had Communist leaders who philosophically opposed racial discrimination. "At the convention level," Homer Stevens, a UFAWU organizer, explained, "the differences in opinion resulting with our union range from extreme anti-Japanese discrimination to that of complete co-operation, harmony and treatment of Japanese Canadians as equals and as brother workers." He recalled how a member at Ladner told him, "I'd made up my mind a long time ago that when the first Jap got back into the fishing industry I was going to take my rifle and shoot him. But I've changed my mind. When the first one of them comes back, I'm coming over [to] shoot you." Less dramatically, an organizer at Stuart Island informed headquarters that, if the executive went "down the line too forcefully" in endorsing the return of the Japanese, members might throw them out since most anti-Japanese fishermen were "totally incapable of taking an un-prejudiced or humanitarian point of view." Contrary to what the union leaders thought, the fishing companies were not anxious to have the Japanese return. An executive of the Canadian Fishing Company said that his firm had found it difficult to control the Japanese, and given the bitterness between white and Japanese fishermen their return to the industry might cause "bloodshed."[63]

Coastal MPs had made it clear in 1947 that they did not want the Japanese in the fisheries. Green wanted them permanently banned; Reid reviewed arguments that he had made since entering Parliament in 1930 and reported that "to a man" white fishermen at Steveston had told him "that if the Japanese came back there would be serious trouble." J.L. Gibson, whose main interest was attacking the CCF, suggested that any Japanese who wanted to fish could fish for whitefish in Manitoba and Saskatchewan. Archibald attacked canners and other "large economic interests" and said that turning the industry "over to the fishermen themselves" would "solve the Jap issue." It was not difficult to imagine what white fishermen might do if they controlled the industry.[64]

Ottawa readily acceded to the wishes of the coastal MPs. Early in 1947, Buck Suzuki, a former fisherman and union organizer, who as a Canadian army veteran could go to the coast, sought a fishing licence. The Department of Fisheries told him that the wartime ban was still in effect. Despite the support of Morris Shumitacher, a prominent civil rights lawyer, and Premier Douglas of Saskatchewan, Suzuki got no satisfaction. BC Minister of Fisheries L.H. Eyres had urged Ottawa to deny such licences. Speaking to constituents, Reid accused the CCF of "championing the cause of the B.C. evacuated Japanese" and promised to do all he could "to prevent any

Japanese from getting a license to fish in B.C. waters." When Reid was appointed parliamentary assistant to the minister of fisheries, the Prince Rupert *Daily News* noted his long-term opposition to the Japanese and argued that, despite what the CCF said, some people in the industry thought that it "has been getting along very nicely" since the Japanese left. The Indians of the area especially feared being displaced by the Japanese. Once he had a position of responsibility, Reid became silent on the fisheries issue, possibly because Minister of Justice Ilsley believed that any law denying Japanese the opportunity to acquire fishing licences might be ruled *ultra vires* as a violation of civil rights. At the same time, the JCCA protested the denial of fishing licences as contrary "to democratic principles and the precepts of Canadian citizenship" and sought support from the UFAWU. Because its members were divided, the UFAWU had no clear policy on the return of Japanese. At the Trades and Labour Congress convention in October 1948, a UFAWU delegate warned, "we've got a job to be done" in overcoming "many prejudices" against the Japanese. The convention opposed all manifestations of racial and religious discrimination, a policy warmly endorsed by a Chinese delegate from the UFAWU.[65]

Even though Suzuki and Tanaka of the JCCA emphasized that no more than 200 or 300 Japanese were likely to re-enter the fisheries, they found that most "white fishermen are taking a very hostile attitude." Tanaka had a "very friendly talk" with Guy Williams of the Native Brotherhood about "understanding and co-operation as between Canadian racial minority groups." To ease any return, Tanaka advised Japanese fishermen to join the UFAWU and not accept any "subservient position through the canneries"; he told a UFAWU convention that Japanese wanted "equal pay" because they were "used to the same standard of living as other Canadians." After little adverse comment, delegates unanimously agreed that Japanese fishermen should belong to the UFAWU and not be segregated by area or type of licence. Without specifying the Japanese or any other racial group, the convention endorsed an overall limit on the number of licences to prevent overcrowding. When Ottawa's emergency powers expired on 31 March 1949, Japanese were again eligible to apply for fishing licences, yet they could not automatically enter the industry. In light of a prewar policy of gradually reducing the number of fishing licences issued to Japanese, the federal cabinet decided that the fisheries minister would maintain his discretion in granting licences, but he said that he would not disqualify an applicant merely because he was of the Japanese race.[66]

The press speculated about their return. The Vancouver *Daily Province* expected few because the industry was overcrowded, and it would take them time to catch up with modern technology; the Prince Rupert *Daily News* thought that they would be better off because with unrestricted licences they would have "just as much freedom as have white fishermen." In any case, only about ten Japanese, including Suzuki, took immediate advantage of the opportunity to get licences. By the end of the 1949 season, however, the UFAWU had seventy-five Japanese Canadian members, who represented about 90 percent of the returning fishermen. To avoid conflict with "gangs of white fishermen" who gave some evidence of exercising "terroristic tactics" against returnees at Steveston, company officials encouraged some returnees to reside in Vancouver and to fish only at night. Nevertheless, the UFAWU persuaded fishermen to vote sixty-seven to six to accept Japanese as "brother union members" and treat them "with the same respect as is accorded other fishermen." Hostility quickly faded. The JCCA retained good relations with the UFAWU by advising members not to become indebted to the canners, who allegedly recruited fishermen in the interior and on the Prairies, and not to fish on the lower Fraser, where the industry was crowded.[67] The combination of a leadership that ideologically eschewed racism, a relatively low number of Japanese who returned to the industry, and practical co-operation that eliminated major grievances about keeping to themselves and working too closely with the canners made the return of Japanese to the fisheries relatively smooth. And, of course, the old bogey that many Japanese fishermen were spies for Japan was quite dead.

Before the war, Japanophobes often complained of Japanese penetration of aspects of agriculture. Early in 1949, the Board of Trade in Maple Ridge, an area that had had a significant Japanese population, unanimously warned of "serious friction" unless the government acted "to prevent a return to the undesirable state of affairs existing in Japanese infested districts pre-war." The board was concerned about the Japanese congregating in small areas, working for lower wages, and being socially inassimilable. Unlike earlier counterparts, the resolution got neither much publicity nor much support. Prince Rupert City Council tabled it; the North Vancouver Board of Trade rejected it after several members recommended making every effort to help Japanese who wished to become Canadians. After a hot debate in which some members revisited ancient arguments against the Japanese while others objected to stirring up race hatred, the Langley and District Board of Trade endorsed the Maple Ridge resolution by one vote. That set the stage for the Annual Meeting of the Associated Boards of Trade of the Fraser Valley and Lower Mainland. At a "heated session" there, Maple Ridge members referred to the prewar "infestation" of their district; other delegates, however, denied any "danger of serious friction" and successfully argued that boards of trade "could not uphold democratic principles and favor restrictive measures at the same time."[68]

No one really knew what to expect when Japanese Canadians returned to the coast. Only a handful had been exempt from the evacuation either because they were married to non-Japanese or because they were hospital patients. The first Japanese to return had received a mixed reception even though they were in Canadian army uniforms. With rare exceptions, Canada did not admit Nisei to its Armed Forces but changed its mind slightly early in 1945 when, at the request of the British and Australian armies, which needed Japanese speakers for psychological warfare and as interpreters and translators, the army secretly began recruiting up to 100 Nisei. Many were so Canadianized that their Japanese-language skills were limited. After basic training in Ontario, sixty-one went to the army's Japanese-language school in Vancouver. Fearing demonstrations, the army gave them no publicity before the end of the war and told them to avoid all public gatherings except religious services. When they ventured downtown, one of them reported, "we have been rather surprised to see the indifference with which we are accepted by the people in the streets. Hardly a soul stares at us – perhaps they actually believed what Mr. Mackenzie said in his election campaign." After the war, three of them in uniform attended a Town Meeting of Canada debate on repatriation featuring Austin Harris of the Japanese Repatriation League and Reverend W.H.H. Norman, an instructor at the language school. From the audience, Private Thomas Shoyama denied Harris' claim that Japanese Canadians had not been loyal to the Allies. The commander of the language school reprimanded the soldiers for disobeying orders to be inconspicuous, but that was the only repercussion.[69]

When the Vancouver Technical School required space for returning soldiers, the language school moved to West Vancouver. The municipal council and local newspaper opposed letting Japanese into the municipality until Major General F.F. Worthington, the head of the school, explained the careful "screening" of the students and the importance of their work. The local MP, James Sinclair, sought to move the school, but its work was done, and it closed in June 1946. West Vancouver high school students, however, had welcomed the Japanese students and organized games with them. Nevertheless, Nisei soldiers heard some insulting remarks and on occasion were refused service in a local restaurant and on a bus. When the "rabid anti-Jap" proprietor of the local theatre refused to admit them, hostile high school students and white soldiers threatened violence against the theatre. The Vancouver *News-Herald* observed that "the Japs who are thus serving in the Canadian army" would "do much to mitigate the all-too-prevalent racial antagonism of which so many Canadians are at present guilty." Yet there were some amusing incidents. One Nisei student reported how people were giving them "the once-over and apparently have found out for the first time that Japs [sic] are all black-haired. One of our blonde students was asked whether he was a Jap or not." In short the mixed response to the Nisei soldiers did not provide a useful indicator of possible reaction to the return of a larger number. When Buck Suzuki, who served with British forces in Southeast Asia, returned to Vancouver in 1946 after his discharge, he found that anti-Japanese feeling had "died down considerably" but was difficult to assess because the only Japanese there were veterans or individuals married to non-Japanese who had seen "little or no discrimination."[70]

Canada's reluctance to recruit Nisei for its Armed Forces and the secrecy of their enlistment differed sharply from the practice of the United States, which had drafted Nisei for military service and publicly honoured their heroics. In addition the American Constitution allowed Nisei to challenge their detention, and civil liberties groups funded their court cases. Canadian civil liberties groups, however, appeared to be unwilling to challenge the relocation of the Japanese, and in any case, under the War Measures Act, such a challenge would probably have been pointless. The court challenges in the United States moved slowly. The Supreme Court did not announce its decision in the *Endo* case, that a "loyal American citizen could not be held in a relocation camp against her will," until 18 December 1944. Acting on advice from Western Defence Command, the government had already decided shortly after the 1944 presidential election to lift the exclusion orders. Anticipating that the Supreme Court would rule that native-born Americans had the right to move freely about the nation, the day before the Supreme Court revealed its decision the American government announced that, effective 2 January 1945, loyal Japanese Americans could return freely to the areas from which they had been removed in 1942. Response to their return was mixed. The *Vancouver Sun* reported without comment in December 1945 that Japanese walked "freely about" Seattle streets, and white people paid little attention to them, but there were some violent incidents, particularly in Oregon. By the spring of 1946, however, over 57,000 relocatees had returned to the American Pacific coast, and except for a "few irresponsible individuals" public opinion was "friendly." From time to time, BC editors pointed to the relative ease with which the American Pacific coast accepted the Japanese but did not pursue the implications. As American citizens by birth, American Nisei had been able to vote once they reached their majority, but the Canadian Nisei veterans had never had that right. As George Tanaka wrote in 1946, "we have never seen or marked a ballot slip; it is taboo by law."[71]

That was not the only disability that the veterans faced. In the spring of 1946, some sought to return to the Fraser Valley. Ottawa officials accepted the claim of Mackenzie, the minister of veterans' affairs, that a Japanese could not succeed in agriculture or business because he would be "ostracized" and might even be "the victim of violence." Reid, in whose New Westminster constituency such settlement was likely to take place, even opposed the return of a few First World War veterans since that might be the harbinger of a mass return. Reid did not have to worry as long as Mackenzie had charge of the Veterans Land Act. In 1947, S.A. Cato, a veteran of the First World War, sought to take up a Fraser Valley holding under the act. Prime Minister King, noting how few Japanese veterans there were, was sympathetic, and the BC Command of the Canadian Legion and Cecil Merritt wrote on Cato's behalf. Merritt pointed out that Cato's son, a member of the Royal Canadian Navy, was boarding in Vancouver with a white family and encountered no prejudice. Nevertheless, Mackenzie still had "misgivings" about placing a Japanese veteran at the coast. He explained that "our duty is to grant the assistance of this Act for the purpose of aiding in the veteran's rehabilitation. If my fears are well grounded – and they are shared by others – we should not be acting in the spirit of the legislation by granting Mr. Cato's application." Recognizing that the situation might be changing, he proposed that a three-man committee composed of a Liberal, a Conservative, and a CCF member from British Columbia advise him. There is no evidence of such a committee being set up.[72]

Those Japanese who were caught in the coastal area without a permit went to jail. One who was found in Vancouver in the fall of 1948 was sentenced to a year at hard labour for his "crime." Another succeeded in posing as a Chinese until he was caught stealing. In addition to a jail term for breaking and entering, he was sentenced to six months for being in a prohibited area. In 1945 and 1946, the government issued very few permits for entry to the coast and enforced the time limit strictly. In the fall of 1945, for example, a Nisei man secured a pass to visit his mother who was critically ill in a Vancouver hospital. The thirty-day pass was extended by a week, but even though his mother's condition worsened it was not extended for a second week, and she died two days after he left. By the end of 1946, however, the government was issuing permits for other than strictly humanitarian reasons. There was, for example, the irony of British Columbia considering itself a Christian community but making a Vancouver-born Nisei and his mother and father, a United Church minister, secure permits to attend his ordination at Canadian Memorial Church in Vancouver. The question of university students was complex. In the fall of 1946, in an almost unanimous resolution, the Parliamentary Forum at the University of British Columbia asked the university administration to facilitate the attendance of Japanese Canadian students. When Brooke Claxton, the minister of national defence, inquired about that possibility, Minister of Labour Mitchell said that any applications would have to be referred to the Cabinet Committee on Japanese Problems. In September 1947, the committee agreed to permit students to attend for the academic year. The students – probably fewer than a dozen – reported that students and faculty were "doing their best" for them. For example, after George Tanaka of the JCCA spoke in February 1948 to a meeting sponsored by the Student Christian Movement, a number of sympathetic campus organizations – including the International Relations Club, the Civil Liberties Unions, the LPP Club, the CCF Club, and the Varsity Christian Fellowship – made plans to protest discrimination against the Japanese. Not to be outdone, the Student Liberal Club warned every Liberal MP and MLA and constituency organization in British Columbia that, by discriminating against the Japanese, they were "in danger of lending a factual basis to the claims of the C.C.F and the L.P.P. that the 'Left' alone is the true and only protector of minorities."[73]

The university was not the only place where Japanese were accepted at the coast, at least in small numbers. At Duncan, Occidentals barely noticed a Japanese who attended to some business matters, although Chinese residents expressed concern about the return of the Japanese. Yet those who visited the coast did not always feel welcome. Six members of the Rutland High School soccer team got permits to attend a tournament in Vancouver. One boy described the "funny feeling" of being in his former hometown. The *New Canadian* reported that everyone who visited the coast "came back with the feeling they just hate the place and just don't want to see or hear about the place." Spokesmen for Japanese Canadians repeatedly told the coastal press that few would return from the interior, where they enjoyed "freedom from the feeling they are shunned on racial grounds." When the University of British Columbia branch of the United Nations Association sought information for a proposed booklet on "how to combat race-haters who may oppose the return of the Japanese Canadians to the coast," Tanaka cautioned against any publicity that might primarily argue "the unlikelihood of any large-scale return of the evacuees."[74]

As it became more possible for Japanese to visit the coast, the executive of the JCCA was "thrilled" by favourable comment even in the Fraser Valley. The *Ladner Optimist,* for example, warned against "flying off the handle" and urged "a sincere and serious effort" to resolve the Japanese question "with all-round fairness." A *Surrey Leader* editorial, reprinted by the *Langley Advance* and the Mission *Fraser Valley Record,* asserted that "the Orientals came here against the expressed will of British Columbians, but we must recognize that today's generation has no other home. They are Canadians; there is no road back to the old land for them. We must accept that, not only in good faith, but in a willingness to have these Canadians of Japanese descent contribute their part to the community – in the schools, sports, business and community affairs," though it cautioned against the re-creation of Japanese enclaves.[75]

G.E. Trueman of the Department of Labour, who had much to do with administering the resettlement of Japanese Canadians, wrote in the *New Canadian* in 1948 that, "tragic as was the consequences to many of the participants, there are few who do not realize that the evacuation has proved to be a blessing in disguise. To a great degree the social and economic restrictions that circumscribed them in the old life and limited their endeavour have disappeared; their children can confidently look forward to a life marked by all the freedoms that should be the heritage of every Canadian citizen." Many Japanese Canadians agreed. For some years, they regarded their removal from the BC coast as a "blessing in disguise" since it allowed them to take up new opportunities in parts of Canada where their activities were not restricted. On the tenth anniversary of Pearl Harbor, Toyo Takata told readers of the *New Canadian* that, "whatever may be said against the mass expulsion, there's no denying that the end has been gratifying. We, during the past decade, have gone down to the depth of futility up to the peak of optimism." Similarly, in an editorial commemorating the conclusion of a peace treaty with Japan in 1953, the *New Canadian* observed that, "strangely enough, the evacuation, though representing a blatant example of an extreme racist attitude without precedent in Canadian history, proved to be a boon ... The relocation and dispersal throughout the country ... has widened their economic security and has resulted in the greater acceptance of Japanese Canadians socially." It was still reporting such a sentiment in 1967 as a spokesman for the Vancouver community said, "in many ways this forced disruption was a blessing in disguise. It speeded up integration by preventing a ghetto-like community from developing."[76]

Despite the paucity of opposition, in 1947 there were doubts about the extent to which the provincial government believed that the new Citizenship Act affected the enfranchisement of Asians. The debate over enfranchising the Japanese suggests that cabinet was unaware of shifts in public opinion. The press speculated on conflict within the Special Committee on Elections. One story intimated that a majority favoured enfranchising all Canadians regardless of their ancestry but that cabinet forced government members to backtrack because of "widespread" dissent on the Japanese issue. Since the franchise issue might be "politically embarrassing," the Vancouver *News-Herald* surmised, the government wanted to be able to say that "it isn't a matter of racial prejudice at all – it is an economic matter. The Japanese present an economic threat to the B.C. coast." The seven-member committee was split. W.T. Straith (Coalition-Liberal, Victoria) joined two CCF members, Harold Winch and Herbert Gargrave, in recommending removing all racial barriers to the franchise. Their minority view had considerable support. The New Westminster *British Columbian* admitted that it was probably the best that could be expected given "race prejudices accentuated by the war" but predicted that people would realize that in a democracy "the vote and citizenship are inseparable." The Vancouver *News-Herald* hoped that the government would find the courage to bring its "laws into harmony with our new national citizenship laws" and eliminate all "discriminatory racial regulations." "Why not let everyone, every race, that is, have the vote?" asked the *Ladner Optimist*. "If we are to move towards a greater measure of democracy, we must avoid racial discrimination of all kinds," said the *Marpole-Richmond Review*. The Vancouver *Daily Province* wondered if the Japanese had been "left out" because of racial or economic prejudice. Either, it contended, was "disgraceful" since "Canadians of Japanese blood are as much Canadian citizens as are Hindus or Chinese," and treating them "differently from other Orientals is to make a mockery of the Citizenship Act." Even T.D. Pattullo, who a year earlier had said that he did not believe in enfranchising "Orientals" for economic and ethnological reasons, now said, "all Orientals properly qualified as Canadians should be given the vote."[77]

The bill presented to the legislature did not mention the Japanese. Harold Winch attacked the omission as "not living up to the principles of Christianity, British justice and democracy," contrary to the Atlantic Charter, the Yalta agreement, and Canadian citizenship, and following lines laid down by Hitler and Mussolini. Straith said that all citizens should have the vote; John MacInnis (CCF, Fort George) contrasted British Columbia's "stupid and short-sighted" policies regarding the Japanese with the "enlightened attitude in the United States." Five MLAs, however, opposed enfranchising the Japanese. R.R. Laird (Coalition, Similkameen) said that the war was too close; A.C. Hope (Coalition, Delta) recounted how Japanese fishing vessels had displayed the Japanese flag when Prince and Princess Chichibu visited in 1937. He did not "think you can ever be a good British Columbian if you're ashamed of the Union Jack." He and Byron Johnson (Coalition-Liberal, New Westminster) recalled their constituents' fears of the Japanese after Pearl Harbor as Coalition members called out "Remember Pearl Harbor – Remember Singapore – Remember Hong Kong." The bill extending the vote to Chinese and "East Indians" was a widely accepted "foregone conclusion" and passed without question, but an amendment to enfranchise the Japanese was defeated.[78]

Given favourable press comment, the relative lack of opposition outside sections of the Coalition caucus, and the lobbying efforts of the JCCA, it seemed likely that the legislature would enfranchise Japanese at its spring 1948 session. Nevertheless, when Winch put forward a proposal to enfranchise all Canadian citizens who had been in the province for six months or more, the Elections Act committee rejected it. In the legislature, Attorney General Wismer said that, as long as Japanese could not live on the coast, the house should not deal with their right to vote. Winch did not pursue the issue. The New Westminster *British Columbian* speculated that the government was standing firm against Japanese enfranchisement "because the CCF urges it." At the 1948 session, however, the JCCA, its allies, and Winch were more concerned with the immediate issue of the employment of Japanese on crown timber lands. Indeed, Tanaka told a Victoria reporter after he met Premier Johnson that he was pleased by plans to lift the employment ban, "the first step in the fight for recognition." He promised to return to seek the franchise.[79]

In the meantime, church and civil liberties groups had waged a low-profile campaign to persuade the federal government to enfranchise Japanese. Early in January 1947, as the federal cabinet considered amendments to the Elections Act, St. Laurent, now secretary of state for external affairs, noted the need to study "the present Federal disfranchisement of certain groups of Orientals in Canada" lest it create difficulties at the United Nations. In response to cabinet's request to appoint a subcommittee of its members to examine the matter, King chose Mackenzie to chair it. Given that, its recommendation that the chief electoral officer make "no proposals respecting disqualifications of certain persons on racial grounds" was no surprise. If the matter arose, the committee advised referring it to a proposed parliamentary committee on human rights. The cabinet agreed. At the Special Parliamentary Committee on the Dominion Elections Act in the spring of 1947, MacInnis argued that a principle of the Citizenship Act was that "every person who was a citizen of Canada would have equal rights with all other citizens regardless of race." For the Liberals, Sinclair suggested that once dispersal of the Japanese was complete it might be "possible" to extend the franchise, but he shared Green's doubts of their past loyalties. The elections committee voted ten to six against enfranchising the Japanese in British Columbia. Over the course of the next year, opposition faded. When the special committee discussed it in June 1948, its short debate dealt only with timing. Should the Japanese be enfranchised immediately or only after the orders in council expired on 31 March 1949? Without debate the House of Commons approved the committee's recommendation to wait, but it was clear that the Japanese would be enfranchised within the year. Nevertheless, there was some truth to the Vancouver *News-Herald*'s cynical comment that "the politicians have been reading the by-election returns from British Columbia."[80]

The press in British Columbia suggested that Ottawa's "eminently sensible and just" action provided "a Gilbertian situation if persons of Japanese ancestry were to be allowed to vote in Federal elections but denied a parallel right in the province." "A section of our citizenry which is regarded as Canadian for national purposes," said the *Victoria Daily Times*, "can no longer remain alien in the provincial field." That too was the opinion of Harold Winch, who suggested that the federal action made the provincial position "even more absurd and glaringly unfair." Provincial cabinet ministers refused to comment. So little was happening that the Vancouver *News-Herald* worried that the CCF might be falling "down in its duty of prodding the government" until the "unfortunate" Japanese minority was enfranchised. Midway through the legislative session, Tanaka went to Victoria. The situation for Japanese Canadians at the coast was clearly improving. A year earlier, when an JCCA delegation sought the advice of influential individuals and organizations in Vancouver about its campaign, it was told to let others "carry the ball" since publicity could arouse antagonism. Now Tanaka himself went to Victoria. There he referred to the United Nations Charter and its clauses on human rights and the Canadian Citizenship Act as he lobbied for the end of various discriminatory laws and practices, including ineligibility for the Old Age Pension bonus, exclusion from employment on public works contracts and the professions of law and pharmacy, and of course the right to vote and stand for office. Less than a week after he spoke to Premier Johnson, the premier introduced an amendment to the Provincial Elections Act to enfranchise all racial groups except Doukhobors. As the premier expected, the bill passed "with very little difficulty." In fact, the only reported comment was that of T.A. Love (Coalition, Grand Forks-Greenwood), who said that the Japanese "were becoming accepted citizens in the interior" and had "earned and won their way into positions that represent education and ability and find themselves readily accepted in society."[81]

Most Asians in British Columbia got their first opportunity to go to polls in June 1949 when there were provincial and federal elections within two weeks of each other. At Lillooet, where there were still some Japanese self-relocatees and a few Chinese, Premier Johnson urged them to "take a keen and active interest" in politics and to treat the franchise as a "sacred possession." At Revelstoke, which had a few Japanese settlers, the political parties invited some of them to serve as scrutineers. In Greenwood-Grand Forks, the Coalition organizer claimed that Japanese leaders said the 370 Japanese voters there would support the Coalition candidate, T.A. Love. When Love lost by forty-nine votes, the organizer claimed that, as in Kaslo-Slocan, where the CCF also won, the Japanese Canadians "voted solidly against Coalition." Because of the secret ballot, it is impossible to know how they voted, although the results suggest that Grace MacInnis of the CCF was correct in predicting that Asians would vote for the CCF because it had "forced the vote to be given to them." Provincially and federally, all three major parties advertised in the *New Canadian*. From its Toronto office, it airmailed copies with provincial election advertisements (including some in Japanese) to British Columbia and carried federal election advertisements for candidates in some Toronto constituencies and around Lethbridge. "For the first time we have felt the full force and significance of newspapers during [the] furor of election time," wrote its columnist, Toyo Takata. Finally in 1949, politicians such as H.H. Stevens could address Asian voters as "fellow Canadian citizens."[82] For Japanese Canadians, there was still some unfinished business; they were not quite yet first-class citizens.

6

Beyond Enfranchisement: Seeking Full Justice for Japanese Canadians

> [There are still] many injustices and hardships against Japanese Canadians arising from their forceful removal from British Columbia in 1942.
>
> Harold Hirose, *National JCCA Bulletin*, 7 November 1949

Cancellation of the "repatriation" policy and the cancellation or expiry of the statutes and regulations restricting the movement and activities of Japanese Canadians marked the end of an important phase of their history, but left them short of full citizenship rights. Although a federal royal commission under Justice H.I. Bird examined property losses and some compensation followed, few Japanese Canadians were satisfied. Canada continued to ban immigration from Japan and made it difficult even for individuals with Canadian citizenship or domicile to enter. Moreover, civil liberties groups gradually lost interest in remedying the remaining problems. With discrimination ending and with Japanese Canadians becoming assimilated into Canadian society and participating in organizations in the general community, many Japanese Canadians saw less relevance for the national Japanese Canadian Citizens Association (JCCA), which claimed to speak for all of them. Even the *New Canadian* suggested that the JCCA should concentrate on promoting social activities. Nevertheless, despite problems in raising funds and maintaining the interest of members and potential members, the JCCA sought the repeal of remaining discriminatory laws, redress for wartime property losses, and equality in immigration, mainly to permit family reunification. In seeking changes in immigration regulations, it sometimes worked jointly with Chinese Canadians and continued to co-operate with like-minded groups in defending human rights.[1]

As of 1 April 1949, people of Japanese ancestry could move freely anywhere in Canada, including the BC coast. As JCCA surveys indicated, relatively few, apart from some fishermen, were likely to return, at least in the immediate

"A Good Year!" *New Canadian,* 24 December 1949. The year 1949 certainly was a good one for Japanese Canadians as they finally gained recognition as full Canadian citizens.

future. The *New Canadian* observed that "the average Japanese Canadian in eastern Canada still remembers the mild B.C. climate and the picturesque scenery. But ask him if he is thinking of returning to B.C. and he is likely to reply: 'What for? What will I do there?' And then after a little thought, he may ask: 'I don't want my children to grow up in an atmosphere of unfriendliness that I grew up in, and where opportunities are so limited.'" It later suggested that apprehension about anti-Japanese elements was less a factor than economic considerations, namely that most Japanese Canadians were "happily resettled." Similarly, George Tanaka told Vancouver reporters that Japanese Canadians had "been absorbed into the economy and social life of eastern Canada and have no intention of returning to the B.C. Coast," where they expected to find "discrimination almost as high as before the war."[2]

Nationally, the Nisei could enter any trade or profession for which they had the necessary qualifications. Both men and women joined the Armed Forces during the Korean War, and some received commissions. As the *New Canadian* remarked in 1951, "ancestry is no longer a handicap to the Nisei in offering his services to his country, which is as it should be." Over the next decade or so, the *New Canadian* reported accomplishments such as the first Nisei to join the Royal Canadian Mounted Police, the first queen's counsel, and elections to municipal councils in both British Columbia and Ontario. In 1960 the *New Canadian,* in reporting that Yasushi Sugimoto had been nominated as the Conservative candidate for Grand Forks-Greenwood in the provincial election, observed that "a profound change has occurred in British Columbia, where ironically enough most of the discrimination against Canadians of Oriental background has existed, when a Canadian Chinese represents Vancouver in the House of Commons and a Canadian Japanese becomes the Conservative candidate in the old Boundary riding."[3]

As discrimination faded, Japanese Canadians established settled communities. In Montreal, the most easterly centre with a significant number of Japanese Canadians, the Nisei reported no discrimination. The husband of a woman who arrived there in 1946 found work as an accountant; she resumed her career as a hairdresser. "Here in this cosmopolitan city," she wrote in an essay prepared in 1971 for a sociology course, "I found a world of difference in attitude towards us ... There was no racial prejudice." The couple regained their "self respect, our dignity as Japanese Canadians." Her five children all had professional careers and "never having known discrimination" saw "racial origin as incidental." Contemporary accounts confirm that. For example, George Tamaki graduated from Dalhousie Law School in 1941 but was not admitted to the Nova Scotia bar because he was a Japanese Canadian. After postgraduate studies at the University of Montreal and working for five years as an adviser to the Government of Saskatchewan, he was admitted to the Quebec bar and joined one of Montreal's most prestigious law firms. Although Montreal's Japanese Canadian community had some internal difficulties coping with an influx of people from the "ghost towns" in 1947, by 1952 it was a stable community.[4]

In smaller Ontario cities too, Japanese Canadians established stable communities. In Fort William, the Great Lakes Lumber Company was their major employer; by 1949 many were buying homes, and a few opened small businesses. In London, although the University of Western Ontario denied a Nisei admission to its medical school because it feared that Asian graduates would have trouble getting internships, the approximately 150 permanent Japanese residents found that initial hostility "was gradually overcome" as they became "a tangible part of its civic society" and had no problem finding employment. In Chatham, which was once hostile to relocatees despite the need for farm labour, the Imperial Order of the Daughters of the Empire chapter admitted as a member an Issei woman who had recently become a Canadian citizen. The largest concentration of Japanese in Canada was in Toronto. At first they tended to settle in the same area, but by 1946 they were buying homes throughout the city and seemed well integrated except at prayer. Both the United and the Anglican Churches had separate Japanese and Caucasian congregations and services even though they might share the same building. Occupationally, the new arrivals found employment in once-closed fields. For example, in 1946 the Toronto Board of Education hired a Japanese Canadian to teach in a public school. Farther west, in Winnipeg, many Japanese Canadians attended their own church services and had some Nisei social and sports activities but otherwise acted much as individuals and integrated with society as a whole. They enjoyed an "almost complete lack of discrimination," rapidly assimilated into the larger community, and bought better homes or improved old ones. Other Manitoba Japanese bought farms. By 1953 members of the Manitoba JCCA expected "a stable future" in the province despite its climate. Two years earlier the Alberta JCCA reported that time had been a "great soother and healer"; older Albertans and new Japanese Canadian settlers had accepted each other and were slowly but surely assimilating socially.[5]

Many of the Japanese Canadians who remained in New Denver and the Slocan Valley were elderly; the *New Canadian* speculated that New Denver had approximately half the elderly Issei in Canada. Yet some of the younger generation stayed. By 1949 they were well established in Kootenay communities, where they played an active role, whether as Queen of the Arrow Lakes at the Dominion Day celebrations in Nakusp, joining service clubs, or setting up businesses, including logging companies, sawmills, farms, retail stores, or professional medical and dental practices. Given the limited economic opportunities in small communities such as New Denver, Greenwood, Grand Forks, and Slocan City, by the mid-1950s some younger Nisei left. The Revelstoke branch of the JCCA complained of "Vancouveritis," a malady whose symptoms were "itchy feet and a desire for the coast climate." Once established elsewhere, the Nisei often sent for their parents. In 1952 the provincial Social Welfare Branch reported a rapid decrease in the number of Japanese in the Slocan Valley.[6]

Nevertheless, at least one former "ghost town," Greenwood, retained a significant Japanese Canadian population; in 1963 it claimed to have more Japanese Canadians per capita than any other city in Canada. Japanese Canadians there worked in a variety of occupations, including the skilled trades and the professions. In Kelowna, some prewar Japanese settlers had become "very wealthy" orchard owners. Both older settlers and their children and wartime arrivals established small businesses or, experiencing no discrimination in employment, found work in stores and offices. When the provincial JCCA met there in 1951, an apologetic Mayor W.B. Hughes-Games recalled a sign nine years earlier that said Japanese were not welcome. He explained: "We were scared because we thought a little Japan would be formed here in Kelowna. I got to admire you people, you are all sincere people and everyone co-operated so splendidly and now the idea of a little Japan is gone." Similarly, in Kamloops, which had also opposed the entry of Japanese, the mayor welcomed the JCCA by saying that "it has been a pleasure to know the Japanese people." Local politicians solicited their votes. The Conservative candidate in the 1952 provincial election expected to win because Dr. Banno was arranging to translate his campaign material into Japanese and circulate it.[7]

Yet delegates to the provincial JCCA convention in January 1950 presented scattered evidence of discrimination. The Grand Forks delegate said that, despite the efforts of Japanese Canadians and their *hakujin* (Caucasian) friends, discrimination continued, but no explanation was recorded. The Okanagan Centre delegate described how his members joined Occidental organizations so that, when discrimination arose, as in the Canadian Legion, they could "squash it" on the spot. At nearby Winfield, the local branch of the International Order of Foresters invited Japanese Canadians to join but had to get its international headquarters in the United States to remove a restrictive clause against Asians.[8]

Although Toyo Takata wrote in the *New Canadian* that inequalities in pay and quibbles about the "Oriental standard of living ... went with the war for us," some discrimination in employment remained. A Kamloops Nisei who sought to article as a chartered accountant was told "in a very subtle way that because of his race it would be rather difficult to place him." Some coastal pulp mills would not employ Japanese. When three Japanese Canadians applied for work in an interior woodworking plant, "race-baiters" fomented a "rumor that a large influx of cheap Oriental labor would displace white labor." The International Woodworkers of America (IWA) immediately advised other workers of the situation. According to the *BC Lumber Worker,* when Japanese workers joined the union, their fellow workers accepted them "on terms of equality." When the Tagami Brothers sought to bid on a parcel of crown timber land in the Slocan Valley in 1951, some of their Caucasian friends urged them not to bid on that parcel since old-time residents wanted it. Determined to demonstrate that they had equal rights, they refused to back down. In the end, their competitor did not submit a bid, and they secured the right to log the land.[9]

The winter of 1949-50, however, was not a good time to return to the coast. An easing of the wartime "boom" economy created an "alarming" degree of unemployment; approximately 8 percent of the labour force in the Lower Mainland was out of work. Not all Vancouver employers would hire Japanese Canadians. The Federation of Telephone Workers asked members if they would work with Chinese or Japanese girls. Most replied negatively; some said that they would quit rather than work with them, but others would welcome them. In any case, the telephone company had no policy on hiring Chinese or Japanese but did not employ any as operators. Even well-qualified automobile mechanics had trouble getting jobs in garages, and not all sawmills employed Japanese. In the summer of 1951, however, the provincial forest service hired a Nisei student as a timber cruiser, and that fall the Vancouver School Board appointed a Nisei teacher. A year later Prince Rupert did the same. Delegates to the provincial JCCA convention early in 1953 claimed that there was no "prejudice as a carry over from the war."[10]

British Columbia was not the only site of discrimination. A Toronto landlord refused to renew the release of a Caucasian woman unless her Japanese Canadian roommate left. Two Japanese Canadians graduated from the University of Toronto with degrees in chemical engineering, but only they and two Jewish classmates could not get suitable employment immediately after graduation. Thus, the JCCA lobbied for a Fair Employment Practice Act in British Columbia and participated in a successful campaign for such a law in Ontario and in the legal challenge to restrictive covenants forbidding the sale or transfer of a property to Asians, Jews, or blacks. It participated in a joint labour institute on race relations in Vancouver that revealed many examples of discrimination. Nevertheless, the *New Canadian* took comfort because problems of racial and religious bias were now "openly regarded as bad."[11]

The Japanese returned slowly to the Vancouver area. By the end of 1949, about half of the approximately 300 there were students either at the University of British Columbia or in various technical and other schools, including St. Paul's Hospital nurses training school. At a meeting to discuss forming a Vancouver branch of the JCCA, the twenty or so individuals present reported that with limited exceptions they were "being accepted as fellow citizens." Occidentals, for example, attended a Valentine's Day dance sponsored by the JCCA. A few merchants returned to Powell Street, but returnees with funds to buy houses did so in various parts of the city, though restrictive covenants still denied them access to some wealthier neighbourhoods. Despite conflicting reports about employment opportunities, the movement back to the coast continued, particularly from the interior. The *New Canadian* also received change of address notices from subscribers who were moving from eastern Canada to the Lower Mainland. Recognizing that by 1952 approximately 2,000 Japanese Canadians lived in Greater Vancouver, including a number who were fishing at Steveston, the JCCA moved its provincial headquarters to Vancouver from Greenwood. The movement to the coast largely ended by 1955, but the population had grown sufficiently to permit the reopening of institutions such as the Anglican Mission and the Japanese Language School. The Anglican Mission, however, had a language problem; older congregants were uncomfortable in English, while younger ones were not familiar with Japanese. Many students at the Japanese Language School were Occidentals who wanted to learn the language for trade purposes. At Steveston the United Church re-established a separate Japanese congregation but in 1953 merged it with its regular congregation at a ceremony attended by church and municipal leaders and announced that henceforth it would hold a common service in English.[12]

Some Japanese returned to the Fraser Valley and re-entered the berry-growing business. Whereas before the war many berry farms were north of the river, the returnees tended to settle on its south side, where land was cheaper, since the only access to the Vancouver market was via a toll bridge or a ferry. Fishing, however, was the main industry to draw Japanese Canadians back to the coast. As explained earlier, both the JCCA and the United Fishermen's and Allied Workers Union (UFAWU) expected some conflict. The 1949 fishing season was a good one, but Japanese fishermen, who had been out of the industry for eight years, found that methods had improved, and white fishermen had used wartime profits to buy better boats and equipment. Nevertheless, the Japanese who operated about twenty-five boats on the Fraser River that season enjoyed good relations with other fishermen, although a rumour that the canneries had invited 250-300 Japanese Canadian fishermen and their families to settle on the coast drew an immediate UFAWU protest. Some canners went to the interior to recruit fishermen but without much success. Indicative of changed opinions in the province, the *Vancouver Sun,* while warning that a large-scale return could "defeat one of the purposes of which the restrictions were imposed in the first place," suggested that if the Japanese re-established "themselves satisfactorily" they might "be allowed to settle down in their new environment and make the most of their new opportunities." Aware of the tenuous relationship with the UFAWU, the JCCA urged members to be careful since the interest-free loans offered by canners were demand notes supported by liens on the boats and equipment. It advised fishermen to join the union and attempt to maintain a standard of living equal to that of other Canadians. In cases of local hostility, the UFAWU made it clear that it would "not tolerate racial strife among its members." Japanese Canadians became active participants in the union. For example, early in 1952, thirty-nine of them were in a 186-member UFAWU delegation that went to Victoria to press for the inclusion of fishermen in the Workmen's Compensation scheme. The number of Japanese fishermen gradually rose but not by the numbers suggested in rumours. Some created a boom for builders of small boats by buying their own boats. A number of women worked in the canneries. By 1957 approximately 1,500 Japanese Canadians resided at Steveston. Most Nisei spoke English; Mitch Mori, a storekeeper, reported a steady decline in sales of Japanese goods. In the early days of the return, some Japanese shops suffered broken windows, but ill feeling and discrimination soon faded. Japanese and white children played with each other, and there was some intermarriage. In 1950, when some Japanese fishermen returned to the up-coast grounds, especially on the Skeena River, Indians were concerned, but the JCCA assured the UFAWU and the Native Brotherhood that Japanese Canadian fishermen would not accept gear or boats that the companies had taken from other fishermen unless they knew why it had been taken. That forestalled trouble. Meanwhile,

Tom Reid (Liberal, New Westminster) turned his attention to the need to conserve the deep-sea fisheries from fishermen from Japan, who, he claimed, had "no sense of conservation of fish."[13]

THE CANADIAN CITIZENSHIP ACT, Canada's subscription to the United Nations Charter and to the Universal Declaration of Human Rights, and enfranchisement still did not give Japanese Canadians in British Columbia full citizenship rights. In its 1949 brief to the provincial government, the JCCA requested the repeal of "all provincial laws that discriminate against Canadian Japanese and render invalid all regulations and conditions." Examples abounded. For instance, in April 1949 the Department of Public Works still honoured the old clause that no Asian might be employed directly or indirectly on government contracts. A Nisei girl who answered an advertisement for student nurses at the Provincial Mental Hospital was told that the civil service did not hire "Asiatics." Sometimes the administration of such laws was not clear. For example, a resident of Grand Forks received a log scaler's licence, but the district forester asked him to return it because his name was not on the provincial voters' list. A JCCA protest revealed that the district forester was misinformed. In any case, such misunderstandings became largely moot as the legislature, by enfranchising Japanese, removed many other disabilities, such as the right to vote for school trustees or for local water districts. By an order in council, the cabinet repealed restrictions on the employment of Chinese and Japanese on public works and contracts but did not apply it retroactively to old contracts. And Asians who were not Canadian citizens were still subject to laws affecting all aliens. The law denying Japanese licences to operate salmon salteries also remained on the statute books. The JCCA was also concerned about elderly Japanese since British Columbia denied them the ten dollars per month of old age pension bonus and would not admit them to the Provincial Home for the Aged. Here too the government seemed to be anxious to make amends. In July it informed the JCCA that effective 1 August 1949 Japanese pensioners, except for the special cases in New Denver and Slocan covered by a dominion-provincial agreement, would be eligible for the ten dollars a month cost-of-living bonus on the same terms as other individuals.[14]

Nevertheless, continued examples of discrimination encouraged the national JCCA to join others to lobby for the inclusion of a Bill of Human Rights in the Canadian Constitution so that "no group of Canadian citizens will again be compelled to undergo similar experiences, or their honour be questioned." In appearing before the Senate Committee on Human Rights and Fundamental Freedoms in 1950, George Tanaka explained that "our most important work ... is still before us, and we are very, very anxious to work with other groups and individuals towards creating a greater citizenship." Tanaka was surprised, however, when, after he explained the discriminatory measures still affecting Japanese Canadians, some senators said that they had been unaware of such problems. The St. Laurent government did not act, so the JCCA continued to participate in delegations that went to Ottawa seeking a Bill of Rights and joined other bodies interested in human rights in sponsoring the publication of a pamphlet, *They Made Democracy Work,* a history of the CCJC. The CCJC argued that its history showed "how individual citizens, by banding together, managed to change the course of events in a very significant way. They made democracy work because they cared enough to make it work." The JCCA also urged the press not to use the derogatory term "Jap" in headlines and complained to Departments of Education about the word *Jap* in textbooks in Alberta and Ontario. In British Columbia, the JCCA joined other groups in seeking a provincial Bill of Rights and a Fair Employment Practices Commission.[15]

Gradually, racist sentiments were abating. In his memoirs, former provincial politician and radio hot-liner Rafe Mair tells of his experience as president of Vancouver's Quilchena Golf Club in the early 1960s. The club accepted Ken Lee as a member before realizing that he was Chinese. Apparently believing that the club had lowered its racial barriers, several Japanese Canadians applied for membership. As Mair recalls, "all hell broke loose." Before the special general meeting called to deal with the situation, two lady members called him. One, an older lady, said that if any "Chinks" or "Japs" were allowed into the club she and forty of her friends would resign; the second, a younger woman, said that if her Japanese friends could not join she and forty of her friends would quit. Silence followed what Mair called his "barnburner of a speech on civil rights" to the crowded meeting. Then a member who had been a prisoner of the Japanese during the war asked, "When are you going to cover that horrible ditch on the seventh and eighteenth holes?" That broke the tension; the club admitted both Chinese and Japanese, and no one quit.[16]

When relocatees went to the interior or beyond in 1942, most could take only very basic personal property: clothing, bedding, and kitchen utensils that would fit into the standard 150-pound baggage allowance permitted by the railways. Some men were even less well off: those sent to work camps could only take clothing and blankets, while internees could take only the clothes that they were wearing, a towel, and a toothbrush. Individuals who owned motor vehicles, cameras, and radios had already had to surrender them. Some sold off personal property, usually at fire-sale prices. Others, expecting to return once the military emergency ended, simply left chattels in their homes or barns and locked doors and windows as they left. Some stored goods with non-Japanese friends or relied on the custodian of enemy property to care for them. Vandals, however, gained access to some storage facilities and so mixed up the property they did not steal that it became impossible to identify its owners. Then in 1943, because vacant houses and farms were deteriorating, the federal government decided to sell them, often by public auction without reserve, thus creating a circumstance in which "the only willing person was the buyer." Given the circumstances and the haste with which everything was done, it was not surprising that the Japanese suffered many losses.[17]

A group calling itself the Japanese Property Owners Association filed a test case against the sale but lost. In any event, the judgment was of academic interest only; the legal process moved so slowly that by the time the decision was announced most of the property had been sold. Individual Japanese Canadians such as Yasuzo Shoji, a veteran of the Canadian Expeditionary Force who got a cheque for $39.32 for his nineteen-acre poultry farm at Whonnock in the Fraser Valley, let the press know of their discontent; former property owners residing in Toronto undertook a survey to demonstrate their losses. Until the repatriation issue was settled, however, compensation for property losses was of secondary interest to the JCCA and the CCJC. Nevertheless, as early as January 1946, the JCCA was thinking of using the public sympathy generated by the campaign against repatriation "to swing in with the property business." That summer the Prime Minister's Office received a large number of mimeographed letters from Japanese persons setting out "almost every possible type of loss sustained through movement" from their homes. In the fall of 1946, the Japanese Canadian Committee for Democracy circulated a survey on property losses. The *New Canadian* expected it to be effective in persuading the government and the public "that the process of evacuation entailed losses extensive and serious enough to justify the establishment of a claims commission."[18]

Not all British Columbians agreed with compensation. In commenting on Shoji's case, R.A. McLellan, the editor of the New Westminster *British Columbian,* noted that Shoji had made no payments on his property since 1939, and because the farm appeared to be uneconomic there seemed "to be no justification for concluding that he was subjected to injustice by reason of his nationality." MP G.A. Cruickshank, who was anxious to have veterans take over former Japanese berry farms, complained of "a group of publishers and professors in the East and some in Vancouver, who were not acquainted with the Jap problem in BC" taking up the issue.[19]

Cabinet was aware of a problem. The press release announcing the end of "repatriation" also asserted that property had been sold at a fair market price, but to ensure fair treatment the government would remedy any demonstrated injustices. A few weeks later Secretary of State Colin Gibson told Parliament that the government contemplated having a commission determine whether "the valuations put on by the government or the valuations put on by the Japanese are current." Over the next few months, cabinet reviewed the kinds of claims to be considered and the setting up of a commission. After a "lively discussion," the Cabinet Committee on Japanese Questions recommended having a commissioner investigate the claims of Japanese who were resident in Canada at the date of its appointment – that is, those who had not been "repatriated." It took time to find a suitable judge and determine the details.[20]

Throughout Canada there was sympathy for property losses. Even before the CCJC began its campaign, the Ontario Older Boys' Parliament, a United Church youth group, passed a resolution deploring the confiscation of property. Similarly, the Canadian Council of Churches and the General Council of the United Church asked the government to provide adequate restitution; District "D" of the Canadian Legion, meeting in Toronto, called for a review of the property situation to ensure that "no Canadian innocents" were deprived of their rights. Newspapers such as the *Toronto Daily Star* referred to the "shocking manner" in which property had been "sold for a song" and urged the government to act quickly and make "proper restitution to these people who have suffered so grievously from racial prejudice." The *Calgary Herald*, using evidence from the CCJC, described "the treatment of Japanese-Canadians by a so-called Liberal government" as "nothing short of disgraceful" and equated the "ridiculously low" selling prices with robbery. Less dramatically, the *Saskatoon Star-Phoenix* said that the government should appoint a commission to compensate Japanese Canadians if the custodian had not taken proper care of their property. A small group of Caucasians in Lethbridge encouraged people to write to their MP and got the local newspaper, radio station, and clergy to publicize the property issue.[21]

Nevertheless, the public was less interested in property than in repatriation, so instead of being a "central player within the Canadian human rights community" the CCJC became a small committee concerned entirely with property rights. It urged compensation at least at the level provided by the United States to its Japanese residents. Although Japanese Americans suffered from sales at fire sale prices, from a lack of resources to pay for mortgages, taxes, or insurance, or from guardians who had not properly cared for property, the government had generally not sold it. *Nisei Affairs* described the Canadian losses, including sentimental treasures, as "an inflicted loss, unjustified, for which restitution we lean heavily on a generous interpretation of the Prime Minister's promise 'to remedy,'" but it warned readers to be honest in their claims.[22]

While cabinet debated how to deal with claims, in May and June 1947 the Public Accounts Committee of the House of Commons investigated the handling of Japanese property and heard testimony from officials from the custodian's office and from a CCJC delegation. The many injustices revealed by this inquiry and a sympathetic press drew public attention to the property question. The Toronto *Globe and Mail*, calling it "one of the most shameful episodes in Canadian history," implied that "the government had deliberately cheated and asked why "so much of the Japanese property was got rid of before the Custodian was given charge of it." Like many other journals, it was particularly shocked by the difference in values paid by the Soldiers Settlement Board to the custodian for Fraser Valley farmland and the amounts that the board's successor, the Veterans Land Act, charged veterans for it. That naturally angered Ian Mackenzie, the minister of veterans' affairs. He attacked the *Globe and Mail*'s editor for making "vile, foul, malicious, meretricious statements" but accepted the paper's reply that it was not an attack on him. Without using words such as "cheating," the other major Toronto dailies agreed with the thrust of the *Globe and Mail*'s attack. The *Evening Telegram* argued that if Japanese property owners were entitled to compensation, they were "entitled to receive the full value of their lands." Until restitution was made, argued the *Toronto Daily Star,* "the wrong done to Japanese Canadians will remain a blot on this country," an "injustice" to Japanese Canadians, and "a challenge to the principles of democratic society." The Montreal *Gazette* dismissed Mackenzie's "fuss and bluster" but was concerned more about the government profiting from selling land to veterans than about Japanese Canadian losses. Other journals simply wanted justice for Japanese Canadians.[23]

BC newspapers also recognized an injustice. The Victoria *Daily Colonist* declared that British Columbians only wanted justice to "be done in connection with their legal holdings." The *Vancouver Sun* saw an "open and shut case"; the government had "the plain duty to pay the losses incurred through no fault of the victims." Its outspoken columnist, Elmore Philpott, said that Canada should "pay proper compensation for the barefaced robbery of these people." While agreeing with the need for compensation, the Vancouver *News-Herald* suggested "that early in the war with Japan, somebody high in official circles at Ottawa had said: 'Let's sell these Japanese boys out fast while we have a chance, so they won't get a chance in B.C. again.'"[24]

So many church and other interested groups wrote to the prime minister that his secretary drafted a form letter indicating that the government was actively considering "methods of dealing with the claim for compensation that persons of Japanese origin may in certain cases wish to make." Finally, in July 1947, the government announced that Justice H.I. Bird would act as a royal commissioner to investigate claims. His frame of reference, probably inspired by advice from the Department of Finance, limited him to recommending compensation only where the custodian failed to act with reasonable care. Those who had called for justice in property claims joined a chorus in calling for an extension of the commission's scope; some noted how the United States seemed to be more generous. The *Vancouver Sun* doubted that Bird would allow the rumoured $5 million claim that the Japanese were seeking and attacked a *Time* magazine report that the government "confiscated" Japanese property and "paid [Japanese] only a small percentage of what the buildings were worth." Nevertheless, as it awaited Bird's report, it admitted that the Japanese were "most certainly ... entitled to every penny that can be proven. They should not suffer through negligent disposal of their assets."[25]

Andrew Brewin of the CCJC explained to the JCCA that the "losses were not a result of exercise of lack of care by the Custodian" but arose from the government's evacuation policy. At its founding convention, the JCCA debated whether to accept Bird's terms of reference or to boycott the commission. On Brewin's advice that a boycott would mean "taking a chance" and require 100 percent unity among claimants, an unlikely possibility, the JCCA asked only that the terms be extended since "a broad means of restitution" for economic losses was necessary to provide the "simple British justice and fair play promised to the Japanese Canadian evacuees." Cabinet widened the terms slightly to free claimants of the need to prove the custodian's negligence. In his history of the redress movement, Roy Miki implies that what "satisfied the CCJC" did not bode well for people who were expecting a broader range of compensation.[26]

Some British Columbians had scant sympathy for any adjustment in the compensation and complained of inflated claims. "After what the Japs did to our men at Hong Kong," the *North Shore Press* said, "it seems a bit strange to read that some people in this country are worrying about the amount realized from the sale of Jap property." An unrepentant Tom Reid told constituents that Conservatives, "aided and abetted by the CCF," and "a group of eastern lawyers are inciting Japanese to demand re-appraisal of their land in B.C. bought by the government at full land values" to hold for veterans. Yet as Justice Bird or one of his subcommissioners visited cities where a significant number of residents had claims, some editors called for the government to rectify any injustices arising from its handling of Japanese property. The *Vernon News* remarked that spectators saw how "injustice had been done." As hearings continued, the New Westminster *British Columbian* defended the "herding" of the Japanese away from the coast in 1942 as a "defensive measure" that might "have saved the Fraser Valley Japanese from unpleasant experiences" and the "forced sale" of their land and equipment as necessary to prevent its deterioration. Nevertheless, it asserted, "it was always assumed that ... they would be given at least bare justice ... Canadians in general will surely endorse measures to rectify this wrong as far as that may be possible."[27]

As the hearings progressed, Justice Bird hastened a slow process by allocating compensation through a sampling technique rather than by dealing with individual claims. On Brewin's advice, the CCJC reluctantly recommended that claimants accept the proposal, "with the prospect of early payment," for refusing it would lead to "heavy expense and delay, and probably a lower overall recovery." Not every claimant agreed, but the JCCA, after receiving further advice that a public campaign on the claims issue "would likely do more harm than good," recommended accepting Bird's offers even though the average return would probably be only 56 percent of the claimants' estimates of the fair market value of their property. That decision, as Roy Miki has documented, caused dissension within the Japanese Canadian community but let Bird complete his recommendations.[28]

Bird submitted his report in mid-April 1950, but not until mid-June, after concerned departments examined it, did the government release his report on 1,434 claims. Bird concluded that, despite heavy responsibilities and an "atmosphere of public hysteria induced by war," the custodian's office had "substantially succeeded" in administering and selling property "with due regard to the owners' interest." He believed that the custodian had secured fair market prices for property in Vancouver but recommended reimbursing owners for costs of the sales that had reduced their returns. Because "circumstances" had not permitted the custodian to secure fair market value for the widely scattered rural properties, he recommended giving their former owners an additional 10 percent of the selling price plus reimbursement of sale costs. As for the 741 parcels of land sold to the Veterans Land Act, Bird recommended increasing the payments to former owners by 80 percent overall. He found that the custodian had largely sold fishing boats at fair market value but proposed compensation for abnormal deterioration between the time they had been surrendered to the navy in December 1942 and their actual sale. Despite difficulties in appraising the value of nets and gear, Bird proposed as "rough justice" a 25 percent increase over the actual selling price, the same average he used for motor vehicles. In the case of missing goods, he used the average price for similar goods as compensation. As for the complicated issue of personal property, Bird rejected claims for goodwill, for goods that had not been declared in 1942 or transferred to the custodian, and a few specific cases. He found that many claimants had not accounted for depreciation in valuing lost property, but he recognized that some property had been pilfered while in the custodian's control. He conceded that his method was not satisfactory but called it "the only practical approach" to calculate fair market values. After considering the report for over a month, cabinet approved the distribution of payments recommended by Bird.[29]

The response, as measured by the mainstream press, was muted. The main interest was the $1,222,829 or total claim in which about 1,200 individuals would share. In British Columbia, neither the Victoria *Daily Colonist* nor the Vancouver *News-Herald* reported the release of the commission's findings; the Vancouver *Daily Province* provided a fairly detailed account of the highlights but made no editorial comment. Elsewhere most newspapers simply provided short wire service reports, if they reported it at all. Editors who did comment were generally favourable. The *Vancouver Sun,* in an editorial titled "Paid in Full," was satisfied with the validation of its earlier comment that the government had "the plain duty to pay the losses incurred through no fault of the victims." In a similar but more sympathetic vein, the *Toronto Daily Star* observed that "what is tardily being done cannot completely cover the suffering and loss involved in Canada's treatment of her Japanese, but it is at least a commendable effort to clear the country's name in the matter of property seizures." The Toronto *Globe and Mail,* after a headline announced that Ottawa would be paying $1,222,829 in "conscience money," suggested that the award would correct "to a large extent" the "grave injustice" done to Japanese Canadian property owners in the Fraser Valley, but overall, it argued, this "measure of restitution" inadequately compensated the victims partly because many losses occurred before the custodian took over. Those, however, were details. "The undying wrong of this episode," it declared, "is the fact that it happened at all," that the government should not have permanently disposed of the property. While satisfied that the losses had been largely repaid, the *Victoria Daily Times* grudgingly opined that "they may write 'finished' to that unhappy chapter and reflect that they were spared the total loss – of life, health, or property – that was the fate of so many in all lands as a result of the conflict."[30]

Not all Japanese Canadians or their friends agreed that the chapter was "finished." The *New Canadian* was gratified that the government intended to honour the awards but complained that its limited terms of reference meant that the report fell "far short of the full and just compensation to which Japanese Canadians are entitled." The CCJC twice complained that Bird's failure to allow interest payments on the difference between the selling price and fair market value was "absolutely inconsistent with the universal practice in compensation cases." The *New Canadian* disputed Prime Minister St. Laurent's claim that the awards were "fair and just" and that "in carrying out the recommendations of Mr. Justice Bird we feel we have discharged our obligations both to the Japanese Canadians and to the general public."[31]

That it had discharged its obligations remained the government's stock answer when a new Toronto-based group, the Evacuation Losses Compensation Committee of Japanese Canadian Citizens, and especially H. Kagetsu raised the issue. Kagetsu, whose father, Eikichi Kagetsu, had owned the Deep Bay Logging Company and its timber limits and property in North Vancouver, claimed that he had received only about 10 percent of its value in compensation. Despite his own interests, in soliciting the support of opposition MPs, Kagetsu declared that his organization was as much concerned with "small losses as ... large." John Diefenbaker promised to raise the matter in Parliament, but private conversations revealed that the ministers concerned would not reopen the issue. Through Brewin and Colin Cameron (CCF, Nanaimo), the JCCA contacted J.W. Pickersgill, the secretary of state, who "in very clear and emphatic tones" said that the government "had done all that was required and all it intended to do in respect to evacuation losses when it paid the amounts" awarded by Bird. Although Brewin and Angus MacInnis (CCF, Vancouver East) saw little hope of reconsideration, MacInnis thought that publicity could be useful and raised the case of Kagetsu and others in

Parliament. Pickersgill was firm; Bird's judgment would not be reviewed.[32]

With such apparent finality and an improving economy, the JCCA's "interest in a 'just and fair' settlement" waned even though in 1960 CCF MP Erhart Regier briefly referred to the property that had been "wrongly taken away" from Japanese Canadians. Many Japanese Canadians just wanted to forget the past. In reporting on a visit to Greenwood in 1954, the *New Canadian* found that, when "queried about their forced migration from their former homes, the response was always the same: 'We try not to think about it. At first we felt that a great injustice had been done. Canada was our home, we worked hard and obeyed the law, yet we were treated as if we had done something wrong.' Then the smiles would return, 'It is all over now and we try not to think of those years again. We are happy here.'" A quarter century later, however, younger Japanese Canadians began to recover their people's past, revived the property issue, and in 1988 secured a redress settlement.[33]

When Mackenzie King outlined a general immigration policy in 1947, he repeated his statement of 1944, namely that "in the years after the war the immigration of Japanese should not be permitted" but indicated that some future Parliament could remove the ban. King worried about the possible embarrassment at the United Nations arising from a policy of permanent exclusion and the possibility that such a policy might lead people in Japan to unite with Russia in resenting Canada.[34]

One of the few editors to remark on the Japanese aspect of the new Asian immigration policy was Georges-Henri Dagneau of Quebec City's *L'Action catholique*. While not favouring massive Japanese immigration and explaining that discrimination against the Japanese was possible because Japan had been defeated, his concern was morality lest exclusion put the Japanese in the same painful position as the Chinese in Canada: that is, they could not have their wives with them. The situations, of course, were not the same; most Japanese immigrants had formed families in Canada before the war. Nationally, the Trades and Labour Congress favoured restrictions on Japanese immigration, but its spokesman was Percy Bengough, a founder of the Asiatic Exclusion League in Vancouver in 1921. In 1947 he told a Senate Standing Committee on Immigration and Labour, "on the Pacific coast we had unions in which Japanese were members and we got on very well with them, but the general picture and the fact that they could not be assimilated certainly showed that we should have restrictions in the future."[35]

British Columbians, who were most likely to be affected by Japanese immigration, said little about the 1947 announcement. Except for Tom Reid and Howard Green, they did not expect the government to change the policy. Indeed, E. Davie Fulton said that the immigration problem "has now been settled." A few editors suggested that Japanese who desired "to become good citizens" and "shoulder their responsibilities as Canadians" could be admitted, but most commentators did not want immigrants from Japan. This sentiment was vividly expressed when, under a banner headline, "Japs Want to Return to Vancouver from Japan: Mass Movement Attempt Likely," the *Vancouver Sun* reported that about 2,500 Canadian-born Japanese, who went to Japan in 1946 under the "Voluntary Repatriation" scheme, wanted to return. It complained of "a new invasion" by individuals who had "merely got an all-expense trip across the Pacific through the generosity of the Canadian Government." This seemed to be only a sensationalist story, but in 1949, when Gordon Sinclair, a Toronto reporter, filed a report from Tokyo that 3,200 Japanese Canadians sought to return, the *Sun* assumed that all were repatriates. It had no sympathy for people who had thought that "Japan would be more congenial" but now believed that Canada was running a "shuttle service."[36]

The first concerns of the JCCA, however, were the estimated 1,692 Japanese Canadians "stranded" in Japan when war broke out who wished to rejoin their families in Canada. Before E.H. Norman returned to Tokyo as Canada's representative in occupied Japan, the Department of External Affairs advised him that, until policy was determined, he should not assist Canadians of Japanese race who wished to return but should refer their inquiries to Ottawa. Some individuals had already applied to return through the United Kingdom liaison mission, then acting for Canada. The department realized that the Canadian born and Japanese nationals or naturalized Canadians with legal domicile in Canada had the right to return, but Hume Wrong of the department recommended against assisting them to secure exit permits, buy passage, or get or renew passports except in special cases such as individuals with family in Canada.[37]

Even strandees with family members in Canada had difficulty returning. The first strandee to return did not arrive until April 1948. She was Mrs. Tsuru Fujiwara (the absent mother in Joy Kogawa's novel *Obasan*), who had come to British Columbia in 1909 as a bride and whose husband, a dentist, and two Canadian-born children, Muriel Kitagawa, a Nisei activist and journalist, and Wes Fujiwara, a Toronto physician, were in Canada. She was visiting Japan when the war broke out. Her daughter launched a campaign to return Mrs. Fujiwara to Canada in April 1946, but the department was reluctant to give her a visa or help her obtain an exit permit and shipping space. More problematic were the more numerous Nisei who had gone to Japan. They had a legal right to return, but the department was uncertain about those who had spent much of their childhoods in Japan since they had been "imbued with the Japanese educational background." The JCCA agreed that such Nisei found "themselves uncomfortable in Canada" and felt "frustrated and left out and their mind is carried back to Japan where they might have suffered privation but not from lack of companionship." By October 1949, fewer than 150 Issei and Nisei had returned. A few more returned in 1950, but the number remained small because few could afford the passage and because the JCCA, though willing to assist, had no travel funds.[38]

While the government readmitted Canadian citizens, it still regarded Japan as an enemy nation and did not permit Japanese nationals, even those with close Canadian relatives, to enter. The JCCA files include cases of children born to Canadians while their parents were visiting Japan before the war, adopted children, the spouses of Canadian citizens, and elderly parents who had lived in Canada (in one case, the father was a veteran of the Canadian Expeditionary Force) before the war but had lost Canadian domicile even though their children resided in Canada. The *New Canadian* welcomed a slight easing of restrictions on Chinese immigration in 1950 and noted that Germans were no longer being classed as enemy aliens. As long as they could not sponsor the entry of close relatives, it declared, Japanese Canadians do not have "the full status of citizenship equal in respects to other Canadians," and it accused Canada of having laws contrary to the Universal Declaration of Human Rights and Freedoms. The JCCA, which also believed that immigration policy meant that Japanese Canadians were not "equal citizens," was already planning to appeal on compassionate grounds for limited immigration for family reunification. In a brief presented to the minister of citizenship and immigration in the summer of 1951, it cited cases of individuals who through accident of birth or location could not join their families in Canada. It reminded the minister that the United Nations had declared the family to be "the natural and fundamental group unit of society and is entitled to protection by society and the State."[39]

Compelling as the arguments might have been, old prejudices in Canada died hard. Late in 1949, Howard Green, an old Japanophobe, had urged the government to define a policy on the re-entry of Japanese to Canada as he suggested that the 165 strandees who sought to return might "be only the forerunner of a very much larger movement." In the parliamentary debate on the peace treaty with Japan, he predicted that ratifying it would lead the JCCA to attempt "to bring about substantial immigration." If these "strandees" and "repatriates" were admitted, he claimed, "they will ask that their families come too, and the first thing we know there may be several thousand covered in the group." Minister of External Affairs Lester B. Pearson assured him that the government had no desire "to make it any easier in the future for them [Japanese] to get here than it has been in the past – and it has not been very easy in the past." The *New Canadian* reiterated that the JCCA request was not for "favored treatment, but only that which we feel we are entitled to on basic grounds." When later that summer the cabinet discussed the peace treaty, Walter Harris, the minister of citizenship and immigration, warned that, once Canada signed it, it would have to consider the general question of immigration and the admission of residents of Japan, including some who "were legally entitled to come to Canada." The potential number of such immigrants was unknown; the liaison mission in Tokyo reported that, of the 1,650 residents of Mio-mura village, colloquially known as America-mura because of its high percentage of prewar emigrants, 729 claimed Canadian status.[40]

Meanwhile, Canada admitted Japanese relatives only on individual and compassionate grounds. In the first eleven months of 1951, that meant three people. The *New Canadian* complained that "the Peace Treaty ... is offering a relative freedom to the Japanese in their country, [yet] Canada's immigration policy still does not recognize this freedom to live in Canada." With the JCCA, it continued to press for the admission of particular individuals, for the removal of race from Canadian immigration law, and for permission to call to Canada immediate family members who were Japanese nationals. "So long as this blot of statutory discrimination remains on the books, we are not Canadians in the truest constitutional sense of the word," wrote Toyo Takata in the *New Canadian*. The JCCA contemplated a campaign to get a mass of letters from Caucasian Canadians to MPs supporting reunification of Japanese families. As for individuals, the JCCA advised members who wanted to bring in relatives to get letters from Canadian friends or employers expressing sympathy and support for the application. For example, the personal appeal of Teiji Kobayashi of Kamloops to J.W. Pickersgill, the minister of citizenship and immigration, included a petition from the local Liberal Association. He was able to bring his Japanese-born daughter to Canada.[41]

Despite considerable sympathy for the Japanese in Canada, including an observation of the Vancouver *Daily Province* that the solution to Japan's population problem was either for other nations to accept large quantities of its manufactures or open their doors to immigrants, Japanophobes were still around. Tom Reid, now a senator, revived ancient prejudices about inassimilability as he complained that the peace treaty could mean the re-entry to Canada of 3,000 Japanese, all of whom would settle in British Columbia. Estimating the potential number of such arrivals was a guessing game. The Department of External Affairs believed that far fewer than 3,000 could return; a JCCA survey completed at the request of the minister of citizenship and immigration suggested that the number of relatives and close friends who were likely to come would "not greatly exceed 1,500." The department, however, calculated that 10,000 to 12,000 people in Japan were admissible by reason of birth in Canada or by being near relatives of Canadian citizens and that many would settle in British Columbia. It recommended delaying "as long as possible" the signing of an immigration agreement with Japan and opposed reviving the Gentlemen's Agreement lest it give former enemies preference over other Asians.[42]

The JCCA lobbied ministers of immigration and MPs for action in individual cases of families "living in forced separation." A few male strandees got themselves and their families to Canada by joining the Canadian Armed

Table 6.1

Japanese immigration to Canada, 1941-63

Year	Immigrants from Japan	Immigrants of Japanese ethnic origin	Immigrants of Japanese citizenship
1941-50	179	42	40
1951	15	3	4
1952	25	7	4
1953	81	49	48
1954	91	73	72
1955	120	102	99
1956	155	124	121
1957	223	185	180
1958	199	193	183
1959	202	197	190
1960	161	169	159
1961	124	116	114
1962	137	153	141
1963	168	199	171

Source: Department of Citizenship and Immigration, Immigration Branch, 1964, copy in DCIR, vol. 128, file 3-38-19.

Forces then fighting in the Korean War. When Japan's Prince Akihoto visited in 1953, CCF MPs such as M.J. Coldwell and Angus MacInnis suggested that "to be friendly" with Japan required justice to those Japanese who wished to return to Canada. R.W. Mayhew, the ambassador to Japan, reported that he was frequently asked, "what is Canada's immigration policy?" He repeatedly sought information. When Prime Minister St. Laurent visited Tokyo in March 1954, a reporter asked, "are you going to encourage or open your gates to Asia as you have done in certain aspects of Europe?" St. Laurent replied, "that is a problem." He explained that Canada had a housing shortage but that several thousand people in Japan with Canadian citizenship were entitled to return as soon as transportation could be arranged. The number of "immigrants" slowly increased; in 1954 there were 91 (see Table 6.1).[43]

The Department of Citizenship and Immigration was becoming more lenient. Following Pickersgill's request for special consideration for close relatives when there were strong humanitarian or compassionate grounds, it almost automatically admitted aged parents of Canadian citizens except for some who lost Canadian citizenship through "repatriation." That affected fewer than fifty individuals. Nisei strandees who had been conscripted into Japanese forces during the war were a particular problem. The JCCA cited several cases of such men who had "faced serious consequences" at the hands of the police and neighbours for themselves and their relatives if they refused military service. An unnamed West Coast newspaper had alleged that Canadians who served in the Japanese military were "nothing less than traitors" and should be tried for treason if they returned to Canada. Only one such Canadian was tried for treason, the notorious "Kamloops Kid," who was hung for his cruelty to Canadian prisoners of war. In March 1953, the minister of citizenship and immigration and the acting minister of external affairs recommended readmitting them, but cabinet did not do so until 1956, when difficulties in securing Japanese war records, the restoration of normal relations between Canada and Japan, and Japan's role as an important market for Canada made it "inappropriate" to retain restrictions against Canadians of Japanese origin residing in Japan. By then there was no evidence of opposition to the Japanese in Canada.[44]

As the government relaxed its immigration policy, the JCCA found declining interest among its members, but the executive maintained close contact with the Department of Citizenship and Immigration. It had the support of church and labour groups for the repeal of racial qualifications from immigration laws, but the *New Canadian* complained that despite denying it the immigration department still discriminated in selecting immigrants, that it sought Europeans, particularly British, but debarred blacks and Asians. "The bar on immigration from Japan," it asserted, "casts a stigma on persons of yellow complexion everywhere" and was the "remaining problem for Niseis in the field of human rights." It noted the Toronto *Globe and Mail*'s endorsement of restrictions on the immigration of "the non-white races" and Pickersgill's statement in a televised debate that English immigrants had less difficulty in assimilating than Japanese and other non-white races, a message echoed by the Department of External Affairs in a brief prepared for C.D. Howe, the minister of trade and commerce, prior to his visit to Japan in the fall of 1956.[45]

The JCCA executive, as politically astute Canadians, realized that interest in promoting trade would probably lead the government to moderate its position on immigration. For example, when the Senate discussed trade relations with Japan, Tom Reid, though not recanting any of his anti-Japanese arguments, said that Canada must treat Japan fairly and equally in order to keep it on "our side." The JCCA also believed that the government would listen to Japanese diplomats. Indeed, those diplomats enquired about apparent special treatment for Chinese in the admission of fiancées and the thousand-fold discrepancy in numbers between the 2,000 to 3,000 Chinese admitted annually and what they said were twenty to thirty Japanese. The Department of External Affairs believed that letting Canadians call fiancées from Japan would improve Canada's "relationship with the Japanese authorities" and prevent the Japanese Embassy from becoming the champion of Japanese Canadians. Pickersgill agreed and announced that Japanese Canadians, both Canadian citizens and landed immigrants of two years standing, could bring fiancées to Canada for marriage. He also lowered the age for parents.[46] This eased immediate concerns of Japanese Canadians but did not give them full equality; like the Chinese and unlike Europeans, they could not sponsor a wide range of relatives.

Although Japanese diplomats complained that Canada seemed to give more favourable treatment to Chinese than to Japanese, Canadian Japanese had initiated co-operation with Canadian Chinese in lobbying for immigration concessions. In 1951 the *New Canadian* had noted that the JCCA and Chinese Canadians had made similar presentations to the minister of citizenship and immigration. Since Canada's ratification of the peace treaty with Japan was then imminent, the *New Canadian* believed that immigrants from Japan would soon be under the general Asian regulations and would thus face the same restrictions as the Chinese, namely that only spouses and minor unmarried children of Canadian citizens would be admissible. That would help few Japanese since most had their spouses and children in Canada. Nevertheless, it suggested that a united appeal would "make a stronger case for the revocation of racial bars in our immigration laws." When JCCA president Ted Aoki visited Vancouver in the summer of 1951, he sought to interest a Chinese Canadian newspaper in working jointly on immigration matters. His approach had some effect; about a year later Foon Sien, the leader of the Chinese Benevolent Association in Vancouver, who claimed to speak for all Canadian Chinese, invited the JCCA to join it and the East Indian Association in a joint presentation to Parliament's immigration committee. The JCCA, however, decided that the time was not opportune for a joint effort, and the groups merely exchanged copies of their briefs to the minister of immigration.[47]

When they did present a joint brief in 1957, both sought the same rights as other Canadian citizens in immigration to "eliminate the stigma of government imposed second-class citizenship" on Canadians of Asian ancestry. In January 1957, the Toronto Immigration Committee of the JCCA and the Chinese Canadian Association (CCA), a group organized during the Korean War by Chinese in Ontario who sought "to assert their rights as Canadian citizens" lest they suffer the fate of Japanese Canadians during the Second World War, had a supper meeting with representatives of the federal Departments of Immigration and of Labour and the Joint Labour Committee to Combat Racial Intolerance. Although the CCA's attempt to promote better relations with the Japanese by inviting Japanese groups to participate in a variety show failed because some Chinese members of the cast did not want to work with the Japanese, co-operation on immigration matters continued. The CCA had determined that past Chinese briefs had "been relatively ineffective because the Chinese alone constitute no strong voting power," so it joined the JCCA in making a presentation to a sympathetic Paul Hellyer (Liberal, Toronto-Davenport) and to Pickersgill. They told Pickersgill that so few Asians could enter that the policy was "serving to eliminate the Canadian citizens of Asian background from the population of Canada." They were pleased by Pickersgill's apparent promise to remove the "unmarried" qualification for children, to lower the age limit for parents, to lift restrictions on fiancées, and to consider grandchildren and children over twenty-one, but they wanted more – that is, to be on an "equal plane" with other Canadian citizens in sponsoring various categories of relatives. Pickersgill, however, advised them that except for fiancées he had only promised to consider change. He explained to Foon Sien after the June 1957 election that he had intended to recommend changes in the policy affecting fiancées, but the election of a minority Conservative government under John Diefenbaker meant that he could no longer do so.[48]

A week before the election the Department of External Affairs prepared a memo reporting three continuing controversies in Canada-Japan relations: trade, fisheries, and immigration. The memo noted that Japan was not concerned about a population problem but wanted "to avoid any appearance of racial discrimination or inferior status." It indicated that Canada had no intention of adopting a quota system for Japanese, as it had established with India, Pakistan, and Ceylon, or to broaden the admissible categories of Japanese apart from an experiment to admit fiancées. In advising the Tokyo embassy, the department warned against any publicity program that might arouse interest in immigration.[49]

The JCCA, whose Toronto branch had reminded candidates of discrimination in immigration, prepared to press the new administration for the removal of "such inequalities" in the Immigration Act that were "inconsistent with the rights of Canadian citizens" and the Universal Declaration of Human Rights. The 1958 election delayed the campaign; in the meantime, the JCCA solicited support outside Parliament from various religious and labour groups. Once the 1958 election confirmed the Progressive Conservatives in office, the CCA and the JCCA sent copies of their brief to Ellen Fairclough, the new minister of citizenship and immigration, to the press gallery, and to MPs. A sympathetic Conservative MP, John Drysdale (Burnaby-Richmond), had already told Parliament of the problems of "repatriates" who wished to return to Canada and of Japanese Canadians who wanted to have their parents who were not yet senior citizens join them. That a Conservative MP from that area would champion the Japanese was telling evidence of changed attitudes in British Columbia. An even greater indication was the presence in the CCA-JCCA delegation to see Fairclough of another BC Conservative MP, Douglas Jung (Vancouver Centre), a Chinese Canadian. He accompanied Roland Michener (Conservative), whose Toronto-St. Paul's constituency included Chinatown, reporters from the Canadian Press, the Toronto *Globe and Mail* and *Le Droit*, and representatives from the Quakers, the YWCA, and the Jewish community. The brief, drafted in consultation with Sid Blum of the Jewish Labour Committee of Canada, again stressed that inequalities in the Immigration Act gave them second-class citizenship. A non-committal Fairclough noted a backlog of 50,000 applicants from all over the world, chiefly from behind the Iron Curtain, but said that cabinet would soon consider revisions in immigration policy. She also "sharply" warned against attempting "to buy favours" from the government. In a press conference immediately afterward, the delegation stressed that it was simply "asking for equal rights and privileges as Canadians."[50]

Their immigration committees still met occasionally to discuss matters such as "the bitter animosity between these two races, especially with the older folks," but the June 1958 presentation appears to have been their last joint venture except for a 1966 conference of the JCCA and the CCA in Toronto to discuss common problems.[51] Differing concerns probably explain the declining interest in co-operation. Because most Japanese had formed family groups in Canada and had secured the return of most strandees and "repatriates" who wished to come back to Canada, family reunification was no longer a major issue, whereas it was in the forefront of Chinese concerns. In addition the Japanese had an ambassador to lobby for changes in immigration laws, whereas Canada did not even recognize the existence of the People's Republic of China.

Indeed, Japan was planning some investments in Canada and wanted to send a limited number of managers and technical personnel to run them, but Canadian immigration policy made that difficult. The prime ministers of Canada and Japan discussed the matter, but the Department of Immigration, though willing to deal with applications sympathetically, insisted that any admissions be made on a case-by-case basis and only as non-immigrants on renewable visas similar to arrangements that it had made for two Christian missionaries and their families and the proxy groom of a Nisei woman who were granted permanent status after some time in Canada. Officials did not want to revive the Gentlemen's Agreement, as suggested by Japan, lest it lead to pressure for a general revision of immigration policy. Japan resented the lack of an arrangement for Japanese other than close relatives to come to Canada and noted how Canada, through its comments on South Africa's apartheid policy, was "developing a reputation as a champion of non-discrimination" yet had not set quotas for Japanese similar to those that it had for immigrants from India, Pakistan, and Ceylon. The embassy did not expect Japan to raise immigration, apart from that of technical personnel, when Prime Minister Diefenbaker visited Japan but recommended considering the whole immigration problem, especially given likely questions from the Japanese press. The embassy suggested that Diefenbaker mention a review of the Immigration Act and the background of the Bill of Rights. It also prepared him for a potentially embarrassing question about the refusal to grant Canadian citizenship to Japanese children adopted by Canadian missionaries. Diefenbaker only announced that Canada would admit managerial and technical personnel required by Japanese firms and grant permanent admission to some. Those "grudging concessions," complained the *Toronto Daily Star,* carried "national self-interest … to the point of lofty arrogance" since they resulted only from Canada's desire to attract Japanese investment. "National self-interest," it argued, "in the long run means that Canada cannot afford racial discrimination in immigration – against the Japanese or anyone else." At the time, however, a slowing of the economy had reduced the interest of Japanese firms in investing in Canada.[52]

When Japan and Canada had formally re-established diplomatic relations with an exchange of ambassadors in 1952, the *New Canadian* admonished readers that the embassy and consulate staffs were representatives of Japan "and we are Canadian citizens" and that while relations should be friendly they should be no different from those that Japanese Canadians might have with diplomats from any other country. Japan's embassy, however, was interested in the social and financial situations of Japanese Canadians and asked the JCCA for the names, addresses, and occupations "of the Japanese [nationals] or the Japanese Canadians" residing in Canada. There is no evidence in the JCCA records of a reply. By 1960, however, the JCCA suggested that Japan should be interested in immigration since most of the relatives that Canadian Japanese wanted were Japanese nationals. Emphasizing that Japan was not seeking to solve "its population problem" through emigration, Ambassador Hagiwara told the *New Canadian* that pressing for the admission of "a wider range of relatives should remain primarily a matter for Canadian citizens of Japanese ancestry." The JCCA told the ambassador of its primary concern with the immigration problems of Japanese Canadians but would co-ordinate its actions on general immigration with those of the embassy. Similarly, the *New Canadian,* though asserting that "as Canadian citizens … we chafe at the discriminatory measure that prevents us from calling over relatives on an equal basis with other Canadian residents of non-Asiatic origins," suggested a limited entry, possibly by a quota, a variation of Hagiwara's suggestion of a formula similar to that of the old Gentlemen's Agreement.[53]

In a new brief to the Canadian government, the JCCA declared that Japanese Canadians, *"as Canadian citizens"* who had readjusted themselves despite past disabilities and "unjust economic, social and political experiences," had "won the right to ask for humane consideration of separated relatives." The modest request stressed that there was no need to worry about the large-scale immigration that Mackenzie King had said in 1947 would "change the fundamental composition of the Canadian population." Fairclough was sympathetic but non-committal, though she noted that unlike the Chinese case there was no evidence of fraud in Japanese immigration. She added, "I think the Japanese had a raw deal in the past." The delegation hit a responsive chord, and Edward Ide's interview on the CBC national news about the submission did no harm. The deputy minister of citizenship and immigration sought further information about the hardship cases cited. That winter Pickersgill, the opposition immigration critic, admitted that he was "not very proud of" cases of Canadian citizens of Japanese origin renouncing their citizenship when they returned to Japan. He asked if anything had been done about the JCCA brief. Fairclough replied that of twelve cases cited some had been admitted, and others were still being reviewed.[54]

If Fairclough chose to reverse the "raw deal" that the Japanese had endured, she did not have to worry too much about Canadian public opinion. Japanese immigration was no longer a live issue, and the handful of comments on it favoured opening the door. A United Church missionary and recent visitor to Japan publicly said that "Communism could gain a foothold" there if Canada shut its doors to immigration and trade; the president of the Canadian Federation of Business and Professional Women's Clubs, after visiting Japan, said that more Japanese should be allowed to emigrate to Canada; and the Hamilton Presbytery of the United Church endorsed a motion noting the "grave injustice" done to Japanese because of Canada's immigration laws. After hearing from the bishop of Osaka that emigration would remedy problems such as abortion, the international Catholic Migration Conference meeting called for Western countries to admit more Japanese. A Liberal MP for Hull, Quebec, told a service club that countries "which call themselves Christian" such as Canada should permit more Japanese farmers to immigrate. The *Star Weekly,* a magazine that circulated widely across Canada, described Canada's policy as one of "injustice to human beings, and folly as far as the national interest is concerned." It argued that the root of the policy was "the notion that this vast country can be kept the exclusive preserve of a relatively few millions of selected whites. What blindness!" "Canada," it concluded, "cannot afford racial discrimination in immigration – against the Japanese or anyone else." Other major newspapers, such as the Montreal *Star* and the Toronto *Globe and Mail,* endorsed the JCCA request. More telling were comments from British Columbia. *Vancouver Sun* columnist James K. Nesbitt was embarrassed when young people in Japan asked him why they could not emigrate to Canada. He concluded that "if the Ottawa government means all it says about brotherly love and world peace it will take its head out of the sand and see to it that the Japanese become our friends, as well as our neighbors across an ever-shrinking Pacific." BC Minister of Mines Kenneth Kiernan, who visited Japan on a trade mission in 1961, found that people there could not "understand our no-Japanese policy." He recommended a small annual quota to relieve discrimination and assist trade.[55]

Early in 1962, Ellen Fairclough announced new immigration regulations: "Any suitably qualified person from any part of the world can be considered for immigration to Canada entirely on his own merits without regard to his race, colour, national origin or the country from which he comes." The policy would reduce the number of unskilled workers entering the country, increase the number of skilled immigrants, and eliminate discrimination based on race, colour, or creed. Although Fairclough claimed that the new policy would benefit Asians, Africans, and nationals of Middle Eastern countries, limitations for classes such as siblings, adult children, orphan nieces, and so on would remain for specified countries based on historical immigration patterns and policies since this could not be changed without "withdrawing privileges which have been enjoyed for many years by close relatives and sponsors from European and western hemisphere countries – those parts of the world from which Canada has traditionally derived the vast majority of its population." As opposition critic Pickersgill observed, the new policy did not abolish discrimination but substituted one set of criteria for another. For the Japanese, the new policy meant that they could be admitted as unsponsored immigrants on the same basis as immigrants from elsewhere if they had the necessary skills. Japanese Canadians could also now sponsor parents of any age. Calling the new policy "only a step," the editor of the *New Canadian* rightly complained that the new policy still included discrimination "against Orientals" since non-Asians could sponsor a wider range of relatives. Edward Ide thought that the new regulations were encouraging. Although it still saw discrimination in the regulations, the Immigration Committee of the JCCA began to focus on assisting new immigrants with settlement and preparation for citizenship. However, few Japanese were anxious to emigrate to Canada – so few in fact that in the next few years the *New Canadian* reported individual arrivals.[56] A rising standard of living in Japan and its acute shortage of skilled workers in most fields reduced interest in emigration.

Further revisions of immigration policy would be the work of Lester Pearson's Liberal government elected in 1963. When René Tremblay, the minister of immigration, visited Tokyo in April 1964, he promised changes in policy and said that Canada was particularly interested in technicians and business experts. He assured the Japanese government that Canada could take care of immigrants. Publicity in the Japanese press surrounding the minister's visit – including headlines such as "Canada Seeking Japan Immigrants" and an editorial in the *Asahi Evening News* indicating that Canada with its high standard of living and small population would be ideal for Japanese farmers – elicited a few inquiries from potential immigrants. In explaining why the number was small, the deputy minister suggested that "face" was the factor since the Japanese were "understandably … somewhat dubious about our intentions to avoid discrimination in the immigration process" and were reluctant to risk being refused a visa. Apparently to obviate that loss of "face," the government of Japan sought some sort of assurance that Canada would accept any qualified applicant whom it had preselected. It also wanted to move its people as a group in a protected environment. Indeed, shortly after Tremblay returned from Tokyo, T. Sharabata, the chief of Japan's immigration bureau, told a Toronto audience that Japan would only send immigrants "of good character who we feel will easily assimilate into the Canadian way of life" and that the flow of immigrants would never be so large that "little Tokyos" would be created in Canada. Some months later Tremblay told Parliament that large-scale immigration from Japan was unlikely because of its good economic circumstances, but he was "confident" that more qualified Japanese professional and technical workers and their families would be coming.[57]

As individuals enquired about immigration, the Department of External Affairs decided to post an immigration officer to the Tokyo embassy. Aware of past sentiments in British Columbia, before making the appointment Ottawa officials asked some BC MPs about the idea. Ron Basford, chairman of the Liberal caucus for British Columbia, thought that such an appointment "would be well received in B.C." The Japanese government was also pleased. Despite complaints from the Tokyo embassy that publicity in Japan about possible immigration had resulted in such a flow of applications that it could not work efficiently, the government did no more than send Vitus Meilus as immigration attaché to Tokyo, where he worked through the embassy's consular section. The inevitable delays in processing applications led T.U. Umeziki, chairman of the Toronto JCCA Citizenship and Immigration Committee, to assert that Canada was encouraging immigration from "white" countries but was neglecting Japan.[58] Why Canada delayed opening the office is unclear, but the delay may have resulted from a relatively rapid turnover of immigration ministers for a variety of reasons that had nothing to do with immigration from Japan.

Finally, in June 1966, Canada opened an immigration office near Tokyo's fashionable Ginza district. In mid-September at the time of the official opening of it and a Government Travel Bureau to promote tourism from Japan, the Canadian Press reported that during the previous year 5,000 Japanese, mainly scientists, engineers, and technicians, had applied, and about 1,000 applications had been processed or were in progress. The report, however, emphasized that Canadian job offers would have to be "attractive." That news, however, was overshadowed by an announcement from Minister of Immigration Jean Marchand that he would soon submit a white paper to Parliament to abolish discrimination in immigration policy. Late in 1964, Prime Minister Lester B. Pearson had asked the immigration department for such a report as the basis for considering immigration policy and administration. That study demonstrated discrimination against "coloured peoples" in immigration policy. The chief theme of the white paper, the prelude to a new Immigration Act, was the abolition of racial and religious discrimination in selecting immigrants. That was of particular relevance to the Japanese. Press reports of Marchand's speech highlighted the features that would most affect immigrants from Japan, namely that they would be eligible for the same assisted passages as immigrants from Europe and that once immigrants were accepted they would have the same rights as Europeans to sponsor relatives. "We are more than satisfied with the calibre of Japanese migrants," he said as he predicted that Canada would soon receive about 1,000 Japanese immigrants per year and that this number would rise to several thousand.[59]

The Canadian press widely reported Marchand's announcement, sometimes with front-page headline news, sometimes with a mere wire service report on an inside page, but with limited comment. The *Ottawa Journal* made a political point by claiming that the previous Conservative government had removed racial and cultural discrimination from immigration policy. Other editors dealt with the principle. The *Calgary Herald* agreed that "racialism must not be permitted to rear its ugly head in Canada" but cautioned that "it would be undesirable and perhaps dangerous for Canada to open its gates wide to unrestricted immigration." The *Toronto Daily Star*, which had been so active in protesting the postwar "repatriation" policy, was sceptical as it asserted that "Japan, the only non white nation with plenty of 20th century skills, should offer a real test of whether Canada means what it says about skill being the basis of choice without regard to colour." From outside Canada, the *Christian Science Monitor* summarized the troubled history of Japanese immigration: "Canada will soon enforce a new immigration policy free of racial prejudice" vividly illustrated "by the proposed admission of Japanese on a substantial scale."[60]

Most striking was the observation of the *Vancouver Sun* that a generation ago Marchand's statement "might have started riots" in Vancouver. While recognizing the symbolism of making the announcement in Tokyo, it noted the strong ties in trade and finance between Canada and Japan as it remarked how "Canadians have grown up" and were internationally minded. Yet it admitted that, while Canada could afford "to be generous and reasonable in taking all who have something to contribute," the new policy would not throw "the doors wide open." The Victoria *Daily Colonist* thought it better to train Canadian-born workers for skilled jobs than to recruit overseas labour but did not specifically refer to Japanese.[61]

Yet some Japanese Canadians were understandably sensitive when Canadian Press erroneously reported that Ralph Loffmark, the provincial minister of trade, had said that the new policy meant that "British Columbia will be flooded with thousands of technically-skilled Japanese." The report of the Loffmark interview appeared on back pages in the local press, but the *New Canadian* and the JCCA thought that his remarks were reminiscent of 1907 and a "Neo-Yellow Peril" campaign. To show that he had been misinterpreted, Loffmark provided the *New Canadian* with clippings from the Victoria papers correctly quoting his saying that the new policy would encourage joint Japanese-Canadian ventures in British Columbia and that the social differences between Japan and Canada were "minimal." The *New Canadian* promptly printed the correct report. There was, in fact, considerable

"Give Me Your Skilled ...," Montreal *Star,* 18 October 1966. Ed McNally pointed out the new limitations in immigration policy.

Japanese investment in BC mines and some secondary industries such as steel and wire plants in Vancouver. Much of this investment took the form of loans to be repaid with production rather than direct investment. In 1967 the *Vancouver Sun* reported that Japanese investors had controlling interest of only one mine in the province.[62]

When Marchand passed through Vancouver en route to Ottawa, a reporter asked if trade had anything to do with the new policy. He said no, "the decision to abolish discrimination is our own." He repeated his predictions about likely numbers and explained that because of its own shortage of skilled manpower, Japan was anxious that Canada be "highly selective" and because of its national pride had asked Canada not to admit "the unskilled and the undesirable." Canada, however, rejected Japan's request that it select emigrants and be allowed to establish a service in Canada to counsel new immigrants and help them find employment. In co-operation with the Canadian government, however, Japan opened an orientation program in Japan, mainly English-language classes, for emigrants; the JCCA planned to assist Japanese immigrants in settlement and the "acquisition of full citizenship." In Vancouver, however, a spokesman for the Japanese Canadian community said that it did not want "wide-open immigration of Japanese" since, if a large number of unskilled workers came, "because of employment and other problems [they] would create a substandard community" that would "plant new seeds of discrimination and block integration." He was pleased that only the skilled would be coming. In fact in 1969, for example, only 765 arrived, and the Canadian immigration office was "one of Canada's most low-keyed immigration promotions anywhere."[63]

Certainly, Canadian attitudes toward Japanese immigration had changed dramatically over the previous two decades. Trade and diplomatic considerations were a consideration and may explain why Marchand chose to announce the new general immigration policy in Tokyo. The policy outlined in the white paper that, at least in theory, removed all racial barriers to immigration was confirmed in the new policy that Canada adopted in 1967, its centennial year. For the Japanese who were enjoying prosperity at home, it was a symbolic victory, but for people from China the new immigration policy marked the beginning of a major change in their history in Canada and in the ethnic composition of Canada's largest cities. While that change is beyond the scope of this book, the evolution of Canada's post-1947 Chinese immigration policy is the subject of the next chapter.

7

Ending Chinese Exclusion: Immigration Policy, 1950-67

All we want is to be on equal terms with other groups.

Foon Sien, in *Vancouver Daily Province*, 19 April 1952

Like Japanese Canadians, Chinese Canadians sought equality in immigration policies. The repeal of the Chinese Immigration Act in 1947 was only a token gesture, for old orders in council limited the entry of Asians to the wives and unmarried children under the age of eighteen of Canadian citizens resident in Canada. Over almost twenty years, Chinese Canadians lobbied successive governments for a relaxation of immigration laws and practices as they called for equality of citizenship and appealed to the humanitarian instincts of other Canadians. Politicians were more amenable to easing immigration laws than officials and slowly eased the regulations. In the meantime, racketeers took advantage of the tight limits on immigration to bring in a number of Chinese through fraudulent means. Yet when the story of massive illegal immigration broke, there was sympathy and amnesty for all but the organizers of the schemes. Not until the 1960s did Canada gradually undertake a major revision of its immigration policies and end exclusionary Chinese immigration practices.

Despite achieving their goal of repealing the Chinese Immigration Act in 1947, the Caucasians who formed the backbone of the Committee for the Repeal of the Chinese Immigration Act remained active and continued to seek the repeal of PC 2115 (the 1931 order in council that required Asians to be Canadian citizens before they could sponsor the admission of relatives). Early in 1950, at the same time as the Chinese Benevolent Association (CBA) submitted a similar brief, the repeal committee told Minister of Immigration Walter Harris that "discrimination against the Chinese on account of race still prevails today in our immigration laws" and made the Chinese in Canada second-class citizens. As well as referring to discrimination, the

CBA's poignant brief noted that the Chinese in Canada were "a rapidly dying racial group" as it asked that Canada admit a few hundred Chinese to give happiness to some men who had lived "an unnatural existence which has probably never been equalled in the history of civilized mankind" and whose children in China were "being raised in the atmosphere of Communism." R.G. Robertson of the Privy Council Office advised the government that Canadian policy was racially discriminatory but observed that the Chinese already in Canada had had ample opportunity to become naturalized and that the CBA seriously underestimated the number of likely immigrants. The briefs had no effect, but the CBA was apparently unaware of the flaws in its argument, for it submitted a virtually identical brief the next year.[1]

Earlier Foon Sien, the chief spokesman for the CBA, had asked that Chinese men be allowed to bring in prospective brides by posting a $1,000 bond to marry within thirty days, but immigration minister Harris flatly rejected the idea. Because China was "rapidly becoming overrun with Communist armies" and "the thought of their children being raised in the atmosphere of Communism and being schooled in its principles is almost unbearable," Foon Sien persisted in seeking changes in the Citizenship Act to reduce the time limits for naturalization and an expansion of the categories for immigrants to include, in certain cases, children up to age twenty-eight, adopted children, orphaned grandchildren, and fiancées. Yet he was a realist. Conscious of old fears of an influx, he noted that 40 percent of the Chinese in Canada were over the age of sixty, that few could afford transportation costs or support for families in Canada, and that most "children" were now adults.[2]

The Chinese had support. The repeal committee criticized Canada's treatment of Chinese "as second-class citizens on account of race." In Parliament, John Diefenbaker, a Progressive Conservative and keen supporter of human rights, and CCFers M.J. Coldwell and Stanley Knowles reminded the government of inequities affecting the Chinese. Citizenship and immigration officials were no longer certain that Canadians opposed Asian immigration since many groups, including the Canadian Congress of Labour, had objected to an immigration policy that discriminated against Asians. Similarly, the National Council of Women's 1950 convention supported the admission of spouses and of children under the age of twenty-one, though a delegate from London, Ontario, citing the likelihood of Chinese immigrants bringing Communism with them, opposed the motion. Officials expected, however, that relaxing immigration policy would help Canada's international relations and enhance its culture without endangering its "fundamental pattern." Moreover, fewer immigrants than expected were arriving probably because of delays in securing citizenship certificates, problems in leaving China, and transportation difficulties.[3]

Cabinet rejected a quota as discrimination "in another form" but late in 1950 agreed to admit husbands as well as wives and children under the age of twenty-one; six months later it extended the age for children to twenty-five. However, it tightened regulations by dating the period for qualification for citizenship not from first arrival in Canada but from the return of the latest visit to China. Recognizing that Canadian citizens were "greatly concerned" about relatives in China, especially since Red China was trying to extort money by threatening their families in China, the Department of Citizenship and Immigration increased its staff in Hong Kong and Ottawa to reduce the processing time. In 1951 about 2,500 Chinese entered the country.[4]

Some Canadian Chinese who sought to bring relatives to Canada, however, complained that officials in the Hong Kong office put the "squeeze" on would-be immigrants. An elderly gentleman who arrived in Duncan, British Columbia, about 1908 and last visited China in 1926 told an interviewer in 1961 that some ten or fifteen years earlier he had tried to get his "No. 3 boy" to Canada, but "the immigration people upside down me. They ask my boy questions, then try to squeeze my boy – that's not good. Oh yeah, the immigration people in Hong Kong, the Chinese interpreter. He say to my boy how old are you, my boy say twenty, he say that's not true, you are thirty – unless you pay. So they try to squeeze him. Not good. Very bad." The dates were vague, but "No. 3 boy" possibly was twenty when he said he was.[5]

Unfortunately, about the time that Foon Sien presented his 1952 brief repeating his earlier requests, a headline story in the Vancouver *Daily Province* criticized a relaxation in immigration practices and alleged that "Canada's Pacific Door" was "practically wide open to any subversive agents or organizers." It cited claims of residents of Vancouver's Chinatown that some of the approximately 3,000 Chinese arrivals in the previous year, including both those who used false papers and the sons of Canadian citizens, were organizing Communists in Canadian Chinatowns. In an advertisement in the Vancouver *News-Herald* and in interviews with journalists, Foon Sien denied the charge, but the *Province* cited the editor of the *New Republic* (the Kuomintang journal published in Victoria) as its authority. The *Province* did not pursue the story. The Royal Canadian Mounted Police (RCMP) found that some had been "trained in subversive activities." Immigration officials determined that some substitutes had been sent for children of Canadian citizens and decided to enforce restrictions on the immigration of children over the age of twenty-one.[6]

Minister of Immigration Harris worried about anti-Asian sentiment in British Columbia. In a draft memo to cabinet, he noted that about 35 percent of the 600 to 800 Chinese immigrants who arrived annually went to British Columbia, and he expected many Japanese Canadians to return to the province. He did not want to admit more than 3,000 Chinese and Japanese annually to the province. In fact BC opinion was less hostile than he thought. The provincial council of the International Woodworkers of America had called for the admission of close relatives of Canadian citizens, and O.L. Jones (CCF, Yale) had raised the cases of constituents who had been unable to bring in relatives because of processing delays and other technicalities. Two Liberals, Arthur Laing (Vancouver South) and James Sinclair (Vancouver North) told Parliament about how well the Chinese had assimilated to Canadian society but stopped short of calling for widening the eligible classes of Chinese immigrants. Although they did not want to see the immigration door opened widely, BC MPs publicized the plights of constituents with close relatives in China. George Pearkes (Progressive Conservative, Nanaimo) and H.W. Herridge (CCF, Kootenay West) criticized the use of x-rays to determine the age of would-be immigrants since an x-ray was not a reliable method of assessing age. One argument for extending the age limit was the slow immigration procedure, which meant that applicants often had their twenty-fifth birthdays before they could reach Canada.[7]

Examples of administrative problems abounded. Acting for the National Council of Chinese Community Centres, Chris Kelly told the Senate Standing Committee on Immigration and Labour about several cases where technicalities or the actions of immigration officials had prevented family reunions. Soon after learning that the age limit had been raised to twenty-five, a Toronto wholesaler and court interpreter who had been naturalized in 1929 applied for the admission of his son, then aged twenty-four; immigration officials were still reviewing his case when he had his twenty-fifth birthday. In another case, when the age limit was eighteen, a mother, siblings, and other relatives came to Canada and left an overage son behind to care for his grandmother and the family's property. The grandmother died, the Communists took over the property, and the son, who escaped to Hong Kong, was the only family member not in Canada. Since he seemed to be ineligible to come, they had not listed him in the original application. In the third case, Chong Ying, the unofficial mayor of Toronto's Chinatown, could not have his twenty-six-year-old son rejoin the rest of his family in Canada because some information was missing from his file.[8]

Because the number of immigrants in the twenty-one to twenty-five age group was not falling as expected, the immigration department suspected that Chinese Canadians were attempting to pass off older children as being under twenty-five. In addition the Hong Kong office warned of an unlimited number of adopted sons under that age. It advised that refusing to accept applications for children over twenty-one would not cause "undue hardship" to Canadian Chinese who had had ample time to become naturalized. The department's policy for twenty-one to twenty-five year olds was not consistent. At times it admitted only those whose absence would cause serious hardship to a Canadian citizen. Thus, it accepted the son of an aging and ailing Okanagan farmer who needed someone to operate the farm but not the son of an elderly man who lived on his pension and had relatives in Canada to care for him. In response to such stories, Laval Fortier, the deputy minister of citizenship and immigration, told the Senate committee that his department rejected applicants from many races, did not rely solely on x-rays, had to be cautious because of individuals falsely presenting themselves as sons or daughters, and, given the situation in China, had to be especially careful to deny entry to impostors who might become "subversive agents."[9]

Foon Sien took note. During a coast-to-coast speaking tour, he declared that "we don't want the door thrown wide open for all Chinese who want to come here, [but] we do feel that complete families should be permitted to join their kin already settled in Canada." His 1954 brief echoed that as it promised there was "absolutely no danger of a flood of Chinese immigrants" following any relaxation of laws affecting the entry of close relatives. Immigration officials were unsympathetic. Citing difficulties in identifying wives and children, they said that it would be even more so for distant relatives and warned of the fiancée clause developing "into a racket." They believed that few bona fide admissible dependents remained in China and that many applicants attempted to misrepresent married or older children. Without providing evidence, the department claimed that Occidentals would not favour an increased number of Chinese immigrants.[10]

On the last point, the department was wrong. After Foon Sien did some lobbying, several MPs expressed sympathy for his cause. A BC Conservative, E. Davie Fulton (Kamloops), reminded Parliament that "we are dealing here, not with Chinese applying to come to Canada, but with people who morally and legally are in fact Canadian citizens because they are the children of Canadian citizens," an argument endorsed by other Conservatives, Walter Dinsdale (Brandon), Roland Michener (Toronto-St. Paul's), H.O. White (Middlesex East), as well as by Coldwell and Herridge of the CCF and, with qualifications, Solon Low of Social Credit. Immigration minister Harris said that the number of applicants had fallen because of difficulties in getting out of China. Under further questioning, he explained that his department had admitted a few hardship cases.[11]

J.W. Pickersgill, who in a cabinet shuffle replaced Harris as minister of citizenship and immigration on 1 July 1954, believed that Canadians still shared King's 1947 sentiment that they did not want immigration "to make a fundamental alteration in the character of our population" despite sympathy for family reunification. He promised no more than "to give some thought" to the admission of parents, grandparents, or grandchildren of Canadian citizens. In fact, between 1947 and the end of 1954, the department processed 16,600 Chinese files; of those 11,404 had arrived, and only 1,576 were rejected. Pickersgill called it a "generous" policy given security concerns because of the Communist takeover in Mainland China and the Korean War. On 10 March 1955, however, the department announced that, since all those who were eligible and who were interested in coming had come or were having their cases resolved, it was cancelling a policy in effect since June 1951 – never a part of the immigration law – of allowing special consideration of "children" aged twenty-one to twenty-five. It could no longer justify giving "Chinese Canadians a preference over other persons of Asian origin" and would give favourable consideration only to the spouses or unmarried children under age twenty-one of a "Canadian citizen resident in Canada who is in a position to receive and care for his dependents" since citizens would be in the best position to assist immigrants in adapting to Canada. Pickersgill justified restoring the age twenty-one limit because of difficulties in determining ages and identities, the belief that some impostors had got through the screening process, and the probability that new immigrants in turn would apply for the entry of other relatives.[12]

Canadians were sympathetic to receiving immigrants from China at least in humanitarian cases, as several complicated cases showed. In 1951 Leong Hung Hing, an elderly Vancouver chef, applied to bring in twenty-year-old Leong Ba Chai, his son by his concubine or second wife. The department refused the application since the son of a concubine was not legitimate in Canadian law. The Supreme Court ruled late in 1952 that under Chinese law the son was legitimate and must be recognized as such. The department accepted that ruling, but in the meantime Leong Hung Hing died. In what a Vancouver lawyer called "bureaucracy at its worst," the department ruled that Leong Ba Chai could not be admitted as the child of a Canadian citizen because his father was no longer in a position to care for a dependent. By an order in council in June 1954, the government announced that it would not admit the children of second wives. This decision, with its implications for adopted children, "bitterly disappointed" Vancouver's Chinese community. Foon Sien complained, "it took a long time and much expense to obtain a favourable ruling from the highest court in the land, and that ruling is now nullified or circumvented. We also feel that a man who admits and tells the truth about the relationship of his children should not be punished. Had he not told the truth, he would have fared well." He would later claim that that order in council was the beginning of a regression in immigration policy. Nevertheless, MPs, even BC Liberals such as Elmore Philpott (Vancouver South), attacked a bureaucratic ruling that demanded "the crossing of the last 't' and the dotting of the last 'i.'" Fulton charged the department with inhumanity and "arbitrary action" in ignoring a Supreme Court ruling. An Alberta Social Credit member, who did not want "mass immigration" to change Canada's "fundamental complexion," thought that denying entry to children whose parents were in Canada undid "much of the good" accomplished by the repeal of the Chinese Immigration Act in 1947. Angus MacInnis cited the hardship of a Chinese national who had resided in Vancouver since 1910 but could not sponsor two grandchildren whom he had supported for many years. Pickersgill answered that the department "assumed that 'child' meant child of father and mother as would be recognized as the wife in Canada" and had not admitted concubines' children.[13]

In the spring of 1955, Pickersgill hinted to Foon Sien that he might consider admitting older children, elderly parents, fiancées, and orphan grandchildren on an individual basis, would sympathetically consider individuals who had entered illegally many years ago, and would favour children whose mothers were in Canada. In fact he suggested that Canada stop accepting applications for children unless their mother, if living, was already in Canada or applied to come at the same time. One of his goals appears to have been a desire to reduce the "disproportionate" amount of time and money that the department was spending on Chinese immigration. Officials warned, however, of problems since there were no vital statistics in China, and husbands who did not want their wives or who could not afford transportation costs for them would say that they were dead or had lost contact with them. In other instances, the deputy suggested, "voluminous correspondence" arose from cases of children who reached Hong Kong but whose mothers could not leave China. As for fiancées, officials saw humanitarian merits but anticipated abuses, including the entry of concubines, "unmarried" children who would bring in their wives as fiancées, and "marriages of convenience." Pickersgill read the comments but still favoured easing the regulations for wives and children and permitting discretion "in cases of special hardship." Through Ralph Campney (Liberal, Vancouver Centre), Pickersgill advised Foon Sien that the regulations were designed to promote "the reunion of families, Canadian style," and that this did not include children of concubines. He had cabinet approve an order in council to admit minor unmarried children only if the parents were already in Canada or landed concurrently with the children. As a concession to Chinese in Canada, he announced, "for humane reasons," a year-long experiment in which Canadians of Asian origin might apply on compassionate grounds for the admission of elderly parents who would pose no security risk.[14]

Foon Sien immediately sought clarification and consideration of his earlier requests for the admission of grandchildren and fiancées; Pickersgill conceded that if the parent was dead this would not prevent the admission of a child who met other qualifications but advised waiting to see the effects of recent changes in regulations before making any other amendments. Reverend J. Lavelle Smith of the Church of All Nations in Toronto commended Pickersgill for liberalizing the immigration rules for Asians, but Fulton praised a journalist who claimed that the minister's purpose was not to keep family groups together but "to maintain the rules which make it almost impossible to emigrate to Canada if you are Asiatic."[15]

Shortly after Pickersgill clarified Chinese immigration policy, the Vancouver *Daily Province* quoted C.E.S. Smith, a senior official in the immigration department, as saying that a "high percentage" of doubtful applicants was being admitted. *Province* reporters had ascertained that at least half and possibly up to 86 percent of Chinese immigrants were guilty of some misrepresentation, usually by purchasing "spurious documents" through what Chinese Canadians referred to as the "squeeze" or "getting a piece of paper." Some documents were forged; others were legitimate ones, such as Canadian birth certificates of Chinese who had died. Bruce Larsen, the reporter, cited the case of a Chinese man who paid $3,000 to bring in a fiancée. He got a Chinese Canadian family to claim her as a daughter. When she arrived, she fell in love with the son of the phoney parents but could not marry him because legally he was her "brother," nor could she ask for help because she was an illegal immigrant. Yet the *Province* was sympathetic to the Chinese. It interviewed several leaders of Vancouver's Chinese community, who agreed that harsh restrictions caused heartbreak and forced some Chinese to resort to "vicious – and illegal – financial squeeze plays." It published their comments that stories about illegal immigration were "fantastic and inaccurate." A Caucasian lawyer who dealt with immigration cases predicted that, unless the reasons for misrepresentation and illegal payments were erased, "the Chinese will gradually be led to believe that in a democracy you buy your way in." Pickersgill dismissed the claim of abuses forming an open door as "rubbish."[16]

Certainly, there was no open door; in his 1956 brief to the minister, Foon Sien complained of "the suffering" of relatives of Canadian Chinese in Communist China who were young enough to take advantage of a "more enlightened" immigration policy. In addition to his usual requests, he suggested a trial period for the admission of unmarried siblings and of up to 500 refugees per year. The Toronto-based National Council of Chinese Community Centres of Canada, which did not recognize the CBA as the head of Chinese organizations in Canada, and whose members were not Canadian citizens, made similar points in its brief. Pickersgill thought that the experiment of admitting parents had succeeded and did not oppose admitting a few orphaned grandchildren and fiancées on compassionate grounds but saw "real dangers in changing the Regulations." His officials agreed but warned of difficulties in identifying children and siblings, in establishing the bona fides of refugees, and of "racketeers" exploiting provisions for the entry of children and fiancées. Noting the shortage of young Chinese women in Canada, C.E.S. Smith had been somewhat sympathetic to an arrangement to obviate the need of Canadians to go to Hong Kong for marriage until he learned "confidentially" from a prominent Chinese Canadian that younger Chinese men wanted to break away from the tradition of an early marriage arranged by parents.[17]

As usual Foon Sien had done his homework to gain support. In his column in *Chinatown News,* he complained that Canada had "done well" by European refugees but "had not recognized that there are Chinese refugees." In the *Vancouver Sun,* Philpott, who was also the Liberal MP for Vancouver South, quoted him as saying, "we do not want an open door but we do want our immediate relatives to come to Canada." Philpott wrote of "increasing esteem" for Chinese Canadians and their legitimate grievance over "pin-pricking laws and regulations which deny their right to equality of treatment." From Vancouver too, the Unitarian Church reminded Pickersgill that by excluding Asians Canada was denying itself talented people who could help to develop the country and was endangering international relations. In Parliament, Harold Winch (CCF, Vancouver East) cited specific hardship cases and asked why the department insisted that Chinese come as a family unit given the difficulty in getting to Hong Kong. Among the cases he cited was a family who got their five-year-old child to Hong Kong but could not get the mother and siblings out of their village and so could not bring in the five year old. He told of a Canadian army veteran who had to hire someone to look after his business while he went to Hong Kong to marry his fiancée. In Parliament, Philpott complained that "the most general grievance" heard by BC MPs was that immigration from Asia was "not treated on the same basis as immigration from other countries," but given the number of entrants he saw "no real cause for complaint." Pickersgill agreed that sentiment in British Columbia had changed but did not think that it would help anyone if Canada admitted "newcomers of any group in such numbers as to create problems, tensions and strains." He explained, "there can be discrimination in immigration but once you let people into this country there should be no discrimination inside the country."[18]

After reviewing policy, Pickersgill reiterated that immigrants should come "as families and bring up their children in this country from the earliest age possible, so that, when they grow up, they will really be Canadians." He also announced that fiancées, if otherwise admissible, could come if the sponsor posted a $1,000 bond and the marriage took place within thirty days. That saved Chinese grooms in Canada the expense of going to Hong Kong to marry. Of 194 fiancées who applied by the end of February 1957, 185 were accepted, and the department recommended extending the program for another year. *Chinatown News* described the new measure as a "welcome improvement," but any credit that Pickersgill may have gained by this concession was lost immediately.[19]

After noting the limited interest of the Chinese in bringing in daughters, the lack of adequate security tests and vital statistics in China, evidence of fraud, attempts to enter the United States via Canada, and the "frightful" workload of Canadian immigration officials in Hong Kong, Pickersgill announced that the department would no longer make a second review of rejected cases unless there was evidence of wrongdoing on its part. Prolonged reviews, he explained, kept officials from dealing with current applications. Privately, he advised officials to be "very careful" in reviewing future cases and not to close files if more information might become available.[20] Winch, Green, and Fulton shouted "unfair" and "terrible." Fulton privately told Foon Sien of his "shock and distress" at the announcement, a stand that garnered considerable attention in the Chinese-language press. Although pleased about the admission of fiancées, Foon Sien protested "most strongly" the "unnecessarily harsh" action of limiting appeals and criticized the government for denying "the moral right of families to be united" for reasons of economy. He had support. The *Vancouver Sun* editorially called Pickersgill's reasoning "bureaucratic arrogance"; the *New Canadian* declared that Chinese Canadians were not "even asking for equality on this particular question. All they want is the unabridged right to enjoy with dignity and pride the full blessing of Canadian citizenship, including the right to appeal in immigration matters." It later joined the CBA in pointing out the irony that in the fall of 1956 Canada accepted refugees from Communist Hungary but denied entry to refugees from Communist China. Unmoved, Pickersgill denied that the situation of refugees in China or Hong Kong was "comparable to the desperate plight of the Hungarian refugees."[21]

While the basic immigration regulations were strictly enforced, Pickersgill extended some leniency to a few individuals who were only slightly overage or had special skills, such as Chinese-language teachers, typesetters, and a sausage maker. His replies to Foon Sien usually indicated that the department would make exceptions on compassionate grounds and reopen cases if new evidence became available. Occasionally, he was tougher than his officials. Although he later said that he regretted that the Liberal Party had implemented an exclusionary Chinese Immigration Act, like his mentor, Mackenzie King, he continued to believe that most Canadians did not want to change immigration policy, and he justified continued restrictions on the difficulty of confirming identities of those who claimed to be relatives of Canadians and the fact that Chinese soldiers had fought Canadians during the Korean War. Although the department recommended letting a farmer bring in his twenty-three-year-old son, Pickersgill said that the farmer should seek the admission of his wife and minor children. Similarly, he apparently denied permission for an overage son in Hong Kong to visit his dying Chinese father even though Winch and other Caucasians were prepared to post a bond to ensure that the young man would return to Hong Kong. Despite such denials, between 31 December 1950 and 30 June 1956, through orders in council, the cabinet admitted 3,126 dependents aged twenty-one and over, of whom 375 were over twenty-five. Pickersgill also sympathetically received a joint delegation of the Chinese Canadian Association (CCA) and the Japanese Canadian Citizens Association (JCCA) in March 1957, but a general election intervened. In reply to an urgent plea in June 1957 from Foon Sien for the admission of fiancé(e)s of both men and women who had been in Canada for at least two years and for a limited number of refugees from Hong Kong, Pickersgill explained that he had intended to recommend some changes, but because the Liberals had lost the recent election he could do nothing.[22]

The election of a minority Progressive Conservative government in June 1957 should have augured well for Chinese Canadians. In opposition, both Prime Minister John Diefenbaker and Davie Fulton, the acting minister of citizenship and immigration, had criticized the Liberals' restrictive Chinese immigration policies. Moreover, Vancouver Centre voters had elected a Chinese Canadian, Douglas Jung, a Progressive Conservative. Foon Sien quickly made representations to the new minister, so many in fact that Fulton's executive assistant said that he had hoped the election would have diminished "Mr. Sien's influence."[23] In the slightly longer run, it did; Sien resigned from the CBA in 1959.

In Parliament Pickersgill and CCF members questioned Fulton about policy changes. Alexander B. Macdonald (CCF, Vancouver-Kingsway) even suggested that, in addition to relatives, Canada should set a quota for admitting "the very best people," such as medical doctors, from Hong Kong, though he stressed that there should be no "flood of immigrants from the Orient" in a time of unemployment. The opposition also reminded Fulton of his previous criticisms of immigration policy. Until the department completed a study, particularly identifying people who claimed to be the children of Canadians, Fulton's only concession was to let Chinese who were not yet citizens apply to bring in relatives.[24]

After the March 1958 election gave the Diefenbaker government a handsome majority, Ellen Fairclough became the minister in charge of immigration. Once again Foon Sien and the CCA circulated briefs to the minister, MPs, and the press gallery. Their separate presentations asked for equality with other Canadian citizens in immigration matters, but only for the removal of specific restrictions, not an open door. Then, on 20 June 1958, the JCCA and the CCA jointly met with Fairclough. Despite his concern to establish a reputation "as a parliamentarian rather than to have others think of me as Chinese," Jung, who had been re-elected in Vancouver Centre, was part of the delegation. The delegates afterward told the press that they were simply "asking for equal rights and privileges as Canadians." When a reporter asked why they didn't ask for more, Ruth Lor of the CCA replied, "if we did, we wouldn't get anywhere – the main thing was getting the family reunited."[25]

That presentation appears to have been the last joint brief. Although the CCA remained active, Foon Sien claimed that the CBA, of which he was still president, represented "practically all" of the 44,000 Chinese in Canada. A month after the CCA and the JCCA presented their brief to Fairclough, Foon Sien made his tenth "pilgrimage" to Ottawa to present his brief on immigration. As in his previous briefs and like the CCA, he called for "equality and nothing more" as he repeated specific requests for changes. A few days later Fairclough told the cabinet immigration committee that the Chinese community was exerting considerable pressure through their MPs for equality in immigration. She noted the humanitarian problem of reuniting families and difficulties in ascertaining identities and obtaining security information from a Communist country. After discussing and rejecting a quota system as discriminatory and revisiting the problems of ascertaining true identities and establishing security, the committee decided to admit married children under twenty-one and to inform Canadian Chinese that they were in a "preferred position re security." After noting that the Chinese population of Canada had actually fallen, the bureaucrats suggested allowing Chinese men in Canada without a son or heir in Canada to bring in adult sons. Meanwhile, in Parliament from time to time, Conservative, Liberal, and CCF MPs praised the good citizenship of their Chinese constituents and asked the minister to be more generous in admitting immigrants. The government remained silent. Pickersgill, the chief opposition critic on immigration, was unwilling to press the issue because of difficulties in preventing fraudulent entries or Communists. Progressive Conservatives in Vancouver passed resolutions favouring more lenient regulations for relatives of Chinese Canadians, and in his eleventh brief to the government Foon Sien cited the endorsement of groups such as the National Council of Women in his request for the admission of children of all ages.[26]

The general issue of Chinese immigration, however, was soon sidetracked by the case of Weldon Chan and family, a government crackdown on illegal Chinese immigrants, and concern about refugees in Hong Kong. Response to Chan's case suggests that Canadians as a whole supported Chinese immigration. Chan, who was born in Hong Kong, went to Vancouver with his wife and five-year-old daughter in April 1959 to visit his wife's parents, who had lived there for many years. When he saw a government announcement that people on tourist visas could apply for permanent residence, he decided to stay. He even became a gunner in the militia. The immigration department, however, ruled him ineligible to apply and ordered him and his family to be deported. The CBA protested. So did members of his regiment. The Vancouver press, referring to his Hong Kong birth, called the situation a "travesty of the Commonwealth concept." Indeed, Ray Perrault, the provincial Liberal leader, urged federal leader Lester B. Pearson to take advantage of an "opportunity for our party to restore good relations with our friends in [the] Chinese community." The *Ottawa Citizen* cited the Chan case as an example of how immigration policy was partly based on racial discrimination and how policies affecting immigrants from Hong Kong conflicted with Canada's preaching about human rights. Before he could be deported, Chan disappeared, leaving his wife and child behind. Mrs. Chan secured an interview in Ottawa with Fairclough, who was not impressed by her claim that returning to Hong Kong would condemn the family to poverty since Mrs. Chan wore a full-length mink coat over an embroidered gown and what appeared to be very large pearl earrings and insisted on having her daughter, then about seven, act as interpreter.[27]

Canadians had humanitarian concerns about refugees in Hong Kong, especially after television programs in World Refugee Year (1960) showed their plight, but Canada regarded them as a British problem. In 1962 the Canadian press gave them wide attention after the Human Rights Council of Hong Kong appealed to Canada and other nations to provide space for people who had fled famine in China and possibly had been driven out by the Chinese government. Reporters for the *Toronto Daily Star* and the *Globe and Mail* despatched a series of illustrated stories about the refugees' difficult living conditions and overcrowding that led the Hong Kong government to return some to China. Jack Brooks told *Vancouver Sun* readers that conditions were so bad that in Canada the SPCA would have prosecuted anyone who kept a dog or a chicken in the dwellings in which some refugees resided. Moreover, he noted that the government had not followed up on its "fatuous" election time offer to take 100 families, a plan that was "like trying to empty the Pacific with a teacup." The *Sun* headlined one of his reports "Canada Is 'Laughing Stock' for Token Refugee Offer."[28]

The refugees became a political issue especially after Fairclough replied to a reporter's question that the refugees "should be resettled in Asia because they would be happiest there." Canadians were more sympathetic. Church groups asked how they could help, the Canadian Council of Churches said that Canada should admit 10,000 Chinese refugees, and the United Church of Canada said that its eleven Chinese congregations would help to bring up to 10,000 refugees if they could include relatives in the group. Later the Anglican Church proposed to sponsor fifty refugee youths. Two prominent rabbis, W. Gunther Plaut and Abraham Feinberg, called on Canada to open its gates to more Chinese refugees. A Caucasian group in Windsor, Ontario, formed a Committee of Concern for Hong Kong Refugees and proposed to assist about a dozen families. Toronto's Chinese Community Centre proposed to raise funds to help the refugees resettle. The Vancouver *Daily Province* asked if Canada could "forever deny the God-given privilege of her vast empty territories to people crippled by the most basic of human needs – hunger." Similarly, the Toronto *Globe and Mail*, after suggesting that Fairclough's idea had "little application" since most refugees could only reclaim "a grave" in China, declared, "we cannot turn our backs on the human misery that exists in Hong Kong."[29] Moreover, the United Nations High Commission on Refugees had asked about Fairclough's statement.

Since the refugee question had arisen in the midst of a federal election campaign, the government had responded quickly, although Grant Deachman, the Liberal candidate in Vancouver-Quadra, said that so many refugees were involved that "Canada could not solve the problem without being inundated and losing her character completely." Fairclough tried to avoid the issue by saying that it was a matter for the Department of External Affairs. Jung, who was seeking re-election in Vancouver-Centre, had quickly urged the prime minister to indicate the government's humanitarian beliefs and set an example for other countries. In reply Diefenbaker announced that Canada would receive about 100 families to assist Britain's difficult situation. Jung was pleased; he did not want Canada to take the entire responsibility for the refugees. The *Toronto Daily Star* initially suggested that "wholesale migration" was not the solution but greeted Diefenbaker's "well-meaning and gracious gesture" even though it underscored Canadians' "race consciousness." Calling on the whole "free world," including Canada, to do more to help the refugees, it later asked, "how much longer can we afford the luxury of believing that Canada can continue to be an exclusive white Anglo-Saxon stronghold?" Its columnist, Pierre Berton, noted the hypocrisy of welcoming white refugees from Europe but not "yellow" refugees. That too was the sentiment of the *Shing Wah Daily News*, although several leaders of Toronto's Chinese community welcomed Diefenbaker's plan.[30]

As soon as Diefenbaker's announcement was reported in Hong Kong, the Canadian immigration office there received calls from long-time residents who wished to be considered as refugees, but the Hong Kong government said that there were no refugees there, only illegal immigrants, and that it would be difficult to find 100 "refugee families." Cabinet decided to subject these families to the usual health checks but to waive normal security checks unless there were adverse reports. It would give preference to families who arrived in Hong Kong as units after 1 May 1962 and whose head had skills that would give him a reasonable chance of finding work in Canada. To avoid providing a back-door method of bringing in relatives, the families would not include those who qualified as relatives of Canadians.[31]

Among Chinese Canadians, views differed. The *Chinese Bulletin* favoured admitting more refugee families as well as those who were waiting to join Canadian relatives. Although anxious to help the recent refugees, others would not give them preference over the relatives of Canadians. At a Conservative election rally in Toronto, Dr. W.H. Lore of the Chinese Community Centre told 1,200 Chinese Canadians that refugees should be admitted only after the relatives of Chinese Canadians. That too was the belief of Reverend Yiu Sing Lee of the Chinese United Church in Toronto. The Canadian-born Jean Lumb of the Chinese Women's Association in Toronto, an active campaigner for immigration reform, told the *Toronto Daily Star*, "it's a crime refugees have been waiting in Hong Kong so long are still there while these recent refugees are admitted." Officials believed that admitting additional refugees would cause protests from Chinese Canadians who wanted to bring in relatives and wondered if the public would view the coming of refugees as "the beginning of the end of 'white Canada' with the attendant implications respecting job security, living standards and so forth" or approve of a humanitarian measure. The selection was so strict – many disappointed applicants claimed of "tough" screening – that Canadian officials could not find 100 eligible families. Of

3,500 applications received by mid-November 1962, the department had approved of fewer than 100 family units and was reluctant to extend the program lest a "tidal wave" of applications delay its regular work and upset Chinese Canadians who resented the slowdown in processing applications from their relatives. Those who came were distributed across the country, and except for some of the later arrivals all were satisfactorily settled and placed in employment.[32]

Interest in the refugee issue waned; concern about illegal immigration gradually arose. A 1955 Vancouver *Daily Province* report that 50 to 85 percent of all Chinese immigrants came under some form of misrepresentation and that Canadian sponsors paid from $500 to $10,000 for spurious documents attracted little attention despite corroboration by the immigration department. Leaders of Vancouver's Chinese community said that new immigration laws might prevent hardship and abuse, but the *Province* and the public apparently accepted Minister of Immigration Pickersgill's dismissal of the claim of abuses constituting "an open door through which any Chinese who wanted to come to Canada as 'rubbish.'"[33]

During the 1950s, the number of immigrants from China averaged about 2,000 per year, and as far as immigration officials could tell they were well documented. In fact many of the documents were fraudulent, or the immigrants were not the individuals to whom the documents applied. In a case heard in the courts in 1961, Wong Yuck Fung was charged with conspiring to bring three people to Canada by unlawful means. In testifying for the crown, Anne May Lee explained how she got to Canada. Her real father, who resided in Portland, Oregon, paid $1,300 to Wong to bring her to Canada. She left Canton in 1954 and went to Hong Kong to meet her "paper mother," who coached her on details about the Wong family. Then Wong tested her "paper mother" and "paper brothers" on their knowledge of the family. When immigration officials in Hong Kong and Vancouver questioned her, she correctly answered questions about the Wong family and was admitted to Canada. Because she could claim Canadian citizenship through her "paper father," she acquired citizenship papers in a few months. Then Wong and her "paper father" took her to Portland, where she met her real father. Other methods included the sale of legitimate Canadian papers. Jean Lumb explained how, for example, someone whose eighteen-year-old son in Hong Kong did not want to come to Canada would, for money or as a favour to a friend, transfer the son's papers to someone whose son was too old to qualify for admission. "These poor kids," she recalled, "had to lie about their age, their surname, their parents, in order to get over ... How could people go through the rest of their lives with the wrong surname, living in fear of being deported? There were also brides who came over with false papers. All kinds of complications! Some of these C.O.D. brides were being sold, brought over and channelled through another man and the agent collected the money." A Toronto informant told a somewhat similar story:

> Our community was small then and everyone knew what was happening. The only bad thing about this practice was ... professional and corrupt middlemen who made great sums of money of such arrangements. The other bad thing was it [the immigration of paper sons] was an enormous cultural shock for young sons to come to Canada and join their fathers who they found working long hours in a 2 by 4 grease joint [laundry]. This was the same man who had been sending money home and writing of the Gold Mountain [Canada], and gave the impression to relatives in China that it was a great land [and] he had a great job.[34]

Not surprisingly, reports of illegal immigration continued. In June 1959, the government sent officials to Hong Kong to investigate. Then, in August, Hong Kong police found information about a well-established illegal immigration operation. Based on this evidence, the RCMP investigated. Almost a year later, Fairclough and Fulton, now justice minister, informed cabinet that suspicions of large numbers of Chinese illegally entering from Hong Kong were "well founded" and that several thousand individuals had entered illegally over the past decade. They told of "paper relatives" and of the coaching of impostors. However, they were less concerned about the entrants than about the organizers of the illegal traffic. Since they believed that large-scale deportation was impossible, officials of the immigration department and the RCMP examined the Chinese confession and "truthful statement" program introduced by the United States in 1956 in connection with an amnesty program. Chinese organizations had accepted that program, which helped to integrate immigrants who no longer lived in constant fear of exposure. Canadian officials did not like the connotations of "confession," so they recommended a status adjustment program. If those who entered illegally before a specified date told the truth, they suggested that the minister should review their cases, and if they were of good character and had not been engaged in systematic illegal immigration they should be permitted to remain in Canada and apply for Canadian citizenship five years after their legal landing. Officials warned that the situation was "extremely complicated" and recommended that simultaneously with the announcement of the program there should be an aggressive field investigation to throw the illegal immigration brokers "off balance" and avoid "adverse publicity from persons not properly informed."[35]

Police charged a few Chinese with assisting illegal immigrants and in October 1959 arrested forty-five people, including immigration brokers, on various charges relating to a scam in which Chinese Canadians were paid large sums to marry "allegedly widowed mothers they had never seen." Those were minor cases; police had bigger plans. They screened about 20,000 names and narrowed them down to 400 to 500 for intensive investigation. Then, on 24 May 1960, in what one reporter described as their "largest peacetime operation," RCMP officers with the assistance of Hong Kong plainclothes police as translators launched simultaneous "lightning" raids on Chinese homes and businesses across Canada in search of evidence such as coaching papers, passports, and visas of an international syndicate or racket engaged in creating "paper families," bringing illegal immigrants to Canada, and exploiting them as "slave labor." The simultaneous raids were headline news across Canada, with newspapers such as Montreal's *La Presse,* the *Winnipeg Free Press,* and the *Calgary Herald* supplementing wire service accounts with stories focusing on local aspects of the raids. The *Free Press* quoted a Chinese physics instructor at Brandon College as saying that, if there were greater equality in immigration laws, there would be no need for rackets. The government promised that illegal immigrants who came forward and helped to convict the "smuggling king-pins" would be eligible for full Canadian citizenship. According to a press report, the RCMP claimed that about 11,000 or half the Chinese immigrants since the war had come illegally, but Fulton denied that this figure had come from the RCMP.[36]

Caucasians had considerable sympathy for the Chinese generally and for illegal immigrants, whom the *Vancouver Sun* described as "victims not only of racketeers but also of Chinese communism" as it noted that most Chinese in Vancouver were hard working and law abiding. The press endorsed Fairclough's promise to take a "humanitarian" approach to the problem and condemned the "racketeers." The Halifax *Chronicle-Herald* urged the immigration department to be more vigilant, but other journals suggested, in the words of the *Winnipeg Free Press,* "once the racketeers have been put out of business let us open our doors a little on the Orient" – in other words, the government should make it easier for Chinese to enter the country legally, and Canada should eliminate racial discrimination in its immigration policy.[37]

When interviewed immediately after the raids, leaders of Chinese communities in Toronto and Montreal said that their people would co-operate with the government since they had to clear their names. And they did. Nevertheless, as they read headlines such as "Onze mille Chinois ont disbourse $44,000,000 pour venir au Canada," "Cross-Country Crackdown: RCMP Raids Closing Net on Chinese Slave Racket," and "Need Payola to Get to Canada – Chinese," resentment grew among Chinese Canadians, but their greatest grievances were the raids themselves, questionnaires about family members, and especially the action of the RCMP of rounding up some Chinese residents and holding them incommunicado while special agents of the Hong Kong police questioned them "in a threatening manner." According to the Emergency Council of Chinese Communities of Canada, a group that included both benevolent and community associations, such measures impugned the loyalty and good citizenship of all and were "tantamount to a form of Apartheid." It worried about Canadian citizens who had acted as benefactors to assist family reunions of friends and relatives. Had Canada's immigration laws been "more humane, just and equitable in the first instance," it suggested that there would have been no misrepresentations. A flier issued by the Chinese Community Centre of Toronto deplored the "extortionists who allegedly take advantage of political refugees from Communist China, people yearning to be re-united with their families in the free world," asked for "fair play," and complained of "A SMEAR AGAINST OUR ENTIRE COMMUNITY IN FICTITIOUS STORIES OF A 44 MILLION DOLLAR 'SMUGGLING RING' AND OF 'SLAVERY' IN OUR COMMUNITY." At a mass meeting in Vancouver, Chinese societies asserted their refusal "to allow the gross insinuation to shake our pride in the achievements of our predecessors" and rejected "an attempt, however well intentioned, to stir up animosities between our community and that of our neighbours with whom we have always had most friendly, enjoyable and comradely relations and with whom we are proud to work together to build a better Canada."[38]

When questioned in Parliament, Diefenbaker denied that the investigation was an "undue reflection" on the "respectable and respected" Chinese people in Canada. Pickersgill doubted stories of widespread bribery or of 11,000 illegal immigrants, referred to the enviable record of the Chinese for obeying the law, and suggested that the government encourage illegal immigrants to come forward by announcing that it would take no action against the children, wives, or parents of Canadian citizens even if they misrepresented themselves. Fairclough assured him that the government had no intention of prosecuting "the victims of these transactions," only of curbing the racketeers. Indeed, she said that complaints of victimization from the Chinese had inspired the investigation and that she had said nothing to reflect unfairly on the "character or integrity of our Chinese Canadians." In the subsequent debate, Liberal and CCF MPs justified the resentment of Chinese Canadians at the procedures used by the police and agreed that it must be made easier for Chinese residents to sponsor their relatives as immigrants.[39]

The MP most concerned was Douglas Jung. Explaining that he had not spoken on "the discriminatory aspects of Chinese immigration regulations" lest he be seen only as a spokesman for minority rights; he chastised the Chinese who had broken the law and urged that they be punished. Nevertheless, he decried the fact that all Chinese had been brought "under a cloak of suspicion" and urged the government to permit dependents, including nephews, nieces, and orphan grandchildren, to join their relatives. "Much of the irregularity in Chinese immigration," he argued, "has sprung from the desire to rejoin loved ones." He called for a quota system for professionals such as doctors, nurses, and skilled technicians without Canadian relatives. Noting that Canada had recently admitted 37,000 Hungarian refugees, he said that if all the Chinese families in Canada were reunited with their kin the number of Chinese in Canada would still be small and that the number of immigrants would drop off. John Taylor, another Vancouver Conservative MP, and several CCF members made similar observations.[40]

Resentment of the registration procedure, doubts about the promised immunity, and the declining but continued influence of the illegal immigration brokers helped to explain reluctance to co-operate with the status adjustment program. Nevertheless, Minister of Justice Fulton, emphasizing that the police were investigating an organized racket and would lay charges as soon as they translated and checked their evidence, expected that once the Chinese got "these racketeers off their backs" they would feel "relief and satisfaction" and that "co-operation will be even more forthcoming." Co-operation, however, was limited. The few who came forward often did not tell the whole truth. Fairclough, disappointed that few people were establishing their correct identities and frustrated by "the mixture of fact and fiction" in many "so-called voluntary truthful statements," conceded that Canada's immigration regulations were partly the problem but argued that the Chinese had been treated more generously in postwar immigration policy than other Asians, Africans, or Latin Americans. She blamed the lack of co-operation on the continued domination of "Chinese 'middlemen' or agents" who were often the English-speaking leaders in Chinese communities.[41]

Jung urged illegal immigrants to come forward, regularize their status, and take advantage of what he called an "amnesty." In Parliament he again explained the difficulty in making a "moral case" against most of them, who were "good and law abiding citizens" whose only motive was to reunite their families and whose problem arose from an "unduly restrictive" Immigration Act, a point endorsed by the *Chinatown News.* He noted that some people interpreted the absence of mass arrests as a lack of strong evidence, while others feared coming forward lest they implicate friends and benefactors. He suggested to Fairclough that regularizing the status of the few who had come forward and letting them bring in wives and children might encourage others to come forward. He worried too that those who obtained citizenship certificates through false identities would be disfranchised and hence unable to vote in the next election. Fairclough replied that only seven cases of revocation of citizenship were being considered. Unlike Fulton she did not believe that a lack of co-operation warranted revocation of citizenship. Stressing that she had never spoken of a general amnesty, she did promise that those who came forward would not be deported or prosecuted for illegal entry if only they or their relatives were involved. That promise of immunity, said the *Vancouver Sun,* was "meaningless," and her claim that the government would not deport anyone whose only misdemeanour was to enter under a false name was, "at best, naïve."[42]

In mid-July 1961, police in Vancouver raided the quarters of several Chinese organizations and the home of Foon Sien as part of the immigration probe. Less than two weeks later, Fulton told a *Vancouver Sun* reporter that, because the Chinese community was not co-operating, the government contemplated using certain powers under the Immigration Act to arrest and question suspects. Fairclough, who had privately debated policies with Fulton, denied considering using such powers. A few days after Fulton spoke, Jack Wasserman, the *Sun* gossip columnist, suggested that Fulton's threat "to invoke sterner laws" was "pretty timid stuff compared to what city Chinese are already suffering at the hands of the RCMP and Hong Kong police"; editorially, the *Sun* called on the government to "Call off the Hounds." Officials in the justice ministry believed that Vancouver Chinese who wanted to slow the investigation inspired the *Sun*'s comments, but the city's Chinese-language press was editorially silent on the raids, and a columnist in the English-language *Chinatown News* reported that the raids made the mood in Chinatown "taut and tense," an observation confirmed by social scientists studying Chinese social organizations in Vancouver. They found that the immigration investigations made many interviewees "wary of answering questions relating even remotely to immigration, organization, or legality." The immigration department was also concerned because a recently arrested immigration agent, after indicating that he would plead guilty, came into some funds from an unknown source and planned to plead not guilty in a jury trial. Moreover, investigations had shown the extent of illegal immigration. An RCMP spot check in the Cariboo city of Quesnel, for example, revealed that two-thirds of its Chinese residents had entered illegally.[43]

Even as the investigations proceeded at a desultory pace, the department considered broader issues and tested public opinion. In the spring of 1961, in Toronto and Montreal, George Davidson, the deputy minister of citizenship and immigration, told public meetings that, given the international situation, Canada might no longer be able to base its immigration policies on "enlightened self-interest" and would have to admit people from overcrowded nations. That, he warned, could require Canadians to change their attitudes toward immigrants. In the summer of 1961, Fairclough told the prime minister that she was willing to make the basis for preferential treatment of relatives not the colour, racial origin, or citizenship of the immigrant but the Canadian citizenship of the sponsor. In January 1962, she announced as part of a general review of immigration policy that "any suitably qualified person, from any part of the world, can be considered for immigration to Canada entirely on his own merit, without regard to his race, colour, national origin or the country from which he comes ... The selection of immigrants, insofar as selection on the basis of skills is concerned, will be done without discrimination of any kind." This, she added, would particularly benefit Asians, Africans, and people from the Middle East and Central and Latin

America. Under persistent questioning, she conceded that some of the new rules still favoured immigrants from "preferred" or mainly white countries, as "it is a case of maintaining the immigration pattern from these countries from which we historically get our immigrants." In her memoirs, she admitted that the changes only "marked the beginning of reform."[44]

The press response varied. In Vancouver, the *Sun* had the headline "Canada Lifts Color Bar from Immigration Rules" and several follow-up articles but no editorial, although its columnist James K. Nesbitt suggested that the new policy merely increased the "accursed policy of sponsored immigration from the Orient." The Vancouver *Daily Province* had only a brief wire service story. Reflecting Toronto's multicultural character, both the *Daily Star* and the *Globe and Mail* gave the announcement front-page attention, as did the Montreal *Star,* while the French-language press did little more than briefly report the story. The *Toronto Daily Star* welcomed the announcement as "a big step" toward eliminating the colour bar in immigration regulations but claimed that few potential immigrants from non-white nations were likely to have the necessary qualifications; the *Globe and Mail* recognized an improvement, "at least on paper," as did the Montreal *Star,* which said that the proof would be in administration of the policy since immigration officials, whose tradition was to exclude people "from 'undesirable' parts of the world," would still decide on admissibility.[45]

The political responses were predictable. Roland Michener told the *Shing Wah Daily News* in Toronto that the new regulations would ease requirements for Chinese and permit an eligible immigrant to bring his wife and minor children with him if he could care for them and that Chinese who were Canadian citizens could now sponsor a much wider range of relatives, but Ian Wahn (Liberal, Toronto-St. Paul's) said that discrimination still applied since Europeans could bring in unmarried grandchildren and orphan nieces and nephews, whereas Chinese could not. Pickersgill, who was visiting the West Coast, described the new policy as "phoney propaganda and camouflage" that was likely to cut immigration. Most significant were Jung's comments. Jung told the *Chinese Times* how the Chinese could benefit from the new policy but admitted to the *Chinatown News* that he did not think the new regulations were "sufficiently adequate to satisfy our Chinese community," a point emphasized by its editor, who noted that Europeans could still sponsor a wider range of relatives than Asians. Nevertheless, the new regulations marked the beginning of an increased number of Chinese immigrants from 876 in 1962 to 5,234 in 1965.[46]

Meanwhile, investigations into illegal immigration dragged on to the consternation of both the Chinese community and the government. Vancouver lawyer Harry Fan told Fairclough that it was "time to make a move when rumors are so convincing that the Racketeers poured a large amount of money into Ottawa and so the Investigation will be dropped soon." In Parliament,

Erhart Regier (NDP, Burnaby-Coquitlam) called on the government to "call off the dogs" but drew more attention and comments of "shame, shame," from other MPs for his comment that one MP "has been aggressive and active in helping to smear people of the same origin as himself." The reference was obviously to Douglas Jung, who, on a question of privilege, denied even entertaining such "preposterous thoughts."[47]

Yet allegations of intrigue within the Chinese community persisted. A sensationalist article in *Maclean's,* a national newsmagazine, "The Criminal Society that Dominates the Chinese in Canada," by Alan Phillips, picked up the story and suggested that Canada's Chinese were controlled by the CBA, which bribed "our politicians with the promise of Chinese votes." Incensed Chinese quickly attacked this slur. At a public meeting in Vancouver, a CBA member called the article "outrageous, slanted, unjustified, biased, ridiculous and a crime." The *Chinese Bulletin* described it as "anti-Chinese" and "preposterous, reckless, baseless, malignant and insolent" and asked how it was possible to accuse an "entire race" because a few members had "committed errors"; the *Chinatown News* suggested that the article was "poppycock" because of its "blanket condemnation of the entire race," its harping on the word *ghetto,* and its failure "to see that Chinese Canadians of second, third, fourth and succeeding generations are traveling on the road to complete integration." Quan Lim of Vancouver, secretary of the Chinese Canadian Citizens Association (CCCA), told Fulton that if there had been any law breaking discriminatory immigration laws were largely to blame, and he accused the police of providing "the trigger to the sensationalism and the implied accusation against our entire people." From its Vancouver headquarters, the CBA issued a circular attacking the article for its "false accusations" about the CBA as a "criminal society" or a "Mafia-like group," its "incorrect facts" that cited "fantastic" numbers about illegal immigrants, and its "racial prejudice and hatred against Canadian Chinese."[48]

The controversy arose just as a federal election campaign began. The *Maclean's* article and its allegations quickly became an issue. Arthur Laing, the Liberal candidate in Vancouver South, called the article "inflammatory and discriminatory" and said that it "smacks of racial hatred." Conservative campaigners replied by calling the article a "Liberal plot." In a letter to the *Chinatown News,* Jung, who was seeking re-election in Vancouver Centre, emphasized that, although *Maclean's* was privately owned, it was known to support the Liberals. He was in a difficult campaign. There were about 3,000 Chinese voters in the constituency, although Liberals accused the Conservatives of using a technicality to leave 500 to 600 of them off voters' lists after the enumerators missed them. The Liberals sought to register them by affidavit. All three national party leaders visited the bellwether constituency, but it was essentially a race between Jung and J.R. Nicholson, the Liberal.[49]

Even though not all those listening to the speeches fully understood English, they greeted the party leaders appreciatively with the traditional Chinese setting off of firecrackers. Liberal leader Lester Pearson got an especially warm welcome as 3,500 people lined both sides of Pender Street between Columbia and Main Streets as he marched through led by a pipe band and followed by the Chinese Lion Dancers. Premier W.A.C. Bennett stood in for the national Social Credit leader. Liberal contender John Nicholson, a lawyer and business executive, was first off the mark in the campaign. With the support of several prominent Chinese Canadians, including Dr. S. Won Leung and Harry Con, as campaign advisers, he phoned and called on "everybody who is anybody" in Chinatown. He had the advantage of being a "star" candidate who, it was suggested, would be in the cabinet if the Liberals formed the government, and Vancouver Centre was accustomed to being represented by cabinet ministers.[50] In an advertisement in *Chinatown News,* Nicholson described himself as a "long time friend of the Chinese Canadian Community" and noted that the Liberals understood the needs of ethnic groups, had enfranchised Chinese Canadians, and, though the claim was dubious, had "handled Chinese immigration fairly and justly." Among Liberal objectives, he cited "fair treatment to immigrants and all others in Canada."[51]

Jung, on the other hand, faced several handicaps. His campaign was slow to start, he seemed to be "far less aggressive" than Nicholson in gaining individual support, and the apparent breakdown of his marriage had not helped him politically. He may have gained some credit by going to Hong Kong and bringing to Canada a twelve-year-old boy whose parents had left him behind when they separately entered Canada under false identities. After regularizing their status, they faced red tape in bringing in their son, but Jung overcame it. However, the Conservatives had the burden of being responsible for immigration policy and for the investigation of illegal immigration. When Fairclough visited, several lawyers attempted to lobby her to review individual cases. She was also involved in a blunder in the eyes of the *Chinatown News* and a Conservative organizer when her entourage pushed aside the seven-year-old daughter of Weldon Chan, who attempted to present her with a bouquet at the airport, and she said that she was too busy to talk to Mrs. Chan.[52]

The Conservatives, however, had an announcement designed to please Chinese voters. Several supporters carried banners thanking the government for its recent announcement that it would admit 100 Hong Kong refugee families. When Diefenbaker visited, he announced that Canada would send $500,000 worth of food to Hong Kong as refugee aid. The *Vancouver Sun* welcomed the gift but thought that it might have been larger and cynically suggested that the announcement was "deliberately timed to help Douglas Jung." Jung denied that, but in a two-page advertisement in the *Chinatown News* the only point in capital letters was "THE ANNOUNCEMENT MADE BY

THE PRIME MINISTER WAS AGAIN THE DIRECT RESULT OF MY REPRESENTATIONS," and it gained a favourable comment from that journal. Liberals were less impressed. When Pickersgill visited, he said that the 100 refugee families would be a "drop in the bucket" and correctly observed that immigration from China had dropped since the Conservatives came to power.[53]

The results demonstrated what the campaign had shown – no party could count on the Chinese as a bloc vote – and proved what the *Chinatown News* had observed in mid-campaign: "Chinese Canadians are politically maturing, as manifested in their active participation in the public affairs of this country. Today we have Chinese Canadians either belonging to or showing preference for one of the four political parties." There was no ethnic solidarity. Nicholson gained 7,697 votes to Jung's 6,803. In an election postmortem, the now saddened *Chinatown News* rued Jung's defeat and its implications for "the political future of Chinese Canadians as a minority group." It described Jung as "a symbol of our new status in a land where our people are not yet entirely free from such blemishes as pigeon-English wisecracks and Chinese exclusion-law psychoses" as it criticized those Chinese voters who, by voting for other candidates, had defeated Jung. A bitter Jung angrily told reporters, "I'm so damned mad. I was beaten by my own people ... I'm the fall guy for this Chinese immigration investigation." The *Vancouver Sun,* however, saw the split as a sign of the political maturity of Chinese Canadians, who "voted as adult, independent thinking individuals, not as a minority group. As Canadians among Canadians." Mor Cheolin, in the *Chinese Bulletin,* blamed the Conservative "witch hunting" of illegal immigrants and an attack in the Chinese-language press on Jung's lack of a Chinese education and his views on Taiwan. Although regarding the failure of his "countrymen" to support him as a "great tragedy," Jung claimed to bear "no grudge or ill will" against them and vowed to come back for the next campaign, which was expected within the year.[54]

The other Canadian city with a significant Chinese population was Toronto. Nevertheless, the *Toronto Daily Star,* in reviewing the Conservative record, noted that the government had modified "to a considerable extent" the racial bias in immigration policy but warned that its effects would depend on the administration of the policy. A few weeks later it suggested that the immigration department was still practising racial discrimination since Chinese had to wait twelve to eighteen months to have their applications processed, whereas Europeans had only a four- to five-month wait. It also documented the case of an immigrant from Hong Kong who applied for citizenship at the same time as two Hungarian co-workers. The Hungarians got their papers within weeks; Mrs. Ko had to wait over a year and got her papers only after a lawyer intervened. Most of the scattered mentions of the Chinese on the hustings concerned Hong Kong refugees. Conservatives were not of one mind. The candidate in Trinity praised Diefenbaker for setting a fine example; the candidate in York South, who had recently visited China, said that bringing in 100 families "just isn't enough." Roland Michener, whose downtown St. Paul's riding had some Chinese voters, joined other Conservatives at a rally attended by 1,200 Chinese Canadians where he agreed that the investigations and prosecutions relating to illegal immigration had been disturbing and suggested that Canada could halt the flow of millions of dollars annually to Hong Kong by admitting refugees with Canadian relatives. Walter Gordon, the high-profile Liberal candidate in Davenport, thought 100 families an "insignificant" number but did not suggest an alternative until Canada solved its unemployment problem. In championing the case of a Toronto resident who had been able to bring in his bride from Hong Kong only after spending $4,000 over ten months and having her case raised in Parliament, Ian Wahn, a Liberal, accused the immigration department of "holding Chinese brides as 'hostages' until citizens tell all to the RCMP." Although the Chinese vote was only a minor factor in the election, Wahn defeated Michener, the incumbent. New Democratic Party (NDP) candidates interviewed by the *Daily Star* called Diefenbaker's plan a "vote catcher" and said that more refugees could be absorbed.[55]

After the June 1962 federal election returned a minority Conservative government, Diefenbaker shuffled his cabinet. Fairclough, who did not believe that they had "quite got to the bottom of the problem" of illegal Chinese immigration, was moved to another portfolio. Donald Fleming was now minister of justice, while Richard Bell became minister of citizenship and immigration. They recognized that the status adjustment program had "fallen far short of expectations" since, as of September 1962, only 1,295 statements had been given, many had contained falsehoods, and all but 112 had been given only when individuals expected that the police would soon be calling. The new ministers simplified the status adjustment procedures and required a full investigation only if those who had had their status adjusted later sought to sponsor relatives as immigrants. Should that investigation reveal fraud, they would be prosecuted and not be allowed to sponsor immigrants. Diefenbaker, who blamed the investigations for Jung's defeat, said that the investigators had sometimes "behaved disgracefully" by taking actions such as interrupting a large banquet and taking its chairman into custody. The police explained that they had sent a message that they wanted to see him after the banquet, but he feigned drunkenness and tried to escape, as he had done on previous occasions. The prime minister was also upset by the failure to stop such "untoward incidents" and planned to meet representatives of Chinese communities from across Canada. Some cabinet ministers, believing that the Conservatives had permanently lost the support of Chinese Canadians because of the investigations, suggested that there was no reason to halt them. The investigations had reduced the number of fraudulent entries from an estimated 50 percent to an estimated 15 percent and had resulted in the conviction of twenty-eight agents for ninety-nine offences, several other cases were before the courts, and "very lenient courts" had acquitted some. Cabinet also discussed the eleven Hong Kong police hired by the RCMP on contract because most Chinese in Canada "were so completely dominated by their community leaders that they would not translate accurately." The RCMP wanted to retain some of the Hong Kong police for other work, but cabinet decided to send them home immediately since the Chinese community regarded them as "spies" and resented that the government seemed to be spying only on the Chinese. Cabinet agreed to continue the prosecutions then under way.[56]

A senior immigration department official believed that the new policy would not solve the Chinese immigration problem since "the vast majority of the Chinese sponsors and their agents will not respect our immigration laws if there is any way to get around them" and argued that the "many thousands" of illegal entrants were unlikely to come forward but would attempt to sponsor family members and fiancées. "When discovered," he claimed, "they will bring all kinds of pressure to bear to avoid exposure," such as questions in the House of Commons, allegations of "third degree methods" in immigration offices, suggestions of bribery to government officials, and "the cry of discrimination." The only solution, he believed, "is to resolutely stick to our guns and show the Chinese that we mean business."[57]

The *Chinese Voice* newspaper, however, felt "joy and relief" at the sudden end of "the 907 days of fear." Ian Wahn congratulated the minister on the new policy, which he thought would "go a long way toward solving the outstanding problems." Yet difficulties persisted. As for the investigations, the CBA noted that only about a dozen Chinese had been convicted of immigration offences since the investigation began, that they had been found guilty of individual cases and were not part of a ring. The *Chinese Bulletin,* noting the "inward fear" felt by Chinese Canadians because of intimidation and RCMP raids, suggested that many who could have come to Canada legally had not done so because of "abusive tests." "Canadian law," it concluded, "can continue to wipe out racketeers of all kinds – but do let good innocent people alone!" A commentator in the *New Republic* observed continuing uncertainties. It would be some time before a "bill of pardon" was discussed in Parliament, and the future of those whose cases were still under investigation was unknown. Would they be given a "clean bill"? Moreover, contradictory government policies contributed to the reluctance of Chinese to adjust their status. The Chinese-language press reported how a young man in Vancouver voluntarily confessed that he had lied about his age but instead of having his status "adjusted" as promised was ordered deported. In the meantime, a few cases went through the courts. Despite sensational evidence such as that of a woman who entered as the wife of her father or of witnesses's changing their testimony about pretending to be relatives when they were not, the stories were buried in the back pages of journals such as the *Vancouver Sun*.[58]

Concerned about the election that was soon anticipated, Jack L. Eng, a Conservative, invited several of "Chinatown's bedrock citizens" to act as a temporary Chinese Canadian Advisory Committee to ascertain viewpoints on Chinese immigration. Observing that the need for equality was paramount in order to remove the "bad effect" of being regarded as "second-class citizens" and that the administration of the Immigration Act needed streamlining, they concluded that "the whole community" was happy with the government's new stand. That was not quite so. Writing in the *New Republic,* Ng Toy Win suggested that Chinese people had sufficient brains to tell if the committee was "truly an effort to improve the situation of the Chinese or simply a gimmick to help the [Conservative] candidate in the next general election." The party, however, was not that helpful to Jung, who was running again. When he asked about discrimination against Chinese in the matter of sponsorship, Minister of Immigration Bell sent him what was almost a form letter claiming that Chinese had been "given very special consideration since 1947" despite "the almost impossible task of verifying identity and relationship[s]" and that, even though China was a Communist country, security screens had not been as strict for Chinese as for others. Because difficulties in verifying identities made it almost impossible to control the movement, Bell was unwilling to enlarge the admissible classes lest that increase "opportunities for fraudulent entry." Although Bell gave Jung little helpful material, Prime Minister Diefenbaker visited the constituency, where, amid the noise of firecrackers and a kilted pipe band, fifty Chinese supporters carrying a banner bearing Chinese characters for the slogan "Work under Diefenbaker" paraded down the street to greet him as he stopped for an hour to speak to 1,400 Chinese Canadians gathered in a banquet room where the mother of one of the "100 refugee families" presented flowers to Mrs. Diefenbaker and where two members of the CBA spoke for the community. In a somewhat generic speech, the prime minister spoke of his many Chinese friends and the role of the Chinese in building the country. On the hustings, Jung took credit for the 1962 change in immigration regulations that substituted skill for race as a major consideration for eligibility for admission and cited a *Time* article that credited him for it. Since the new immigration regulations affected more than Chinese, Jung's claim was based more in election rhetoric than in fact. He accused Nicholson of mentioning the Chinese only once in Parliament and that in his maiden speech, where he described his constituency.[59]

A major problem for Jung in 1963 was Nicholson's "iron corps of Chinatown supporters" headed by many of the same community leaders who had organized his 1962 campaign. During the campaign, Nicholson told the Chinatown Lions Club of his intention "to fight for a better immigration deal" for Chinese Canadians seeking to bring in relatives, including sons and daughters, no matter their ages. He claimed that the number of Chinese immigrants had declined from about 3,000 a year when the Liberals were in office to fewer than 1,000 in recent years. Admitting that he spoke of the Chinese only once in Parliament, he stressed his work behind the scenes with the authorities who could solve problems of individual constituents. During the campaign, federal leader Lester B. Pearson told 3,500 Chinese Canadians at an open-air rally that he could make no promises about immigration quotas, but the Liberals were the "Party of Immigration," and he had urged the government to admit 500 refugee families rather than 100. He vowed that a Liberal government would "encourage family unity regardless of age, ethnic origin or religion," "ensure that the decisions of immigration officials are subject to review by appropriate and independent tribunals," and do something about processing delays. Nicholson won with a larger margin than in 1962 and became minister of forests in Pearson's new minority Liberal government.[60]

No Chinese Canadian was elected to the new Parliament, but Ian Wahn, the Liberal MP for Toronto-St. Paul's, became the chief advocate of the Chinese on the government side. Although references to "the ethnic vote" in Toronto still largely referred to Europeans, that a Toronto MP should take on this role was quite appropriate as the city had a substantial population of Chinese ethnic origin. As soon as the new Parliament met, Wahn introduced a bill "to grant amnesty and to confirm the rights of Asians, Africans and other persons subject to racial discrimination whose admission to Canada may have been irregular or illegal." During the throne speech debate, he welcomed the government's announcement that it would undertake a major review of immigration policy. Shortly thereafter, he joined representatives of Chinese community and benevolent associations of Toronto, Hamilton, Ottawa, and Montreal when they presented a brief to Guy Favreau, the new immigration minister. They asked that, "to permit family unity," sons and daughters of Chinese residents should be admitted no matter their age or marital status, that procedures relating to immigration and status adjustment be speeded up, and that investigations and prosecutions for past entries be stopped. In a follow-up letter to "Dear Mike," K. Dock Yip and Harry Litt Lam, Toronto lawyers, expressed their hope that the new prime minister would implement his promises about "citizenship in practice." The other follow-up was a question from Paul Martineau, a Quebec Conservative, about the brief. Favreau replied that he was studying the problems and might go to Hong Kong to see how problems in handling cases there could be overcome. Two Toronto dailies commented on the request. The *Evening Telegram* conceded that legal immigrants should be able to sponsor immediate relatives and that others who could usefully contribute to Canada should be admitted. However, it suggested that the Chinese community should help to legalize the position of illegal immigrants. The *Globe and Mail* went further and recommended looking "to the Orient" for people who, by increasing Canada's population, would "guarantee its economic and political future." The latter comment was well received by *Chinatown News,* which called the initial requests "mild and reasonable."[61]

A short time later Favreau told Vancouver's Chinese community of the recent brief from Ontario and Quebec Chinese and reiterated his support for "the reunification of families, regardless of race, creed, colour or age." He promised to eliminate any prejudice in immigration matters. He had already made several gestures in that direction, including issuing a special permit to Weldon Chan and family; making arrangements to admit as a landed immigrant Mrs. Louie Yuet Sun, who had been ordered deported even though she had a five-year-old Canadian-born son; and admitting the son, daughter-in-law, and family of Lee Gan, the proprietor of Victoria's Don Mee restaurant. Nevertheless, he stressed that the problem of illegal immigration must be solved. In Parliament, Prime Minister Pearson said that his government, "like its predecessor," was "firmly opposed in principle and in practice to racial discrimination."[62]

While in Vancouver, Favreau heard representations from several individuals, including Foon Sien, and representatives of the CBA, the CCCA, and the Chinese unit of the Army, Navy, and Air Force Veterans. They sought to bring in a broader range of relatives, including the families of their siblings, the removal of age limits for children, a clarification of definitions, greater courtesy at the Hong Kong office, streamlining of procedures, easier access to naturalization, implementation of the promise to bring in 500 refugee families a year for five years, and an annual quota of 1,000 Chinese immigrants. The political import of the situation was underlined when Weldon Chan's daughter presented bouquets to Mrs. Favreau and Mrs. Nicholson. A delegation that met the minister in Victoria made similar representations, as did a letter from the Manitoba CBA.[63]

Favreau's Vancouver audience waited for some concrete action such as the implementation of a campaign promise to admit 500 families. Some MPs, including some Liberals, were also impatient. From time to time, they asked the government when it would change the Immigration Act to eliminate discrimination. Marcel Lambert (Conservative, Edmonton West) reflected the sentiment well when he complained about how applicants in Hong Kong were told to return in four or five months. He suggested "that so far as Chinese immigrants are concerned we in western cities would welcome a lot more." He explained that the Chinese in Edmonton were professionals and excellent businessmen and that the second generation were among "the very best citizens" of the city. The MPs cited individual hardships such as those of Wong Hong Taw, of Kootenay West, a once prosperous market gardener who relied on welfare because of illness. Fifty local residents, including the mayor of Trail, and prominent businessmen had signed a petition supporting his request to bring his son from Hong Kong. Officials in the department's Nelson office said that Wong Hong Taw was in no position to sponsor an immigrant; the Hong Kong office said that the son's limited qualifications meant that he could not qualify as an unsponsored immigrant.[64]

Even applicants with political friends in high places could not speed up the process, though through political channels they could sometimes gain admission. A file in Lester Pearson's papers illustrates the process well. It began with a letter dated 27 November 1963 from the immigration department to an executive of the Saskatchewan Liberal Association. The department agreed that the son of a resident of a small Saskatchewan town met the occupational requirements, and the father had the means to support him, his wife, and his children, but stated that the department could not complete "certain necessary inquiries" before the following May. The provincial Liberal informed the prime minister that the applicant was one of the party's best friends among the Chinese population, had initially applied in August 1962, and was having to send $200 a month to support the family in Hong Kong. If the whole family could not be admitted immediately, he proposed admitting the son so that he could earn money to help support the family. When the prime minister inquired, departmental officials mentioned the need to make "certain inquiries" and the need for the entire family to pass medical examinations before they could consider granting temporary admission to the son. Finally, in July 1964, the department decided to give visas to the family if they passed the medical exams, but it did not call the family for those exams until the Prime Minister's Office again intervened. That did the trick. The exams were scheduled quickly, the family passed them, and they arrived in Canada in November 1964.[65]

Yet political pressure did not always succeed. Another Saskatchewan case concerned the proprietor of a small-town restaurant who wanted to bring in his thirty-four-year-old married son to take over the business. Although Wilf Gardiner, Saskatchewan's Liberal minister of public works, championed the case, the immigration department ruled that the son, who was overage, married, had only six years of primary schooling, and earned his living by painting toys, gave no evidence of having any skills or other qualifications that would qualify him for admission. In passing that information on to Gardiner, Prime Minister Pearson noted, "I am afraid that for the time being this is the situation."[66]

Officials in the immigration department did not share the same liberal ideas as the politicians. "Traditionally," the acting director of immigration reported in 1963, "Canada's immigration policy, however enunciated, has been based on the premise that immigration should help maintain the essentially occidental character of the Canadian population." He explained, in connection with a proposal from the Anglican Church to sponsor fifty youths in the care of the Anglican bishop of Hong Kong whom the church would educate and integrate in Canada,

> the idealist does not believe in the innate superiority of the white man or the white man's culture as is implied by the laws governing sponsorship. The pragmatist does not believe that any democratic government can ignore the demands of the Canadian-Chinese community, supported as it is by a vocal and seemingly increasing body of public opinion, for equal sponsorship rights, or completely resist the external pressures being applied by the newly emergent nations in the Caribbean area who are attempting to use Canada as an outlet for their largely unskilled and uneducated surplus population.

He warned that "unbridled immigration" from Asia and Africa could "swamp" Canadian culture, mores, and customs. Although he admitted that gauging public responses was necessary, he warned that "there is a large segment of the Canadian public heretofore silent, who *may* endorse non-racial discrimination in principle but who would probably react violently if they thought that Immigration were to threaten their jobs, their living standards or their way of life." This specific case, the official warned, posed a particular dilemma: if the minister refused the Anglicans, they would accuse him of racial prejudice; if he accepted their plan, they would regard him as "an enlightened man," but other groups would make similar proposals, and the Chinese community might be upset because it was more interested in sponsoring family members. These were the views of only one individual and do not seem to have been passed on, but they were consistent with the department's sentiment that as Canada's gatekeeper it was responsible for protecting the status quo. Moreover, as one official wrote, "this branch is and always has been doubtful about the advisability of expanding the basis of Chinese immigration and the fraud associated with it." Thus, when the new minister proposed to allow Canadian citizens to sponsor their sons and daughters and their families and fiancées regardless of country of origin, the department warned of even greater opportunities for fraud than had been uncovered during the recent investigations.[67]

Although many senior officials in the immigration department were serving on an acting basis during most of 1963 and 1964, and the deputy minister during much of 1963 was in an acting position only, the department had considerable influence because the prime minister, for reasons unrelated to Chinese immigration, shuffled his cabinet on several occasions, so no minister held the portfolio for very long. Soon after becoming minister in February 1964, René Tremblay made a fact-finding trip to Hong Kong. His report that procedures in the office there were being reformed encouraged the Chinese community to expect improved practices. In July, after tracing the history of the Chinese in Canada and admitting that both Chinese and other Canadians were responsible for the past isolation of the Chinese in Canada, he told a Toronto audience that his department's responsibility was to seek immigrants who would help "to create a greater Canada" through their skills and knowledge.[68]

The changes in Chinese immigration policy announced in the summer of 1964 were not inconsistent with this practice but fit the ideas of departmental officials and did little to increase the number of immigrants. Tremblay explained that the refugee problem in Hong Kong was over, that the people trickling in from China were economic and not political refugees, and that they must be treated as ordinary immigrants. He told Parliament that extending sponsorship to cover siblings and more distant relatives would interfere with the processing of immediate dependents and increase problems of detecting and controlling impostors. Specifically denying "any desire to discriminate against Chinese," he claimed that his decision was "dictated solely by the facts of the situation." He hoped that once the Hong Kong office could be expanded it would be possible to consider applications from skilled but unsponsored immigrants. In any case, he argued that there was no "impossible barrier to the reunion of Chinese families in Canada" and that the number of Chinese immigrants had increased from 876 in 1962 to 1,571 in 1963. His only concession was to permit the entry of fiancés. That disappointed Chinese Canadians. As a petition from members and friends of the Chinese Evangelical Baptist Church in Toronto told Prime Minister Pearson, "there are not too many Chinese women who are in this category [to sponsor their fiancés], and this change would not be of too much help."[69]

Several Liberal MPs also complained about the limits of the change. Joseph Macaluso (Hamilton West) told Parliament that discrimination had been practised in Hong Kong and that ministerial discretion was using the interpretation of the regulations "as a smokescreen." Wahn privately reminded the minister and the prime minister that the caucus immigration committee had recommended changing the Immigration and Citizenship Acts to remove injustices affecting Chinese. While Tremblay was concerned about inequality and humanitarian considerations, he was unwilling to make changes until the "important and unique problems pertaining to Chinese immigration, namely, identification and equitable enforcement of Canadian laws," had been resolved. Indeed, one of his officials described the history of postwar Chinese immigration as "a series of minor concessions" that added up to major changes, and he complained that, "as soon as one concession is granted, pressure is applied for another" and that many of these concessions had simply permitted "the admission of impostors." Another official warned that any concessions for sponsored relatives would lead to pressure from certain Europeans and provide opportunities for more fraud among the Chinese. Moreover, he noted that, given limited travel between Canada and China in the early 1940s, there were few sons aged twenty-one to twenty-five eligible for admission. The official's most telling argument was a calculation that, during trips to China between 1926 and 1958, Chinese in Canada claimed to have fathered 15,233 children of whom 12,883 were boys, nearly all of whom survived. Allowing even generous conception and survival rates,

"Immigration Dept.," *Toronto Daily Star,* 7 January 1965. By using exaggeration and stereotypes of the corrupt Mafia and the downtrodden Chinese, Macpherson criticized the Immigration Department for its methods of investigating illegal Chinese immigration. By permission of the *Toronto Star.*

he calculated that no more than 7,450 children could have been born.[70]

One example of the pressure to increase immigration was the request of the British Columbia Lower Mainland Farmers' Co-Operative Association to bring in up to 200 farm workers. The association's sixty-two Chinese members collectively produced about 80 percent of the fresh vegetables grown in Greater Vancouver. In a lengthy brief to the immigration minister, Douglas Jung, their solicitor, explained that Canadians and younger Chinese would not do such work because of its long hours, poor pay, and lack of opportunity for advancement. So short was the labour supply that the farmers feared having to go out of business unless they paid "exorbitant wages." Anticipating arguments against inferior accommodation, the brief suggested that even the humblest accommodation offered was "paradise" compared to conditions in Hong Kong and China, and the labourers could improve their housing in the winter off-season. Association members would guarantee a minimum one-year contract including fair wages and board. They would offer a longer contract but did "not want to be accused of holding these people in bondage." They would, however, post a bond that the workers would not leave their employ until their contracts expired. In any case, the labourers did not speak English and thus would not compete for jobs with the unemployed in the "white" sector. Although the brief suggested that these workers would be "responsible heads of families" whose main interest was giving "their children a better opportunity," the association asked that immigration officials not apply the usual "strict and high standard." The brief noted that many farm operators had only recently been reunited with their families because of Canadian immigration laws and hoped to increase production to improve their families' standards of living, but the labour shortage meant that they had to employ family members, including young children and elderly pensioners. Supporting the brief were various fruit and vegetable wholesalers in Vancouver, mainly Chinese, but also the produce manager of W.H. Malkin Company, one of the largest food wholesalers in Vancouver. Although the Chinese farmers needed labour for the spring planting, as of 19 June they had received no reply. Explaining that Jung advised them not to make the matter a political issue, James Chan, the president, said that the matter had not been raised in Parliament, as some members had wanted, but implied that they would make their plea public.[71]

The matter was becoming political. Minister of Immigration Tremblay told Chan that he could not lower normal immigration selection standards, but if the association found workers who could meet those standards he would consider their applications. He explained to Prime Minister Pearson that living and working conditions and wages were so poor that even Chinese workers would not accept them for very long. Moreover, said the minister, the RCMP was investigating a complaint that it was a scheme to bring in inadmissible relatives. Rumours circulated about a scheme to bring in "coolie labour," a point that Harold Winch mentioned in Parliament and a charge that Jung immediately denied as he noted that the government was letting Quebec farmers bring in labour from Algeria. Hal Dornan, one of Pearson's assistants, noted that admitting "cheap labour" would leave the government open to criticism, but denying labour to Chinese farmers might cost the government the support of Chinese voters. In Vancouver, a CBC Television program featured a debate between Jung and Winch in which Jung criticized certain residents of Chinatown for not helping the farmers who had received support from the Chamber of Commerce in Kelowna, where crops were rotting because of a shortage of pickers. After Jung spoke to its convention, the British Columbia Federation of Agriculture endorsed the import of Chinese temporary workers, who would be paid standard wages, but the BC Federation of Labour argued that if farmers paid reasonable wages they would have no difficulty getting labour. The provincial ministers of labour and of agriculture thought importing temporary workers impractical, and if properly dispersed there was no shortage of farm workers. Immigrants, Chinese or otherwise, they said, must come as permanent settlers. Eventually, the federal government rejected the plan to bring in the agricultural labourers.[72]

The Liberal government had also inherited the status adjustment program, which officials described as "a flop" because there had been few prosecutions. Even though extensive RCMP investigations had revealed the extent of the conspiracy and identified large numbers of agents and fraudulent immigrants, only fifty-eight, chiefly agents, had been prosecuted, and they had received light sentences. In addition, since no clear cut-off date for amnesty had been announced, illegal immigrants seemed to think that they need not confess until they thought they might be detected, and no penalties were imposed on those who did not come forward or who gave false statements. In Parliament Arnold Peters (NDP, Timiskaming, Ontario) complained that "a multi-million dollar racket" had not been stopped, that the RCMP had not been allowed to prosecute any illegal actions, and that, by issuing an amnesty through an order in council, the government had "legalized any action that may have occurred illegally." Several months later he repeated his charges and urged bringing the matter into the open in order to correct flaws in the immigration system, especially as they affected Asians.[73]

Thus, in August 1964, at the same time as he announced that fiancés could be eligible for immigration, Tremblay dealt with the question of illegal immigration. Noting the existence of "a highly efficient System" for forging documents and photographs and coaching schools, he reported that "contrary to popular belief" most illegal immigrants were not relatives of Canadians but were being brought in for the "profit" of immigration agents. That, he asserted, tarnished the reputation of Chinese Canadians as good citizens and made it more difficult for them to bring in "true relatives." After explaining that the status adjustment program had been designed to benefit the Chinese, who now complained about it, he said that it had been misunderstood and had achieved limited success even though it had lasted longer than anticipated. Since he believed that its four-year duration had given people adequate time to put their affairs in order, he announced that as of 1 September the RCMP and immigration officers would apply the same laws to Chinese as to other residents. In other words, the status adjustment program would end in little more than two weeks, though under questioning in Parliament he agreed that the deadline could be extended.[74]

MPs, including Liberals such as John Turner (Montreal, St. Lawrence-St. Georges) and Ian Wahn, immediately attacked the timetable. They argued that the number of applications for adjustment had been steadily increasing in Toronto and that people had been reluctant to file because the slow process left them without documents or the ability to sponsor relatives for some months. They did not question the need to end the program but called for a longer warning period. In its protest, the CCCA in Vancouver quoted Jung as denying that overall the status adjustment program had failed. In fact Jung believed that, while the Chinese initially hated the RCMP and were unwilling "to act as stool pigeons on their friends," they now realized that no one would be arrested or deported, so they were "coming forward in a steady stream." The Vancouver-based CBA also called for a postponement of the deadline. Department officials did not interpret these protests as worthy of a change in policy. They noted Jung's indication that cancellation was "inevitable." While denying having any views on the relations between the minister and his party's backbenchers, they suggested that the "exaggerated" feelings of some of them may have whipped up opposition in the Chinese community. They wanted to clarify that the status adjustment program and not the amnesty was being terminated, and they were concerned about the effects of future arrangements for Chinese on other ethnic groups. The situation was complicated when J.R. Nicholson, then postmaster general, allegedly told a public meeting of the CBA in Vancouver that the government had temporarily removed the amnesty deadline and would extend it to include ship deserters and other illegal immigrants who entered before 31 August 1964. According to R.B. Curry of the department, that statement (which Nicholson later denied making) was "dangerous" because it did not indicate that agents and racketeers were exempt from the amnesty and would probably lead to requests for similar amnesties from Greeks, Italians, and Portuguese and other ethnic groups who had ship deserters and illegal entrants who "would completely negate immigration legislation and procedures." Because he thought that questions would arise and that the minister in charge should make important policy statements in Parliament, Curry drafted a statement for Tremblay that distinguished between status adjustment and amnesty.[75]

In Parliament, Tremblay explained the differences and recalled that, when the plans were announced in 1960, it was clearly stated that the amnesty did not apply to those who had engaged in illegal immigration for profit or who had helped immigrants other than their own relatives. It was intended to apply only to those who arrived before 1 July 1960, but ministers had been lenient. However, such tolerance could not continue without "seriously weakening the application of, and the respect for, our laws." Responding to criticism, Tremblay had earlier announced that the adjustment program would continue indefinitely for illegal immigrants who arrived before 1 September 1964. Those who arrived after that date would be subject to the same laws as any other immigrants, and the amnesty would not be extended to others. The Chinese community was pleased with the time extension. *Chinatown News* called it "an act of wisdom, compassion and understanding," though it pointed out that immigration policies were still discriminatory. While somewhat sceptical of the general amnesty, it noted that many people were going to the immigration offices to "give themselves up."[76]

Thus, the status adjustment program continued, and the amnesty was generally given to those who arrived before 1 September 1964, except for agents or racketeers and ship deserters. Both the number of applications received and the number processed were rising, but the department did not know how many persons whose status should be adjusted had not applied. By late 1966, 10,533 Chinese had applied for adjustment, 9,962 had been processed, and the department expected to clear the backlog in a few months. By then departmental officials, who had earlier suggested letting it run its course without a formal termination that might be misunderstood, were generally satisfied that the program had removed the "agents" from the scene and was giving the government better control over Chinese immigration.[77]

Early in 1965, as part of a cabinet shuffle, Nicholson became minister of citizenship and immigration. Some constituents were cautiously optimistic, but Andrew Lam, a columnist in *Chinatown News*, was less sanguine. When Nicholson first visited the constituency as minister, leaders of many community organizations met him. The CBA, acting for forty-one organizations, presented the main brief showing how Canadian Chinese had contributed to the growth and welfare of "our country" and wanted to "be placed on equal footing" in matters of citizenship and immigration by eliminating the "immoral and insulting" colour bar that limited the close relatives whom Asians and Africans could sponsor. The CBA reminded Nicholson of Pearson's 1963 promise to admit 500 families and sought an easing of requirements so that sponsored relatives could learn skills in Canada or relieve labour shortages in agriculture, garment factories, laundries, and domestic service. Referring to the concern of "some narrow minded citizens" about a flood of Chinese swamping the country, it said that there would be no "mass influx" because of the immigration department's limited processing facilities and the need to raise over $1,000 for transportation, fees, and other expenses and to arrange housing, employment, and finances. It pointed out that newcomers brought capital into the country and created new jobs. Recognizing the political nature of immigration policy, it added, "let the Liberal Party liberalize the immigration laws, for it would further support the Liberals' policy statement of 'all citizens are equal' ... wherever they were born, whatever their racial origins and creed." In a poignant plea for the admission of a broader range of relatives, the CCCA asked, for example, that men without heirs because they had been unable to visit China be permitted to bring in adopted relatives. Nicholson was impressed, particularly with the argument about inequality in sponsoring relatives, but finding an alternative that would retain "one of the basic tenets of immigration, that of admission by selection," represented "probably the toughest problem" of an immigration minister. His only immediate action was to announce that Chinese Canadians would probably soon have the same passports as other Canadian citizens and, responding to a request from the Army, Navy, and Air Force Veterans, that Chinese Canadians need no longer fill out special forms on returning from visits to the Orient. However, he also indicated that the amnesty would be lifted in the near future.[78]

While the immigration branch underwent an internal reorganization and eliminated much red tape that shortened the waiting time for sponsored relatives in Hong Kong, both it and a special cabinet committee considered immigration policy generally. They gave "special attention" to economic factors, particularly a shortage of willing, well-qualified immigrants, and to difficulties in "assimilating large numbers of immigrants of alien colours and creeds" if a non-discriminatory policy was adopted. The committee working on social and cultural issues drafted a statement: "Discrimination is wrong when it is irrational, arbitrary, and based on such irrelevant factors as race," but social and cultural characteristics affecting an immigrant's ability to become established in Canada "are a legitimate factor in selection." In dealing specifically with Asians, the department considered ways of preventing an influx if a non-discriminatory immigration policy was adopted. Sponsored immigrants tended to be less educated than others but had a support system. "Devising a politically acceptable solution" that did not discriminate against certain sponsors but retained government control was difficult. Officials saw administrative problems in extending sponsorship privileges for Chinese, but the minister opposed such restrictions. One division of the department suggested limiting the "privilege of sponsorship" of other than spouses and minor children to Canadian citizens. After discussion, the minister and senior department members decided that "universal sponsorship" for Canadian citizens would create serious problems in identifying Chinese and others for whom reliable records could not be obtained. The solution was to let Canadians from Asia and Africa sponsor a wider variety of relatives but to limit numbers by imposing a minimal educational requirement that "would be especially relevant to Chinese immigration."[79]

Meanwhile the federal election of November 1965 intervened. At the Chinese Community Centre in Vancouver, Nicholson described the immigration question as "a situation where both the Government of Canada, and the members of the Chinese community in this country have been put in an embarrassing position, and where no easy solution could be found." Pointing to a "satisfactory trend," he suggested that the arrival of 7,316 immigrants in the previous three years indicated the "growing esteem" of other Canadians for the Chinese. Yet he admitted that much had "to be done before Chinese Canadians can feel fully at home in this land. Much distrust will have to be dissipated. Much suspicion will have to be overcome. Much prejudice will have to be set aside." In a full-page advertisement in *Chinatown News,* he described himself as "the man chosen to introduce changes and update the Canadian Immigration Act and regulations." Recognizing the importance of the Chinese vote, Pearson again came to a street rally in Chinatown, where bands and fireworks greeted him. Nicholson's chief opponent was again Douglas Jung, who advertised his accomplishments: cancelling the age limit for parents, removing the $1,000 deposit required for fiancées, and making it possible for non-citizens to sponsor dependents. In his many speeches, he blamed the illegal immigrant problem on the previous Liberal government, reminded voters that a Conservative government had created the amnesty program, and argued that the Liberals had not fulfilled a promise to bring in 500 refugee families and to admit agricultural labourers. He promised that a

Conservative government would improve the immigration laws. *Chinatown News,* however, suggested that despite his slick campaign Jung was fighting an uphill battle against Nicholson, who had "built up a tremendous following" by attending every function in Chinatown or sending a representative or a wire, of never failing to deal with a constituent's problems, and of representing a party whose policies were closer to those of most residents of Chinatown than those of the Conservative Party. When the ballots were counted, Nicholson won more than 50 percent of the vote in the polls in Chinatown, while Jung and the NDP candidate split the rest.[80]

Nationally, the Liberals won another minority government. Before the election, the immigration department had drafted a white paper on policy that Tom Kent, who became deputy minister after the election, described as "largely a defence of existing policy." Nevertheless, during the campaign, Ian Wahn, who was seeking re-election, admitted that there was "some discrimination towards colored people in our immigration policies," but the Liberals had done much to improve the situation and, if re-elected, would soon issue a white paper that would "go a long way to liberalizing immigration." Under the direction of Kent and a new minister, Jean Marchand, the department revised the draft to make it less defensive and "more related to economic policy." Although Kent later admitted that the published paper did little more than propose a tightening of the sponsorship program, when it was announced in October 1966, it promised to "create uniformity of standards for admission for all countries" and let Canadian citizens sponsor, "on a universal basis, a broader range of relatives than at present." *Chinatown News,* while observing that the white paper proposals still discriminated against the unskilled, regarded the new plan as "at least an improvement since it gives the Oriental Canadian an equal chance to compete, and it goes far in removing the worst of the inequities." Yet to assuage any fears about a massive influx of Chinese, Marchand said that the new policy would not mean mass migration from Hong Kong because education levels there were low. Like his predecessors, Marchand was unnecessarily cautious: the records of politicians and the immigration department and press comment are surprisingly bereft of the racist letters and propaganda that had been so common before the war.[81]

After the influential parliamentary committee on immigration considered the white paper, the government amended the immigration regulations. It retained the sponsorship system, but without geographic or racial restrictions, and introduced a "points system" to judge most potential immigrants. In Vancouver, the new policy elicited little comment in the general press, but *Chinatown News* commended Marchand "for his realistic approach to the problem of immigration … [that would] … only redound to Canada's benefit." In Montreal the *Gazette* welcomed the new policy but did not specifically mention Asians. Henceforth "Chinese were now on the same basis as all other immigrants," and "A New Kind of Chinese" immigrant began coming to Canada, individuals who were able to enter Canada not because of their family relationships but because of their skills and the capital that they had for investment.[82] That, however, is another story.

Conclusion

The euphoria that Canadians felt at the time of their centennial in 1967 reflected pride in their nation. As they remembered how previous generations had built a nation from sea to sea, had established Canada's place in the world, and had given Canadians a high standard of living, they could also congratulate themselves on having largely overcome "racism," at least as it applied to their citizens of Chinese and Japanese descent and in immigration policies. The latter accomplishments, however, had occurred only in the previous quarter century. What had happened? How? Describing "how" was the burden of this and the previous two volumes of this trilogy; it remains to summarize "why" British Columbians and other Canadians changed their minds and began including the Japanese and Chinese as full Canadian citizens.

Today it is widely understood that race is socially constructed. That was not always so. Until at least the 1940s, "race" was often defined largely in physical, especially physiognomic, terms or what James St. G. Walker has called a "common sense" explanation that racial differences were self-evident. That idea found expression in British Columbia. In trying to explain why there was agitation for the "mass deportation" of Japanese and not for "nationals of other war-mongering nations," a Kelowna newspaper, for example, suggested that "the only reason seems to be that the Japanese have an oriental facial countenance, whereas the Europeans look like any other white skinned person." The notion of "race," however, was rapidly falling out of fashion in the Western world, where rooting out the evils of racism and the horrors that it had wrought had been a major reason for fighting a world war. As the Prince Rupert *Daily News* commented early in 1946, "we have had enough of segregation, of narrow prejudice and discrimination. It works like a slow poison on the minds of men, and the terrifying success of Nazi propaganda should be enough to show how easy it is to make it grow and fester."[1]

The most authoritative debunking of the "myth" of race was the statement made in June 1950 by the United Nations Educational, Scientific, and Cultural Organization (UNESCO) Committee of Experts on Race Problems.

These physical and social scientists, observing that "the term 'race' as used in popular parlance is perhaps the most confused and most confusing term in the language," pointed out that "members of different races resemble each other vastly more closely than they differ from each other" and that "environmental influences, history and opportunity," not genetics, explained cultural differences. They unequivocally declared that "'race' is not so much a biological phenomenon as a social myth." The UNESCO committee argued that, "in popular parlance, it would be better when speaking of human races to drop the term 'race' altogether and speak of *ethnic groups*."[2] Even before the war, many Canadians were paying attention to ethnic origin rather than the "common sense" idea of "race." Whereas they once referred to Asians collectively as Orientals" or "Asiatics" or even earlier "Mongolians," by 1941 "nation" had become a more useful concept, and Canadian Caucasians expressed sympathy for the Chinese and suspicion of the Japanese. The war accentuated that perception of difference.

The disappearance of "race" as a biological concept also undermined a stock argument against the Asian presence before the Second World War, namely the fear that propinquity would lead to miscegenation. Neither Asians nor Occidentals liked the idea, and interracial marriages were few. As notions of race faded, intermarriages increased, especially among Japanese Canadians. In 1950, noting the 150 intermarriages over the previous decade, Toyo Takata suggested that such unions would "eventually wipe out physical traces of race and color and with it will go all the drum-beating of the race-purists," but it would be a slow process: "We won't be around when the disappearance of racial identity will become a biological fact."[3]

At the same time as a United Nations agency sponsored a study on "race," the United Nations as a whole used the evils of the recent war to build on the Atlantic Charter to draw attention to the need to protect human rights and included "fundamental human rights" in its charter and most clearly articulated the concept in the preamble of the Universal Declaration of Human Rights, proclaimed in December 1948. The declaration averred that "disregard and contempt for human rights have resulted in barbarous acts which have outraged the conscience of mankind." Its text referred to civil rights as recognition of "a person before the law," "freedom of movement within the state," and the rights to leave from and return to one's own country, not to "be arbitrarily deprived of [one's] nationality," to own property, and to participate in government through equal suffrage. Because of Canada's concern for its international reputation, it had granted those rights to all of its citizens or, in the case of Japanese Canadians, was about to grant them.[4] The Chinese had already benefited. During the war, governments slowly eliminated legal disabilities on the Chinese: they returned their firearms, which had been confiscated in 1940, they called up eligible Chinese Canadians for military service in 1944, and Saskatchewan enfranchised the

Chinese that year. The major changes came in 1947, when British Columbia enfranchised Chinese Canadians and began repealing discriminatory laws and Ottawa repealed the exclusionary Chinese Immigration Act. Those protesting proposals to "repatriate" the Japanese, the sale of Japanese property, and the unequal treatment of the Chinese had appealed to the Atlantic Charter during the war. Afterward, with their civil libertarian allies, Japanese Canadians fought the "repatriation orders" not only on grounds of justice, human rights, and the need to abandon "racialism" but also on the basis of Canadian citizenship. The last argument was especially compelling because Canada had finally defined Canadian citizenship with legislation in 1946. The BC legislature narrowly rejected the enfranchisement of the Japanese in 1947, but two years later it readily granted them that right. In 1949 too, the federal government, finally realizing that most British Columbians no longer regarded the Japanese as a "problem," removed a major civil disability on Japanese Canadians, the ability to move freely within Canada. Ever cautious, however, it did not remove practices that discriminated against immigrants from Asia until 1967, when it adopted a general immigration policy that built on immigrants' skills rather than their origins.

Change had come slowly, for there was little inclination to relax immigration barriers more than a token amount. The ancient fear that by their sheer numbers Asians could swamp a "white Canada" survived the war in the minds of many BC MPs and lasted even longer among the bureaucrats in charge of immigration policy. While Canadians were confident that they could assimilate a small addition to their Asian population, immigration officials doubted their ability to deal with a large number and preserve a white society. Even the Asian Canadian community understood that an open door policy was not practical. Nevertheless, many Caucasians sympathized with Chinese and Japanese Canadians who wanted to bring their relatives to Canada. Moreover, in British Columbia, where that fear had been strongest, migration from elsewhere in Canada and from Europe had strengthened its population base. Whereas the province had only 817,961 residents in 1941, by 1951 it had 1,165,210 and was growing rapidly; by 1961 the population was 1,590,268. That almost doubling of the population in twenty years reduced apprehension of being overwhelmed.

British Columbians also felt more secure because they no longer had to worry about Japan as a threat. Building on fears that developed during Japan's search for a Greater East Asian Co-Prosperity Sphere, many Canadians saw Japan's attack on Pearl Harbor as a prelude to a military attack on western North America. The Allies' trouncing of Japan and the demilitarization clauses in the subsequent peace treaty removed Japan as a military threat. That and the demonstrated loyalty to Canada of Japanese Canadians made it possible for Canada to extend the rights of citizenship to them. Until the peace treaty was signed and Canada re-established diplomatic relations with

Japan in 1952, Canada could ignore Japan in shaping its immigration policy. As the revival of Japan's economy made it an important country for trade and ultimately a source of investment in Canadian industry, Japan became a partner and friend, not a foe. Thus, Canada had to pay attention to Japan's interests in shaping its immigration policies and symbolically announced the revisions of 1967 in Tokyo. Of course Japan's prosperity meant that relatively few Japanese wanted to emigrate to Canada.

Changed views of "race," concerns for human rights, and a growing sense of security were important factors in changing attitudes toward Asians, but they were not the only ones. As pointed out in previous volumes, among the oldest objections to the Asian presence in Canada were economic ones. Anti-Asian agitators alleged that, by remitting funds to families in Asia or only coming as sojourners, Asians did not contribute to the growth of the Canadian economy. As the Chinese population declined and as Japanese Canadians established families in Canada, that complaint largely disappeared by 1941. Another common charge against Asians was that, by accepting lower wages and poorer working conditions, their "cheap labour" took jobs from white people and undermined their standards of living. Even before the war, provincial laws regulating minimum wages and working conditions and the co-operative marketing of agricultural products had largely eliminated charges of "unfair" competition, though it persisted in the fisheries and in Vancouver in small business. When the war began, Caucasian and First Nations fishermen welcomed the departure of their Japanese competitors, and some Caucasians expressed interest in acquiring property owned by the Japanese. Despite that, there is no evidence that removing economic competition was the motive for removing the Japanese from the coast.

Most laws restricting Asian activities remained on the statute books throughout the war years. During and immediately after the war, general prosperity and shortages of labour meant that the economic argument against Asians no longer carried much weight. Yet in 1946 and 1947, when Ian Mackenzie sought to prevent the return of the Japanese to the coast, he cited economic reasons. He was not totally inconsistent; in 1942 he had mentioned the desire of British Columbians to be free of Japanese competition but had stressed national security as the main argument for sending the Japanese inland. That Mackenzie was out of touch with BC opinion is well shown by the protest in 1948 when the BC government tried to deny employment to Japanese on crown lands. The old spectre of "cheap labour" was not a persuasive argument, and opening employment opportunities to Asians fit well with concerns about human rights.

Toleration was a two-way street, but the lanes were not even. Caucasians only had to set aside their prejudices; Asians had to be good citizens and had to campaign actively to secure the rights due to them as Canadian citizens. As Japanese Canadians were dispersed, Caucasians who had not previously known them recognized their good qualities, their loyalty to Canada, their good citizenship, and their willingness to contribute to the community despite the inequities under which they laboured. Their co-operation with dispersal and their use of democratic political means to fight involuntary repatriation gradually won over all but the most hardened Japanophobes to accept them as fellow citizens. This appreciation first appeared in the "ghost towns" of the West Kootenay and the Boundary Districts of the BC interior but also developed wherever significant numbers of Japanese were able to settle east of the Rockies. Thus, for example, the *Ottawa Citizen* opined early in 1946 that "only by release from fear and hatred can race prejudice be cured. A willingness to live and let live in friendliness within the same community with a share of the same education and interests is the answer to those who assert that Canadians of Japanese origin cannot be assimilated into the work and life of the only country they know." As the Vancouver *Daily Province* noted in 1949, "the Japanese have purged themselves. They have accepted the principle of dispersal and have so conducted themselves in the interior of the province that they are not only accepted but are welcomed and admired." Even more striking, because of its source, was the comment by the *Vancouver Sun:* "Seven years have brought a radical change in the situation. The Japanese themselves are scattered all across Canada, instead of being congested in a special area around Vancouver. They are willing and anxious to be Canadian, owing this country their first loyalty. We shall do well to accept their resolve at its face value and to remove all obstacles from their path to citizenship."[5]

Several years later *Vancouver Sun* columnist James K. Nesbitt reflected the idea of inclusion well when he wrote in 1955 how "racial prejudice is slowly but surely disappearing from British Columbia ... Canadians of Japanese, Chinese and East Indian ancestry are accepted in all walks of life, like Canadians of any other ancestry ... The color of a citizen's skin, the race of his ancestors, are becoming less important. What matters is the individual living in B.C. today, and how he behaves himself."[6]

In the first decades after the war, Japanese Canadians had disagreed on how to deal with their wartime experiences. The articulate Muriel Kitagawa, who, with her husband and small children, self-evacuated to Toronto, told the Toronto Council of Women in 1948 that "the majority of my people are glad to be out of B.C. and not even the tourist climate can lure them back to the scenes of their humiliation. But that does not excuse the evacuation." She reminded the council, "this forced removal of a racial minority from their homes and birthplaces was the proof positive that a vociferous group of race-baiters can upset the just balance of a normally sane people."[7] At the same time, others understood that the "mass evacuation was a political necessity in the spring of 1942, in view of feeling prevailing in British Columbia. Then too, the fact that the United States had apparently already decided to evacuate its Japanese from the West Coast would have left Canada in a rather awkward position had she not done likewise."[8] Others simply wanted to forget their wartime experiences. After interviewing almost 500 people about their wartime experiences as part of the research for the history of the Japanese in Canada, Ken Adachi reported in 1960 that "people were reluctant to discuss this phase of their lives for fear of repercussion and hesitated to give names or details."[9]

The wartime experiences of the Chinese Canadians were much less dramatic. They too had long made an effort to be good citizens; their contributions to the war effort through the voluntary military service of their young men, their work in the munitions industry, and their purchase of war bonds did no harm to their reputations. Thus, because of their own merits as well as awareness of human rights, after the war British Columbia readily repealed its discriminatory laws and practices that applied to them. Canada's establishment of diplomatic relations with China in 1943 helped to explain the relaxation of Chinese immigration regulations in 1947, but diplomatic relations ended in 1949 with the Communist takeover of China, and it was left to Chinese Canadians themselves and their friends to lobby for further easing of immigration regulations. The fact that they were accepted as fellow Canadian citizens was well demonstrated after 1949 when rumours that some immigrants were Communist agents did not elicit widespread hostility to the Chinese already in Canada, again suggesting that Canadians were judging people not by their ethnicity but by their individual merits.

The question, however, was no longer just a BC one. Because of the self-dispersal of the Chinese and the forced dispersal of the Japanese, the treatment of Asians had become a national question.[10] In the early years of the Pacific War, there was little difference across Canada in attitudes toward accepting the Japanese, and one of the most widely quoted of the fearmongers in early 1942 was Premier Mitchell Hepburn of Ontario. Yet it was Canadians east of the Rockies, especially in Toronto and Winnipeg and to a lesser extent Montreal, where civil libertarians particularly in the churches and in the press successfully appealed to Canadian and international values of human rights. That work in persuading the government to modify and then end the "repatriation" policy for Japanese and to ease immigration regulations for both Chinese and Japanese, and the decision to remove the Japanese from the coast, illustrate how governments respond to public opinion. Paradoxically, the BC MPs who so effectively conveyed their constituents' antipathy to the Japanese in January and February 1942 failed to recognize the waning of that hostility. In the 1950s, however, a new generation of BC MPs was much more amenable to relaxing immigration regulations.

Although politicians made immigration policy, bureaucrats in the immigration department long discouraged them from opening the doors to Chinese and Japanese. Despite extensive turnover in the personnel of the Department of Citizenship and Immigration both in the bureaucratic and in the ministerial ranks, officials saw themselves as gatekeepers and were much more cautious in easing regulations than their political ministers, who generally yielded to their advice.[11]

In the process of consolidating their "White Man's Province" in the interwar years, British Columbians largely eliminated any danger of the Asian population growing through immigration or that Asians in their midst would be "unfair" economic competitors. Yet like other Canadians, they held to their notion that these people of a different "race" must be excluded from full membership in Canadian society. Despite some sympathy for Canadian-born Asians, they were unwilling to grant them the basic right of citizenship, the franchise. And when the Pacific War began, long-held but unfounded fears that the ethnicity of the Japanese in Canada would trump their Canadian citizenship came to the fore with calamitous consequences for them. By the end of the war, Canadians realized the evils of racism and the need to respect human rights. With the twin concepts of civil rights and citizenship in the forefront, though not without some debate, Canadians gradually accepted the full inclusion of people of Chinese and Japanese ancestry in the Canadian polity. Over time, too, Canadians adopted an immigration policy that, while controlling numbers, dropped practices that excluded people by ethnic origin and included them by what they might contribute to the nation. Inclusion replaced exclusion as Canada's policy toward its citizens and people of Chinese and Japanese ancestry.

The persistent campaigning of Japanese and especially Chinese Canadians for equality in treatment paid off. Because of discriminatory franchise laws before the war, Japanese and Chinese Canadians had limited experience in Canadian electoral politics, but they learned quickly and patiently used those skills to secure widespread political support in their quest for full equality with other Canadian citizens. It was a sense of inclusion that they desired to share. In preparing a presentation for the Royal Commission on Bilingualism and Biculturalism in 1964, the Japanese Canadian Citizens Association declared that "we are for the multi-cultural society where a Canadian citizen is recognized as a national of Canada."[12] For both the Japanese and the Chinese, citizenship had trumped ethnic or "racial" origin.

Epilogue

The history of the Chinese and Japanese in Canada continued, of course, after 1967. In the case of the Chinese, it was marked by massive immigration not only from Hong Kong and the People's Republic of China but also from the Chinese diaspora throughout Asia. Between 1968 and 1994, 398,579 individuals arrived from China and Hong Kong, and an additional number of ethnic Chinese came from other parts of the world (see Table E.1). The majority settled in Greater Toronto and Greater Vancouver. Although legal discrimination had long since disappeared, some old complaints reappeared with a twist. Whereas in the early decades of the twentieth century complaints about Asians often referred to their low standards of living and crowded housing, now the objection was to the conspicuous consumption of Chinese immigrants. The wealthy newcomers, mainly from Hong Kong, were actually a very small number of the arrivals, but many Chinese, including the Canadian born, suffered from this new stereotype. As journalist Margaret Cannon explained in relation to Toronto in the late 1980s, "formerly the Chinese had been thought of as 'good' immigrants – that is as poor, humble, eager to please and so on. The new Chinese became the focus of local wrath, with earlier residents complaining about everything from parking foul-ups to noise at a local plaza catering to their Oriental neighbors."[1] Another complaint concerned the fast luxury cars that some Chinese parents, some of them absentees, gave to undisciplined young sons. A larger issue was the ability of the wealthy to pay high prices for houses in prime residential areas – often to demolish them and build new "monster" houses on lots that had been bulldozed to remove the trees, apparently to conform to principles of *feng shui*. The "monster" houses were a particular issue in Vancouver but also appeared in some Toronto suburbs. In Vancouver, municipal bylaws controlling the design of houses and protecting trees defused the agitation. Nevertheless, in both Vancouver and Toronto, the new immigrants were often blamed – rightly or wrongly – for escalating real estate values so much that middle-class people could no longer afford to buy houses in the city.[2]

Table E.1

Immigration to Canada by country of last permanent residence

Year	People's Republic of China	Hong Kong	Taiwan
1947-62	21,877	n/a	n/a
1964-67	18,716	n/a	n/a
1968	8,382	n/a	n/a
1969	177	7,301	n/a
1970	119	4,509	n/a
1971	47	5,009	n/a
1972	25	6,297	859
1973	60	14,662	1,372
1974	379	12,704	1,382
1975	903	11,132	1,131
1976	833	10,725	1,178
1977	798	6,371	899
1978	644	4,740	637
1979	2,056	5,966	707
1980	4,936	6,309	827
1981	6,550	6,451	834
1982	3,571	6,542	560
1983	2,217	6,710	570
1984	2,214	7,696	421
1985	1,883	7,380	536
1986	1,902	5,893	695
1987	2,625	16,170	1,467
1988	2,778	23,281	2.187
1989	4,430	19,908	3,388
1990	7,989	29,261	3,681
1991	13,915	22,340	4,488
1992	10,429	38,910	7,456
1993	9,466	36,576	9,867
1994	12,486	44,169	7,441
1995	13,291	31,746	7,691
1996	17,516	29,966	13,207
1997	18,526	22,250	13,224
1998	19,700	8,087	7,193
1999	29,150	3,671	5,483
2000	36,750	2,865	3,535
2001	40,365	1,965	3,114
2002	33,307	1,541	2,910
2003	36,116	1,472	2,126
2004	36,429	1,547	1,992
2005	42,291	1,784	3,092

Sources: Data for China (including Hong Kong) for 1947-67: Alan B. Simmons, "Globalization and Backlash Racism in the 1990s: The Case of Asian Immigration to Canada," in *The Silent Debate: Asian Immigration and Racism in Canada,* ed. Eleanor Laquian, Aprodicio Laquian, and Terry McGee (Vancouver: Institute of Asian Research, University of British Columbia, [1998]), 38. Data for all countries for 1968-2005: Department of Immigration, *Immigration Statistics* (annual reports, published under the department's various names, including Manpower and Immigration, Employment and Immigration Canada, and Citizenship and Immigration), www.gdsourcing.com/works/Immigrat.htm.

Caucasians also alleged that Chinese students through their hard work scored high marks and were able to secure a disproportionate share of scarce places in university programs such as pharmacy. That issue came to a head in 1979 when *W-5*, a CTV program, ran the story "Campus Giveaway," which alleged that 100,000 foreign students were pushing Canadians out of professional schools. The camera showed a classroom at the University of Toronto full of Chinese pharmacy students. In fact the program admitted only Ontario residents and certainly not foreign or visa students. Activist Chinese Canadian students launched a protest. Eventually, they gained the support both of Chinese Canadians across the country and of Caucasian politicians, including Toronto City Council. As historian Anthony Chan observed, "the Chinese community, once stereotyped as passive and docile, was now action-oriented and conscious of its own democratic rights." Eventually, the network apologized for a presentation that appeared to be racist, for depicting Chinese Canadians as foreigners (the main grievance), and for stereotyping them.[3]

Moreover, some newcomers were sojourners. Some Hong Kong residents, encouraged by the special consideration that Canadian immigration policy gives to entrepreneurs and investors, "hedged their bets" before the transfer of Hong Kong from British to Chinese control in 1997 by acquiring Canadian citizenship but maintaining their business interests in Hong Kong as "astronauts" who crossed the Pacific on a regular basis. Others came from Taiwan and the People's Republic of China. Indeed, after 1997, immigration from Hong Kong fell off so sharply that it was no longer in one of the "top ten" sources of immigrants, while immigration from the People's Republic of China rose. Others came to attend Canadian universities or one of the many private English-language schools that sprang up in many Canadian cities or even public high schools, which recruited them as tuition-paying students to fill classrooms that would otherwise be vacant because of a declining population of teenagers in Canada. Yet school boards complained of the cost of educating immigrant children who often required specialized instruction in English as a second language, though others, through native intelligence and hard work, often won scholarships.

Evidence of racism appeared in the form of graffiti and the outbursts of extreme right-wingers, but the common reaction was more restrained, although some authors have suggested that Canadians are reticent to speak out on matters relating to Asian immigration and racism.[4] Exploring the reasons for this and the dramatic contrast between the situation of sixty years ago is beyond the scope of this book, but a hypothesis can be put forward, namely that several generations have passed and that younger generations have grown up in a world that understands the importance of human rights and of treating all people as equals. Thus, when racism appeared, those who expressed it, not its targets, were the villains. For example, when a suburban Vancouver branch of the Canadian Legion refused to let some Sikh veterans attend a reception after a Remembrance Day parade because their turbans violated the Legion's "no hats" policy, the *Vancouver Sun* ran a cartoon of the Legion headquarters with a sign at the door, "as a gesture of allegiance to outmoded traditions please check your brains at the door."[5]

For students of the last third of the twentieth century and the early years of the twenty-first, another subject requiring fuller examination is the relationship within ethnic groups. Wing Chung Ng has begun such a study, but his intensive work goes only to 1980 and, of course, deals only with Vancouver. Nevertheless, what he has found in his analysis of that city's Chinese community and the contest between different groups over "the meaning of being Chinese in Canada" indicates that there is room for further investigation.[6] Many newcomers, who were themselves culturally diverse, had little in common with the second, third, and fourth generations of Canadian-born Chinese. Many of the latter no longer spoke Chinese, or if they did it was Cantonese, whereas many newcomers were Mandarin speakers. In 1961, when MP Douglas Jung welcomed a trade delegation from China in Cantonese, the interpreter asked if his speech should be translated into Chinese. Jung switched to English.[7]

Many newcomers did quickly adapt to Canadian life and society. While some who came through family reunification schemes lacked the marketable skills or knowledge of English to get more than menial jobs, the unsponsored immigrants had the human and financial capital necessary to establish prosperous enterprises or secure good jobs in business or the professions. Once they qualified for Canadian citizenship, they joined mainstream political parties. Both the Canadian born and immigrants have held high political office. Raymond Chan, an immigrant from Hong Kong, served in the Liberal cabinets of Jean Chrétien and Paul Martin. Bob Wong, a Canadian-born Chinese, served in the cabinet of Ontario premier David Peterson. Hong Kong immigrant David Lam was one of British Columbia's most successful lieutenant governors, while a Canadian-born Chinese and former football star, Norman Kwong, holds a similar office in Alberta. And, of course, a wartime refugee from Hong Kong, Adrienne Clarkson (née Poy), served as governor general after a distinguished career in journalism.[8]

A few Japanese Canadians have been elected to municipal office in various cities throughout the country, but given their small numbers they have had a limited impact on provincial or national electoral politics. In the federal election of 2004, however, Beverley (Bev) Oda, a Sansei, born in 1944 in Thunder Bay, Ontario, where her father worked in a mill, was elected as the Conservative member of Parliament for Clarington-Scugog-Uxbridge in Ontario. She was re-elected in 2006 and appointed minister of heritage. And Thomas Shoyama, a leader of the prewar Nisei community, held one of the most senior positions in the federal civil service, that of deputy minister of finance.

Given their anxiety to rebuild their lives in their new Canadian homes, it is not surprising that from approximately 1949 to 1977 Japanese Canadians did little as a group to seek recompense for their wartime sufferings. Yet the Canadian government realized that it had committed an injustice during the war. At the opening of the Japanese Canadian Cultural Centre in Toronto in 1964, Prime Minister Lester B. Pearson said that Canada's wartime treatment of its Japanese residents during the war was "a black mark against Canada's traditional fairness and devotion to the principle of human rights," but he did not follow with a formal apology or an offer of compensation.[9]

In the early 1980s, younger Japanese Canadians, having taken great pride in their heritage through the 1977 celebration of a century of Japanese settlement in Canada and undoubtedly aware of the friendly reception given to the publication of Shizuye Takashima's brief memoir, *A Child in Prison Camp,*[10] began a campaign for redress, as was happening in the United States. The early stages of the redress campaign were fraught by divisions among Japanese Canadians between those who wanted to forget the past and those who insisted that justice be done. The settlement, as finally negotiated, saw individual grants of $21,000 to survivors of the relocation, a formal condemnation by the government of its "unjust treatment" of Japanese Canadians during and after the Second World War, $15 million to establish a "community fund" mainly for community projects and for implementation of the settlement, and opportunities for those who had been convicted under the War Measures Act to apply for pardons and for those who had lost their Canadian citizenship (and their children born in Japan) through deportation to regain it.[11] That redress settlement with its provision for "repatriates" to regain their Canadian citizenship was a strong symbol of the full inclusion of Japanese Canadians in Canadian life.

The success of Japanese Canadians in securing redress encouraged Chinese Canadians to seek redress for their head tax payments. That, and especially the adoption of the Canadian Charter of Rights in 1982, inspired Shack Jang Mack, who had paid the head tax in the early 1920s, to seek the advice of his MP, Margaret Mitchell (NDP, Vancouver East). In Parliament, she asked if the government had any intention of redressing the head tax and exclusion issues. She did not get a satisfactory answer. The Chinese Canadian National Council (CCNC), took up the cause and drew up a list of over 4,000 head tax payers, their widows, and their descendants. However, after granting redress to Japanese Canadians, the federal government announced that it would not consider requests for redress from other groups. Yet the head tax issue raised significant legal issues, and with funding from the Court Challenges Program, the CCNC launched a class action on behalf of Mack, Quan Ying Lee, the widow of a head tax payer, and Yew Lee, the descendant of one. They sought a return of the monies paid and alleged that the head tax had violated the equality provisions of the charter and international principles of human rights. The courts in Ontario, where the case was

"Shares in Toyota," Victoria *Times-Colonist,* 1 April 1984. During the 1980s, Japanese Canadians lobbied the federal government for redress for their wartime losses. By that time, of course, the economy of Japan was booming and Japanese automobile manufacturers were doing very well in North American markets and were investing in Canada. Courtesy of Raeside.

heard and appealed, admitted that discrimination had existed and that the Chinese Immigration Act was a "stain" on Canadian history. Nevertheless, the courts ruled that, because the discrimination occurred before the charter was enacted, there was no legal basis for the claim. As well, the courts noted that international principles of human rights did not come into use until after the Chinese Immigration Act was repealed. Moreover, the courts pointed out that at the time Canada had the legal right to collect the tax. The Supreme Court of Canada denied the plaintiffs the right to appeal. Like the courts, the press recognized that a great wrong had been imposed on the head tax payers. Editors called for the government to make a formal apology. Two BC newspapers, the *Vancouver Sun* and the *Victoria Times-Colonist,* argued that doing so would discharge its obligations, whereas the Toronto *Globe and Mail* asserted that the government should give a modest monetary payment to the survivors.[12]

The issue festered, and shortly before the Liberal government fell in the fall of 2005 Minister of Multiculturalism Raymond Chan announced that the government would set aside $2.5 million as an acknowledgment that the head tax had been wrongly collected. How the funds would be spent was not specified, but it was suggested that they might go toward an educational program, perhaps in a museum. That satisfied the National Congress of Chinese Canadians, which also accepted Chan's argument that an apology might be perceived as an acknowledgment of guilt and lead to a number of legal claims. Other Chinese Canadians, however, claimed that the National Congress was a front for Liberals in Toronto's Chinatown. Members of the CCNC and the Association of Chinese Canadians for Equality and Solidarity complained that they had not been consulted even though they had been calling for individual compensation and an apology since the mid-1980s. The federal New Democratic Party, whose leader, Jack Layton, is married to Olivia Chow, a Chinese Canadian who was elected to Parliament in a Toronto constituency in 2006, supported the CCNC in arguing for a compensation package. Realizing that the head tax was becoming an issue in several Vancouver- and Toronto-area constituencies, where Chinese Canadians formed a significant portion of the electorate, Prime Minister Paul Martin, in an interview on Fairchild Radio, a Chinese-language broadcaster, said that he regretted the head tax and apologized for it but that the government would not provide individual compensation. Chan and David Emerson, a cabinet minister, whose Vancouver-area constituencies had a population that was over 40 percent Chinese, later explained that the apology was given after the government received further legal advice that an apology would not trigger lawsuits. On the Conservative side, several BC candidates said that the government should renegotiate the agreement and try to bring the Chinese factions together, but Conservative multicultural critic Bev Oda and immigration critic Inky Mark, the descendant of head tax payers, said that they and their leader, Stephen Harper, agreed with the Liberal plan.

Even so, Harper told a radio interviewer that it was "time for Parliament and the government of Canada to recognize this grave injustice, and to apologize for it." A few days after the election, as prime minister designate, Harper repeated his belief that the Chinese Canadian community deserved an apology and appropriate redress for the head tax. Although nationally the Conservatives won more seats than the Liberals, in Vancouver and Toronto they were shut out. Raymond Chan was re-elected in Richmond and David Emerson in Vancouver-Kingsway. Nevertheless, as *Vancouver Sun* reporter Miro Cernetic observed, "Canada's Chinese community has flexed its political muscle in a way that hasn't been seen before and it won't be corralled into positions by a powerful cabinet minister or the leaders of a single interest group."[13] The head tax was an issue in the 2006 federal election. Subsequently, in June 2006, Prime Minister Stephen Harper accepted Canada's "moral responsibility," though not its "liability," issued a formal apology to Chinese Canadians, and announced "symbolic payments" to the handful of surviving head tax payers or to their surviving spouses. That announcement, a move that was endorsed by the leaders of all three opposition parties, demonstrated clearly that Chinese Canadians are fully included in Canadian political life, that their Canadian citizenship had triumphed.[14]

Notes

Abbreviations

Note: Collections cited only once or twice have not been abbreviated.

BCA	British Columbia Archives
BCLJ	*British Columbia Legislative Journal*
BCSCR	British Columbia Security Commission Records, LAC
CCRC	Chinese Canadian Research Collection, UBC
CCAR	Chinese Canadian Association Records, LAC
CCJC	Co-Operative Committee on Japanese Canadians, LAC
CEPR	Custodian of Enemy Property Records, LAC
CNSP	C.N. Senior Papers, BCA
CVA	City of Vancouver Archives
CWCR	Cabinet War Committee Records, LAC
DC&I	Department of Citizenship and Immigration, LAC
DCER	*Documents on Canadian External Relations*
DEAR	Department of External Affairs Records, LAC
DFin	Department of Finance Records, LAC
DImm	Department of Immigration Records, LAC
DLab	Department of Labour Records, LAC
DNDR	Department of National Defence Records, LAC
EDFP	E. Davie Fulton Papers, LAC
FABP	F. Andrew Brewin Papers, LAC
FDP	Francis Dickie Papers, BCA
GGMcGP	G.G. McGeer Papers, BCA
GR	Government Records, BCA
GTP	Grace Tucker Papers, LAC
HCD	Canada, Parliament, House of Commons, *Debates*
HCGP	Howard Green Papers, CVA
HCGFP	Howard Green Family Papers, Add Mss 1034, CVA
HDWP	Halford Wilson Papers, BCA
HDWPV	Halford Wilson Papers, CVA
HDP	Hugh Dobson Papers, BCA
HLKP	H.L. Keenleyside Papers, LAC
HRMacMP	H.R. MacMillan Papers, UBC
HWHP	H.W. Herridge Papers, LAC
IAMP	Ian Alistair Mackenzie Papers, LAC
JBP	John Bracken Papers, LAC
JCCA	Japanese Canadian Citizens Association, LAC
JDP	John Diefenbaker Papers, LAC (microfilm)

JLRP	J.L. Ralston Papers, LAC
JWPP	J.W. Pickersgill Papers, LAC
KP	W.L.M. King Papers, LAC
LAC	Library and Archives Canada
LBPP	Lester B. Pearson Papers, LAC
LSt.LP	Louis St. Laurent Papers, LAC
MFP	Margaret Foster Papers, LAC
MJCP	M.J. Coldwell Papers, LAC
MMC	MacInnis Memorial Collection, UBC
MTP	Minoru Takada Papers, LAC
PCOR	Privy Council Office Records, LAC
PP	Premiers' Papers, GR 1222, BCA
PPR	Provincial Police Records, BCA
PSP	Provincial Secretary's Papers, BCA
RBHP	R.B. Hanson Papers, LAC
RCMPR	Royal Canadian Mounted Police Records, LAC
RGRP	R.G. Robertson Papers, LAC
RLMP	Royal Letherington Matland Papers, BCA
SD	Canada, Parliament, Senate, *Debates*
SFU	Simon Fraser University Archives
TDPP	Thomas Dufferin Pattullo Papers, BCA
TWPP	T.W. Parsons Papers, BCA
UBC	University of British Columbia, Special Collections
UCCA	United Church of Canada Archives, Toronto
UFAWUR	United Fishermen and Allied Workers Union Records, UBC
VWOP	V.W. Odlum Papers, LAC
WACBP	W.A.C. Bennett Papers, SFU
WMS/HM	Women's Mission Society, Home Missions, UCCA
WNSP	Walter N. Sage Papers, UBC

Introduction

1 David J. Mitchell, *W.A.C. Bennett and the Rise of British Columbia* (Vancouver: Douglas and McIntyre, 1983), 397. They probably did not meet in high school since Wing graduated in 1929 and Shoyama, who graduated in 1933, probably entered Kamloops High School the following September. Given that Kamloops was not large (its total population in 1931 was 6,167), they probably knew of each other.

2 Patricia E. Roy, *A White Man's Province: British Columbia Politicians and Chinese and Japanese Immigrants, 1858-1914* (Vancouver: UBC Press, 1989), and *The Oriental Question: Consolidating a White Man's Province, 1914-41* (Vancouver: UBC Press, 2003).

3 Toronto had 2,326 Chinese residents, while Montreal had 1,708. Edgar Wickberg, ed., *From China to Canada: A History of the Chinese Communities in Canada* (Toronto: McClelland and Stewart, 1982), 303; Ken Adachi, *The Enemy that Never Was* (Toronto: McClelland and Stewart, 1976; reprint, with an afterword by Roger Daniels, 1991), 423.

4 This point is also discussed in José E. Igartua, *The Other Quiet Revolution: National Identities in English Canada, 1945-71* (Vancouver: UBC Press, 2006), 36-49.

5 Patricia E. Roy, "British Columbia's Fear of Asians, 1900-1950," *Histoire sociale/Social History* 13 (1980): 163.

6 Suzanne Morton, *At Odds: Gambling and Canadians, 1919-1969* (Toronto: University of Toronto Press, 2003).

7 Constance Backhouse, *Colour-Coded: A Legal History of Racism in Canada, 1900-1950* (Toronto: Osgoode Society, 1999), 8. For a brief discussion of the varying definitions of the terms "race" and "racism," see Roy, *The Oriental Question*, 7-11.

8 James St.G. Walker, *"Race," Rights and the Law, and the Supreme Court of Canada* (Toronto: Osgoode Society, 1997), 6.

9 Ross Lambertson, *Repression and Resistance: Canadian Human Rights Activists, 1930-1960* (Toronto: University of Toronto Press, 2005), 107, 140. See also Stephanie D. Bangarth, "The Politics of Rights: Canadian and American Advocacy Groups and North America's Citizens of Japanese Ancestry, 1942-1949" (PhD diss., University of Waterloo, 2003).

10 F.H. Soward and Edgar McInnis, *Canada and the United Nations* (New York: Manhattan, 1956), 200-2; George Egerton, "Entering the Age of Human Rights: Religion, Politics, and Canadian Liberalism, 1945-50," *Canadian Historical Review* 83 (2004): 470. See also Christopher MacLennan, *Toward the Charter: Canadians and the Demand for a National Bill of Rights, 1929-1960* (Montreal and Kingston: McGill-Queen's University Press, 2003).

Even the Australians, who built "a great white wall" to keep out Asian immigrants, bowed to ideas of human rights as in the United Nations Charter, to the need for good relations with Asian nations, and to domestic lobbying from churches, socialists, and liberals. In the 1960s and 1970s, Australia slowly dismantled "White Australia" laws. Australians accepted the idea that race was not a barrier to assimilation. See Sean Brawley, *The White Peril: Foreign Relations and Asian Immigration to Australasia and North America 1919-78* (Sydney: University of New South Wales Press, 1995), and Gwenda Tavan, *The Long, Slow Death of White Australia* (Melbourne: Scribe Publications, 2005).

Although the civil rights movement that led to the end of legal segregation of blacks in the United States did not come to fruition until the 1960s, American moves to relax exclusionary legislation regarding Chinese in 1943 and to allow residents of Japanese ancestry to move freely about the country early in 1945 influenced Canadian policy, though Canada delayed adopting these policies for several years.

11 *Canada Year Book, 1948-49* (Ottawa: King's Printer, 1949), xxxi. See, for example, Victoria *Daily Colonist* (hereafter the *Colonist*), 27 February 1947; Prince Rupert *Daily News,* 30 November 1945; *Vancouver Sun,* 17 December 1945; *Nanaimo Free Press,* 25 March 1946; *Victoria Daily Times* (hereafter *Times*), 1 November 1946; Toronto *Telegram,* 16 May 1947; *Winnipeg Free Press,* 7 May 1947; Toronto *Globe and Mail,* 8 June 1950.

12 Forrest E. La Violette, *The Canadian Japanese and World War II: A Sociological and Psychological Account* (Toronto: University of Toronto Press, 1948).

13 Ann Gomer Sunahara, *The Politics of Racism: The Uprooting of Japanese Canadians during the Second World War* (Toronto: Lorimer, 1981); W. Peter Ward, *White Canada Forever: Popular Attitudes and Public Policy toward Orientals in British Columbia* (Montreal and Kingston: McGill-Queen's University Press, 1978; reprint 1990, 2002); Roy Miki, *Redress: Inside the Japanese Canadian Call for Justice* (Vancouver: Raincoast, 2004).

Some other accounts of the redress campaign are Maryka Omatsu, *Bittersweet Passage: Redress and the Japanese Canadian Experience* (Toronto: Between the Lines, 1992), and Roy Miki and Cassandra Kobayashi, *Justice in Our Time: The Japanese Canadian Redress Settlement* (Winnipeg: NAJC; Vancouver: Talonbooks, 1991).

14 Patricia E. Roy et al., *Mutual Hostages: Canadians and Japanese during the Second World War* (Toronto: University of Toronto Press, 1990).

15 Denise Chong, *The Concubine's Children: Portrait of a Family Divided* (Toronto: Viking, 1994); Anthony Chan, *Gold Mountain: The Chinese in the New World* (Vancouver: New Star, 1983); Peter S. Li, *The Chinese in Canada,* 2nd ed. (Toronto: Oxford University Press, 1998); Wickberg, ed. *From China to Canada;* David Chuenyan Lai, *Chinatowns: Towns within Cities in Canada* (Vancouver: UBC Press, 1988); Kay Anderson, *Vancouver's Chinatown: Racial Discourse in Canada, 1975-1980* (Montreal and Kingston: McGill-Queen's University Press, 1991); Wing Chung Ng, *The Chinese in Vancouver, 1945-80: The Pursuit of Identity and Power* (Vancouver: UBC Press, 1999); Paul Yee, *Saltwater City: An Illustrated History of the Chinese in Vancouver* (Vancouver: Douglas and McIntyre, 1988; rev. ed. 2006).

16 In their analysis of the press mainly in the 1990s, Frances Henry and Carol Tator concluded that readers usually were sympathetic to the editorial position of the newspaper that they read. Frances Henry and Carol Tator, *Discourses of Domination: Racial Bias in the Canadian English-Language Press* (Toronto: University of Toronto Press, 2002), 7. See also Foon Sien, "Past Achievements: Future Aspirations," *Chinatown News,* 3 January 1956.

17 Toyo Takata, *Nikkei Legacy: The Story of Japanese Canadians from Settlement to Today* (Toronto: NC Press, 1983); Louis Fiset and Gail M. Nomura, *Nikkei in the Pacific Northwest: Japanese Americans and Japanese Canadians in the Twentieth Century* (Seattle: University of Washington Press, 2005); *Nikkei Images: National Nikkei Museum and Heritage Centre Newsletter,* 1995-.

In 1965, the JCCA began a campaign to eliminate the term "Jap" from the media and daily usage. The *Chinatown News* called for the obliteration of the equally racist terms "Chink" and "Chinaman." *Chinatown News,* 3 October 1965.

18 Miki, *Redress,* 2, 50-53. For an informed comment on the misuse of the term in the United States, see

Roger Daniels, "Words Do Matter: A Note on Inappropriate Terminology and the Incarceration of Japanese Americans," in Fiset and Nomura, *Nikkei in the Pacific Northwest,* 190-214.

Chapter 1: A Civil Necessity

1 J.L. Granatstein and Gregory Johnson note that military and police authorities had limited intelligence about both Japan's military plans and activities within the Japanese community in British Columbia. J.L. Granatstein and Gregory Johnson, "The Evacuation of the Japanese, 1942: A Realist Critique of the Received Version," in *On Guard for Thee: War, Ethnicity, and the Canadian State, 1939-1945,* ed. Norman Hillmer, Bohdan Kordan, and Lubomyr Luciuk (Ottawa: Canadian Committee for the History of the Second World War, 1988), 101-29. Canada, Department of Labour, *Report on Re-Establishment of Japanese in Canada, 1944-1946* (Ottawa: Department of Labour, 1947), 5; *Vancouver Sun,* 18 October 1961.

2 Department of Labour, *Re-Establishment of Japanese,* 24; Alfred Rive to Consul General of Spain, 29 May 1942, BCSCR, vol. 15; Chiefs of Staff Appreciation, 19 February 1942, JLRP, vol. 72; 144th Meeting of the Chief of Staffs Committee, 17 February 1942, DNDR, MfC8340; Joint Services Committee, Pacific Command, Minutes, 19 February 1942, DNDR, MfC8369. Some American military leaders wanted to exclude all Japanese from the coast.

In prewar planning, Department of National Defence officials had no indication of any Japanese on the west coast of Vancouver Island being likely saboteurs. Nevertheless, given the ease of sabotaging the Ucluelet air station, they recommended removing residents on its outskirts and demolishing their buildings. That these people were Japanese was "entirely incidental." J.F. Preston, Colonel, General Staff Pacific Command, plus senior officers of RCN, RCAF, and RCMP, meeting at Victoria, 3 September 1941, DEAR, vol. 2859, file 1698-B-40; Vancouver *Daily Province* (hereafter *Province*), 14 February 1942.

3 *Trail Daily Times*, 6 December 1941; W.L.M. King, Diary, 7 December 1941; W.L.M. King to T.D. Pattullo, 7 December 1941, KP, #264813 [not sent]; CWCR, Minutes, 7 December 1941; W.L.M. King, Radio Speech, 8 December 1941, NAC, audiotape R8171. A provincial Liberal convention on 2 December, against the wishes of Pattullo, voted to form a coalition with the Conservatives. Pattullo's resignation and the formation of a coalition government of Liberals and Conservatives were imminent. The coalition remained in office until it disintegrated in 1952. See Robin Fisher, *Duff Pattullo of British Columbia* (Toronto: University of Toronto Press, 1991), 346-51; B. Hethey, circular, 8 December 1941, GR 1222, vol. 157; and *Times,* 8 December 1941. In the summer of 1941, the Department of External Affairs drafted a letter to Pattullo noting the importance of avoiding anti-Japanese demonstrations but did not send it. External Affairs to T.D. Pattullo, 25 July 1941, DEAR, vol. 2859, file 1698-B-40.

4 This committee was composed of representatives of government departments concerned with the Japanese and of British Columbians known for their different views on the situation. It was established in January 1941 to keep the federal government informed on the Oriental situation. See Patricia E. Roy, *The Oriental Question: Consolidating a White Man's Province* (Vancouver: UBC Press, 2003), 217, 220.

5 In October 1941, the Cabinet War Committee approved the internment of those Japanese whom the Department of Justice and the RCMP thought should be interned for cause but not the wholesale internment of Japanese. J.E. Read to Commissioner, RCMP, and others, 29 October 1941, DEAR, vol. 2859; S.T. Wood, CBC broadcast, c. 8 December 1941, DEAR, vol. 2007; F.J. Hume to W.L.M. King, 9 December 1941, DEAR, vol. 2978; C.H. Hill, Acting Commissioner, BC Division, to Commissioner, 8 December 1941, and C.H. Hill, to Commissioner, 9 December 1941, RCMPR, vol. 3564; H.L. Keenleyside to Yoriki Iwasaki, 7 February 1942, DEAR, vol. 3004; *Province,* 8 December 1941; Vancouver *News-Herald,* 11 December 1941. Ottawa formally authorized the indefinite detention of the fishing vessels on 9 December 1941. N.A. Robertson to W.L.M. King, 10 December 1941, KP, #C249381. Hill had some compassion for the fishermen. He ascertained that all the boat owners had homes on shore and that none was likely to suffer financial hardship until the beginning of the spring fishing season. C.H. Hill to R.R. Tait, 11 and 12 December 1941, RCMPR, vol. 3564. Details of prewar planning about the Japanese-Canadian situation may be found in Roy, *The Oriental Question,* ch. 7.

6 C.H. Hill to Commissioner, 11 December 1941, RCMPR, vol. 3564; *Vancouver Sun,* 8 December 1941. Lawyers for the BC Plate Glass Insurance Company complained that "misguided patriots" broke windows in eight Japanese stores in December. The police chief blamed "a few half-crazy people" and reported that vandalism, peaking shortly after Pearl Harbor, was abating. *Province,* 8 and 9 December 1941, 10 February 1942; Maurice Pope to Chief of the General Staff, 9 December 1941, DNDR, vol.

2725. For example, Thomas Shoyama to W.L.M. King, 7 December 1941, and K. Rikimaru, Northern BC Residential Fishermen's Association, to W.L.M. King, 12 December 1941, DEAR, vol. 2942; Vernon and District Japanese Community to W.L.M. King, 9 December 1941, KP, #271142; T. Mitsui to W.L.M. King, 10 December 1941, KP, #264101-2; *Chilliwack Progress,* 10 December 1941; *Comox Argus,* 11 December 1941; *Vancouver Sun,* 11 December 1941; *Maple Ridge-Pitt Meadows Weekly Gazette* (hereafter *Gazette*), 12 December 1941; the *New Canadian,* 12 December 1941; Port Alberni *West Coast Advocate,* 17 December 1941; *Kelowna Capital News,* 17 December 1941; *Kelowna Courier,* 18 December 1941; Vancouver *News-Herald,* 24 December 1941; *Vernon News,* 25 December 1941.

7 Lew Gordon, Memo, 8 December 1941, PCOR, vol. 5960. The JCCA thanked Vancouver newspapers for their tolerance. JCCA, Minute Book, 16 December 1941, Vancouver Chapter, vol. 1; *Vancouver Sun,* 8 December 1941; Vancouver *News-Herald,* 8 December 1941; *Province,* 8 December 1941; *Federationist,* 11 December 1941; *Comox District Free Press,* 11 December 1941. Harold Ede, the postmaster, informed the RCMP on 13 December that two Japanese families had moved into the area and with a Japanese already there made "a chain of points towards Trail." Ede was reported to be a lieutenant in the army. His letter was eventually forwarded to RCMP headquarters in Ottawa, which passed it to the army and Canada Post with the request that they take any possible disciplinary action. Ede to Constable Newington, 13 December 1941, and S.T. Wood to Deputy Chief of the General Staff, 5 January 1942, DNDR, C8366, Headquarters 8613. *Vernon News,* 11 and 18 December 1941; *Kelowna Courier,* 11 and 18 December 1941.

8 Emphasis added. Prince Rupert *Daily News,* 11 December 1941; *Penticton Herald,* 11 December 1941; *Nanaimo Free Press,* 8 December 1941; *Kamloops Sentinel,* 11 December 1941; *Ladysmith Chronicle,* 12 December 1941; *Creston Review,* 12 December 1941. A month later the *Creston Review* declared that "the authorities are fully aware of the treacherous temperament and mentality of the Japs. Nothing should be left to chance – intern all suspects immediately, – move others to safe places." *Creston Review,* 16 January 1942; *Times,* 12 December 1941; *Colonist,* 8 December 1941.

9 The censor "killed" or modified some stories, but given some *Sun* editorials he does not seem to have interfered with editorials or letters to the editor. *Times,* 9 December 1941; Prince Rupert *Evening Empire,* 9 December 1941; *Colonist,* 9 December 1941; G.W. McPherson to the Custodian, 21 December 1941, CEPR, vol. 2; Lew Gordon to W. Eggleston, 15 December 1941, PCR, vol. 5977; W. Hutcherson, *Landing at Ladner* (New York: Carlton, 1982), 176.

10 Ian Mackenzie to John Hart, 11 December 1941, G.G. McGeer to Ian Mackenzie, 13 December 1941, and R.W. Mayhew to Ian Mackenzie, 12 December 1941, IAMP, vol. 26. Mayhew told Mackenzie that the government must make greater efforts to convince people to prepare to defend their homes against incendiary bombs.

11 *Times,* 18 December 1941; *Vancouver Sun,* 18, 19, 22, and 23 December 1941; *Province,* 10 December 1941; J.W. Cornett to Ian Mackenzie, 16 December 1941, and Austin Taylor to Ian Mackenzie, IAMP, vol. 26; Conference in Mayor's Office, 24 December 1941, CVA, Vancouver Board of Trade, Special Minute Book; L. Gordon to W. Eggleston, 15 December 1941, PCOR, vol. 5977; Prince Rupert *Daily News,* 18 and 19 December 1941. Colonel J.W. Nicholls reported that Prince Rupert was "exceedingly vulnerable" and recommended better defences or arrangements to evacuate women, children, the aged, and the infirm. The Cabinet War Committee had him interview the chief of the general staff. CWCR, 14 January 1942.

12 R.H.B. Ker to Ian Mackenzie, 11 December 1941, IAMP, vol. 24; Angus Macdonald to W.L.M. King, 16 December 1941, DEAR, vol. 2935; M. Reynolds to W.L.M. King, 2 January 1942, DEAR, vol. 2798; *Province,* 15 and 19 December 1941; G.W. McPherson to Custodian, 21 December 1941, CEPR, vol. 2; Harry Phelan to Ian Mackenzie, 21 December 1941, IAMP, vol. 24; Harry Phelan to W.L.M. King, 21 December 1941, KP, #264895-96; William McDermott to George Cruickshank, 22 December 1941, DNDR, MfC8366. Over thirty years later, a graduate student who interviewed residents of Maple Ridge reported that they remembered the Japanese as good, honest, and hard-working people but believed that some were heavily armed and would fight for Japan if the opportunity arose. John M. Read, "The Pre-War Japanese Canadians of Maple Ridge" (MA thesis, University of British Columbia, 1975), 69. At the request of the commissioner, F.J. Mead of the RCMP inquired of J. Edgar Hoover and Edgar Tamm of the FBI about fifth column activities in Hawaii as described by Knox. Hoover replied that the statement was incorrect and was made to divert attention from the failures of the US Navy. Mead asked the commissioner to treat the information "with discretion." F.J. Mead to Commissioner, 29 December 1941, DEAR, vol. 2930, file 2860-40.

13 Minutes, Joint Services Committee, Pacific Coast, 19 December 1941, DHist 193.009 (D3); F.J. Hume to W.L.M. King, 20 December 1941, DEAR, vol. 1867; *Province,* 19 December 1941; J.R. Radford, circular, 20 December 1941, RCMPR, vol. 3564.

14 C.H. Hill to Commissioner, 20 December 1941, RCMPR, vol. 3564; *Vancouver Sun,* 16, 19, and 26 December 1941; *Colonist,* 30 December 1941; *Chilliwack Progress,* 24 December 1941; *Province,* 19 December 1941; Vancouver *News-Herald,* 13 and 20 December 1941.

15 *Times,* 30 December 1941; Ian Mackenzie to W.L.M. King, 22 December 1941, CNSP, vol. 2; H. Green to S.H. Green, 28 and 31 December 1941, HCGP, vol. 3; *Province,* 22 December 1941.

16 Cabinet War Committee, 29 December 1941; R.O. Alexander to Chief of the General Staff, 30 December 1941, IAMP, vol. 32; John Hart to W.L.M. King, 31 December 1941, GR 1222, vol. 100; H.L. Keenleyside to M.A. Pope, 3 January 1942, RCMPR, vol. 3564; M.A. Pope to R.O. Alexander, 4 January 1942, DEAR, vol. 2978.

17 C.R. Peters to Officer Commanding, E Division, 31 December 1941, RCMPR, vol. 3564; Gwen Cash, *A Million Miles from Ottawa* (Toronto: Macmillan, 1942), viii. Some of these observations are drawn from H.T. Matson to W.L.M. King, 12 January 1942, KP, #281549-51, and from Al Williamson in Vancouver *News-Herald,* 12 January 1942.

18 On 5 March 1942, A. McGillivray of the Vancouver Zone Council of the Canadian Legion told the fisheries minister, "the Japanese fishing fleet off the coast of British Columbia was mastered and manned by fully qualified Japanese Naval officers – men who had been familiarizing themselves with every inch of our coastline." The Legion sought access to the Japanese fishing fleet as a way of rehabilitating ex-servicemen. A. McGillivray to J.E. Michaud, 5 March 1942, DFish, vol. 1643; "Text of Resolution Regarding the Japanese Situation Adopted by the Victoria, B.C., Kiwanis Club, in Regular Meeting Assembled, December 30th, 1941," copy in DEAR, vol. 2798. The resolution also demanded that Japanese be deprived of all cameras, radio equipment, and firearms. It did not specify internment but asked Ottawa to take steps "to eradicate this danger." *Times,* 30 December 1941, 10 and 13 January and 16 February 1942. The Native Sons sent an open letter with similar ideas to King a month later. *Colonist,* 6, 7, and 11 January 1942; *Province,* 8 January 1942; A.H. Adams to W.L.M. King, 7 January 1942, KP, #271872; P.T. Stern to Ian Mackenzie, 10 January 1942, C.E. Giles to Ian Mackenzie, 8 January 1942, Duncan and Cowichan District Committee to Ian Mackenzie, 14 January 1942, and T.P. McConnell to Ian Mackenzie, 10 January 1942, IAMP, vol. 24; *Cowichan Leader,* 8 and 15 January 1942; *Ladysmith Chronicle,* 9 January 1942.

19 *Times,* 5, 13, and 22 January 1942. The censor killed a British United Press story suggesting that Japanese bombers could burn British Columbia's forests and asked the press to delete references to saboteurs in the report of the forestry committee of the legislature. By May, when the chief forester told the Victoria Rotary Club that incendiary fire raids could make the forthcoming forest fire season dangerous, the censor let the story pass. Lew Gordon, Memos, 27 and 28 January and 21 May 1942, PCOR, vol. 5960; H.T. Matson to W.L.M. King, 12 January 1942, KP, #281549-51; *Colonist,* 6 January 1942; O.J. Wales to Maurice Bernier, 7 January 1942, RCMPR, vol. 3564; R.W. Mayhew to W.L.M. King, 8 January 1942, KP, #281592-93; note signed "JAG" [J.A. Gibson] on R.W. Mayhew to W.L.M. King, 8 January 1942, DEAR, vol. 2798.

20 *Times,* 10 January 1942; *Ubyssey,* 9 January 1942; *Peace River Block News,* 22 January 1942. McClung's essay also appeared in the Regina *Leader-Post,* 10 January 1942.

21 On British purchases, see Dianne Newell, "The Politics of Food in World War II: Great Britain's Grip on Canada's Pacific Fishery," Canadian Historical Association, *Historical Papers* (1987): 178-97. The fisheries minister later reported that there were plenty of fishermen because the industry had been overcrowded. J.E. Michaud to J.C. Thorson, 4 March 1942, DFish, vol. 1643. Canada, Department of Fisheries, *Annual Report for the Year 1941-42* (Ottawa: King's Printer, 1942), 31; A.W. Neill to Francis Dickie, 15 December 1941, FDP; J.A. Motherwell to D.B. Finn, 16 December 1941, DFish, vol. 1627; A.J. W[hitmore], Memo, 7 January 1942, PCOR, vol. 25, file J-25-1; F.J. Hume to W.L.M. King, 20 December 1941, DEAR, vol. 1867; W.T. Burgess to Ian Mackenzie, 31 December 1941, IAMP, vol. 19; George North and Harold Griffin, *A Ripple, a Wave* (Vancouver: Fisherman Publishing Society, 1974), 13; *Fisherman,* 9 December 1941, cited in Werner Cohn, "The Persecution of Japanese Canadians and the Political Left in British Columbia, December 1941-March 1942," *BC Studies* 68 (1985-86): 5-6; Minutes, Joint Services Committee, Pacific Coast, 19 December 1941, DHist, 193.009 (D3); Hutcherson, *Landing at Ladner,* 178; H.E. Beyer, Secretary, Kyoquot Trollers Co-Operative Association, to W.L.M. King, 15 January 1942, IAMP, vol. 19; *Federationist,* 8 January 1942. The *Winnipeg Free Press,*

7 January 1942, suggested making Japanese fishing equipment available to surplus fishermen from Manitoba. F. Rolley, Secretary, Fishermen's Protective Association (Gillnetters), to J.E. Michaud, 5 January 1942; Ole Stegavig, Secretary, Canadian Halibut Fishing Vessel Owners Association, to J.E. Michaud, 12 January 1942, and A. McGillivray to Minister of Fisheries, 5 March 1942, DFish, vol. 1643; *Times,* 29 December 1941; *Vancouver Sun,* 30 December 1941; *Penticton Herald,* 1 January 1942.

22 *Vancouver Sun,* 18 December 1941; *Ladysmith Chronicle,* 24 December 1941; *Federationist,* 24 December 1941; *Nanaimo Free Press,* 18 December 1941; F.J. Hume to W.L.M. King, 20 December 1941, DEAR, vol. 1867; *Province,* 23 December 1941 and 8 January 1942; Lew Gordon to W. Eggleston, 18 December 1941, PCR, vol. 5979; Lew Gordon, Memorandum, 19 December 1942, PCOR, vol. 5960; R. Bell-Irving to Millar Freeman, 5 January 1942, Millar Freeman Papers, University of Washington Library (thanks to Roger Daniels for this reference). Toronto *Globe and Mail,* 4 February 1942. In June, Bell-Irving reported that the absence of Japanese had not affected the business. Ralph S. Plant to V.W. Odlum, 13 June 1942, VWOP, vol. 10; Alfred Adam Bailey to W.L.M. King, 28 February 1942, KP, #271872ff. Several individuals and groups with no direct connection to the industry protested any return of fishing licences or boats to Japanese fishermen. See correspondence in DEAR, vol. 2798, file 773-B-40.

23 K.C. Stuart to H.L. Keenleyside, 26 December 1941, DEAR, vol. 3004, file 3464-H-40C; Lew Gordon to W. Eggleston, 18 December 1941, PCOR, vol. 5979; *Province,* 17 December 1941; *Times,* 27 December 1941; *Vancouver Sun,* 23 and 31 December 1941; Prince Rupert *Daily News,* 15 January 1942.

24 Commissioner Wood of the RCMP asked the FBI if the United States was letting American citizens of Japanese origin operate their vessels. S.T. Wood to J.E. Hoover, 5 January 1942, RCMPR, vol. 3564. Hoover replied that commandants of each naval district made local policy, and some let Japanese fish under certain restrictions. John Shirras to Commissioner, 29 and 30 December 1941, PPR, vol. 163; *Province,* 2 and 3 January 1942; *Vancouver Sun,* 30 December 1941; F.J. Hume to W.L.M. King, 2 January 1942, DEAR, vol. 1867. The photograph of the fishing fleet appeared in many newspapers both in British Columbia and beyond.

25 A copy of the petition is in IAMP, vol. 25; *Langley Advance,* 15 and 22 January 1942; Kaslo Board of Trade, Minute Book, 22 January 1942, BCA; *Colonist,* 20 January 1942; *Province,* 16 January 1942; *Fraser Valley Record,* 22 January 1942; Prince Rupert *Evening Empire,* 29 January 1942; *Cowichan Leader,* 15 January 1942.

26 *Federationist,* 11 December 1941 and 8 January 1942; *Province,* 5, 6, and 12 January 1942.

27 H.F. Angus to N.A. Robertson, 2 January 1942, DEAR, vol. 1867; H.F. Angus to N.A. Robertson, 24 December 1941, DEAR, vol. 3004; F.J. Mead to Commissioner, 27 December 1941, RCMPR, vol. 3564; N.A. Robertson to John Hart, 3 January 1942, KP, #276652; N.A. Robertson to Ian Mackenzie, 5 January 1942, IAMP, vol. 24; T.W.S. Parsons, Diary, 4 and 7 January 1942, TWPP, vol. 1.

28 A collection of these letters and wires may be found in DEAR, vol. 2798. All the resolutions called for interning Japanese; many referred to possible fifth column activity. *Comox Argus,* 1 January 1942; *Cowichan Leader,* 1 January 1942; *Ladysmith Chronicle,* 2 January 1942; *Nanaimo Free Press,* 6 January 1942; *Times,* 5 January 1942; L.F. Stevenson to Secretary, Department of National Defence for Air, 2 January 1942, DHist, 181.009 (D5546); Vancouver *News-Herald,* 3 January 1942.

29 C.H. Hill to Commissioner, 3 January 1942, RCMPR, vol. 3564; *Vancouver Sun,* 3 January 1942.

30 *Times,* 5 and 7 January 1942; *Colonist,* 4 January 1942.

31 *Province,* 2, 3, and 5 January 1942; *Vancouver Sun,* 2, 3, 5, and 8 January 1942 (the editorials of 2 and 8 January were reprinted in the *Times*); Lew Gordon, Memo, 3 January 1942, and Lew Gordon to W. Eggleston, 3 January 1942, PCOR, vol. 5960. A Vancouver neighbourhood newspaper, the *Highland Echo,* advised readers on 8 January 1942 to act with justice and reason and let the police and military authorities handle the situation. Thomas Shoyama, editor of the *New Canadian,* replied on 12 January that he could not apologize for Japan "because we are Canadians." The censor reviewed the *New Canadian*'s copy before publication because he feared "some bit of ignorant arrogance [on its part] might arouse Vancouverites to violence." R.W. Baldwin, Memo re the *New Canadian,* 12 March 1942, PCOR, vol. 5977; New Westminster *British Columbian* (hereafter *Columbian*), 6 and 7 January 1942; Vancouver *News-Herald,* 5 January 1942. On 9 January 1942, both Prince Rupert dailies made restrained comments on possible fifth column activities and the need for government action.

32 Lew Gordon, Memos, 3 and 8 January 1942, PCOR, vol. 5960; *Vancouver Sun,* 3 January 1942; Charles Bishop in *Calgary Herald,* 5 January 1942. When the Kiwassa Club asked the city not to issue trade licences to Japanese, the licence committee replied that it did not have such powers. Vancouver *News-Herald,* 27 January 1942; *Province,* 3 January 1942. The letters to Wilson from the first week of

January are located in HDWP. The censor "killed" Wilson's unfounded story of two navy men and three Japanese fishermen being killed in a skirmish at Prince Rupert. Lew Gordon, Memo, 8 January 1942, PCOR, vol. 5960; Joint Services Committee, Pacific Coast, 9 January 1942, DHist, 193.009 (D3). The RCMP objected to Wilson trying to spread the rumour but did not think it possible to stop him under the Defence of Canada Regulations. C.H. Hill to S.T. Wood, 12 January 1942, and S.T. Wood to H.L. Keenleyside, 20 January 1942, DEAR, vol. 1867. For Wilson's earlier activities, see Roy, *The Oriental Question,* 221-25.

33 *Province,* 5, 6, 7, and 8 January 1942; Vancouver *News-Herald,* 5 and 9 January 1942; *Vancouver Sun,* 5 January 1942; Ira Dilworth to Gladstone Murray, 6 January 1942, Ira Dilworth to H.F. Angus, 6 January 1942, and Grey Turgeon to W.L.M. King, 6 January 1942, DEAR, vol. 2798. Turgeon represented Cariboo but resided in Vancouver.

34 When the United Fishermen's Union denied being associated with the group, Burnett explained that he had given the press a list of invitees, not attendees. Vancouver *News-Herald,* 10, 12, and 13 January 1942; *Province,* 10 January 1942. The press censor considered that Maddison was "well off his mental base." Lew Gordon to W. Eggleston, 21 May 1942, PCOR, vol. 5979. After the evacuation was announced, Mackenzie wired Maddison, hoping that "you and other experienced men will have sufficient influence to restrain any excitable elements." Ian Mackenzie to C.W. Maddison, 2 March 1942, IAMP, vol. 25.

35 *Province,* 9 January 1942; *Times,* 12 January 1942.

36 *Province,* 5, 7, and 9 January 1942; *Times,* 5 and 6 January 1942; *Colonist,* 6 January 1942.

37 In addition to Mackenzie, Keenleyside, Angus, Norman Robertson, and W.J. Coupar, an assistant to the deputy minister of labour, had lived in British Columbia.

38 Minutes, Meeting to Consider Questions Concerned with Canadian Japanese and Japanese Nationals in British Columbia, 8 January 1942, DLab, vol. 174. During a break in the meeting, an unnamed politician said that "for years his people had been telling themselves that war with Japan would afford them a Heaven-sent opportunity to rid themselves of the Japanese economic menace for ever more." Cited in Maurice A. Pope, *Soldiers and Politicians: The Memoirs of Lt.-Gen. Maurice A. Pope* (Toronto: University of Toronto Press, 1962), 177. A few weeks later, presumably in reference to the same meeting, H.L. Keenleyside recalled that the representative of the provincial government indignantly denied "any wish to use this opportunity to separate Canadian Japanese from their normal livelihoods or to uproot them economically so that they might be eliminated from our national life." H.L. Keenleyside to A.D.P. Heeney, 27 January 1942, PCOR, vol. 25. Canadian officials continued to pay attention to what the Americans were doing through their legation in Washington. Canadian Minister to W.L.M. King, 2 February 1942, DLab, vol. 655.

39 Agenda, Meeting to Consider Questions Concerned with Canadian Japanese and Japanese Nationals in British Columbia, 8 January 1942, and Ian Mackenzie to W.L.M. King, 10 January 1942, IAMP, vol. 32. PC 251, 13 January 1942, KP, #C249388; *Province,* 14 January 1942. For a brief history of the Japanese in the Canadian Armed Forces, see Patricia E. Roy, "The Soldiers Canada Didn't Want: Her Chinese and Japanese Citizens," *Canadian Historical Review* 59 (1978): 341-58.

40 Pope, *Soldiers and Politicians,* 177; Hugh L. Keenleyside, *Memoirs, Volume 2: On the Bridge of Time* (Toronto: McClelland and Stewart, 1982), 173; H.F. Angus to H.L. Keenleyside, 6 October and 6 November 1977, HLKP, vol. 20; Escott Reid, "The Conscience of a Diplomat: A Personal Statement," *Queen's Quarterly* 74 (1967): 587. Reid said that four years later General Pope said he "came away from that meeting feeling dirty all over."

41 The main report is in DLab, vol. 174. The Standing Committee claimed that British Columbians opposed military service, and Mackenzie did not favour it. Ian Mackenzie to W.L.M. King, 10 January 1942, IAMP, vol. 32. The unsigned handwritten memo (IAMP, vol. 32) may have been written by Mackenzie. In the meantime, J.E. Read, legal adviser of the Department of External Affairs, prepared a memorandum in case of the "mass evacuation of Japanese nationals from the British Columbia coastal area" in which he urged making "every effort ... to avoid unnecessary sacrifice" of Canadian or British prisoners of the Japanese. To avoid singling out Japanese, he suggested making the coast a "defence area" from which all able-bodied male enemy aliens, including Germans and Italians, might also be removed. J.E. Read, Memorandum Concerning Measures Directed Against Japanese in B.C., 12 January 1942, IAMP, vol. 32; H.F. Angus, note for Mr. Robertson concerning publicity of the results of the meeting to discuss Japanese in British Columbia, 8 January 1942, DEAR, vol. 2978; Meeting to Consider Questions Concerned with Canadian Japanese and Japanese Nationals in British Columbia,

8 January 1942. The addenda to this report is in IAMP, vol. 32.

42 Vancouver *News-Herald,* 9 and 10 January 1942; *Province,* 8 and 9 January 1942; *Vancouver Sun,* 10 January 1942.

43 Vancouver *News-Herald,* 12 and 19 January 1942; *Province,* 19 January 1942; *Times,* 19 January 1942. Hume's endorsement of Mackenzie led the *Province* of 20 January 1942 to accuse him of trying "to make political capital." T.W.S. Parsons privately echoed this view. T.W.S. Parsons to Norman Senior, 14 January 1942, IAMP, vol. 25.

44 Bruce Hutchison to J.W. Dafoe, [14] January 1942, Dafoe Papers (I am indebted to J.L. Granatstein for this reference). Hutchison said that Mackenzie claimed Keenleyside "made a mess of it." Ian Mackenzie to John Hart, 15 January 1942, IAMP, vol. 32. Note on H.L. Keenleyside to W.L.M. King, 13 January 1942, KP, #277510-16; H.L. Keenleyside to T. Shoyama, 26 January 1942, HLKP, vol. 20; H.L. Keenleyside to Ian Mackenzie, 26 January 1942, DLab, vol. 174. The unedited release is in the *Colonist,* 15 January 1942, under a CP byline. Most papers printed only a summary; *Province,* 14 January 1942.

45 *Province,* 14 and 15 January 1942. The Vancouver *News-Herald* of 15 January 1942 called the policy "reasonable"; *Vancouver Sun,* 14 January 1942; *Times,* 14 January 1942; *Comox Argus,* 15 January 1942; *Nanaimo Free Press,* 15 January 1942; *Cowichan Leader,* 15 January 1942; Prince Rupert *Daily News,* 16 January 1942.

46 *Province,* 14 and 20 January 1942; W. Eggleston, Memo, 23 January 1942, PCOR, vol. 5960.

47 Earle Dunsmuir to R.B. Hanson, 10 January 1942, RBHP, vol. 79; *Province,* 12 January 1942; *Colonist,* 13 January 1942.

48 Vancouver *News-Herald,* 13 January 1942; *Province,* 14 January 1942; Howard Green to his parents, 15 and 18 January 1942, HCGP, vol. 3. Green maintained these views. In 1967, he responded to an allegation that British Columbia coerced Ottawa into removing the Japanese: "It was a matter of life and death. These fellows back east ... completely overlooked the situation people on the coast faced." *New Canadian,* 7 October 1967.

49 *Vancouver Sun,* 15 and 19 January 1942; W.C. Stevens, North Lonsdale Liberal Association, to Ian Mackenzie, 12 January 1942; John K. Wills, Burnaby Liberal Association, to Ian Mackenzie, 13 January 1942; Nora Hutchings, North Burnaby Liberal Association, to Ian Mackenzie, 6 February 1942; Mary Knorr, West Burnaby Liberal Association, to Ian Mackenzie, 4 February 1942; R.W. Mayhew to Ian Mackenzie, 17 January 1942; J. Price to R.W. Mayhew, 16 January 1942; and R.H.B. Ker to Ian Mackenzie, 22 January 1942, all in IAMP, vol. 24; *Province,* 15 January 1942; *Nanaimo Free Press,* 21 January 1942; *Times,* 14 and 16 January 1942; Reginald Hayward to W.L.M. King, 17 January 1942, DEAR, vol. 2798. T.W. Goode to H.D. Wilson, 15 January 1942, HDWP; R.T. Osborne to W.L.M. King, 24 January 1942, KP, J2, vol. 295; *Colonist,* 15 January 1942; *Comox District Free Press,* 29 January 1942; Prince Rupert *Evening Empire,* 15 January 1942. Tom Reid's proposal to send all Japanese to Japan was "too sweeping" for the Conservative New Westminster *British Columbian* of 20 January 1942. Never a supporter of Reid, it argued that not all Japanese were as treacherous as those who planned Pearl Harbor.

50 Ken Adachi, *The Enemy that Never Was: A History of the Japanese Canadians* (Toronto: McClelland and Stewart, 1976), 209; H.L. Keenleyside to W.L.M. King, 6 February 1942, KP, #C249449; Vancouver *News-Herald,* 22 January 1942; Bryce M. Stewart to Ian Mackenzie, 26 January 1942, IAMP, vol. 32; Under-Secretary of State for External Affairs to Deputy Minister of National Defence for Air, 11 February 1942, DEAR, vol. 2859, file 1698-B-40.

51 There is no mention of the Japanese question in the New Westminster *British Columbian*'s account of the election, but its reports were brief, and three proposed all-candidates' meetings were cancelled because of blackouts.

52 N.A. Robertson to W.L.M. King, 20 January 1942, KP, #C249391; E. Reid to W.L.M. King, 21 January 1942, KP, #383503. Tom Reid blamed "some of the Ottawa officials" for not consulting the BC MPs. *HCD,* 2 February 1942, 225; A.W. Neill to H.L. Keenleyside, 21 January 1942, KP, #C249431-32; H.F. Angus to A.W. Neill, 20 January 1942, DEAR, vol. 2798; E. Reid to Ian Mackenzie, 21 January 1942, and Ian Mackenzie to R.G. Robertson, 22 January 1942, IAMP, vol. 32.

53 Among those suggested as replacements by the Department of External Affairs were Brigadier W.W. Foster, Reverend W.G. McWilliams, a United Church clergyman who had worked in Japan, and Laura Holland, a social worker, because of the questions likely to arise respecting the wives and children of Japanese nationals. N.A. Robertson to W.L.M. King, 14 January 1942, and N.A. Robertson to Ian Mackenzie, 22 January 1942, DNDR, vol. 895, file 570, MfT1809.

54 H.L. Keenleyside to N.A. Robertson, 27 January 1942, DLab, vol. 174; *New Canadian,* 13 February 1942; Vancouver *News-Herald,* 10 February 1942. When Mackenzie suggested Macintosh as head of the corps, a horrified Keenleyside replied that, after Alderman Wilson, Macintosh had been "the most outspoken opponent of the Japanese in British Columbia" in the past decade and had publicly favoured deporting all Japanese in Canada to Japan. "It would be impossible," Keenleyside warned, "to expect ... the native-born and other Canadian nationals" to enlist in a corps under his command. H.L. Keenleyside to Ian Mackenzie, 23 January 1942, IAMP, vol. 32. On second thought, Mackenzie agreed that "antipathy" to Macintosh would reduce enthusiasm for enlistment. H.L. Keenleyside to N.A. Robertson, 27 January 1942, DLab, vol. 174.

55 Ian Mackenzie to B.M. Stewart, 23 January 1942, DLab, vol. 174; H.L. Keenleyside, "The Japanese Problem," 26 January 1942, IAMP, vol. 32. He noted that Japan had enquired through Spain, the protecting power, about Canada's treatment of Japanese. In a memo to the prime minister, Norman Robertson pointed to the need to treat Japanese nationals who were enemy aliens under international law and to treat Canadian nationals separately. He believed that the Canadian Japanese were more likely to volunteer for the corps if their services could be used on work directly associated with the war. N.A. Robertson to W.L.M. King, 20 January 1942, PCOR, vol. 25, file J-25-1.

56 H.L. Keenleyside[?], "Memorandum on Progress with Relation to the Japanese Problem in British Columbia," c. 26 January 1942, KP, #C249422-29.

57 Ian Mackenzie to N.A. Robertson, 28 January 1942, IAMP, vol. 32; *HCD,* 23 January 1942, 5 (Stirling); *HCD,* 26 January 1942, 19 (Reid).

58 J.H. McVety to A. MacNamara, 28 January 1942, and H.C. Bray to Director, Military Operations and Intelligence, 29 January 1942, DLab, vol. 174; J.L. Ralston to H. Mitchell, 5 February 1942, DNDR, vol. 2672.

59 George Murray to W.L.M. King, 15 January 1942, KP, #282146-47; John Hart to Ian Mackenzie, 28 January 1942, IAMP, vol. 25; *Penticton Herald,* 25 December 1941; *Grand Forks Gazette,* 29 January 1942; Prince Rupert *Evening Empire,* 6 January 1942; Prince Rupert Chamber of Commerce to W.L.M. King, 15 January 1942, DEAR, vol. 2798. T.D. Pattullo to Ian Mackenzie, 20 January 1942; Terrace and District Board of Trade to Olof Hanson, 19 January 1942; and E.T. Kenney to Ian Mackenzie, 23 February 1942, in IAMP, vol. 25; R.W. Calderwood, Secretary, Smithers District Chamber of Commerce, resolution, 12 February 1942; D.K. Kerr, Secretary, Terrace and District Board of Trade, to Olof Hanson, 6 February 1942; and D.B. Johnston to H. Mitchell, 24 January 1942, in DLab, vol. 655; Nelson *Daily News,* 30 January 1942; *Province,* 27 January 1942; Vancouver *News-Herald,* 29 January 1942; Ian Mackenzie to R.G. Robertson, 22 January 1942, IAMP, vol. 32; H.F. Angus to R.G. Robertson, 22 January 1942, DEAR, vol. 8805, file 580, MfT1809.

60 *Maclean's,* 1 February 1942; *Saturday Night,* 28 February 1942; Montreal *Gazette,* 12 February 1942; *Ottawa Journal,* 19 December 1941 and 21 and 25 February 1942; *Globe and Mail,* 6 and 16 January and 4 February 1942; *Le Devoir,* 9 February 1942; *Winnipeg Free Press,* 12 and 16 January and 27 February 1942; Regina *Leader-Post,* 16 January 1942; *Saskatoon Star-Phoenix,* 9 January and 23 February 1942; *Calgary Herald,* 6, 15, and 20 January and 6 and 17 February and 4 and 11 March 1942; *Brantford Expositor,* 16 January and 2 March 1942.

British Columbians did not want to discourage potential tourists. At the peak of the agitation, the Montreal *Star* of 20 February 1942 editorially noted a message from British Columbia's deputy minister of trade and industry that "we continue to find life very pleasant, and to enjoy our outdoor recreations, our mild winter and early spring." On tourism in British Columbia during the war, see Michael Dawson, "From 'Business as Usual' to 'Salesmanship in Reverse': Tourism Promotion in British Columbia during the Second World War," *Canadian Historical Review* 83 (2002): 230-54.

61 Peter Heenan to A. MacNamara, and A. MacNamara to N.A. McLarty, 6 February 1942, IAMP, vol. 32; A. MacNamara to J.L. Ralston, 5 February 1942, DNDR, MfC8340; H.L. Keenleyside to W.L.M. King, 6 February 1942, KP, #C249450-52: *Vancouver Sun,* 7 February 1942; *Province,* 7 and 10 February 1942; F. Blackburn to F.W. Gershaw, 3 February 1942, DLab, vol. 655.

62 *Province,* 14 and 15 February 1942; the *Nanaimo Free Press* of 18 February 1942 complained of other provinces "murmuring" about accepting some Japanese and failing to learn what "the real viewpoint of the average oriental is to occidental civilization."

63 *Penticton Herald,* 15, 22, and 29 January and 5 March 1942. After the BCFGA endorsed the limited use of Japanese labour, the Board of Trade and the Canadian Legion in Oliver passed resolutions in opposition. *Penticton Herald,* 19 February 1942. For the earlier story, see Patricia E. Roy, *A White Man's*

Province: British Columbia Politicians and Chinese and Japanese Immigrants, 1958-1914 (Vancouver: UBC Press, 1989), 176-77; F.J. Nixon to W.A.C. Bennett, 16 January 1942, WACB, vol. 9; *Province,* 5 February 1942; J.R. Butler to H. Mitchell, 6 February 1942, DLab, vol. 655; J.R. Wiglesworth to Ian Mackenzie, 15 January 1942, IAMP, vol. 25. Census Division 3, which included the whole of the Okanagan and Similkameen Valleys and the Shuswap area, had a total Japanese population of 779 in the spring of 1941. The published census does not have a detailed breakdown, but it is clear that the Japanese were concentrated around Kelowna and Vernon.

64 See Patricia E. Roy, "A Tale of Two Cities: The Reception of Japanese Evacuees in Kelowna and Kaslo, B.C.," *BC Studies* 87 (1990): 23-47; *Kelowna Capital News,* 14 January 1942; *Kelowna Courier,* 15 and 22 January 1942. Several boards of trade and municipal councils suggested that such work could include building the Hope-Princeton and other highways. For example, E.W. Barton to Ian Mackenzie, 9 January 1942, IAMP, vol. 25; W. Metcalfe to W.A.C. Bennett, 23 January 1942, WACBP, vol. 13; *Kelowna Courier,* 12, 19, and 26 February 1942; E.W. Barton to W.L.M. King, 17 February 1942, KP, #272276-81; G.H. Dunn to Ian Mackenzie, 18 February 1942, IAMP, vol. 24; *Penticton Herald,* 19 February 1942.

65 *Vernon News,* 8, 15, 22, and 29 January and 5 and 26 February 1942; J. Wright to Grote Stirling, 20 February 1942, and Ian Mackenzie to *Kelowna Courier,* 23 February 1942, IAMP, vol. 25.

66 BC Interior Vegetable Marketing Board to Ian Mackenzie, 27 January 1942, and W.A.C. Bennett et al. to A.C. Taylor, 28 February 1942, IAMP, vol. 25; *Province,* 29 and 30 January 1942; *Penticton Herald,* 29 January 1942; *Vernon News,* 5 February 1942; C.A. Hayden to A. MacNamara, 9 February 1942, DLab, vol. 174; Nelson *Daily News,* 28 January and 28 February 1942; *Grand Forks Gazette,* 19 February 1942.

67 H.M. Levey, City Clerk, Kamloops, to John Hart, 6 February 1942; John Hodgson to W.L.M. King, 20 February 1942; and H.M. Levey to W.L.M. King, 21 February 1942, in DLab, vol. 655. Stirling quoted the resolution in Parliament, *HCD,* 19 February 1942, 706; G. Copithorne to Ian Mackenzie, 21 February 1942; Ian Mackenzie to L.S. St. Laurent, 23 February 1942; and T.J. O'Neill to Ian Mackenzie, 23 February 1942, in IAMP, vol. 25; *Kamloops Sentinel,* 12 and 26 February 1942.

68 Memo to H. Mitchell, 17 February 1942, DLab, vol. 174; R.C. Vaughn to P.J.A. Cardin, 17 February 1942, and S.T. Wood to J.M. Bernier, 25 February 1942, RCMPR, vol. 3553; Lew Gordon, Memo, 18 February 1942, PCOR, vol. 5960.

69 *Cowichan Leader,* 22 January 1942; *Times,* 29 January 1942; *Province,* 12 and 13 February 1942; *Globe and Mail,* 13 February 1942; Marion Green to Howard Green, 19 February 1942, HCGFP, vol. 7; *Vancouver Sun,* 31 January and 3 February 1942; J.W. Cornett to J.L. Ralston, 31 January 1942; J.L. Ralston to J.W. Cornett, 5 February 1942; and J.W. Cornett to J.L. Ralston, 6 February 1942, in CVA, Mayor's Correspondence, "War Years."

70 For example, *Brantford Expositor,* 21 January and 2 March 1942; *Saskatoon Star-Phoenix,* 27 January 1942; *Winnipeg Free Press,* 13 February 1942; Winnipeg *Tribune,* 20 February 1942; and *Le Droit,* 22 February 1942. In press reports, Hepburn's comment was overshadowed by his simultaneous criticism of the American Navy. Among the newspapers in which the advertisement appeared were the Vancouver *News-Herald,* 9 February 1942; *Saskatoon Star-Phoenix,* 9 February 1942; *Le Devoir,* 9 February 1942; and *Le Droit,* 20 February 1942.

71 *HCD,* 29 January 1942, 151-57.

72 *HCD,* 29 January 1942, 158; 2 February 1942, 226-27; 3 February 1942, 257; 9 February 1942, 435; Grey Turgeon to W.L.M. King, 6 February 1942, KP, #288155-56.

73 Port Alberni *West Coast Advocate,* 4 February 1942; *Vancouver Sun,* 3 and 14 February 1942; *Trail Daily Times,* 10 February 1942; *Times,* 11 February 1942; *Cowichan Leader,* 12 February 1942. The editorial was reprinted in the *Vancouver Sun,* 14 February 1942; Prince Rupert *Evening Empire,* 3 February 1942; and Kaslo *Kootenaian,* 12 February 1942.

74 J.A. Paton, speech, 28 January 1942, WACBP, vol. 15; *Times,* 30 January and 13 and 14 February 1942; Vancouver *News-Herald,* 31 January 1942; *Province,* 31 January 1942; British Columbia, Legislative Assembly, *Votes and Proceedings,* 12 February 1942.

75 W.N. Sage to H.F. Angus, 17 February 1942, WNSP, box 3; *Vancouver Sun,* 14, 16, 18, and 19 February 1942; *Province,* 18, 19, 20, 24, and 25 February 1942; *Trail Daily Times,* 21 February 1942; Howard Green to "Dear Folks'n," 22 February 1942, HCGP, vol. 3; Canadian Brotherhood of Railway Employees and other Transport Workers, Pacific Division, no. 59, resolution, 20 February 1942, DLab, vol. 655; Arthur Turner to W.L.M. King, 21 February 1942, KP, #288386.

76 *Vancouver Sun,* 13, 17, and 18 February 1942; *Times,* 18 February 1942; Ian Mackenzie to W.L.M. King,

14 February 1942, CNSP, vol. 2; Howard Green to "Dear Folks'n," 18 January 1942, HCGP, vol. 2; *Brantford Expositor,* 21 January 1942.

77 Chiefs of Staff Appreciation, 19 February 1942, Ralston Papers, v. 72; Notes for Ralston's Speech to Secret Session of Parliament, 24 February 1942, JLRP, v. 72; *Sun,* 23 and 25 February 1942. Hutchison expressed similar concerns less colourfully in the *Times* (17 and 18 February 1942); *Times,* 23 and 25 February 1942; *News-Herald,* 27 February 1942; *Nelson Daily News,* 27 February 1942.

78 Greg Robinson, *By Order of the President* (Cambridge, MA: Harvard University Press, 2001), 102. Lippmann's column appeared in American newspapers such as the *Washington Post* and the same day in the Montreal *Gazette. HCD,* 9 February 1942; *Province,* 14 February 1942. The *Province* ran a photograph of several Japanese reading the notice; J.H. King to W.L.M. King, 2 February 1942, KP, #277592-93.

79 R.O. Alexander to Secretary, DND, 11 February 1942, DNDR, MfC8366; Joint Services Committee, Pacific Coast, Minutes, 13 February 1942, DNDR, vol. 2688. P.A. Hoare, Senior Officer (Prince Rupert), in his report for 15-22 February 1942, suggested that removing all Japanese from coastal areas would relieve "a very dangerous situation from the point of view of sabotage and aid to the enemy as well as the great danger of development of inter-racial strife." DNDR, vol. 11757. His report did not reach Esquimalt until 9 March 1942! In the meantime, Mackenzie asked Ralston to issue instructions to remove all Japanese from places such as Ucluelet. Ian Mackenzie to J.L. Ralston, 12 February 1942, IAMP, vol. 32; Joint Services Committee, Pacific Coast, Minutes, 19 February 1942, DNDR, vol. 2688. General Stuart thought that went beyond the policy announced in mid-January. K.C. Stuart to J.L. Ralston, 14 February 1942, DNDR, MfC8340. Under the Defence of Canada Regulations, Canadian nationals could not be required to leave a protected area, but the military could establish specific "controlled areas" where it could regulate the conduct of residents. T.W.S. Parsons to R.L. Maitland, 17 February 1942, and R.L. Maitland to Ian Mackenzie, 17 February 1942, IAMP, vol. 42; *Colonist,* 21 February 1942; *Times,* 16 and 23 February 1942; G.S. Pearson to A. MacNamara, 17 February 1942, DLab, vol. 174; Vancouver *News-Herald,* 24 February 1942.

80 W.C. Woodward to W.L.M. King, 11 February 1942, KP, #288847-49; Vancouver *News-Herald,* 13 and 14 February 1942; M. Macintosh to W.L.M. King, 20 February 1942, DEAR, vol. 2798.

81 Hugh Dalton to C.N. Senior, 19 February 1942, IAMP, vol. 25; Vancouver *News-Herald,* 21 February 1942. McVety suggested advancing the date for compulsory departure to 1 March to conform with American policy. J.H. McVety to A. MacNamara, 18 February 1942, DLab, vol. 174. Observing the public demand, MacNamara recommended setting the evacuation date as soon as work camps were ready. A. MacNamara to Ian Mackenzie and to H. Mitchell, 19 February 1942, IAMP, vol. 32.

82 *Times,* 11 February 1942. In editorials on 17 and 19 February, the *Times* presented variations on this theme; *Colonist,* 11 February (reprinted in the *Trail Daily News,* 13 February 1942), 13, 14, 15, 17, 20, and 21 February 1942; *Nanaimo Free Press,* 18 February 1942; *Comox Argus,* 12 and 19 February 1942; *Cowichan Leader,* 19 February 1942; *Ladysmith Chronicle,* 20 February 1942; *Trail Daily News,* 24 February 1942; Prince Rupert *Daily News,* 25 and 27 February 1942; Prince Rupert *Evening Empire,* 26 February 1942; *Vernon News,* 26 February 1942; *Columbian,* 21 February 1942; *Chilliwack Progress,* 18 February 1942; W. Nichols to H.L. Keenleyside, 9 February 1942, DEAR, vol. 2978; *Province,* 17 February 1942; Vancouver *News-Herald,* 17, 20, 21, and 23 February 1942; *Vancouver Sun,* 17 and 20 February 1942. It suggested that wives and children could follow once arrangements were made.

83 Many such letters can be found in IAMP, vols. 24 and 25; Prince Rupert *Daily News,* 4 February 1942; M.C. Ironside to R.W. Mayhew, 11 February 1942, KP, #277169-72; *Nanaimo Free Press,* 11 February 1942; J. Hillas to W.L.M. King, 11 February 1942, DEAR, vol. 2798; *Province,* 7, 19, and 23 February 1942; T.P. McConnell to Ian Mackenzie, 7 February 1942, Fraternal Council of B.C. to W.L.M. King, 13 February 1942, and Prince Rupert Chamber of Commerce to Ian Mackenzie, 19 February 1942, IAMP, vol. 24; Vancouver Kinsmen Club, resolution, 10 February 1942, H.L. Comely-Combe to W.L.M. King, 21 February 1942, United Commercial Travellers, Vancouver Council, 17 February 1942, C. MacDonald to Ian Mackenzie, 20 February 1942, A.R. Harvey to Ian Mackenzie, 23 February 1942, A.R. Bernard to Ian Mackenzie, 23 February 1942, W.M. Hawley, British Columbia Poultry Industries Committee to Ian Mackenzie, 18 February 1942, and B.O. Moxon to Ian Mackenzie, 20 February 1942, IAMP, vol. 25; *Times,* 17 February 1942; J.D. Allen, Prince Rupert Group Toc H, to W.L.M. King, 12 February 1942, N. Longton to W.L.M. King, 19 February 1942, G.G. Hotby to W.L.M. King, 24 February 1942, M. Chatfield to W.L.M. King, 24 February 1942, B. Friesen to W.L.M. King, 23 February 1942, and J.R. Burnes to W.L.M. King, 21 February 1942, DLab, vol. 655; Frank Boyd to H.D. Wilson, 20 February

1942, HDWP; T.M. Sullivan to W.L.M. King, 20 February 1942, DEAR, vol. 2798; *Columbian,* 21 February 1942; *Powell River Town Crier,* 23 February 1942.

84 M.F. Hunter to Municipal Councils, 14 February 1942, H. Hackwood to W.L.M. King, 24 February 1942, and W.E.B. Monypenny to W.L.M. King, 23 February 1942, DLab, vol. 655; E.S. Fox to W.L.M. King, 20 February 1942, KP, #275711; *Cowichan Leader,* 19 February 1942; *Colonist,* 20 and 25 February 1942; *Chilliwack Progress,* 18 February 1942; J. Edward Sears to J.L. Ralston, 19 February 1942, and C.N. Senior to *Times,* 24 February 1942, IAMP, vol. 25; *Nanaimo Free Press,* 24 February 1942; *Prince George Citizen,* 26 February 1942. Copies of many resolutions can be found in DLab, vol. 655, and DEAR, vol. 2798. Cumberland, which filed the resolution, was an exception. *Comox District Free Press,* 19 February 1942; A. McGavin to W.L.M. King, 20 February 1942, KP, #279336; *Times,* 24 and 28 February 1942; M.F. Hunter to W.L.M. King, 24 February 1942, KP, #277046-47.

85 R.W. Mayhew to Hubert Savage, 11 February 1942, KP, #281597-612; *Times,* 20 February 1942. Those signing the resolution were Youth Victory Club, Defence of Canada League, Native Sons of Canada, CCF District Council, Chinese Canadian Club, Royal Antediluvian Order of Buffaloes, Immediate Action Committee, IODE, Machinists Local No. 456, Saanich Board of Trade, Island Fruitgrowers' Association, Victoria Longshoremen's Association, Knights of Pythias, Lodge 61, Women's Institute of Colwood, Britannia and Pro Patria branches of Canadian Legion, Greater Victoria Teachers' Association, Toastmasters International, Gyro, Kiwanis, Kinsmen, Victoria Auxiliary to Canadian Forestry Corps, Canadian Auxiliary Territorial Services, and Industrial Defence Workers. J. Price to Grant MacNeil, 25 February 1942, and J. Price to Speaker and Members of Parliament, 23 February 1942, BCSCR, vol. 2; *Colonist,* 24 and 28 February 1942.

86 Hubert Savage to "Dear Sir," 24 February 1942, DLab, vol. 655. Savage continued to demand that the Japanese be interned or put under guard and suggested placing them in the camps used for the unemployed during the Depression and hiring Chinese guards! H. Savage to A. Taylor, 9 March 1942, BCSCR, vol. 2; *Times,* 26 February 1942; Montreal *Gazette,* 3 March 1942; *Brantford Expositor,* 13 March 1942.

87 J.K. Johnson to W.L.M. King, 26 February 1942, DLab, vol. 655; *Colonist,* 27 February 1942; Ian Mackenzie to J.R. Bowler, 26 February 1942, and Ian Mackenzie to J.L. Ralston, 26 February 1942, IAMP, vol. 32; *Times,* 2 March 1942.

88 *Province,* 3, 11, 17, and 21 February 1942; *Vancouver Sun,* 10 February 1942. J.W. Cornett to J.L. Ralston, 10 February 1942, IAMP, vol. 24; Resolution, 16 February 1942. Copy in HDWP; Vancouver *News-Herald,* 21 and 25 February 1942.

89 Report of meeting of 11 February 1942, HDWP; *Province,* 12 February 1942; *New Canadian,* 31 July 1940.

90 M.C. Robinson et al. to W.L.M. King, 24 February 1942, DLab, vol. 655. A slightly different version of the resolution and covering letter is in BCSCR, vol. 2. Robinson, a blinded veteran of the First World War, was the western superintendent of the Canadian National Institute for the Blind. *Province,* 26 February 1942. David McKee to Executive and Branch Secretaries, 25 February 1942, KP, #C249456; M.C. Robinson to H.F.G. Letson, 24 February 1942, BCSCR, vol. 2. The Vancouver manager of a national firm reported to his superior in Ottawa that it was "only because of a few level heads ... that a certain number of excitable people who may have started a riot were held back." W.J. Wellwood to E.A. Pickering, 27 February 1942, IAMP, vol. 25; T.A. Barnard to Ian Mackenzie, 19 February 1942, and W.F. Whebell to Ian Mackenzie, 10 February 1942, IAMP, vol. 24; H.D. Wilson to A.W. Neill, 24 February 1942, HDWPV, 551-A-7.

91 Ian Mackenzie to J.L. Ralston, 26 February 1942, IAMP, vol. 32; S. Mussallem to Ian Mackenzie, 21 February 1942, and Ian Mackenzie to S. Mussallem, 22 February 1942, IAMP, vol. 25; H.M. Davenport to Ian Mackenzie, 23 February 1942, IAMP, vol. 24; *Gazette,* 27 February 1942.

92 *Cowichan Leader,* 26 February 1942; *Province,* 25 February 1942.

93 On behalf of Chambers, the Nanaimo MP who was overseas, Mayhew later presented a petition from 1,100 Saanich residents asking for "immediate steps to eliminate all possibility of subversive acts by the resident Japanese in this province." *HCD,* 19 February 1942, 768. The petition was rejected on a technicality; it was addressed to the prime minister, not the House of Commons. *Times,* 20 February 1942; W.L.M. King, Diary, 19 February 1942. Not all spoke in the debate. James Sinclair (Liberal, Vancouver North) was also serving in the Armed Forces. *HCD,* 2 February 1942, 226; 5 February 1942, 342; 9 February 1942, 433-43; 17 February 1942, 640; 19 February 1942, 711-20. G.G. McGeer to W.L.M. King, 13 February 1942, KP, #279354-56. McGeer suggested isolating "all Japanese" but did not say where. G.G. McGeer to W.L.M. King, 5 March 1942, IAMP, vol. 19. Mayhew suggested putting

Mackenzie in charge of moving the Japanese. R.W. Mayhew to W.L.M. King, 12 and 17 February 1942, KP, #281597 and #281603-4; J.H. King to Ian Mackenzie, 20 February 1942, and C.N. Senior to Hugh Dalton, 25 February 1942, IAMP, vol. 25; Ian Mackenzie to L.S. St. Laurent, 14 February 1942, IAMP, vol. 24; Bruce Hutchison in *Times,* 16 February 1942.

94 [BC Members] to Ian Mackenzie, 21 February 1942, IAMP, vol. 32; Olof Hanson et al. to W.L.M. King, 21 February 1942, DLab, vol. 174; *Province,* 24 February 1942.

95 *Toronto Daily Star,* 23 February 1942; Winnipeg *Tribune,* 22 February 1942; *Vancouver Sun,* 23 February 1942.

96 W.L.M. King, Diary, 19 and 20 February 1942; Ian Mackenzie to J.L. Ralston, 23 February 1942, RCMPR, vol. 3563; Ian Mackenzie to J.L. Ralston et al., 24 February 1942, IAMP, vol. 25; *Times,* 24 February 1942. On prewar concern about riots, see Roy, *The Oriental Question,* Chapter 7. Ann Gomer Sunahara oversimplifies by saying that Mackenzie, whose goal was "the obliteration of the Japanese problem in British Columbia," "lied about the demands of public opinion in B.C." The volume of resolutions and their sources – the provincial government, municipal councils, boards of trade, service clubs, mainstream newspapers, and other responsible bodies – gave them greater impact than their numbers suggest. In any case, under the War Measures Act, the prime minister, with the concurrence of the Cabinet War Committee, made policy. Moreover, like President Franklin D. Roosevelt, whose early experiences and prejudices, as Greg Robinson has persuasively argued, led him to accept unquestioningly the claim of military officials that Japanese Americans threatened national security, Mackenzie King had had early experiences with the Japanese. He may not have had the same prejudices, but as Stephanie Bangarth observes, his first experience with the "Oriental Question" was an investigation of damage claims following the 1907 anti-Asian riot in Vancouver. Thus, he could easily conclude that removing the Japanese from the coast was a lesser evil than possible mob action. And, like Roosevelt, King was preoccupied with the larger issues of the war. Ann Gomer Sunahara, *The Politics of Racism: The Uprooting of Japanese Canadians during the Second World War* (Toronto: Lorimer, 1981), 47; Robinson, *By Order of the President;* Stephanie Bangarth, "Mackenzie King and Japanese Canadians," in *Mackenzie King: Citizenship and Community,* ed. John English, Kenneth McLaughlin, and P. Whitney Lackenbauer (Toronto: Robin Brass Studio, 2002), 119.

97 W.L.M. King, Diary, 24 February 1942; *HCD,* 25 February 1942, 810. Howard Green told his parents, "it is quite an accomplishment and on the Q.T. I feel that if I had not been so fighting mad about the thing we would have got far less." Howard Green to "Dear Folks," 1 March 1942, HCGP, vol. 3. Some months later the Spanish consul, acting as protecting power for Japan in Canada, complained of discrimination against the Japanese by race since other enemy aliens were not being moved. The Department of External Affairs, concerned that Japan might use unequal treatment as an excuse for reprisals against Canadian nationals, recommended stating that the evacuation was only from the restricted area, applied to all enemy aliens, and was being done for military rather than racial or economic reasons. N.A. Robertson to A. MacNamara, 5 June 1942, DLab, vol. 655. No such statement was made in Parliament.

98 W.L.M. King to V.B. Harrison, 30 October 1940, DNDR, vol. 805, file 571, MfT1809; Permanent Joint Board on Defence, Journal of Discussions and Decisions, 10-11 November 1941, copy in KP, J4, vol. 320; H.F. Angus, "My First Seventy-Five Years (1891-1966)," copy in BCA MS0775, 320.

99 *Nanaimo Free Press,* 26 February 1942; *Columbian,* 28 February and 2 March 1942; *Colonist,* 27 February 1942; *Vancouver Sun,* 26 February 1942; *Times,* 27 February 1942; Port Alberni *West Coast Advocate,* 5 March 1942; *Province,* 2 March 1942; *Marpole-Richmond Review,* reprinted in *New Canadian,* 17 March 1942; A. MacInnis to M.C. Robinson, 25 February 1942, BCSCR, vol. 2.

100 Prince Rupert Rotary Club to W.L.M. King, 6 March 1942, KP, #284317; Prince Rupert Junior Chamber of Commerce to W.L.M. King, 7 March 1942, and Prince Rupert Gyro Club to W.L.M. King, 11 March 1942, KP, J2, vol. 295. Branches of the Canadian Legion; the Women's Canadian Club of Vancouver; the Canadian Pensioners Association, Victoria; the North Shore Lady Laurier Club; the New Westminster and Cranbrook Gyro Clubs; the Native Brotherhood of BC; the Vancouver and District Lawn Bowling Club; the Vancouver Local Council of Women; and the City Councils of Nanaimo, Victoria, and Enderby passed or endorsed similar resolutions. The 50,000 copies of a petition for the removal of all Japanese distributed by the IODE provincial chapter were redundant. *Times,* 1 March 1942; IODE to Ian Mackenzie, 1 March 1942, and Ian Mackenzie to C.W. Maddison, 2 March 1942, IAMP, vol. 25; Joint Services Committee, Pacific Command, 27 February 1942, DNDR, MfC8369; R.W. Mayhew to W.L.M. King, 25 February 1942, KP, #281609-10; M.C. Robinson to L.S. St. Laurent, [25 February 1942], Minutes

of Meeting of Citizens' Defence Committee, 27 February 1942, and press release, [c. 26 February 1942], BCSCR, vol. 2; *Province,* 27 February and 3 March 1942; E.B. McMaster to W.L.M. King, 10 March 1942, DLab, vol. 655; *Vancouver Sun,* 28 February 1942.

101 *Times,* 28 February and 2 March 1942; *Province,* 2 March 1942; *Gazette,* 13 March 1942; Canadian Legion, Mission City, to W.L.M. King, 2 March 1942, DLab, vol. 655. Some of the Victoria groups reconstituted themselves as the United Organizations' Security Council and suggested that the Security Commission report to them on its work in removing Japanese. *Colonist,* 3 March 1942. Collins attacked the Pacific Co-Operative Union for attempting "to whitewash a group of residents who are here to exploit the natural resources of this province for their own benefit." He concluded, "as far as the Fraser Valley is concerned it is time for pruning in a drastic manner. Keep the province Christian and British." *Columbian* and Mission *Fraser Valley Record,* 25 February 1942.

102 Montreal *Gazette,* 11 March 1942. Tom Reid said that the Canadian government could not retaliate. Charles Bishop in Winnipeg *Tribune,* 10 March 1942; N.A. Robertson to S.T. Wood, 9 March 1942, RCMPR, vol. 3567, and KP, #283922; Lew Gordon, Memo, 11 March 1942, PCOR, vol. 5960; Ian Mackenzie to L.S. St. Laurent, 10 March 1942, IAMP, vol. 24.

103 *Colonist,* 11, 17, and 19 March 1942; Powell River *News,* 12 March 1942; *Vancouver Sun,* 10 March 1942; *Kelowna Capital News,* 11 March 1942; *Ladysmith Chronicle,* 13 March 1942; *Cowichan Leader,* 12 March 1942; Nelson *Daily News,* 13 March 1942; C.N. Senior to Ian Mackenzie, 10 March 1942, KP, #C249463; *Province,* 11 March 1942; *Trail Daily Times,* 11 March 1942; *Salmon Arm Observer,* 12 March 1942; *Prince George Citizen,* 19 March 1942; *Vernon News,* 12 March 1942; *Nanaimo Free Press,* 12 March 1942.

104 Shortly after the war, the *Vancouver Sun* argued on 29 December 1948 that "the evacuation was a military necessity"; H.F. A[ngus], draft for Undersecretary of State for External Affairs, 27 March 1944, DEAR, vol. 3005, file 3464-AD-40C; John Shirras to O.G. Estabrook, 12 May 1942, BCSCR, vol. 3; NAJC, *Democracy Betrayed: The Case of Redress* (Winnipeg: NAJC, 1984), 15.

At its meetings in July 1941, the Special Committee on Measures to Be Taken in the Event of War with Japan noted "with satisfaction" that military and police authorities in British Columbia "had taken and were continuing to take precautions" against possible attacks on the Japanese population of Vancouver and other cities "by irresponsible elements of the white population." Report of Special Committee on Measures to Be Taken in the Event of War with Japan, 28 July 1941, DEAR, vol. 2859, file 1698-A-40. In the United States, too, concerns about protecting the local Japanese were advanced as a reason for removing them from the coast. In 1942, for example, John McCloy, assistant secretary of war, claimed that the Japanese "were moved largely because we felt we could not control our own white citizens in California." However, after a comprehensive examination of the documents and an interrogation of over 750 witnesses, including some surviving officials, the United States Congressional Commission on Wartime Relocation and Internment of Civilians concluded in 1981 that protecting Japanese from vigilantes was a "lame" explanation. The commission also rejected the argument of "military necessity" as it noted the failure of anyone in Washington to question that argument. Instead, it concluded that "the broad historical causes that shaped" the decision to exclude Japanese Americans from the coast "were race prejudice, war hysteria and a failure of political leadership," and it noted the failure of civil libertarians to speak out against exclusion of the Japanese. Commission on Wartime Relocation and Internment of Civilians, *Personal Justice Denied* (Seattle: University of Washington Press, 1997) [first published by the US Government Printing Office, 1982 and 1983], 8, 83, 89, 459. John McCloy to Robert Patterson, 23 July 1942, Library of Congress, Robert Patterson Papers, file 137. (I am indebted to Greg Robinson for this reference). American historians have also argued that the prejudices of certain military leaders influenced policy. Klancy Clark De Nevers, *The Colonel and the Pacifist: Karl Bendetsen, Perry Saito, and the Incarceration of Japanese Americans during World War II* (Salt Lake City: University of Utah Press, 2004); Peter Irons, *Justice at War* (New York: Oxford University Press, 1983), 31.

105 Angus, "My First Seventy-Five Years," 319; *Lethbridge Herald,* 31 March 1942; Paul D. Murphy, "Memorandum re Japanese Evacuation," 2 May 1942, KP, #282078; "C.C.F. Policy Statement for Guidance of Speakers," November 1942, MacInnis Memorial Collection, vol. 41B/14; *Western Recorder,* November 1942, 9. In the House of Commons in 1947, Angus MacInnis said that the Japanese had been removed "not only for the protection and security of the west coast, but also for their own protection," though he contended that they should have been treated as "wards of the state" rather than as "enemy aliens." *HCD,* 24 April 1947, 2317; Interviews with F.J. Mead, 2 September 1943, F.H.

Soward, 14 September 1943, and A.W. Sparling, 15 March 1944, DHist, 322.009 (D358); Hugh L. Keenleyside, *Memoirs of Hugh L. Keenleyside: On the Bridge of Time* (Toronto: McClelland and Stewart, 1982), 175; *Nisei Affairs*, 20 August 1945. Many years later J.W. Pickersgill told an interviewer that King and other cabinet ministers had feared that "there might be a pogrom." Sunahara, *The Politics of Racism*, 47; *HCD*, 24 April 1947.

106 In an article written for the *New Canadian* of 16 June 1948, Trueman said that the evacuation had been undertaken because of what had been termed a "military necessity." He explained that such concerns had proved baseless, but "the fear and apprehension felt at the time by British Columbia residents were undoubtedly genuine." Before joining the commission, Trueman was executive secretary of the Central YMCA in Montreal. He had spent twenty years with the YMCA in Japan and spoke Japanese. R.S. Hosking to A. MacNamara, 13 April 1942, BCSCR, vol. 10; *Province*, 6 January 1943; *Columbian*, 7 January 1943. The council of the Vancouver Board of Trade wondered how the federal government would discipline Trueman. Humphrey Mitchell interpreted Trueman's statement as being designed to create "an attitude of mind which would be helpful in obtaining employment for the Canadian Japanese in Eastern Canada." Trueman said that he spoke on the subject for only a minute and a half in a half-hour speech and used American examples to show an eastern audience that they had nothing to fear from saboteurs. He asserted, "I certainly had no thought whatever of 'paddling' British Columbia or any other region ... It is quite likely that had I been on the West Coast at the time of Pearl Harbor I would have joined in the demand for mass evacuation." He claimed to be one of the "best friends" of the BC people, for he was "definitely committed to the dispersal idea." W.E. Payne to Ian Mackenzie, 11 January 1943, H. Mitchell to Ian Mackenzie, 25 January 1943, and G.E. Trueman to A. MacNamara, 13 January 1943, IAMP, vol. 25; *Times*, 7 January 1943; *Cowichan Leader*, 14 January 1943; *Vancouver Sun*, 6, 7, and 9 January and 7 May 1943; Vancouver *News-Herald*, 7 January 1943; *Province*, 6 and 7 February 1943; *HCD*, 4 February 1943, 133. In later debate, Reid repeated his attack on Trueman. *HCD*, 30 June 1943, 4221. A.W. Neill and T.J. O'Neill agreed; *Times*, 20 and 23 February 1942.

107 Adachi, *The Enemy that Never Was*, 218; J.B. Shimek to N.A. McLarty, 5 January 1942, DEAR, vol. 2798; Leo Sweeney to H.M. Doggon, 7 January 1942, HDWPV, 551-A-7.

108 Hugh Dobson to W.L.M. King, 9 January 1942, DEAR, vol. 2798; William Deans to W.L.M. King, 13 January 1942, KP, #274093-94; *Province*, 14 and 19 January 1942; *Ladysmith Chronicle*, 23 January 1942; Francis Northcote to Ian Mackenzie, 9 January 1942, IAMP, vol. 24. The Woman's Christian Temperance Union in Vancouver also expressed the hope that "in a Christian nation" the Japanese would be moved "in an orderly manner, with proper consideration for humane treatment in the matter of accommodation and other services." Mrs. R.C. Weldon to W.L.M. King, 26 February 1942, KP, #288684.

109 NAJC, *Democracy Betrayed*, 15; Austin Taylor to John Godwin, 6 May 1942, KP, #776221-26.

Chapter 2: Adverse Sentiments beyond the Coast

1 Cabinet War Committee, 26 February 1942; S.T. Wood to L.S. St. Laurent, 26 February 1942, RCMPR, vol. 3563; W.L.M. King, Diary, 26 and 27 February 1942. Attorney General R.L. Maitland consulted his counterpart, Earl Warren, in California to ascertain what was being done there and found that the United States was no further ahead. R.L. Maitland to Ian Mackenzie, 16 March 1942, KP, #279793-94.

2 Austin Taylor suggested including the local commanders of the army, navy, and air force; presumably to make it a civilian committee, they were not appointed. Ian Mackenzie to W.L.M. King, 1 March 1942, KP, #279777-79. The advisory board was active in the early stages of the evacuation but, according to George Pearson, met only when convenient for Taylor. Birt Showler, another member, reported in September that the board had met only three times. *Vancouver Sun*, 2 September 1942. Technically, the Security Commission ceased to exist in 1943 when its responsibilities were transferred to the Department of Labour, but there was little change in personnel, and it used Security Commission stationery. Thus, the "commission" remained the term in common use for what became the Japanese Division of the Department of Labour. For simplicity's sake, "commission" is used throughout this chapter.

3 Acting on suggestions from other members, Mackenzie recommended appointing Mrs. Percy B. Scurrah and Mrs. Mary Sutherland. Ian Mackenzie to W.L.M. King, 1 March 1942, KP, #279777-79; Ian Mackenzie to Austin Taylor, 16 and 19 March 1942, IAMP, vol. 24; *Federationist*, 26 March 1942. *Province*, 2, 11, and 19 March 1942.

4 *Province*, 11, 18, 25, and 26 March 1942; *Vancouver Sun*, 13, 19, 20, 21, 23, and 26 March 1942; *Colonist*,

17 March 1942; John Hart to W.L.M. King, 16 March 1942, GR 1222, vol. 100/1. The deputy minister of trade and industry assured a national magazine that tourists were welcome! E.G. Rowebottom to Editor, *Saturday Night,* 7 March 1942. *HCD,* 23 March 1942, 1559; Howard Green to "Folk's," 22 March 1942, HCGP, vol. 3.

5 *Trail Daily Times,* 23 May 1942; W.L.M. King, Diary, 19, 26, 27, 30, and 31 May and 1 June 1942; *Saskatoon Star-Phoenix,* 27 May 1942; C.P. Stacey, *Six Years of War: The Army in Canada, Britain, and the Pacific* (Ottawa: Queen's Printer, 1966), 173; *Times,* 1, 4, 5, 11, and 22 June 1942; *Province,* 4 and 6 June 1942; Ian Mackenzie to R.G. Robertson, 7 July 1942, DEAR, vol. 3027. R.W. Mayhew had suggested making arrangements to evacuate children from the island. R.W. Mayhew to L.S. St. Laurent, 2 March 1942, BCSCR, vol. 10/305.

6 *Colonist,* 4 and 23 June 1942; *Vancouver Sun,* 2 and 4 June, 23 July, 10, 12, and 14 August 1942; *Calgary Herald,* 22 June 1942; *Trail Daily Times,* 4 and 27 June 1942; *Times,* 3 and 4 June 1942; *Province,* 3 and 6 June 1942; *New Canadian,* 6 April 1942. Lew Gordon, Memo, 21 July 1942, PCOR, vol. 5960; Edmonton *Bulletin,* 12 June 1942; Calgary *Albertan,* 5 June 1942. Occasional references to possible Japanese attacks continued, possibly to rekindle waning interest in air raid precautions. *Vancouver Sun,* 5 May 1943 and 20 January 1944; *Colonist,* 14 April 1944.

7 *Trail Daily Times,* 18 September 1942; *Grand Forks Gazette,* 16 July 1942; *Prince George Citizen,* 5 March 1942; *Penticton Herald,* 23 April 1942; H. Mitchell to Austin Taylor, 5 March 1942, BCSCR, vol. 2/35; *Similkameen Star,* 30 April 1942; A.W. Neill to H. Mitchell, 9 May 1942, and S.T. Wood to L.S. St. Laurent, 5 June 1942, DLab, vol. 175; T.F. McWilliams, "The New Japanese Menace," *Kelowna Courier,* 6 August 1942; Vancouver *News-Herald,* 20 March 1942; Journal of Discussions and Decisions, Permanent Joint Board on Defence, 26-27 May 1942, KP, #C220372; H. Mitchell to J.L. Ralston, 27 May 1942, and Extract from Minutes, Joint Chiefs of Staff, 7 July 1942, DNDR, C5394; Acting Minister of National Defence to H. Mitchell, 1 June 1942, DHist, 314.009 (D17); G.W. Daniels, Revelstoke Branch, Canadian Legion, to W.L.M. King, 2 March 1942, H. Mitchell to L.S. St. Laurent, 13 June 1942, and S.T. Wood to L.S. St. Laurent, 8 June 1942, DLab, vol. 655; Nisei Mass Evacuation Group to Austin Taylor, 15 April 1942, BCSCR, vol. 3; Meeting of Cabinet Sub-Committee on Japanese, 10 June 1942, PCOR, vol. 25, file J-25-1; *New Canadian,* 17 March 1954. For details on the Mass Evacuation Group, see Ann Gomer Sunahara, *The Politics of Racism: The Uprooting of Japanese Canadians during the Second World War* (Toronto: Lorimer, 1981), 66-71; and Roy Miki, *Redress: Inside the Japanese Canadian Call for Justice* (Vancouver: Raincoast, 2004), Chapter 3. As employment opportunities opened, more men left the camps. The program ended in the summer of 1944. *New Canadian,* 5 August 1944. In October on behalf of the Government of Japan, the Spanish consul complained about the "severing [of] men from their wives and children." By then most families had been reunited. Pedro E. Schwartz to N.A. Robertson, 20 October 1942, DEAR, vol. 3005, file 3464-AD-40C.

8 Almost every account of the evacuation includes descriptions of conditions at Hastings Park. Fred Howlett to Ian Mackenzie, 4 March 1942, IAMP, vol. 25; Vancouver *News-Herald,* 31 March 1942; *Province,* 4, 14, and 20 April 1942; J.W. Cornett to H. Mitchell, 29 April 1942, BCSCR, vol. 9; *New Canadian,* 6 April 1942; *Lethbridge Herald,* 4 April 1942; *Federationist,* 19 March and 16 April 1942. Austin Taylor to A. MacNamara, 4 April 1942, BCSCR, vol. 2. Mackenzie said he meant only that Hastings Park would not become a permanent abode. He endorsed Taylor's policy of dealing with Japanese in "the British way" and denied any thought of permanently separating families. Draft press release, c. 5 April 1942, BCSCR, vol. 2; *Province,* 6 April 1942; Vancouver *News-Herald,* 6 April 1942.

9 Wilson's outbursts led the press censor to suggest that, since he had recently joined the reserves, the army should send him "to some point in Northern British Columbia where he could not make a nuisance of himself." Lew Gordon to W. Eggleston, 21 April 1942, PCOR, vol. 5979. H.D. Wilson to A.I. McKinley, 18 May 1942, HDWPV, 551-A-7. Vancouver *News-Herald,* 15, 16, 20, and 29 May and 2 June 1942; C.H. Hill to Commissioner, 28 April 1942, DEAR, vol. 3004; Austin Taylor to A. MacNamara, 27 May 1942, and Ian Mackenzie to H. Mitchell, 29 May 1942, DLab, vol. 175; *Calgary Herald,* 14 May 1942; Calgary *Albertan,* 14 May 1942; *Province,* 14 May 1942.

10 *Province,* 2, 4, and 6 March 1942; Vancouver *News-Herald,* 24 July and 11 and 12 August 1942; *Vancouver Sun,* 23 July and 11 August 1942; Lew Gordon to W. Eggleston, 24 July 1942, PCOR, vol. 5979; Fred Howlett to H. Mitchell, 18 August 1942, DLab, vol. 655; Ian Mackenzie to H. Mitchell, 24 August 1942, DLab, vol. 176.

11 George Cruickshank to A. MacNamara, 1 May 1942, R.W. Mayhew to H. Mitchell, 1 June 1942, and Austin Taylor to A. MacNamara, 4 June 1942, DLab, vol. 175; G.G. McGeer to W.L.M. King, 29 May

1942, GGMcGP, vol. 2; R.W. Mayhew to Ian Mackenzie, 15 May 1942, IAMP, vol. 24. A spokesman for the Japanese also complained of delays in designating areas for evacuees. *Province,* 2 and 11 June 1942.

12 David McKee to Ian Mackenzie, 16 July 1942, IAMP, vol. 175; Grey Turgeon, *HCD,* 18 June 1942, 3448; T.J. O'Neill, *HCD,* 19 June 1942, 3479-90. Neill attributed delays to "two officials at Ottawa, deeply entrenched in the government offices, whose souls seem to be bound up in the prosperity and happiness of the Japanese in British Columbia." The reference was to H.L. Keenleyside and H.F. Angus, against whom Neill had privately campaigned for some months. Prime Minister King instantly defended their right to entertain "humane feelings." A.W. Neill to Halford Wilson, 10 March 1942, HDWP. *Vancouver Sun,* 15 and 20 July 1942.

13 Two Liberals, James Sinclair and Alan Chambers, were in the Armed Forces; G.G. McGeer was absent.

14 Minutes of Meeting of BC Members of Parliament with Ian Mackenzie, J.G. Gardiner, and George Black in the Office of Humphrey Mitchell, 21 July 1942, DLab, vol. 175; *HCD,* 29 July 1942, 4936-57. In June the prime minister's office proposed asking the Security Commission for advice about the long-term settlement of the Japanese, but Norman Robertson recommended delaying the request since bitterness might lead to suggestions to repatriate all persons of Japanese origin. H.L. Keenleyside to H.F. Angus, 27 June 1942, DEAR, vol. 3005, file 3464-V-40.

15 Andrew McGavin et al. to R.W. Mayhew, and R.W. Mayhew to W.L.M. King, 1 August 1942, KP, #281619-21; *Cowichan Leader,* 13 August 1942; Minutes, 39th Annual Convention, Union of BC Municipalities, Kamloops, 15-16 September 1942.

16 *Vancouver Sun,* 4 June, 30 July, and 26 September 1942; *Province,* 6 June 1942. The rector of St. James' Anglican Church, which was adjacent to "Little Tokyo," attacked delegates, including Alderman Wilson, for their "lack of Christian kindness" toward local Japanese. G.G. McGeer did not think that the *Sun*'s editorial comment was "sincere." G.G. McGeer to W.L.M. King, 26 September 1942, KP, #279557. Privately, Taylor defended the commission by noting that the consul general for Spain and a representative of the International Red Cross had said that their recent inspection would not give any excuses to Tokyo for reprisals. Austin Taylor to A. MacNamara, 30 July 1942, DLab, vol. 176. E. Maag of the Red Cross was willing to be quoted that the suggestion of BC members to turn the evacuation over to the military would be "an international calamity." E. Maag to F.J. Mead, 3 August 1942, BCSCR, vol. 15; *Province,* 30 July and 15 December 1942; *Chilliwack Progress,* 1 and 8 April 1942; Mission *Fraser Valley Record,* 16 April 1942.

17 Austin Taylor to Ian Mackenzie, 9 March 1942, BCSCR, vol. 11; Minutes of Meeting of Advisory Board to BC Security Commission, 13 March 1942, BCSCR, vol. 7. BC Security Commission, *Removal of Japanese from Protected Areas, March 4, 1942, to October 31, 1942* (Vancouver: BC Security Commission, 1942), 9. At one point, the commission considered using Indian residential schools to house women and children and putting Indian children in day schools. In the United States, the unwillingness of western governors to accept Japanese Americans except in camps under guard led the government to build, in isolated areas, ten large internment or "concentration camps" surrounded by barbed wire fences and patrolled by armed guards. Apart from teachers and War Relocation Authority officials, the Japanese had little contact with Caucasians. Both nations, however, encouraged people to leave their interior homes and head farther east, where, because of the war, their labour was in demand.

18 *Cowichan Leader,* 26 March 1942; Prince Rupert *Evening Empire,* 14 March 1942; Vancouver *News-Herald,* 18 March 1942; *Langley Advance,* 30 April 1942; *Province,* 24 April 1942; *New Canadian,* 30 May 1942; N.F. Black et al. to Reverend A.E. Whitehouse, 14 September 1942, HDP, Mf808a. *Vancouver Sun,* 4 July 1942.

19 This discussion is based on a perusal of *Le Devoir* and *La Presse* in February and early March 1942; BC Security Commission, *Removal of Japanese,* 11; Adelard Godbout to Ian Mackenzie, 18 May 1942, IAMP, vol. 25; *New Canadian,* 16 October 1943 and 18 February 1944. The Drummondville United Church opposed any plan to have Japanese offset a scarcity of farm labour; such protests were rare. G.E. Hamel, circular letter, 26 April 1942, DLab, vol. 655.

20 Vancouver *News-Herald,* 19 March 1942; *Columbian,* 9 March 1942; *Maclean's,* 15 March 1942; *Lethbridge Herald,* 6 June 1942; *Ottawa Journal,* 17 June 1942.

21 Stephanie Bangarth, "The Long, Wet Summer of 1942: The Ontario Farm Service Force, Small-Town Ontario, and the Nisei," *Canadian Ethnic Studies,* 37, 1 (2005): 41; *Brantford Expositor,* 13 March 1942; Jarnal Singh, "Wartime Toronto and Japanese Canadians," *Polyphony* 6, 1 (1984): 199-200. At http://collections.ic.gc.ca/magic/mt71.html (viewed 6 December 2005); J.W. Buckley, Secretary, Toronto District Labour Council, to W.L.M. King, 7 March 1942, DLab, vol. 655; *Toronto Daily Star,* 22 April

1942; Beatrice Barber to W.L.M. King, 6 June 1942, KP, #272261-64; *Province,* 23 April, 8 June, and 10 July 1942; *Vancouver Sun,* 27 October 1942; Vancouver *News-Herald,* 3 June 1942; *Ottawa Journal,* 5 June 1942; Patrick Boyer, *A Passion for Justice: The Legacy of James Chalmers McRuer* (Toronto: Osgoode Society, 1994), 165. Even a senior civil servant who needed household help for his ailing wife could not get permission to bring in a Japanese maid. H.R. MacMillan to Hector McKinnon, 21 September 1942, HRMacMP, vol. 8.

22 A. MacNamara to Austin Taylor, 17 June 1942, DLab, vol. 24; Sudbury City Council to W.L.M. King, 5 March 1942, KP, #279942; Edmonton *Bulletin,* 26 March 1942; A. McNaughton to H. Mitchell, 11 November 1942, C.E. Lenton to W.L.M. King, 24 November 1942, E.F. Kearney to H. Mitchell, 5 December 1942, DLab, vol. 655; *Province,* 2 April, 24 August, and 24 September 1942; BC Security Commission, *Removal of Japanese,* 11; *Vancouver Sun,* 1 February 1943; Graham Pipher to F.J. Mead, 3 July 1942, BCSCR, vol. 11.

23 William R. Young, "Chauvinism and Canadianism: Canadian Ethnic Groups and the Failure of Wartime Information," in *On Guard for Thee: War, Ethnicity, and the Canadian State, 1939-1945,* ed. Norman Hillmer, Bohdan Kordan, and Lubomyr Luciuk (Ottawa: Canadian Committee for the History of the Second World War, 1988), 45-46; Forrest E. La Violette, "Social Psychological Characteristics of Evacuated Japanese," *Canadian Journal of Economics and Political Science* 11 (1945): 420.

24 G.E. Trueman to W.A. Eastwood, 21 June 1943, A. MacNamara to George Collins, 19 May 1943, W.S. Roome, RCMP, report, 10 June 1943, W.J. Butt, RCMP, report, 11 June 1943, G.E. Trueman to W.A. Eastwood, 21 June 1943, G.E. Trueman to C.V. Booth, 16 August 1943, BCSCR, vol. 10; Vancouver *News-Herald,* 25 September and 3 October 1944.

25 E. Eggington to W.L.M. King, 18 January 1944, KP, #311486; *New Canadian,* 7 April 1945; G.E. Trueman to C.V. Booth, 20 August 1943, BCSCR, vol. 10. The RCMP report on an incident at Beamsville was removed from the file because of privacy legislation.

26 Co-Operative Committee on Japanese-Canadian Arrivals in Toronto, 8 June 1943, CCJC, vol. 1; Combined Report of the Men's and Women's Subcommittees to the Co-Operative Committee on Japanese-Canadian Arrivals in Toronto, 1 November 1943, CCJC, vol. 2; G.E. Trueman to A. MacNamara, 16 August 1943, G.E. Trueman to W.A. Eastwood, 27 August and 19 November 1943, DLab, vol. 180; G.E. Trueman to A. MacNamara, 8 February 1944, J.W. Somers to N.A. Robertson, 24 March 1944, DLab, vol. 181; Ken Adachi, *The Enemy that Never Was* (Toronto: McClelland and Stewart, 1976), 287; *New Canadian,* 29 April 1944; *Province,* 4 March 1944; Vancouver *News-Herald,* 6 April 1945; F. DesBrisay and J. Lister to George Collins, 26 March 1943, DLab, vol. 169; Department of Labour, *Report on the Administration of Japanese Affairs in Canada, 1942-1944* (Ottawa: Department of Labour, 1944), 41, 44; Department of Labour, *Report on the Re-Establishment of Japanese in Canada, 1944-46* (Ottawa: Department of Labour, 1947), 20; Rev. K. Shimizu, "Resettlement of Japanese Canadians," 21 June 1944, CCJC, vol. 2.

27 John Bracken to H. Mitchell, 25 March 1942, BCSCR, vol. 2; *Winnipeg Free Press,* 20, 21, and 27 February and 26 and 28 March 1942; Winnipeg *Tribune,* 9 February and 7 March 1942; *Lethbridge Herald,* 23 April 1942; T. Queen to Austin Taylor, 6 April 1942, BCSCR, vol. 9; *Province,* 29 April and 6 May 1942 and 8 August 1944; George Murton to A. MacNamara, 2 March 1942, and John Bracken to Austin Taylor, 23 June 1942, DLab, vol. 170; *Calgary Herald,* 22 April 1942; W.A. Eastwood to R.C. Brown, 28 August 1942, BCSCR, vol. 16; BC Security Commission, *Removal of Japanese,* 10. Two Manitoba market gardening communities did not want any Japanese. *Province,* 29 April 1942; Manitoba Japanese Canadian Citizens' Association, *The History of Japanese Canadians in Manitoba* (Winnipeg: Manitoba Japanese Canadian Citizens' Association, 1996), 11-12. Before the war, Manitoba had forty-two residents of Japanese ancestry, of whom twenty-one were in Winnipeg. They included red caps at the Canadian National Railway station, a member of the Canadian Army Dental Corps, a lampshade maker, a tailor, and an elevator operator at the Royal Alexandra hotel. Winnipeg *Tribune,* 8 December 1942.

28 W.J. Patterson to A. MacNamara, 21 April 1942, and Regina Subdivision, RCMP, report, 7 April 1942, BCSCR, vol. 2; Vancouver *News-Herald,* 15 September 1942; *Saskatoon Star-Phoenix,* 19 June, 6 and 28 July, and 15 September 1942. As of October 1941, 107 residents of Saskatchewan had registered as Japanese. Survey of Registration, DEAR, vol. 2909.

Despite fine academic credentials, Tamaki could not get permission from the city to attend the University of Toronto, where he had been accepted to do graduate studies in law. In 1943, however, the Board of Control reversed its decision and Tamaki was admitted as a British subject who was not under

RCMP supervision. He wrote a thesis on the law relating to nationality under Bora Laskin's direction and became a leading tax lawyer in Montreal and later in Toronto. Philip Girard, *Bora Laskin: Bringing Law to Life* (Toronto: Osgoode Society, 2005), 144.

29 Summary of Registrations of Japanese, 1 March-20 October 1941, DEAR, vol. 2509. For a brief history of the Japanese in Alberta, see Ann Gomer Sunahara and David Sunahara, "The Japanese in Alberta," in *Peoples of Alberta: Portraits of Cultural Diversity*, ed. Howard Palmer and Tamara Palmer (Saskatoon: Western Producer, 1985), 394-412, and Howard Palmer, "Patterns of Racism: Attitudes towards Chinese and Japanese in Alberta 1920-1950," *Histoire sociale/Social History* 13 (1980): 150-54; Edmonton *Bulletin*, 9 and 30 December 1941; Calgary *Albertan*, 3 January 1942; *Lethbridge Herald*, 8, 13, and 30 December 1941 and 2 January 1942.

30 Edmonton *Bulletin*, 9 and 12 December 1941, 16 and 19 February 1942; *Lethbridge Herald*, 5 February 1942; *Calgary Herald*, 6, 15, and 20 January and 6, 17, and 18 February 1942.

31 Edmonton *Bulletin*, 16, 21, and 26 January 1942 and 4 and 11 February 1942.

32 *Lethbridge Herald*, 23 January 1942; *Calgary Herald*, 12 February 1942; Edmonton *Bulletin*, 24 February 1942.

33 Edmonton *Bulletin*, 26 and 27 February and 12 March 1942; *Calgary Herald*, 26 February and 10 March 1942; Forrest E. La Violette, *The Canadian Japanese and World War II: A Sociological and Psychological Account* (Toronto: University of Toronto Press, 1948), 122.

34 *Calgary Herald*, 14 March 1942; *Lethbridge Herald*, 14, 20, and 25 March 1942; Philip Baker to H. Mitchell, 16 March 1942, DLab, vol. 174.

35 *Calgary Herald*, 4 and 5 March 1942; *Lethbridge Herald*, 4, 7, 10, and 11 March 1942. The Hutterites, members of a religious sect, held land communally and efficiently farmed it. Living in largely self-contained colonies, they had little contact with surrounding communities and did not patronize local merchants to any extent.

36 *Lethbridge Herald*, 14, 16, 18, 19, and 31 March 1942.

37 A.H. Avery, Secretary, Taber Citizens Committee, to Minister of National Defence, 16 March 1942; CIB (Criminal Investigation Branch), Lethbridge, 16 March 1942, DLab, vol. 174; *Calgary Herald*, 11 and 19 March 1942; *Taber Times*, reprinted in *Lethbridge Herald*, 9 March 1942; *Lethbridge Herald*, 9, 11, 16, and 25 March and 29 April 1942; W.R. Tucker, President, Taber Branch, Canadian Legion, to W.L.M. King, 29 August 1942, DLab, vol. 655.

38 William Aberhart to A. MacNamara, 17 March 1942, William Aberhart to W.L.M. King, 27 March 1942, William Aberhart to John Shirras, 31 March 1942, H. Mitchell to William Aberhart, 22 April 1942, William Aberhart to H. Mitchell, 23 May 1942, DLab, vol. 170; *Calgary Herald*, 19 March 1942; *Lethbridge Herald*, 20 March 1942; Austin Taylor to William Aberhart, 23 March 1942, DLab, vol. 174. PC 3213 (21 April 1942) authorized the Security Commission to make agreements with the provinces. PC 3903 (11 May 1942) dealt with Ontario, while PC 4615 (2 June 1942) dealt with Alberta.

39 *Calgary Herald*, 14, 28, and 31 March, 1, 11, and 14 April, 27 May, and 3 and 5 June 1942; G.G. Cushing, Secretary, Calgary Trades and Labour Council to W.L.M. King, 7 April 1942, DLab, vol. 655; J.M. Miller, City Clerk, Calgary, to W.L.M. King, 24 April 1942, KP, #281738. Calgary *Albertan*, 12 June 1942.

40 *Calgary Herald*, 18 February 1942; *Lethbridge Herald*, 11, 12, 17, 20, and 31 March 1942; *Vancouver Sun*, 12, 18, and 21 August 1942; Edmonton *Bulletin*, 9 April 1942. Chinese restaurateurs in Lethbridge said that they would prefer not to have Japanese customers, but only one said that he would refuse to serve them. Calgary *Albertan*, 8 April 1942.

41 Edmonton *Bulletin*, 2, 9, 13, 14, and 24 April and 12 June 1942; L.S. St. Laurent to R.T. Rose, Executive Secretary, Edmonton Chamber of Commerce, 13 April 1942, Austin Taylor to R.T. Rose, 15 April 1942, and R.T. Rose to Austin Taylor, 23 April 1942, BCSCR, vol. 9. When eight students from the University of British Columbia applied to the University of Alberta, the university noted Edmonton's strategic location and the need of the students to gain the permission of the Security Commission. Edmonton *Bulletin*, 30 June 1942. The city objected, so the university only admitted Japanese students who were Alberta residents or had been previously enrolled. La Violette, *The Canadian Japanese and World War II*, 306. The Cabinet War Committee decided to let the universities decide on the acceptance of Japanese students. A. Rive to Registrar, McGill University, 15 September 1942, DEAR, vol. 3005, file 3464-W-40.

42 Vancouver *News-Herald*, 3 April 1942; Director, Parks and Forests Branch, to J.M. Wardle, 20 March 1942, LAC, Records of Canadian Parks Service, vol. 175; L.A. Nelmes, Jasper Detachment, RCMP, report, 7 May 1942, BCSCR, vol. 9; J.A. Wood to Controller, National Parks Bureau, 24 June 1942, DLab, vol. 655; *Lethbridge Herald*, 25 March 1942; Edmonton *Bulletin*, 3 April 1942.

43 *Province,* 5 and 20 March, 27 June, and 24 July 1942; Austin Taylor to A. MacNamara, 9 March 1942, BCSCR, vol. 2; Agreement between BC Security Commission and Government of Alberta, 6 May 1942, and Austin Taylor to A. MacNamara, 29 August 1942, DLab, vol. 170; *Vancouver Sun,* 12, 18, and 21 August 1942; G.G. Cushing to W.L.M. King, 7 April 1942, DLab, vol. 655; Minister of Justice to R.T. Rose, 12 April 1942, BCSCR, vol. 9; "Japanese Movement-Pacific Coast (Period Ending October 31, 1942)," BCSCR, vol. 1.

44 Austin Taylor to A. MacNamara, 29 August 1942, DLab, vol. 170; E.C. Manning to W.L.M. King, 26 March 1945, PCOR, vol. 26, file J-25-1; A. MacNamara to J.W. Pickersgill, 3 April 1945, DLab, vol. 639; *New Canadian,* 19 June, 11 September, and 23 October 1943; Minutes of Southern Alberta Youth Council, 20 January 1946, Minuro Takada to Kyoto Shigeshiro, 31 October 1946, Minuro Takada to Hunter Lewis, 19 February 1946, W.S. Wallace to Ruby Miuma, n.d., and Minutes of Southern Alberta Youth Council, 9 February 1947, LAC, Minuro Takada Papers; Edmonton *Bulletin,* 10 February 1943; *Province,* 27 June and 8 December 1942 and 18 April and 15 August 1944; Vancouver *News-Herald,* 9 March 1944; W.S. Wallace to Mark Hopkins, 12 September 1977, CCJC, vol. 1.

45 *Kelowna Courier,* 11 June 1942; *Penticton Herald,* 18 June 1942; *Vernon News,* 5 March 1942; *Province,* 23 April and 8 June 1942; *Vancouver Sun,* 6 March 1942; T.J. O'Neill to A. MacNamara, 31 July 1942, DLab, vol. 175; Colin Clifford, Slocan District Board of Trade, to A. MacNamara, 5 September 1942, DLab, vol. 655; W.A.C. Bennett to H.B. Morley, 10 June 1942, WACBP, vol. 1; Williams Lake Board of Trade to R.W. Bruhn, 7 April 1942, BCWSC, vol. 7; *Similkameen Star,* 12, 19, and 26 March 1942.

46 S.T. Wood to F.J. Mead, 4 March 1942, RCMPR, vol. 3563; W.A.C. Bennett to Ian Mackenzie, 2 March 1942, DLab, vol. 174; *Kelowna Courier,* 5 and 12 March 1942; Ian Mackenzie to L.S. St. Laurent, 3 March 1942, IAMP, vol. 24; *Vernon News,* 5 and 12 March 1942; E.W. Barton to W.L.M. King, 5 March 1942, KP, J2, vol. 295; Vancouver *News-Herald,* 6 March 1942. Mackenzie urged Taylor to stop the independent movement of Japanese by taking their automobiles and immediately gathering up men before sending them to work camps or farm colonies. Ian Mackenzie to Austin Taylor, 5 March 1942, DLab, vol. 174.

47 E.W. Barton to W.L.M. King, 11 March 1942, KP, #272278; *Penticton Herald,* 12 March 1942; *Vernon News,* 12 and 19 March 1942; R.G. Rutherford to BC Security Commission, 11 March 1942, BCSCR, vol. 4; *Province,* 6, 10, and 16 March 1942; *Kelowna Courier,* 12 and 19 March 1942; T. Wilkinson to Austin Taylor, "re Attorney-General," 16 March 1942, RLMP. For further details, see Patricia E. Roy, "A Tale of Two Cities: The Reception of Japanese Evacuees in Kelowna and Kaslo, B.C.," *BC Studies* 87 (1990): 23-47.

48 The Penticton Board of Trade called for continuous supervision of all Japanese in Canada to prevent them from aiding the enemy but regarded suggestions of internment and expatriation as too strong. *Penticton Herald,* 12 March and 16 April 1942; *Vernon News,* 12 March 1942; *Kelowna Courier,* 12 and 19 March 1942. *The Japanese Contribution to Canada* (Vancouver: Canadian Japanese Association, 1940), 23. Kelowna City Council relented slightly in mid-December by letting the Buddhist church have light and water until the end of the month provided that it was used only under police supervision and by Canadian-born Japanese who had been in Kelowna before 7 December 1941. *Kelowna Courier,* 17 and 24 December 1942.

49 Message telephoned by R.G. Rutherford from Vancouver to E.W. Barton, 19 March 1942, WACBP, vol. 13; Vancouver *News-Herald,* 23 March 1942. R.P. MacLean, manager and editor of the *Kelowna Courier,* apologized to Taylor, explaining that "the Japanese situation was simply too much" to handle for the acting editor. R.P. MacLean to Austin Taylor, 25 March 1942, BCSCR, vol. 10; *Province,* 20, 26, and 30 March 1942; *Kelowna Courier,* 19 and 26 March 1942; *Vernon News,* 26 March 1942; *Penticton Herald,* 2 April 1942; Grote Stirling to A. MacNamara, 1 May 1942, DLab, vol. 175. Rutherford and the Okanagan and Kamloops area branches of the Canadian Legion seemed to be satisfied, although legionnaires wanted Japanese-owned vehicles to be immobilized.

50 *Province,* 31 March 1942; *Salmon Arm Observer,* 2 and 16 April and 13 and 27 May 1942; 28 September, 12 October, 23 November, and 14 December 1944; and 5 July 1945.

51 *Kelowna Courier,* 5 March and 7 May 1942; *Vernon News,* 23 April, 7 and 14 May 1942; *Province,* 6 March 1942; Thomas Wilkinson to Austin Taylor, "re Attorney-General," 16 March 1942, RLMP; Grote Stirling to A. MacNamara, 2 June 1942, DLab, vol. 175.

52 *Penticton Herald,* 14 and 21 May 1942; *Kelowna Courier,* 14 and 21 May 1942; *Province,* 18 May 1942; Austin Taylor to A. MacNamara, 20 May 1942, DLab, vol. 175.

53 Austin Taylor to F. DesBrisay, 30 May 1942, Austin Taylor to A. MacNamara, 20 May 1942, A. MacNamara

to F. DesBrisay, 13 July 1942, DLab, vol. 175; F. DesBrisay to A. MacNamara, 28 July 1942, DLab, vol. 176; H. Mitchell to F. DesBrisay, 1 June 1942, BCSCR, vol. 9; *Vernon News,* 11 June, 6 August, 5 and 12 November 1942; Vancouver *News-Herald,* 22 August 1942; *Kelowna Courier,* 19 November 1942; *Province,* 22 August 1942.

54 *Vernon News,* 27 August, 3, 10, and 24 September 1942; 10 February, 15 June, 10, 17, and 31 August, 7 and 14 September 1944; and 15 February 1945; *Kelowna Courier,* 6 May 1943; David Howrie to A. MacNamara, 6 September 1944, DLab, vol. 655.

55 *Kelowna Courier,* 26 November and 3 December 1942; *Penticton Herald,* 3 and 10 December 1942; *Vernon News,* 3 December 1942 and 1 July 1943. Kelowna City Council refused to accept Pettigrew's resignation as its representative on the committee.

56 *Kelowna Courier,* 19 November 1942 and 14 January 1943; *Vernon News,* 3 December 1942; *Penticton Herald,* 26 November, 10 and 31 December 1942, and 7, 14, and 21 January 1943; *Grand Forks Gazette,* 14 January 1943; *Province,* 26 November 1942; Naramata Local, BCFGA, 6 January 1943, and A.L. King, Memo, 29 January 1943, DLab, vol. 655. Both the CPR and the CNR had great difficulty getting labour and employed Japanese in their roundhouses, much to the consternation of the railway brotherhoods. *Province,* 19 January 1944.

57 *Penticton Herald,* 9 July 1942 and 21 January 1943; *Kelowna Capital News,* 26 August, 23 September, 10 and 31 December 1942, and 4 February 1943; *Kelowna Courier,* 20 and 27 August, 10 September, 10 and 31 December 1942, and 4 February 1943; *Vancouver Sun,* 11 December 1942.

58 *Kelowna Courier,* 8 and 15 April 1943; *Province,* 15 April 1943; *Vernon News,* 6 May 1943; *Penticton Herald,* 6 May 1943; W.A. Eastwood to George Collins, 13 May 1943, BCSCR, vol. 7. Stirling also complained about infiltration. Grote Stirling to A. MacNamara, 12 April 1943, DLab, vol. 177.

59 *Kelowna Courier,* 29 April, 13 May, and 3, 10, 17, and 24 June 1943; *New Canadian,* 1 May 1943; *Province,* 11 May 1943; *Vernon News,* 10 and 17 June 1943; G.A. McKay to W.L.M. King, 28 May 1943, DLab, vol. 655.

60 *Kelowna Courier,* 24 June, 1, 22, 29 July, and 3 August 1943; *Province,* 26 June 1943; *Kelowna Capital News,* 21 July 1943.

61 *Kelowna Courier,* 12 August, 28 October, and 18 November 1943, 3, 10, and 17 February 1944; T. Wilkinson et al. to W.A.C. Bennett, 9 August 1943, WACBP, vol. 13.

62 J.K. Barnes to C.I.B., Vancouver, 8 June 1944, DLab, vol. 178; *Kelowna Courier,* 14 December 1944 and 11, 18, and 25 January 1945; *Kelowna Capital News,* 31 January 1945; *Province,* 20 January 1945; E.W. Barton to H. Mitchell, 23 January 1945, DLab, vol. 655; Kelowna Board of Trade, circular, 19 January 1945, IAMP, vol. 24.

63 *Kelowna Courier,* 1 and 22 February, 1 March, and 18 October 1945; *Kelowna Capital News,* 14 March 1945; T.B. Pickersgill to A. MacNamara, 17 February 1945, BCSCR, vol. 2.

64 A.L. Baldock to W.L.M. King, 15 January 1946, KP, J2, vol. 473. *HCD,* 12 February 1943, 386. See Chapter 4 of this text.

65 *Kamloops Sentinel,* 5, 12, and 26 March 1942 and 17 November 1943; Mass Meeting of Kamloops Residents Called by the Municipal Council, 3 March 1942, DLab, vol. 655; *Province,* 4 March 1942; R.E. White to T.J. O'Neill, 8 March 1942, IAMP, vol. 24.

66 *Chinese Times,* 11 and 15 June 1942; *Kamloops Sentinel,* 7, 14, and 21 May, 4 and 25 June, and 2 July 1942; *HCD,* 19 June 1942, 3480; N.C. DeWitt to F.J. Mead, 23 May 1942, DLab, vol. 175; D.B. Johnston to Ian Mackenzie, 15 May 1942, IAMP, vol. 25; F.A. MacCallum to L.S. St. Laurent, 16 June 1942, DLab, vol. 655. The Vernon Board of Trade rejected the resolution except for the land ownership clause. *Vernon News,* 21 May 1942. The Associated Boards of Trade of the Fraser Valley and Lower Mainland tabled the land ownership resolution on a technicality. Vancouver *News-Herald,* 6 June 1942. The Nanaimo and Cranbrook boards endorsed it. W.D. Gilroy to W.L.M. King, 27 July 1942, KP, #276032-33. The Canadian Chamber of Commerce, at the request of H.L. Keenleyside, kept the resolution from public discussion at its annual general meeting. D.L. Morell to H.L. Keenleyside, 18 December 1942, DEAR, vol. 2798.

67 R.W. Bruhn to Austin Taylor, 4 August 1942, DLab, vol. 176; *Kamloops Sentinel,* 4 June, 12 and 26 November, and 10 and 17 December 1942; 17 March, 5 May, 20 October, and 17 November 1943; and 23 February 1944; J.W. Hooker, in charge Yale District, BC Provincial Police, to Officer Commanding, Kamloops, 15 May and 24 November 1943, BCSCR, vol. 5; *Vancouver Sun,* 28 March 1944; T.J. O'Neill to H. Mitchell, 22 July 1942, DLab, vol. 655; B. Johnstone to D.L. Morell, 4 December 1942, DEAR, vol. 2798. When a Monte Lake lumber operator brought in Japanese loggers and their families,

fifty residents signed a petition for their removal. Residents of Monte Lake, BC, to BC Security Commission, 19 May 1943, DLab, vol. 655.

68 J. Fripps to Commissioner, 28 March 1944, and J.K. Barnes to C.I.B., Vancouver, 14 April 1944, DLab, vol. 178.

69 The Security Commission believed that the total Japanese population of the Kamloops district was 229, of whom 39 were residents before the evacuation. George Collins to A. MacNamara, 15 March 1944, DLab, vol. 655; C.K. Gray, Superintendent, Kamloops, to Commissioner, RCMP, 20 March 1944, DLab, vol. 178; *Kamloops Sentinel,* 8, 15, and 22 March 1944; *Province,* 1, 14, and 27 March 1944; *HCD,* 5 May 1944, 2691.

70 The designation of an area around an ammunition dump required long-time resident George Oishi and his family to move in the fall of 1943. Oishi asked that he be allowed to lease his farm so that he could return after the war, but the custodian would not give him special treatment. Oishi sold his farm and home privately to Peter Wing, a prominent Chinese resident. With permission from the minister of justice, he bought a farm outside the protected area. *Kamloops Sentinel,* 27 October 1943 and 10 May 1944; G.W. McPherson to A. MacNamara, 18 October and 3 November 1943, and Hugh Dalton to H. Mitchell, 5 April 1944, DLab, vol. 655; J.K. Barnes to C.I.B., 4 April 1944, and H. Mitchell to T.J. O'Neill, 5 June 1944, DLab, vol. 178; *Kamloops Sentinel,* 22 and 29 March 1944.

71 *Kamloops Sentinel,* 20 September, 4 October, and 13 December 1944; Petition, 9 December 1944, DLab, vol. 655; T.B. Pickersgill to A. MacNamara, 3 March 1945, BCSCR, vol. 2.

72 *Kelowna Courier,* 13 September 1945; *Kamloops Sentinel,* 19 September 1945.

73 On Tashme and the other dwellings built for the evacuees, see Patricia E. Roy et al., *Mutual Hostages: Canadians and Japanese during the Second World War* (Toronto: University of Toronto Press, 1990), Chapter 5. *Bridge River-Lillooet News,* 20 March and 24 April 1942; J.A. MacLennan to F.J. Mead, 25 March 1942, BCSCR, vol. 7; W.A. MacBrayne to W.A. Eastwood, 17 August and 24 October 1942, BCSCR, vol. 4.

74 Austin Taylor to R.L. Maitland, 14 April 1942, BCSCR, vol. 7; *Bridge River-Lillooet News,* 10 April and 1, 8, 15, and 22 May 1942; Vancouver *News-Herald,* 29 April 1942; *Vancouver Sun,* 26 August 1942; J.G. Turgeon to A. MacNamara, 5 May 1942, DLab, vol. 175 (the letter was published in the *Bridge River-Lillooet News,* 22 May 1942); E.A. Jarvis to Officer Commanding, Provincial Police, Kamloops, 14 August 1942, E.A. Jarvis to Officer Commanding, Kamloops, 1 April 1943, and C.G. Barber to Commissioner, C.I.B., BC Provincial Police, 5 April 1943, BCSCR, vol. 5; G.G. Estabrook to Austin Taylor, 7 May 1942, BCSCR, vol. 4; *Province,* 20 August 1942; W.A. Eastwood, report, 8 March 1943, BCSCR, vol. 34.

75 Austin Taylor to Ian Mackenzie, 4 March 1942, Ian Mackenzie to Austin Taylor, 5 March 1942, H. Mitchell to Austin Taylor, 6 March 1942, A. MacNamara to Austin Taylor, 10 March 1942, DLab, vol. 174.

76 Meeting of the Joint Committee of the Four Christian Churches Working among the Japanese at Hastings Park, 8 April 1942, John Shirras to J.A. Tyrwhitt et al., 29 April 1942, BCSCR, vol. 7. For further details, see Patricia E. Roy, "The Christian Churches and the Japanese Canadians," in Ludgard De Decker, ed., *Toward a Just Society: The Interplay of Power and Influence* (Victoria: Centre for Studies in Religion and Society, 1998), 27-52.

77 Austin Taylor to J. Wilson, 17 April 1942, and C.L. Herridge to Austin Taylor, 7 April 1942, BCSCR, vol. 7; *Grand Forks Sun,* 17 April 1942; B.H. Smith to Ian Mackenzie, 26 February 1942, and W.A. Gordon to W.L.M. King, 20 March 1942, IAMP, vol. 25; J. Abrahamson to W.L.M. King, 8 March 1942, and Nakusp Board of Trade to H. Mitchell, 18 August 1942, DLab, vol. 655; *Vernon News,* 15 March and 18 June 1942; Vancouver *News-Herald,* 21 July 1942; *Times,* 5 June 1943; Nakusp *Arrow Lakes News,* 19 March and 23 April 1942.

78 Ian Mackenzie to J.L. Ralston, 27 February 1942, IAMP, vol. 32; S.G. Blaylock to Austin Taylor, 16 March 1942, BCSCR, vol. 2; Austin Taylor to A. MacNamara, 29 March 1942, BCSCR, vol. 22; A. MacNamara to Ian Mackenzie, 21 March 1942, BCSCR, vol. 7; S.G. Blaylock to C.D. Howe et al., 31 July 1942, and F.J. Mead to A. MacNamara, 4 August 1942, DLab, vol. 176; S.G. Blaylock to W.L.M. King, 5 December 1942, KP, #272307-13; S.G. Blaylock to J.L. Ralston, 27 January 1943, KP, #289781-82; *Trail Daily Times,* 20 March and 26 September 1942; A.D. Turnbull to R.M. Hayland, 19 March 1942, BCA, A.D. Turnbull Papers, vol. 1; R.M. Hoyland to H. Mitchell, 20 March 1942, DLab, vol. 655. Trail had a spy scare when Saburo Takahashi, a twenty-two-year-old Japanese national, was arrested as he drove through nearby Rossland. His new car was equipped with a radio and a stock of canned goods,

and he carried a sketch showing industrial plants and the radio station. The *Trail Daily Times* of 21 and 23 March 1942 cited his presence as evidence of the government's "laxity" in handling the situation and wondered what proof there was that hundreds of Japanese were not doing the same. Investigation revealed that Takahashi, an engineering student at the University of British Columbia, was moving to the University of Alberta. A classmate had asked him to visit his parents in Trail and drew the map to show the way to their home. Takahashi was allowed to proceed. *Province,* 27 March 1942.

79 *Creston Review,* 20 March 1942; *Trail Daily Times,* 14 July 1942; *Nelson Daily News,* 10 April and 17 June 1942.

80 *Province,* 20 August 1942; Nakusp *Arrow Lakes News,* 8 and 22 October 1942; J.C. Harris, "Notes and Memories of the Coming of the Japanese to the Slocan Lake Country, 1942 ... 28 March 1944," BCA, J.C. Harris Papers, vol. 3; W.K. Esling to A. MacNamara, 28 September 1942, and R.W. Crellin to W.K. Esling, 13 September 1942, DLab, vol. 655. For a detailed account of the experience of the Japanese in New Denver, see Patricia E. Roy, "If the Cedars Could Speak: Japanese and Caucasians Meet at New Denver," *BC Studies* 131 (2001): 81-92.

81 BC Security Commission, *Removal of Japanese,* 24; *Nelson Daily News,* 30 January and 11 December 1943; Nakusp *Arrow Lakes News,* 15 July and 16 December 1943; W.G.C. Lanskail to H. Mitchell, 16 November 1943, DLab, vol. 655; Colin Clifford to W.G.C. Lanskail, 2 December 1943, BCSCR, vol. 4.

82 *Nelson Daily News,* 14 and 26 August 1943, 9, 13, and 26 October 1943, and 9 May 1944; W.G.C. Lanskail to H. Mitchell, 28 January 1944, W.K. Esling to A. MacNamara, 17 March 1944, H.B. Gore to H. Mitchell, 31 January 1944, and W.K. Esling to H. Mitchell, 6 June 1944, DLab, vol. 655.

83 Kaslo *Kootenaian,* 19 August and 25 November 1943; *Nelson Daily News,* 21 November 1943; *Colonist,* 12 January 1944. Another delegate suggested that farmers in his district had had no opportunity to work with Japanese "and consequently could not know them." *Vancouver Sun,* 11 January 1944.

84 Kaslo Board of Trade, Minute Book, 4 March 1942, BCA, AMss 1691; H. Hartin to Security Commission, 13 March 1942, BCSCR, vol. 7; Kaslo *Kootenaian,* 19 March 1942; Howard Green to "Folks'n," 22 March and 29 April 1942, and Howard Green to Mother, April 1942, HCGP, vol. 3; Roy E. Green to R.L. Maitland, 29 April 1942, GR 1222, vol. 163.

85 Kaslo Board of Trade, Minute Book, 26 March 1942, BCA, MfA01691; Kaslo *Kootenaian,* 23 and 30 April 1942.

86 Kaslo *Kootenaian,* 28 May, 9 July, 18 September, and 15 October 1942; 12 October 1944; 15 March and 5 and 19 April 1945; F. McGibbon to W.K. Esling, 20 June 1942, KP, #275455-59. For further details, see Roy, "A Tale of Two Cities," 23-47; David McKee to Ian Mackenzie, 24 June 1942, and David McKee to J.C.G. Herwig, 8 July 1942, IAMP, vol. 25.

87 Kaslo Board of Trade, Minute Book, 10 November 1944, BCA, MfA01691; C.R. Fahrni to W.L.M. King, 10 November 1944, KP, #311597; R.D. Gardner to H. Mitchell, 3 October 1944, DLab, vol. 655; Kaslo City Council, 2 October 1944, DLab, vol. 660; *New Canadian,* 25 November 1944; Kaslo *Kootenaian,* 2 November 1944 and 21 June 1945; A. MacNamara to H.W. Herridge, 13 March 1946, HWHP, vol. 42; The Historical Committee, *History of Kaslo* (Kaslo: Historical Committee, 1943), 59-60. When Green's father was seriously ill, Dr. Shimo-Takahara saved his life. H.T. Abey to H. Mitchell, 17 November 1944, DLab, vol. 655.

88 *Grand Forks Gazette,* 12 March, 1 May, 2, 16, and 30 July 1942; H.C. Clark to W.L.M. King, 14 March 1942, DLab, vol. 655; R.F. Sander to Austin Taylor, 15 July 1942, DLab, vol. 175.

89 *Penticton Herald,* 19 March and 18 June 1942; *Grand Forks Gazette,* 26 March and 2, 9, and 30 April 1942; *Grand Forks Sun,* 10 April 1942; Inter-Church Committee Minutes, 23 April 1942, BCSCR, vol. 7; *Similkameen Star,* 25 June 1942; A. Katsuyoshi Morita, *Powell Street Monogatari* (Burnaby, BC: Live Canada Publishing, 1988), 8.

90 *Grand Forks Gazette,* 9 September and 30 December 1943; *New Canadian,* 2 September 1944; Vancouver *News-Herald,* 21 March 1945.

91 *Grand Forks Sun,* 1 May 1942; *Grand Forks Gazette,* 7 May, 11 June, 20 August, 30 September, 8 October, and 3 December 1942; 18 February and 7 October 1943; 17 February, 23 March, and 25 May 1944; *New Canadian,* 28 July 1948; J.E. Murton, report, 8 September 1942, DLab, vol. 176; RCMP, New Denver, to Office Commanding, E Division, 10 May 1943, BCSCR, vol. 9; J.E. Murton, report, 3 March 1943, BCSCR, vol. 4. At least one Japanese family settled there before Pearl Harbor. Several Sugimoto children were listed in school promotion lists in June 1941 but not in 1940.

92 *Grand Forks Sun,* 4 and 18 August 1943; *Grand Forks Gazette,* 13 and 27 January and 8 and 15 June 1944.

93 *New Canadian,* 8 January 1944.

Chapter 3: "Repatriation" to Japan and "Non-Repatriation" to British Columbia

1 *HCD,* 4 August 1944, 5915-17; W.L.M. King to H.P. Hodges, 7 August 1944, KP, #312955.

2 *Colonist,* 24 March 1942. Government liquor stores and beer parlours were the only legal sources of alcoholic beverages. J.A. Tyrwhitt to J.A. Hutton, 23 September 1942, BCSCR, vol. 12; George Collins to Arthur MacNamara, 1 March 1943, C.V. Booth, Monthly Education Report, May 1943, H.G.T. Perry to J.A. Tyrwhitt, 15 August 1942, and H.G.T. Perry to J.A. Tyrwhitt, 28 August 1942, BCSCR, vol. 13; J.E. Murton, RCMP, reports, 31 January and 3 March 1943, BCSCR, vol. 4; H.N. MacCorkindale to S.J. Willis, 19 December 1941, and H.N. MacCorkindale to Principals, 29 August 1942, CVA, Vancouver School Board fonds, series 314, war files, location 56-E-4; S.J. Willis to J.A. Tyrwhitt, 6 October 1942, BCA, BC High School Correspondence Branch Records, vol. 1. The correspondence school offered to enrol high school students, but the fee of nine dollars per course plus two dollars for registration was beyond the means of most. E.E. Lucas, director of the high school correspondence branch, suggested that six to ten students could share the cost and submit only one lesson. After the course, they could write the matriculation examinations for one dollar per subject. E.E. Lucas to J.A. Tyrwhitt, 29 October 1942, BCA, BC High School Correspondence Branch Records, vol. 5. For details on education, see Patricia E. Roy, "'Due to Their Keenness Regarding Education, They Will Get the Utmost out of the Whole Plan': The Education of Japanese Children in the Interior Housing Settlements during World War Two," *Historical Studies in Education/Revue d'histoire de l'education* 4 (1992): 211-31. Many Nisei who taught in these schools recalled their memories in Frank Moritsugu and the Ghost Town Teachers Historical Society, *Teaching in Canadian Exile* (Toronto: Ghost Town Teachers Historical Society, 2001); *Vancouver Sun,* 29 January and 6 February 1943; *Kelowna Courier,* 11 February 1943; Vancouver *News-Herald,* 30 January and 1 February 1943; *Province,* 30 January and 1, 2, and 16 February 1943, 14 March 1945. Arthur MacNamara, the deputy minister of labour, proposed disallowance. A. MacNamara to Minister of Labour, 9 February 1943, W.L.M. King to John Hart, 12 February 1943, John Hart to W.L.M. King, 16 February 1943, IAMP, vol. 25; J.E. Read to W.L.M. King, 10 February 1943, KP, #C249486-87; A. MacNamara to George Collins, 28 April 1943, BCSCR, vol. 28.

3 H.G.T. Perry to W.A.C. Bennett, 16 April 1943, W.A.C. Bennett to H.G.T. Perry, 7 May 1943, A.S. Matheson to H.G.T. Perry, 17 April 1943, H.G.T. Perry to A.S. Matheson, 16 April and 5 May 1943, WACBP, 2/11; C.V. Booth, Memo, 6 November 1942, BCSCR, vol. 11. Ratepayers in Lumby, near Vernon, voted twenty-six to twelve against admitting Japanese children. In 1943 the federal government established this commission under F.W. Jackson to investigate complaints about welfare and maintenance in the interior settlements. In 1946 the Department of Labour said that the province should reassume its educational responsibilities under the BNA Act but agreed to pay for education in settlements still under its administration. A. MacNamara to T.B. Pickersgill, 8 June 1946, BCSCR, vol. 12. Several Christian churches established kindergartens and high schools in the Japanese settlements. *Vancouver Sun,* 19 May 1944; *Times,* 13 March 1945.

4 Despite conflicting press reports about the views of BC MPs, only Howard Green disapproved of Ottawa overriding the provincial regulation. Given "very alarming" rumours of Japanese buying sawmills in the interior, Attorney General R.L. Maitland urged the federal government "to prevent this sort of thing occurring." Minister of Labour Mitchell suspected that it was only a rumour but placated Maitland by having the RCMP investigate. Howard Green to "Folks," 21 March 1943, HCGP, vol. 3; R.L. Maitland to Ian Mackenzie, 5 June 1942, DLab, vol. 175; H. Mitchell to Ian Mackenzie, 13 June 1942, IAMP, vol. 25. In June 1942, the Interior Lumbermen's Association almost unanimously opposed using Japanese labour but changed its view by October as the labour shortage worsened. *Vernon News,* 4 June 1942; *Vancouver Sun,* 9 and 10 October 1942; *Province,* 13 October 1942 and 18 February 1943; J.H. King to H. Mitchell, 13 October 1942, Wilfred Hanbury to E.M. Little, 10 October 1942, A. Wells Gray to C.D. Howe, 23 October 1942, G.S. Pearson to A. MacNamara, 26 October 1942, Wilfred Hanbury to L.M. Crandall, 21 December 1942, Wilfred Hanbury to Ian Mackenzie, 7 November 1942, Ian Mackenzie to H. Mitchell, 24 November 1942, and John Hart to Ian Mackenzie, 17 February 1943, IAMP, vol. 25; Okanagan Federated Shippers Association and BCFGA to Mitchell, 6 November 1942, DLab, vol. 655; Minutes of Meeting, 6 November 1942, W.A.C. Bennett to R.L. Maitland, 7 November 1942, and R.L. Maitland to W.A.C. Bennett, 10 November 1942, WACBP, MG1/2, vol. 10; Kaslo *Kootenaian,* 14 January 1943; Kaslo Board of Trade, Minute Book, 14 January 1943, BCA, MfA01691; *Nelson Daily News,* 6 and 20 February 1943; *Vernon News,* 19 November and 24 December 1942; PC 1422, CWCR, 11 March 1943; *Times,* 24 February 1943.

5 *Province,* 17 October and 20 November 1942, 24 February and 17 December 1943; *Vancouver Sun,* 24 February 1943; *Kelowna Courier,* 11 March 1943; *Nelson Daily News,* 14 August and 14 December 1943.

6 *Vancouver Sun,* 10 September and 26 October 1942; A.L. Hager to V.W. Odlum, 6 July 1942, VWOP, vol. 5; H.E. Beyer, Secretary, Kyoquot Trollers Co-Operative Association, to W.L.M. King, 22 December 1942, IAMP, vol. 25; *Province,* 11 and 12 December 1942, 24 February and 22 March 1943; Vancouver *News-Herald,* 4 August 1942, 13 February 1943, and 14 October 1944; *Maple Ridge-Pitt Meadows Weekly Gazette,* 18 December 1942.

7 J.B. Shimek to Austin Taylor, 7 March 1942, and L.A. Shepherd, MLA, Memo re Japanese Farms in the Fraser Valley, 7 March 1942, BCSCR, vol. 16; *Province,* 18 February and 4 March 1942; *Surrey Leader,* 11 March 1942; *Columbian,* 19 November and 3 December 1942; *Vancouver Sun,* 3 October 1942 and 2 March 1943; Vancouver *News-Herald,* 6 March and 16 September 1942; Minutes, 39th Annual Convention, Union of BC Municipalities, Kamloops, 15-16 September 1942; *Gazette,* 11 September 1942. The Maple Ridge Board of Trade suggested paying Japanese owners a fair price in the form of Victory Bonds, the cost of which could be recovered through postwar reparations from Japan. The *Gazette* of 13 March 1942 agreed with paying a fair price but questioned using Victory Bonds since the Japanese would need ready cash. For hostility to the Mennonites acquiring Japanese farms, see T.D. Regehr, *Mennonites in Canada, 1939-1970: A People Transformed* (Toronto: University of Toronto Press, 1996), 110-12.

8 G. Murchison to T.A. Crerar, 22 April 1942, T.A. Crerar to Ian Mackenzie, 27 April 1942, E.H. Coleman to Secretary of State, 3 June 1943, G. Murchison to Crerar, 8 and 16 September 1942, and Ian Mackenzie to T.A. Crerar, 14 April 1942, IAMP, vol. 25; PC 5523, 29 June 1942. Someone in the Department of External Affairs, possibly H.F. Angus, questioned the constitutionality of the order in council that affected provincial rights over property. Memo for Mr. Robertson, 7 July 1942, DEAR, vol. 3121. The SSB paid taxes to municipalities. One Japanese Canadian farmer, a veteran of the Canadian Expeditionary Force, who acquired his farm through the SSB after the First World War, regained it with difficulty after the Second World War. See Peter Neary, "Zennosuke Inouye's Land: A Canadian Veterans Affairs Dilemma," *Canadian Historical Review* 85 (2004): 423-50.

9 C.L. Drewry to Under-Secretary of State, 26 June 1942, CEPR, vol. 2; *Vancouver Sun,* 29 August, 1 September, and 14 November 1942; M. Wright to G.W. McPherson, 16 October 1942, IAMP, vol. 24; E.H. Coleman to Secretary of State, c. December 1942, IAMP, vol. 25. Not all Japanese property in Vancouver was in Little Tokyo. In 1944 the custodian sold a parcel of view property occupying the equivalent of two city blocks in the fashionable Dunbar district for $28,000, the assessed value. *Province,* 14 February 1944; E.H. Coleman to Secretary of State, 16 March 1942, and J.E. Read to N.A. Robertson, 19 March 1942, DEAR, vol. 3121. Given the limited demand for Japanese stores, the custodian's office suggested moving their owners and merchandise to self-supporting communities to reduce storage charges and provide the evacuees with a living, but that was not done.

10 Cabinet Committee on Japanese Problems, 11 January 1943, IAMP, vol. 24. The Department of Labour feared that once the Japanese learned their property was to be liquidated they would become "very difficult to manage" and might engage in sit-down strikes and sabotage. A. MacNamara to H. Mitchell, 18 January 1943, IAMP, vol. 25; H. Mitchell to N. McLarty, 20 January 1943, DLab, vol. 177. In an interview almost twenty years later, Louis St. Laurent admitted that mistakes had been made in handling the possessions of the Japanese but added that "they couldn't take their landed possessions with them when they were moved" and claimed that adequate compensation had been given. *Vancouver Sun,* 18 October 1961. In prewar planning, the custodian of enemy property indicated that in the case of war with Japan all property in Canada of people residing in Japanese territory would come under his department but made no mention of the property of the Japanese in Canada. G.W. McPherson, Memo, 30 July 1941, DEAR, vol. 2859, file 1698-A-40. *Vancouver Sun,* 26 January, 6 and 20 February 1943, and 7 February 1944; Alfred Rive to Consul General of Spain, Montreal, 8 April 1944, DEAR, vol. 3005, file 3464-Ad-40C; *New Canadian,* 20 February and 10 April 1943; Vancouver *News-Herald,* 8 February 1944; *Province,* 8 and 11 February 1943.

11 "Memo Re Japanese in the Interior, 1943," United Church Archives, Toronto; W.H.H. Norman to W.L.M. King, 4 March 1943, and Frances Horning to W.L.M. King, 3 May 1943, DLab, vol. 2798; Mildred Fahrni to W.L.M. King and Ian Mackenzie, 9 March 1943, and H. Ballantyne, Religious Education Council of Canada, to Ian Mackenzie, 7 July 1943, IAMP, vol. 25. H.F. Angus prepared a memorandum that was forwarded to the prime minister doubting the validity of a policy that repudiated the government's promise of "just treatment." H.F. Angus to N.A. Robertson, 13 March 1943,

DEAR, vol. 3121. Other protesters included the BC Conference and the General Council of the United Church of Canada, the Vancouver-based Consultative Council for Co-Operation in Wartime Problems of Canadian Citizenship, and the National Council of Women. "MAB" to R.G. Robertson, 20 July 1943, and G.R. Trench to W.L.M. King, 3 January 1944, DEAR, vol. 2798; *Marpole-Richmond Review,* 28 February 1945; W.W. Judd et al. to W.L.M. King, 27 June 1944, KP, #C349524-27; "Horace" to G.H. Villett, 11 April 1943, and A.W. Neill to Rev. Charles Finnemore, 17 June 1943, HDP, Mf842A.

12 *Kelowna Courier,* 4 February 1943; *Cowichan Leader,* 2 December 1943; Vancouver *News-Herald,* 27 March 1944; *Province,* 21 March 1943, 28, 30, and 31 March 1944, and 22 March 1945; H. Mitchell to L.S. St. Laurent, 10 November 1943, and L.S. St. Laurent to H. Mitchell, 20 December 1943, DLab, vol. 178; *BCLJ,* 21 March 1945; *Nelson Daily News,* 31 May 1944; *Times,* 10 April 1943 and 23 February 1945; *Colonist,* 24 May 1944; *Vancouver Sun,* 16 March 1945.

13 A.L. Drake to H.D. Wilson, 14 May 1942, HDWP; *Province,* 16 July 1942, 7 and 9 March and 1 May 1944; *Vancouver Sun,* 14 October 1942 and 13 June 1944.

14 G.E. Trueman, "Evacuation Issues," *New Canadian,* 23 June 1948.

15 The self-proclaimed "group of public-spirited men and women," including civil libertarians such as Dr. Norman Black, Laura Jamieson, and Protestant clergy such as W.H. Norman, G. Hayden Stewart, and Hugh McLeod, formed the Consultative Council for Co-Operation in Wartime Problems of Canadian Citizenship soon after the evacuation was announced. W.H. Norman, circular letter, [March 1942]; Meeting of Consultative Committee, 30 March [1942], MFP. R.L. Maitland to C. Than, 9 April 1942, RLMP, vol. 4; R.H.B. Ker to Ian Mackenzie, 17 November 1942, IAMP, vol. 25; R.H.B. Ker to H. Mitchell, 19 February 1943, DLab, vol. 655; *Colonist,* 16 October 1943; *Vancouver Sun,* 20 June, 31 August, 5 and 10 September, and 21 October 1942. When the mayor of Nanaimo suggested repatriating all Japanese in 1940, Prime Minister King said that was neither "practical nor feasible." W.L.M. King to V.B. Harrison, 30 October 1940, DNDR, MfT1809. The Kyoquot Trollers Co-Operative, which had long complained about Japanese fishermen, called for the repatriation of "all people of Japanese birth and descent at the end of the war." H.E. Beyer to W.L.M. King, 22 December 1942, DEAR, vol. 3005, file 3464-V-40. Vancouver *News-Herald,* 10 September and 14 and 21 October 1942; Resolution of Vancouver City Council, 20 October 1942, copy in IAMP, vol. 25. Halford Wilson, who favoured repatriation, was absent on army duty.

16 Ian Mackenzie to Fred Howlett, 26 October 1942, IAMP, vol. 25; Vancouver *News-Herald,* 17 November 1942; *Vancouver Sun,* 17 November 1942. Stirling thought it "a difficult problem," Hanson promised to study it, and O'Neill thought that the resolution would be favourably received. The Typographical Union and the Native Sons of BC publicly praised Cornett's stand. *Province,* 21 September 1942; Vancouver *News-Herald,* 2 October 1942.

17 Vancouver *News-Herald,* 7 and 8 December 1942; *Province,* 4 and 10 December 1942; *Vancouver Sun,* 25 January 1943.

18 S. Mussalem to W.L.M. King, 29 September 1942, DEAR, vol. 3005, file 3464-V-40; *Cowichan Leader,* 17 September 1942; Union of BC Municipalities, Resolutions to Be Considered by the Convention, Port Alberni, 16-17 September 1943; Resolution Adopted at the 7th Annual Conference of the Canadian Federation of Mayors and Municipalities, June 1944, for Presentation to the Government of Canada, KP, #307497. Among the organizations were boards of trade, the Native Sons of British Columbia and the Native Sons of Canada, Farmers' Institutes, the Orange Order, the Canadian Daughters' League, the Native Sisterhood, the Kyoquot Trollers Co-Operative, the boatbuilders' section of the Canadian Manufacturers' Association in Vancouver, the Army and Navy Veterans Association, and the national Canadian Legion convention. A copy of the leaflet, dated 25 July 1942, is in the CVA pamphlet file; Mrs. B.M. Steeves to Minister of Immigration, 28 May 1943, and W.P.J. O'Meara to Minister of Mines and Resources, 30 September 1942, DImm, MfC4752; *Province,* 13 April, 27 May, and 8 November 1942; 7 June 1943; 28 February and 24 and 28 April 1944; H.E. Beyer to W.L.M. King, 22 December 1942, IAMP, vol. 25; *Times,* 11 June 1942, 4 March 1943, 17 and 21 August 1943, and 12 July 1944; R.D. Cameron to Ian Mackenzie, 17 May 1944, and Army and Navy Veterans in Canada, BC Provincial Command, to Ian Mackenzie, 6 March 1944, IAMP, vol. 24; Port Alberni *West Coast Advocate,* 2 April 1942; *Kelowna Courier,* 9 April 1942; *Vancouver Sun,* 20 October 1942, 20 April 1943, 22 and 24 April and 17 May 1944; *Nanaimo Free Press,* 17 June 1943; Vancouver *News-Herald,* 20 October 1942; 4 March, 1, 4, and 21 May 1943; 25 March and 15 April 1944; C.V. Sayer to John Hart, 21 May 1943, KP, #293667; R.D. McLachlan to W.L.M. King, 8 February 1944, KP, #316659-61; Mary Paterson to W.L.M. King, 30 May 1942, KP, #282693; John Grant to W.L.M. King, 21 July 1943, KP, #293364; District Farmers' Institute

(Kamloops), Resolution, July 1944, DLab, vol. 655; *Colonist,* 11 January 1944; *Gazette,* 14 August and 11 September 1942; J.T. Gawthorp to W.A.C. Bennett, 5 March 1943, WACBP, 1/12, vol. 13; John Hart to W.L.M. King, 22 May 1943, KP, #293666. Others included S. Evans (International Alliance of Theatrical Stage Employees and Moving Picture Machine Operators, Victoria) to Ian Mackenzie, 2 January 1943, IAMP, vol. 25, and Tofino Board of Trade to A.W. Neill, 27 February 1943, DLab, vol. 2798.

19 *Columbian,* 3 December 1942; A.H. Richmond to Ian Mackenzie, 28 April 1942, and J.K. Wills to Ian Mackenzie, 3 January 1943, IAMP, vol. 25; Executive Committee of the British Columbia Liberal Association, Vancouver, 11 April 1944 (copy in TDPP, vol. 58/20), endorsed the resolution and forwarded it to Mackenzie. Ann Thompson to Ian Mackenzie, 22 May 1944, IAMP, vol. 24; Annual Meeting of the British Columbia Conservative Association and Executive, Vancouver, 23-24 October 1942, copy in WACBP, MG 1/1, 6/10; A.R. MacDougall to John Bracken, 28 April 1943, H.M. Woodward to John Bracken, 23 April 1943, and A.W. Neill to H.H. Stevens, 10 December 1943, JBP, vol. 120; Oak Bay District Conservative Association to W.L.M. King, 1 September 1942, DLab, vol. 655; *Cowichan Leader,* 7 October 1943; Vancouver *News-Herald,* 10 April 1944; *Province,* 20 July 1944; *Vancouver Sun,* 26 and 27 April 1943; *Times,* 12 and 14 October 1943 and 17 August 1944; *Colonist,* 6 October 1943.

20 Hodges also believed that repatriates might "inculcate into the Japanese people a concept of the democratic point of view ... [that would] help offset the false doctrines of the militarists." *Province,* 18 November 1942, 9, 13, and 16 February and 2 March 1943; E.C. Kenney to Thiselton Mark, 15 March 1943, DLab, vol. 2798; *Times,* 10 February and 2 and 4 March 1943.

21 *Vancouver Sun,* 6 and 17 February 1943; Vancouver *News-Herald,* 6 and 13 February 1943; *Province,* 6 and 13 February and 4 March 1943; *Times,* 10 February 1943.

22 Vancouver *News-Herald,* 1 November 1943 and 14 and 18 April 1944; *Vancouver Sun,* 19 and 21 February 1943 and 18 April 1944; *Cowichan Leader,* 20 April 1944; *Province,* 15, 17, 19, and 27 April 1944.

23 *Vancouver Sun,* 18 April, 20 May, and 7 and 8 July 1944; *Colonist,* 18 June and 19 July 1944; *Kelowna Courier,* 20 July 1942; *Trail Daily Times,* 5 July 1944; *Penticton Herald,* 13 July 1944; Vancouver *News-Herald,* 30 May 1944; *Province,* 12 April 1943 and 19 April 1944; *Times,* 30 June 1944.

24 *HCD,* 1 March 1943, 796-99, and 30 June 1943, 4208-9. The *Vernon News* of 8 July 1943 praised British Columbia's MPs for reminding colleagues that the Japanese question was a national issue but attacked Neill's secession threat for throwing away seventy-five years "of struggling towards a common goal as a free and united people." *HCD,* 30 June 1943, 4206-23; 12 July 1943, 4657; and 29 June 1942, 4170; Howard Green to Folks, 4 July 1943, HCGP, vol. 3. Other MPs also doubted the loyalty of the Japanese, but Reid showed his prejudice by explaining, "we have hundreds and thousands of people in this country who are of German and Italian descent, but who in the second or third generation have become good Canadians. But who is going to marry into the oriental group? If they do, what will their progeny be? They will be oriental because that is what has happened whenever mixed marriages have taken place." *HCD,* 30 June 1943, 4222. Reid suggested leaving the postwar fate of British Columbia's Japanese "to the men returning from our fighting fronts – especially to those who have suffered at the hands of the Japanese in Hong Kong." *Vancouver Sun,* 17 January 1944.

25 *Vancouver Sun,* 6 and 19 February 1943; *Nanaimo Free Press,* 29 October 1943; *Times,* 16, 17, and 25 February and 22 April 1943; *Province,* 8 and 16 February, 3 March, 14 and 23 July 1943; Vancouver *News-Herald,* 3 March and 3 July 1943 and 14 June 1944.

26 Report of the Post-War Rehabilitation and Reconstruction Committee of the New Westminster Board of Trade, March 1944, copy in IAMP, vol. 21; D.B. Johnstone to Ian Mackenzie, 15 May 1942, IAMP, vol. 24; *Vernon News,* 21 May 1942; R.C. Ironside to W.L.M. King, 20 July 1942, KP, #277171; W.D. Gilroy to W.L.M. King, 27 July 1942, KP, #276032-33; *Trail Daily Times,* 27 May 1942; *Nelson Daily News,* 27 May 1942; *Province,* 17 June 1943; *Penticton Herald,* 29 June 1944; *Vancouver Sun,* 27 June 1944.

27 *Penticton Herald,* 5 August 1943; *Nelson Daily News,* 26 August 1943; Kaslo *Kootenaian,* 11 May 1944; Colin Clifford to W.G.C. Lanskail, 2 December 1943, DLab, vol. 655; S.G. Blaylock to W.L.M. King, 12 July 1944, DEAR, vol. 3004.

28 *Nelson Daily News,* 14 August 1943; *Trail Daily Times,* 9 June 1944; *Vancouver Sun,* 17 May 1943;

Rev. C.R. Trench to John Bracken, 3 January 1944, JBP, vol. 22. In 1944 its Evangelical and Social Services Committee protested deportation as "un-British and above all un-Christian," Nazi-like policy that could play into "Japan's ambition for a unification of the coloured races against the white." British Columbia Conference, United Church of Canada, Evangelism and Social Services Committee, Report, May 1944, HDP, Mf843A. The whole conference deleted specific references to the Japanese but hoped that the government would "live up to the spirit of its agreements affecting minority groups in Canada." *Vancouver Sun,* 25 May 1944. *Province,* 22 and 25 May 1944; *Western Recorder,* October 1944. After preparing the resolution, Dr. Black realized that the council had not invited representatives of the Presbyterian Church to sign. He invited five Presbyterian clergymen in Vancouver to participate in the council. N. Black to Five Presbyterian Clergymen, 2 June 1944, HDP, Mf808A; N. Black et al. to W.L.M. King, 29 May 1944, KP, #308236-38.

29 *Vancouver Sun,* 18 May and 15 June 1943, 20 April and 8 and 12 July 1944; *Colonist,* 1 June and 12 July 1944; *Kelowna Courier,* 17 February 1944. *Province,* 8 December 1943. When some people accused him of Jap-baiting for saying that "once a Japanese, always a Japanese," Stevens looked again at Japan's naturalization laws. He skirted the question of dual nationality but cited Japanese statutes to show that naturalized citizens of Japan lacked full civil rights. *Province,* 2 March 1944. V.W. Odlum to Ralph Plant, 4 September 1943, VWOP, vol. 10.

30 *Vancouver Sun,* 14 December 1943, 1, 2, 3, 14, 15, and 27 June 1944; Vancouver *News-Herald,* 6 June 1944; Ian Mackenzie to John Godwin, 7 December 1942, IAMP, vol. 25; *Lethbridge Herald,* 27 May 1942; Ian Mackenzie to Dominion Command, Canadian Legion, Vancouver, 5 June 1944, text as amended at Vancouver, IAMP, vol. 9. When the *New Canadian* accused Cornett of blowing "a Nazi tune," both he and the *Vancouver Sun* called for its suppression. That amused the censor but not some city councillors, who, possibly "needled" by the *Vancouver Sun,* called it "saucy abuse." John Graham to R.W. Baldwin, and John Graham, Memo, 14 June 1944, PCOR, vol. 5980.

31 *Vancouver Sun,* 5 June 1944; *Province,* 5 June 1944; Vancouver *News-Herald,* 11 July 1944.

32 *Province,* 4 and 11 March 1942; *Cowichan Leader,* 7 October 1943; Vancouver *News-Herald,* 23 March and 14 December 1942; *Kelowna Courier,* 18 June 1942. *Vancouver Sun,* 2 July and 23 November 1942, 11 May 1943. The *Bridge River-Lillooet News* of 24 December 1942 echoed these sentiments.

33 Department of Labour, *Report on the Administration of Japanese Affairs in Canada* (Ottawa: Department of Labour, 1944), 39; A. MacNamara to Austin Taylor, 13 July 1942, BCSCR, vol. 4; S.T. Wood to A. MacNamara, 28 November 1942, DLab, vol. 639; *New Canadian,* 6 March 1943; Utaka Uyeda to W.L.M. King, 2 August 1944, DEAR, vol. 3005, file 3464-V-40; Slocan Valley Nisei Organization to T. Takada, LAC, Minuro Takada Papers. See also Patricia E. Roy et al., *Mutual Hostages: Canadians and Japanese during the Second World War* (Toronto: University of Toronto Press, 1990), Chapter 6.

34 J.L. Granatstein, *A Man of Influence: Norman A. Robertson and Canadian Statecraft, 1929-1968* (Ottawa: Deneau, 1981), 163; N.A. Robertson to W.L.M. King, 20 August 1943, KP, #C194881-83; N.A. Robertson to Leighton McCarthy, 11 October 1943, KP, #C194880.

35 Cited in Sandra C. Taylor, "Evacuation and Economic Loss: Questions and Perspectives," in *Japanese Americans: From Relocation to Redress,* ed. Roger Daniels, Sandra C. Taylor, and Harry H.L. Kitano (Seattle: University of Washington Press, 1991), 163; A.H. Brown to A. MacNamara, 20 July 1944, DLab, vol. 639. The Department of Labour wanted the Japanese question put on the agenda of a proposed dominion-provincial conference, but the Privy Council Office said that it might cause so much controversy it would impede discussion of other problems. N.A. Robertson to A. MacNamara, 4 April 1944, DLab, vol. 639.

36 *Times,* 6 November 1943; *Vancouver Sun,* 29 December 1943; W.L.M. King to Bruce Hutchison, 29 December 1943, University of Calgary Library, Bruce Hutchison Papers, vol. 2; Thomas Wayling, *Vancouver Sun,* 29 January 1944; London Japanese Advisory Committee to W.L.M. King, 29 June 1944, DEAR, vol. 3005, file 3464-V-40; *Globe and Mail,* 23 and 30 November 1943.

37 R.G. Robertson to W.L.M. King, 27 March 1944, KP, #C249497-100; R.G. Robertson to N.A. Robertson, 20 March 1944, H.F. A[ngus], Memo, 22 March 1944, and A.R. Menzies, Memo, 22 March 1944, DEAR, vol. 5761; H.T. Pammett, Memo, 12 October 1943, George Collins, Memo of Recommendations of BC Security Commission Advisory Board, 5 November 1943, and R.G.

Robertson to N.A. Robertson, 11 April 1944, DLab, vol. 639; F.J. Mead to F.P. Varcoe, 10 April 1944, RCMPR, vol. 3568. Gordon Robertson did not think that segregation had to be physical as in the United States, where certain centres were designated for the disloyal. He proposed that individuals could be removed from the "disloyal" category if they showed reasons why they should be considered loyal. CIPO poll, released 16 February 1944, copy in DEAR, vol. 3005, file 3464-Y; *Province,* 16 February 1944; *Times,* 16 February 1944. A poll two months earlier that did not distinguish between Canadian citizens and others revealed that 54 percent of Canadians would send Japanese back to Japan, while 39 percent would let them remain. In that poll, 60 to 70 percent of British Columbians favoured sending the Japanese to Japan and that generally, "the further an area is from the Pacific Coast, the smaller the majority which favors repatriation." *Province,* 22 December 1943.

38 *Nanaimo Free Press,* 29 January 1944; *Colonist,* 1 February and 11 March 1944; *Times,* 29 January and 18 and 20 February 1944; *Kelowna Courier,* 3 February 1944. While condemning the "horrible" atrocities, its competitor, the *Kelowna Capital News* of 16 February 1944 noted that the Japanese in Canada had nothing to do with them. Both the *Vancouver Sun* and the *Province* had editorials on the atrocities but did not allude to Japanese Canadians; *Province,* 29 January 1944; *Vancouver Sun,* 28 January 1944. Austin Taylor to A. MacNamara, 4 March 1944, DLab, vol. 178; *Vancouver Sun,* 15 June 1944.

39 Interdepartmental Meeting, 11 April 1944, DLab, vol. 639; George Collins to A. MacNamara, 3 February 1944, BCSCR, vol. 4; Cabinet War Committee, 19 April 1944; *HCD,* 5 May 1944, 2669-87; *Times,* 12 May 1944; *Vancouver Sun,* 18 January 1944; *Saturday Night,* 24 June 1944; James Dyer, *Vancouver Sun,* 26 May 1944; Montreal *Star,* 17 May 1944. *Sherbrooke Record,* 13 May 1944; cited in *Vancouver Sun,* 23 May 1944. *Maclean's,* a national news magazine, published on 1 December 1943 a debate between Angus MacInnis and Howard Green.

40 N.A. Robertson to W.L.M. King, 13 June 1944, KP, #C249502-4.

41 *Times,* 6 January 1944 and 14 February 1945; *Marpole-Richmond Review,* 12 January 1944; *Vancouver Sun,* 6 January 1944 and 28 February 1945; *Province,* 3 March and 17 April 1944.

42 The 1917 Wartime Elections Act disfranchised individuals from enemy alien countries who had been naturalized in Canada after 1902. Most of those affected were Liberal voters. *HCD,* 17 July 1944, 4918-20; W.L.M. King, Diary, 13 July 1944; J.W. Pickersgill to W.L.M. King, [early July 1944], DEAR, vol. 5761; Pickersgill's memo appears to have been based in part on a message from Senator Norman Lambert. W.J. Turnbull to J.W. Pickersgill, 6 July 1944, KP, #C189134; J.L. Granatstein, *Canada's War: The Politics of the Mackenzie King Government, 1939-1945* (Toronto: Oxford University Press, 1975), 264-65, 284; J.M. Beck, *Pendulum of Power: Canada's Federal Elections* (Scarborough: Prentice-Hall, 1968), 251.

43 Forrest E. La Violette to Norman Black, 19 June 1944, HDP, Mf808A; Roger Obata and George Tanaka, Brief in the Matter of the War Services Electors Bill, 24 June 1944, CCJC, vol. 1; W.J. Turnbull to W.L.M. King, 21 June 1944, KP, #C249512-13; National Interchurch Advisory Committee to W.L.M. King, 20 June 1944, KP, J2, vol. 295. Copies of the various protests may be found in this volume; H.C. Bray to Director, Military Intelligence, 15 July 1944, DNDR, vol. 2640; Hugh Dobson to W.L.M. King, 20 June 1944, HDP, Mf808A; *United Church Observer,* 1 July 1944; *Toronto Daily Star,* 21 June 1944; Toronto *Globe and Mail,* 4 July 1944.

44 Norman Lambert, *SD,* 28 June 1944, 246; *SD,* 30 June 1944, 268-84, and 19 July 1944, 308; J.W. Pickersgill to W.L.M. King, 11 July 1944, KP, #C249533-34; Arthur Beauchene, Memo, 13 July 1944, KP, #C249536-39; N. McClarty to Ian Mackenzie, 10 July 1944, IAMP, vol. 9; *HCD,* 17 July 1944, 4921, 4937; W.L.M. King, Diary, 17 July 1944. Angus MacInnis was in Australia as part of a parliamentary delegation.

45 *Vancouver Sun,* 5 July 1944; *Penticton Herald,* 13 July 1944; *Province,* 30 June and 6 July 1944.

46 Toronto *Globe and Mail,* 4 July 1944; *Vancouver Sun,* 30 June and 6 and 11 July 1944; *Trail Daily Times,* 18 July 1944; *Ladysmith Chronicle,* 4 August 1944; *Saturday Night,* 1, 8, and 22 July 1944; *Colonist,* 4 and 19 July 1944; *Times,* 6 July 1944; *Vancouver Sun,* 20 June and 10 and 18 July 1944; Vancouver *News-Herald,* 3 July 1944.

47 R.G. Robertson, "Policy with Regard to Japanese Persons in Canada," 15 July 1944, DEAR, vol. 5761; W.L.M. King to R.W. Brown, 20 July 1944, KP, #308499; Gordon Robertson, *Memoirs of a Very Civil Servant* (Toronto: University of Toronto Press, 2000), 41.

48 *HCD,* 4 August 1944, 5925, 5943, 5948; 12 August 1944, 6397; Vancouver *News-Herald,* 5 August 1944; A.D. Dunton to Cabinet Members, 7 August 1944, KP, #311250-51.

49 Mrs. L.B. Smart to W.L.M. King, 13 November 1944, DEAR, vol. 3005, file 3464-V-40; *Times,* 5 August

1944; *Nanaimo Free Press,* 18 August 1944; *Province,* 5 August 1944; R.H. Hiscocks to H. Mitchell, 14 September 1944, and David Howrie to A. MacNamara, 6 September 1944, DLab, vol. 655; Vancouver *News-Herald,* 12 December 1944.

50 C.E. Hope, the founder of the White Canada Association in 1929, in a private letter to an American colleague questioned the loyalty of all Japanese. C.E. Hope to Miller Freeman, 12 August 1944, University of Washington Library, Miller Freeman Papers. Thank you to Roger Daniels for this reference.

Federal officials admitted that they did not know how to prevent a "wholesale movement" of Japanese to the coast after the war but hoped that they would not be anxious to return to an "unfriendly" atmosphere. H.L. Keenleyside to E. Reid, 27 October 1944, DEAR, vol. 5761. Officials discussed the loyalty commission and its composition from time to time, but it was never established. *Province,* 4 and 5 August 1944; *Colonist,* 5, 6, and 12 August and 4 October 1944, 7 March 1945; *Marpole-Richmond Review,* 13 September 1944; *Vancouver Sun,* 9 August 1944 and 18 January and 10 February 1945.

51 *Vancouver Sun,* 4, 5, and 12 August 1944; *Ladysmith Chronicle,* 11 August 1944; *Province,* 16 August 1944; *Kelowna Courier,* 10 August 1944; *Vernon News,* 10 and 24 August 1944; W.J. Hamilton to W.L.M. King, 18 September 1944, DEAR, vol. 3005, file 3464-V-40.

52 *Colonist,* 5 and 8 August 1944; *Times,* 5 August and 13 September 1944; *Province,* 5 August 1944; Union of BC Municipalities, Resolutions to Be Considered by the Convention at Nelson, BC, 12-13 September 1944. In an interview with the *Province,* Thomas Shoyama, a Kaslo resident and editor of the *New Canadian,* expressed satisfaction with dispersal, which he expected would lead to full and equal rights of citizenship for loyal Japanese Canadians. *Province,* 5 August 1944. The Kaslo *Kootenaian,* a good friend of the Japanese in Kaslo, said on 10 August 1944 that the Japanese welcomed dispersal "because they are ambitious to be accepted as full-fledged Canadians."

53 Among Bracken's reasons for sending the Japanese at least 500 miles inland or to Japan was the possibility that after the war they might be considered disloyal if they visited Japanese ships in BC ports! *Times* and *Colonist,* 18 August 1944. Vancouver *News-Herald,* 15 and 18 August 1944 and 8 March 1945; Mission *Fraser Valley Record,* 21 September 1944; *Penticton Herald,* 16 November 1944; *Province,* 22 November 1944; *Times,* 31 October 1944 and 20 February 1945; *Colonist,* 7 March 1945; "Memo for Mr. Bracken – B.C. Trip, 8 August 1944," JBP, vol. 45; E.C. Carson to W. Rigby, 6 March 1945, UFAWUR, vol. 83. Social Credit was not a factor in BC politics, but national leader Solon Low and an Alberta cabinet minister visited in October 1944. Low believed that the Japanese could not be forcibly ejected because many were Canadian citizens but thought that most wanted to go to Japan and favoured inducing them to do so. *Province,* 10 October 1944; *Kelowna Courier,* 12 October 1944 and 1 February 1945; Mission *Fraser Valley Record,* 9 November 1944 and 8 March 1945.

The story about Japanese characters on Mount Douglas may date to the 1920s, when a Chinese resident took a bucket of whitewash up the mountain and wrote some Chinese characters on the mountainside. See the essay by Candace Yip, "The Legend of Lore Neen: The Life of My Grandfather," in Brandy Liên Worrall, ed., *Finding Memories, Tracing Routes: Chinese Canadian Family Stories* (Vancouver: Chinese Canadian Historical Society, 2006), 51. I am indebted to Henry Yu for this reference.

54 *Penticton Herald,* 10 August 1944; Vancouver *News-Herald,* 7 November 1944; W. Gray to T.B. Pickersgill, 22 March 1945, BCSCR, vol. 16; J.W. de B. Farris to Edna P. Gordon, 17 April 1945, JWdeBFP, vol. 10; R. Gibbons to C.N. Senior, 10 September 1944, IAMP, vol. 2; *Province,* 31 August and 11 and 17 October 1944; *Fraser Valley Record,* 24 August and 12 October 1944; W.A.C. Bennett to J.A. Paton, 30 September 1944, WACBP, vol. 1/2, 2/1; *Vancouver Sun,* 8 December 1944.

55 *Province,* 9 and 19 September and 8 December 1944; *Colonist,* 10 and 12 September 1944; H. Mitchell to R.B. Hiscocks, 26 September 1944, DLab, vol. 655; Ian Mackenzie, speech to Vancouver Centre Liberal Nominating Convention, 18 September 1944, BCA, C.N. Senior Papers, vol. 1; Ian Mackenzie to Cairine Wilson, 26 September 1944, IAMP, vol. 24. Fergus MacKean, provincial leader of the Labour-Progressive Party (Communist), also attacked the CCF for raising the franchise issue. He wanted to ban Japanese from the coast but called Mackenzie's slogan "an appeal to racial prejudice."

56 *Vancouver Sun,* 22 September 1944; *Province,* 26 and 28 September and 12 October 1944; Vancouver *News-Herald,* 14 October 1944; *Penticton Herald,* 28 September 1944; *Kelowna Courier,* 28 September 1944; W.A.C. Bennett to J.A. Paton, 20 September 1944, WACBP, vol. 1/2, 2/1.

57 Fahrni had taught Japanese high school students at New Denver for the United Church. Her experiences there are recounted in Nancy Knickerbocker, *No Plaster Saint: The Life of Mildred*

Osterhout Fahrni (Vancouver: Talon, 2001), Chapter 10.

58 Mission *Fraser Valley Record,* 12 October 1944; *Vancouver Sun,* 22 February 1945; *Province,* 4 and 5 October 1944; Vancouver *News-Herald,* 7 and 14 October 1944; *Kamloops Sentinel,* 4 October 1944; J. Greenall to G.G. McGeer, 18 January 1945, GGMcGP, vol. 1; *BC Lumber Worker,* 15 January 1945; *Nanaimo Free Press,* 13 March 1945; *Fisherman,* 20 March 1945.

59 *Province,* 18 December 1944; *Vancouver Sun,* 18 December 1944 and 2 January and 10 February 1945; *Colonist,* 20 December 1944; Mission *Fraser Valley Record,* 15 February 1945.

60 D.B. Johnstone to W.L.M. King, 21 October 1944, KP, #313454; *Kamloops Sentinel,* 1 November 1944; *Kelowna Courier,* 23 November and 14 December 1944; *Province,* 16 December 1944; Kelowna Board of Trade circular, 19 January 1945, copy in IAMP, vol. 24. J.O.C. Kirby to W.L.M. King, DEAR, vol. 3005, file 3464-V-40. See also Patricia E. Roy, "A Tale of Two Cities: The Reception of Japanese Evacuees in Kelowna and Kaslo, B.C.," *BC Studies* 87 (1990): 23-47.

61 *Province,* 2, 8, and 21 March 1945; *Penticton Herald,* 1 March 1945; Vancouver *News-Herald,* 21 March 1945; *Times,* 27 February 1945; Mission *Fraser Valley Record,* 1 and 15 March 1945; *Cowichan Leader,* 8 March 1945; *Ladysmith Chronicle,* 2 March 1945; M.F. Hunter to R.W. Mayhew, 27 February 1945, KP, #344028. Victoria sent its version to all cities and municipalities; twenty-one replied, but only seven endorsed it. Mayhew sent it to the prime minister with a covering note saying that it was "exceedingly stupid." R.W. Mayhew to W.L.M. King, 2 March 1945, KP, #348258; M.F. Hunter to John Hart, 27 April 1945, GR 1222, vol. 174; *Colonist,* 27 February 1945.

62 *Comox District Free Press,* 1, 8, and 15 March 1945; *Kelowna Courier,* 1 March 1945; Prince Rupert *Daily News,* 6 March 1945. Nanaimo City Council rejected Victoria's call for a referendum but a week later endorsed a resolution from the local Moose Lodge opposing the return of Japanese to the coast. *Nanaimo Free Press,* 27 February and 6 and 13 March 1945.

63 A few critics, including some University of British Columbia students, and Colonel H.E. Lyon, who condemned racial intolerance, attended the founding meeting. Moncton Resolution, 15 November 1945, DEAR, vol. 3554. The Port Arthur City Council declined to act because it was a national and not a municipal issue. *Saskatoon Star-Phoenix,* 5 September 1945; John Graham to R.W. Baldwin, 7 March 1945, PCOR, vol. 5979; C.E. Hope to "Dear Sir," 2 October 1945, HWHP, vol. 42; Vancouver *News-Herald,* 3 and 23 February 1945; *Marpole-Richmond Review,* 7 February 1945; *Vancouver Sun,* 23 February and 10 September 1945; *Province,* 16 March 1945; S.W. Mulholland to Ian Mackenzie, 28 March 1945, Ian Mackenzie to S.W. Mulholland, 4 April 1945, and V.H. Johnson to Ian Mackenzie, 16 April 1945, IAMP, vol. 24; RCMP Intelligence, Vancouver, report, 21 May 1945, BCSCR, vol. 9; Moncton City Council to W.L.M. King, 15 November 1945, DLab, vol. 655.

64 [Grace Tucker] to H.G. Watts, 27 March 1945, GTP; *Vancouver Sun,* 19 September 1944; Vancouver *News-Herald,* 13 September 1944 and 14 March 1945; *Province,* 13 September 1944 and 22 May 1945.

65 Vancouver *News-Herald,* 25 November 1944; N.F. Black to W.L.M. King, 13 January 1945, KP, #C249575-77; *Nanaimo Free Press,* 28 February 1945; *Vancouver Sun,* 19 March 1945; Interview with Dr. N.F. Black on CKWX, 20 March 1945, transcript in DEAR, vol. 3005; W.H. Norman, *What about the Japanese Canadians?* (Vancouver: Vancouver Consultative Council for Co-operation in Wartime Problems of Canadian Citizenship, 1945).

66 *Times,* 17 January 1945; A.H. Brown to T.B. Pickersgill, 20 March 1945, DLab, vol. 639; "Notice to All Persons ... ," 12 March 1945, and T.B. Pickersgill to Editor, *Fraser Valley Record* [and other editors], 15 March 1945, BCSCR, vol. 16. A poll taken by the Wartime Information Board in April 1945 revealed that 49 percent of the Canadian public was unwilling to have a Japanese Canadian family in their neighbourhood. In British Columbia, the figure was 57 percent. Wartime Information Board, *Survey,* no. 66, 30 June 1945.

67 For details on the response of the Japanese, see Roy et al., *Mutual Hostages,* Chapter 6. In March 1945, the editor of the *Fisherman* asked a number of MLAs for their opinion on the return of the Japanese. All who replied, including E.C. Carson, Tilly Rolston, J.A. Paton, K.C. MacDonald, and E.C. Kenney, opposed their return. The letters are in UFAWUR, vol. 83. Examples include Canada Pensioners' Association of the Great War (Victoria branch) to W.L.M. King, 24 March 1945, KP, #344553; Fraternal Council of British Columbia to J.W. de B. Farris, 14 April 1945, JWdeBFP, vol. 6; Native Sons of British Columbia, Resolution, 6-7 April 1945, copy in HWHP, Japanese Canadians-General; *Legion Letter,* BC Command, Canadian Legion, BESL, 1 (June 1945); Skeena Federal Liberal Association to W.L.M. King, 22 March 1945, IAMP, vol. 24; Vancouver North Federal Liberal Association to W.L.M. King, 8 April 1945, KP, #350098; *Vancouver Sun,* 15 March, 9 April, and 1 May 1945; *Colonist,* 20 March, 15 May, and

15 June 1945; *Times,* 17 March 1945; *Surrey Leader,* 5 April 1945; Vancouver *News-Herald,* 17 March and 30 April 1945. *Province,* 23 February, 17, 19, and 20 March, 30 May, and 16 June 1945. The *Marpole-Richmond Review* of 6 June 1945 approved the United Nations resolution opposing racial persecution.

68 *Vancouver Sun,* 17 and 23 May 1945; *Province,* 31 May and 1 June 1945; Vancouver *News-Herald,* 22, 23, 26, and 30 May 1945; *Columbian,* 25 and 30 May 1945; *Times,* 6 June 1945; *Marpole-Richmond Review,* 6 June 1945; *Langley Advance,* 21 May 1945; Vancouver *News-Herald,* 31 May and 6 June 1945; Mission *Fraser Valley Record,* 17 May 1945; *Kamloops Sentinel,* 30 May 1945.

Reid added his own twist, a suggestion that King's civil service advisers had enjoyed "fine trips to Japan and were bribed by the Japanese previous to the war," a point that he subsequently raised in Parliament. *Province,* 31 May 1945. His Conservative opponent, George Twiss, turned it against him by advertising, "a vote for Reid means a vote for King ... who – according to Tom Reid – is 'advised by Jap Bribed Men.'" *Langley Advance,* 7 June 1945. Keenleyside told Coldwell that if Reid had named names he and H.F. Angus would have taken him to court. H.L. Keenleyside to M.J. Coldwell, 13 September 1945, HLKP, vol. 20. Prince Rupert Liberals withdrew the nomination of James A. Donnell, pastor of First United Church, after he refused to endorse a resolution favouring the deportation of the Japanese from Canada. Prince Rupert *Daily News,* 14 March 1945.

69 *Kamloops Sentinel,* 6 June 1945; Speeches by John Bracken, Vancouver, 28 May 1945, and Kamloops, 30 May 1945, JBP, vol. 110; *Times,* 30 May 1945; Vancouver *News-Herald,* 18 and 29 May 1945; *Vancouver Sun,* 17 May 1945; *Province,* 11, 17, and 25 May 1945; *Langley Advance,* 3 May 1945; *Colonist,* 10 May 1945; *Marpole-Richmond Review,* 6 June 1945; *North Shore Press,* 8 June 1945; *Nanaimo Free Press,* 22 May and 9 June 1945; *Comox District Free Press,* 23 April and 17 and 31 May 1945. The Social Credit candidate in Yale would rehabilitate the Japanese and give them fair value for their land. *Kelowna Courier,* 17 May 1945.

70 Harold Griffin, speech, CKNW, 26 February 1945, UFAWUR, vol. 83; *Vernon News,* 10 May 1945; Prince Rupert *Daily News,* 4 June 1945.

71 The advertisements appeared in a number of provincial newspapers, including the *Times,* 2 June 1945.

72 *Vancouver Sun,* 16 and 23 May and 2, 4, 5, and 6 June 1945; Vancouver *News-Herald,* 4, 15, 26, and 30 May and 2 June 1945; *Times,* 28 May 1945; *Salmon Arm Observer,* 31 May 1945; *Cowichan Leader,* 17 and 31 May 1945; *Province,* 22 May 1945; *Nanaimo Free Press,* 28 May and 7 June 1945; *Colonist,* 30 May 1945.

73 Prince Rupert *Daily News,* 24 March, 22 and 30 May, 4 and 13 June 1945. G.G. McGeer to W.L.M. King, 28 July 1945, KP, #346331.

74 Examples of conflict among Japanese Canadians may be found in Roy et al., *Mutual Hostages,* 162-66, and Ann Gomer Sunahara, *The Politics of Racism: The Uprooting of Japanese Canadians during the Second World War* (Toronto: Lorimer, 1981), 121-23. *Province,* 14 April and 16 and 31 May 1945; *Vancouver Sun,* 7 March and 27 April 1945; *Nisei Affairs* 1, 1 (20 July 1945); John Graham, Memo, 10 March 1945, and R.W. Baldwin to John Graham, 15 March 1945, PCOR, vol. 5980. See Patricia E. Roy, "The Soldiers Canada Didn't Want: Her Chinese and Japanese Citizens," *Canadian Historical Review* 59 (1978): 341-58.

75 J.A. G[ibson] to W.L.M. King, 16 July 1945, KP, #C249496; N.A. R[obertson] to W.L.M. King, 16 July 1945, KP, #C249592-95; *Toronto Daily Star,* 7 August 1945; *Vancouver Sun,* 1 and 14 August 1945. Thomas Socknat, *Witness against War: Pacifism in Canada 1900-1945* (Toronto: University of Toronto Press, 1987), 276-79. For the work of the CCJC and a comparison with its counterpart, the American Civil Liberties Union, see Stephanie D. Bangarth, "The Politics of Rights: Canadian and American Advocacy Groups and North America's Citizens of Japanese Ancestry, 1942-1949" (PhD diss., University of Waterloo, 2003), especially Chapter 2.

76 *Times,* 29 November 1943; Vancouver *News-Herald,* 27 November 1944; *Vancouver Sun,* 2 February 1945.

Chapter 4: The Effects of the War on the Chinese

1 Cited in Kwok B. Chan and Lawrence Lam, "Chinese in Timmins, Canada, 1915-1950: A Study of Ethnic Stereotypes in the Press," *Asian Profile* 14 (1985): 579; James W.F. Chin, "The Chinese Canadian," *Chinatown News,* 18 March 1966; *Vancouver Sun,* 14 July 1958.

2 *Times,* 16 August 1945; *Colonist,* 17 August 1945; Prince Rupert *Daily News,* 11 August 1945; *Vernon News,* 16 August 1945; *Kelowna Capital News,* 13 August 1945; *Columbian,* 16 August 1945; *Trail Daily Times,* 11 August 1945. In New Westminster, Chinese set off firecrackers to the delight of this small observer. *Province,* 15 August 1945; Denise Chong, *The Concubine's Children: Portrait of a Family Divided* (Toronto: Viking, 1994), 152.

3 *Halifax Herald*, 15 August 1945; Montreal *Star*, 15 August 1945; Toronto *Globe and Mail*, 15 August 1945; Hamilton *Spectator*, 16 August 1945; Regina *Leader-Post*, 16 August 1945; *Winnipeg Free Press*, 17 August 1945; *Calgary Herald*, 15 August 1945.

4 British Columbia, Department of Trade and Industry, *Annual Report*, 1945 (Victoria: King's Printer, 1947), R5, and *Annual Report*, 1948, DD5; Forest Service Department, *Annual Report*, 1947 (Victoria: King's Printer, 1948), 31; Department of Mines, *Annual Report*, 1948 (Victoria: King's Printer, 1950), A13; Public Utilities Commission, *Annual Report*, 1948 (Victoria: King's Printer, 1949), 131.

5 *Chinese Times*, 12, 23, and 26 December 1941; *Times*, 8 January 1942; *Vancouver Sun*, 26 February 1942. In Vancouver the Women's International Freedom and Peace Association objected to Chinese schoolchildren wearing such "buttons" lest it breed racial discrimination. *Chinese Times*, 8 January and 11 and 16 March 1942; *Kamloops Sentinel*, 19 February 1942.

6 Vancouver *News-Herald*, 12 January 1942; *Toronto Daily Star*, 5 and 6 January 1942; *Kamloops Sentinel*, 12 February 1942, 21 January and 11 August 1943, and 11 October 1944; Vancouver *News-Herald*, 24 February 1942; *Cowichan Leader*, 12 February 1942; *Cranbrook Courier*, 26 February 1942; *Kelowna Capital News*, 18 February 1942; *Times*, 10 March 1943; *Colonist*, 17 March and 11 April 1944; *Nanaimo Free Press*, 7 July 1944; *Nelson Daily News*, 17 February 1942, 23 and 27 August and 6 September 1943; *Trail Daily Times*, 6 March 1943; *Salmon Arm Observer*, 2 November 1944; *Grand Forks Gazette*, 12, 26, and 29 August 1943; *Grand Forks Sun*, 27 August 1943; Edmonton *Bulletin*, 12 February 1942; *Saskatoon Star-Phoenix*, 5 August 1942; *Toronto Daily Star*, 5 and 29 January and 13 February 1942; *Halifax Herald*, 16 January 1942; Montreal *Star*, 10 January 1942; Montreal *Gazette*, 12 February 1942; Toronto *Globe and Mail*, 3 and 27 February 1942; Regina *Leader-Post*, 7 February 1942; *Calgary Herald*, 6, 12, and 14 February 1942; *Ottawa Journal*, 20 February 1942; Chinese Minister to Ross McLean, 23 September 1942, LAC, China, Consulate (Canada), vol. 4.

7 *Colonist*, 29 January 1944; *Columbian*, 25 August 1944; *Vancouver Sun*, 8 August 1944; Vancouver *News-Herald*, 10 and 12 April 1943 and 15 August 1944; *Province*, 22 February 1944. In 1944, when a Canadian-born Chinese woman on *Citizens' Forum* spoke against racial discrimination, the Anti-Oriental Penetration League demanded equal time. The CBC wisely rejected its request. *Colonist*, 14 March 1944. *Colonist*, 29 July 1944; *Vancouver Sun*, 8 August 1944; *Nanaimo Free Press*, 17 January 1945; *Times*, 22 March 1945.

8 *Chinese Times*, 11 May 1942, 19 July 1943, and 1 March 1944; Vancouver *News-Herald*, 25 February and 23 November 1943; *Colonist*, 11 April 1944; *Province*, 19 March 1942.

9 *Colonist*, 13 April 1944; *Times*, 14 March 1944; *Chinese Times*, 5 and 7 July 1943; *BC Lumber Worker*, 9 August and 1 November 1943, 20 March and 17 April 1944; *Nanaimo Free Press*, 8 July 1943; Alicja Muszynski, *Cheap Wage Labour: Race and Gender in the Fisheries of British Columbia* (Montreal and Kingston: McGill-Queen's University Press, 1996), 192; *Province*, 9 and 10 March 1944.

10 Bing-shue Lee to Fung Kat-shau, 25 August 1942, LAC, China, Consulate (Canada), vol. 3; Vancouver *News-Herald*, 23 February 1943; *Province*, 13 March 1943. Ontario repealed its White Women's Labour Law in 1947.

11 Mrs. H. Joe to Editor, *Vancouver Sun*, 21 July 1944; *Vancouver Sun*, 25 August 1942 and 3 August 1944; *Colonist*, 2 June and 4 November 1944; *Province*, 12 January 1942; *Vancouver Sun*, 13 December 1941; *Trail Daily Times*, 26 February 1943; *Salmon Arm Observer*, 22 March 1945; Prince Rupert *Daily News*, 13 June 1945.

12 *Times*, 5 February 1942; W.B.T. Seto to Major General R.O. Alexander, 15 April 1942, J.C. Murchie to R.O. Alexander, 13 April 1942, and C.Y. Hsie to R.O. Alexander, 21 and 23 April 1942, DHist 322.009 (D814); Frank Ho Lem to George Pearkes, 6 December 1942, DHist 322.009 (D478); A.M. Manson to Arthur MacNamara, 3 May 1944, DLab, vol. 127a. In 1946 the refusal of the Royal Canadian Navy to enlist a highly trained Chinese Canadian caused brief political controversy. The navy said that he was rejected because of his age, but some editors accepted his claim that racism was the explanation and criticized what they perceived as discrimination. Toronto *Globe and Mail*, 13 April 1946; *Nelson Daily News*, 19 April 1946, quoting the *Windsor Star*. For a fine account of the Chinese who served in Canada's Armed Forces, see Marjorie Wong, *The Dragon and the Maple Leaf: Chinese Canadians in World War II* (London, ON: Pirie Publishing, 1994).

13 *Chinese Times*, 12 December 1942; *Times*, 10 December 1942; *Province*, 31 July 1942 and 14 July 1943; Vancouver *News-Herald*, 14 July 1943; *Nanaimo Free Press*, 2 September 1944; *HCD*, 30 June 1943, 4214; P.W. Dempson, "Chinese Get Their First Vote in Saskatchewan," *Saturday Night*, 13 May 1944, 24; Regina *Leader-Post*, 4 April 1944.

14 Hayne Wai, "Three Voices: A Wong Family Album," in Brandy Liên Worrall, ed., *Finding Memories, Tracing Routes: Chinese Canadian Family Stories* (Vancouver: Chinese Canadian Historical Society of British Columbia, 2006), 46; Mor Cheolin to W.L.M. King, 16 August 1944, DEAR, vol. 3282; Vancouver *News-Herald,* 16, 18, and 23 August 1944 and 27 March 1945; *Chinese Times,* 24 August and 25 September 1944; Wong Kung Lai to John Hart, 16 October 1944, Chinese Canadian Association to Hart and Members of the Council, 16 February 1945, and "A Brief Prepared in Conjunction with a Petition to the Governments of the Province of British Columbia and the Dominion of Canada for the Granting of the Franchise of Canadian Citizens of Chinese Descent in the Province of British Columbia," Vancouver, 16 February 1945, Chinese Canadian Association, "For the Franchise," [c. 15 February 1945], BCA, GR 1222, vol. 176; Foon Sien, "Past Achievements, Future Aspirations," *Chinatown,* 3 January 1956; *Vernon News,* 14 September 1944. A man who did not feel obliged to serve since he could not vote was found guilty of failing to report for military service and was given a week to settle his affairs before reporting for training. *Colonist,* 8 June 1945. In Chapter 5 of "From Diaspora to North American Civil Rights: Chinese Canadian Ideas, Identities, and Brokers in Vancouver, BC, 1924-1960" (PhD diss., University of Toronto, 2002), Lisa Rose Mar used interviews and contemporary Chinese-language newspapers to examine attitudes within the Chinese community toward military service and the experiences of some of those who served.

15 George Pearkes to Brigadier K. Adam, 25 August 1944, George Pearkes to R.B. Gibson, 4 September 1944, Frank Ho Lem to George Pearkes, 4 and 20 September 1944, and J.C. Murchie to George Pearkes, 23 September 1944, DHist 322.009 (478); A.C. Spencer to George Pearkes, 12 October 1944, DHist 112.352D09 (D191); Cabinet War Committee, minutes, 13 December 1944; Colonel H.R.W. Allan to Foon Sien, 27 January 1945, UBC, Foon Sien Scrap Book, vol. 1; *Vancouver Sun,* 17 November 1945.

16 *Cowichan Leader,* 31 August 1944; *Vancouver News-Herald,* 24 August 1944 and 4 January 1946; *Vancouver Sun,* 23 August 1944; *Nanaimo Free Press,* 2 September 1944; *Province,* 22 August 1944 and 28 March 1945.

17 W.S. Chow to Minister of Finance, 6 December 1940, and Chief Controller to W.S. Chow, 13 January 1941, DImm, MfC10661; A.D.P. Heeney to W.L.M. King, 24 December 1941, PCOR, vol. 2, file I-50-3.

18 H. Jack to W.L.M. King, 29 April 1942, KP, 277215-18; Bing-Shuey Lee to E.C. Mark, 14 August 1942, LAC, China, Consulate (Canada), vol. 3.

19 T.A. Crerar to W.L.M. King, 17 September 1942, KP, #273822-23; W.L.M. King to T.A. Crerar, 17 September 1942, KP, #273824; W.L.M. King, Diary, 7 October 1942; N.A. Robertson to E.H. Coleman, 19 May 1942, DEAR, vol. 4261; N.A. Robertson to W.L.M. King, 28 October 1942, KP, #C192730-32; H.L. Keenleyside to W.L.M. King, 3 October 1942, note on copy of N.A. Robertson to W.L.M. King, 28 October 1942, and H.L. Keenleyside to V.W. Odlum, 5 March 1943, DEAR, vol. 3193; A.L. Jolliffe to H.L. Keenleyside, 10 December 1942, DImm, Mf10661; H.L. Keenleyside to N.A. Robertson, 17 November 1942, DImm, MfC4785. Diplomatic and other factors leading to the repeal of the Chinese Immigration Act are well described in F.J. McEvoy, "'A Symbol of Racial Discrimination': The Chinese Immigration Act and Canada's Relations with China, 1942-1947," *Canadian Ethnic Studies* 14, 3 (1982): 24-42. Keenleyside first proposed a reciprocal arrangement in 1933; see Patricia E. Roy, *The Oriental Question: Consolidating a White Man's Province, 1914-41* (Vancouver: UBC Press, 2003), 200. Outside the government, there was some support for a reciprocal arrangement. A conference of the western Canadian branches of the Canadian Institute of International Affairs in October 1943 noted that "the most reasonable approach to the vexed question of Oriental immigration would seem to be to put it on a footing of reciprocity" in which possibly the number of Asians entering Canada might be set as equal to the number of Canadians emigrating to those Asian countries. The study group suggested that approach would remove "the invidious element of race discrimination" while ensuring a small number of entrants since few Canadians were likely to emigrate to Asia. W.L. Morton, *Building Post War Canada: Some Factors and International Aspects: A Western View* (Toronto: Canadian Institute of International Affairs, 1943), 27.

20 *Vancouver Sun,* 12 January 1943; *Province,* 4 March 1943; Vancouver *News-Herald,* 15 April 1943; *Times,* 15 April and 11 May 1943; *Chinese Times,* 12 April and 3 May 1943.

21 Vancouver *News-Herald,* 14 July 1943; *Province,* 17 June 1943; *Vancouver Sun,* 18 October 1943; W.L.M. King, Diary, 30 July 1943; *HCD,* 12 July 1943, 4582-83.

22 *Times,* 2 November 1943; *Vancouver Sun,* 25 June 1943; *Ottawa Journal,* 13 October 1943; V.W. Odlum to W.L.M. King, 9 October 1943, 1 December 1943, and 9 October 1945, DEAR, vol. 3193; V.W. Odlum to W.L.M. King, 30 December 1943, DImm, vol. 587; V.W. Odlum to Department of External Affairs,

7 August 1945, KP, #C192765-66. F.W. Eggleston, Australia's representative in China, sent similar messages about modifying the "White Australia" policy to avoid alienating an ally. Gwenda Tavan, *The Long, Slow Death of White Australia* (Melbourne: Scribe, 2005), 37-38.

23 Significantly, the memo originally referred to British Columbia, but that was crossed out and replaced with "Canada." N.A. Robertson to W.L.M. King, [17] January 1944, KP, #C192756; Minutes of Meeting on Chinese Immigration in Norman Robertson's Office, 6 December 1943, DImm, vol. 2365; W.L.M. King to N.A. Robertson, 3 January 1944, DEAR, vol. 3193; Vancouver *News-Herald*, 19 April 1944; *Times*, 23 May 1944. The removal of a Chinese American woman from a train passing through Canada garnered much unfavourable publicity, especially in the United States. Canada subsequently eased provisions for transients of Chinese ancestry. See McEvoy, "'A Symbol of Racial Discrimination,'" 30-32; H.L. Keenleyside to W.L.M. King, 2 June 1944, KP, #192761-63; V.W. Odlum to W.L.M. King, 22 August 1944, DEAR, vol. 3193.

24 Vancouver *News-Herald*, 19 April 1944; *Times*, 28 April and 23 May 1944; *Toronto Daily Star*, 21 April 1944; Toronto *Globe and Mail*, 6 April 1944; *Saturday Night*, 8 April 1944; *Winnipeg Free Press*, 19 April 1944.

25 Foon Sien to W.L.M. King, 29 August 1945, DEAR, vol. 3193; Dong Wong Jung and Foon Sien to W.L.M. King, 5 December 1946, KP, #366715-16; *Province*, 6 December 1945. Vancouver *News-Herald*, 30 August 1945; Ottawa *Morning Journal*, 31 August 1945; *Chinese Times*, 17 and 29 January 1947. Letters from Chinese Canadian organizations are in KP, J2, vol. 430. Stephanie D. Bangarth, "'We Are Not Asking You to Open Wide the Gates for Chinese Immigration': The Committee for the Repeal of the Chinese Immigration Act and Early Human Rights Activism in Canada," *Canadian Historical Review* 84 (2003): 412.

26 Gerald E. Dirks, *Canada's Refugee Policy: Indifference or Opportunism?* (Montreal and Kingston: McGill-Queen's University Press, 1977), 140; G.S. Patterson, Memo of Conversation with A.L. Jolliffe, 16 November 1945, DEAR, vol. 3193; N.A. Robertson to V.W. Odlum, 31 January 1946, KP, #370925ff.; Chinese Ambassador to Department of External Affairs, 31 May 1946; J.A. G[ibson] to N.A. Robertson, 9 July 1946, KP, #C192767. The relevant intradepartmental correspondence is in DEAR, vol. 3193.
An exceptional case was that of Charlie Toy of Wadena, Saskatchewan, and his wife. He went to China shortly before the war and married her but returned to Canada, joined the Canadian army, and served in the European theatre. When the Japanese took over Hong Kong, his wife was forced to flee along with her infant, who later died of exposure. Just before the government announced that it would be repealing the Chinese Immigration Act, she arrived in Saskatoon. *Saskatoon Star-Phoenix*, 8 January 1947.

27 For population statistics, see Edgar Wickberg, ed., *From China to Canada: A History of the Chinese Communities in Canada* (Toronto: McClelland and Stewart, 1982), 302. Quoted in *Province*, 27 December 1946; *Vancouver Sun*, 5 January and 27 December 1946; *Nelson Daily News*, 7 December 1946; Vancouver *News-Herald*, 27 December 1946.

28 *Calgary Herald*, 19 December 1946; *Peterborough Examiner*, 14 February 1948, cited in Zhongping Chen, "The Chinese Minority and Everyday Racism in Canadian Towns and Small Cities: An Ethnic Study of the Case of Peterborough, Ontario, 1892-1951," *Canadian Ethnic Studies* 36 (2004): 87; Regina *Leader-Post*, 7 December 1945; *Kamloops Sentinel*, 26 February 1947; *Kelowna Courier*, 27 February 1947; *Surrey Leader*, 18 June 1947.

29 *Colonist*, 6 December 1946 and 17 July 1947; *Vancouver Sun*, 5 August 1947; *Province*, 1 November 1945 and 7 July 1948; Vancouver *News-Herald*, 27 August 1945; *Nanaimo Free Press*, 24 October 1945.

30 Cabinet Committee on Immigration Policy, 20 December 1946, PCOR, vol. 32, file I-50-M.

31 Other nationalities mentioned and the percentages opposed to their immigration were Japanese, 60 percent; Jewish, 49 percent; German, 34 percent; Russian, 33 percent; Negro, 31 percent; Italian, 25 percent; Middle European, 16 percent; Ukrainian, 15 percent; and Polish, 14 percent. Canadian Institute of Public Opinion, news release, 30 October 1946.

32 A.E. Armstrong and S.K. Ngai to J.A. Glen and Louis St. Laurent, 21 December 1946, DEAR, vol. 3193; Committee for the Repeal of the Chinese Immigration Act to W.L.M. King, 24 January 1947, KP, #381092-94; J.H. Sansome to W.L.M. King, 23 December 1946, KP, #373698. On the Committee for the Repeal of the Chinese Immigration Act, see Bangarth, "'We Are Not Asking,'" 395-422; *Toronto Daily Star*, 16 January 1947. In introducing the legislation in Parliament, J.A. Glen, whose Ministry of Mines and Resources was responsible for immigration, noted "considerable agitation in the minds of many people in Canada" for its repeal. *HCD*, 11 February 1947, 307; W.J. Gallagher to W.L.M. King, 20

January 1947, KP, #384705-7; *Toronto Daily Star,* 16 December 1946; Winnipeg *Tribune,* 18 December 1946. In Australia Christian churches and Communists also criticized the ban on Chinese immigration. Tavan, *The Long, Slow Death,* 45-46.

33 *Nelson Daily News,* 7 December 1946; *Vancouver Sun,* 27 December 1946; *Toronto Daily Star,* 16 January 1947; *Nanaimo Free Press,* 22 November 1946; *Saturday Night,* 14 December 1946; *Winnipeg Free Press,* 18 December 1946; Winnipeg *Tribune,* 5 April and 19 and 27 December 1946; Montreal *Star,* 27 December 1946; Montreal *Gazette,* 1 and 22 January 1947; David Croll to W.L.M. King, 15 November 1946, KP, #362761; Toronto *Globe and Mail,* 27 November 1946; North Bay *Daily Nugget,* 24 January 1947; *Ottawa Citizen,* reprinted in *Calgary Herald,* 13 December 1946; Toronto *Evening Telegram,* 25 January 1947.

34 Cabinet Committee on Immigration Policy, 6 and 20 December 1946, PCOR, vol. 82-I-50-M; "Government Consideration of the Chinese Immigration Position," [c. February 1947], KP, #C192812; R.G. Robertson to W.L.M. King, 11 January 1947, KP, #C192902-3; also in *DCER,* vol. 23, 1947, ed. Norman Hillmer and Donald Page (Ottawa: Department of External Affairs and International Trade, 1993), 285-86; W.L.M. King, Diary, 25 January and 14 March 1947. When Liu left Ottawa in 1947 for a new assignment, King sent the "dear little fellow, very true, loyal, fine friend," a handwritten letter and a copy of his book, *Industry and Humanity,* inscribed "with my affectionate regard and esteem." W.L.M. King, Diary, 16 March 1947.

35 The various resolutions may be found in KP, J2, vol. 430; *Brantford Expositor,* 27 January 1947.

36 *Times,* 28 January 1947; *Le Droit,* 27 and 28 January 1947; *Canadian Register,* 1 February 1947; *L'Action catholique,* 27 January 1947; *Toronto Daily Star,* 16 and 28 January 1947; Montreal *Star,* 28 January 1947; Montreal *Gazette,* 28 January 1947; Regina *Leader-Post,* 29 January 1947; *Saskatoon Star-Phoenix,* 30 January 1947; *Ottawa Citizen,* 28 January 1947; *Province,* 29 January and 14 February 1947; Vancouver *News-Herald,* 28 January 1947; Prince Rupert *Daily News,* 28 January 1947; *Colonist,* 28 January 1947. For example, E.D. Murray, Halifax Presbytery, United Church of Canada, to W.L.M. King, 30 January 1947, Ottawa Civil Liberties Association to W.L.M. King, 3 February 1947, and A.H. Agnew, University of Toronto Liberal Association, to W.L.M. King, 15 February 1947, all in KP, J2, vol. 430; Conseil de Ville Québec, 7 February 1947, LSt.LP, vol. 13; Canon W.W. Judd to W.L.M. King, 13 February 1947, KP, #386061-62; *HCD,* 11 February 1947, 307; Waiching Wong, Chin Heehen, and Soon Wintue, Assembly of Chinese Residents of Vancouver, to M.J. Coldwell, 27 January 1947, MJCP, vol. 10. See also Chinese Free Masons of Calgary to W.L.M. King, 28 January 1947, Kingston Chinese Community Centre to W.L.M. King, 29 January 1947, and Saskatchewan Chinese Benevolent Association to W.L.M. King, 29 January 1947, KP, J2, vol. 430.

37 On the same day that Glen introduced the repeal legislation, the cabinet agreed to revoke PC 1378 of 17 June 1931 that required Chinese applying for naturalization to have the approval of the Chinese minister of the interior. "Naturalization of Chinese," 11 February 1947, DEAR, vol. 3193.

38 *HCD,* 11 February 1947, 307-38; *Kamloops Sentinel,* 19 February 1947; Alan Jessup in *Province,* 19 February 1947.

39 In 1945 Reid won by 1,929 votes; Cruickshank, by 1,527; Mackenzie, by 818; and Sinclair, by 664. A.D.P. Heeney to J.A. Glen, 14 February 1947, *DCER,* 1947, 288, and A.D.P. Heeney to N.A. Robertson, 28 February 1947, *DCER,* 1947, 289; L.B. Pearson to Cabinet Committee on Immigration, 26 May 1947, *DCER,* 1947, 293; A.R. Menzies, "Asiatic Immigration into Canada," 1 March 1947, DEAR, vol. 6178; W.L.M. King, Diary, 11, 12, and 14 February 1947. King blamed Glen, "a very poor minister," for not consulting with the BC members in advance. J.W. Pickersgill to W.L.M. King, 13 February 1947, KP, #C192814-15.

40 Vancouver *News-Herald,* 25 February 1947; *Ladner Optimist,* 30 January 1947; Arthur Rayne to John Bracken, 4 February 1947, JBP, vol. 22; *Times,* 10 February 1947; H. Yeulet to W.L.M. King, 21 February 1947, KP, #395982; *Columbian,* 12 April 1947; E. Reid to W.L.M. King, 17 February 1947, KP, #389458-59; *Surrey Leader,* 17 April 1947; *Province,* 9 and 11 April 1947.

41 Jack Greenall, BC Federation of Labour, to W.L.M. King, 19 February 1947, KP, #385169; E. Dalskog, IWA, to W.L.M. King, 21 February 1947, KP, #383351; Robert Metzger, Victoria Labour Council, to W.L.M. King, 13 March 1947, KP, #387211; Nigel Morgan, Labour Progressive Party, to W.L.M. King, 20 February 1947, KP, #387462; Eric Nicol, Canadian Civil Liberties Union, to W.L.M. King, 22 February 1947, KP, #387688; David Owens, Civil Liberties Union of Manitoba to John Bracken, 8 April 1947, JBP, vol. 22; H.E. Thayer, Victoria-Oak Bay CCF, to W.L.M. King, 20 March 1947, LSt. LP, vol. 13; *BC Lumber Worker,* 24 February 1947. When some Vancouver Island IWA members

questioned their leaders, Dalskog replied that the union was not calling for large-scale immigration but merely the end of discrimination against Chinese, some of its best members. *BC Lumber Worker,* 1 May 1947. *Vancouver Sun,* 17 March 1947; Vancouver *News-Herald,* 17 March 1947. *Labour Gazette,* April 1947, 499; W.A. Cameron, General Board of Missions, Presbyterian Church in Canada, to H.L. Keenleyside, 24 April 1947, DC&I, vol. 125; W.W. Judd, Church of England in Canada, Department of Christian Social Service, to John Bracken, 13 February 1947, JBP, vol. 22; Montreal *Gazette,* 18 February 1947; Toronto *Globe and Mail,* 6 March 1947; *Saskatoon Star-Phoenix,* 3 March 1947. Nationally, the executive of the Imperial Order of the Daughters of the Empire asked that the government refuse admission to Chinese and other specified groups until it defined a general immigration policy. Mrs. J.G. Spragge to W.L.M. King, 9 April 1947, KP, #39074-75.

42 For example, Chinese Benevolent Society, Windsor, to L.S. St. Laurent, 14 February 1947, LSt.LP, vol. 13; Hoysun Ninyung Benevolent Association, Victoria, to W.L.M. King, 18 February 1947, Chinese Community of Sudbury to W.L.M. King, 14 February 1947, Halifax Chinese Community to W.L.M. King, 18 February 1947, KP, #386667; Frank Ho Lem, Pacific Unit Number 280 of Army, Navy, and Air Force Veterans, to W.L.M. King, 17 February 1947, KP, #385595; Y.C. Lowe, Chinese Workers Protective Association, Vancouver, to W.L.M. King, 21 February 1947, KP, #385891; Chinese Benevolent Association and Kuo Min Tang, Edmonton, to W.L.M. King, 27 February 1947, KP, #386944; Vancouver *News-Herald,* 17 March 1947.

43 *HCD,* 1 May 1947, 2646; 2 May 1947, 2698-2716; 5 May 1947, 2764, 2787-88, 2791; W.L.M. King, Diary, 2 May 1947; R.G. Robertson to N.A. Robertson, 13 May 1947, RGRP, vol. 1.

44 *HCD,* 11 February 1947, 319, 324, 331, and passim; 2 May 1947, 2710 and passim; 5 May 1947, 2762, 2722, and passim; Regina *Leader-Post,* 15 May 1947.

45 *L'Action catholique,* translated and cited in Montreal *Gazette,* 21 May 1947; *Edmonton Journal,* 3 May 1947; *Calgary Herald,* 7 May 1947; Toronto *Globe and Mail,* 15 May 1947; *Toronto Daily Star,* 7 and 20 May 1947; Regina *Leader-Post,* 9 May 1947.

46 *Vancouver Sun,* 14 June 1947; *Colonist,* 27 June 1947; *Labour Gazette* 47 (1947): 781.

47 Nanking *Central Daily News,* 10 May 1947, translation in KP, #383606-7; Chang Chun, President, Yuan National Government, to W.L.M. King, 19 May 1947, KP, #382406-9; Laurent Beaudry to L.S. St. Laurent, 16 May 1947, and T.C. Davis to L.S. St. Laurent, 19 May 1947, DEAR, vol. 3193.

48 Canadian Ambassador to China to L.S. St. Laurent, 13 May 1947, and H.L. Keenleyside to J.A. Glen, 7 May 1947, DEAR, vol. 3193 (also in *DCER,* 1947, 289-90); L.B. Pearson to Cabinet Committee on Immigration, 10 May 1947, DC&I, vol. 125 (also in *DCER,* 1947, 293-95); H.L. Keenleyside, Memo, 23 May 1947, DC&I, vol. 125.

49 *New Republic,* translated in *Vancouver Sun,* 12 May 1947; *Colonist,* 17 July 1947; *Vancouver Sun,* 5 August 1947; *Times,* 4 October 1947.

50 H.L. Keenleyside to Acting Minister, 14 June 1947, Mr. Siegel, "Chinese Immigration to Canada: Possible Numbers as a Result of the Repeal of the Chinese Immigration Act, and Prospects for Actual Arrivals," 1 December 1947, and W.M. Benidickson to H.L. Keenleyside, 5 November 1947, DC&I, vol. 125; *Times,* 26 February 1948; *Toronto Daily Star,* 7 May 1947; A.E. Armstrong to J.A. Glen, 16 February 1948, KP, #399591-94; A.E. Armstrong et al. to Senate Committee on Immigration and Labour, 10 March 1948; Cabinet Committee on Immigration Policy, minutes, 15 April 1948, PCOR, vol. 82, file I-50-M. The cabinet committee admitted a handful of individuals such as the China-born children of Canadian citizens, the spouses of Canadian citizens or parents of Canadian-born children, a few professionals, and members of Roman Catholic religious orders who were closing their missions in China.

Among the newspapers commenting favourably on the committee's submission either in their editorials or in their news columns were *Ottawa Citizen,* 17 February and 10 March 1948; Toronto *Globe and Mail,* 23 February and 11 March 1948; *Toronto Daily Star,* 24 February 1948; *Colonist,* 28 February 1948; *Times,* 26 February 1948; and *Trail Daily Times,* 6 July 1948.

51 Colin Gibson to K. Dock Yip, 13 April 1949, Colin Gibson to Foon Sien, 19 October 1949, and Director of Chinese Immigration to Deputy Minister, 23 November 1949, DC&I, vol. 125; A.R. Menzies to T.C. Davis, 28 April 1949, DEAR, vol. 3193, file 5068-B-40; *Vancouver Sun,* 22 November 1948. The government may not have had accurate knowledge of the number. A memorandum in December 1949 indicated that 523 Chinese had been admitted to Canada since repeal of the Immigration Act. Minister of Mines and Resources to Cabinet, 10 December 1949, PCOR, file I-50-3; *Times,* 4 October 1947; A.E. Armstrong to J.A. Glen, 16 February 1948, KP, #399591-94; *Toronto Daily Star,* 24 February 1948;

Colonist, 28 February 1948.

52 Director of Chinese Immigration to Deputy Minister, 23 November 1949, Colin Gibson to Cabinet, 10 December 1949, N.A. Robertson to Colin Gibson, 27 December 1949, A.L. Jolliffe to Walter Harris, 26 June 1950, DC&I, vol. 125; *Vancouver Sun,* 15 January 1950; Cabinet Conclusions, 8 February 1950, PCOR, MfT2366. After the Communist takeover of China, cabinet agreed to give temporary entry permits to officials of the former Nationalist government and to other Chinese citizens who were in Canada but to discourage them from coming to Canada, though it would entertain individual applications for admission. Cabinet Conclusions, 1 February 1950, PCOR, MfT2366; *Vancouver Sun,* 7 December 1950.

53 Foon Sien, "Past Achievements"; *Province,* 23 October 1945; *Vernon News,* 16 January 1947; *CCF News,* 7 November and 19 December 1946; Vancouver *News-Herald,* 9 September and 8 and 30 November 1946; *Vancouver Sun,* 23 October and 27 December 1946 and 22 January 1947. Jack Scott, in *Vancouver Sun,* 24 January 1947; *Times,* 26 March 1947. *Statutes of British Columbia,* 11 Geo. 6, c. 28.

The question of dual citizenship arose in the fall of 1947 when it was reported that Chinese Canadians, including those born in Canada, could vote for a new Chinese National Assembly and be elected to it. The Victoria *Daily Colonist* thought it anomalous that the Chinese who had recently gained the right to vote in British Columbia could also vote in China; the Vancouver *News-Herald* declared, "in citizenship, as at the table, you can't have your cake and eat it too." While older Chinese residents of Victoria "flocked" to the poll to vote for Canadian representatives to the assembly, the younger Canadian-born Chinese showed little interest in the election. *Colonist,* 7 November 1947; Vancouver *News-Herald,* 1 December 1947; *Times,* 22 November 1947.

For a comprehensive account of the Chinese Canadian campaign for enfranchisement, see Carol F. Lee, "The Road to Enfranchisement: Chinese and Japanese in British Columbia," *BC Studies* 30 (1976): 44-76. The smaller "East Indian" community also sought enfranchisement. See J.F. Hilliker, "The British Columbia Franchise and Canada's Relations with India in Wartime, 1939-1945," *BC Studies* 46 (1980): 40-60.

54 *Province,* 7 and 9 September and 1 November 1948, 9 March 1949; *Vancouver Sun,* 3 September 1948; *Nanaimo Free Press,* 9 September 1948; Vancouver *News-Herald,* 30 September 1946, 9 March 1949; Prince Rupert *Daily News,* 9 March 1949; *Columbian,* 10 March 1949; *Times,* 8 March 1949; *Colonist,* 9 March 1949; Calgary *Albertan,* 16 March 1949; Foon Sien, "Past Achievements." *Statutes of British Columbia,* 13 Geo. 6, c. 18, s. 2 (Municipal Elections Act), and c. 73, s. 4 (Vancouver Incorporation Act). Vancouver, which had its own charter, replaced the "No Asian" clause with a requirement that voters have "an adequate knowledge of either the English or the French language." After Chinese and "East Indians" were enfranchised provincially, some municipalities let local taxpayers vote on by-laws but not for municipal council.

55 Initially, Chinese Canadians showed little interest in Vancouver municipal politics. Although the city set up a special registration office on East Pender Street, few registered, possibly because they did not understand regulations about tenants and property owners. *Province,* 11 July 1949; *Vancouver Sun,* 13 and 14 July 1949. In 1965 the Chinese Canadian Citizens Association endorsed Halford Wilson, who had led the anti-Asian campaign before the war, for alderman. Foon Sien to H.D. Wilson, HDWP, 551-D-2. *Chinese Times,* 27 and 29 May and 2 and 3 June 1948; Flyer "Announcing Oct 8th, Mr. Foon Sien, Outstanding Chinese Canadian Leaders as Guest Speaker," copy in UBC, Foon Sien Scrapbook, vol. 1; *Vancouver Sun,* 2 August 1948; *Province,* 22 June 1949. Stevens' chances in the election were slim, especially after a bitter internecine dispute within the Progressive Conservative Party over the nomination. Ralph Campney, a Liberal, won with 10,102 votes; Rodney Young, the CCF incumbent, gained 6,364, and Stevens received 5,933. An LPP and an independent candidate each won fewer than 1,000 votes. *Vancouver Sun,* 4 and 28 June 1949. Campney remained the MP until a Progressive Conservative, Douglas Jung, defeated him in 1957.

56 *Revised Statutes of British Columbia* (1936), c. 1888, s. 6; *Statutes of British Columbia,* 12 Geo. 6 (1948). Vancouver *News-Herald,* 6 November 1945 and 24 June 1947; *Nanaimo Free Press,* 27 September 1945; *Trail Daily Times,* 27 October 1945; *Cowichan Leader,* 28 February and 26 September 1946; *Province,* 22 October 1945, 29 January, 9 April, 7 and 16 July, and 14 October 1948; *Vernon News,* 27 February 1947; *Kamloops Sentinel,* 2 January 1946 and 22 October 1948; *Vancouver Sun,* 14 August 1948 and 26 May 1961; *Times,* 9 June and 13 December 1947; *Colonist,* 13 June 1947; *New Canadian,* 15 February and 15 and 29 March 1950; *Chinatown News,* 3 June 1961.

57 Foon Sien, "Past Achievements"; *New Canadian,* 2 December 1950 and 21 March 1956; Chinese

Canadian Association, Minute Book, 11 January 1957, CCAR; Chinese Benevolent Association, "A Brief Concerning Human Rights and Fundamental Freedoms for Presentation to the Right Honourable John G. Diefenbaker, Prime Minister of Canada," 25 June 1959, JDP, #46753ff.; *Colonist,* 21 May 1948; *Chinese Times,* 9 and 28 January 1959; *Chinese Bulletin,* July-August 1962; *Chinatown News,* 3 November 1963.

58 *New Canadian,* 4 June and 30 July 1949, 28 March 1956; *Province,* 1 June 1949; *Colonist,* 20, 21, and 22 March 1947; *Times,* 18, 19, and 21 March 1947; *Chinatown News,* 3 February 1956. *Statutes of British Columbia,* 4-5 Eliz. 2, c. 16. About the same time, Denise Chong's mother was told that even the top Chinese graduates of the Grandview High School of Commerce in Vancouver could not get secretarial jobs. Chong, *The Concubine's Children,* 163.

59 *Columbian,* 21 and 22 March 1956; *New Canadian,* 28 March 1956; *Chinatown News,* 3 April 1956.

60 Prince Rupert *Daily News,* 13 June 1945; *Kamloops Sentinel,* 20 February, 6 March, 1 May, and 2 October 1946; *Vancouver Sun,* 7 November 1947 and 2 and 5 November 1948; David Ricardo Williams, *Mayor Gerry: The Remarkable Gerald Grattan McGeer* (Vancouver: Douglas and McIntyre, 1986), 282; *Chinese Times,* 29 and 31 March and 1 April 1947. The phenomenon was not confined to Vancouver. About the same time in Toronto the owner of a Chinese gambling house was charged with bribing the police. *Chinese Times,* 5 May 1947.

61 *Vancouver Sun,* 13 September 1949 and 26 October 1964; *Chinatown News,* 3 May 1965; Toronto *Globe and Mail,* cited in *Chinatown News,* 3 June 1967. Suzanne Morton, *At Odds: Gambling and Canadians, 1919-1969* (Toronto: University of Toronto Press, 2003), 152-57.

62 *Kelowna Capital News,* 17 October 1945; *Kamloops Sentinel,* 2 January 1946; Vancouver *News-Herald,* 6 November 1945 and 24 June 1947; *Nanaimo Free Press,* 27 September 1945; *Trail Daily Times,* 27 October 1945; *Cowichan Leader,* 28 February and 26 September 1946; *BC Catholic,* 9 May 1946; *Province,* 22 October 1945 and 29 January, 9 April, 16 July, and 14 October 1948; *Vernon News,* 27 February 1947; *Kamloops Sentinel,* 2 January 1946 and 22 October 1948; *Vancouver Sun,* 14 August 1948.

63 Mor Cheolin, "Bright Children of Inter-Marriages," *Chinese Bulletin,* December 1964; *Chinatown News,* 18 August 1961; 18 September, 3 and 18 October, and 18 December 1963; 3 July 1964; 18 April 1965; and 18 January 1967; *Province,* 28 July 1962.

64 Wing Chung Ng, *The Chinese in Vancouver, 1945-80: The Pursuit of Identity and Power* (Vancouver: UBC Press, 1999), 93-96; Elections British Columbia, *Electoral History of British Columbia 1871-1986* (Victoria: Elections British Columbia, 1988), 264; *Chinatown News,* 3 and 18 January 1956; *New Canadian,* 5 June 1957; Douglas Jung to "Dear Friend," 24 May 1957, JDP, #10655; Douglas Jung to J.G. Diefenbaker, 2 June 1959, JDP, #244670ff.; John Meisel, *The Canadian General Election of 1957* (Toronto: University of Toronto Press, 1962), 301.

65 *SD,* 10 July 1958, 306; Tom Gould in *Vancouver Sun,* 11 July 1958; *Vancouver Sun,* 12 and 22 July 1958. A systematic study of newspapers in the northern Ontario community of Timmins found in the mid-1940s that the paper began referring to Chinese as "Chinese man" or occasionally "Chinese gentleman" rather than "Chinaman." Chan and Lam, "Chinese in Timmins," 579.

66 *Chinese Bulletin,* April 1961.

67 *BC Lumber Worker,* 30 June 1947, 25 February and 29 November 1948; Muszynski, *Cheap Labour,* 192-95; *Vancouver Sun,* 16 February 1948.

68 *Chinese Times,* 4 February 1943 and 24 January 1945; *Province,* 1 November 1945; *Vernon News,* 11 May 1944; Visit to Ashcroft by Berching Ho, Stanford Lyman, and William Wilmott, September [1961?], CCRC, vol. 11.

69 Chinese Canadian Association, Minutes of General Meeting, 1 April 1951, and Chinese Canadian Association, Journal [c. 1971], CCAR, vol. 1; *Vancouver Sun,* 9 December 1950.

70 British Columbia, Registrar of Vital Statistics, *Annual Report,* 1952 (Victoria: Queen's Printer, 1953), W48; David Chuenyan Lai, *Chinatowns: Towns within Cities in Canada* (Vancouver: UBC Press, 1988), 122-26, *Province,* 3 October 1960; *Chinatown News,* 18 January 1967, reprinted from *Edmonton Journal.*

71 For a brief account of Toronto's Chinatowns, see Lai, *Chinatowns,* 146-49, 164-74. Toronto *Globe and Mail,* 2 and 5 April 1955; *Chinatown News,* 18 November 1964, 18 February and 18 September 1965, 3 July 1966, and 3 April 1967; Nancy Collins, in *Toronto Daily Star,* reprinted in *Chinatown News,* 18 February 1967; *CCA Journal,* 5 March 1968.

72 Chong, *The Concubine's Children,* 137; *Vancouver Sun,* 26 June 1958.

73 Kay Anderson, *Vancouver's Chinatown: Racial Discourse in Canada, 1875-1980* (Montreal and Kingston: McGill-Queen's University Press, 1991), 179; *Province,* 26 September 1960, cited in Anderson,

Vancouver's Chinatown, 193; *Vancouver Sun,* 7 August 1961 and 1 April 1963; *Chinatown News,* 18 August 1961; Lai, *Chinatowns,* 128; Ng, *The Chinese in Vancouver*, 97-99.

74 *Vancouver Sun,* 27 November 1961; *Chinatown News,* 3 November 1962.

75 *Vancouver Sun,* 9 January 1962, 23 January and 1 and 27 April 1963; *Province,* 28 January 1963; *Chinatown News,* 18 March and 19 July 1964; Anderson, *Vancouver's Chinatown,* Chapter 6; Lai, *Chinatowns,* 126-35.

76 *Chinatown News,* 18 November 1964; *Vancouver Sun,* 3 February and 18 April 1966.

77 *Chinatown News,* 18 April and 3 May 1966, 3 and 18 November 1967.

78 *Chinatown News,* 3 November 1967.

Chapter 5: Toward First-Class Citizenship for Japanese Canadians, 1945-49

1 Ross Lambertson, *Repression and Resistance: Canadian Human Rights Activists, 1930-1960* (Toronto: University of Toronto Press, 2005), 5-6.

2 B.K. Sandwell et al. to L.S. St. Laurent, 17 December 1948, PCOR, vol. 162, file H-11; Citizens' Forum, *Is There a Deepening Crisis in Civil Liberties in Canada* (Toronto: Canadian Association for Adult Education, 1946); Douglas G. Anglin to W.L.M. King, 16 June 1947, and W.L.M. King to Douglas G. Anglin, 25 June 1947, DLab, vol. 639; *Washington Post,* 10 June 1946.

3 The constitution and an outline of the institute's history may be found in HDP, box 27-18; *Vernon News,* 19 July 1945; Mrs. Hugh MacMillan et al. to W.L.M. King, 25 July 1945, DLab, vol. 657; Montreal *Gazette,* 4 January 1946. Only eleven newspapers published the letter. Sandra Djwa, *The Politics of Imagination: A Life of F.R. Scott* (Vancouver: Douglas and McIntyre, 1987), 238. Commenting on the letter, Norman Robertson told the prime minister, "until my native province of British Columbia achieves some change of heart, I do not see what we can do about it except strive to limit and lessen the discriminations every time an opportunity offers." N.A. Robertson to W.L.M. King, 5 January 1946, KP, #C194932.

4 Department of Labour, *Report on the Re-Establishment of Japanese in Canada, 1944-1946* (Ottawa: Department of Labour, 1947), 27; Memo from Department of Labour on Program for Repatriation and Relocation of Persons of Japanese Race in Canada, 4 September 1945, PCOR, vol. 26, file J-25-1; R.G. Robertson to Hume Wrong, 24 October 1945, KP, #C249600-6; A.H. Brown to R.G. Robertson, 13 September 1945, and A.H. Brown to H.T. Pammett, 24 October 1945, DLab, vol. 657. That volume and DEAR vol. 3554 contain many resolutions. M.J. Coldwell to Louis St. Laurent, 15 October 1945, DLab, vol. 659. A brief history of the CCJC is in Edith Fowke, *They Made Democracy Work* (Toronto: CCJC and JCCA, 1951). As of 15 October 1945, 2,056 Japanese had sought to cancel their requests for repatriation; by 31 December 1945, the number had risen to 4,720, with the majority being Canadian born and their children. "Number of Japanese Requesting Repatriation on Official Declaration Forms, as at 31st December, 1945," and "Reasons for Cancellation of Requests for Repatriation as of October 15th, 1945," DLab, vol. 1529. *Saturday Night,* 1 September 1945; *Winnipeg Free Press,* 7 September and 6 October 1945. *Ottawa Journal,* 23 October 1945; *Orillia Packet and Times,* 11 October 1945; Lorne Green, "Around the World," 1 September 1945, copy in CCJC, vol. 2.

5 *Nanaimo Free Press,* 16 October 1945; *Kamloops Sentinel,* 30 October 1945; *Colonist,* 19 and 29 December 1945. Atrocity stories continued until at least 1947; returnees were popular service club speakers. *Times,* 6 and 7 September 1945.

6 *Winnipeg Free Press*, 14 and 19 September and 18 October 1945. The Vancouver *Daily Province* mildly rebuked the UBCM for venturing into a federal responsibility, lacking patience with dispersal, and lumping together Japanese nationals and loyal Canadian citizens of Japanese ancestry and noted the lack of co-operation of other provinces with dispersal. 7 September 1945. *Vancouver Sun,* 15 and 25 September and 29 December 1945; *Halifax Herald,* 1 November 1945; *Province,* 26 November and 28 and 29 December 1945; *Colonist,* 30 December 1945 and 20 January 1946; *Saturday Night,* 13 and 27 October 1945; Prince Rupert *Evening Empire,* 11 January 1946; A.H. Brown to George Collins, 18 January 1946, DLab, vol. 658; *Ottawa Evening Citizen,* 25 January 1946.

7 *Halifax Herald,* 3 June 1946, reprinted in *Vancouver Sun,* 13 June 1946; Saint John *Telegraph Journal,* 29 August 1945; *Vancouver Sun,* 31 August 1945; E.J. Mooney to A. MacNamara, 29 August 1945, DLab, vol. 657.

8 Vancouver *News-Herald,* 29 August and 26 September 1945 and 14 December 1946; *Vancouver Sun,* 31 August 1945 and 1 February 1946; *Nelson Daily News,* 26 January 1946; *Calgary Herald,* 7 December 1945; *Nisei Affairs,* 9 February 1946; A. MacNamara to J.E. Davidge, 22 May 1946, DLab, vol. 657.

In the spring of 1946, the dispersal program was going so slowly that Minister of Justice St. Laurent suggested making each province accept a quota but did not indicate how it could be enforced. A.H. Brown of the Department of Labour cynically suggested that without agreements the government would have "to put the balance of the Japanese apparently in the Northwest Territories." At least one draft of the Repatriation and Resettlement Bill had a clause prohibiting Japanese settlement in the coastal area, an idea that Mackenzie liked but that Brown thought "entirely wrong" and Norman Robertson politically unwise since it "might be regarded as discriminatory or as limitations upon the rights of a citizen." A.H. Brown to A. MacNamara, 30 April and 2 May 1946, and N.A. Robertson to B.F. Wood, 7 May 1946, DLab, vol. 661.

9 Vancouver *News-Herald,* 6, 16, and 24 October 1945; *Nanaimo Free Press,* 19 and 22 October 1945; *Vernon News,* 25 October 1945; *Colonist,* 19 September 1945; *Vancouver Sun,* 20 and 22 October 1945; *Ladysmith Chronicle,* 5 and 12 October 1945; *Cowichan Leader,* 11 and 25 October 1945; *Province,* 10, 13, and 22 October 1945; *Langley Advance,* 18 October 1945; *Comox District Free Press,* 11 October 1945; Prince Rupert *Daily News,* 18 and 24 October 1945; G.W. Nickerson to Tom Reid, 1 May 1947, IAMP, vol. 25. Successful Coalition candidates, including Nancy Hodges (Victoria), J.H. Cates (North Vancouver), H.J. Welch (Comox), and R.C. MacDonald (Dewdney), made similar comments, but in no case was the Japanese question a major campaign issue. During the June 1945 federal election, Prince Rupert Liberals had Muriel Cordeaux, a war correspondent, who was "stripped, beaten and injured" by the Japanese, as a featured speaker. She said that what "she had learned of the Japanese" led her to volunteer support for the Liberals and their policy of exclusion. Prince Rupert *Daily News,* 9 June 1945. Cordeaux, the widow of Captain Hoskin of the Empress of Canada, also spoke at a ladies' Liberal meeting in New Westminster. *Columbian,* 4 June 1945.

10 *Penticton Herald,* 18 October 1945; *Ladysmith Chronicle,* 19 October 1945; *Vancouver Sun,* 20 February 1945; C.G. MacNeil to David Lewis, 26 October 1945, and C.G. MacNeil to A.O. Smith, 29 October 1945, MMC, vol. 17. The advertisement appeared in the *Times* and the *Colonist,* 24 October 1945.

11 Frank Rasky to the *Varsity,* 30 October 1945; Minutes of a Meeting, 26 March 1946, KP, #C194959; *Ladner Optimist,* 31 January, 7 March, and 11 October 1946; *Surrey Leader,* reprinted, *Ladner Optimist,* 14 February 1946; *Vancouver Sun,* 22 May 1946. *Grand Forks Gazette,* 17 January 1946; Vancouver *News-Herald,* 14 and 26 November 1946.

12 *Province,* 7 September and 30 November 1945, 6 February 1946; Courtenay-Comox Board of Trade to W.L.M. King, 29 October 1945, DEAR, vol. 2798; *Vancouver Sun,* 23, 27, and 29 November 1945; L.S. Daynes to Minister of Justice, 26 January 1946, KP, #370389; R.C. Perkins to W.L.M. King, 17 March 1946, KP, #371960; *Surrey Leader,* 21 February 1946; Prince Rupert *Daily News,* 26 October 1945; G.R. Pearkes to H. Mitchell, 10 April 1946, DLab, vol. 657; *Trail Daily Times,* 5 October 1946; *Penticton Herald,* 4 October 1945; C.V. Sayer to Ian Mackenzie, 24 September 1945, IAMP, vol. 24.

13 *Vancouver Sun,* 23 November and 12 December 1945, 1 February 1946; Vancouver *News-Herald,* 15 November 1945; *Columbian,* 18 January 1946; Army and Navy Veterans in Canada, BC Command, to W.L.M. King, 3 May 1946, KP, #379821-22; Army and Navy Veterans in Canada, Lower Mainland Council, to United Fishermen and Allied Workers Union, 6 June 1946, UFAWUR, vol. 83; Howard Green to John Bracken, 22 January 1946, JBP, vol. 48; Ian Mackenzie to W.L.M. King, 7 January 1946, KP, #368736-38; *Province,* 15 January 1946.

14 Mrs. Hugh Macmillan and James M. Finlay, to All Members of Parliament, 29 October 1945, KP, #C249611. Copies of some letters and petitions are in DLab, vol. 660; George T. Tamaki, "Deportation by Order-in-Council," and editorial, *Nisei Affairs,* 29 October 1945 (Tamaki was possibly the only Japanese Canadian to hold a law degree); M.J. Coldwell to L.S. St. Laurent, 15 October 1945, DLab, vol. 659; *Ottawa Journal,* 23 October 1945.

15 *HCD,* 21 November 1945, 2376; Special Cabinet Committee, 12 September 1945, DLab, vol. 639; H.A. Brown to T.B. Pickersgill, 16 October 1945, DLab, vol. 1529; R.G. Robertson to W.L.M. King, 28 November 1945, KP, #350125; J.D. Herbert, "Canadian Intolerance," Regina *Leader-Post,* 1 and 22 December 1945; Civil Rights Defence Committee to H. Mitchell, 10 December 1945, DLab, vol. 1529. The *New Canadian,* 24 November 1945; *Toronto Daily Star,* 3 December 1945; W.W. Judd for Department of Christian Social Service, Church of England in Canada, to Members of Senate and Commons, 7 December 1945, KP, #344498ff.; *Winnipeg Free Press,* 4 December 1945; *Times,* 24 December 1945. The poll was reported in a number of newspapers but not broken down by province or region.

16 Hugh Dobson to W.L.M. King, 29 October 1945, HDP, file B24; Laura McKenzie to W.L.M. King, 20

December 1945, KP, #344366; L.H. Ward to W.L.M. King, 6 December 1945, KP, J2, vol. 472. Many letters and resolutions can be found in KP, J2, vol. 472; *Vernon News*, 15 November 1945; *Grand Forks Gazette*, 8 November 1945; *Vancouver Sun*, 5 December 1945. Among the protesters were a missionary rally of Anglican, Presbyterian, Baptist, and United Church youth, the Student Christian Movement at the University of British Columbia, the Social Service Committee of the Women's Board of Baptist Missions in British Columbia, various congregations, women's auxiliaries, and youth groups from throughout the province.

17 A.D.P. Heeney to W.L.M. King, 13 December 1945, KP, #C249646-47; A.D.P. Heeney to H. Mitchell, 17 December 1945, DLab, vol. 639; *HCD*, 17 December 1945, 3698. A brief analysis of the legal arguments made by the CCJC and of the courts' judgments may be found in Stephanie D. Bangarth, "The Politics of Rights: Canadian and American Advocacy Groups and North America's Citizens of Japanese Ancestry, 1942-1949" (PhD diss., University of Waterloo, 2003), 240-49.

18 *Nisei Affairs*, 19 January 1946; *Toronto Daily Star*, 22 December 1945; Toronto *Globe and Mail*, 21 December 1945; *Maple Leaf*, 25 January 1946.

19 PC 45, 8 January 1946; *Saturday Night*, 22 December 1945; Winnifred Thomas to W.L.M. King, 27 December 1945, DLab, vol. 657; F.A. Brewin to L.S. St. Laurent, 24 December 1945, FABP, vol. 1; Donalda Macmillan to W.L.M. King, 11 January 1946, KP, #363519; J.S.M. Finlay and D. MacMillan to Ministers of Toronto and District, 14 January 1946, CCJC, vol. 2; R.G. Robertson to W.L.M. King, 4 March 1946, KP, #C194952. The work of the churches in protesting deportation is examined in Bangarth, "The Politics of Rights," 109-13.

20 The observations in the previous two paragraphs are drawn mainly from letters and petitions scattered through the King Papers. *CCF News*, 3 January 1946; R.G. Robertson to W.L.M. King, 4 March 1946, KP, #C194952; R.G. Robertson to A.H. Brown, 14 January 1946, KP, #361222; R.G. Robertson to G.R. Hunter, 19 February 1946, KP, #365328-29; C.H. Millard to David Croll, 26 November 1945, JBP, vol. 22; C.H. Millard to W.L.M. King, 23 February 1946, KP, #378774; Albini Lafortune to W.L.M. King, 4 March 1946, KP, #367094-95.

T.B. Pickersgill of the Department of Labour suggested that replies to certain letters and delegations protesting repatriation include extracts from wartime censored letters showing what both naturalized and Canadian-born Japanese citizens thought before Japan's defeat. T.B. Pickersgill to A. MacNamara, 2 March 1946, DLab, vol. 1528. Nothing seems to have come of this idea.

21 *Colonist*, 26 January 1946; *Vancouver Sun*, 23 January 1946; Prince Rupert *Evening Empire*, 2 February 1946; *Western Business and Industry*, cited in *Langley Advance*, 14 February 1946; Toronto *Evening Telegram*, 14 January 1946.

22 R.W. Brown, "Political Deal Gives Japs 'New Life' in Canada," *Vancouver Sun*, 14 December 1945 and 26 January 1946; *Province*, 5 January 1946; *Times*, 25 January and 20 February 1946; R.L. Maitland to H. Mitchell, 20 February 1946, DLab, vol. 659.

23 *Province*, 21 February 1946; *Times*, 9 April 1946; *Nanaimo Free Press*, 22 December 1945; *Colonist*, 21 February 1946; *Vancouver Sun*, 20 February and 1 March 1946; Prince Rupert *Daily News*, 21 February 1946; Montreal *Gazette*, 21 February 1946; *La Presse*, 21 February 1946; *Toronto Daily Star*, 28 February 1946; *CCF News*, 21 February 1946.

24 *Reference re the Validity of Orders in Council of the 15th Day of December 1945 in Relation to Persons of the Japanese Race* [1946], *Canada Law Reports, Supreme Court of Canada, 1946* (Ottawa: King's Printer, 1946), 248-327. The Saskatchewan government showed its commitment to justice for Japanese Canadians by hiring a Nisei physician at its cancer clinic and a Nisei lawyer for the attorney general's office. *Toronto Daily Star*, 21 January 1947. In 1950 it appointed Thomas Shoyama as economic adviser to the premier, a position that he held until he moved to the federal government in 1964. *Saskatoon Star-Phoenix*, 29 October and 22, 23, and 30 November 1945, 20 March 1947. The Saskatchewan Bill of Rights, "Canada's first comprehensive human rights legislation," prohibited racial segregation in hotels, restaurants, theatres, and other public places as well as in employment, housing, and education. Constance Backhouse, *Colour-Coded: A Legal History of Racism in Canada, 1900-1950* (Toronto: Osgoode Society, 1999), 251. A fine account of its origins is Carmela Patrias, "Socialists, Jews, and the 1947 Saskatchewan Bill of Rights," *Canadian Historical Review* 87 (2006): 265-92.

25 G.S. Wismer to Ian Mackenzie, 6 May 1946, IAMP, vol. 24; *Trail Daily Times*, 16 May 1946; A. Brooksbank to G.S. Wismer, 24 June 1946, KP, #361217; H. Edwards to W.L.M. King, 14 June 1946, KP, J2, vol. 473. Coalition members A.C. Hope and R.C. MacDonald called for repatriating all Japanese because they were dual nationals and belonged to a race that was "entirely unassimilable with any

white race." Their motion died on the order paper. *Province,* 9 and 10 April 1946. *Province,* 16 May 1946; Vancouver *News-Herald,* 18 and 20 March 1946; *Nanaimo Free Press,* 30 April 1946; *Comox District Free Press,* 25 July 1946; Laura Hardy to W.L.M. King, 4 March 1946, DLab, vol. 655; Wilhelmina Hopkins to W.L.M. King, 25 March 1946, KP, #365939-40.

26 Statement of the Co-Operative Committee on Japanese Canadians, 20 February 1946, KP, #C194954; R.G. Robertson to W.L.M. King, 22 February 1946, KP, #C194947-48; Ian Mackenzie to H. Mitchell, 25 February 1946, and N.A. Robertson to A. MacNamara, 1 March 1946, DLab, vol. 639; N.A. Robertson to W.L.M. King, 27 February 1946, KP, #C194949-51; Cabinet Conclusions, 6 March 1946, press release, 13 March 1946PCOR, MfC, copy in DLab, vol. 658; *Province,* 13 and 22 March 1946; Toronto *Globe and Mail,* 29 March 1946.

27 Minutes of a Meeting Concerning the Problem of Japanese in Canada, 26 March 1946, copy in KP, #C194959ff.; Andrew Brewin, cited in newsletter issued 28 March 1946 by Kunio Hidaka; revised version issued 3 April 1946; copy in MTP; CCJC, Memorandum for the Members of the House of Commons and the Senate of Canada, April 1946, copy in JBP, vol. 22.

28 *Nisei Affairs,* 20 August 1945, 16 September and 16 December 1946; CCJC, *Our Japanese Canadians: Citizens Not Exiles* (Toronto: CCJC, 1946).

29 D. Badger, "Passing Judgement on B.C. and the Japanese," *Western Miner* (October 1945): 56; *Grand Forks Gazette,* 8 November 1945; Donald J. McIntosh, petition, 28 August 1946, DLab, vol. 655. Other petitions may be found in DLab, vol. 657, and in KP, #C194996. An international workshop of Canadian and American teachers, students, and public-minded citizens at the University of British Columbia sent similar concerns to the prime minister. W.E. Tomlinson to W.L.M. King, 21 August 1946, KP, #378433.

30 *HCD,* 2 April 1946, 502-3; 5 April 1946, 618-19, 624-25; 9 April 1946, 703-4, 716-17, 719-20, 725-26; 11 April 1946, 795, 802; 30 April 1946, 1082; 2 May 1946, 1152; 3 May 1946, 1209; 13 May 1946, 1492; 14 May 1946, 1503-5. *Colonist,* 9 April 1946; *CCF News,* 11 April 1946.

Later, after seconding John Diefenbaker's motion to include a Bill of Rights in the citizenship legislation, Davie Fulton attacked orders in council limiting the rights of Canadians but did not mention any relating to the Japanese. Paul Martin chided Fulton for having earlier defended the orders providing for the deportation of Japanese on the grounds that most of those affected were not citizens of Canada. Despite disagreeing with past policies that admitted Japanese to Canada, Fulton conceded that, if the Japanese were fit to be citizens and permitted to stay, they must have "full rights of citizenship." *HCD,* 7 May 1946, 1303-10.

C.E. Hope of the White Canada Research Committee, who had urged the government to outlaw dual citizenship, alleged that the Canadian-born Japanese were "much more dangerous than the older ones" and conjectured that there would have been sabotage "if an invasion had taken place." C.E. Hope to H. Mitchell, 2 January 1946, DLab, vol. 657. Arguments about dual citizenship impressed St. Laurent, who did not advocate deportation but who suggested that it might be necessary to depart from the "principle of equal rights and self-determination of peoples." *HCD,* 8 May 1946, 1335.

31 *Province,* 3 December 1946, reprinted in *Calgary Herald,* 7 December 1946; *CCF News,* 19 December 1946; Montreal *Star,* 4 and 9 December 1946; *Ottawa Evening Citizen,* 3 December 1946; Toronto *Globe and Mail,* 4 December 1946; *Toronto Daily Star,* 3 December 1946; Calgary *Albertan,* 5 December 1946; *Lethbridge Herald,* 13 December 1946; Regina *Leader-Post,* 5 December 1946; *Winnipeg Free Press,* 7 December 1946; R.G. Robertson to W.L.M. King, 7 December 1946, KP, #C194976.

32 *Province,* 3 December 1946; *CCF News,* 5 December 1945; *Colonist,* 4 December 1945; *Vancouver Sun,* 3 and 13 December 1946; J.W. P[ickersgill] to W.L.M. King, 26 December 1946, RGRP, vol. 1.

33 Among the papers in which the Canadian Press report appeared were the *Brantford Expositor,* 15 January 1947 and the *Saskatoon Star-Phoenix,* 15 January 1947; R.G. Robertson to W.L.M. King, 3 December 1946, PCOR, file J-25-1; Committee on Japanese Problems, Secret Memo to Cabinet, 13 January 1947, KP, #C194839; W.L.M. King, Diary, 22 January 1947; R.G. Robertson to W.L.M. King, 1 February 1947, KP, J4, vol. 361. In September 1947, the government ended financial assistance to any Japanese going to Japan.

34 *Saskatoon Star-Phoenix,* 5 June 1947. The Regina *Leader-Post* of 20 May 1947 noted the irony of Mackenzie introducing the resolution. In a long speech that traced the history of human rights from the Magna Carta to the United Nations Charter, which King read in advance (W.L.M. King, Diary, 15 May 1947), Mackenzie suggested that given the common law tradition Canada should not "tamper with her heritage of liberty by seeking to inscribe in statutes the freedom that is inherently ours." *HCD,* 16

May 1947, 3148-49. With relatively little debate, the House of Commons approved the committee, though Alistair Stewart, Stanley Knowles, and Angus MacInnis of the CCF noted that Japanese Canadians did not enjoy the same freedoms as other Canadians. *HCD,* 16 May 1947, 3161, and 19 May 1947, 3120 and 3123.

35 For details, see Patricia E. Roy, "Lessons in Citizenship: The Delayed Return of the Japanese to Canada's Pacific Coast," *Pacific Northwest Quarterly* 93 (2002): 69-80, reprinted in *Nikkei in the Pacific Northwest: Japanese Americans and Japanese Canadians in the Twentieth Century,* ed. Louis Fiset and Gail Nomura (Seattle: University of Washington Press, 2005), 254-77.

36 *Winnipeg Free Press,* 20 October 1945 and 22 April 1947; *Medicine Hat Daily News,* 20 December 1945; *Vancouver Sun,* 21 December 1945; Citizens' Forum, "Is There a Deepening Case for Civil Liberties in Canada?" (draft, 1946-47), and *Do We Need a Bill of Rights in Canada?* (1946-47), copies in JDP, #1192ff. and #6270-71; J.A. Macdonald to L.S. St. Laurent, 15 January 1948, LSt.LP, vol. 15; B.K. Sandwell and Andrew Brewin, to Senate Committee on Human Rights and Fundamental Freedoms [c. 1948], HWHP, vol. 22; S.H. Hatcher (First Unitarian Congregation, Toronto) to L.S. St. Laurent, 8 March 1950, PCOR, vol. 152, file H-11; *Nisei Affairs,* January 1947; JCCA, Minutes of Meeting, 30 August-2 September 1947, JCCA, file 12-1; Report of Executive Secretary to the Second National [JCCA] Conference, 2 September 1947 to 30 March 1948, MTP.

On 27 December 1948, *Vancouver Sun* columnist Elmore Philpott, in urging Canada to incorporate the Universal Declaration of Human Rights into its Constitution, cited the "exile" of "Canadians of Japanese ancestry for no other reason than that they were of such ancestry" as one of many examples of discrimination. His editors disagreed and claimed that no Japanese Canadian had been coerced to return to Japan and that their removal from the coast in 1942 had been a "military necessity." *Vancouver Sun,* 29 December 1948. That was the last gasp of the paper's anti-Japanese campaign. A full account of the campaign for a Bill of Rights is Christopher MacLennan, *Toward the Charter: Canadians and the Demand for a National Bill of Rights, 1929-1960* (Montreal and Kingston: McGill-Queen's University Press, 2003). On Ontario's Racial Discrimination Act, see James St. G. Walker, *"Race," Rights, and the Law in the Supreme Court of Canada* (Toronto: Osgoode Society; Waterloo: Wilfrid Laurier University Press, 1997), 197 and passim. *HCD,* 1 July 1960, 5647; 4 July 1960, 5690 and 5699; 7 July 1960, 5906-8.

37 Prince Rupert *Evening Empire,* 3 January 1947; *Vancouver Sun,* 9 September 1946; *New Canadian,* 4 May 1946; *Province,* 27 January 1947; A. MacNamara to T.B. Pickersgill, 9 May 1946, DLab, vol. 658; Department of Labour, *Report on the Re-Establishment of Japanese,* 25.

38 Recommendations of Department of Labour to Cabinet Committee on Japanese Problems for Meeting of 13 December 1946, and "Press Release for Prime Minister's Office," 23 January 1947, RGRP, vol. 1; *Vancouver Sun,* 13 and 24 January 1947; *Calgary Herald,* 27 January 1947; Regina *Leader-Post,* 28 January 1947; *Toronto Daily Star,* 24 January 1947; Toronto *Globe and Mail,* 28 January 1947; *Saturday Night,* 1 February 1947; *Province,* 27 January 1947; Vancouver *News-Herald,* 25 January 1947.

39 *Canadian Jewish Review,* 3 January 1947; *Calgary Herald,* 3 and 27 January and 5 February 1947; *Toronto Daily Star,* 18 and 25 January 1947; Montreal *Star,* 27 January 1947; Toronto *Globe and Mail,* 28 January 1947; *Saskatoon Star-Phoenix,* 28 January and 1 May 1947; Regina *Leader-Post,* 28 January 1947.

40 *Calgary Herald,* 29 March 1948.

41 *Colonist,* 25 January and 2 March 1947; Vancouver *News-Herald,* 21 January 1947; *Vancouver Sun,* 24 January and 7 March 1947; West Burnaby Liberal Association to W.L.M. King, 31 January 1947, KP, #383097; Hazel Woodward to John Bracken, 25 February 1947, and Vancouver South-Point Grey Progressive Conservative Association, Meeting, 11 February 1947, JBP, vol. 22; *Nanaimo Free Press,* 12 April 1947; *Province,* 15 February 1947; Mrs. G.F. Stuart to Ian Mackenzie, 24 February 1947, IAMP, vol. 25; *Vernon News,* 15 May 1947. The Canadian Legion national convention that spring censured the denial of civil rights to Japanese during the war and called for a review of property sales after Jewish war veterans from Ontario lobbied for such a resolution. Carmela Patrias and Ruth A. Frager, "'This Is Our Country, These Are Our Rights': Minorities and the Origins of Ontario's Human Rights Campaigns," *Canadian Historical Review* 82 (2001): 22.

42 Norman F. Black to Ian Mackenzie, 25 March 1947, Hunter Lewis to W.L.M. King, 25 March 1947, IAMP, vol. 25; A.J. MacLachlan to W.L.M. King, 26 June 1947, DLab, vol. 657; Vancouver *News-Herald,* 21 February and 12 September 1947; *Columbian,* 3 December 1946. Lengthy reports of the Vancouver Civil Liberties pamphlet or editorials based on it appeared in Regina *Leader-Post,* 7 May 1947; *Calgary Herald,* 12 May 1947; *Saskatoon Star-Phoenix,* 5 May 1947; and *Winnipeg Free Press,* 20 May 1947.

43 *Vancouver Sun*, 11 April and 9 May 1947; *Colonist*, 24 April 1947; Vancouver *News-Herald*, 14 and 22 November 1946; *HCD*, 27 March 1947, 1806.

44 *HCD*, 22 April 1947, 2315-27; 23 April 1947, 2334, 2336, 2343-52; 24 April, 2361-77; Senate, *Debates*, 8 May 1947, 324. C.E. Hope clearly expressed this notion when he wrote to Humphrey Mitchell of his conviction that the RCMP and External Affairs knew more about Japanese spying than they let on. "It is a self-evident fact," he claimed, "that the Japs as a whole are not a civilised race and because of the undoubted existence of this fifth column that we have been so insistent about sending them all back to Japan or at least ... keeping them all out of British Columbia." C.E. Hope to H. Mitchell, 4 June 1947, DLab, vol. 657. In September 1947, an unscientific public opinion poll sponsored by a local department store chain reported that 87.6 percent of the population did not believe that Japanese who were naturalized Canadians should be permitted to return to British Columbia. *Province*, 11 September 1947.

45 *Colonist*, 24 April and 10 May 1947; Vancouver *News-Herald*, 28 April 1947; *Vancouver Sun*, 1 April 1947; *HCD*, 23 April 1947, 2345.

46 R.G. Robertson of the Prime Minister's Office reported "receiving a number of letters from various parts of the country, protesting at continued restrictions on Japanese." R.G. R[obertson] to W.L.M. King, 12 May 1947, KP, J2, vol. 473. Examples of organizations sending letters of protest include the Canadian Council of Churches, the University of Toronto Liberal Association, and the National Council of Jewish Women. The *Comox District Free Press* of 8 May 1947 agreed with the continued exclusion of Japanese from the coast, described the Japanese question as a "national problem," and ascribed it mainly to the lower standard of living of the Japanese. *CCF News*, 1 May 1947; *Toronto Daily Star*, 26 April 1947; *Saturday Night*, 26 April 1947; *Calgary Herald*, 29 April 1947; *Winnipeg Free Press*, 9 May 1947 (also in Regina *Leader-Post*, 15 May 1947). The *Vancouver Sun* of 2 May 1947 responded to *Saturday Night* by pointing out that the dispersal program was not yet complete. *Nisei Affairs*, February 1947; D. MacMillan to W.L.M. King, 28 February 1947, KP, #388610; Dr. G.A. Ishiwara to W.L.M. King, 8 May 1947, KP, #C11038. At the time, the registrar of Canadian citizenship was not considering applications from Japanese nationals for Canadian citizenship. Paul Deziel to Southern Alberta Youth Council, 13 February 1947, MTP.

47 Privy Council Office, Memo, 10 January 1948, DLab, vol. 639; Cabinet Committee on the Japanese Question, 15 January 1948, PCOR, vol. 84; R.G. Robertson to W.L.M. King, 15 January 1948, KP, #C195009; W.L.M. King, Diary, 30 January, 3 and 18 February 1948; Vancouver *News-Herald*, 31 January 1948; *Province*, 2 February 1948. John Hart retired at the end of December 1947 and was immediately succeeded by Johnson.

Caucus does not appear to have considered an idea of C.N. Senior, Mackenzie's secretary, that the government take advantage of the absence of a BC representative in the cabinet to end restrictions on Japanese. J.W. Pickersgill endorsed the idea because he believed that continuing the orders would embarrass Liberal MPs elsewhere, especially in Manitoba and Ontario, and that in British Columbia, where attitudes seemed to be changing, the CCF, not the Tories, was the political threat. He warned that "many genuine Liberal votes would be thrown to the C.C.F. on a fundamental issue like this." Moreover, he concluded, "on grounds of justice" the orders should be repealed. C.N. Senior to W.L.M. King, 7 February 1948, KP, #401090; J.W. Pickersgill, Memo, 12 February 1948, KP, #C195016-18. Dillon O'Leary reported the concerns, including the by-election, expressed by the BC Liberals in caucus. *Vancouver Sun*, 8 March 1948.

48 *Province*, 2 March 1949; *Colonist*, 12 March 1948; Davie Fulton to George Tanaka, 9 March 1948, JCCA, vol. 9; *HCD*, 15 March 1948, 2216-18.

49 PC 804, 2 March 1948; *HCD*, 15 March 1948, 2217-44.

50 *Vancouver Sun*, 22 March, 28 May, and 11 June 1948; *Winnipeg Free Press*, 17 and 20 March 1948; Toronto *Globe and Mail*, 17 March 1948; Toronto *Globe and Mail*, reprinted in *Trail Daily Times*, 6 July 1948.

51 *Columbian*, 10 January 1946; Kaslo *Kootenaian*, 27 December 1945.

52 J.C. Harris to W.L.M. King, 23 February 1946, KP, #365411; S.N. Ross et al. to W.L.M. King, 12 March 1946, KP, #370086-370092; *HCD*, 22 April 1947, 2326; *Times*, 2 March 1949; *Nanaimo Free Press*, 6 February 1946. For details, see Patricia E. Roy, "A Tale of Two Cities: The Reception of Japanese Evacuees in Kelowna and Kaslo, BC," *BC Studies* 87 (1990): 23-47, and "If the Cedars Could Speak: Japanese and Caucasians Meet at New Denver," *BC Studies* 131 (2001): 81-92.

53 *Bridge River-Lillooet News*, 24 January and 7, 14, and 21 February 1947; *Ashcroft Journal*, 25 January 1947

54 *Nelson Daily News,* 8 October 1945 and 5 April 1946.

55 *Kamloops Sentinel,* 21 November 1945; 16 January and 17 July 1946; 26 November 1947; 27 October and 5 November 1948; 23 February and 4 July 1949; *Province,* 5 March and 29 April 1946, 20 and 22 January 1947; Laura T. Hardy to W.L.M. King, 4 March 1946, DLab, vol. 655; Kamloops Local Council to Mrs. G.D. Finlayson, 17 April 1946, KP, #371050; W. Hopkins to W.L.M. King, 25 March 1946, KP, #365939; Margaret Taylor to W.L.M. King, 5 January 1946, KP, #366720; Tom Reid, Joint Committee of the Senate and the House of Commons (re) the Indian Act, 11 March 1947, 33.

56 *Vernon News,* 10 January 1946; 26 June, 30 October, and 6 November 1947; and 3 March 1949; *Nelson Daily News,* 5 April 1946; *Times,* 4 April 1947.

57 *Kelowna Courier,* 24 January 1946, 16 January 1947, and 11 April 1949; W.A.C. Bennett to John Hart, 23 January 1946, WACBP, vol. 13; W.A.C. Bennett to R. Rutherford, 4 April 1947, WACBP, MG1/2, vol. 8; D.M. Disney to W.L.M. King, 14 December 1946, IAMP, vol. 25; *Province,* 17 January and 8 February 1947; *HCD,* 24 April 1947, 2361; JCCA, Founding Convention, 11 September 1947, JCCA, file "JCCD Newsletter."

58 *Vancouver Sun,* 24 September 1945, 27 and 28 January and 28 May 1948; *Colonist,* 15 October 1947; Mrs. Nora Hutchings, North Burnaby Liberal Association, to W.L.M. King, 5 February 1948, KP, #C11048; E.T. Applewhite, Prince Rupert Liberal Association, to H. Mitchell, 6 April 1948, DLab, vol. 655; *Province,* 6 April 1948; *BC Lumber Worker,* 18 June, 24 September, and 8 October 1945; E. Dalskog to W.L.M. King, 16 February 1948, KP, #398184-85; *CCF News,* 28 January 1948; Hugh M. Rae to B.I. Johnson, 29 January 1948, HDP; C.G. McMynn to E.T. Kenney, 29 January 1948, GR 1222, vol. 206; Vancouver *News-Herald,* 28 January 1948. In Ottawa Angus MacInnis suggested that the action might violate the United Nations Charter and the Canadian Citizenship Act; Senator Mackenzie said that there was "no new policy," and Green preferred not to discuss "a provincial matter." *Province,* 28 January 1948.

59 Vancouver *News-Herald,* 28 January and 12 February 1948; *Province,* 30 January 1948; *Times,* 30 January 1948; Prince Rupert *Daily News,* 28 January 1948; *Vancouver Sun,* 27 January 1948.

60 J.K. Nesbitt, in Vancouver *News-Herald,* 30 January 1948; Vancouver *News-Herald,* 2 February 1948; *Vancouver Sun,* 31 January and 7 April 1948; *Columbian,* 3 February 1948; Elmore Philpott, in *Vancouver Sun,* 5 February 1948; *Vernon News,* 5 February 1948; *BC Lumber Worker,* 19 February 1948; *Toronto Daily Star,* 5 February 1948.

61 Vancouver *News-Herald,* 16 February 1948; *Province,* 9 and 22 April 1948; *Vancouver Sun,* 7 April 1948; *BCLJ,* 21 April 1948; *Winnipeg Free Press,* 16 April 1948. Many of the letters and resolutions are in GR 1222, vol. 206.

62 *Province,* 23 April 1948; *Times,* 22 April 1948; *Nanaimo Free Press,* 22 April 1948; Vancouver *News-Herald,* 22 April 1948.

63 Ucluelet Residents to W.L.M. King, 11 December 1945, KP, J2, vol. 473; *Nanaimo Free Press,* 12 December 1945; Minutes of Sunbury Local UFAWU, 14 April 1946, and [signature missing, Stuart Island] to Bill Rigby, 28 April 1946, UFAWUR, vol. 83; J. Cameron to W.L.M. King, 6 January 1947, IAMP, vol. 25; J.E. Eckman to H. Mitchell, 14 December 1946, DLab, vol. 657; Homer Stevens to George Tanaka, 15 February 1948, JCCA, vol. 13, MfC12830; Homer Stevens and Rolf Knight, *Homer Stevens: A Life in Fishing* (Madeira Park, BC: Harbour, 1992), 58-59.

64 Gibson referred to a Tofino fisherman who "conveniently disappeared" to Japan just before the war. The fisherman, K. Nakai, informed Prime Minister King that he had moved to Vancouver, where his daughters were attending high school, and was evacuated to Greenwood before relocating to Toronto. K. Nakai to W.L.M. King, 27 June 1947, KP, #C11037. *HCD,* 22 April 1947, 2323, 23 April 1947, 2337, 2340.

65 T. Buck Suzuki to M. Shumitacher, 3 February 1947, and T.C. Douglas to Ian Mackenzie, 5 March 1947, JCCA, file 25-1-P; M.F.C. Suzuki to G. Tanaka, 4 February 1949, JCCA, file 15-7, MfC12832; G. Tanaka to Hunter Lewis, 9 February 1949, JCCA, file 15-6, MfC12832; *Vancouver Sun,* 19 April, 2 May, and 26 November 1947; Prince Rupert *Daily News,* 23 and 26 April 1948 and 7 February 1949; R.G. Robertson to W.L.M. King, 15 January 1948, RGRP, vol. 1; G. Tanaka to W.L.M. King, 23 January 1948, DLab, vol. 657; *Colonist,* 14 and 17 October 1948.

66 H.H. Stevens to U. Sakamoto, 19 January 1949; G. Tanaka to Third Provincial Convention of JCCA, Greenwood, BC, 26-27 February 1949; and G. Tanaka to H.H. Stevens, 28 March 1949, UFAWUR, vol. 83; Question Period after Speech by G. Tanaka, 22 March 1949, UFAWUR, vol. 220; T.B. Suzuki to G. Tanaka, 4 February 1949, G. Tanaka to Hunter Lewis, 9 February 1949, and H.H. Stevens to G. Tanaka, 31 March 1949, JCCA, vol. 15, MfC12830; *Vancouver Sun,* 18 March 1949; *Fisherman,* 1 and 8 April 1949; Cabinet Minutes, 4 April 1949, PCOR, MfT2366. For the prewar policy, see Roy, *The Oriental Question,* 103-10.

67 Theodore T. Hirota, "The Times They Are Changin'," *Nikkei Images* 9 (2004): 7; *Province,* 7 April 1949; Prince Rupert *Daily News,* 9 April 1949; Vancouver *News-Herald,* 11 April 1949; *Fisherman,* 21 June 1949; JCCA press release to *New Canadian* and *Continental Times,* 28 November 1949; H.H. Stevens to A.J. Turner, 23 February 1950, UFAWUR, vol. 83.
68 H. Allen, Maple Ridge Board of Trade, to L.S. St. Laurent, 16 February 1949, DLab, vol. 657; Mission *Fraser Valley Record,* 16 February 1949; Prince Rupert *Daily News,* 8 March 1949; Vancouver *News-Herald,* 19 March 1949; *North Shore Press,* 18 March 1949; *Langley Advance,* 10 March 1949; *Vancouver Sun* (New Westminster ed.), 24 and 25 March 1949.
69 On recruiting Nisei for the army, see Roy Ito, *We Went to War: The Story of the Japanese Canadians Who Served during the First and Second World Wars* (Etobicoke, ON: S-20 and Nisei Veterans Association, 1984), and Roy, "The Soldiers Canada Didn't Want." *Nisei Affairs,* 20 August 1945; *Province,* 27 August 1945; *Vancouver Sun,* 15 September 1945.
70 Vancouver *News-Herald,* 23 October 1945 and 4 March 1946; Vancouver *Lions Gate Times,* 15 and 22 November 1945; A.P. McKenzie, "Report of S-20 Japanese School – Winter Term – October to December 1945," DHist, 171.009 (D192); F.F. Worthington to Secretary, DND, 6 March 1946, DHist, 322.009 (D586); *Vancouver Sun,* 23 November 1945; Buck Suzuki, "Operation Resettlement," *Nisei Affairs,* 16 December 1946.
71 Lambertson, *Repression and Resistance,* 102; Commission on Wartime Relocation and Internment of Civilians, *Personal Justice Denied* (Seattle: University of Washington Press, 1997) [first published, Washington, DC: Government Printing Office, 1982 and 1983], 239 and passim; *Vancouver Sun,* 3 December 1945; Ian Mackenzie to H. Mitchell, 20 May 1946, IAMP, vol. 79; Ian Mackenzie to H. Mitchell, 17 October 1946, IAMP, vol. 25; *Province,* 30 January 1948; Vancouver *News-Herald,* 28 January 1948; *Nisei Affairs,* November-December 1945; George Tanaka, "A Matter of Birth and Ballot," *Nisei Affairs,* 7 October 1946.
72 E. Reid to Ian Mackenzie, 4 March 1947; R.G. Robertson to Ian Mackenzie, 26 February 1947; Ian Mackenzie to H. Mitchell, 11 March 1947; David McKee to T.D. Anderson, 18 April 1947; C.N. Senior to W.C. Bethune, 6 May 1947; C. Merritt to Ian Mackenzie, 20 September 1947; Ian Mackenzie to C. Merritt, 14 October 1947, all in IAMP, vol. 25. Zennosuke Inouye, another First World War veteran, had secured land under the Soldiers Settlement Act. Angus MacInnis raised his case in Parliament (*HCD,* 24 April 1947, 2379), but Inouye's persistence largely explained his success in reclaiming his farm. See Peter Neary, "Zennosuke Inouye's Land: A Canadian Veterans Affairs Dilemma," *Canadian Historical Review* 85 (2004): 423-50.
73 *Vancouver Sun,* 15 November 1945, 17 May 1947, and 10 November 1948; *Nisei Affairs,* November-December 1945; T.B. Pickersgill to A. MacNamara, 29 January 1945, Brooke Claxton to H. Mitchell, 27 March 1947, and H. Mitchell to Brooke Claxton, 5 April 1947, DLab, vol. 655; Vancouver *News-Herald,* 22 November 1946 and 26 February 1948; Minutes of Cabinet Committee on Japanese Problems, 3 September 1947, RGRP, vol. 1; S. Takata to George Tanaka, 30 September 1948, JCCA, vol. 4.; Frank G.P. Lewis, open letter, 13 March 1948, DLab, vol. 657.
74 *Cowichan Leader,* 27 March 1947; *Kelowna Courier,* 20 December 1948; *Vancouver Sun,* 17 December 1948; *Kamloops Sentinel,* 7 January 1948; *Nanaimo Free Press,* 26 February 1949; Eric Broderick to George Tanaka, 22 November 1948, and George Tanaka to Eric Broderick, 30 December 1948, JCCA, vol. 15, MfC12832.
75 National Executive Committee, JCCA, to George Tanaka, 28 March 1949, JCCA, vol. 15, MfC12832; *Ladner Optimist,* 24 March 1949; *Surrey Leader,* 21 April 1948, reprinted in *Langley Advance,* 12 May 1949, and Mission *Fraser Valley Record,* 4 May 1949; C.V. Booth to A.H. Brown, 14 April 1949, DLab, vol. 655.
76 *New Canadian,* 30 June 1948, 1 December 1951, 30 April 1952, and 6 September 1967, quoting *Province,* 4 September 1967.
77 *BCLJ,* 19 February 1947; *Columbian,* 23 January 1947; Vancouver *News-Herald,* 11, 22, and 24 January and 2 March 1947; *Ladner Optimist,* 30 January 1947; *Marpole-Richmond Review,* 12 February 1947; *Province,* 23 May 1946 and 7 and 22 January 1947; *Vancouver Sun,* 22 January 1947. A national affairs columnist in the *BC Catholic* of 30 January 1947 used similar phrasing in reporting on the failure of the provincial legislature to enfranchise Japanese.
78 *Times,* 20 and 26 March 1947; Vancouver *News-Herald,* 20 March and 3 April 1947; *CCF News,* 3 April 1947; T.D. Pattullo to W.G. Wilson, 8 August 1946, TDPP, vol. 66. In several editorials, the *Winnipeg Free Press* of 7 and 9 April and 7 May 1947 condemned the provincial legislature for not enfranchising Japanese. The BC press attacked the paper for interfering in other questions relating to the Japanese

but did not on this question presumably because it had similar views.

79 *Vancouver Sun,* 3 February 1948; Vancouver *News-Herald,* 2, 16, and 24 March 1948; *Columbian,* 5 March, 17 and 19 April 1948; *Province,* 16 April 1948.

80 Cabinet Conclusions, 7, 14, and 28 January 1947, PCOR, MfT2365; E.W. Mackay to W.L.M. King, 31 January 1947, KP, #388307; Hunter Lewis to W.L.M. King, 25 March 1947, KP, #386750; *Province,* 28 March 1947; Canada, House of Commons, *Special Committee on Dominion Election Act, 1938* (Ottawa, 1947), 197 and 241-49, and *Special Committee* (Ottawa, 1948), 39-42; *Vancouver Sun,* 30 May 1947; *HCD,* 15 June 1948, 5258; Vancouver *News-Herald,* 17 June 1948.

81 *Colonist,* 17 June 1948 and 23 March 1949; *Times,* 15 June 1948 and 8 March 1949; *Province,* 17 June 1948 and 2 March 1949; *Vernon News,* 24 June 1948; *CCF News,* 24 June 1948; *Vancouver Sun,* 16 June 1948; Vancouver *News-Herald,* 16 June 1948; JCCA, Minutes of National Conference, 30 August 1947, JCCA, vol. 2, MfC12819; George Tanaka to Premier and Government of British Columbia, 4 March 1949, JCCA, vol. 9, MfC12825; Byron Johnson to George Tanaka, 11 March 1949, JCCA, vol. 15, MfC12832. *Statutes of British Columbia,* 13 Geo. 6, c. 19, s. 2. The Doukhobors were disfranchised in 1931 for refusing to accept military service. Their franchise was restored in 1957.

82 A total of 2,089 votes were cast in Grand Forks-Greenwood and 3,070 in Kaslo-Slocan. *Vancouver Sun,* 19 May and 9 and 20 June 1948; Vancouver *News-Herald,* 9 June 1948; *Province,* 4 May and 22 June 1949; *Kamloops Sentinel,* 6 May 1949; *CCF News,* 6 and 25 May and 1 June 1949; *New Canadian,* 18 June 1949; Calgary *Albertan,* 16 March 1948; Report of provincial JCCA meeting, 22 January 1950, JCCA, file 12/11, MfC12829. Stevens' chances were slim, especially after a bitter dispute within the Conservative Party over the nomination. Ralph Campney (Liberal) won with 10,102 votes; Rodney Young, the CCF incumbent, gained 6,364, and Stevens received 5,933. An LPP and an independent candidate each won fewer than 1,000 votes. *Vancouver Sun,* 4 and 28 June 1949.

Chapter 6: Beyond Enfranchisement

1 Harold Hirose, in *National JCCA Bulletin,* 7 November 1949. Concern about maintaining membership runs through JCCA records and the *New Canadian;* for example, Report of the BC Chapter to the JCCA Conference, September 1961, JCCA, vol. 12-18, MfC12829, and *New Canadian,* 7 June 1950. A brief biography of Hirose and his work among the Japanese Canadians in Manitoba may be found in Peter T. Nunoda, "Harold Hirose on Integration and Citizenship for Japanese Manitobans, 1942-52," *Prairie Forum* 27 (2002): 209-39.

2 *New Canadian,* 20 April and 11 May 1949; *Vancouver Sun,* 3 March 1949.

3 *New Canadian,* 8 August 1951, 3 September 1960, 25 April 1964, and 6 January 1967. Sugimoto's 202 votes were just under 8 percent of those cast, but he ran ahead of the party, which secured less than 7 percent of the popular vote province-wide. About 500 Japanese Canadians, including children, lived in the constituency.

4 June Tanaka, "Discrimination and Prejudice as They Affected the Japanese in Canada," LAC, June Tanaka Papers; Jessie Nishiata, ed., "The Japanese in Montreal: An Economical and Sociological Survey," copy in JCCA, vol. 14-37, MfC12831; *New Canadian,* 2 July 1952.

5 *New Canadian,* 7 December 1949, 18 February and 1 July 1950, 10 February and 16 June 1951, and 2 and 30 June 1956; *Vancouver Sun,* 14 May 1946; Toronto *Globe and Mail,* 5 January 1958; George Tanaka to Roy Shinobu, 8 August 1950, JCCA, vol. 9-6, MfC12825; Manitoba Report, 4-7 November 1949, JCCA, vol. 12-20, MfC12830; Manitoba Report, 1953, JCCA, vol. 12-13, MfC12829; Fourth National Conference of the JCCA, 23-27 March 1951, JCCA, vol. 12-10, MfC12829.

6 *New Canadian,* 13 July and 7 December 1949; 4 February, 19 July, 2 September, and 22 November 1950; 14 February and 25 July 1951; 2 October 1954; and 29 December 1956; British Columbia, Social Welfare Branch, *Annual Report,* 1952 (Victoria: Queen's Printer, 1953), W21. So many left the self-supporting settlement of East Lillooet that the water supply was cut off, and it "ceased to exist." *New Canadian,* 5 May 1951. At New Denver, the province acquired the buildings from the federal government and transferred them without charge to their occupants in 1960. *New Canadian,* 18 May 1960.

7 Mor Cheolin, in *Chinese Bulletin,* June 1963; Fifth Provincial Conference of BC JCCA, 2-4 February 1951, and Provincial Meeting, JCCA, 22 January 1950, JCCA, file 12-11, MfC12829; George H. Green to Davie Fulton, 10 May 1952, EDFP, vol. 2. It is unknown whether he got the Japanese Canadian vote. It was a poor year for Conservatives; P.A. Gagliardi of the upstart Social Credit Party won the seat.

8 Provincial Meeting, JCCA, 22 January 1950, JCCA, vol. 12-11, MfC12829.

9 Kar Kobayashi to George Tanaka, 18 October 1951, JCCA, vol. 8-28, MfC12825; *BC Lumber Worker,*

reprinted in *New Canadian,* 3 August 1948; Tom I. Tagami, "The Story of Tagami Bros. Lumber," *Nikkei Images* 10 (2005): 1-3.

10 *New Canadian,* 4 and 18 March and 12 April 1950, 26 May, 15 August, 26 September, and 3 October 1951; and 6 June 1952; *Province,* 28 February 1953.

11 George Tanaka, "Examples of Discrimination Based on Race Encountered by Japanese Canadians," JCCA Meeting, 24 February 1950, JCCA, vol. 14-7, MfC12831; *New Canadian,* 21 April 1950 and 14 March 1951; Ross Lambertson, *Repression and Resistance: Canadian Human Rights Activists, 1930-1960* (Toronto: University of Toronto Press, 2005), 224. The *Beach O' Pines,* the Ontario case, is explained in James St. G. Walker, *"Race," Rights, and the Law in the Supreme Court of Canada* (Toronto: Osgoode Society, 1997), Chapter 4.

12 *New Canadian,* 15 October and 2 November 1949; 15 and 18 February, 10 May, 8 November, and 6 December 1950; 17 January, 15 August, and 3 October 1951; 20 February and 18 March 1952; 11 September 1954; and 12 January and 11 May 1955; George Tanaka to Nobby Ogura, 9 December 1949, JCCA, vol. 4-20, MfC12821; Kar Kobayashi to George Tanaka, 15 March 1952, JCCA, vol. 4-19, MfC12821; *Province,* 16 February 1953; R. Thompson to L.S. St. Laurent, 13 February 1950, and A.D. Darlington to L.S. St. Laurent, 13 January 1950, PCOR, series 18, vol. 199, file U-II-1.

13 *New Canadian,* 4 February 1956; 3 September 1949; 8 March, 20 May, and 23 September 1950; 17 and 21 March 1951; 23 March 1952; and 23 October 1957; *Vancouver Sun,* 25 November 1949 and 7 January 1950; National JCCA to National Executive, 29 November 1949, JCCA, vol. 3, MfC12820; George Tanaka to Ted Aoki, 14 August 1951, JCCA, vol. 4-27, MfC12821. Tension between Japanese Canadian fishermen at Port Edward on the Skeena River and the UFAWU apparently ended when the former abandoned the idea of having a separate union. *New Canadian,* 24 July and 18 August 1954. *HCD,* 15 February 1951, 104-5. Buck Suzuki complained of the Kika Nisei (Canadian-born Japanese who had spent some years in Japan) interfering with radio use by trivial chatter in Japanese. *New Canadian,* 12 December 1959.

14 George Tanaka to Premier, 4 March 1949, JCCA, vol. 9-8, MfC12825; N.W. Macpherson to George Tanaka, 22 April 1949, JCCA, vol. 9-6, MfC12825; H.C. Anderson to T. Tanaka, 23 December 1948, and George Tanaka to Premier of BC, 22 February 1949, JCCA, vol. 15-6, MfC12832; National Executive Committee, minutes, 8 February 1949, JCCA, vol. 2, MfC12819; National JCCA Bulletin, 11 February 1949; *Chinese Times,* 28 February 1947; R.W. Griffith to George Tanaka, 8 July 1949, JCCA, vol. 9-25, MfC12826.

15 *New Canadian,* 12 April 1950, 2 May 1951, 3 May 1952, and 23 March 1962; Submission of National JCCA to the Special Senate Committee on Human Rights and Fundamental Freedoms, May 1950, JCCA, vol. 3, MfC12820; Senate, Proceedings of the Special Committee on Human Rights and Fundamental Freedoms, 10 May 1950; JCCA Executive Meeting, 14 May 1950, JCCA, vol. 2, MfC12819; Seventh Annual BC JCCA Convention, 27 February-1 March 1953, JCCA, vol. 12-13, MfC12829. Edith Fowke, *They Made Democracy Work: The Story of the Co-Operative Committee on Japanese Canadians* (Toronto: CCJC and JCCA, [1951]), 32.

16 Rafe Mair, *Canada: Is Anyone Listening?* (Toronto: Key Porter, 1998), 39.

17 JCCA submission to Royal Commission on Japanese Canadian Property, 12 November 1948, signed by T.K. Shoyama and George Tanaka, CCJC, vol. 1. See Roy Miki, *Redress: Inside the Japanese Canadian Call for Justice* (Vancouver: Raincoast, 2004), 100-1, and Ken Adachi, *The Enemy that Never Was* (Toronto: McClelland and Stewart, 1976), 322-23; JCCA Submission to Royal Commission on Japanese Canadian Property, 12 November 1948, JCCA, vol. 1. A Department of External Affairs official suggested that, to protect the property of Canadians in the Far East, the personal property of Japanese in Canada should be properly stored and protected at government expense and sold only with the owner's consent. There is no evidence of any heed being paid to this recommendation. S.M. Scott, Memo, 15 June 1943, and Under-Secretary of State for External Affairs to Consul General of Spain, 12 July 1943, DLab, vol. 655. Hugh Keenleyside to Peter Loudon, 8 November 1967, HLKP, vol. 20.

18 Lieutenant L.C. Fletcher advised Nisei serving with Canadian forces in Malaysia that as soldiers they could not "take part in public agitation of any sort" but could appeal to MPs such as M.J. Coldwell for help in gaining redress for properties lost by their families; George Tanaka to "Kasey," 30 January 1946, JCCA, vol. 7-2, MfC12823; *Columbian,* 1 November 1946; D. Badger, "Passing Judgment," *Western Miner* (1946): 35; [George Tanaka?] to "Kasey," 30 January 1946, JCCA, vol. 2-7.

19 *Columbian,* 1 November 1946; R.G. Robertson to A. MacNamara, 9 July 1946, BCSCR, vol. 34-2201; Lieutenant L.C. Fletcher to all Nisei in Draft, *RULLP Newsletter,* 30 July 1946. See also Roy Ito, *We*

Went to War: The Story of Japanese Canadians Who Served during the First and Second World Wars (Etobicoke, ON: S-20; Nisei Veterans Association, 1984), 273. *New Canadian,* 9 and 16 November 1946; *Ladner Optimist,* 31 January 1946.

20 *Vancouver Sun,* 23 January 1947; Cabinet Conclusions, 10 March, 30 April, and 12 July 1947, PCOR, MfT2365; Special Cabinet Committee on Claims by Japanese Evacuees, 24 March 1947, BCSCR, vol. 35-2203; Cabinet Committee on Japanese Questions, 21 April 1947, DLab, vol. 639; *HCD,* 18 February 1947, 539; A.R. Menzies to Under-Secretary of State for External Affairs, 21 April 1947, DEAR, series G-1/263-38.

21 Robert Edmonds and R.M. King to W.L.M. King, 31 December 1945, KP, #344885-86; W.J. Gallagher to John Bracken, 8 May 1947, JBP, vol. 22; *Toronto Daily Star,* 19 February, 28 April, and 8 and 15 May 1947. *Nisei Affairs,* 28 February 1947; *Calgary Herald,* 3 January 1947; *Saskatoon Star-Phoenix,* 4 June 1947; W.S. Wallace to Mark Hopkins, 12 September 1977, CCJC, vol. 1.

22 Lambertson, *Repression and Resistance,* 139. Andrew Brewin to W.L.M. King, 21 April 1947, KP, #381827-28; *Nisei Affairs,* 28 February 1947. Japanese American property losses are summarized in Commission on Wartime Relocation and Internment of Civilians, *Personal Justice Denied* (Seattle: University of Washington Press, 1997) [first published, Washington: Government Printing Office, 1982 and 1983], Chapter 4.

23 Toronto *Globe and Mail,* 14, 15, and 24 May 1947; Toronto *Evening Telegram,* 12 May 1947; *Toronto Daily Star,* 6 and 15 May 1947; *HCD,* 14 May 1947, 3085; Montreal *Gazette,* 16 May 1947; *Saskatoon Star-Phoenix,* 4 June 1947.

24 *Colonist,* 15 May 1947; *Vancouver Sun,* 10 May and 5 June 1947, 22 March 1948; Vancouver *News-Herald,* 12 May 1947.

25 A representative letter is G.J. Matte to Hazel M. Journier, 28 May 1947, KP, J2, vol. 473, file P-30-9; W.G. Clark to Douglas Abbott, 19 April 1947, DFin, vol. 3986, file P-2-S; Toronto *Globe and Mail,* 19 June and 3 July 1947; *Toronto Daily Star,* 26 July, 6 September, and 17 September 1947; N.F. Black to W.L.M. King, 21 August 1947, KP, #381612-16; Civil Liberties Union, Vancouver Branch, to W.L.M. King, 23 August 1947, KP, #382546-57; *Vancouver Sun,* 25 July 1947; Cabinet Conclusions, 11 September 1947, PCOR, series A-5-a, vol. 2640, MfT2365.

26 Report of discussion between Brewin and delegates, 2 September 1947, and Minutes of JCCA Meeting, 30 August-2 September 1947, JCCA, vol. 1-8; Roger Obata to W.L.M. King, 10 September 1947, KP, #387775ff.; Miki, *Redress,* 114.

27 *North Shore Press,* 1 August 1947; *Columbian,* 1 November 1946, 26 November 1947, and 5 February 1948; *Vancouver Sun,* 25 July and 1 October 1947; *Vernon News,* 19 February 1948. Descriptions and critiques of the Bird Commission may be found in Adachi, *The Enemy that Never Was,* 325 ff., and Miki, *Redress,* 111-27.

28 Andrew Brewin to CCJC, 13 April 1949, Margaret Boos to Claimants, 16 April 1949, and George Tanaka to Executive of Local JCCA Chapters, 18 March 1950, JCCA, vol. 4-29, MfC12821; Miki, *Redress,* 116-25. Adachi, *The Enemy that Never Was,* 133, has a fairly detailed account of the conflict.

29 H.I. Bird, report, 6 April 1950, 14, 24, 25, 39, 49, 50, 60. A typescript of this report is in LAC, Records of Parliament (RG 14 D2), vol. 559; Cabinet Conclusions, 21 April and 19 June 1950, MfT2366.

30 Cabinet Conclusions, 19 June 1950, PCOR, MfT2366; Toronto *Globe and Mail,* 14 and 15 June 1950. Many newspapers (e.g., Montreal *Star,* 14 June 1950; *Calgary Herald,* 14 June 1950; *Halifax Herald,* 14 June 1950, and Regina *Leader-Post,* 13 June 1950) published wire service reports without comment and mainly in inconspicuous positions. Surprisingly, neither the *Winnipeg Free Press* nor the *Ottawa Journal* reported it. *Vancouver Sun,* 14 June 1950; *Toronto Daily Star,* 14 June 1950; *Times,* 14 June 1950.

31 *New Canadian,* 21 June and 18 October 1950; James M. Finlay to L.S. St. Laurent, 14 July 1950, and L.S. St. Laurent to James M. Finlay, 3 August 1950, FABP, vol. 2; James M. Finlay to L.S. St. Laurent, 24 October 1950, and L.S. St. Laurent to George Tanaka, 5 October 1950, PCOR, vol. 167, file J-25-1.

32 E. Kagetsu to John Diefenbaker, 16 March 1954, JGDP, #47163, and E. Kagetsu to John Diefenbaker, 26 March 1954, JGDP, #47166-68. The stock answer remained on government files. In 1968, when the Committee on Evangelism and Social Action of the BC Synod of the Presbyterian Church asked John Turner, the minister of justice, to create a commission to take further measures for redress, Turner replied with a copy of the recommendations of the Bird Commission. D.J.M. Corbett to Grace MacInnis, 10 May 1969, LAC, Grace MacInnis Papers, vol. 10; John Diefenbaker to E. Kagetsu, 27 March 1954, JGDP, #47173; E. Kagetsu to Julian Ferguson, 31 March 1954, JGDP, #47181; T. Shata, Executive Secretary, JCCA, to Provincial Liaison Officers, 31 March 1954, JCCA, MfC12819; *HCD,*

16 June 1954, 6094, 6098. Fulton agreed with MacInnis that the Japanese had not had full justice but noted that Canadians who had suffered because of internment of themselves or close relatives had not had "full justice" either. Two years later, in July 1956, D.L. Jones (CCF, Okanagan-Boundary) and Erhart Regier (CCF, Burnaby-Coquitlam) raised the matter, but then Secretary of State Roch Pinard merely said that he would try to get information about the property claims of Japanese Canadians. *HCD,* 4 July 1956, 5655, 5659.

33 *HCD,* 5 July 1960, 5743; Miki, *Redress,* 126; *New Canadian,* 2 October 1954. The government flatly rejected the claim of Hokuro Hirai, a Japanese national, who had operated a silk store and hosiery factory in Toronto and had returned to Japan because "the Peace Treaty with Japan makes no provision for the consideration of claims for compensation to Japanese nationals, formerly resident in Canada, whose properties were confiscated during the war." It suggested that he seek compensation from the government of Japan. J.S. Cross to Hokuro Hirai, 14 July 1954, PCOR, vol. 103, file W-20-2-H.

34 *HCD,* 1 May 1947, 2646; W.L.M. King, Diary, 22 January and 1 May 1947, King Papers, LAC. Before the war, Canadian missionaries and traders in Japan saw it as a bulwark against Communism. John D. Meehan, *The Dominion and the Rising Sun: Canada Encounters Japan, 1929-1941* (Vancouver: UBC Press, 2004), 97.

35 *L'Action catholique,* 2 May 1947; Senate Standing Committee on Immigration and Labour, 25 July 1946.

36 Roy W. Brown of the *Vancouver Sun* remained concerned about the possible return of what he erroneously claimed were 12,000 Canadian-born Japanese. Toronto *Financial Post,* 3 January 1953. Although Fulton said that the Japanese immigration question was closed, Green demanded that the government state how it would prevent it. S.S. McKeen (Liberal), the only BC senator to refer to Japanese immigration, repeated stories of the military ambitions of the Japanese in British Columbia, their lower standards of living, and their concentration in the province and warned of the possibility of riots and bloodshed if they returned to the West Coast. *HCD,* 11 February 1947, 316-19; 1 May 1947, 2646; 2 May 1947, 2699; 5 May 1947, 2784-85; *SD,* 8 May 1947, 324; *Langley Advance,* 2 January 1947; *Times,* 2 May 1947; Prince Rupert *Daily News,* 5 May 1947; *Vancouver Sun,* 14 and 21 May 1947 and 1 March 1949.

37 George Tanaka to Deputy Minister of Mines and Resources, 8 December 1947, JCCA, MfC12827; *New Canadian,* 26 May 1948; N.A. Robertson to E.H. Norman, 3 and 5 July 1946, and Hume Wrong to Acting Secretary of State for External Affairs, 10 August 1946, DEAR, vol. 3766, file 7648-K-40C. The Department of External Affairs opposed a British suggestion that for security reasons the control authority in Japan should "control all forms of emigration." R.E. Collins to A.R. Menzies, 18 September 1947, DEAR, vol. 4613, file 50051-40, part 3.

38 Mrs. E. Kitagawa to N.A. Robertson, 4 April 1946, LAC, N.W. Fujiwara-M. Kitagawa Collection; H.H. Wrong to Minister of Immigration, 15 August 1946, DEAR, vol. 3766, file 7648-K-40-C; Report to Provincial JCCA Chapters, 5 July 1948, JCCA, file 10-14, MfC12827; *New Canadian,* 12 May 1948; 1 June, 27 July, and 1 October 1949; and 25 August 1950.

39 *New Canadian,* 10 January, 21 February, and 14 March 1951. Canada did not officially terminate a state of war with Germany until July 1951; JCCA, National Executive Minutes, 21 January 1951, JCCA, MfC12819; JCCA President's Message, Third Annual Conference, 22 April 1950, JCCA, vol. 12-20, MfC12829; George Tanaka to Minister of Citizenship and Immigration, 27 June 1951, JCCA, MfC12826.

40 *HCD,* 10 December 1949, 3143, and 16 June 1951, 3300-1; *New Canadian,* 11 July 1951; Cabinet Conclusions, 2 August 1951, in Greg Donaghy, ed., *Documents on Canadian External Relations,* vol. 17, 1951 (Ottawa: Department of Foreign Affairs and International Trade, 1996), 1828; A.R. Menzies to Under-Secretary of State for External Affairs, 10 August 1951, DEAR, vol. 3622, file 2722-AH-40.

41 *New Canadian,* 5 December 1951, 2 and 20 February and 8 March 1952, and 1 December 1956; George Tanaka to Ted Aoki, 3 February 1952, JCCA, MfC12821. A fisherman born in Steveston married a Japanese woman in Japan in 1940. He applied to bring her to Canada, but the war intervened. Once he was permitted to resume fishing, he returned to Steveston, but despite favourable letters from three Caucasians – the managers of the cannery and the Royal Bank in Steveston and a building contractor – the Department of Immigration ruled that his wife was a Japanese citizen and therefore non-admissible, but their sons born in 1941 and after his 1950 visit were. The correspondence is in JCCA, MfC12827.

42 *Province,* 6 January 1950; *SD,* 2 April 1952, 146-47; C.S. Gadd to Mr. McCardle, 23 April 1952, DEAR, vol. 128; George Tanaka to W. Harris, 23 June 1952, JCCA, MfC12825; C. Isbister to Secretary of State for External Affairs, 5 June 1964, LBPP, vol. 207.

43 *New Canadian,* 7 April 1954; *HCD,* 24 April 1953, 4354, and 24 March 1955, 2331; R.W. Mayhew to Under-Secretary of State, 7 January 1954, and Press Conference, St. Laurent, Tokyo, 11 March 1954, DEAR, vol. 6153, file 11563-5-11-40; Minister of Citizenship and Immigration to Cabinet, 18 April 1955, DEAR, vol. 3977.

44 JCCA Meeting, 28 April 1952, JCCA, MfC12819; *New Canadian,* 16 July 1952; Cabinet Conclusions, 12 March 1953, PCOR, MfT2369; Ministers of Citizenship and Immigration and of External Affairs to Cabinet, 23 February 1956, *DCER,* vol. 23, 1390; Laval Fortier to C.E. Smith, 26 March 1956, DC&I, vol. 128.

45 T. Ebata to M. Sumiya, 10 March 1955, JCCA, MfC12819; *New Canadian,* 22 October 1955, and 1, 18, and 29 February 1956; Toronto *Globe and Mail,* 2 January 1956; "Japanese Immigration, Prepared for Mr. Howe's Visit," 8 October 1956, DEAR, vol. 3977.

46 *SD,* 20 May 1954, 492-98; JCCA, Executive Committee Meeting, 6 November 1955, MfC12819; Jules Leger to Laval Fortier, 4 March 1957, DC&I, vol. 128. The embassy carefully noted that it had nothing to do with JCCA petitions and that "the legal ties of the Japanese Canadians with Japan are completely broken" when it complained informally about long delays in approving the entry of Japanese nationals, including relatives of Japanese Canadians and Japanese businessmen. Japanese Embassy, aide memoire, July 1958, DC&I, vol. 128; *New Canadian,* 23 March 1957.

47 As early as 1946, Canadians of Japanese and of Chinese descent in Toronto had some joint social activities, such as a badminton competition. *Nisei Affairs,* 16 December 1946. The JCCA considered working with the Chinese in 1948. National Executive Meeting, 16 June 1948, JCCA, MfC12819; *New Canadian,* 18 and 21 July 1951; Ted Aoki to George Tanaka, 15 August 1951, JCCA, MfC12821; JCCA, Minutes of Meeting, 6 June 1952, JCCA, MfC12819. The co-operation of the Japanese and the Chinese in lobbying for immigration reforms appears to belie Freda Hawkins' observation that ethnic groups seldom had much concern for other groups. However, the comparative brevity of their formal association suggests that her general observation holds. Freda Hawkins, *Canada and Immigration* (Montreal and Kingston: McGill-Queen's University Press, 1972), 248.

48 General Meeting of Chinese Canadian Association, 9 February 1958, Minutes, Executive Meeting, 16 November 1956, and "Report on the Variety Show of CCA, January 1957," CCA; Report of the Toronto Immigration Committee, March 1956-December 1957, in JCCA, MfC12826; *New Canadian,* 13 March 1957; Chinese Canadian Association and Japanese Canadian Citizens Association to J.W. Pickersgill, 9 March 1957, JCCA, MfC12826; Stan Hiraki and Ruth Lor to J.W. Pickersgill, 9 March 1957, and J.W. Pickersgill to Stan Hiraki and Ruth Lor, 12 March 1957, JWPP, vol. 45; J.W. Pickersgill to Foon Sien, 18 June 1957, JWPP, vol. 46; Minutes, Executive Meeting, 16 November 1956, CCRA, vol. 1. When it seemed that the Korean War might lead to a full-scale war with China, some Vancouver Chinese feared being "uprooted from their homes as were the Japanese Canadians during World War II." *New Canadian,* 24 January 1951. At hearings of an Ontario Royal Commission on Civil Rights in 1965, the JCCA said that in a war against China the Chinese might experience the same "harsh treatment" that its members had faced. *New Canadian,* 5 May 1965; *Chinatown News,* 18 May 1965.

49 Memo on Canada-Japan Relations, 2 June 1957, DEAR, vol. 6872, file 4606-C-21-40; Information Division to Far Eastern Division, 19 September 1954, DEAR, vol. 6830, file 2727-AH-40.

50 *New Canadian,* 5 June 1957; JCCA, Executive Meeting, 19 February 1958, JCCA, MfC12819; *HCD,* 21 May 1958, 329; CCA and JCCA to Minister, June 1958, copy in HWHP, vol. 40; Report of Delegation, 20 June 1958, JCCA, MfC12826.

51 Executive Minutes, 2 December 1958 and 4 November 1965, CCA; *Chinatown News,* 18 April and 3 May 1966; *New Canadian,* 23 March 1966.

52 *HCD,* 25 January 1960, 258; Memo, Visit to Ottawa of Japanese Foreign Minister, Zentaro Kosaka, 14-16 September 1960; I.M. Teackles to Far East Division, 8 May 1961; Embassy, Tokyo, to External, 10 and 21 October 1961; G.A. Cowley to B.A. Keith, 27 October 1961; and W.F. Bull to Zentaro Kosaka, 28 October 1961, DEAR, vol. 5081, file 4606-C-21-40; *New Canadian,* 4 March 1959; *Toronto Daily Star,* 30 October 1961. In 1960 Japan sent five engineers to explore copper deposits in the Highland Valley near Kamloops; in 1962 several whalers came to teach British Columbians how to track whales and prepare them for human food. *Winnipeg Free Press,* 24 May 1960; *Vancouver Sun,* 17 November 1961 and 31 March 1962.

53 *New Canadian,* 18 June 1952 and 16 January 1960; K. Sumiya, Vice Consul, Vancouver, to George Tanaka, 24 February 1953, JCCA, vol. 14-2, MfC12831; Toru Hagiwara to Editor, *New Canadian,* 6 February 1960; JCCA, Executive Meeting, 23 March 1960, JCCA, MfC12819.

54 JCCA to Ellen Fairclough, 19 July 1960, JGDP, #102886. The brief was widely circulated. Copies are in HWHP and LBPP; JCCA, Executive Meeting, 13 November 1960, 24 September 1963, 29 April and 20 May 1965, JCCA, MfC12819; *HCD*, 10 February 1961, 1946. *New Canadian*, 23 July 1960.

55 National Report to the Sixth JCCA Conference, Toronto, 1-3 September 1961, JCCA, file 12-18, MfC12829; *New Canadian*, 28 November 1959, 10 June 1959, 9 March and 24 August 1960, and 11 February 1961; "Lower the Color Barriers," *Star Weekly*, 20 August 1960; *Vancouver Sun*, 24 and 29 June 1961.

56 *HCD*, 19 January 1962, 9-11; *New Canadian*, 27 January 1962.

57 *New Canadian*, 8 April and 27 May 1964, 19 January 1966; *HCD*, 14 August 1964, 6823-24; Tokyo to Ottawa, 8 May 1964, R.B. Curry to Under-Secretary of State, 22 May 1964, Tokyo to Department of External Affairs, 1 and 24 December 1964, H.F. Clark to Tokyo, 2 December 1964, DEAR, vol. 10192, file 83-6-Japan-1; C. Isbister to Minister, 5 June 1964, LBPP, vol. 207-572; *Maclean's*, 6 June 1964, 2-3.

58 C. Isbister to Minister, 6 December 1964, DC&I, vol. 128; Tokyo to Under-Secretary of State, 29 July 1965, DEAR, vol. 10192, file 83-6-Japan-1; *New Canadian*, 2 June 1965 and 19 January 1966.

59 *Times*, 20 and 21 September 1966; L.B. Pearson to R. Tremblay, 30 December 1964, LBPP, vol. 723, file 551-25; *New Canadian*, 15 June 1966; *Province*, 1 October 1966.

60 *Ottawa Journal*, 21 September 1966; *Calgary Herald*, 21 September 1966; *Toronto Daily Star*, 21 September 1966; *Christian Science Monitor*, reprinted in Regina *Leader-Post*, 20 September 1966.

61 *Vancouver Sun*, 21 September 1966; *Colonist*, 22 September 1966.

62 *New Canadian*, 11 March 1964, 21 and 28 September and 5 October 1966; JCCA Meeting, 16 November 1966, JCCA, MfC12819. Jack Brooks, in *Vancouver Sun*, 7 October 1967.

63 *Province*, 1 October 1966; R.B. Curry to Under-Secretary of State for External Affairs, 22 November 1966, and R. Goldsclag to R.B. Curry, 12 December 1966, DEAR, vol. 10192, file 83-6-6-Japan-1; *New Canadian*, 25 January, 27 May, and 6 September 1967; *Financial Post*, 22 August 1970. The last quotation is from a reprint of a Vancouver *Daily Province* article.

Chapter 7: Ending Chinese Exclusion

1 W. Noyes to W.E. Harris, 22 March 1950, HWHP, vol. 40; CBA, Brief Concerning Immigration Laws Submitted to the Cabinet, 24 March 1950, JCCA, MfC12826; R.G. Robertson to J.W. Pickersgill, 29 March 1950, PCOR, vol. 166, file I-50-3.

2 Walter Harris to Foon Sien, 14 February 1950, and Foon Sien to Walter Harris, 5 March 1952, DC&I, vol. 125; CBA, Brief Concerning Immigration Laws Submitted to the Cabinet, 24 March 1950 [resubmitted 18 April 1951], JCCA, MfC12826.

3 *HCD*, 23 June 1950, 4048-50; Deputy Minister of Citizenship and Immigration [Laval Fortier] to Walter Harris, 26 June 1950, and Jean Boucher to Laval Fortier, 30 November 1950, DC&I, vol. 125; Toronto *Globe and Mail*, 2 June 1950.

4 Cabinet Conclusions, 21 December 1950; PC 6229, 28 December 1950, Laval Fortier to Director of Immigration, 26 June 1951, DC&I, vol. 125. The Asian-language press was notified of the change in a press release on 22 March 1951; *Times*, 22 November 1950; *HCD*, 6 December 1951, 1634.

5 Interview by W.E. Wilmott, Duncan, BC, 15 April 1961[?], CCRC, vol. 11.

6 Foon Sien to Walter Harris, 5 March 1952, and Walter Harris to Cabinet, 10 June 1952, DC&I, vol. 125; *Province*, 8 and 10 April 1952; Vancouver *News-Herald*, 10 April 1952; *Vancouver Sun*, 12 April 1952.

7 Walter Harris to Cabinet, draft, 13 November 1952, DC&I, vol. 128; IWA to Government of Canada, 19 March 1952, PCOR, file I-50-12; *HCD*, 28 March 1952, 906; 4 July 1952, 4271-72; 24 April 1953, 4354-55, 4363, and 4384. Two Newfoundland Progressive Conservative MPs made similar pleas on behalf of the close relatives of Chinese. Harris claimed that x-rays were useful to about age twenty-three, and Hong Kong staff used them only after they rejected an applicant as a result of other investigations.

8 Minutes of Senate Standing Committee on Immigration and Labour, 15 April 1953, PCOR, file I-50-12.

9 C.E. Smith to Deputy, 23 June 1954; Director, Immigration Branch, to Deputy, 21 May 1954; and Laval Fortier to J.W. Pickersgill, 27 September 1954, JWPP, vol. 46.

10 *London Free Press*, 11 April 1954; Wong Foon Sien to Walter Harris, 29 April 1954, JWPP, vol. 47; P.S. Baldwin, Director of Citizenship and Immigration, to Chief, Admissions Division, 13 May 1954, and C.E. Smith to Deputy Minister, 22 June 1954, JWPP, vol. 46. Such cases were handled by the Superintendent in Hong Kong, who acted as consul. Between 1948 and 1954, there were 109 such cases. In nine the applicant was given the benefit of the doubt, and seventeen cases were still under review. Forty-five were impostors, thirty-three did not pursue the matter after being refused, and five women

had lost their citizenship through marriage. C.E. Smith to Deputy Minister, 21 September 1954, JWPP, vol. 46.

11 *HCD,* 26 June 1954, 6790-6834.

12 J.W. Pickersgill, "The Place of Immigration in National Development," Speech at Dauphin, Manitoba, 3 November 1954, Mabel Timlin Papers, University of Saskatchewan Archives, vol. 8; *HCD,* 17 February 1955, 1243; Quoted in J.W. Pickersgill to Cabinet, 12 October 1955, and J.W. Pickersgill to Vaughan Lyon, 22 May 1956, JWPP, vol. 45; J.W. Pickersgill to Foon Sien, 7 October 1954; Director to Deputy, 7 January 1966; R. O'Connor, Memorandum, c. 10 March 1955; M.C. Hoey to J. Ross Ker, 15 June 1955; and J.W. Pickersgill to Robert Harvey, 28 March 1956, JWPP, vol. 46.

13 Thomas C. Marshall, quoted in *New Canadian,* 5 January 1955. *New Canadian,* 23 October 1954; Foon Sien to Ralph Campney, 30 May 1955, JWPP, vol. 46; Foon Sien, "Yesterday, Today, Tomorrow," *Chinatown News,* 3 November 1956; *HCD,* 15 February 1955, 1165, 1168, 1175, 1191, and 1193, and 17 February 1955, 1243.

14 J.W. Pickersgill to Deputy Minister, 30 May 1955, DC&I, vol. 125; Laval Fortier to J.W. Pickersgill, 6 June 1955, with notes by Pickersgill; J.W. Pickersgill to Foon Sien, 8 June 1955; and M.C. Hoey to J. Ross Ker, 11 June 1955, JWPP, vol. 46; J.W. Pickersgill to Cabinet, 12 October 1955, and press release, 17 October 1955, JWPP, vol. 45; PC 1955-521, 12 October 1955.

15 Foon Sien to J.W. Pickersgill, 17 November 1955, and J.W. Pickersgill to Foon Sien, 26 November 1955, JWPP, vol. 45; Davie Fulton to Anthony J. Wright, 27 October 1955, and Anthony J. Wright to Davie Fulton, 14 October 1955, EDFP, vol. 12.

16 *Province,* 29 October and 1 and 3 November 1955; *Ottawa Citizen,* 2 November 1955; *Chinatown News,* 18 January 1956.

17 CBA to Pickersgill, 25 May 1956, DC&I, vol. 125; Minutes, Executive Meeting, CCA, 16 November 1956, CCAR. In 1945 the Chinese Community Centre of Ontario changed its name from the Chinese Protection Federation, which had been concerned with helping China in the war against Japan. Richard H. Thompson, *Toronto's Chinatown: The Changing Social Organization of an Ethnic Community* (New York: AMS Press, 1989), 69-71. J.W. Pickersgill to Deputy, 26 May 1956, DC&I, vol. 125; C.E. Smith to Deputy Minister, 18 July 1956, and Laval Fortier to J.W. Pickersgill, 27 July 1956, JWPP, vol. 46.

18 Foon Sien, "'The Waiting People': Do They Hope in Vain?" *Chinatown News,* 18 April 1956; *Vancouver Sun,* 29 May 1956. Also quoted in *New Canadian,* 5 June 1956; Vaughan Lyon to J.W. Pickersgill, 4 May 1956, JWPP, vol. 45; *HCD,* 7 August 1956, 7167, and 8 August 1956, 7201, 7205.

19 *HCD,* 8 August 1956, 7209; C.E. Smith to J.W. Pickersgill, 2 March 1957, JWPP, vol. 46; *Chinatown News,* 18 August 1956.

20 The RCMP refused the request of the immigration department that it screen Canadian sponsors of immigrants, saying that it was short-handed and believed that "the security benefits derived would be almost negative and would not justify the extra work involved." Laval Fortier to J.W. Pickersgill, 28 December 1956, and J.W. Pickersgill to Deputy Minister, 11 August 1956, JWPP, vol. 46; *HCD,* 8 August 1956, 7207-13.

21 *HCD,* 8 August 1956, 7208; Davie Fulton to Foon Sien, 9 August 1956, Foon Sien to Davie Fulton, 27 August 1956, and J.W. Pickersgill to Robert Harvey, 10 January 1957, EDFP, vol. 12; Foon Sien to J.W. Pickersgill, 27 August and 17 December 1956, JWPP, vol. 46; *Vancouver Sun,* 13 August 1956; *New Canadian,* 1 September 1956 and 5 January 1957.

22 Recommendation to Council, 23 February 1955, J.W. Pickersgill to Foon Sien, 8 September 1956, Laval Fortier to J.W. Pickersgill, 5 July 1955, Foon Sien to J.W. Pickersgill, 15 June 1957, and J.W. Pickersgill to Foon Sien, 18 June 1957, JWPP, vol. 46; *HCD,* 9 June 1960, 4714-15; 7 August 1956, 7166; and 9 August 1956, 7348.

23 For Jung and the 1957 election, see Chapter 4. Ian G. Pyper to Lyle Justley, 9 October 1957, EDFP, vol. 35.

24 Minutes, Executive Meeting, 13 November 1957, and Sid Blum, Director, Jewish Labour Committee of Canada, to Ruth Lor, 17 December 1957, CCAR; *HCD,* 15 January 1958, 3385; 25 January 1958, 3840; and 30 January 1958, 4061. The joint CCA-JCCA delegation is discussed above, pp. 253-55.

25 CBA, Brief, to Ellen Fairclough, 25 July 1958, DC&I, vol. 125; CCA and JCCA to the Minister of Citizenship and Immigration, June 1958, copy in LBPP, vol. 47; Report of Delegation, 20 June 1958, JCCA, MfC12826. D. Jung to J.G. Diefenbaker, 2 June 1959, JGDP, #244670ff. On Pickersgill's advice, the Liberals made no comment. General Meeting of CCA, 9 February 1958, CCAR, vol. 1.

26 CBA, Brief Concerning Immigration Law for Presentation to the Honourable Ellen Fairclough, 25 July 1958, DC&I, vol. 125; Cabinet Committee on Immigration, 29 July 1958, DC&I, vol. 128. Phrases that questioned "Chinese standards of truth and morality" were crossed out. C.E. Smith to Deputy Minister of Citizenship and Immigration, 7 August 1958, DImm, vol. 223; Ellen Fairclough to Cabinet, 8 August 1958, PCOR, file I-50-12; *HCD,* 23 August 1958, 4027, 4030, and 4037; and 4 and 5 March 1959, 1618, 1636, 1639, 1643, and 1645; J.W. Pickersgill to Miss McQuarrie, 7 October 1959, LBPP, vol. 40; *Chinese Times,* 31 March 1958, DC&I, vol. 125 (translation); CBA, Brief, to Ellen Fairclough, 24 June 1958, HWHP, vol. 22. On 1 May 1960, the Joint Committee of Oriental Associations of Calgary presented a brief to Fairclough recommending an annual quota of 500 Oriental persons, including refugees, plus 500 orphans who would be sponsored by relatives who were Canadian citizens. Calgary City Council, various Progressive Conservative associations, church groups, and chambers of commerce in Calgary supported them. Copy in JGDP, #48168ff.

27 Ray Perrault to L.B. Pearson, 22 October and 5 November 1959, and James Bissett to M. Macdonald, 2 November 1958, LBPP, vol. 40; *Vancouver Sun,* 26 October 1959; *Ottawa Citizen,* 22 October 1959. Chan later sued Jung for libel because Jung questioned how a man who deserted his family could be a good citizen. The case was eventually dismissed. *HCD,* 9 June 1960, 4720-21. Ellen Louks Fairclough, *Saturday's Child: Memoirs of Canada's First Female Cabinet Minister* (Toronto: University of Toronto Press, 1995), 113.

28 *Vancouver Sun,* 1 June 1962; *Toronto Daily Star,* 11 and 22 May and 11 June 1962; Toronto *Globe and Mail,* 18, 21, 22, and 28 May 1962.

29 *Toronto Daily Star,* 26 and 30 May and 4 June 1962; Toronto *Globe and Mail,* 14 and 25 May 1962; Erhart Regier, *HCD,* 15 July 1960, 6388-89; *Chinese Times,* 9 May 1962; *Province,* 10 May 1962, quoted in *Chinatown News,* 18 May 1962; Geneva to Ottawa and G.S. Murray, 18 May 1962; Department of External Affairs to London, 23 May 1962; G.F. Davidson to Director, 28 May 1962; and D.M. Sloan, Memo to File, 12 June 1962, DImm, vol. 914.

30 *Province,* 15 and 23 May 1962; *Chinatown News,* 3 June 1962; *Toronto Daily Star,* 19, 23, and 24 May 1962.

31 Superintendent of Immigration, Hong Kong, to Chief of Operations, Ottawa, 25 May 1962; Record of Cabinet Decision, Meeting of 28 May 1962; and F.W. Millard to Superintendent, Hong Kong, 5 June 1962, DImm, vol. 914; Acting Director of Immigration to Acting Deputy Minister, 18 October 1963, DC&I, vol. 125.

32 D.M. Sloan, Memo for File, 12 June 1962; Acting Director of Immigration to Deputy Minister, 14 November 1962; and G.F. Davidson to Minister, 14 November 1962, DImm, vol. 914; *Chinese Bulletin,* July-August 1962. The *Chinatown News* said that the *Bulletin,* though claiming to be politically neutral, promoted Communist ideas in its Chinese-language pages. *Chinatown News,* 18 July 1961; *Toronto Daily Star,* 3 and 11 June and 30 July 1962; Toronto *Globe and Mail,* 15 November 1962.

33 *Province,* 29 October and 3 November 1955.

34 *Vancouver Sun,* 26 August 1961; Jean Lumb, in *Jin Guo: Voices of Chinese Canadian Women,* ed. Momoye Sugiman and Women's Book Committee, Chinese Canadian National Council (Toronto: Women's Press, 1992), 49; Thompson, *Toronto's Chinatown,* 104.

35 Ellen Fairclough and Davie Fulton to Cabinet, 24 March 1960, DC&I, vol. 125; J.K. Abbott, Director of Inspection Services, Department of Citizenship and Immigration, to Sub-Inspector G.N. Jones, Passport and Visa Fraud Section, RCMP, Memo, 12 April 1960, EDFP, vol. 35. Some details on the background of the breakup of illegal immigration may be found in Freda Hawkins, *Canada and Immigration: Public Policy and Public Concern* (Montreal and Kingston: McGill-Queen's University Press, 1972), 131-32. A brief account of the American confession program and its background may be found in Mae M. Ngai, *Impossible Subjects: Illegal Aliens and the Making of Modern America* (Princeton: Princeton University Press, 2004), Chapter 6.

36 *Chinese Times,* 12 and 13 April and 13 May 1960; Bruce Larsen, in *Vancouver Sun,* 24 May 1960; Toronto *Globe and Mail,* 25 May 1960; *Province,* 25 May 1960; Montreal *Star,* 24 May 1960; *Toronto Daily Star,* 25 May 1960; *La Presse,* 25 May 1960; *Calgary Herald,* 25 May 1960; *Winnipeg Free Press,* 25 May 1960; *HCD,* 25 May 1960, 4221, and 6 June 1960, 4533; Interview with S.P. Spalding, RCMP, n.d., copy in EDFP, vol. 35.

37 *Vancouver Sun,* 25 May 1960; Halifax *Chronicle-Herald,* 26 May 1960; *Toronto Daily Star,* 26 May 1960; *Winnipeg Free Press,* 25 and 26 May 1960; Toronto *Globe and Mail,* 27 May 1960.

38 *Le Devoir,* 25 May 1960; *Toronto Daily Star,* 26 May 1960; *Vancouver Sun,* 24 May 1960; W.C. Wong,

Chinese Community Centre of Ontario, "The Chinese Community Centre Association Asks Fair Play for a Minority Group," copy in LBPP, vol. 78 (capitals in original); Chinese Communities of Canada to Prime Minister and Minister of Citizenship and Immigration, n.d., CCAR (this appears to be another version of Emergency Council of Chinese Communities of Canada [Toronto] to John Diefenbaker, 20 June 1960, JGDP, #190098; Chinese Community Centre of Toronto, "The Chinese Community Centre Association Asks Fair Play for a Minority Group," LBPP, vol. 78; *Toronto Daily Star,* 27 May 1960; Montreal *Gazette,* 27 May 1960; CBA, National Headquarters, to H.W. Herridge, 3 June 1950, HWHP, vol. 40. In response to Pearson's question, Fulton said that complaints of mistreatment were unfounded and that the Hong Kong police had been carefully instructed in Canadian police methods and laws. *HCD,* 23 June 1950, 5285.

39 *HCD,* 6 June 1960, 4533; 9 June 1960, 4710, 4716, 4723, and 4759; 5 July 1960, 5810-12.

40 *HCD,* 9 June 1960, 4720-22, 4736; 16 June 1960, 5000-1 and 5007.

41 *HCD,* 6 July 1960, 5815, and 8 February 1961, 1912; Ellen Fairclough to John Diefenbaker, 4 July 1961, EDFP, vol. 35; Ellen Fairclough to John Diefenbaker, 4 July 1961, DC&I, vol. 125.

42 *HCD,* 25 May 1961, 5490-91; Ellen Fairclough to John Diefenbaker, 4 July 1961, and Ellen Fairclough to Davie Fulton, 24 July 1961, EDFP, vol. 35; Ellen Fairclough to John Diefenbaker, 4 July 1961, DC&I, vol. 125; *Vancouver Sun,* 31 August 1961, reprinted in *Chinatown News,* 18 September 1961; *Chinatown News,* 3 September 1961.

43 *Vancouver Sun,* 15, 21, 26, and 28 July 1961; Ian G. Pyper to J. Macaulay, Executive Assistant to Minister of Justice, 4 August 1961, EDFP, vol. 35; "Progress Report on Research into Chinese Social Organization in Vancouver, September 1961," CCRC, vol. 6; *Chinatown News,* 3 August 1961.

44 *New Canadian,* 29 March and 31 May 1961; Ellen Fairclough to John Diefenbaker, 4 July 1961, JGDP, #244630-32; "Statement by the Honourable Ellen L. Fairclough ... 19 January 1962," copy in LBPP, vol. 78; *Toronto Daily Star,* 20 and 22 January 1962; Ninette Kelley and Michael Trebilcock, *The Making of the Mosaic: A History of Canadian Immigration Policy* (Toronto: University of Toronto Press, 1998), 332-33; Fairclough, *Saturday's Child,* 119.

45 *Vancouver Sun,* 19 and 24 January 1962; *Province,* 20 January 1962; *Toronto Daily Star,* 20 and 22 January 1962; Toronto *Globe and Mail,* 20 and 22 January 1962; Montreal *Star,* 19 and 22 January 1962; *La Presse,* 20 and 24 January 1962; *Windsor Star,* quoted in *Le Droit,* 29 January 1962; J.K. Nesbitt, in *Vancouver Sun,* 23 January 1962. Two years later Nesbitt upset the *Chinatown News* when he seemed to say that recent Hong Kong immigrants were setting the Chinese community back several generations because they only worked in vegetable and grocery stores. The paper attacked the stereotyping, noted that the offspring of many grocery operators were business and professional people, and argued that admitting only technicians was neither realistic nor a measure of equality. Nesbitt replied that he was not denigrating grocers but saying that language problems forced the Hong Kong immigrants into the business. He believed that people of good health and reputation who could speak English should be able to come from anywhere and take any job for which they were qualified. He agreed with the *Chinatown News* in giving priority to "applicants who are willing to learn our official language, once admitted; and have the ability to acquire skills." *Chinatown News,* 18 April and 3 May 1964.

46 Edgar Wickberg, ed., *From China to Canada* (Toronto: McClelland and Stewart, 1982), 244 and 298; *Chinese Times,* 22 January 1962; *Chinatown News,* 3 February 1962; Toronto *Globe and Mail,* 22 January 1962; *Province,* 26 January 1962; Hawkins, *Canada and Immigration,* 131.

47 Harry E.S. Fan to Ellen Fairclough, 15 January 1962, EDFP, vol. 35; *HCD,* 25 January 1962, 203, and 26 January 1962, 235.

48 *Vancouver Sun,* 6 April 1962; Quan Lim to Davie Fulton, 7 April 1962, EDFP, vol. 35; Alan Phillips, "The Criminal Society that Dominates the Chinese in Canada," *Maclean's,* 7 April 1962, 49; Lam Tong et al., Chinese Benevolent Association, Circular, 11 April 1962, copy in JGDP, MfM9302; *Chinatown News,* 3 April 1962; *Chinese Bulletin,* April 1962.

49 *Province,* 5 April 1962; *Vancouver Sun,* 28 May and 4, 6, and 9 June 1962; *Chinatown News,* 3 and 18 May 1962.

50 H.H. Stevens (1921, 1926), Ian Mackenzie (1930, 1935-48), and Ralph Campney (1952-57).

51 *Province,* 1 June 1962; *Vancouver Sun,* 1, 15, and 16 June 1962; *Chinatown News,* 18 May 1962.

52 *Province,* 5 June 1962; *Vancouver Sun,* 1, 21, and 28 May and 16 June 1962; *Chinatown News,* 3 and 18 May 1962; Toronto *Globe and Mail,* 23 May 1962; LeRoy L. Brown to Davie Fulton, 10 August 1962, EDFP, vol. 35. A few days before the Fairclough incident, Diefenbaker accepted flowers from Chan's daughter, which led Ron Basford, the Liberal candidate in Vancouver-Burrard, to declare that it was

"cruel and heartless" for Diefenbaker "to play politics with little children and the sufferings of the Chan family." *Vancouver Sun,* 8 June 1962.

53 *Vancouver Sun,* 4 June 1962; *Chinatown News,* 2 and 3 June 1962.

54 *Chinatown News,* 3 June and 3 July 1962; *Chinese Bulletin,* July-August 1962. The latter editorial was reprinted in the *Vancouver Sun,* 10 July 1962. *Vancouver Sun,* 16 July 1962, reprinted in *Chinatown News,* 3 August 1962; *Vancouver Sun,* 19 June 1962. The CCF candidate, Margaret Erickson, secured 5,113 votes; the Social Crediter, George Hahn, 1,779; and an independent, Burton White, 224.

55 *Toronto Daily Star,* 14 and 28 May and 1, 4, 8, and 9 June 1962; Toronto *Globe and Mail,* 21 and 24 May and 11 June 1962. The New Democratic Party (NDP) was the new name of the Co-Operative Commonwealth Federation (CCF).

56 Fairclough, *Saturday's Child,* 114; R.A. Bell and Donald Fleming to Cabinet, 28 September 1962, DC&I, vol. 125; John Diefenbaker, *One Canada: Memoirs of the Right Honourable John G. Diefenbaker,* vol. 3 (Scarborough: Signet, 1978), 125; Cabinet Decision, 8 November 1962, copy in DImm, vol. 877, and at www.collectionscanada.ca/archivianet/020150_e.html (viewed 30 July 2006). In light of this policy, the RCMP discontinued its "massive investigation ... of all suspect cases which entered Canada prior to the announcement of the amnesty." G.F. Davidson to Minister, 4 December 1962, DImm, vol. 877.

57 J.K. Abbott to Deputy Minister, 20 December 1962, DImm, vol. 877.

58 *Chinese Voice,* 26 November 1962, translation in CCRC, vol. 12; Ian Wahn to R.A. Bell, 22 November 1962, and S. Yuen to A.M. Patton, 6 November 1962, DImm, vol. 877; Lam Tong et al., Chinese Benevolent Association, Circular, 11 April 1952, JGDP, MfM9302; *New Republic,* 18 December 1962, translation in DImm, vol. 877; *Chinese Bulletin,* June 1962; *Chinese Times,* 24 September 1962; *Vancouver Sun,* 10, 11, and 17 October 1962.

59 Jack L. Eng to R.A. Bell, 14 January 1963; Report from Ng Toy-win, *New Republic,* 18 December 1962; and R.A. Bell to Douglas Jung, 6 March 1963, DC&I, vol. 125; *Vancouver Sun,* 11 March 1963; *Columbian,* 28 March 1963. The Conservatives also ran Gladys Chong, a native of Victoria and a clothing designer, in the neighbouring constituency of Vancouver East, which had some Chinese voters but, since its creation in 1935, had always elected a CCF MP. Harold Winch, the incumbent who succeeded Angus MacInnis in 1953, held the constituency through four elections. When Chong accused him of racial discrimination, he referred to the CCF record on Asian enfranchisement. *Vancouver Sun,* 22 March 1963; *Province,* 27 March 1963. Nicholson won 9,472 votes; Jung, 7,353; Margaret Erickson, NDP, 5,826; and Bevis Walters, Social Credit, 1,430.

In a provincial election in September, the candidates of the major parties in the two-member constituency of Vancouver Centre "went all out to woo Pender St. support." Leslie Peterson, a cabinet minister, who had the editorial support of the *Chinatown News* because of his championing of civil rights issues, was one of the two successful Social Credit candidates. *Chinatown News,* 18 September and 3 October 1963.

60 *Province,* 1 March 1963; *Chinatown News,* 3 March 1963; Wing Chung Ng, *The Chinese in Vancouver, 1945-80: The Pursuit of Identity and Power* (Vancouver: UBC Press, 1999), 96. *Vancouver Sun,* 12 March and 2 April 1963; L.B. Pearson to Chinese Canadians, Vancouver, 1 April 1963, DC&I, vol. 125.

61 *HCD,* 20 May 1963, 30; 4 July 1963, 1840; and 30 July 1963, 2796; K. Dock Yip and Harry Litt Lam to L.B. Pearson, 25 July 1963, LBPP, vol. 207; Toronto *Evening Telegram,* 28 August 1963; Toronto *Globe and Mail,* quoted in *Chinatown News,* 3 September 1963; *Toronto Daily Star,* 30 May 1962.

62 Guy Favreau to Chinese Community, Vancouver, 23 September 1963, DC&I, vol. 125. A week later Robert Prittie (NDP, Burnaby-Richmond) commended the proposals and urged Favreau and the cabinet to review procedures for citizenship applications that gave arbitrary powers to officials in the Department of Citizenship and Immigration. *HCD,* 3 October 1963, 3192, and 18 October 1963, 3738. Jung later wrote to the *Chinatown News* (3 October 1962) explaining that he had arranged with the immigration minister for the admission of Lee Gan's family the previous March but admitted that the *Vancouver Sun,* not Favreau, was probably responsible for the conclusion. However, the issue did not go away from the Chinese-language press as Harry Fan claimed that the Liberal government admitted the family. *Chinatown News,* 18 October 1963.

63 *Chinatown News,* 3 October and 18 November 1963.

64 *Chinatown News,* 18 January 1964; *HCD,* 14 December 1963, 5883-85, and 20 December 1963, 6237-59.

65 The detailed correspondence is in LBPP, vol. 269. For privacy reasons, some details have been omitted.

66 L.B. Pearson to Wilf Gardiner, 1 February 1965, LBPP, vol. 269.

67 Acting Director of Immigration to Acting Deputy Minister, 18 October 1963, J.K. Abbott to Deputy

Minister, 2 December 1963, and D.M. Sloan to Deputy Minister, 3 December 1963, DC&I, vol. 125. Officials in Hong Kong believed that students from Communist universities were "particularly dangerous security risks" and denied them student visas. An applicant who won a scholarship to the University of British Columbia had his case reviewed and was admitted subject to passing a medical examination. He had the support of Dr. Leslie Kilborn, a Canadian medical missionary, professor of physiology at the University of Hong Kong, and former dean of Medicine at West China University, an institution sponsored by the United Church of Canada, who wrote to Prime Minister Pearson on his behalf. Leslie Kilborn to L.B. Pearson, 29 August and 14 December 1963, and René Tremblay to L.B. Pearson, 24 February 1964, LBPP, vol. 208.

68 *Chinatown News,* 2 and 18 April and 18 July 1964.

69 *HCD,* 14 August 1964, 6821; Fifty-seven members and friends of the Chinese Evangelical Baptist Church to L.B. Pearson, 21 August 1964, and R.G. R[obertson] to L.B. Pearson, 30 December 1964, LBPP, vol. 207.

70 *HCD,* 23 June 1964, 4608; Ian Wahn to L.B. Pearson, 14 October 1964, and René Tremblay to L.B. Pearson, 4 November 1964, LBPP, vol. 207; R.B. Curry to Minister, 12 March 1965, and K.M. Davidson, Memo, 4 and 5 March 1965, DImm, vol. 877.

71 Lower Mainland Farmers' Co-Operative Association to René Tremblay, 26 February 1964, and James Chan to René Tremblay, 19 June 1964, LBPP, vol. 269.

72 René Tremblay to James Chan, 15 September 1963, René Tremblay to L.B. Pearson, 16 September 1964, and Hal Dornan to Mary Macdonald, 8 October 1964, LBPP, vol. 269; *HCD,* 25 September 1964, 8456; *Chinatown News,* 3 and 18 October 1964, and 18 January, 3 February, and 22 March 1965; *Times,* 12 and 14 January 1965.

73 Acting Director of Immigration to Deputy Minister, 26 November 1963, DC&I, vol. 125; *HCD,* 20 December 1963, 6238, and 2 April 1964, 1723-25.

74 *HCD,* 14 August 1964, 6821-22, and 19 August 1964, 7019.

75 *HCD,* 14 August 1964, 6846-47 and 6867, and 18 August 1964, 6950; *Chinatown News,* 3 September 1964; Quan Lim to Minister, 17 August 1963, C.M. Isbister to Minister, 18 August 1964, and R.B. Curry to Minister, 9 and 10 September 1964, DImm, vol. 877; Roy Mah, in *Vancouver Times,* 8 September 1964.

76 *HCD,* 19 August 1964, 7019, and 11 September 1964, 7877-78; *Chinatown News,* 3 and 18 September 1964.

77 R.B. Curry to Commissioner, RCMP, 23 September 1964; R.B. Curry to Minister, 17 March 1965; L.E. Hawkins to Director, 11 February 1966; and A.L. May to Mr. Stirling, 15 March 1966, DImm, vol. 877; *HCD,* 23 September 1964, 8347, and 16 November 1966, 9951. The program ended in 1973.

78 Among those presenting briefs were the Lower Mainland Farmers' Co-Operative Association, the CCCA, and the Chinese Army, Navy, and Air Force Veterans. *Chinatown News,* 18 February, 18 March, and 3 and 18 April 1965; *Province,* 20 March 1965; *Vancouver Sun,* 20 and 22 March 1965. Quon H. Wong to J.R. Nicholson, 19 March 1965, LBPP, vol. 207; J.R. Nicholson to Ian Wahn, 12 April 1965, DImm, vol. 877.

79 G. R[obertson] to L.B. Pearson, 30 December 1964, LBPP, vol. 207; René Tremblay to L.B. Pearson, 22 January 1965; Draft Memo, 18 January 1965; "The Sponsorship Problem, by JLM," n.d.; R.B. Curry to Minister, 18 March 1965; Director, Policy and Planning Directorate, to Chief, Policy and Planning Division, c. August 1965 and 11 August 1965; Project 1, "Social and Cultural Aspects of Immigration," 10 November 1965; Memo to Cabinet, 22 June 1966, all in DImm, vol. 723. The reorganization of the department is described in Hawkins, *Canada and Immigration,* Chapter 6.

80 *Chinatown News,* 3 October and 3 and 18 November 1965. Toronto's Chinese had a low profile in the 1965 election.

81 Tom Kent, *A Public Purpose: An Experience of Liberal Opposition and Canadian Government* (Kingston: McGill-Queen's University Press, 1988), 409-10; *Toronto Daily Star,* 30 October 1965; *HCD,* 8 July 1966, 7377; *Chinatown News,* 3 November 1966; *Province,* 1 October 1966. One of the few examples of anti-Asian propaganda was an advertisement in a Vancouver neighbourhood newspaper, the *West Ender,* in April 1965. Headed "Our Nation in Danger ... Changes in Immigration Laws Will Destroy Canada," the advertisement was accompanied by the picture of a group of "coolies" and the caption "They want to come to Canada." The text repeated old shibboleths about a high "Oriental" birth rate and the creation of a "race problem," as in the United States. When *Chinatown News* brought it to his attention, the editor of the *West Ender* apologized for "gross carelessness" in publishing an ad that was

in "bad taste" and "rife with racial hatred." Nicholson, the postmaster general, appreciated the apology and noted that David Stanley, who sponsored the advertisement, had been running "practically a private vendetta against the Post Office" for its refusal to distribute his hate literature. *Chinatown News*, 3 and 18 May and 3 June 1965. In April 1967, the *Vancouver Sun* published a letter to the editor filled with "yellow peril" ideas but had an editorial on the first-class citizenship of Chinese Canadians and a column by Mamie Maloney describing Chinese contributions to Canadian society. *Chinatown News*, 18 April 1967.

82 A Vancouver *Daily Province* editorial of 15 September 1967 made no comment about Asian immigrants and suggested that the new policy might mean few changes since officials still had discretion and since the "real test" of the immigration system would be its success in "bringing into Canada enough people in terms of our national needs who possess the qualities of good citizenship." In a brief news report, the *Vancouver Sun* of 12 September 1967 suggested that the new regulations would mean only a marginal increase in immigration. *Chinatown News*, 18 May and 18 September 1967; Montreal *Gazette*, 15 September 1967; Wickberg, *From China to Canada*, 244-45.

Conclusion

1 James St. G. Walker, *'Race,' Rights, and the Law in the Supreme Court of Canada* (Toronto: Osgoode Society, 1997), 13; *Kelowna Capital News*, 2 January 1946; Prince Rupert *Daily News*, 24 January 1946.

2 Ashley Montagu, *Statement on Race* (New York: Henry Schuman, 1951), 45, 61, 87, 116, 73.

3 *New Canadian*, 25 November 1950 and 19 March 1952. By 1955 the *New Canadian* regularly reported the marriages of Nisei to Occidentals, although a columnist suggested that intermarriage still set one apart. *New Canadian*, 24 December 1955. Intermarriage was less common among Chinese Canadians.

4 Those who argued for better treatment of the First Nations made similar references to the Atlantic Charter and the UN declaration. See R. Scott Sheffield, *The Red Man's on the Warpath: The Image of the "Indian" and the Second World War* (Vancouver: UBC Press, 2004), 146 and passim.

5 *Ottawa Citizen*, 25 January 1946; *Province*, 9 March 1949; *Vancouver Sun*, 11 March 1949.

6 *Vancouver Sun*, 8 November 1955.

7 *New Canadian*, 2 June 1948.

8 *New Canadian*, 6 October 1948.

9 JCCA Meeting, 20 January 1960, JCCA, MfC12819. A Sansei (third-generation) student once thanked me because a lecture on the wartime treatment of the Japanese Canadians had solved a mystery. His parents had talked of their high school days in the West Kootenay but had never explained why they were there.

10 In 1941, 53.8 percent of the Chinese in Canada lived in British Columbia; in 1951, 49 percent; in 1961, 41.6 percent; and in 1971, 37.3 percent. Jin Tan and Patricia E. Roy, *The Chinese in Canada* (Ottawa: Canadian Historical Association, 1985), 17. The changes in the Japanese population were much more dramatic. In 1941, 95.4 percent resided in British Columbia; in 1951, 33 percent; in 1961, 35.7 percent; and in 1971, 36.4 percent. Calculated from Ken Adachi, *The Enemy that Never Was: A History of the Japanese Canadians* (Toronto: McClelland and Stewart, 1976), 423.

11 Freda Hawkins, *Canada and Immigration: Public Policy and Public Concern* (Montreal and Kingston: McGill-Queen's University Press, 1972), 141, 353, and 377. Hawkins concluded that before 1967 bureaucrats made immigration policy.

12 JCCA Meeting, 17 June 1964, JCCA, vol. 2, MFC12819.

Epilogue

1 Margaret Cannon, *China Tide: The Hong Kong Exodus to Canada* (Toronto: HarperCollins, 1989), 12.

2 For details of conflicts especially over housing and related issues in Vancouver, see Katharyn Mitchell, *Crossing the Neoliberal Line: Pacific Rim Migration and the Metropolis* (Philadelphia: Temple University Press, 2004), and David Ley, "The Rhetoric of Racism and the Politics of Explanation in the Vancouver Housing Market," in *The Silent Debate: Asian Immigration and Racism in Canada*, ed. Eleanor Laquian, Aprodicio Laquian, and Terry McGee (Vancouver: Institute of Asian Research, [1998]), 331-48. Ley notes contradictory studies of the role of the Chinese in inflating house prices and argues that many complaints about prices preceded the large-scale immigration of wealthy Chinese. A brief mention of the issue in Toronto may be found in Cannon, *China Tide*, 168, 176-79.

3 Anthony B. Chan, *Gold Mountain: The Chinese in the New World* (Vancouver: New Star, 1983), 175. This account is based on Chan's Chapter 9.

4 Aprodicio A. Laquian and Eleanor R. Laquian, "Asian Immigration and Racism in Canada: A Search for Policy Options," in Laquian, Laquian, and McGee, *The Silent Debate,* 21.
5 The cartoon by "King" appeared in the *Ottawa Citizen,* 2 June 1994, and was reprinted in the *Vancouver Sun,* 6 June 1994.
6 Wing Chung Ng, *The Chinese in Vancouver,* 1945-80 (Vancouver: UBC Press, 1999), 4 and passim.
7 *Vancouver Sun,* 14 October 1961; *Chinatown News,* 18 November 1961.
8 Peter Li, *The Chinese in Canada* (Toronto: Oxford University Press, 1998), 152-53.
9 *New Canadian,* 10 June 1964.
10 Shizuye Takashima, *A Child in Prison Camp* (Toronto: Tundra, 1971). It was probably the first published English-language personal memoir of the wartime experiences of Japanese Canadians and has been republished several times.
11 Several leading participants in the redress campaign have published histories of it: Roy Miki, *Redress: Inside the Japanese Canadian Call for Justice* (Vancouver: Raincoast, 2004); Roy Miki and Cassandra Kobayashi, *Justice in Our Time: The Japanese Canadian Redress Settlement* (Vancouver: Talonbooks, 1991); and Maryka Omatsu, *Bittersweet Passage: Redress and the Japanese Canadian Experience* (Toronto: Between the Lines, 1992). The agreement is summarized in Miki, *Redress,* 306-7.
12 The legal issues raised by the case are examined in *Calling Power to Account: Law, Reparations, and the Chinese Canadian Head Tax Case,* ed. David Dyzenhaus and Mayo Moran (Toronto: University of Toronto Press, 2005). *Vancouver Sun,* 13 July 2001; *Victoria Times-Colonist,* 20 December 2001; Toronto *Globe and Mail,* 13 July 2001.
13 Robert Matas, "Redress Plan Lacks Apology," Toronto *Globe and Mail,* 12 November 2005; Gloria Galloway, "Head-Tax Debate Heats up on Hustings," Toronto *Globe and Mail,* 29 December 2005; Peter O'Neil, "3 Tories Break with Party on Chinese-Canadian Issue," *Vancouver Sun,* 7 December 2005; Peter O'Neil, "PM Apologizes for Head Tax on Chinese Immigrants," *Vancouver Sun,* 6 January 2006; Peter O'Neil, "Harper Courts Chinese, Cities," *Vancouver Sun,* 27 January 2006; Miro Cernetic, "Gin Wong's Motorcycle Diaries," *Vancouver Sun,* 14 January 2006. Elected as a Liberal, Emerson switched parties within days of the election and was sworn in as a minister in the Conservative government.
14 *HCD,* 22 June 2006, 1510. Several of the party leaders said a few words in Chinese, which the Hansard reporters recorded phonetically.

Index